A COMMENTARY ON
MICAH

A COMMENTARY ON
MICAH

Bruce K. Waltke

WILLIAM B. EERDMANS PUBLISHING COMPANY
GRAND RAPIDS, MICHIGAN / CAMBRIDGE, U.K.

Published 2007 by

Wm. B. Eerdmans Publishing Co.

2140 Oak Industrial Drive N.E., Grand Rapids, Michigan 49505 /

P.O. Box 163, Cambridge CB3 9PU U.K.

Paperback edition 2008

Printed in the United States of America

13 12 11 10 09 08   8 7 6 5 4 3 2

Library of Congress Cataloging-in-Publication Data

Waltke, Bruce K.

A commentary on Micah / Bruce K. Waltke.

p.   cm.

Includes bibliographical references and indexes.

ISBN 978-0-8028-6412-3 (pbk.: alk. paper)

1. Bible. O.T. Micah — Commentaries.   I. Title.

BS1615.53.W35 2007

224.93077 — dc22

2006014246

www.eerdmans.com

To Bill Reimer, Bernard Bell, and the Eerdmans editors,

Who gave me a voice

CONTENTS

vii

Contents

Contents

PREFACE

This book aims in the first place to interpret the book of Micah by the grammatico-historical method. This method entails determining a book's historical context, its text, the meaning of every word and their syntactical relationship, its figures of speech, its rhetorical techniques, and its literary forms.

In the second place, the book aims to interpret what the book of Micah means to the contemporary church. This is achieved by considering its role and contribution within the canon of Holy Scripture and, related to that, how its historical horizon interfaces with the church's contemporary horizon.

Each of these endeavors in turn entails subdisciplines. For example, to determine Micah's historical horizon one must engage in asking introductory questions about the author and his date and the book's integrity and structure. To determine its text one must carefully evaluate readings found in ancient Hebrew texts and in ancient versions. To assure an accurate interpretation of its grammar, I first wrote *An Introduction to Biblical Hebrew Syntax* (1990). To interpret figures of speech one must first identify a figure, then label it, and finally determine its true significance. By employing rhetorical criticism one can gain new insights into the biblical writers' techniques and thus give their works deeper meaning and coherence.

The book is divided into two major parts: Introduction and Commentary. With regard to the former I need mention here only that in deciding matters such as author and date, I followed the scientific method of allowing the book's own data to guide me. I reject the secular prejudice that prophecy is *vaticinium ex eventu* ("proclamation after the event"), and its corollary that supernatural prophecy is not possible. These secular dogmas are as religiously binding in secular scholarship as the dogma of some Fundamentalists that the

Bible comes to us by divine dictation. Neither of these prejudices can be squared with the content of the Bible.

The Commentary consists of three parts: translation, exegesis, and exposition. The notes to the translation contain the mass of text-critical matters. Not everyone has a taste for textual criticism, but a comprehensive study of all textual variants is as essential as roots to a flower. These notes are for those who question the reliability of a given reading.

The exegesis contains the bulk of historical and philological analyses. Not everyone has a taste for these details either, but they are the stem that carries the flower, the exposition of the text.

Form-critical analysis yields about twenty-one distinct oracles, and rhetorical criticism shows that these are divided into three cycles of judgment oracles followed by salvation oracles. The first cycle, 1:2–2:13, begins with two judgment oracles predicting the destruction of Samaria in the North (1:2-7) and the House of David going into exile in the South (1:8-16). The next two judgment oracles (2:1-5, 6-11) condemn the venal land barons and the lying prophets whom they bribed. The cycle closes with a remnant emerging triumphant from an implicitly besieged Jerusalem.

The second cycle begins with three judgment oracles (3:1-4, 5-8, 9-12) condemning and sentencing Israel's three kinds of leaders: magistrates, prophets, and priests. They reach a climax with the prediction that Jerusalem and its temple will be devastated. But in a breathtaking switch, Micah predicts the exaltation of a future Zion and temple that are destined to be the center for the salvation of the nations. The following oracles develop the fact that this will be accomplished through a remnant that survives both the Assyrian siege of Jerusalem and Israel's exile into Babylon. This remnant will give birth to the Messiah, who will establish peace. Its last two oracles picture God's covenant people ruling the nations and God protecting his kingdom.

The third cycle begins with the Lord's call that Israel repent (6:1-8). Israel's implicit rejection of his call leads to oracles predicting the infliction of Israel's covenant curses (6:9-16) and social anarchy (7:1-6/7). The cycle and book are drawn to conclusions with a song of victory (7:6/7-20). The victory song concludes with the exclamation, "Who is a God like you *(mî-'el-kāmôkā)?*" Thus the book begins with Micah's name and ends with an etymological explanation of its significance: there is no God like Israel's covenant-keeping God.

*   *   *

In the early 1980s Inter-Varsity Press honored me with an invitation to write a commentary on Micah for their distinguished Tyndale Old Testament Commentaries, edited by Professor D. J. Wiseman, a dear friend of mine and an internationally esteemed colleague on the committee that is responsible for the text of the New International Version of the Bible. That series of commentaries, one of the finest in the English-speaking world, aims to be a "handy" exegetical commentary on each book of the Bible. In spite of my best efforts to keep it "handy," however, one anonymous referee said of it before its publication in 1988: "The itsy-bitsy book of Micah. Nobody reads it anyway. So we might just as well have one erudite work in our series."

At about the same time as that publication, the editors at Baker Book House invited me to write an in-depth exegetical commentary of Micah for their anticipated three-volume work, *The Minor Prophets,* edited by the late Thomas E. McComiskey. I had learned to respect Tom in the early 1960s as a fellow church member while he was working toward his Ph.D. at Brandeis University and I working toward mine at Harvard. Having just completed essential research on Micah and wanting to taste more, I readily accepted the invitation. Perhaps because of my Teutonic blood — or is it my insecurity? — when taking on an assignment like that, I research each pericope as though I were writing a doctoral dissertation. So I set about to appraise critically every Hebrew text and ancient version of Micah that I could lay my hands on. After writing the first chapter and forwarding it to the editors of Baker to get their go-ahead, I received the green light to proceed. However, by the time I was into chapter 5 — I had been forwarding the work to Tom chapter by chapter — they realized that my commentary was totally out of balance in length, not quality, with the other commentaries in that three-volume work, necessitating that I cut it in half. That work divides the commentaries into exegesis for the scholar-pastor and exposition for the busy pastor. Since it is written primarily for pastors, not for scholars, I mostly trimmed the exegetical portion. But I must admit that I felt like a fool who had put on a diver's suit to pull the stopper out of a bathtub.

Several years later Bill Reimer, the Regent College bookstore manager, knowing the situation, asked me to hand over the full commentary to him, and, after reading it, committed Regent College bookstore to its publication. By now the manuscript, like an ancient scroll, had lost its last several pages on Mic 7:8-20. Bill hired Regent students Charles Yu, Rob Clements, and Bernard Bell to transform my hard copy into electronic form for publication. Bernard, who had become a highly respected close friend, did the lion's share of the work. Meanwhile I pursued writing commentaries on Genesis (Zondervan, 2001) and on Proverbs (Eerdmans, two vols., 2004, 2005). Before publishing the commentary on Micah by the Regent College Press, Bill took it upon himself to send the electronic version of the manuscript to the editors at the Eerdmans Publishing Company to test their interest. To my astonished delight, this "Cadillac" of publishers agreed to give me a voice, and Baker Book House graciously gave them permission to publish the full work. Though I have dedicated the work to Bill Reimer, Bernard Bell, and the Eerdmans editors, I express my sincere gratitude to all who helped to make this book possible.

Though I have not brought my research up to date as much as I would have liked, I trust that the scholar, pastor, teacher, and layperson will find the work profitable, whether they read the exegetical sections, the expository sections, or both.

BRUCE K. WALTKE

ABBREVIATIONS

AB	Anchor Bible
AnBib	Analecta biblica
ANEP	*The Ancient Near East in Pictures Relation to the Old Testament*, ed. J. B. Pritchard, 2d ed. Princeton: Princeton University Press, 1969
ANET	*Ancient Near Eastern Texts Relating to the Old Testament*, ed. J. B. Pritchard, 3d ed. Princeton: Princeton University Press, 1969
AnOr	Analecta orientalia
AJSL	*American Journal of Semitic Languages and Literature*
ATR	*Anglican Theological Review*
Aug Rom	*Augustinianum Roma*
AUSS	*Andrews University Seminary Studies*
BA	*Biblical Archaeologist*
BAR	*Biblical Archaeology Review*
BASOR	*Bulletin of the American Schools of Oriental Research*
BDB	F. Brown, S. R. Driver, and C. A. Briggs, *A Hebrew and English Lexicon of the Old Testament*. Oxford: Clarendon, 1907
BHK	*Biblia Hebraica*, ed. R. Kittel. Stuttgart, 1905-6, 1973[16]
BHS	*Biblia Hebraica Stuttgartensia*, ed. K. Elliger and W. Rudolph. Stuttgart: Deutsche Bibelgesellschaft, 1983
Bib	*Biblica*
BJPES	*Bulletin of the Jewish Palestine Exploration Society*
BKAT	Biblischer Kommentar: Altes Testament
BTB	*Biblical Theology Bulletin*
BZ	*Biblische Zeitschrift*
BZAW	Beihefte zur *Zeitschrift für die alttestamentliche Wissenschaft*
CAT	Commentaire de l'Ancien Testament
CBQ	*Catholic Biblical Quarterly*
CBQMS	Catholic Biblical Quarterly Monograph Series
DJD	Discoveries in the Judaean Desert of Jordan

EncJud	*Encyclopedia Judaica*
EvQ	*Evangelical Quarterly*
La Formation	B. Renaud, *La Formation du Livre de Michée: Tradition et Actualisation,* Études Bibliques. Paris: Gabalda, 1947
GB	*Wilhelm Gesenius' Hebräisches und Aramäisches Handwörterbuch über das Alte Testament,* ed. F. Buhl. Berlin/Göttingen/Heidelberg: Springer, 1962
GKC	*Gesenius' Hebrew Grammar,* ed. E. Kautsch, tr. A. E. Cowley, 2d ed. Oxford: Clarendon, 1910
HALOT	L. Koehler, W. Baumgartner, et al., *The Hebrew and Aramaic Lexicon of the Old Testament,* tr. M. E. J. Richardson et al., 4 vols. Leiden: Brill, 1994-99
HAT	Handbuch zum Alten Testament
HKAT	Handkommentar zum Alten Testament
Holladay	W. Holladay, *A Concise Hebrew and Aramaic Lexicon of the Old Testament.* Grand Rapids: Eerdmans, 1971
HSM	Harvard Semitic Monographs
HSS	*Harvard Semitic Studies*
HTR	*Harvard Theological Review*
HUCA	*Hebrew Union College Annual*
IB	*Interpreter's Bible*
IBHS	B. K. Waltke and M. P. O'Connor, *Introduction to Biblical Hebrew Syntax.* Winona Lake, Ind.: Eisenbrauns, 1989
ICC	International Critical Commentary
IDB	*The Interpreter's Dictionary of the Bible,* ed. G. A. Buttrick, 4 vols. Nashville: Abingdon, 1962
IDBSup	*Interpreter's Dictionary of the Bible, Supplementary Volume.* Nashville: Abingdon, 1976
IEJ	*Israel Exploration Journal*
JAOS	*Journal of the American Oriental Society*
JBL	*Journal of Biblical Literature*
JJS	*Journal of Jewish Studies*
JNES	*Journal of Near Eastern Studies*
JPOS	*Journal of the Palestinian Oriental Society*
JSOT	*Journal for the Study of the Old Testament*
JSOTSup	*Journal for the Study of the Old Testament* Supplement Series
JSS	*Journal of Semitic Studies*
JTS	*Journal of Theological Studies*
K	*Kethib*
KAT	Kommentar zum Alten Testament
KBL	L. Koehler and W. Baumgartner, *Lexicon in Veteris Testamenti libros,* 2d ed. Leiden: Brill, 1958
KHC	Kurzer Hand-Commentar zum Alten Testament
KJV	King James Version

KS	Karl Elliger, *Kleine Schriften zum Alten Testament.* Munich: Kaiser, 1966
L	Codex Leningradensis
Lis	G. Lisowsky, *Konkordanz zum Hebräischen Alten Testament,* 2d ed. Stuttgart: Württembergische Bibelanstalt, 1958
LXX	Septuagint
LXX^A	Codex Alexandrinus
LXX^B	Codex Vaticanus
LXX^L	Lucianic recension
LXX^Q	Codex Marchalianus
LXX^R	Codex Veronensis
MT	Masoretic Text
NAC	New American Commentary
NBD	*New Bible Dictionary,* ed. J. D. Douglas. Downers Grove, Ill.: InterVarsity, 1982
NICOT	New International Commentary on the Old Testament
NIDOTTE	*New International Dictionary of Old Testament Theology and Exegesis,* ed. W. A. VanGemeren, 5 vols. Grand Rapids: Zondervan, 1997
NIV	New International Version
NIVAC	New International Version Application Commentary
NRSV	New Revised Standard Version
OTL	Old Testament Library
OTS	*Oudtestamentische Studiën*
PEQ	*Palestine Exploration Quarterly*
PJ	*Palästina-Jahrbuch*
Q	*Qere*
RB	*Revue Biblique*
RechScRel	*Recherches de Science Religieuse*
RevSém	*Revue de Sémitique*
RSV	Revised Standard Version
SBLDS	Society of Biblical Literature Dissertation Series
SBT	Studies in Biblical Theology
SEÅ	*Svensk Exegetisk Årsbok*
Sym	Symmachus
Syr	Syriac
TDNT	*Theological Dictionary of the New Testament,* ed. G. Kittel and G. Friedrich. Grand Rapids: Eerdmans, 1964-76
TDOT	*Theological Dictionary of the Old Testament,* ed. G. J. Botterweck, H. Ringgren, and H.-J. Fabry. 10 vols. Grand Rapids: Eerdmans, 1974-
Tg	Targum
THAT	*Theologisches Handwörterbuch zum Alten Testament,* 2 vols. Munich: C. Kaiser, 1971
Theod	Theodotion

TLOT	*Theological Lexicon of the Old Testament*, ed. E. Jenni and C. Westermann, tr. M. E. Biddle, 3 vols. Peabody, Mass.: Hendrickson, 1997
TNIV	Today's New International Version
TOTC	Tyndale Old Testament Commentaries
TThSt	Trierer theologische Studien
TWOT	*Theological Wordbook of the Old Testament*, ed. R. L. Harris, G. L. Archer, and B. K. Waltke. Chicago: Moody, 1980
Vg	Vulgate
VT	*Vetus Testamentum*
VTSup	*Vetus Testamentum*, Supplements
WBC	Word Biblical Commentary
WMANT	Wissenschaftliche Monographien zum Alten und Neuen Testament
WTJ	*Westminster Theological Journal*
ZAW	*Zeitschrift für die Alttestamentliche Wissenschaft*
ZDPV	*Zeitschrift des Deutschen Palästina-Vereins*
ZTK	*Zeitschrift für Theologie und Kirche*

Hebrew Transliteration Scheme

Consonants

א	ʾ	ʾālep
ב	b	bêt
ג	g	gîmel
ד	d	dālet
ה	h	hê
ו	w	wāw
ז	z	zayin
ח	ḥ	ḥêt
ט	ṭ	ṭêt
י	y	yôd
כ ך	k	kāp
ל	l	lāmed
מ ם	m	mêm
נ ן	n	nûn
ס	s	sāmek
ע	ʿ	ʿayin
פ ף	p	pê
צ ץ	ṣ	ṣādê
ק	q	qôp
ר	r	rêš
שׂ	ś	śîn
שׁ	š	šîn
ת	t	tāw

Vowels

בָ	ā	qāmeṣ
בַ	a	pataḥ
בֶ	e	sĕgôl
בֵ	ē	ṣērê
בִ	i	short ḥîreq
בִ	ī	long ḥîreq written defectively
בָ	o	qāmeṣ ḥāṭûp
בוֹ	ô	ḥôlem written fully
בֹ	ō	ḥôlem written defectively
בוּ	û	šûreq
בֻ	u	short qibbûṣ
בֻ	ū	long qibbûṣ written defectively
הַ	a	furtive pataḥ
בָה	â	final qāmeṣ hâ
בֵי	ey	sĕgôl yôd (בֵי = ey)
בֵי	ê	ṣērê yôd (בֵי = êy)
בִי	î	ḥireq yôd (בִי = îy)
בָיו	āyw	qāmeṣ yôd wāw (בָיו = āu)
בֲ	ă	ḥāṭēp pataḥ
בֱ	ĕ	ḥāṭēp sĕgôl
בֳ	ŏ	ḥāṭēp qāmeṣ
בְ	ĕ	vocal šĕwāʾ
בְ	–	silent šĕwāʾ

INTRODUCTION

I. THE PROPHET

The book of Micah's superscription attributes its authorship to Micah the Moreshtite and identifies its literary genre as "the word of *I AM* . . . which he prophesied" (or "saw" as a divine vision or audition; cf. 1:1). Two prophets bear the common biblical name of Micah: Micaiah son of Imlah, a prophet in the Northern Kingdom at the time of Ahab, ca. 874-852 B.C. (1 Kgs 22:8-28; 2 Chr 18:7-27), and Micah of Moresheth Gath, a Southern prophet who ministered between ca. 740 and 690 B.C. (cf. 1:1, 14). "Mi-ca-iah" is a sentence name, meaning "Who [Heb. *mi*] is like [*k*] Yah [*iah*]?" (cf. 1:1). By this naming his parents constantly praised *I AM* as being incomparable to any other deity. It also portends the prophet's message. By artfully inserting his name in the people's hymn of praise at the end of his book, their prophet-son added luster to *I AM*'s glory: Who like *I AM*[1] forgives his guilty people to be true to his covenant promises to the patriarchs? (7:18). God's memorial name initially became famous when he hurled the Egyptian army into the depths of the sea to keep covenant fidelity with the patriarchs. He will, however, add even greater luster to his name in the last days when he hurls Israel's iniquities into the depths of the sea to be true to his covenant with Abraham and Jacob (7:19-20).

Micah does not recount his initial call to ministry as do Isaiah (ch. 6), Jeremiah (ch. 1), Ezekiel (ch. 2), and Amos (ch. 7). The claim that "the word of *I AM*" came to him and that he "prophesied" his "vision" (Mic 1:1) gives him the status of *I AM*'s plenipotentiary. As a messenger from the heavenly court, he was invested with all its authority in his addresses to Israel's royal capitals of

---

1. In this book I am using "*I AM*" rather than "Yahweh" for Heb. *yhwh*.

Samaria and Jerusalem. The prophetic commissioning and messenger formula, "Thus says *I AM*," reflects the image of ancient Near Eastern diplomatic protocol (cf. Isa 21:6). In Hebrew *mal'āk* means either "messenger" or "angel." Both divine "angels" and human "prophets" serve as messengers of revelation (cf. the *angelus interpres* of Zech 1:4; 2:7[3]). Isaiah received his initial call to his ministry of judgment in his temple vision of the heavenly court amid the fiery seraphim. When *I AM* asked the gathered host, including Isaiah, "Who will go for us?" Isaiah responded, "Here am I. Send me [and not an angel]" (Isa 6:1-10). Likewise, when he received his second call vis-à-vis the end of the exile, the visionary once again found himself in *I AM*'s heavenly court, hearing *I AM*'s commission, "comfort [Heb. pl.] my people." Whereupon Isaiah hears the voice of a prophet on earth crying in the desert, "Prepare the way for *I AM*" (Isa 40:1-10). Although Micah, Isaiah's contemporary, does not recount such an experience, he nevertheless hears the word of *I AM* as though he were in the heavenly court: "Listen to what *I AM* says: 'Stand up, [Micah], plead the case before the mountains.'" Whereupon the obedient prophet addresses earth's mountains, "Hear, mountains, *I AM*'s accusation." Like Isaiah, Micah announces on earth oracles of doom and of salvation beyond judgment in skillfully arranged collections.

Although Micah veils his autobiographical information, his messages of judgment rest on the lofty ethical standards given to Israel on Sinai (Mic 6:1-8), his messages of hope on God's unchanging faithfulness to Abraham. Rebuffed by his audience (2:6; 6:6-11), this flashing preacher lifted his almost solitary voice from the highest peaks of ethical standards above the clamorous masses. Even his prophecies of doom must be valued as *I AM*'s gift to his people (cf. Num 23:23; Deut 18:14). Silence is a worse form of judgment (cf. Ezek 7:26; Amos 8:2; Ps 74:9). But even worse are preachers who preach only that God is love and will not judge sinners (cf. Mic 2:11; 3:11).

But tragically, prophets and priests in Micah's time were in cahoots with the corrupt bureaucrats in the royal court (Mic 2:6-11; 3:6-7). Their villainy infected the entire nation, making it cynical and corrupt (6:9-16). Micah removed his veil of modesty only in order to contrast himself with the false prophets against whom he, Isaiah, and some anonymous prophets had to contend. This true representative of heaven distinguished himself by speaking the truth (cf. 2:6-11) and by upholding the values of the Mosaic covenant (cf. 3:5-8). Because true prophets differ from false prophets in character, they also differed in their messages. In order to ingratiate themselves with the rich and ruling classes, the hireling prophets fatally preached *I AM*'s gracious attributes at the expense of his righteousness and justice. Micah, filled with the spirit of justice, preached judgment upon sin and grace for the repentant. Whereas his depraved rivals were filled with lust, greed, and self-ambition, Micah was filled with zeal for the oppressed, the telltale sign that he was full of *I AM*'s spirit (3:8). He has often been called "the prophet of the poor," but in fact he is a prophet of the middle class, which he saw being reduced to intractable poverty by the rich (2:1-5, 6-11). Micah was a person in his own right, not merely *I AM*'s megaphone.

Micah was identified by his place of origin rather than by his family, in contrast, for example, to Isaiah son of Amoz. Amos, the prophet to the Northern Kingdom a generation earlier, was known by his home as well as by his vocation, "Amos, one of the shepherds of Tekoa." To judge from these parallels, Micah's identification as a Moreshtite (Mic 1:1, 14; see the commentary) implies that he was an outsider to the capitals. Were he ministering in his hometown, he would probably have been called, "Micah son of so and so." Unlike Amos, who did not regard himself and was not regarded by others as a prophet but as a shepherd, Micah had the identity of a "professional" prophet, that is, he belonged to a recognized class of charismatic figures in Israel who shaped the nation's foreign policies through their prophecies. Micah's powerful voice changed Hezekiah's heart, reshaped Judah's policies, and so saved the nation from immediate catastrophe (cf. Jer 26:17-19).

II. HISTORICAL BACKGROUND

Micah delivered his messages of doom and hope to Samaria and Jerusalem during the reigns of Jotham (742-735 B.C.), Ahaz (735-715 B.C.), and Hezekiah (715-686 B.C.). In his lifetime two volatile forces were at work in Israel's history: moral corruption within and the rising Neo-Assyrian Empire without. This aggressive, ruthless state was bent on subduing its neighbors to enrich itself with their taxes. In a world under *I AM*'s moral sovereignty the mix was unstable; *I AM*'s threatened curses for covenant infidelity were about to be fulfilled in Micah's lifetime. We turn first to consider the moral corruption within Israel and then to the imperial Assyrian state without.

Amos (ca. 775-743 B.C.) gives us eyewitness testimony to the moral rot at work inside Samaria a generation before Micah (cf. Amos 2:6-7; 4:6-9; 5:10-12; 8:4-6). Hosea, who bridged the generations between Amos and Micah (ca. 760-725), testifies that the same sorry situation continued to obtain in Samaria. From Hosea's successors, Micah and Isaiah, we learn that the contagious social injustices that prevailed in Samaria now prevailed in her prostitute sister Jerusalem as well. Egregious injustices by rich landowners against stalwart farmers whom the rich were driving off their land and into an unrelieved, dependent

3

economic status (Mic 2:1-3, 8-9; 3:1-3, 9-10) were producing a shocking contrast between extreme wealth and dire poverty. Dishonest practices prevailed everywhere. Since judges and prophets were venal, the poor had no redress and no voice (6:10-11; 7:1-4a). *I AM* had entrusted political power to the royal court system to safeguard his holy nation against injustices, sanctioned prophets to stand above the judges and hold them accountable to *I AM*, and elected priests to teach them covenant values. But the royal judges "despised justice and distorted all that is right" (3:9); the gifted prophets became hirelings: "if one feeds them, they proclaim 'peace'; if he does not, they prepare to wage war against them" (3:5); and the educated priests only "taught for a price" (3:11). Blinded by their own cupidity, the false prophets saw no connection between Israel's sin and the rampaging Assyrian army, but the true prophet saw the holy Sovereign marching above the Assyrian juggernaut (cf. 1:3-7). When Israel's social safety nets broke, *I AM* himself stepped in to right the wrong and fulfill the covenant curses (6:1-5, 13-16). The nation that bore *I AM*'s name looked religious as it thronged the temple and offered lavish gifts to buy off *I AM* (6:1-8). But because they replaced the moral covenant, which mandated love to God (Deut 6:5) and love for neighbor (Lev 19:18), with a covenant among the powerful to despoil the weak, judgment was inescapable.

The Assyrian army became "the rod of my [*I AM*'s] anger" (cf. Isa 10:5) and stomped through "the pleasant land" during the second half of the eighth century, casting one city after another into exile (cf. Mic 1:10-19). The arrogant and ruthless Tiglath-pileser III (744-727 B.C.) (= Pul, his Babylonian throne name, 1 Chr 5:26) launched the Neo-Assyrian Empire on its ambitious policy of imperial expansion. In 743 or 738, he demanded tribute from Menahem, among other western rulers. At about the same time a certain "Azriyau of Yaudi," who some think is Azariah (i.e., Uzziah) of Judah,[2] instigated a short-lived revolt (cf. 2 Kgs 15:4). In 734 Tiglath-pileser III penetrated into Israel's coastal plain, marched through Philistia, and reached the Wadi el-'Arish in the Sinai (2 Kings 16; 2 Chronicles 28). About 736-732 B.C., he conquered Damascus and organized North Syria into an Assyrian province, occupied and cut off Galilee and Transjordan from Israel, and confirmed Hoshea on the throne of the rump state of Israel after the latter had assassinated Pekah.

Prior to the rise of the Neo-Assyrian Empire oppressors had plundered Israel for centuries. But now Tiglath-pileser III inaugurated a new political policy of the gravest theological concern to Israel. The Assyrian was appropriating to himself Israel's sworn land (cf. Deut 6:1-3). As Isaiah saw it, since Galilee was

---

2. Cf. H. Tadmor, "Azriayu of Yaudi," *Scripta Hierosolymitana* 8 (1961) 232-42 versus S. Hermann, *A History of Israel in Old Testament Times*, tr. J. Bowden (London: SCM, 1975), 244.

the first of the land to fall into this darkness, it would also be the first to see the light of God's salvation after judgment (Isa 9:1-2). The new Assyrian nemesis signaled that the covenant had been so broken that its intended curses, including exile, were now being fulfilled (Lev 26:26-46, esp. vv 27-33; Deut 28:15-68, esp. vv 36-37, 49-57).

The Assyrian king enjoyed military superiority because his troops were well disciplined; "not a sandal thong is broken" (cf. Isa 5:26-29).[3] Moreover, his was a standing army, unlike the conscripted levies that the western states relied upon. He employed professional mercenaries of various nationalities whom he paid from the huge tributes he exacted from them. In other words, the conquered nations supported the international army that raped them (cf. Mic 4:11, 13).[4] The Assyrian king was content to accept tribute until a rebel king, such as Hoshea, withheld it and cherished ideas of rebellion. Then he would reduce the rebel king, deport his nation's leadership, appropriate the land, and govern it. The kings of Israel foolishly tried to match strength with strength and false religion with false religion (cf. 5:9-14[10-15]). The reforming prophets, however, knew that salvation belonged to *I AM*, and he demanded repentance, remembrance of their covenant beginnings, and renunciation of sin (cf. 6:1-8).

When Tiglath-pileser III was succeeded by his son Shalmaneser V in 726 B.C., the time seemed opportune for Hoshea, the last Northern king, to rebel. He formed an alliance with the king of Egypt and withheld his annual tribute. The Bible matter-of-factly describes what happened in 2 Kgs 17:5-6. It correctly attributes the siege to Shalmaneser V, though his successor, Sargon II, claimed credit for the capture of Samaria. Exacting the extreme measure of subjugation in order to neutralize the land against further revolts, he deported Israel's upper classes — the large property holders, rulers, and religious leaders against whom true prophets had inveighed. The once proud kingdom of the North now became just another Assyrian province named Samaria. *I AM* had dropped the curtain upon his final act of judgment on the polluted kingdom (cf. Mic 1:3-7). In the debris at Samaria excavators found richly decorated ivory fragments, mute testimony to the ostentatious luxury denounced by the prophets.

Periodic rebellions by the petty nations in Syria-Palestine against the tributes the Assyrian exacted from them kept them in constant dread of Assyria's reprisals. Sargon's armies conducted four campaigns to whip the rebel-

---

3. Hermann, *History of Israel*, 244, said of the text: "Every detail in this saying of Isaiah is based on exact observation of Assyrian techniques and practices in war."

4. J. Lindblom, *Micha literarisch untersucht*, Acta Academiae Aboensis, Humaniora, 6/2 (Åbo: Åbo Akademi, 1929). He compares Isa 22:6; 29:7-8; cf. Hos 10:10, cited by L. C. Allen, *The Books of Joel, Obadiah, Jonah, and Micah*, NICOT (Grand Rapids: Eerdmans, 1976), 247 n. 28.

lious western states into line in 720, 716, 713, and 712 B.C. In 720 Sargon annexed Hamath wholly into the empire, and Gaza in southwest Palestine became another Assyrian province. Shortly after Hezekiah had fully assumed the throne, Ashdod refused to pay the tribute, stirred up Edom and Moab to join the coalition, and looked to Hezekiah to reverse his father's pro-Assyrian policy. Isaiah influenced official policy in Judah against joining the folly by going around Jerusalem barefoot and stripped, dramatizing the plight of an exile. In 713 Sargon deposed the ruler of Ashdod and took other cities along the Philistine plain.

For Hezekiah, however, "might was not necessarily right," and a line had to be drawn between prudent submission and moral rectitude. He was willing to pay the tribute but not to sell his soul. He initiated sweeping reforms to purify the temple worship (2 Kgs 18:3-6; 2 Chronicles 29–31), restored the Passover (2 Chr 29:20-31), and repented for the social corruptions in response to Micah's preaching against the turpitude, venality, and injustices that characterized Judah (Jer 26:18). Perhaps Micah drew a veil over the king in his denunciations against the nation because of these reforms (cf. 3:1; 4:14[5:1]; 7:3).[5]

Nevertheless, against prophetic advice he refused to pay the tribute. In ca. 705, when Sennacherib (705-686) succeeded his father Sargon II to the Assyrian throne, the time seemed propitious for Hezekiah to withhold the hated tribute. From a political viewpoint his judgment seemed sound. Merodach-baladan had successfully reestablished himself as king of Babylon and encouraged the western states to join his rebellious coalition. He sent his envoys to Hezekiah (cf. 2 Kgs 20:1-21; Isaiah 39). Hezekiah succumbed to the blandishments of the Babylonians and showed off his armory and treasury, two essentials to support a revolt. Moreover, Shabaka (ca. 710/9-696/5 B.C.), an energetic king, ruled Egypt. But spiritually Hezekiah was wrong, for Isaiah had denounced the rebellion (cf. Isa 30:1-2). In a prophecy whose fulfillment did not have particular bearing on the revolt in 701, but would have a catastrophic effect on Israel's future, Isaiah forewarned that as a result of Hezekiah's folly Babylon would one day carry Judah off into captivity (cf. Isa 39:6-8). Micah confirmed Isaiah's dire predictions. In an oracle wherein *nomen est omen*, he pictured the Assyrian taking captives from city after city through his homeland in his march to Jerusalem (cf. 1:10-16). Micah mimed the captives' fate by himself going about stripped and wailing (cf. Mic 1:8-9). But the two great reforming prophets, Isaiah and Micah, saw beyond the Babylonian captivity. A large section of Isaiah (chs. 40–55) is addressed to these exiles. With amazing and brilliant prophecies he comforted the discouraged Judean exiles with glorious visions of a new exo-

---

5. David W. Baker, T. Desmond Alexander, and Bruce K. Waltke, *Obadiah, Jonah, Micah,* TOTC 23a (Downers Grove, Ill.: InterVarsity, 1988) = Waltke, *Micah,* 141.

dus from there (Isaiah 40–55). Micah also addressed them, and he too predicted their return from Babylon (cf. Mic 4:9-10; 5:1-5[2-6]).

Occupied at first in Babylon, Sennacherib finally appeared on the Judean scene in 701 B.C. (cf. 2 Kgs 18:17–19:37; 2 Chr 32:1-12; Isaiah 30–31; 36–37[6]). He rushed through Syria, Phoenicia, and the plain of Sharon, encountering very little opposition. Once he had captured Joppa, at the southern end of the Sharon, he moved through the Philistine coastal plain at will. Padi, king of Ekron in Philistia, wanted to submit, but his officials handed him over as a prisoner to Hezekiah. At this time Sennacherib stormed and overthrew the major defensive cities in the Shephelah (Judah's western foothills) that protected Jerusalem. Of that campaign Sennacherib boasted:

> As for Hezekiah, the Jew, he did not submit to my yoke. I laid siege to 46 of his strong cities, walled forts, and to the countless small villages in their vicinity, and conquered [them] by means of well-stamped [earth-]ramps, and battering-rams brought [thus] near [to the walls] [combined with] the attack by foot soldiers, [using] mines, breeches as well as sapper work. I drove out [of them] 200,150 people, young and old, male and female, horses, mules, donkeys, camels, big and small beyond counting, and considered [them] booty.[7]

The forty-six "strong cities" included the nine mentioned by Micah in 1:10-15.[8] The most important was Lachish (cf. 1:13), as evidenced by its size and the prominence given to it in the reliefs in Sennacherib's palace.[9] Excavations there uncovered a huge pit into which the Assyrians, presumably, dumped some 1,500 bodies, covering them with pig bones and other rubbish, presumably the Assyrian army's garbage dump.

No human defense or political alliance could halt the Assyrian tide. At the same time he was besieging Lachish, Sennacherib also hemmed in Jerusalem with an overwhelming army (2 Kgs 18:17; 2 Chr 32:9; Isa 36:2). Jerusalem at this time had mushroomed to over three or four times its former size and was thronged with refugees both from fallen Samaria and from the conquered cities of Judah (cf. Mic 2:12). After Lachish fell, the Assyrians turned to Libnah (2 Kgs

---

6. *ANET*, 287-88.

7. *ANET*, 288.

8. A. F. Rainey, "The Biblical Shephelah of Judah," *BASOR* 251 (1983) 2.

9. Archaeologists are divided over the dating of the destruction of Lachish III. Recent excavations there under D. Ussishkin seem to have shifted the balance in favor of the Assyrian date; see D. Ussishkin, "Answers at Lachish," *BAR* 5/6 (1979) 16-39; W. H. Shea, "Nebuchadnezzar's Chronicle and the Date of the Destruction of Lachish III," *PEQ* 111 (1979) 113-16.

19:8-9; Isa 37:8). At this point Tarhaqah, brother of Shabaka, led the combined forces of Nubia and Egypt to intervene, but Sennacherib decisively defeated them in the plain of Eltekeh, a part of the coastal plain level with Jerusalem. Only *I AM* could save the besieged city. Isaiah joined a repentant Hezekiah in prayer (cf. 2 Kgs 19:1-19) for the temple-city's deliverance and boldly predicted the city's miraculous deliverance (2 Kgs 18:17–19:34; 2 Chr 32:1-23). Both Micah and Isaiah, serving as prophetic witnesses to each other, predicted the impossible (2 Kgs 18:17; 19:31-34; 2 Chr 32:1-23). *I AM* responded, according to the Bible's prophet-historians. Sennacherib unwittingly confirms their veracity. His boast that he shut up Hezekiah as a prisoner in Jerusalem, "like a bird in a cage," actually testifies to his failure to take the city and authenticates Micah and Isaiah as true prophets of *I AM*. The biblical historian-theologians attribute the blow that devastated Sennacherib's besieging horde to the angel of *I AM* (2 Kgs 19:35; 2 Chr 32:22-23). From a political perspective — and the two perspectives should not be pitted against each other — a bubonic plague killed them, an inference drawn from Herodotus's account that in a dream Pharaoh Sethos was promised the help of a deity against Sennacherib, and during the night an army of field mice destroyed the Assyrian equipment so that they had to flee without their weapons. The outcome validates the prophetic message that it is folly to try to match strength with strength and false religion with false religion (cf. Mic 5:9-14[10-15]). (The comments above are developed on pp. 41-43.)

III. Date and Authorship

Many biblical critics assume the liberal posture of putting the canon of historical criticism above the biblical canon to determine what actually occurred in Israel's history. By historical criticism I mean the critical posture that determines the accuracy of biblical statements about the date, authorship, unity, and historical veracity of the biblical books on the basis of the Enlightenment's dictates: skepticism,[10] analogy,[11] and coherence.[12] Historical critics approach their labors of deciding these issues with the same skepticism with which they approach any other ancient Near Eastern myth. Their skepticism and their faith that we live in a closed universe, where every effect has a natu-

10. By "skepticism" I mean reading the Bible as one would read any other ancient myth.

11. By "analogy" I mean testing the historical accuracy of the Bible by modern experience. For example, if people are not raised from the dead in the present time, they were not raised from the dead in the past.

12. By "coherence" I mean that every event has a natural, historical cause without positing divine intervention.

ral cause, pushes them to restrict the prophetic gift. In their restricted view of prophecy, prophets cannot address future generations and their predictions must be dated to the time of their fulfillment. In other words, the alleged prophetic proclamation of a future event actually occurred after the event, *vaticinia ex eventu* ("proclamation after the event"). If this is true, the Holy Bible is stained with a serious moral stain of deception, at the worst, or of obfuscation, at the least.

By observing abrupt transitions of themes and jerkiness of style, and thinking it improbable that a prophet would have weakened the effect of his messages threatening doom by introducing oracles of hope, these critics first analyze the oracles into diverse literary types, then group them into appropriate forms such as oracles of doom and hope, and finally date their content on the assumption of *ex eventu*. Before the rise of the biblical theology movement (ca. A.D. 1930-70), historical critics for the half-century from ca. 1880 to 1930 sought to control their datings of biblical books and their sources by correlating the theological content of the oracles and/or books with the evolution of Hebrew religion as drawn up by J. Wellhausen.[13] The biblical academy today mostly rejects this evolution, due to the flood of data turned up by the spade of archaeologists who refuted it, but it still assumes the so-called scientific principles of historical criticism. Some scholars try to support the *ex eventu* assumption by the disciplines of linguistics, theology/philosophy, and psychology. With regard to the first two, they try to construct a typological grid of linguistic and theological developments and to date the oracles by pegging them on the basis of their internal data into their typological-chronological grid.

Before critically appraising the literary approaches and the scientific data that allegedly validate the theory of *ex eventu*, let us first look at the history of biblical criticism based on the foundation of faith in *ex eventu* rather than faith in the biblical witness. Von Ewald[14] in 1867 initiated the literary-historical approach to Micah even before Wellhausen's classic *Geschichte Israels* (1878) appeared. In 1881 Stade,[15] in an epoch-making article, by systematically employing the literary-historical approach, laid the foundation for all future research. On the bases of historical criticism, there is now a widely held consensus that Micah is not the author of 2:12-13; 4:1–5:9; 7:8-20. Assuming the principle of *ex eventu*, this consensus is inevitable, for in these passages one finds that the ora-

---

13. J. Wellhausen, *Geschichte Israels*, Vol. 1 (Berlin: Heimer, 1878).

14. G. H. A. von Ewald, *Jesaja mit den Übrigen älteren Propheten erklärt: Die Propheten des Alten Bundes erklärt*, 2d ed. (Göttingen: Vandenhoeck & Ruprecht, 1867), 1:523. Ewald later retracted this position.

15. B. Stade, "Bemerkungen über das Buch Micha," *ZAW* 1 (1881) 161-72.

cles of salvation that contain theological and historical material are after the time when Micah lived.

In the decade 1915-24, the form-critical approach supplemented the literary-historical approach in deciding the date of the oracles in Micah. Form critics identify the literary genre of the isolated units and imaginatively reconstruct the setting-in-life in which they originated and were circulated. Tradition critics build on the results of literary and form critics and imaginatively reconstruct the development of the oracle from its brief (usually thought to be) oral form to its final form. In 1915 H. Schmidt[16] initiated the form-critical approach to Micah, and in 1929 J. Lindblom[17] wrote the most influential work from this viewpoint. According to Lindblom, among other things, 1:2-7, 8-16; 6:9-16; 7:1-4; and 7:13 were originally written perhaps as pamphlets and disseminated among the people at appropriate places. Lindblom dealt extensively with the delimitation and type of each oracle in Micah. Recent form critics, such as A. Weiser,[18] assign the life setting of as many oracles as they can to Israel's cultus. This approach led A. S. Kapelrud[19] to defend the traditional authorship of many more oracles than the oracles of doom. For example, he assigns the hope oracles in chapters 4–5 to the autumnal new year festival before the destruction of the temple.

Redaction criticism picks up where literary criticism and/or form criticism and tradition criticism leave off and seeks to understand the reamplification, rearrangement, and reapplication both of individual oracles and of the final form of the book in the life of the community that held it sacrosanct. Critics today mostly date the final form of Micah to the exilic[20] or the postexilic period,[21] before the dynamic activity of Ezra and Nehemiah. For example, B. Renaud,[22] who in my opinion wrote the best work on Micah apart from his historico-critical bias, thinks that 5:2(3) is a redactional gloss in order to justify

---

16. H. Schmidt, "Micha," in *Die Schriften des Alten Testaments* (Göttingen: Vandenhoeck & Ruprecht, 1915), 2:130-53.

17. Lindblom, *Micha literarisch untersucht*.

18. A. Weiser, "Micha," in *Das Buch der zwölf kleinen Propheten*, Das Alte Testament Deutsch 24 (Göttingen: Vandenhoeck & Ruprecht, 1963), 228-90.

19. A. S. Kapelrud, "Eschatology in the Book of Micah," *VT* 11 (1961) 392-405.

20. R. Ungerstern-Sternberg, *Der Rechtsstreit Gottes mit seiner Gemeinde, Der Prophet Micha* (Berlin: Calwer, 1958); W. Harrelson, *Interpreting the Old Testament* (New York: Holt, Rinehart & Winston, 1964), 362; John T. Willis, "The Structure, Setting, and Interrelationship of the Pericopes in the Book of Micah" (Ph.D. diss., Vanderbilt University, 1966), 303.

21. B. Renaud, *Michée, Sophonie, Nahum* (Paris: Gabalda, 1987); Allen, *Micah*, 252.

22. B. Renaud, *La Formation du Livre de Michée: Tradition et Actualisation*, Études Bibliques (Paris: Gabalda, 1977) (hereafter *La Formation*), 246-47.

to restored Israel the delay in the fulfillment of the eschatological-messianic promises found in 4:9–5:5(6) and to renew their hope in them.

We now turn to appraise the three modes of criticism. Literary and form-critical analysis, by observing in the text abrupt changes in the form, mood, vocabulary, and content of Micah's oracles, have done yeoman service in showing that the book consists of at least nineteen or twenty oracles. But critical reconstructions of their internal development and external redaction are highly speculative and doubtful, without a smidgen of hard evidence. Not surprisingly, whereas a large consensus has been reached about the boundaries of the oracles, only little consensus has been reached regarding their life settings and/or development — aside from the superscription's claim that they were addressed to Samaria and Jerusalem. There is no consensus about their prehistorical development or their posthistorical redaction into the extant book, aside from the fact the book reached its final form in the exilic or the postexilic communities. Of course, this consensus is the inevitable conclusion that must be drawn if one assumes the principle of *ex eventu.*

But let us leave speculation aside and turn to address linguistic typology and theological typology, and the alleged psychological improbability of mixing hope oracles with doom oracles. We will pay attention particularly to the oracles that scholars have been prone to deny to Micah, and to the academic consensus that the book of Micah reached its final form in the exilic or the postexilic communities.

The grammar of Micah is preexilic, displaying none of the characteristic features of postexilic Hebrew.[23] Moreover, vocabulary tests are extremely difficult to control because texts can be archaized or modernized, and words can disappear from the limited texts reflecting a dead language and then later reappear.[24]

Most of the allegedly later religious ideas in Micah are found in preexilic Jeremiah. Willis in fact collected some thirty-one parallels between the two.[25] Critics are prone to assume that this means that Micah borrowed from Jeremiah. For example, Renaud thinks that he can establish the exilic date of 2:12 with the following argument: "Jer 23:1-6 is the only passage to make God say [in the first person as in Micah]: 'And I, I will gather the remnant of my ewes' (Jer 23:3), and to link therefore the three concepts of reassembling, of herd, and of remnant." But how can he be sure that Micah depended on Jeremiah, especially

---

23. D. A. Robertson, *Linguistic Evidence in Dating Early Hebrew Poetry,* SBLDS 3 (Missoula, Mont.: Scholars Press, 1972), 154.

24. R. Polzin, *Late Biblical Hebrew: Toward an Historical Typology of Biblical Hebrew Prose,* HSM 12 (Missoula, Mont.: Scholars Press, 1976), 7; K. A. Kitchen, "Egypt," *NBD,* 350.

25. Willis, "Structure, Settings, and Interrelationships," 306-10.

since Micah is explicitly quoted in Jer 26:18?[26] Willis reached the opposite conclusion. According to him, the verse looks back to the Davidic tradition because the verbs "gather" and "bring together" occur in passages in which David gathers Israel to fight.[27]

Allen[28] cogently rebutted the psychological argument about mixing oracles of hope and doom as follows: "Certainly a message of comfort would weaken one of condemnation if both were uttered in the same situation to the same audience, but literary juxtaposition is no proof of contemporaneity. Oracles collected from years of prophetic ministry and different spiritual climates can reasonably range over a host of prophetic moods from stormy to fair." Besides, the double focus of the prophet on destruction and renewal is succinctly summarized in Jer 1:10, and both moods find expression in Lamentations 3, a poem unified by a strict acrostic structure. Finally, the announcement of hope in 5:8-14(9-15) is so closely connected with Isa 2:6-8, dated by all to the late eighth century B.C., that most critics do not deny it to Micah.

Let us now look more particularly at the disputed oracles of hope. In the commentary we argue with Allen that the setting of 2:12-13 is the time of Sennacherib's invasion in 701 B.C.

Micah 4:1-5 so dovetails with Micah's denunciation of Jerusalem and his threat that Jerusalem would become a heap of rubble (3:9-12) that it probably predates preexilic Isa 2:2-4. (Jerusalem did not fall because Hezekiah repented [Jer 26:18-19].) We argue the case more fully in the commentary.

Allen[29] further notes that 4:6-8 shares in common with 2:12-13 the motifs of the remnant, sheep, and divine kingship, but denies the oracle to Micah because here "remnant" appears as a technical term full of hope for the elect who survive God's judgment. He awards the first use of the term in this sense to Jeremiah. But Amos 5:15 represents the first appearance of this technical meaning. Why could not Micah be among the earliest prophets to use the term in this way? In fact, he was one of the elect who survived the Assyrian onslaught that took thousands of Judeans into captivity and left only a remnant in Jerusalem. In fact, preexilic Isaiah (Isa 37:32 = 2 Kgs 19:31; Isa 37:4 = 2 Kgs 19:4) uses the term in precisely this connection. Surprisingly, Allen says about 5:6-8(7-9), where "remnant" occurs with the same sense as in 4:6-8, that "there is nothing in the oracle to rule out an eighth-century provenance."[30]

The "now" of distress in 4:9-14(4:9–5:1) fits well into the Assyrian crisis.

26. Renaud, *La Formation*, 112.
27. Willis, "Structure, Setting, and Interrelationships," 200.
28. Allen, *Micah*, 251.
29. Allen, *Micah*, 244.
30. Allen, *Micah*, 248.

The reference to nations in 4:11 is not apocalyptic (a literary genre that arose in Israel after Micah), as some have assumed, but probably refers to the nations comprising the Assyrian imperial army. Note that the restoration from Babylon in 4:10 is seen as something remote in time and place. In sum, the provenance of these oracles is implicitly Jerusalem in the preexilic epoch.

The date of 4:14–5:5(5:1-6) can be determined by the mention of Assyria and the land of Nimrod in 5:4-5(5:5-6). Even Renaud, who denies the integrity of the oracle, is forced to concede that 5:4b-5(5b-6) "comes from a time when Asshur reigned over Babylonia, which would really correspond to the epoch of Isaiah and of Micah."[31]

There is nothing in 5:6-8(7-9) and 7:8-20 to rule out an eighth-century provenance. Allen bows to the scholars who assign 7:8-20 to an exilic or postexilic date, but offers no evidence to validate his skepticism.[32]

In brief, if one rejects the posture of skepticism and faith in *ex eventu*, there is no compelling reason to urge against the authenticity of any oracle to the prophet Micah in the book that bears his name. Unlike Isaiah 40–55, its provenance is consistently Palestinian at the time of the Assyrian invasions. Moreover, the book's artful structure (see below, "Form and Structure") demonstrates the book's unity. The editorial notice in 1:1 (note the sing., "the word of *I AM*," *contra* Jer 1:1; Amos 1:1) and the editorial suture "Then I said" in the first person in 3:1 together suggest that Micah had a hand in editing the unified book traditionally assigned to him.

IV. FORM AND STRUCTURE

Luther complained about the prophets: "They have a queer way of talking, like people who, instead of proceeding in an orderly manner, ramble off from one thing to the next, so that you cannot make head or tail of them or see what they are getting at."[33] These abrupt transitions reflect the manner in which the prophet or his disciples edited the book. About twenty once-independent oracles comprise the book. These include doom oracles threatening judgment (e.g., a proclamation of *I AM*'s epiphany [1:2-7], lament song [1:8-16], funeral lament [2:1-5], reproach [3:1-5], lawsuit [6:1-8]), proclamations of salvation (2:12-13), prayer and praise (7:14-19), and so on. The book is Micah's file of sermons delivered on different occasions. But his sermon files have been skillfully

31. Renaud, *La Formation*, 253.
32. Allen, *Micah*, 251.
33. Cited by Allen, *Micah*, 257 n. 56.

fitted together like pieces of a rose window in a cathedral, pieced together by catchwords and logical particles.[34]

Apart from its superscription, which, like the other superscripts in the Twelve, sets Micah apart from them, the design or scheme of the book of Micah is unique. Instead of moving from large collections of doom oracles to large collections of salvation oracles, Micah collects the two types of oracles into three cycles of doom and hope. Some analyze Micah's scheme as chapters 1–3 (threat), 4–5 (hope), and 6–7 (threat). D. G. Hagstrom, like his teacher J. L. Mays at Union Theological Seminary in Virginia, proposes a two-part structure of the final form of the book: chapters 1–5 and 6–7. Hagstrom detects coherence "when there are features within the text [such as consonance] that hold it together"[35] and helpfully notes: "there are degrees of coherence."[36] M. H. Jacobs, depending on conceptual coherence, regards the book of Micah as "Yahweh's disputes with Israel concerning Israel's fate" and sees its macrostructure as consisting of two disputes, chapters 1–5 and 6–7. But an intractable oracle of hope (2:12-13) favors reckoning with a dominant conceptual alternating pattern of doom (A) and hope (B): A (1:1–2:11)–B (2:12-13), A' (3:1-11)–B' (4:1–5:14[4:1–5:15]), and A" (6:1–7:6)–B" (7:7-20).[37] J. T. Willis in his doctoral dissertation defended and developed this old scheme. In short, I analyze the book as having three coherent sections of doom and hope: 1:2–2:13; 3:1–5:14(3:1–5:15) and 6:1–7:20.[38] Jacobs agrees that these are the dominant concepts: "What then constitutes the conceptuality of the book of Micah? Is it judgment or hope? The fact of the matter is that it is both. . . . The final word . . . is not the judgment, but the hope that beyond the judgment lies a future in which the existence of Israel is a reality. . . . Within the dynamics of that relationship, the sin-judgment and promise-hope dynamics are to be understood as the conceptual framework of God's justice in judgment and God's mercy in preserving and forgiving Israel."[39]

In the first cycle, Micah's oracles of doom threaten the capitals of both Samaria and Jerusalem with exile on account of their venality (1:2–2:11). These oracles begin with *I AM*'s punitive epiphany (1:2-7), followed by a lament song (1:8-16), a funeral lament (2:1-6), and a controversial saying (2:7-11). He draws

---

34. For an excellent survey of a history of research on the construction of Micah see M. R. Jacobs, *The Conceptual Coherence of the Book of Micah*, JSOTSup 322 (Sheffield: Sheffield Academic Press, 2001), 14-45.

35. D. G. Hagstrom, *The Coherence of the Book of Micah: A Literary Analysis*, SBLDS 7 (Atlanta: Scholars Press, 1988), 3.

36. Hagstrom, *Coherence*, 125.

37. Jacobs, *Conceptual Coherence*, 63-76.

38. Willis, "Structure, Setting, and Interrelationships."

39. Jacobs, *Conceptual Coherence*, 222-23.

this section to a close, however, with a short oracle of hope, proclaiming that *I AM* will gather his elect remnant into Jerusalem to survive the Assyrian siege and will become their Warrior-King to lead them out (2:12-13).

The second cycle, marked off from the first by the editorial suture, "then I said," moves from three oracles of reproach threatening to dismantle Jerusalem for its failed leadership (3:1-12) to a number of diverse oracles promising the nation salvation "in that day" (4:1–5:14[4:1–5:15]). In that day *I AM* will exalt Jerusalem high above the nations (4:1-5) and there reassemble the afflicted remnant, who will restore God's dominion over the earth (4:6-8). Although Israel's failed leadership could not save itself from invaders and from exile in Babylon (4:9-14 [4:9–5:1]), God will transform their extreme pain of exile into birth pangs that introduce a new age with the birth and reign of Messiah. He will regather the purged remnant, defend them against the "Assyrian" when he invades our land, and lead them to victory (5:1-14[2-15]). Importantly, for our analysis, Willis has demonstrated beyond reasonable doubt the unity of 3:9–4:3, linking the oracles of judgment in chapter 3 with those of hope in chapters 4–5. Some scholars have mistakenly interpreted 5:9-14(10-15) as an oracle of doom, but in fact it is a promise that God will rid Israel of her besetting sins.

The third cycle, which is marked off by an editorial anacrusis (cf. the commentary at 6:1a), also moves from diverse doom oracles — beginning with a legal lawsuit (6:1-8) and concluding with a lament song (7:1-7) — to a victory song, a composite of hymns of confidence and praise (7:8-19). The motif of confidence (7:7), present in most lament songs, forms a transition to the final song of victory. *I AM* will snatch from the spiritually depraved (6:1-16) and disintegrating nation (7:1-7), an elect remnant of chosen people whom he will forgive and save (7:8-20).

Coherence is achieved through a variety of phenomena: vocabulary, grammar and syntax, logical connectives, thematic development, recurrence of motifs, logical connections, and patterns of structure. Jacobs emphasizes conceptual coherence.[40] On the vertical axis, within the cycles techniques of coherence such as catchwords and logical particles link its oracles together. On the horizontal axis, striking affinities bind the three sections, which are structured according to an alternating A-B pattern. Suffice it here to note that each section commences with the imperative "hear" or "listen" (1:2; 3:1; 6:1) and that the hope sections all contain the motif of shepherding (2:12; 4:8; 5:3[4]; 7:14) and, more importantly, mention the remnant (2:12-13; 4:6-7; 5:6-7[7-8]; 7:18). The vertical and horizontal axes combine to give the apparently disjointed oracles a remarkable coherence. Micah's "rosette window," while containing distinct

---

40. Jacobs, *Conceptual Coherence*, 46-57.

pieces, has an artful coherence proclaiming *I AM*'s covenant. On the one hand, the faithful covenant partner, *I AM*, will fulfill his threatened curses if unfaithful Israel does not repent. On the other hand, as a faithful covenant keeper, he will cleanse his unfaithful partner by hurling their iniquities into the depths of the sea if they return to him.

V. TEXT

Emanuel Tov in his magisterial *Textual Criticism of the Hebrew Bible*[41] provides an excellent introduction to the texts and versions of the OT. Siegfried J. Schwantes in his Johns Hopkins doctoral dissertation, "Critical Study of the Text of Micah," provides helpful data, but his evaluations of individual texts are often less than convincing; he fails to develop adequately a method of textual criticism that is appropriate to Micah by not considering the historical background of the texts and versions. In the following list of the texts and versions used in the preparation of this commentary, I supplement Tov's work only as necessary for the text of Micah.

1. *Masoretic Text* (designated MT). *BHS* (in which Elliger edited the Minor Prophets) constitutes its basic text. In this commentary, I correct the diplomatic text of *BHS* (i.e., L = the Leningrad Codex) with the Dead Sea Scrolls, the versions, and emendations.

2. *Qumran Cave 1*. Designated 1QpMic or 1Q14, the Hebrew manuscript of Micah discovered in Cave 1 at Qumran consists of twenty-three fragments containing citations of Mic 1:2-9; 6:14-16; 7:17 (and possibly 4:13 and 7:6, 8-9).[42] Maurya P. Horgan draws the conclusion that "the text of Micah was interpreted both eschatologically . . . and in terms of the history of the sect [at Qumran]."[43]

3. *Qumran Cave 4*. Designated 4QpMic (?) or 4Q168, the number of fragments comprising this manuscript is debated because the same scribe produced a *pesher* (i.e., a commentary) on Hosea.[44] Allegro assigns four fragments under this title. Strugnell,[45] followed by Horgan,[46] adds Allegro's fragment 2 to

---

41. E. Tov, *Textual Criticism of the Hebrew Bible* (Minneapolis: Fortress, 1992).

42. D. Barthélemy and J. T. Milik, *Qumran Cave I*, DJD 1 (Oxford: Clarendon, 1955), 77-80 and pl. xv.

43. M. P. Horgan, *Pesharim: Qumran Interpretations of Biblical Books*, CBQMS 8 (Washington, D.C.: Catholic Biblical Association, 1979).

44. J. M. Allegro, *Qumrân Cave 4*, vol. 1: *4Q158–4Q186*, DJD 5 (Oxford: Clarendon, 1968), 36 and pl. xii.

45. J. Strugnell, "Notes en Marge du Volume V des 'Discoveries in the Judaean Desert of Jordan,'" *Revue de Qumran* 7 (1969-71) 204.

46. Horgan, *Pesharim*, 261-62.

4QpHos[b] and places fragments 9 and 36 of 4QpHos[b] with 4QpMic. The document cites Mic 4:8-12 without commentary, making it questionable whether the document is a *pesher*. Horgan cautions that the reconstruction of the text is uncertain. It contains one material variant from MT (cf. commentary at 4:9).

4. *Wadi Murabba'at.* Designated Mur 88 or Mur XII and written about the time of the Second Jewish Revolt, this long scroll of the Minor Prophets found in Wadi Murabba'at Cave 5 contains portions from Joel 2:20 to Zech 1:4, including almost all of Micah.[47] Virtually identical with the text printed in *BHS*, its nine variants from the 1,600 words of the *BHS* are incidental: the change of a single consonant and the presence or absence of *matres lectionis,* a preposition, or the conjunction *wāw.* Its divisions match those of MT.

5. *Quotations and Allusions from Nonbiblical Texts.* Rabin[48] enumerates eight references to Micah in the Zadokite Documents, half of which represent a text different from MT, but supported by one of the ancient versions. Carmignac[49] prepared a scriptural index to the *Hodayoth,* or Psalms of Thanksgiving, containing quotations or allusions from Micah.

6. *Septuagint* (designated LXX). The text used in this commentary is the critical edition of the Göttingen Septuagint, superbly edited by Joseph Ziegler. Ziegler[50] demonstrated through strict linguistic controls that one translator produced LXX of the Minor Prophets. Regarding LXX of Hosea, Nyberg[51] finds that "it is overly composed of gross misunderstandings, unfortunate readings, and superficial lexical definitions that often are simply forced into conformity to similar Aramaic cognates. Helplessness and arbitrary choice are the characteristic traits of this interpretation." Unaware of Ziegler's study demonstrating the unity of LXX in the Minor Prophets, Gerleman[52] not surprisingly reaches the same conclusions: "The *Vorlage* of the Greek translator was not identical

---

47. P. Benoit, J. T. Milik, and R. de Vaux, *Les Grottes de Murabba'ât,* 2 vols., DJD 2 (Oxford: Clarendon, 1961), 181-205 and pls. xvi-lxxiii.

48. C. Rabin, *The Zadokite Documents* (Oxford: Clarendon, 1954), 79.

49. J. Carmignac, "Les Citations de l'Ancien Testament, et Spécialement des Poèmes du Serviteur, dans les Hymnes de Qumran," *Revue de Qumran* 2 (1959-60) 357-94.

50. J. Ziegler, "Die Einheit der Septuaginta zum Zwölfprophetenbuch," *Verzeichnis der Vorlesungen an der Staatlichen Akademie zu Braunsberga* (1934-35), 1-16; repr. in Ziegler's *Sylloge: Gesammelte Aufsätze zur Septuaginta,* Mitteilungen des Septuaginta-Unternehmens der Akademie der Wissenschaften in Göttingen 10 (Göttingen: Vandenhoeck & Ruprecht, 1971), 29-42.

51. H. S. Nyberg, *Studien zum Hoseabuche: Zugleich ein Beitrag zur Klärung des Problems der alttestamentlichen Textkritik,* Uppsala Universitets Årsskrift 1935/6 (Uppsala: Almqvist & Wiksells, 1935), 116.

52. G. Gerleman, *Zephanja textkritisch und literarisch untersucht* (Lund: Gleerup, 1942), 85-86.

with the consonantal text of the MT but close to it. The *Vorlage* had neither vowel signs nor vowel letters. . . . The translator is very free in his interpretation of the MT. His work points to an innumerable number of wrong vocalizations, unfortunate divisions of the text, and superficial lexical definitions. . . . Finally, it seems fairly clear that the capabilities of the translator were not always up to mastering certain words and expressions that are difficult to translate. Therefore he occasionally resorted to conjecture." Independently, I reached the same conclusions for LXX of Micah.

7. *Kaige-Theodotion.* Barthélemy[53] demonstrates that the Greek OT manuscript found at Naḥal Hever — representing a text widely used during the first century A.D. — was characterized by an attempt to bring LXX more in line with the standardized text type used by the Masoretes.

8. *Aquila* (A.D. 130), *Symmachus* (Sym; 170), *Theodotion* (180), and *Origen* (230) conformed the Greek text even more closely to the proto-MT.[54]

9. *Syriac Peshitta* (Syr). For the text of the relatively late version of the OT Syriac I used the Brill critical edition, *The Old Testament in Syriac according to the Peshitta Version* (in which Gelston prepared the Minor Prophets). Schwantes[55] agrees with Nyberg[56] that on the whole MT is better than the Peshitta; that the Peshitta stands closer to MT than to LXX; and that MT preserves a feeling for rhythm that is absent from Syriac.

10. *Old Latin.* Lacking a critical edition of the Old Latin version (or versions?) of Micah, I depended on the critical notes in *BHS*, which are based on several manuscripts.[57]

11. *Latin Vulgate* (Vg). For Jerome's translation of the Hebrew Scriptures into Latin, which was prepared about A.D. 400, I used Weber's *Biblia Sacra iuxta Vulgatam Versionem.* The Vulgate is of very limited value in recovering the original text of Micah. It mostly agrees with the official Hebrew text, and when it agrees with LXX or later versions against MT, it may not represent an independent witness to a different Hebrew text because it was influenced by them.

12. *Aramaic Targums (Tg).* For the official Aramaic Targum of Micah, I relied on the critical edition edited by Sperber *(Bible in Aramaic).*

---

53. D. Barthélemy, *Les Devanciers d'Aquila: Première Publication Intégrale du Texte des Fragments du Dodécaprophéton,* VTSup 10 (Leiden: Brill, 1963).

54. F. Field, *Origenis Hexaplorum quae supersunt; sive Veterum Interpretum Graecorum,* 2 vols. (Oxford: Clarendon, 1875; repr. Hildesheim: Olms, 1964).

55. S. J. Schwantes, "A Critical Study of the Text of Micah" (Ph.D. diss., Johns Hopkins University, 1962), 13.

56. Nyberg, *Studien zum Hoseabuche,* 253-54.

57. E. Würthwein, *The Text of the Old Testament: An Introduction to the Biblia Hebraica,* tr. E. F. Rhodes (Grand Rapids: Eerdmans, 1979), 88-90.

13. *Emendation.* When no text or version satisfied exegetical expectations, I emended the text.

VI. Select Bibliography

Abou-Assaf, Ali, Pierre Bordreuil, and Alan R. Millard. *La Statue de Tell Fekherye et Son Inscription Bilingue Assyro-Araméenne.* Recherche sur les Civilisations, Cahier 7. Paris: ADPF, 1982.

Aharoni, Miriam, and Yohanan Aharoni. "The Stratification of Judahite Sites in the 8th and 7th Centuries B.C.E." *BASOR* 224 (1976) 73-90.

Aharoni, Yohanan. *The Land of the Bible: A Historical Geography.* Translated and edited by Anson F. Rainey. 1st ed. Philadelphia: Westminster, 1967. 2d ed., 1979.

————. "Trial Excavation in the 'Solar Shrine' at Lachish: Preliminary Report." *IEJ* 18 (1968) 157-69.

Ahlström, G. "Is Tell ed-Duweir Ancient Lachish?" *PEQ* 112 (1980) 7-9.

————. "Tell ed-Duweir: Lachish or Libnah?" *PEQ* 115 (1983) 103-4.

Albright, W. F. *Archaeology and the Religion of Israel.* Baltimore: Johns Hopkins University Press, 1942.

Allegro, John M. *Qumrân Cave 4,* Vol. 1: *4Q158–4Q186.* DJD 5. Oxford: Clarendon, 1968.

Allen, Leslie C. *The Books of Joel, Obadiah, Jonah, and Micah.* NICOT. Grand Rapids: Eerdmans, 1976.

Alonso-Schökel, Luis. *Estudios de Poética Hebrea.* Barcelona: Flors, 1963.

————. "Is. 10:28-32: Análisis Estilístico." *Bib* 40 (1959) 230-36.

Alt, Albrecht. "Micha 2:1-5: *Gēs Anadasmos* in Juda." *Interpretationes ad Vetus Testamentum Pertinentes Sigmundo Mowinckel Septuagenario Missae,* 13-23. Edited by Nils A. Dahl and Arvid S. Kapelrud. Oslo: Land og Kirche, 1955. Reprinted in Alt's *Kleine Schriften zur Geschichte des Volkes Israel,* 3:373-80. Munich: Beck, 1959.

Alter, Robert. *The Art of Biblical Poetry.* New York: Basic Books, 1985.

Andersen, Francis I., and David Noel Freedman. *Micah: A New Translation with Introduction and Commentary.* AB 24E. New York: Doubleday, 2000.

Anderson, Bernhard W. *Out of the Depths: The Psalms Speak for Us Today.* Philadelphia: Westminster, 1974. Rev. ed. 1983.

Baker, David W., T. Desmond Alexander, and Bruce K. Waltke. *Obadiah, Jonah, Micah.* TOTC 23a. Downers Grove, Ill.: InterVarsity, 1988.

Barker, Kenneth L. *Micah, Nahum, Habakkuk, Zephaniah.* NAC. Nashville: Broadman & Holman, 1998.

Barthélemy, Dominique. *Les Devanciers d'Aquila: Première Publication Intégrale du Texte des Fragments du Dodécaprophéton.* VTSup 10. Leiden: Brill, 1963.

Barthélemy, Dominique, and Jozef T. Milik. *Qumran Cave I.* DJD [of Jordan] 1. Oxford: Clarendon, 1955.

Bartlett, J. R. "The Use of the Word *rōʾš* as a Title in the Old Testament." *VT* 19 (1969) 1-10.

Bauer, Hans, and Pontus Leander. *Historische Grammatik der hebräischen Sprache des Alten Testamentes.* Halle: Max Niemeyer, 1918-22. Reprinted Hildesheim: Olms, 1962.

Beauchamp, P. *Le Deutero-Isaïe dans le Cadre de l'Alliance.* Lyon: Cours de la Faculté de Théologie de Fourvière, 1970.

Begrich, Joachim. "Die priesterliche Tora." Pp. 63-88 in *Werden und Wesen des Alten Testaments: Vorträge gehalten auf der Internationalen Tagung alttestamentlicher Forscher zu Göttingen vom 4.–10. September 1935.* Edited by Paul Volz, Friedrich Stummer, and Johannes Hempel. BZAW 66. Berlin: Töpelmann, 1936.

Benoit, P., Jozef T. Milik, and Roland de Vaux. *Les Grottes de Murabbaʿât.* 2 vols. DJD 2. Oxford: Clarendon, 1961.

Ben Zvi, Ehud. *Micah.* The Forms of the Old Testament Literature XXIB. Grand Rapids: Eerdmans, 2000.

Bentzen, Aage. *King and Messiah.* London: Lutterworth, 1955.

Berdyaev, Nicolas. *Freedom and the Spirit.* Translated by Oliver F. Clarke. New York: Scribner/London: Bles, 1935.

Bewer, J. W., and Zeev Vilnay. "The Topography of Israel in the Book of the Prophet Micah [Hebrew]." *BJPES* 19 (1939) 1-19.

Boer, Pieter A. H. de. "The Counsellor." Pp. 42-71 in *Wisdom in Israel and in the Ancient Near East: Presented to Professor Harold Henry Rowley.* Edited by Martin Noth and D. Winton Thomas. VTSup 3. Leiden: Brill, 1955.

Bordreuil, P. "Michée 4:10-13 et Ses Paralleles Ougaritiques." *RevSém* 21 (1971) 21-38.

Brongers, H. A. "Alternative Interpretationen des sogenannten *Waw Copulativum*." *ZAW* 90 (1978) 273-77.

———. "Die Partikel *lĕmaʿan* in der biblisch-hebräischen Sprache." *OTS* 18 (1973) 84-96.

Brooks, Beatrice A. "Fertility Cult Functionaries in the Old Testament." *JBL* 60 (1941) 227-53.

Brown, Michael A. "'Is It Not?' or 'Indeed!': *HL* in Northwest Semitic." *Maarav* 4 (1987) 201-19.

Brueggemann, Walter. "'Vine and Fig Tree': A Case Study in Imagination and Criticism." *CBQ* 43 (1981) 188-204.

Buchanan, George W. "Eschatology and the 'End of Days.'" *JNES* 20 (1961) 188-93.

Budde, Karl. "Das Rätsel von Micha 1." *ZAW* 37 (1917-18) 77-108.

Bullinger, E. W. *Figures of Speech.* Grand Rapids: Baker, 1968.

Byington, Steven T. "Plow and Pick." *JBL* 68 (1949) 49-54.

Calvin, John. *Commentaries on the Twelve Minor Prophets,* Vol. 3: *Jonah, Micah, Nahum.* Translated by John Owen. Edinburgh: Calvin Translation Society, 1847. Reprinted Grand Rapids: Baker, 1981.

Carmignac, Jean. "Les Citations de l'Ancien Testament, et Spécialement des Poèmes du Serviteur, dans les Hymnes de Qumran." *Revue de Qumran* 2 (1959-60) 357-94.

———. "Notes sur les Peshârîm." *Revue de Qumran* 3 (1963) 505-38.

Casanowicz, Immanuel M. *Paronomasia in the Old Testament.* Boston: Cushing, 1894.

Cassuto, Umberto. *A Commentary on the Book of Exodus.* Translated by Abraham Israels. Jerusalem: Magnes, 1967.

Cathcart, Kevin J. "Micah 5:4-5 and Semitic Incantations." *Bib* 59 (1978) 38-48.

Cazelles, H. "La Fille de Sion et Théologie Mariale dans la Bible." *Bulletin de la Société Française d'Études Mariales* 1 (1965) 51-71.

Childs, Brevard S. *Memory and Tradition in Israel.* SBT 37. Naperville, Ill.: Allenson/London: SCM, 1962.

Clements, Ronald E. *God and Temple.* Philadelphia: Fortress/Oxford: Blackwell, 1965.

———. "Patterns in the Prophetic Canon." Pp. 42-55 in *Canon and Authority: Essays in Old Testament Religion and Theology.* Edited by George W. Coats and Burke O. Long. Philadelphia: Fortress, 1977.

Clifford, Richard J. *The Cosmic Mountain in Canaan and the Old Testament.* HSM 4. Cambridge, Mass.: Harvard University Press, 1972.

———. "The Use of *hôy* in the Prophets." *CBQ* 28 (1966) 458-64.

Clowney, Edmund P. "Israel and the Church: The New Israel." Pp. 207-20 in *Dreams, Visions, and Oracles: The Layman's Guide to Biblical Prophecy.* Edited by Carl E. Armerding and W. Ward Gasque. Grand Rapids: Baker, 1977.

Collin, Matthieu. "Récherches sur l'Histoire Textuelle du Prophète Michée." *VT* 21 (1971) 281-97.

Craigie, Peter C. *Psalms 1–50.* WBC 19. Waco, Tex.: Word, 1983.

Crenshaw, J. L. "*Wᵉdōrēk ʿal-bāmŏtê ʾāreṣ.*" *CBQ* 34 (1972) 39-53.

Cross, Frank M. "The Council of Yahweh in Second Isaiah." *JNES* 12 (1953) 274-77.

Dahood, Mitchell. *Psalms,* Vol. 1: *1–50.* AB 15. Garden City, N.Y.: Doubleday, 1966.

———. *Psalms,* Vol. 3: *101–150.* AB 17. Garden City, N.Y.: Doubleday, 1970.

———. "Some Ambiguous Texts in Isaiah." *CBQ* 20 (1958) 41-49.

Davies, Graham I. "Tell ed-Duweir = Ancient Lachish: A Response to G. W. Ahlström." *PEQ* 114 (1982) 25-28.

Deissler, Alfons, and Mathias Delcor. *La Sainte Bible,* Vol. 8: *Les Petits Prophètes.* Paris: Letouzey & Ane, 1964.

Demsky, A. "The Houses of Achzib: A Critical Note on Micah 1:14b." *IEJ* 16 (1966) 211-15.

Derousseaux, Louis. *La Crainte de Dieu dans l'Ancien Testament.* Paris: Cerf, 1970.

Dever, William C. "Iron Age Epigraphic Material from the Area of Khirbet el-Kôm." *HUCA* 40-41 (1969-70) 139-204.

De Vries, Simon J. *Yesterday, Today and Tomorrow: Time and History in the Old Testament.* Grand Rapids: Eerdmans, 1975.

Diringer, David. "The Early Hebrew Weights Found at Lachish." *PEQ* 74 (1942) 82-103.

Donner, H. *Israel unter den Völkern.* VTSup 11. Leiden: Brill, 1964.

Driver, G. R. "Birds in the Old Testament." *PEQ* 87 (1955) 5-20, 129-40.

———. "Linguistic and Textual Problems: Minor Prophets, II." *JTS* 39 (1938) 260-73.

Duhm, Bernhard. "Anmerkungen zu den zwölf Propheten, III: Das Buch Micha." *ZAW* 31 (1911) 161-204.

Durham, John I. "*Šālôm* and the Presence of God." Pp. 272-93 in *Proclamation and Presence: Old Testament Essays in Honour of Gwynne Henton Davies.* Edited by John I. Durham and J. Roy Porter. Richmond, Va.: John Knox/London: SCM, 1970.

Edelkoort, A. H. "Prophet and Prophet (Micah 2:16-11; 3:5-8)." *OTS* 5 (1948) 179-89.

Ehrlich, Arnold B. *Randglossen zur hebräischen Bibel,* vol. 5: *Ezechiel und die kleinen Propheten.* Leipzig: Hinrichs, 1912.

Ehrman, Albert. "A Note on *yešaḥ* in Mic. 6:14." *JNES* 18 (1959) 156.

———. "A Note on Micah II,7." *VT* 20 (1970) 86-87.

———. "A Note on Micah 6:14." *VT* 23 (1973) 103-5.

Elliger, Karl. "Die Heimat des Propheten Micha." *ZDPV* 57 (1934) 81-152. Reprinted in Elliger's *Kleine Schriften zum Alten Testament,* pp. 9-71. Edited by Hartmut Gese and Otto Kaiser. Theologische Bücherei 32. Munich: Kaiser, 1966.

Fairbairn, Patrick. *Prophecy Viewed in Respect to Its Distinctive Nature, Its Spe-*

cial Function, and Proper Interpretation. Edinburgh: T&T Clark, 1865. Reprinted Grand Rapids: Baker, 1976.

Feuillet, A. "Un Sommet Religieux de l'Ancien Testament: L'Oracle d'Isaïe XIX (v 16-25) sur la Conversion de l'Egypte." *RechScRel* 39 (1951) (*Mélanges Lebreton* I) 63-87.

Field, Frederick. *Origenis Hexaplorum quae supersunt; sive Veterum Interpretum Graecorum.* 2 vols. Oxford: Clarendon, 1875. Reprinted Hildesheim: Olms, 1964.

Finkelstein, Jacob J. "The Middle Assyrian *Sulmānu*-Texts." *JAOS* 72 (1952) 77-80.

Finley, Thomas. *Micah.* Everyman's Bible Commentary. Chicago: Moody, 1996.

Fisher, Loren R. "The Temple Quarter." *JSS* 8 (1963) 32-41.

Fitzmyer, Joseph A. "*Lĕ* as a Preposition and a Particle in Micah 5:1 (5:2)." *CBQ* 18 (1956) 10-13.

Fohrer, G. "Micha 1." In *Das ferne und nahe Wort: Festschrift L. Rost.* Edited by F. Maas. BZAW. Berlin: A. Töpelmann, 1967.

Follis, Elaine R. "The Holy City as Daughter." Pp. 173-84 in *Directions in Biblical Hebrew Poetry.* Edited by Elaine R. Follis. JSOTSup 40. Sheffield: JSOT Press, 1987.

Fuente, G. de la. "Notas al Texto de Miqueas." *Aug Rom* 7 (1967) 145-54.

Gaster, Theodor H. "Notes on the Minor Prophets, 2: Micah V.13." *JTS* 38 (1937) 163-65.

Gerleman, Gillis. *Zephanja textkritisch und literarisch untersucht.* Lund: Gleerup, 1942.

Gordis, Robert. "A Note on *ṭôb*." *JTS* 35 (1934) 186-88.

————. "Quotations as a Literary Usage in Biblical, Oriental, and Rabbinic Literature." *HUCA* 22 (1949) 157-219.

Graetz, H. *Emendations in plerosque Sacrae Scripturae Veteris Testamenti libros.* Edited by W. Bacher. Breslau: Schlesische Buchdruckerei, 1895.

Graham, W. C. "Some Suggestions towards the Interpretation of Micah 1:10-16." *AJSL* 47 (1930-31) 237-58.

Gray, John. *I & II Kings: A Commentary.* 2d ed. OTL. Philadelphia: Westminster, 1970.

Gunkel, Hermann. *Einleitung in die Psalmen: Die Gattungen der religiösen Lyrik Israels.* Edited by Joachim Begrich. Göttingen: Vandenhoeck & Ruprecht, 1933.

Haak, Robert D. "A Study and New Interpretation of *qṣr npš*." *JBL* 101 (1982) 161-67.

Hackett, Jo Ann. *The Balaam Text from Deir 'Allā.* HSM 31. Chico, Calif.: Scholars Press, 1984.

Hagstrom, David Gerald. *The Coherence of the Book of Micah: A Literary Analysis.* SBLDS 89. Atlanta: Scholars Press, 1988.

Halévy, J. "Le Livre de Michée." *RevSém* 12 (1904) 97-117.

Halpern, Baruch. "Jerusalem and the Lineages in the Seventh Century B.C.E.: Kinship and the Rise of Individual Moral Liability." Pp. 11-107 in *Law and Ideology in Monarchic Israel.* Edited by Baruch Halpern and Deborah W. Hobson. JSOTSup 124. Sheffield: Sheffield Academic Press, 1991.

Harris, R. Laird. "The Last Days in the Bible and Qumran." In *Jesus of Nazareth: Saviour and Lord.* Edited by Carl F. H. Henry. Grand Rapids: Eerdmans, 1966.

Harvey, Julien. *Le Plaidoyer Prophétique contre Israël après la Rupture de l'Alliance: Étude d'une Formule Littéraire de l'Ancien Testament.* Bruges/Paris: Desclée de Brower/Montreal: Bellarmin, 1967.

———. "Le 'Rîb-Pattern,' Réquisitoire Prophétique sur la Rupture de l'Alliance." *Bib* 43 (1962) 172-96.

Hasel, Gerhard F. *The Remnant: The History and Theology of the Remnant Idea from Genesis to Isaiah.* Berrien Springs, Mich.: Andrews University Press, 1974.

Haupt, Paul. "The Book of Micah: A New Metrical Translation with Restoration of the Hebrew Text." *AJSL* 26 (1909-10) 201-52; 27 (1910-11) 1-63.

Hermann, S. *A History of Israel in Old Testament Times.* Translated by J. Bowden. London: SCM, 1975.

Herntrick, V. *Der Prophet Jesaja, kap. 1–12.* Das Alte Testament Deutsch. Göttingen: Vandenhoeck & Ruprecht, 1950.

Heschel, Abraham J. *The Prophets.* New York: Harper & Row, 1962.

Hillers, Delbert R. *Covenant: The History of a Biblical Idea.* Baltimore/London: Johns Hopkins University Press, 1969.

———. "*Hôy* and *Hôy*-Oracles: A Neglected Syntactic Aspect." Pp. 185-88 in *The Word of the Lord Shall Go Forth: Essays in Honor of David Noel Freedman.* Edited by Carol L. Meyers and Michael P. O'Connor. Winona Lake, Ind.: Eisenbrauns for the American Schools of Oriental Research, 1983.

———. *Micah: A Commentary on the Book of the Prophet Micah.* Hermeneia. Philadelphia: Fortress, 1984.

Hitzig, Ferdinand. *Die zwölf kleinen Propheten.* Kurzgefasstes exegetisches Handbuch zum Alten Testament 1. Leipzig: Weidmann, 1852.

Honeyman, A. M. "*Merismus* in Biblical Hebrew." *JBL* 71 (1952) 11-18.

———. "The Pottery Vessels of the Old Testament." *PEQ* 71 (1939) 76-90.

Hoonacker, Albin van. *Les Douze Petits Prophètes.* Études Bibliques. Paris: Gabalda, 1908.

Horgan, Maurya P. *Pesharim: Qumran Interpretations of Biblical Books.* CBQMS 8. Washington, D.C.: Catholic Biblical Association, 1979.

Horst, Friedrich. *Hiob.* BKAT 16/1. Neukirchen-Vluyn: Neukirchener, 1968.

Huffmon, Herbert B. "The Covenant Lawsuit in the Prophets." *JBL* 78 (1959) 285-95.

Hyatt, J. Philip. "On the Meaning and Origin of Micah 6:8." *ATR* 34 (1952) 232-39.

Innes, D. K. "Some Notes on Micah, Chapter 1." *EvQ* 39 (1967) 126-28.

————. "Some Notes on Micah." *EvQ* 41 (1969) 10-13, 109-12, 169-71, 216-20.

Jacob, E. *Theology of the Old Testament.* New York: Harper & Row, 1958.

Jacobs, Mignon R. *The Conceptual Coherence of the Book of Micah.* JSOTSup 322. Sheffield: Sheffield Academic, 2001.

Jagersma, Henk. *A History of Israel in the Old Testament Period.* Translated by John Bowden. Philadelphia: Fortress, 1983.

Janzen, Waldemar. *Mourning Cry and Woe Oracle.* BZAW 125. Berlin: de Gruyter, 1972.

Jeppesen, Knud. "Micah 5:13 in the Light of a Recent Archaeological Discovery." *VT* 34 (1984) 462-66.

Jeremias, Joachim. "Moreseth-Gath, die Heimat des Propheten Micha." *PJ* 29 (1933) 42-53.

————. *Theophanie: Die Geschichte einer alttestamentliche Gattung.* WMANT 10. Neukirchen-Vluyn: Neukirchener, 1965.

Joüon, P. *Grammaire de l'Hebreu Biblique.* Rome: Pontifical Biblical Institute, 1923.

Junker, H. "Sancta Civitas, Jerusalem Nova: Eine formkritische und überlieferungsgeschichtliche Studien zu Is 2." in *EKKLESIA: Festschrift für Bischof Dr. Matthias Wehrer.* TThSt 15. Trier: Paulinus, 1962.

Kapelrud, Arvid S. "Eschatology in the Book of Micah." *VT* 11 (1961) 392-405.

Kedar-Kopfstein, Benjamin. "Semantic Aspects of the Pattern *Qôṭel.*" *Hebrew Annual Review* 1 (1977) 155-76.

Keel, Othmar. *The Symbolism of the Biblical World: Ancient Near Eastern Iconography and the Book of Psalms.* Translated by Timothy J. Hallett. New York: Seabury, 1978.

Kellermann, D. "Überlieferungsprobleme alttestamentlicher Ortsnamen." *VT* 28 (1978) 428.

Kenyon, Kathleen M. *Jerusalem: Excavating 3000 Years of History.* New York: McGraw-Hill/London: Thames & Hudson, 1967.

————. *Royal Cities of the Old Testament.* London: Barrie and Jenkins, 1971.

Kirkpatrick, Alexander F. *The Book of Psalms.* Cambridge Bible for Schools and Colleges. Cambridge: Cambridge University Press, 1906.

Kleinert, Paul. *Micah.* Translated by George R. Bliss. Lange's Commentary on the Holy Scriptures 14. Edited by Philip Schaff. New York: Scribner, Armstrong, 1874. Reprinted Grand Rapids: Zondervan, n.d.

Knauf, Ernst A. "Dagesh Agrammaticum im Codex Leningradensis." *Biblische Notizen* 10 (1979) 23-25.

Knierim, Rolf. *Die Hauptbegriffe für Sunde im Alten Testament.* Gütersloh: Mohn, 1965.

Koch, Klaus. "Tempeleinlassliturgien und Dekaloge." Pp. 45-60 in *Studien zur Theologie der alttestamentlichen Überlieferungen: Festschrift für Gerhard von Rad.* Edited by Rolf Rendtorff and Klaus Koch. Neukirchen-Vluyn: Neukirchener, 1961.

König, Eduard. *Historisch-kritisches Lehrgebäude der hebräischen Sprache,* Vol. 2: *Historisch-Comparative Syntax der hebräischen Sprache.* Leipzig: Hinrichs, 1897.

Kopf, Lothar. "Arabische Etymologien und Parallelen zum Bibelwörterbuch." *VT* 8 (1958) 161-215.

Krinetzki, L. "Zur Poetik und Exegese von Ps. 48." *BZ* 4 (1960) 70-92.

Kugel, James L. *The Idea of Biblical Poetry: Parallelism and Its History.* New Haven: Yale University Press, 1981.

Kutzsch, Ernst. *"miqrā'."* *ZAW* 65 (1953) 247-53.

Labuschagne, Casper J. "Amos' Conception of God and the Popular Theology of His Time." *Proceedings of Die Ou-Testamentiese Werkgemeenskap in Suid-Afrika* (1966) 122-33.

———. *The Incomparability of Yahweh in the Old Testament.* Pretoria Oriental Series 5. Leiden: Brill, 1966.

Laetsch, T. *Bible Commentary: The Minor Prophets.* St. Louis: Concordia, 1956.

Lagarde, Paul de. *Onomastica Sacra.* Göttingen: D. L. Horstmann, 1887.

Lambdin, Thomas O. *Introduction to Biblical Hebrew.* New York: Scribner, 1971.

Lefèvre, André. "L'Expression 'en ce jour-là' dans le Livre d'Isaïe." Pp. 174-79 in *Mélanges Bibliques Rédigés en l'Honneur de André Robert.* Paris: Bloud & Gay, [1957].

Lemaire, André. "L'Inscription de Balaam Trouvée à Deir 'Alla: Épigraphie." Pp. 313-25 in *Biblical Archaeology Today: Proceedings of the International Congress on Biblical Archaeology, Jerusalem, April 1984.* Jerusalem: Israel Exploration Society/Israel Academy of Sciences and Humanities/American Schools of Oriental Research, 1985.

Lescow, Theodor. "Das Geburtsmotiv in den messianischen Weissagungen bei Jesaja und Micha." *ZAW* 79 (1967) 172-207.

———. *Micha 6:6-8: Studien zur Sprache, Form, und Auslegung.* Stuttgart: Calwer, 1966.

————. "Redaktionsgeschichtliche Analyse von Micha 6–7." *ZAW* 84 (1972) 182-212.

Leslie, Elmer A. *The Prophets Tell Their Own Story.* New York: Abingdon, 1939.

Lestienne, M. "Les 'Dix Paroles' et le Décalogue." *RB* 79 (1972) 484-510.

Ligier, L. *Péché d'Adam, Péché du Monde.* Paris: Aubier, 1960.

Limburg, James "The Root *ryb* and the Prophetic Lawsuit Speeches." *JBL* 88 (1969) 291-304.

Lindblom, Johannes. *Micha literarisch untersucht.* Acta Academiae Aboensis, Humaniora, 6/2. Åbo: Åbo Åkademi, 1929.

————. *Prophecy in Ancient Israel.* Philadelphia: Fortress/Oxford: Blackwell, 1962.

Lindenberger, James. "Micah 2:12-13: A Promise or Threat." Paper read at the Centre for the History of Biblical Interpretation, Vancouver School of Theology, November 1985.

Lipiński, E. "*B'ḥryt hymym* dans les Textes Preéxiliques." *VT* 20 (1970) 445-50.

Lohfink, Norbert. *Das Hauptgebot: Eine Untersuchung literarischer Einleitungsfragen zu Dtn 5–11.* AnBib 20. Rome: Pontifical Biblical Institute, 1963.

Lutz, Hanns-Martin. *Jahwe, Jerusalem und die Völker: Zur Vorgeschichte von Sach 12:1-8 und 14:1-5.* WMANT 27. Neukirchen-Vluyn: Neukirchener, 1968.

McComiskey, Thomas E. "Micah." Vol. 7, pp. 393-445 in *Expositor's Bible Commentary.* Edited by Frank E. Gaebelein. Grand Rapids: Zondervan, 1985.

Macholz, Georg C. "Die Stellung des Königs in der israelitischen Gerichtsverfassung." *ZAW* 84 (1972) 157-82.

McKane, William. *Proverbs: A New Approach.* OTL. Philadelphia: Westminster/ London: SCM, 1970.

Marti, Karl. *Das Dodekapropheton.* KHC 13. Tübingen: Mohr, 1904.

Martin-Achard, R. "An Exegete before Gen 32,23-33." In *Structural Analysis and Biblical Exegesis: Interpretational Essays.* Pittsburgh: Pickwick, 1974.

Mason, Rex. *Micah, Nahum, Obadiah.* Old Testament Guides. Sheffield: Sheffield Academic, 1991.

May, Herbert C. "The Fertility Cult in Hosea." *AJSL* 48 (1931-32) 73-98.

Mays, James L. *Micah: A Commentary.* OTL. Philadelphia: Westminster, 1976.

Meek, T. J. "Some Emendations in the Old Testament." *JBL* 48 (1929) 162-73.

Melamed, Ezra Z. "Break-up of Stereotype Phrases as an Artistic Device in Biblical Poetry." Pp. 115-53 in *Studies in the Bible.* Edited by Chaim Rabin. Scripta Hierosolymitana 8. Jerusalem: Magnes, 1961.

Mendenhall, George E. *Law and Covenant in Israel and the Ancient Near East.* Pittsburgh: Biblical Colloquium, 1955. Offprinted from *BA* 17 (1954) 26-46, 49-76.

————. *The Tenth Generation: The Origins of the Biblical Tradition*. Baltimore: Johns Hopkins University Press, 1973.

Miller, Patrick D., Jr. "Synonymous-Sequential Parallelism in the Psalms." *Bib* 61 (1980) 256-60.

Moran, William L. "The Ancient Near Eastern Background of the Love of God in Deuteronomy." *CBQ* 25 (1963) 77-87.

Morgenstern, Julian. "The *Ḥᵃsîdîm* — Who Were They?" *HUCA* 38 (1967) 59-73.

Mowinckel, Sigmund. *He That Cometh*. Translated by C. W. Anderson. Nashville: Abingdon/Oxford: Blackwell, 1956.

Nägelsbach, C. *Der Prophet Jesaja*. Bielefeld: Velhagen & Klasing, 1877.

Neiderhiser, Edward A. "Micah 2:6-11: Considerations on the Nature of the Discourse." *BTB* 11 (1981) 104-7.

Nicole, Roger. "Old Testament Quotations in the New Testament." Pp. 43-53 in *Hermeneutics*. By Bernard L. Ramm et al. Grand Rapids: Baker, 1971.

Nielsen, Eduard. *Oral Tradition: A Problem in Old Testament Introduction*. SBT 11. Naperville: Allenson/London: SCM, 1954. 4th ed. 1961.

Noth, Martin. "Jerusalem und die israelitische Tradition." *OTS* 8 (1950) 28-46.

Nowack, Wilhelm. "Bemerkungen über das Buch Micha." *ZAW* 4 (1884) 277-91.

————. "Micha." Pp. 195-238 in *Die kleinen Propheten*. HKAT. Göttingen: Vandenhoeck & Ruprecht, 1922.

Nyberg, Henrik S. *Studien zum Hoseabuche: Zugleich ein Beitrag zur Klärung des Problems der alttestamentlichen Textkritik*. Uppsala Universitets Årsskrift 1935/6. Uppsala: Almqvist & Wiksells, 1935.

O'Connor, Michael P. *Hebrew Verse Structure*. Winona Lake, Ind.: Eisenbrauns, 1980.

Orlinsky, Harry M. "The Textual Criticism of the Old Testament." Pp. 113-32 in *The Bible and the Ancient Near East: Essays in Honor of William Foxwell Albright*. Edited by G. Ernest Wright. Garden City, N.Y.: Doubleday, 1961.

Otto, Rudolf. *The Idea of the Holy: An Inquiry into the Non-rational Factor in the Idea of the Divine and Its Relation to the Rational*. Translated by John W. Harvey. Oxford: Oxford University Press, 1923.

Peiser, F. E. "Micha 5." *Orientalistische Literaturzeitung* 10 (1917) 363-67.

Ploeg, Johannes P. M. van der. "Les Chefs du Peuple d'Israël et Leurs Titres." *RB* 57 (1950) 40-61.

Polzin, R. *Late Biblical Hebrew: Toward an Historical Typology of Biblical Hebrew Prose*. Missoula, Mont.: Scholars Press, 1976.

Pope, Marvin H. *El in the Ugaritic Texts*. VTSup 2. Leiden: Brill, 1955.

Proksch, O. "Gath." *ZDPV* 66 (1943) 174-91.

Pusey, Edward B. "Micah." Vol. 2, in *The Minor Prophets with a Commentary Ex-*

planatory and Practical and Introduction to the Several Minor Prophets. Oxford: Parker 1860. Reprinted Grand Rapids: Baker, 1950.

Rabin, Chaim. *The Zadokite Documents.* Oxford: Clarendon, 1954.

Rad, Gerhard von. *Holy War in Ancient Israel.* Translated by Marva J. Dawn. Grand Rapids: Eerdmans, 1991.

─────. "Die Stadt auf dem Berge." *Evangelische Theologie* (1948) 439-47.

Rainey, Anson F. "The Biblical Shephelah of Judah." *BASOR* 251 (1983) 1-22.

Ramsey, George W. "Speech-Forms in Hebrew Law and Prophetic Oracles." *JBL* 96 (1977) 45-58.

Reicke, Bo. "Liturgical Traditions in Mic. 7." *HTR* 60 (1967) 349-67.

Reinke, Lorenz. *Der Prophet Micha.* Giessen: Roth, 1874.

Relandi, Adriani. *Palestina ex Monumentis Veteribus Illustrata.* Trajecti Batavorum: Broedelet, 1714.

Renaud, Bernard. *La Formation du Livre de Michée: Tradition et Actualisation.* Études Bibliques. Paris: Gabalda, 1977.

─────. *Structure et Attaches Litteraires de Michée IV-V.* Paris: Gabalda, 1984.

─────. *Michée, Sophonie, Nahum.* Paris: Gabalda, 1987.

Ringgren, Helmer. "König und Messias." *ZAW* 64 (1952) 120-47.

Robertson, D. A. *Linguistic Evidence in Dating Early Hebrew Poetry.* Missoula, Mont.: Society of Biblical Literature, 1972.

Robinson, Theodore. "Micha." Pp. 127-52 in *Die zwölf kleinen Propheten.* By Theodore H. Robinson and Friedrich Horst. 1st ed. HAT 14. Tübingen: Mohr, 1938. 2d ed. 1954.

Rudolph, Wilhelm. *Micha, Nahum, Habakuk, Zephanja.* BKAT 13/3. Gütersloh: Mohn, 1975.

Ryder, Stuart A., II. *The D-Stem in Western Semitic.* Janua Linguarum, Series Practica 131. The Hague/Paris: Mouton, 1974.

Ryssel, Victor. *Untersuchungen über die Textgestalt und die Echtheit des Buches Micha.* Leipzig: Hirzel, 1887.

Saarisalo, A. "Topographical Researches in the Shephelah." *JPOS* 11 (1931) 98-99.

Sakenfeld, Katharine D. *The Meaning of Ḥesed in the Hebrew Bible: A New Inquiry.* HSM 17. Missoula, Mont.: Scholars Press, 1978.

Saphir, Athialy P. "The Mysterious Wrath of Yahweh: An Inquiry into the Old Testament Concept of the Suprarational Factor in Divine Anger." Ph.D. diss., Princeton Theological Seminary, 1965.

Sasson, Jack M. "Flora, Fauna and Minerals." Vol. 1, pp. 383-452 in *Ras Shamra Parallels: The Texts from Ugarit and the Hebrew Bible.* Edited by Loren R. Fisher. AnOr 49. Rome: Pontifical Biblical Institute Press, 1972.

Sawyer, John. "What Was a *Mošia*?" *VT* 15 (1965) 475-86.

Schmidt, H. "Micha." Vol. 2, pp. 130-53 in *Die Schriften des Alten Testaments*. Göttingen: Vandenhoeck & Ruprecht, 1915.

———. "Micha." In *Die grossen Propheten*. Göttingen: Vandenhoeck & Ruprecht, 1915.

Schwantes, Siegfried J. "Critical Notes on Micah 1:10-16." *VT* 14 (1964) 454-61.

———. "A Critical Study of the Text of Micah." Ph.D. diss., Johns Hopkins University, 1962.

Sellin, Ernst. "Micha." Pp. 254-303 in *Das Zwölfprophetenbuch*. KAT 12. Leipzig: Deichert, 1911.

Smith, Gary. *Hosea, Amos, Micah*. NIVAC. Grand Rapids: Zondervan, 2001.

Smith, John M. P. *A Critical and Exegetical Commentary on the Books of Micah, Zephaniah, and Nahum*. ICC. Edinburgh: T&T Clark/New York: Scribner, 1911.

Speiser, E. A. "'People' and 'Nation' of Israel." *JBL* 79 (1960) 156-63.

Sperber, Alexander. *The Bible in Aramaic Based on Old Manuscripts and Printed Texts*, Vol. 3: *The Latter Prophets according to Targum Jonathan*. Leiden: Brill, 1962.

Stade, Bernhard. "Bemerkungen über das Buch Micha." *ZAW* 1 (1881) 161-72.

———. "Miszellen: Mich 2,4." *ZAW* (1886) 122-23.

Strugnell, John. "Notes en Marge du Volume V des 'Discoveries in the Judaean Desert of Jordan.'" *Revue de Qumran* 7 (1969-71) 163-276.

Tasker, Randolph V. G. *The Biblical Doctrine of the Wrath of God*. London: Tyndale, 1956.

Taylor, John. *The Massoretic Text and Ancient Versions of the Book of Micah*. 2d ed. London: Williams & Norgate, 1891.

Thomas, D. Winton. "The Root ṣnʿ in Hebrew, and the Meaning of *qdrnyt* in Malachi 3:14." *JJS* 1 (1948-49) 182-88.

Tournay, R. "Bulletin." *RB* 72 (1965) 303.

Tov, Emanuel. *Textual Criticism of the Hebrew Bible*. Minneapolis: Fortress, 1992.

Ungerstern-Sternberg, R. *Der Rechtsstreit Gottes mit seiner Gemeinde, Der Prophet Micha*. Berlin: Calwer, 1958.

Ussishkin, David. "Excavations at Tel Lachish, 1973-1977." *Tel Aviv* 5 (1978) 1-97.

———. "Lachish." Vol. 3, pp. 735-53 in *Encyclopedia of Archaeological Excavations in the Holy Land*. Edited by Michael Avi-Yonah and Ephraim Stern. 4 vols. Englewood Cliffs, N.J.: Prentice-Hall/Jerusalem: Israel Exploration Society/Massada, 1977.

Vaux, Roland de. *Ancient Israel: Its Life and Institutions*. Translated by John McHugh. New York: McGraw-Hill, 1961.

———. *The Early History of Israel*. Translated by David Smith. Philadelphia: Westminster, 1978.

————. "Le 'Reste d'Israël' d'après les Prophètes." *RB* (1933) 526-39.

Vos, Geerhardus. *The Pauline Eschatology*. Princeton: Princeton University Press, 1930.

Vuilleumier, René. "Michée." Pp. 1-92 in *Michée, Nahoum, Habacuc, Sophonie*. By René Vuilleumier and Carl A. Keller. CAT 11b. Neuchâtel: Delachaux & Niestlé, 1971.

Waltke, Bruce K. "Aims of Old Testament Textual Criticism." *WTJ* 51 (1989) 93-108.

————. "The Authority of Proverbs." *Presbyterion* 13 (1987) 77-78.

————. *The Book of Proverbs*. NICOT. 2 vols. Grand Rapids: Eerdmans, 2004, 2005.

————. "Kingdom Promises as Spiritual." Pp. 263-87 in *Continuity and Discontinuity: Perspectives on the Relationship between the Old and New Testaments: Essays in Honor of S. Lewis Johnson, Jr.* Edited by John S. Feinberg. Westchester, Ill.: Crossway, 1988.

————. "The Reliability of the Old Testament Text." Vol. 1, pp. 63-67 in *NIDOTTE*.

Wanke, G. *Die Zionstheologie der Korachiten*. BZAW. Berlin: Töpelmann, 1966.

Watson, Wilfred G. E. "Allusion, Irony, and Wordplay in Micah 1:7." *Bib* 65 (1984) 103-5.

————. "Reclustering Hebrew *l'lyd-*." *Bib* 58 (1977) 213-15.

Weber, Robert, et al., eds. *Biblia Sacra iuxta Vulgatam Versionem*, Vol. 2. 3d ed. Stuttgart: Deutsche Bibelgesellschaft, 1983.

Weiden, W. A. van der. *Le Livre des Proverbes*. Biblica et Orientalia 23. Rome: Pontifical Biblical Institute, 1970.

Weippert, Helga. "Pferde und Streitwagen." Pp. 250-55 in *Biblisches Reallexikon*. Edited by Kurt Galling. 2d ed. HAT 1. Tübingen: Mohr, 1977.

Weiser, Artur. "Micha." Vol. 1, pp. 227-89 in *Das Buch der zwölf kleinen Propheten*. 4th ed. Das Alte Testament Deutsch 24. Göttingen: Vandenhoeck & Ruprecht, 1963.

————. *The Psalms*. OTL. Philadelphia: Westminster, 1962.

Wellhausen, Julius. *Die kleinen Propheten*. Berlin: Georg Reimer, 1898. Reprinted Berlin: de Gruyter, 1963.

Welten, P. *Die Königs-Stempel*. Abhandlungen des Deutschen Palästinavereins. Wiesbaden: Harrassowitz, 1969.

Westermann, Claus. *Basic Forms of Prophetic Speech*. Translated by Hugh C. White. Philadelphia: Westminster, 1967. Reprinted Louisville: Westminster/John Knox and Cambridge: Lutterworth, 1991.

————. *Isaiah 40–66: A Commentary*. Translated by David M. G. Stalker. OTL. Philadelphia: Westminster, 1969.

———. *The Old Testament and Jesus Christ*. Translated by Omar Kaste. Minneapolis: Augsburg, 1970.

———. *Praise of God in the Psalms*. Richmond, Va.: John Knox, 1965.

Wijngaards, J. "*ḥwṣy*' and *h'lh*: A Twofold Approach to the Exodus." *VT* 15 (1965) 91-102.

Wildberger, Hans. *Jesaja*. BKAT 10. Neukirchen-Vluyn: Neukirchener, 1966.

———. "Die Völkerwallfahrt zum Zion: Jes. 2:1-5." *VT* 7 (1957) 62-81.

Williams, James G. "The Alas-Oracles of the Eighth Century Prophets." *HUCA* 38 (1967) 75-91.

Willi-Plein, Ina. *Vorformen der Schriftexegese innerhalb des Alten Testaments: Untersuchungen zum literarischen Werden der auf Amos, Hosea und Micha zurückgehenden Bücher im hebräischen Zwolfprophetenbuch*. BZAW 123. Berlin: de Gruyter, 1971.

Willis, John T. "The Authenticity and Meaning of Micah 5:9-14." *ZAW* 81 (1969) 353-68.

———. "Micah 2:6-8 and the 'People of God' in Micah." *BZ* 14 (1970) 72-87.

———. "Micah 4:14–5:5 — A Unit." *VT* 18 (1968) 529-47.

———. "*mmd ly yṣ*' in Micah 5:1." *Jewish Quarterly Review* 58 (1967-68) 317-22.

———. "A Note on *w'mr* in Micah 3:1." *ZAW* 80 (1968) 50-54.

———. "On the Text of Micah 2:1aα-β." *Bib* 48 (1967) 534-41.

———. "Review of *Micha 6:6-8*, by Theodor Lescow." *VT* 18 (1968) 273-78.

———. "Review of *Structure et Attaches Litteraires de Michée IV–V*, by Bernard Renaud." *VT* 15 (1965) 400-403.

———. "Some Suggestions on the Interpretation of Micah 1:2." *VT* 18 (1968) 372-79.

———. "The Structure of Micah 3–5 and the Function of Micah 5:9-14 in the Book." *ZAW* 81 (1969) 191-214.

———. "The Structure of the Book of Micah." *SEÅ* 34 (1969) 5-42.

———. "The Structure, Setting, and Interrelationships of the Pericopes in the Book of Micah." Ph.D. diss., Vanderbilt University, 1966.

———. "Thoughts on a Redactional Analysis of the Book of Micah." Pp. 87-107 in Vol. 1 of *Society of Biblical Literature Seminar Papers*. Edited by Paul J. Achtemeier. Missoula, Mont.: Scholars Press, 1978.

Wolfe, Roland E. "Micah: Introduction and Exegesis." Vol. 6, pp. 901-49 in *IB*. Edited by George A. Buttrick. Nashville: Abingdon, 1956.

Wolff, Hans W. *Dodekapropheten 4: Micha*. BKAT 14/4. Neukirchen-Vluyn: Neukirchener, 1982.

———. *Micah: A Commentary*. Translated by Gary Stansell. Continental Commentaries. Minneapolis: Augsburg/Fortress, 1990.

————. *Micah the Prophet.* Translated by Ralph D. Gehrke. Philadelphia: Fortress, 1981.

Woude, Adam S. van der. "Micah in Dispute with the Pseudo-Prophets." *VT* 19 (1969) 244-60.

————. *Micha.* De Prediking van het Oude Testament. Nijkerk: Callenbach, 1976.

Wright, G. Ernest. "The Lawsuit of God: A Form-Critical Study of Deuteronomy 32." Pp. 26-67 in *Israel's Prophetic Heritage: Essays in Honor of James Muilenburg.* Edited by Bernhard W. Anderson and Walter Harrelson. New York: Harper/London: SCM, 1962.

————. *The Old Testament against Its Environment.* SBT 2. Chicago: Regnery/London: SCM, 1950.

Würthwein, Ernst. *The Text of the Old Testament: An Introduction to the Biblia Hebraica.* Translated by Erroll F. Rhodes. Grand Rapids: Eerdmans, 1979.

————. "Der Ursprung der prophetischen Gerichtsrede." *ZTK* 49 (1952) 1-16.

Yadin, Yigael. *The Art of Warfare in Biblical Lands in the Light of Archaeological Study.* 2 vols. New York: McGraw-Hill/London: Weidenfeld & Nicolson, 1963.

Zevit, Ziony. "A Chapter in the History of the Israelite Personal Names." *BASOR* 250 (1983) 1-16.

Ziegler, Joseph. "Beiträge zum griechischen Dodekapropheton." *Nachrichten der Akademie der Wissenschaften in Göttingen, philologisch-historische Klasse* (1943) 345-412. Reprinted in Ziegler's *Sylloge: Gesammelte Aufsätze zur Septuaginta,* 71-138. Mitteilungen des Septuaginta-Unternehmens der Akademie der Wissenschaften in Göttingen 10. Göttingen: Vandenhoeck & Ruprecht, 1971.

————. *Duodecim Prophetae.* 3d ed. Septuaginta Vetus Testamentum Graecum 13. Göttingen: Vandenhoeck & Ruprecht, 1984.

————. "Die Einheit der Septuaginta zum Zwölfprophetenbuch." *Verzeichnis der Vorlesungen an der Staatlichen Akademie zu Braunsberga* (1934-35) 1-16. Reprinted in Ziegler's *Sylloge: Gesammelte Aufsätze zur Septuaginta,* 29-42. Mitteilungen des Septuaginta-Unternehmens der Akademie der Wissenschaften in Göttingen 10. Göttingen: Vandenhoeck & Ruprecht, 1971.

COMMENTARY

SUPERSCRIPTION (1:1)

1   The word of *I AM* that came to Micah the Moreshtite in the days of Jotham, Ahaz, and Hezekiah, kings of Judah, which he prophesied concerning Samaria and Jerusalem.

EXEGESIS

1 *dĕbar (word)* is a collective singular, gathering up into itself about twenty oracles contained in this book, which is edited as a unified whole and so refers to the whole book. Elsewhere the singular may designate individual prophecies (cf. Isa 1:10; 28:13; Jer 1:4; Amos 7:16). *yhwh* (of *I AM*) is a genitive of authorship. G. Gerleman[1] noted that this singular construct chain occurs 242 times in the OT and almost always (225 times) appears as a technical form for the prophetic revelation.

'ăšer (that) introduces the first of two relative clauses modifying the topic of this title, "the word of *I AM*." *hāyâ (came)*, a qal constative perfective,[2] also represents as a singular event the many revelations that came to Micah during the days of Jotham, Ahaz, and Hezekiah. *hyh* commonly designates an event coming into being. *mîkâ (Micah)* is a sentence name consisting of three parts,

---

1. G. Gerleman, *Theologisches Handwörterbuch zum Alten Testament*, 2 vols. (München: C. Kaiser, 1971) (hereafter *THAT*), 1:439.

2. B. K. Waltke and M. P. O'Connor, *Introduction to Biblical Hebrew Syntax* (Winona Lake, Ind.: Eisenbrauns, 1989) (hereafter *IBHS*), §31.1.

mî "who," *kā* "is like," and [*yā*]*h* "Yah" (cf. *mîkāyh* in Jer 26:18). In the Bible, 194 names terminate in either a short form, -*yâ*, or a long form, -*yāhû*, both theophoric suffixes for *yhwh (I AM)*. The name of Micah of Moresheth (ca. 725 B.C.), which through syncopation develops from *mîkāyâ* to *mîkâ*, exhibits the short form in contrast to the long form found in the name of Micaiah (*mîkāyĕhû*) ben Imlah, a Northern prophet at the time of Elijah (ca. 850 B.C.; 1 Kgs 22:8; 2 Chr 18:7). This difference between the long and short forms is consistent with Ziony Zevit's conclusion,[3] which was drawn from both biblical and extrabiblical evidence, that the shorter form developed in Israel by the beginning of the eighth or the end of the ninth centuries and in Judah by the second half of the eighth century.

LXX[B] et al. *ton tou mōrasthi* "the one of Morashti," with the Coptic, Ethiopic, and Arabic, understand *hammōraštî* (the Morashtite) as the name of Micah's father. Syriac (hereafter Syr) and Tg and most LXX recensions more properly interpret the definite noun as a place name with a gentilic suffix[4] (so also Jer 26:18). The full name of Micah's hometown was probably Moresheth Gath (cf. 1:14), and so close to that celebrated city in the Philistine pentapolis.

bîmê yôtām 'āḥāz yĕḥizqîyâ (in the days of Jotham, Ahaz, and Hezekiah) consists of a construct governing a coordinate noun phrase,[5] a temporal genitive.[6] *yĕḥizqîyâ (Hezekiah)*, meaning "May *I AM* strengthen," has the form found in Isa 1:1; Hos 1:1; 1 Chr 4:41; 2 Chr 28:27 in contrast to *ḥizqîyāhû* "My strength is *I AM*" (2 Kgs 16:20; 18:1; Jer 26:18-19). It is unnecessary for the interpretation of the book to untangle the bramble patches in the complex history of the second half of the eighth century, especially with reference to Hezekiah. Roughly speaking, these Judean kings and their dates are Jotham (740-733), Ahaz (735-715), and Hezekiah (715-687) (cf. 2 Kgs 15:5–20:21 and 2 Chr 27:1–32:33), which give the maximum limit for Micah's ministry as fifty-three years and the minimum limit as twenty years. Since Sennacherib's invasion of Jerusalem in 701 B.C. is certainly in view in such prophecies as 1:8-16, Micah's ministry should be extended down to at least that date. His earliest datable prophecy, the downfall of Samaria (1:2-7), must antedate 722 B.C.

malkê yĕhûdâ (kings of Judah) stands as a qualifying apposition to the three mentioned kings. LXX's *hyper hōn* relates the second relative clause to "the kings of Judah," the nearer antecedent, rather than to "the word of *I AM*."

---

3. Z. Zevit, "A Chapter in the History of Israelite Personal Names," *BASOR* 250 (1983) 14-15).

4. *IBHS* §5.7.

5. *IBHS* §9.3.

6. *IBHS* §9.5.1.

Vg rightly relates it to the latter (cf. its parallel use even to the addition with *'al* in Isa 1:1; 2:1; Amos 1:1; cf. Isa 13:1; Hab 1:1).

Whereas in English syntax the first relative *'ăšer (that)* introduces a restrictive clause that modifies "the word of *I AM*," the second *'ăšer (which)* introduces a nonrestrictive clause, also modifying the same topic. Once again, the qal constative perfective singular *ḥāzâ (prophesied)* represents the revelations that came to Micah over a span of about fifty years as a single event. This verb occurs in twenty-four out of about fifty usages with reference to the prophetic experience and in that connection means to experience passively and/or deliver actively a revelatory vision and/or audition. In the passive sense of receiving the vision it can be rendered by "saw" (cf. Num 24:4, 16) and/or possibly by "heard" (cf. Isa 2:1, where "word," as here, is the subject) and in the active sense by "prophesy" (cf. Isa 30:10). This verb for "seeing" is used with reference to an auricular experience because the Hebrew associates diverse sorts of vivid sensations with the eyes (cf. Exod 5:21). An uninterpreted visual image is never mentioned with this word.[7] Balaam describes his revelation as both visual and auricular (Num 24:4-5, 15-16). Probably this title does not intend to distinguish precisely between the prophet's passive experience, whether it be visual (cf. Mic 1:3) and/or auricular, and the active sense of revealing the word of *I AM* (cf. 2:6).

The adverbial preposition *'al (concerning)* introduces the addressees, *Samaria and Jerusalem*, a metonymy for the leaders, civic rulers, ecclesiastical priests, and gifted prophets (cf. ch. 3), and a synecdoche for both nations (cf. 6:1–7:8). In only one prophecy, 1:2-7, are both capitals singled out. Elsewhere, Jerusalem and so Judah are principally in view but called "Israel" and treated as representative of the whole nation (see 1:1).

EXPOSITION

Either Micah himself or a later editor adds the prose narrative title, which in syntax and theme is unrelated to the rest of the book. It is the sixth book among the twelve Minor Prophets according to the essentially chronological arrangement in the Hebrew canon, Peshitta, Vg, and English versions. In the LXX it stands third after Amos, probably on account of its length. Micah's prose form is well suited to state particular, historical information in contrast to the poetry found in the rest of the book, which is best suited to elevate the audience into cosmic, universal truth.

7. Cf. A. Jepsen, *"chāzāh,"* TDOT 4:283, and A. S. van der Woude, *"ḥzh,"* THAT 1:536.

This title, lacking a predicate, contains a topic, "the word of *I AM*," quali-fied by two relative clauses indicating first the human author and his times and secondly the manner of communication between the divine author and the human author and the addressees. In this way it succinctly states the divine author, the human author, the mode of communication between them, the historical situation, and the addressees. In Hos 1:1, Joel 1:1, and Zeph 1:1 (cf. Jo-nah 1:1; Hag 1:1; Zech 1:1) only the revelatory event is mentioned, and in Isa 1:1 (cf. Hab 1:1) only the mode of communication qualifies the topic, "the vision of Isaiah."

Most emphatically the book's audience is told that it is about to hear "the word of *I AM*," its divine author. In contrast to Isa 1:1, Jer 1:1, Amos 1:1, and Nah 1:1, which read "the words/vision of so and so," putting the accent on the prophet and/or the diversity of his messages, in Mic 1:1 the focus is on the di-vine origin of the prophet's message. The collective singular has the book as a whole in view. In this book the invisible God becomes audible.[8]

The expression "that came" underscores the kerygmatic dynamics of the revelatory experience. In contrast to Isaiah, Jeremiah, Ezekiel, and Amos, Micah gives us no autobiographical account of his call to ministry. B. Renaud,[9] though aiming to show a later Deuteronomistic influence in the composition of the ti-tle, judiciously commented regarding the topic and this modifier: "It places the accent upon the divine origin of the prophetic word — it is the very word of God — and, as a consequence, upon its embracing [*englobante*] value: one does not speak . . . of words in the plural or of such and such a prophet, but of the Word of *I AM*, which almost takes the figure of a hypostasis and which happens as an event in the life of the prophet." The book is not only the word of *I AM* in the sense that Micah bears witness to his experience but more importantly in the sense that the triune God bears witness to himself through that revelation. Were that not so, the book would be neither revelatory nor Holy Scripture. For saints, on the one hand, God speaks with authority (cf. 2 Cor 4:20; 1 Thess 1:5), and so the Word of God also comes to them as a kerygmatic event. For them, as in the case of Hezekiah, it brings repentance (cf. Jer 26:18-20). For others, on the other hand, it hardens judgment, as *I AM* said to Isaiah, Micah's contemporary in Jerusalem (Isa 6:9-13). In either case it will not return to him empty but will accomplish what he wills (Isa 55:10-11).

One must not introduce pagan mythological thinking about words here. According to an almost universally held opinion among OT scholars, the bibli-

---

8. Cf. A. J. Heschel, *The Prophets* (New York: Harper & Row, 1962), 22.

9. B. Renaud, *La Formation du Livre de Michée: Tradition et Actualisation*, Études Bibliques (Paris: Gabalda, 1977) (hereafter *La Formation*), 5.

cal writers held the magical view that, as E. Jacob[10] put it, "A spoken word is . . . an operative reality whose action cannot be hindered once it has been pronounced." Note, however, that according to Deut 18:21-22 one could distinguish *I AM*'s words from false words by whether or not what a prophet proclaimed came true or not. Also, Isa 55:10-11 assigns the power of God's words not to the words themselves but to God, who sovereignly uses them according to his own pleasure. Finally, Jer 18:5-10 says that the fulfillment of the prophecy depends on the response of the audience. A threat of judgment will not land if the cursed repent, and a promised blessing will not happen if the blessed apostatize. This very thing happened in Micah's preaching. He predicted the downfall of Jerusalem (Mic 3:12), but Hezekiah repented and *I AM* relented. To be sure, sometimes the word of *I AM* is personified (cf. Isa 9:8; Ps 107:20), but as G. Gerleman suggests,[11] this usage is nothing more than the normal tendency of poets to enliven and personify abstractions. On the other hand, in biblical theology "words" function differently than they do in the view of most moderns. In their worldview, words can influence the minds of hearers and, in that sense, historical events. In biblical theology, by contrast, God's words are both creative and destructive. By his word he brought the earth into existence (Gen 1:3 passim; Ps 33:6), and that same word guides the course of history by uprooting some nations and planting others (Jer 1:9-10). God's word is powerful not because it has magical potency but because he sovereignly uses it.

The pattern of Micah's hymnic name is common in pagan literature; for example, one commonly meets in Akkadian reports a name like, "Who is like Sin [the moon-god]." The sentence name of the human author, "Who is like Yah?" is more than a label for identification; it reveals the essence of his parents' faith, who wished above all to praise *I AM*, and it portends our prophet's message. He artfully plays upon his name and its significance when he alludes to *I AM*'s incomparability in pardoning sin: "Who is a God like you, who forgives iniquity?" (7:18). Although Micah does not include autobiographical material about his call, he does tell us that in contrast to false prophets, who like most men were filled with self-ambition, he was filled with zeal for the oppressed, the telltale sign that he was filled with *I AM*'s spirit (3:8). He is not merely *I AM*'s megaphone but a person. He delivered his messages of judgment through tears (1:7-8) and with earnest pleading (6:1-8). He preached, as H. Jagersma[12] noted, with Amos's passion against injustice and Hosea's heart of love. Micah con-

---

10. E. Jacob, *Theology of the Old Testament* (New York: Harper & Row, 1958), 127.

11. *THAT* 1:442.

12. H. Jagersma, *A History of Israel in the Old Testament Period* (Philadelphia: Fortress, 1983), 152.

cludes his book not with dark gloom but with bright hope. As God hurled the Egyptian army into the depths of the sea at the founding of the nation, even more miraculously he will hurl its sins into its depths to be remembered no more (Mic 7:8-20). His messages of judgment rest on the lofty ethical standards given to Israel on Sinai (6:1-8); his messages of hope on God's unchanging faithfulness to Abraham (7:20). As *I AM's* plenipotentiary, Micah was holy; he was *I AM's* property, and touching him incurred God's anger.[13] Rebuffed by his audience (6:6-11), this flashing preacher lifted his almost solitary voice, setting forth the highest ethical standards. Even his prophecies of doom must be valued as *I AM's* gift to his people (cf. Num 23:23; Deut 18:14). Silence is a worse form of judgment (cf. Ezek 7:26; Amos 8:2; Ps 74:9).

Micah was identified by his place of origin rather than by his family, in contrast, for example, to his contemporary, Isaiah son of Amoz. Amos, the prophet to the Northern Kingdom a generation earlier, was known both by his home and by his vocation, "Amos, one of the shepherds of Tekoa." To judge from these parallels, Micah's identification as a Morashtite implies that he was an outsider to the capitals. Were he ministering in his hometown, he would probably have been called "Micah son of so-and-so." Unlike Amos, who did not regard himself and was not regarded by others as a prophet but as a shepherd, Micah had the identity of a "professional" prophet, that is, he belonged to a recognized class of charismatic figures in Israel who shaped the nation's foreign policies through their prophecies. His inspired voice shattered Hezekiah's heart, reshaped Judah's policies, and saved the nation from immediate catastrophe (Jer 26:17-19).

Moresheth is mentioned already in the Tell el-Amarna correspondence (ca. 1350 B.C.), and even, as in Mic 1:13-14, with Lachish. If Moresheth Gath is its full name, it is identical with Morashti of the Byzantine sources, a village east of Beth Guvrin. It has been identified both with Tell ej-Judeideh, a rather imposing mound 32 km. southwest of Jerusalem and 10 km. northeast of Lachish, and with Tell el-Menshiyeh, about 7 km. southwest of Tell ej-Judeideh and 10 km. west of Beth Guvrin. In either case, it lay about halfway between Jerusalem and Gaza, near the ancient Philistine city of Gath (modern Tell eṣ-Ṣâfî) and the ancient Judean stronghold of Lachish, which guarded the southwestern approach into the Shephelah.

The Shephelah ("Lowland"), a homogeneous zone of Eocene limestone, plays a prominent role in Micah's oracles against the towns located there (cf. Mic 1:8-16). The Negev lies just south of it, separated from it by the narrow pass formed by a break in the Eocene ridges just north of Tel Halif. Moresheth Gath

---

13. Cf. J. Lindblom, *Prophecy in Ancient Israel* (Philadelphia: Fortress, 1962), 203.

stands on the edge of the Shephelah, nearly a thousand feet above the sea, over-looking the undulating coastal plain to its west, dotted with fortified cities. The northern vestiges of the Shephelah's outcrop are the foothills around Gezer and Gimzo (cf. 2 Chr 28:18). On the east it is separated from Judah's high Cenomanian limestone ridges, called "The Hill Country" in the OT, by a long, narrow trough created by the exposure of Senonian chalk. This north-south line of lower hills formed a geographical buttress for the Judean hill country east of it. Its geopolitical importance was enhanced by several valleys that traversed it from east to west, giving access to the higher terrain and especially to Jerusalem, located on one of the summits. A foreign army aiming to capture Judah's king in his mountain must first remove the pawn-like towns in the Shephelah. Solomon fortified Gezer, and his son Rehoboam fortified many other towns in the Shephelah, in order to guard the western approaches to Jerusalem. Assyrian reliefs picture the invader assailing Gezer and Lachish. Micah's homeland bore the brunt of successive Assyrian invasions during his lifetime. In contrast to Amos's home, which, lying just on the eastern summits of Judah's central ridge, is bare desert, the broad traversing valleys separating the irregular chalk hills of the Shephelah are rich and red with alluvial soil, with room for grainfields on either side of the perennial or almost perennial streams. Growing up with stalwart men who owned and farmed these fields, Micah sympathized profoundly with their sufferings and the wrongs done to them by oppressive tyrants. In corrupt courts these bureaucratic sharks finagled the farmers' patrimonies away from them. Micah fearlessly championed their cause (cf. Mic 2:1-11). He has often been called "the prophet of the poor"; more accurately, he is a prophet of the oppressed, which in his days included the middle class (cf. 2:6-11). He gave voice to the sighs of the oppressed, too weak to have a voice.

By mentioning the kings of Judah by name while also indicating that he is addressing the Northern Kingdom, Micah conspicuously omits mention of their contemporary peers in the North, Menahem (745-737 B.C.), Pekaiah (737-736), Pekah (736-732), and Hoshea (732-724). Like the other prophets of the second half of the seventh century B.C., Isaiah and Hosea, he omits their names because they usurped *I AM*'s throne through assassinations; they set themselves up but not by *I AM*'s prophetic designation (Hos 8:4). This interpretation finds confirmation in the mention by Amos and Hosea of Jeroboam II, a Northern king who had prophetic endorsement by reason of his being the third generation in Jehu's lineage (2 Kgs 10:30; 15:10-12). By specifying the time of revelation, the title rules out the notions of most modern higher critics that some of the prophecies date from after the time of Micah (see the Introduction, pp. 8-13).

The second half of the eighth century was an extremely troubled time in Israel's history. The Assyrian kings, in carrying out their policy of imperialistic expansion, one after another stomped through the pleasant land and successively lopped off portions of it. In contrast to the freestanding armies of the Western States, the Assyrian kings maintained an imperial army of professional mercenaries paid for by the tribute they demanded from their conquered subjects. States that refused to pay were ruthlessly smashed. In ca. 740 B.C. Tiglath-pileser III (= Pul, his Babylonian throne name; 1 Chr 5:26) (745-727 B.C.) received a crushing tribute from Rezin of Damascus and from Menahem of Samaria (2 Kgs 15:17-22) and shortly after this organized North Syria into an Assyrian province. Menahem, to secure the Assyrian king's favor and confirm him on the throne, gave him a thousand talents of silver. In 734 Tiglath-pileser penetrated Israel's coastal plain, marched through Philistia close to Micah's hometown, and reached the Wadi el-Arish in the Sinai. Pekah, having assassinated Pekaiah son of Menahem and follower of his father's pro-Assyrian policy, allied himself with Rezin to throw off the Assyrian yoke. Together they put pressure on Ahaz to compel him to join them and also to secure their southern flank. Following his refusal, they marched up to Jerusalem to depose him in order to put Tabeel, a Syrian pawn of their own, on the Judean throne. In spite of Isaiah's objections (Isaiah 7), Ahaz enlisted Tiglath-pileser's help by voluntarily becoming his vassal, that is, by submitting himself to his religion and offering him a huge tribute. The Assyrian king, all too glad to intervene further in Palestinian affairs, responded quickly. He devastated Damascus in 732 B.C., occupied Galilee and Trans-jordan, and confirmed Hoshea on the throne of the rump state of Israel after the latter had assassinated Pekah. This profaning of the holy land clearly signaled that *I AM* was exacting the curses threatened in his covenant with Israel (Leviticus 26; Deut 28:15-68). When Shalmaneser V (726-722) succeeded his father Tiglath-pileser, the time seemed opportune for Hoshea to rebel. He formed an alliance with So, king of Egypt, and withheld the despised tribute. Shalmaneser besieged the city in 724, and his successor, Sargon (721-705), finished mopping up the city. In order to neutralize the land against further revolts, Assyria deported Israel's upper classes and imported other races to take their place. The once-proud kingdom of the North now became incorporated as an Assyrian province under the name of Samaria. Prophets such as Jeremiah (31:20), Ezekiel (37:15), and Nahum (2:2) sustained the hope that the Northern Kingdom would be restored to a theocracy in Israel's golden future. Whereas others used the name "Israel" as a theological term for the whole nation, Micah used it as a political term for Judah as well, reflecting his political views for a unified Israel. Hezekiah tried but failed to make it a historical reality (2 Chr 30:1-12).

As we noted on pp. 6-8, in 720 Sargon annexed Hamath wholly into the empire, and Gaza in southwest Palestine became an Assyrian province. Shortly after Hezekiah had fully assumed the throne, Ashdod refused to pay the tribute, stirred up Edom and Moab to join the coalition, and looked to Hezekiah to reverse his father's pro-Assyrian policy. Isaiah influenced official policy in Judah against joining the folly by going around Jerusalem barefoot and stripped, dramatizing the plight of an exile. In 713 Sargon deposed the ruler of Ashdod and took other cities along the Philistine plain. Although Hezekiah initiated sweeping reforms to purify the temple worship (2 Kgs 18:3-6; 2 Chr 29:1-19), restored the Passover (2 Chr 29:20–31:23), and repented for the social corruptions against which Micah preached (Jer 26:18), against prophetic advice he refused to pay the tribute. When Sennacherib (705-686) succeeded his father Sargon, Hezekiah joined a coalition of several states, including Merodach-baladan who had reestablished himself in Babylon (2 Kings 20; Isaiah 39), and withheld the tribute. He also probably counted on Judah's favored position in occupying both the Shephelah and high central ridge that towered over the Philistine plain. As part of his defense he also dug a tunnel to ensure water supplies in case of siege (2 Kgs 20:20). In addition, he relied on Egypt, "a broken reed," according to Isaiah (Isa 30:1-5; 31:18). Isaiah predicted that as a result of Hezekiah's folly in joining Merodach-baladan, involving his folly of succumbing to the blandishments of the Babylonians and in showing off his military might and his wealth, Judah would one day fall to the Babylonians.

Micah was in total agreement with Isaiah that Judah would be punished for this folly (Mic 1:8-16), including deportation to Babylon (cf. Mic 4:9-10). Occupied in Babylon, Sennacherib did not respond until 701 B.C. He rushed through Syria, Phoenicia, and down the plain of Sharon, encountering very little opposition. Once Joppa, at the southern end of the Sharon, had been subdued, he directed his full force against the cities lying along the coastal plain. He then moved into the Shephelah, taking forty-six strong cities, including the nine mentioned in Mic 1:10-15, the most important of which was Lachish. Excavations there uncovered a huge pit into which the Assyrians had dumped some 1,500 bodies and covered them with pig bones and other debris, presumably the Assyrian army's garbage. At the same time that he was besieging Lachish he also hemmed in Jerusalem with an overwhelming army (2 Kgs 18:17; Isa 36:2; 2 Chr 32:9). Jerusalem at this time had mushroomed to over three or four times its former size and was thronged with refugees from both fallen Samaria and from the conquered cities of Judah (cf. Mic 2:12). After Lachish fell, the Assyrians turned to Libnah (2 Kgs 19:8-9; Isa 37:8). At this point Tarhaqah, brother of Shabaka, led the combined forces of Nubia and Egypt to intervene (2 Kgs 19:9; Isa 37:9), but Sennacherib decisively defeated them in the plain of Eltekeh, a part of the coastal plain level with Jerusalem. Hezekiah now repented and with Isaiah prayed for a miraculous deliverance. Both Micah and Isaiah boldly predicted the impossible (2 Kgs 18:17–19:34; 2 Chr 32:1-23). The Bible attributes Hezekiah's deliverance to the angel of *I AM* (2 Kgs 19:35-36; Isa 37:36-37; 2 Chr 32:22-23), whose earthly instrument was probably a bubonic plague carried by rats, an inference drawn from Herodotus's account that in a dream Pharaoh Sethos was promised the help of a deity against Sennacherib and that during the night an army of field mice destroyed the Assyrian equipment so that they had to flee without their weapons.

The manner of revelation, "saw/heard/prophesied," has important hermeneutical implications. God spoke at many times and in diverse ways in the OT (Heb 1:1); to Moses he spoke face to face (Exod 33:11; Deut 34:11), and to his inspired sages through their observations of the created order and their reflections upon it (cf. Prov 2:6; 24:32). To prophets he communicated his message through dreams and visions, that is, through revelatory, dream-like visions and auditions, which they in turn delivered to their audiences (cf. Num 24:3-4, 15-16). The difference is important in interpreting Holy Scripture. Inferior forms of revelation, such as the riddle-like visions of the prophets in contrast to the clear, face-to-face encounters of God with Moses, carry less weight than superior forms of revelation, as God makes clear to the prophet Aaron and the prophetess Miriam in Num 12:6-8. So also, the clearest revelation of God in his Son, Jesus Christ, has priority over all OT revelations. As I have argued,[14] if there be any tension between our interpretation of the OT and of the NT, priority must be given to the New. More specifically, as I argued elsewhere,[15] the NT does not teach a millennium in which Israel will be reconstructed as a political kingdom once again, but rather a realized eschatology in which Christ's kingdom has come in fulfillment in the church today and will come in consummation in the new cosmos. Micah's prophecies regarding the Messianic Age must be interpreted according to the lucid teachings of the NT, which excludes the symbolic book of Revelation, and not according to a premillennial model, which is built on OT prophecy and apocalyptic literature instead of on the plain teachings of Christ and his apostles. After Pentecost the apostles never mention the national restoration of political Israel. Instead, Paul foresees ethnic Israel's restoration to the kingdom in Christ (Rom 11:1-26).

With regard to the addressees, we need to distinguish two audiences. In the pre-literary stage Micah addressed his oracles to Israel's leadership (magistrates, priests, prophets), especially in Jerusalem. On the literary level (see 3:1 and 6:1), Micah's audience is the covenant community throughout her history. Note that

14. B. K. Waltke, "The Authority of Proverbs," *Presbyterion* 13 (1987) 77-78.
15. B. K. Waltke, "Kingdom Promises as Spiritual," in *Continuity and Discontinuity,* ed. J. S. Feinberg (Westchester, Ill.: Crossway, 1988), 1263-87.

prophecy is the Eternal's word and so continues to endure and live forever (cf. Isa 40:8). Roger Nicole[16] with insight noted that our Lord Jesus Christ and his apostles often cited the OT by using the present tense "he says" rather than "he said," and reinforced its present relevance by the use of the pronouns "we" and "you" instead of "they" and "them." As a result God sovereignly used his message through Micah in his original addressees just as he wields this word in us, as a fragrance of life or death (cf. John 3:8; 1 Pet 1:23-25), through sovereignly endowed men in the church with gifts of utterance (1 Cor 12:1–14:39).

I. First Cycle: God Gathers the Elect Remnant into Jerusalem (1:2–2:13)

A. God Punishes Samaria and Judah (1:2-16)

1. Judgment on Samaria (1:2-7)

2   Hear, O peoples, all of you,
        make yourself attentive, O earth, and its fullness;
    for *I AM* will become a witness against you,
        the Lord from his holy palace!

3   For look! *I AM* is about to come forth from his place;
        and he will come down and tread upon the high places of the earth.

4   And the mountains will melt beneath him,
        and the valleys will split apart,
    like wax melting before a fire,
        like water pouring down a mountain gorge.

5   On account of Jacob's rebellion is all this,
        on account of the sins of the house of Israel.
    What is Jacob's transgression?
        Is it not Samaria?
    And what is Judah's great high place?
        Is it not Jerusalem?

6   Therefore I will make Samaria into a heap of rubble in the field,
        into a place for planting vineyards.
    I will pour down into the valley her stones,
        and her foundations I will lay bare.

---

16. R. Nicole, "Old Testament Quotations in the New Testament," in *Hermeneutics*, ed. B. Ramm et al. (Grand Rapids: Baker, 1971), 46.

7   And all her idols will be broken to pieces;
    and all her prostitute wages will be burned with fire;
        and all her images I will make a shocking devastation.
    Since from the wages of prostitutes she collected them,
        they will again be used as wages for prostitutes.

EXEGESIS

2 Micah the Moreshtite's introductory summons; *šim'û 'ammîm kullām (Hear, O peoples, all of you)* seems to echo precisely the concluding summons of Micah son of Imlah. More probably, however, a scribe, perhaps mistaking the two Micahs, glossed the expression into the mouth of the earlier prophet; it is not in the original LXX of either 1 Kgs 22:28 or 2 Chr 18:27. In any case, the two identical expressions have different senses. Whereas Micah son of Imlah summoned the nations to confirm the truthfulness of his prophecy of doom against Israel, Micah of Moresheth summoned them to hear it because it was a witness against them. Hebrew *kullām (all of you)*, woodenly, "all of them," is a genitive of measure.[1] LXX's *akousate, laoi, logous* possibly read *kullām* as *millîm* "words," in which case it attests a final *lm*, not *km*, disallowing one to smooth the text to *kúllĕkem* "all of you" (cf. Syr). The resemblance of *kāp* and *mêm* in both the paleo-Hebrew and early Aramaic square scripts supports this understanding of LXX. S. J. Schwantes[2] notes the same confusion in Mic 1:12; 5:11, 13; 7:20.

The "unexpected" third-person plural pronominal suffix (but see Job 17:10 and, above all, 1 Kgs 22:28 [= 2 Chr 18:27]) may have contributed to the confusion. Hebrew (and classical Arabic) syntax regularly employs the third person in modifying clauses after the vocative.[3] LXX more probably added *logous* and syntactically related *kullām* to the next clause: *kai pantes hoi en autē*. H. W. Wolff[4] is probably right in suggesting that LXX circumvents the syntactical problem entirely by linking "all of them" with the next clause: *kai prosechetō hē gē kai pantes hoi en autē* "And let the earth give heed, and all those in it." The article indicating the vocative is omitted from both *'ammîm (O peoples)* and *'ereṣ (O earth)* in terse prophetic style. *'ammîm (peoples)* denotes a community

---

1. *IBHS* §9.5.2.

2. S. J. Schwantes, "A Critical Study of the Text of Micah" (Ph.D. diss., Johns Hopkins University, 1962), 20.

3. See D. R. Hillers, *Micah* (Philadelphia: Fortress, 1984), 16.

4. H. W. Wolff, *Dodekapropheten 4: Micha*, BKAT 14/4 (Neukirchen-Vluyn: Neukirchener, 1982), 10.

of people, often larger than a clan but less numerous than a race, who are related and unified in some way, by blood, history, and/or culture.[5] Here communities outside of Israel are in view: note both the plural form and the parallel *'ereṣ (earth)*. Hillers[6] thinks that the oracle was addressed originally to the heavenly court, but the text in hand does not represent a mythological background. L. C. Allen[7] helpfully compares Isa 3:13-14.[8] *haqĕšîbî (make yourself attentive)* denotes a conscious, willing, and attentive use of the ears and may be more emphatic than *šim'û (hear)* (cf. Isa 32:3). *'ereṣ (earth)* can denote "earth" in a cosmological sense or, more restrictedly, the "land" of Israel. The latter is screened out by the parallel *'ammîm (peoples)*, a plural, and by the qualifying compound *ûmĕlō'āh*, dwellers capable of hearing as in Isa 23:1.

Wāw with the jussive in *wîhî (for . . . will become)* may or may not be consequential (temporal or logical);[9] a logical connection is probably in view (*contra* NRSV), for the report in v 2B seems to give the basis for the summons in v 2A. *I AM*'s witness against them is a matter of life and death. 1QpMic and Mur 88 read *yhwh 'dny yhyh* "*I AM* the Lord will become" instead of MT's *wîhî 'ădōnāy yhwh* "the Lord *I AM* will become." *'ădōnāy yhwh* is the more frequent reading, 293 times, of which 217 are in Ezekiel, whereas *yhwh 'ădōnāy* occurs only five times (Hab 3:19; Pss 68:20[19]; 109:21; 140:8[7]; 141:8), making the Q reading statistically more difficult. Nevertheless, MT would be preferred because the other reading is found exclusively in hymns. More probably, however, *'ădōnāy* has been glossed from v 2Bb in differing ways in Q and MT, even though it has the support of Vg, Syr, and Tg. Its omission in v 2Ba in LXX further corroborates this suggestion. It seems strange that *I AM* should become *bākem lĕ'ēd (a witness against you)* with reference to the nations, since *I AM* will accuse Samaria and Jerusalem (v 5) and sentence Samaria (vv 6-7). One could ease the tension by rendering *bākem* "among you" (cf. LXX *en hymin*). But B. Renaud[10] rightly disallows this translation because (1) in the expression *lĕ'ēd . . . bĕ* (Exod 20:16; Deut 31:26; Jer 42:5; Prov 25:13) and its related form *'ēd . . . bĕ* (Num 5:13; Deut 31:19; Josh 24:22; 1 Sam 12:5; Mal 3:5; Prov 24:28) *bĕ* always means "against," and (2) "the expression 'among you' would seem to grant to the earth the role of

5. G. Van Groningen, "'*mm*," *TWOT* 2:676; E. A. Speiser, "'Peoples' and 'Nation' of Israel," *JBL* 79 (1960) 156-63.

6. Hillers, *Micah*, 18-19.

7. L. C. Allen, *The Books of Joel, Obadiah, Jonah, and Micah*, NICOT (Grand Rapids: Eerdmans, 1976), 269-70.

8. For an exhaustive survey of the history of interpretation see J. T. Willis, "Some Suggestions on the Interpretation of Micah 1:2," *VT* 18 (1968) 372-79.

9. *IBHS* §35.4.2.

10. *La Formation*, 12.

judge, with *I AM* limiting himself to that of accuser." In fact, however, *I AM* assumes both functions, as accuser (v 5) and as judge (vv 6-7). In Micah 4–5 the sins and salvation of the nations come more clearly into focus.

'ădōnāy (the Lord) is a title denoting sovereignty, a notion reinforced by its suffix, a *status emphaticus,* "Lord of all."[11] The preposition *min* in *mēhêkal (from his holy palace)* implies a verb of motion, namely, *yōṣē' (comes forth)* in v 3. "Palace" signifies a royal residence. Although this makes it a "temple" (cf. NRSV), that rendering obscures the prophet's emphasis on God's royalty and lordship over the earth. J. L. Mays[12] accurately paraphrases "holy palace" in this attributive genitive construction by ". . . the royal residence sanctified by his presence." Although elsewhere this language could denote *I AM's* temple on Zion, the imagery of *I AM's* descent in v 3 shows that the heavenly palace of the Lord of all is in view (cf. 1 Kgs 8:30; Ps 11:4), and Mic 3:12 designates the earthly mount as profane and about to be leveled. *I AM's* holiness prompts his epiphany in holy war in v 3.

3 *kî (for)* logically introduces the reason (vv 3-7) for the summons. *hinnēh (look!)* may either emphasize "the immediacy, the here-and-now-ness," of the situation or function "to introduce a fact upon which a following statement . . . is based."[13] In the latter sense it would mean, "For since *I AM* is coming forth . . . , the mountains melt. . . ." The former nuance is preferred because it commonly occurs with participles, as here, and the latter nuance is probably contradicted by the verse divisions. *BHS* for metrical reasons arbitrarily,[14] against all textual witnesses, emends *hinnēh yhwh* into *hinnēhû.* The participial form *yōṣē' (is about to come forth),* with *hinnēh* normally denotes imminent future.[15] Oracles ordinarily predict the future, and the literal counterpart of this figurative epiphany (see vv 6-7) is future. "Come forth" in the language of epiphany means to march out for battle (cf. Judg 5:4; Isa 26:21; Zech 14:3; Ps 68:8[7]). *mimměqômô (from his place)* commonly signifies sanctuary,[16] a meaning certified by "holy palace" in v 2.

LXX[A] omits *wĕyārad (and he will come down),* and LXX[L] and 1QpMic omit *wĕdārak (and tread).* H. M. Orlinsky[17] argues in the light of the use of *drk*

---

11. *IBHS* §6.3.5.3.

12. J. L. Mays, *Micah: A Commentary,* OTL (Philadelphia: Westminster, 1976), 40.

13. T. Lambdin, *Introduction to Biblical Hebrew* (New York: Scribner, 1971), 168-69, §135; cf. *IBHS,* 618.

14. So also Wolff, *Micha,* 10.

15. *IBHS* §36.6.4.3.

16. S. Amsler, *"qūm," THAT* 2:369.

17. H. M. Orlinsky, "The Textual Criticism of the Old Testament," in *The Bible and the Ancient Near East,* ed. G. E. Wright (Garden City, N.Y.: Doubleday, 1961), 129 n. 25.

with *'al-bāmŏtê* plus *'āb* (Isa 14:14), *'ereṣ* (Amos 4:13), *yām* (Job 9:8), "it would seem more likely that the Micah fragment has preserved the secondary of the two readings." The Lucianic recension may have lost the second verb by homoioteleuton, for both verbs end with *-bēsetai*. Mur 88, a large number of MSS of LXX, and R read with MT. Without emendation MT has 4/4 meter and presents YHWH's stately march from heaven to the high places of earth. J. L. Crenshaw[18] notes: "Both [verbs] are integral to theophanic depictions, and Micah elsewhere uses double verbs in this fashion (1:8; 2:11, 13; 4:10, 13; 5:4, 5, 6, 8 [MT 3, 4, 5, 7]). The fact that 5:4f have *dārak* as the second verb speaks in favor of its originality in 1:3." Finally, the shorter reading can be explained easily as due to haplography, for the two verbs share three of their four consonants. The *waw*-relatives with the two verbs *(and . . . will)* signify sequential actions.[19] *Kethib bāmŏtê/Qere bāmŏtê*, with no difference in meaning *(high places)*, designates either geographical "heights" or, better, as in Amos 4:13, "slopes," or the cultic shrines located on them. Here the focus is on the earth. This report of *I AM*'s epiphany in holy war corresponds to Judg 5:4-5; Isa 26:21; Jer 25:30-31; Ps 18:8-16(7-15). The language would also have been familiar to Micah's pagan audience, to judge from scenes of Baal astride mountains[20] and similar ancient Near Eastern expressions of theophanies.[21] The expression "tread upon the high places" "conveys the notion of possessing key terrain and so possessing the earth."[22] 1QpMic reads *h'rṣ* instead of *'āreṣ (the earth)*. H. L. Orlinsky observes that the anarthrous construction in the compound *bāmŏtê 'āreṣ* is idiomatic Biblical Hebrew (cf. Deut 32:13; Isa 58:14; Amos 4:13). LXX consistently uses the article according to its own idiom.

4 Verse 4Ba/b constitutes emblematic parallels to v 4Aa/b, making a linear reading of the verse impossible. LXX uniquely relieves the incoherence by changing "melt" to *saleuthēsetai* "shake" (its rendering for **nāmôṭ* [niphal of **môṭ* "be shaken"; cf. Isa 40:20; Ps 46:6(5); 82:5] or *nāmôg* [niphal of *mûg* "melt away"; Nah 1:5]) and by omitting "split apart," leaving the coherent reading in v 4Ab-4Ba, "the valleys will melt like wax before fire." The *waw*-relative in *wěnāmassû (And . . . will melt)* indicates that v 4 is (con)sequential to v 3. The niphal stem signifies middle voice.[23] The figurative images of *I AM*'s epiphany are drawn from volcanic eruptions and/or earthquakes (cf. Isa 64:1-2[2-3]; Amos 4:13; Hab 3:6; Pss 50:3; 97:5). The literal events being signified are the As-

18. J. L. Crenshaw, "*Wᵉdōrēk 'al-bāmŏtê 'āreṣ*," *CBQ* 34 (1972) 44-45.

19. *IBHS* §30.4.5.3.2.

20. Cf. J. T. Whitney, "High Place," *NDB*, 483.

21. Wolff, *Micha*, 24.

22. E. A. Martens, "*bāmâ*," *TWOT* 1:113.

23. *IBHS* §21.2.1.

syrian invasions, especially that of Shalmaneser V (see v 1). The articles with *hehārîm (the mountains)* and *wĕhāʿămāqîm (and the valleys)* are definite in the imagination.[24] H. Wolff[25] notes that "the high places of the earth" in v 3 now become "the mountains," and that they, the original foundations of the earth, represent endurance, height, and majesty (Zech 4:7; Pss 90:2; 95:4). On the other hand, he suggests, "the valleys" or "the plains" stand for the favored fruit-bearing areas where humans live. These parallel members constitute a merismus, a trope of inclusion encompassing the whole topography, where "gods" and "men" dwell.[26] *I AM* will eradicate everything. *yitbaqqāʿû (will split apart)* is a hithpael denoting a direct reflexive and not the passive voice (*contra* RSV, corrected in NRSV). *taḥtāyw (beneath him)* is gapped in v 4Ab.

nāmassû (melting) is gapped in v 4Ba. *kaddônag (like wax)* and *kĕmayim (like water)* have the article of class, and so are left untranslated. When mountains melt like wax before fire, they are no more (Ps 97:5). The hophal participle *muggārîm (pouring down)* of the root *ngr* has a causative notion that can scarcely be translated. The verb *ngr (pour down)* with the noun *ʾēš (fire)* links the figurative epiphany and the historical reality of v 6. B. Renaud[27] made these observations about *bĕmôrād (in a mountain gorge)*:

> On the basis of a comparison of Hebrew *môrād* with Arabic *maurid,* R. Köbert translated *bmwrd* "at the watering place." The second comparison would be, he thinks, in full harmony with the first: both would be borrowed from everyday life. According to O. Garcia de la Fuente, *môrād* means rather "descent," "slope." He proposed the translation *cañada* "gorge of a mountain." In effect, it is a matter of the deepest part of a valley that serves both as a trail for herds during their migration and as a natural channel for waters during the rainy season. In Palestine many trails, especially those that lead to mountain pastures, are nothing but intermittent torrents of water. The Arabic *maurid,* invoked by Köbert, would also have the sense of "ditch." The comparison here concerns much more the image of the descent and of the slope wherein the water runs than of the water itself.

When *I AM* pours down the fertile valleys into deep canyons, like cascading waterfalls down a rocky slope, then man's place of life and hope is entirely removed from him.

---

24. *IBHS* §11.5.5.
25. Wolff, *Micha,* 25.
26. See A. M. Honeyman, "*Merismus* in Biblical Literature," *JBL* 71 (1952) 11-18.
27. Renaud, *La Formation,* 13.

5 *bĕ (on account of)* has a causal force.[28] *pešaʿ (rebellion)* means "a willfully criminal infraction of covenant" (cf. 1 Kgs 12:19; Jer 2:29; Amos 5:12), and *ḥaṭṭōʾwt (sins)* means an objective deviation from and deterioration of its stipulations (Judg 20:16; Prov 19:2). The pair, according to J. L. Mays,[29] "constitute a comprehensive characterization of the people's conduct." *yaʿăqōb (of Jacob)*, a genitive of agent,[30] refers to the Northern Kingdom because *šōmrôn (Samaria)* stands parallel to it in v 5Ba (cf. v 6A). *kol-zōʾt (all this)*, a genitive of measure,[31] according to Renaud[32] always refers to what precedes, validating the view that the epiphany is punitive. LXX, Syr, and Tg read singular "sin," but MT's incongruous plural with singular is preferred. In v 13 MT reverses the singular and plural of these same parallel nouns, and in 3:8, a close parallel to 1:5, both nouns are singular. This plural in v 5Ab matches the intensified plural parallel, "great high place," in v 5B. There is no need to emend conjecturally with BHS *yiśrāʾēl (Israel)* to *yĕhûdâ* "Judah." In this book "Israel" is, or better includes, "Judah" (cf. 1:1, 14, 15; 3:9; 5:1). These verses show that *bêt yiśrāʾēl (house of Israel)*, a genitive of association,[33] refers to the Southern Kingdom; the parallel in v 5Bb confirms it. Together "Jacob" and "house of Israel" form a merismus, so that the whole nation is indicted.

1QpMic and Syr read the easier *mâ* "what" instead of *mî (what)*, literally "who," of MT (cf. *tis* of LXX) (twice in v 5Ba/b). The more difficult and figurative "who" personifies sin and its appositives, "Samaria" and "Jerusalem." By such questions the prophet prepares his audience to agree with him that the two capital cities, metonymies for their leaders, are in fact the covenant breakers worthy of the death inflicted upon Samaria in vv 6-7 and Judah in vv 8-16. Since the judicial sentence in this particular pericope, vv 6 and 7, is handed down against Samaria alone, the accusation against Judah in v 5Bb seems out of place. Many critics think that a later redactor added it. According to J. Jeremias,[34] the style of v 5B is not the style of Micah but reflects the processes of late exegesis, and, according to J. Lindblom,[35] Micah uses Judah only one other time (1:9) and in a geographic sense, not ethnic as here. Our knowledge of

28. BDB 90, §5.
29. Mays, *Micah*, 4.
30. *IBHS* §9.5.1.
31. *IBHS* §9.5.3.
32. *La Formation*, 30.
33. *IBHS* §9.5.3.
34. J. Jeremias, *Theophanie: Die Geschichte einer alttestamentliche Gattung*, WMANT 10 (Neukirchen-Vluyn: Neukirchener, 1965), 331-32.
35. J. Lindblom, *Micha literarisch untersucht*, Acta Academiae Aboensis, Humaniora 6/2 (Åbo: Åbo Åkademi, 1929), 149 n. 1.

Micah's style, however, is too limited to make such judgments, and indeed Judah is used in 1:9. B. Renaud[36] makes a strong case for thinking that originally 1:2-7, "the Fall of Samaria," and 1:8-16, "the Fall of the Shephelah," were originally separate oracles and that a redactor later combined them into a unified whole by adding among other things v 5Bb. It may be that Micah himself secondarily added it, as J. T. Willis[37] suggested.

In any case, we need an accusation against Judah here to warrant the lament threatening the judgment of Judah in 1:8-16 in this unified chapter. Our expectation is realized in all texts and versions. LXX fully harmonizes v 5Bb with 5Ab by reading *hē hamartia oikou Iouda* "the sin of the house of Judah." *bāmôt (great high place)* may be a plural of intensification;[38] a countable plural would be unacceptable with the singular appositive noun, "Jerusalem." RSV, following LXX, Syr, and Tg, reads *ḥaṭṭaʾt bêt*, "sin of the house of . . ." instead of "great high place" of MT and Vg. MT can hardly have been a copyist's mistake, either intentionally or unintentionally, whereas *ḥaṭṭaʾt* is almost certainly an attempt to align v 5Bb to v 5Ab, even as *pešaʿ* in v 5Ba is parallel to *pešaʿ* in v 5Aa. Also, *bāmôt* "great high place as a cultic site" constitutes a fine pun, a common trope in Micah, with *bāmŏtê* ("high places as geographical sites") in v 3. Pagan cultic "high places" were usually located on natural heights (1 Sam 9:14; 10:5; 1 Kgs 11:7; 2 Kgs 17:9, 29; 23:5, 8), supplied with idols (2 Chr 33:19), an *ʾašērâ* — a live tree (cf. Mic 5:13) or perhaps a pole — symbolizing the female fertility goddess, and a *maṣṣēbâ* — one or more stone pillars — symbolizing the male fertility deity (2 Kgs 3:2). An altar (2 Kgs 21:3; 2 Chr 14:2), built of stones, was either separate from the *bāmâ* or part of it. The *bāmâ* contained a tent or room where the cultic vessels were stored and where sacrificial meals were eaten (1 Kgs 12:31; 13:32; 2 Kgs 17:29; 23:19).[39] Penitent Hezekiah removed them from Jerusalem (2 Kgs 18:1-6; cf. Amos 7:9).

6 The *wāw*-relative with *wěśamtî (therefore I will make)* signifies logical consequence after the accusation (v 5).[40] The tense is future; note the parallel nonperfect form without *waw* in vv 6-7. Though the sentence lacks the formula announcing the divine speech, often followed by a participle (cf. 2:3; 3:5, 12), only *I AM* could speak of inflicting the catastrophic blow that knocked out the grandiose city famous for its incomparable walls. The expected formula may have been removed in the editing of the book.

šōmʿrôn (Samaria) clearly links the judicial sentence with the accusation. Its celebrated walls would now be reduced to *lěʿî haśśādeh (a heap of rubble in*

---

36. *La Formation*, 50.
37. Willis, "Some Suggestions on the Interpretation of Micah 1:2," 374.
38. *IBHS* §7.3.5.
39. Cf. K.-D. Schunck, *"bāmāh," TDOT* 2:142-43.
40. *IBHS* §32.1.3.

the field). LXX has instead of "heap of rubble" *opōrophylakion* "a hut to keep fruit" (cf. Isa 1:8), and is followed by Syr "field house." Renaud[41] plausibly suggests that the two versions wanted to attenuate the brutal text of 3:12, so that, instead of being reduced to a heap of rubble, Jerusalem becomes a hut in the field, and that, by analogy, the same Hebrew word was translated by the same Greek word in 1:6. Three arguments can be raised against Vuilleumier's suggestion that *haśśādeh (field)*, a genitive of location,[42] means here "vicinity, suburb, neighborhood," so that, according to her, v 6A should read "I will make Samaria into a ruin, her vicinity into a vineyard": (1) cultural — one cannot project on ancient cities the modern situation; (2) lexical — the supporting text she cites uses *śādeh* for lands administratively dependent on the cities around which they are located; (3) tradition — MT links *haśśādeh* with the preceding, not the following, word. *haśśādeh (field)* is a genitive of location[43] and depicts the open country (cf. 1 Sam 27:5 for a similar expression).

Moreover, Samaria will revert to its formerly unsettled situation, *lĕmaṭṭā'ê kārem (a place for planting vineyards)*, before Omri acquired the virgin site. LXX smooths the text by adding *kai* "and" to "plantings." *maṭṭā'ê (planting)* is a plural of indetermination.[44] There is no need to appeal to Akkadian *karmu* "ruin"[45] with respect to *kerem (vineyard)* against all Hebrew evidence. The foundation of the royal residence on the city's acropolis will become a heap of rubble, and the rest of the city will again become a place for planting vineyards.

The *waw*-relative *wĕhiggartî (for I will pour down)* introducing v 6B must be a logical sequence explaining the situation in v 6A.[46] As noted in v 4, the root *ngr* links *I AM's* punitive epiphany with this literal judicial sentence. By comparing the philology of v 6A with Ps 79:1 and of v 6B with Ps 137:7, H. Wolff[47] draws the proper conclusion against J. Lindblom, E. Sellin, and W. Beyerlin that *I AM* is not comparing himself to an earthquake but to a conquering invader. *I AM* used the battering rams of the Assyrian army under Shalmaneser V (2 Kgs 17:3-6) to carry out his sentence against *'ăbāneyhā (her stones)*, the proud stones of her retaining walls and royal residence.[48] The chiastic construction *wîsōdêhā*

41. *La Formation*, 14.

42. *IBHS* §9.5.2.

43. *IBHS* §9.4.2.4; G. R. Driver, "Linguistic and Textual Problems: Minor Prophets, II," *JTS* 39 (1938) 264.

44. *IBHS* §7.6.3.7.

45. So S. J. Schwantes, "Critical Notes on Micah 1:10-16," *VT* 14 (1964) 454-61.

46. *IBHS* §32.3.3.4.

47. Wolff, *Micah*, 26.

48. See Y. Yadin, *The Art of Warfare in Biblical Lands in the Light of Archaeological Study*, 2 vols. (New York: McGraw-Hill, 1963), 1:313-20.

'ăgalleh (and her foundations I will lay bare) represents not the chronological sequence of v 6ʙa and v 6ʙb but the two aspects involved in dismantling Samaria's fortifications and royal quarters. The figurative language, "lay bare,"
may evoke notions of public shaming (cf. Ezek 16:37; Hos 2:14[12]).

7 *wĕkol (and all)* can be qualitative (i.e., "all kinds of") or quantitative
(i.e., "all," "every"); the threefold repetition in v 7ᴀ supports the latter. Not a
remnant of the false religion will survive. The pronominal suffix in *pĕsîlêhā (her
idols)* links v 7 with v 6. With the loss of her fortifications (v 6), Samaria also
lost her cult; her gods could not defend her. The root *psl* "to hew into shape"
designates "carved images." R. L. Harris[49] writes:

> There is not any one word for "idol" in the OT. The idols are named vari-
> ously by the prophets depending on the characterization they felt would be
> most effective. Five words are mainly used: (1) *gillûl* "logs, blocks" (though
> KB suggests that it is a pejorative word calling idols dung pellets) . . . ,
> (2) *pesel* "carved image," (3) *massēkâ* "cast image," (4) *maṣṣēbâ* "standing
> stone image," (5) *'āṣāb* "thing of grief" [*sic!* see below]. . . . The prophets
> scorned the idols as things made by the hand of men . . . (e.g., Isa 2:8). They
> did not admit that the idol was a mere representation of the god. They de-
> clared that the material object itself was the pagan's god — and with the
> prevailing animism, they were doubtless correct.

S. Schwantes[50] suggests that the form *yukkattû (will be broken to pieces)* is not
the hophal of *ktt* but the old qal passive, in which case it would mean "crushed."
Since the verb also occurs in the piel/pual and hiphil, that option is better ruled
out because the old qal passive is best restricted, among other things, to verbs
not otherwise occurring in the hiphil.[51] It probably means "be hammered to
pieces." The passive is impersonal (cf. LXX *katakopsousin,* opting for the impersonal construction of the indefinite subject with the active verb; cf. also its
emprēsousin "they will burn" for *yiśśārĕpû).*

Scholars have stumbled over *'etnanneyhā (prostitute wages)* in 7ᴀaβ because it is not a semantic parallel to "images" (7ᴀaα/7ᴀb). *BHS* regards 7ᴀaβ as
an addition, but our knowledge of Hebrew meter is too insecure to destroy the
fine parallelism we hope to show; also *'ēš (fire)* provides a crucial verbal link with
v 4. J. Wellhausen wants the word to be *'ăšērêhā* "her asheras"; W. Rudolph[52] and

---

49. R. L. Harris, *"gillûl," TWOT* 1:163-64.
50. Schwantes, "Critical Notes on Micah 1:10-16," 27.
51. Cf. GKC §53u.
52. W. Rudolph, *Micha, Nahum, Habakuk, Zephanja,* KAT 13/3 (Gütersloh: Mohn, 1975),
33.

R. Vuilleumier[53] omit it. G. R. Driver[54] thinks *'etnan* in this verse derives from two distinct roots and means "effigy" in v 7Aαβ and "prostitute's hire" in v 7B. He also cites[55] B. Halpern as referring to Arabic *tanna* "compared," whence *tinnu(n)* "likeness" and *tinanu(n)* "effigy." The excellent pun would match Micah's fondness for that figure to express poetic justice, but it lacks lexical support in Hebrew. W. G. E. Watson[56] thinks that it is a variant of *tannîn* "sea serpent" (i.e., "perhaps, images of snakes"). Two arguments invalidate Wellhausen's often-followed proposal: (1) textual — no support; and (2) contextual — metonymy prepares the way for the remainder of the sentence where the idols are regarded as produced from the revenues derived from cult-prostitution. Watson argues against himself by conceding that in v 7B the same word means "prostitute's price." Other suggestions are also gratuitous, for they fail to take note that the prophet could be using metonymy. The suffix *-êhā (her)* is an objective genitive, "wages paid to a prostitute." The idols in view here were constructed from silver and gold paid to cult prostitutes. This debauchery and debasing of mankind enriched the temples with splendid images. Micah mentions this source rather than the effect for the play he intends in v 7B. Though the form *yiśśārĕpû (will be burned)* is an impersonal passive, the agent, according to the parallels, is *I AM*. What Israel failed to do according to the Law (Deut 7:15, 25; 9:21; 12:3; cf. 2 Kgs 18:4) *I AM* will carry out.

Although R. L. Harris implied that *'ăsabbeyhā (her images)* derives from root I *'ṣb* "to grieve,"[57] more probably it derives from II *'ṣb* "to shape, fashion."[58] If so, all five principal words for idols refer to their physical nature. With *'āśîm (I will make)* the impersonal constructions of v 7Aα/β give way to the more emphatic personal construction, "I." *I AM*, not Assyria in the final analysis, overthrows the pagan cult and thereby upholds his holy Law. *šĕmāmâ (a shocking devastation)* designates an area so devastated that it arouses horror, terror, awe. Each of the succeeding parts of v 7A becomes more emphatic.

kî (since) introduces the causal protasis in v 7Ba to the apodosis in v 7Bb. The substantiation for the overthrow is stated in the accusation (v 5). *mē'etnan*

53. R. Vuilleumier and C.-A. Keller, *Michée, Nahoum, Habacuc, Sophonie,* CAT XIb; (Neuchâtel: Delachaux & Niestlé, 1971), 18 n. 2.

54. Driver, "Problems and Solutions," *VT* 4 (1954) 242.

55. Driver, "Problems and Solutions," 242 n. 7.

56. W. G. E. Watson, "Allusion, Irony and Wordplay in Micah 1:7," *Bib* 65 (1984) 103-5.

57. So also *Wilhelm Gesenius' Hebräisches und Aramäisches Handwörterbuch über das Alte Testament,* ed. F. Buhl (Berlin/Göttingen/Heidelberg, 1962) (hereafter GB) 609 and KBL 726.

58. So BDB 781; L. G. Lisowsky, *Konkordanz zum hebräischen Alten Testament,* 2d ed. (Stuttgart: Württembergische Bibelanstalt, 1958; hereafter Lis), 1104-5; R. B. Alden, "'āṣab," *TWOT* 2:688.

(*from the wages of prostitutes*) lexically and grammatical conforms with *'etnanneyhā* in v 7A. The personification of Samaria *qibbāṣâ (she collected them)* is replaced in Syr and Tg (Vg) by the easier impersonal passive, "they were gathered." "Gather" demands an object, the "idols" mentioned in v 7A, and suggests that Samaria had the purchasing power from its extensive and flourishing "trade" to bring the most expensive and potent idols into the capital. The money to hire these cult prostitutes had come from the conquest of neighbors and from the exploitation of the common man (cf. Mic 2:1-2).

The conquering Assyrian army, parading under the symbols of the Assyrian pantheon, would use the precious metals of gold and silver that formerly overlaid Samaria's rich idols (cf. Isa 40:19-20) to pay the Assyrian cult prostitutes, providing revenue for their cultic centers, and so *wě'ad-'etnan zônâ yāšûbû (they will again be used as wages for prostitutes)*. The *wāw* is an apodosis *wāw*. The repetition of *'etnan zônâ (wages for prostitutes)* denotes poetic justice; as Israel had secured its money to support sacred courtesans by exploiting others, so the Assyrians would support theirs by robbing Israel. The subject of *yāšûbû (they will again)* refers to the "idols" of v 7A, more specifically the gold and silver that decorated them (cf. Isa 46:1, 2; Dan 1:3). T. Laetsch[59] calls attention to Cyrus's edict, "speaking of the gods placed in Babylon's temples by former kings as having been returned by him to their former shrines."

EXPOSITION

C. Westermann[60] established that the basic judgment oracle, such as is found in 1:2-7, consists of three elements: introduction (address) (= v 2), accusation (= v 5A) with development (= v 5B), the messenger formula (missing in v 6A), and announcement of judgment (the intervention of God) (= v 6) with results of intervention (= v 7). This oracle varies the pattern by altering the address from naming the original culprit, principally Samaria, and summoning instead all the nations to the Heavenly Prosecutor's accusation against Samaria and Jerusalem and his announcement of judgment against the former and by adding to it the prophet's vision of *I AM* coming in a punitive epiphany as a conqueror of all the earth. All nations are summoned, for judgment against the chosen nations entails their judgment as well. It also differs in lacking the messenger for-

---

59. T. Laetsch, *Bible Commentary: The Minor Prophets* (St. Louis: Concordia, 1956), 249.
60. C. Westermann, *Basic Forms of Prophetic Speech,* tr. H. C. White (Philadelphia: Westminster, 1967; repr. Louisville: Westminster/John Knox, 1991), 169-75.

mula before the announcement of judgment, "thus says *I AM*," probably because the original prophecy was reworked to dovetail in this literary framework.

B. Renaud[61] faults G. Fohrer[62] for suggesting that the summons reflects the "covenant lawsuit form" (cf. 6:1-8) in which *I AM* summons the cosmic elements to hear as witnesses his case against Israel because v 2 differs from this form in that the nations, not the cosmic elements, are addressed and are summoned as defendants themselves, not as witnesses. Renaud's first argument, however, is based on content, not form, but his second objection is cogent. According to J. Jeremias,[63] the primitive structure of the theophanic genre consists of two elements: (1) the coming of *I AM* from a determined place (= v 3) and (2) cosmic disturbances that accompany this coming from afar (= v 4). On a form-critical basis the prophecy against Samaria can be confidently analyzed as follows:

I. Address: All peoples are summoned to hear the Heavenly Prosecutor's case (v 2).
   A. All peoples are summoned to the trial (v 2A).
   B. *I AM* prosecutes all nations (v 2B).
II. Epiphany: The heavenly and holy Judge descends in punitive epiphany (vv 3-4).
   A. *I AM* descends from his celestial, holy palace (v 3).
   B. Earth undergoes a cosmic reversal (v 4).
III. Accusation: The house of Israel broke covenant (v 5).
   A. Summary: Jacob and Judah broke covenant (v 5A).
   B. Development: Samaria and Jerusalem broke covenant (v 5B).
IV. Sentence: *I AM* decrees annihilation of Samaria (vv 6-7).
   A. Its fortifications will be destroyed (v 6).
   B. Its idols will be reused in another cult (v 7).

These four main elements are linked by logical particles: "for" (v 3, i.e., the punitive epiphany gives the reason why the nations are summoned to the Prosecutor's case), "all this" (v 5, i.e., the accusation explains the punitive epiphany), and "therefore" (v 6, i.e., the sentence is the result of the accusation).

Micah jolts his audience (v 2), all peoples, with the message that Samaria, Israel's majestic capital, will be leveled to the ground because of her idolatry. As

---

61. *La Formation*, 28.

62. G. Fohrer, "Micha 1," in *Das ferne und nahe Wort: Festschrift L. Rost*, ed. F. Maas, BZAW (Berlin: A. Töpelmann, 1967), 82.

63. Jeremias, *Theophanie*, 11-13, 15; cf. C. Westermann, *Praise of God in the Psalms* (Richmond, Va.: John Knox, 1965), 98.

Jesus in his famed Sermon on the Mount addressed the onlookers in an outer circle and his disciples in an inner circle (cf. Matt 5:1-2), so also Micah intends his messages for two audiences, the non-covenant and covenant people. That still holds true. The judicial sentence decreed against Samaria serves as a paradigm for *I AM*'s judicial sentence against all idolaters. J. Willis[64] wrote: "The prophets consider Yahweh's punishment of Israel a model or pattern for Yahweh's future punishment of the nations." E. B. Pusey[65] said: "Every judgment is an earnest, a forerunner, a part, of the final judgment and an ensample of its principles. It is but 'the last great link in the chain' which unites God's dealings in time with eternity. God's judgments on one imply a judgment on all. His judgments in time imply a Judgment beyond time."

Micah underlines *I AM*'s sovereignty over all nations by summoning all nations on earth without exception and by matching his universal summons (v 2A) with his universal rule (v 2B), calling him "Lord of all," referring to God's residence as a "palace," and inferring its heavenly character ("he comes down"). To *I AM*'s sovereignty Micah adds his sublime holiness ("holy palace," v 2B) and power (vv 3-4). No one escapes God's scrutiny, justice, and power. The summons implies a biting indictment against the sons of the covenant. They had been chosen to be a light to the nations and to bring them salvation, but the sons of darkness have so overwhelmed them that now all come under divine wrath. How ironic that whereas at one time *I AM*'s wrath against the Canaanites served as a warning to Israel (cf. Lev 18:28), now Israel becomes a warning to others. All threatened judgments, let it be recalled, are conditional. If sinners repent beforehand, they will be saved (Jer 18:7-8; Jonah 3:4, 10; 4:1). This principle is still valid (2 Cor 6:2).

The World Ruler is now (vv 3-4) envisioned as a victorious conqueror, as he rises from his heavenly throne, marches forth from his holy sanctuary, and strides upon the earth's high places. Under the heat of his glowing wrath and under his heavy tread the eternal and majestic mountains melt and flow like hot wax, and the arable plains where man finds his immediate source of life split apart like waterfalls roaring down a rocky gorge. Nothing escapes nor remains. When this majestic God suddenly erupts with justice, puny man's proud walls and fortifications crumble and fall into the ravines. Humans feel secure as long as the long-suffering God remains in heaven, but when he marches forth in judgment, they are gripped by the stark reality and gravity that they must meet the holy God in person (cf. Amos 4:2). The blind eyes of unbelievers saw only the immediate cause of Samaria's fall, the inexorable march of Assyria's

---

64. Willis, "Some Suggestions on the Interpretation of Micah 1:2," 378.
65. E. B. Pusey, "Micah," in *Minor Prophets* (London: Parker, 1860), 295.

57

crack international army under the leadership of its brilliant kings. But Micah's open eyes saw behind the juggernaut the invincible march of God. Julia Ward Howe caught a similar vision while on a visit during the American Civil War to the Federal army encamped near Washington and gave expression to it in the stirring lines of "The Battle Hymn of the Republic":

> Mine eyes have seen the glory of the coming of the Lord;
> He is trampling out the vintage where the grapes of wrath are stored;
> He hath loosed the fateful lightning of his terrible quick sword:
> His truth is marching on. . . .
>
> I have seen him in the watchfires of a hundred circling camps;
> They have builded him an altar in the evening dews and damps;
> I have read his righteous sentence by the dim and flaring lamps;
> His day is marching on. . . .

Unbelieving secular humans sees no connection between their immoral behavior and the cycles of depression, increasing crime, politicians instead of statesmen to guide them, ceaseless war, and venereal diseases. If they would "see" God ruling earth's affairs, and tremble before him, they would have nothing to fear.

God accuses Israel of breaking covenant (v 5). His relationship to Israel was not by contract but in covenant, a matter of the heart. In contrast to contracts, which are essentially based on distrust, a covenant is based on an "I-thou" commitment to one another, which is conceived in love and brought forth through faith. Micah will later explicate specifically how Israel broke covenant (chs. 2–3; 6:1–7:7). Samaria and Jerusalem serve by metonymy for the nation's leadership (ch. 3). What awesome responsibility they bear!

At about 880 B.C. Omri acquired Samaria as a virgin site, established it, and together with his successor, Ahab, built it up into a splendid royal residence. Though lower than less imposing mountains to its north, east, and south, it was located on a mount over a hundred meters high, which commanded a view over the Plain of Sharon in the West, it was impregnable except by a prolonged siege cutting it off from the trade routes bringing food from the Valley of Esdraelon, and it was oriented toward the advanced culture of Phoenicia and Syria rather than toward the temple on Mount Zion. Archaeologists have uncovered the exquisitely dressed stones with which these two scions built the city; according to K. M. Kenyon,[66] its "earliest supporting wall was in a style of masonry dressing which was not equaled in Palestine, or indeed anywhere

---

66. K. M. Kenyon, *Royal Cities of the Old Testament* (London: Barrie & Jenkins, 1971), 76.

else in the Near East." But instead of becoming a light set on a hill, it plunged the privileged nation into utter moral darkness with its licentious prostitution. The professing church faces a similar danger. Instead of conforming the world to the image of Christ, some expressions of it are being conformed to its adulterous ways. It may be that the time has come for judgment to begin with the house of God (1 Pet 4:17).

Speaking with all the authority of an invincible king, the heavenly Judge who has come to earth sentences guilty Samaria to utter ruin (v 6) and her precious idols, covered with silver and gold, to plunder (v 7). The imagery of *I AM's* punitive epiphany (v 4), making mountains melt as before fire, now finds its historical counterpart in the crashing down of Samaria's strongholds into the valleys, and its idols burned in fire. The slopes of its proud hill will revert to vineyards; its carefully guarded foundations will be shamefully denuded; and its exquisite stones will be torn down until its formerly splendid buildings remain only a heap of rubble. The scene resembles the situation of apostate churches throughout the world that have become pagan temples or at best museums. Their lampstands have been removed (cf. Revelation 2–3).

The prophecy has been reaching toward the grand finale, the destruction of Samaria's idols and her cult-prostitution (v 7). J. L. Mays[67] commented: "It is remarkable that, in a prediction of the devastation and disappearance of such a great city, only the fate of idols should be mentioned. The fact shows that these representations of other gods are the real target of *I AM's* action." These idols were the tangible symbols of her pagan worldview, and from that worldview sprang her twisted value system (cf. Rom 1:18-31). These idols, so attractive to the flesh and demanding no moral rectitude, seduced Samaria to break covenant and to commit crimes, just as Mammon, Sex, and Drugs are seducing humanity today away from God.

The cult prostitute's wages were analogous to a bride price and provided the chief source of revenue for the shrines.[68] Payment from her patrons consisted of money, food, and clothing (Gen 38:17, 18; Ezek 16:10-11; Hos 2:11[9]). The Law strictly forbade cultic prostitution and especially the use of such profits on behalf of the temple cultus (Deut 23:17-18[16-17]). Cultic prostitution finds its basis in the idea that the forces of life in nature, especially at the spring season, were revived through the union of a god and goddess (e.g., Isis-Osiris, Ininni-Dumuzi, Ishtar-Tammus, and Astarte-Adonis cults) and that this divine union, insuring fertility of the crops and of the wombs, was effected through

---

67. Mays, *Micah,* 47.

68. See H. G. May, "The Fertility Cult in Hosea," *AJSL* 48 (1931-32) 92-93; E. A. Leslie, *The Prophets Tell Their Own Story* (New York: Abingdon, 1939), 131.

sympathetic magic and celebration involving the enactment of sexual intercourse with a sacred votary. The licentious rites of sympathetic magic are described by various Greek historians — Herodotus, Strabo, Lucian, and the like — and the important role they played in temple affairs is confirmed and illustrated by hundreds of liturgical texts and legal codes from the ancient Near East and by thousands of nude, plump female figurines from sites scattered widely all over the area.[69] Concerning the female votaries or *zônâ*, Beatrice Brooks,[70] without carefully distinguishing between secular and sacred prostitution — they went together hand in hand (cf. Jer 3:2; Amos 2:7-8) — said this:

> They arrayed themselves elaborately and flashily with scarlet garments and much jewelry and cosmetics (Jer 4:30; Ezek 23:40). . . . Possibly they sang to attract attention (Isa 23:16), and had a special mark on the forehead (Jer 3:3). . . . They were found by the wayside (Tamar [Gen 38:19], Ezek 16:25 and Prov 7:12), "on every high hill and under every green tree" (Jer 2:20), by the shrines (Ezek 16:23), and at the threshing floor (Hos 9:1). . . .

Sacral prostitution did not come into Israel like Pallas, "full-grown from the head of the Olympian Zeus," but spread like a pernicious cancer from various Canaanite cults just as quickly as the new morality is destroying modern society. More specifically, Ahab introduced licentious Baal worship into Samaria (1 Kgs 16:31-33); it spread so rapidly that within Elijah's lifetime only 7,000 had not bowed the knee to Baal (1 Kgs 18:18-22; 19:13-18), implying that the rest succumbed to the sensual allurement his worship demanded. Ahaziah, the son-in-law of Ahab, officially introduced it into Jerusalem (2 Kgs 8:25; cf. 2 Kgs 23:7; Ezek 8:1-14); earlier kings tolerated the "high places" with their shameful rites (1 Kgs 11:1-18; 14:21; 15:14; 22:43; 2 Kgs 12:3[2]) contrary to the Law (Deut 17:17-18). "The prophets combatted both [secular and sacred prostitution] as strenuously as they could, Am 2:7; Jer 5:7; etc."[71] Church leaders who are more indebted to psychology than to the Scriptures in their endeavor to make their parishioners happy instead of holy today condone all sorts of sexual immorality.

In contrast to the abiding presence of a believing remnant representing the true religion, nothing remains of the false religion. Because Israel's leader patronized puny rivals of the living God instead of smashing and burning

---

69. See W. F. Albright, *Archaeology and the Religion of Israel* (Baltimore: Johns Hopkins University Press, 1942).

70. B. A. Brooks, "Fertility Cult Functionaries in the Old Testament," *JBL* 60 (1941) 236-37.

71. F. Hauck and S. Schulz, *"pornē," TDNT* 6:585.

them, they were crushed along with them. Unless nations dethrone the new temples erected to Mammon in the great metropolises of the world, they will all fall together at last when the figurative language of *I AM's* epiphany in vv 3-4 shall be most exactly fulfilled at the appearing of the Lord Jesus Christ in blazing fire with his powerful angels from heaven (2 Thess 1:7-10). The idols in which Samaria trusted, though so popular, far from protecting her brought its judgment. So also modern man's trust in his defense budgets and technological skills, instead of in the living God, will actually destroy him. Poetic justice awaited the idols. Just as they had been constructed from the silver and gold paid to cult votaries, so also their precious metals were broken down by the Assyrian soldiers and reused to hire cult prostitutes in Nineveh, from which, we may suppose, new idols, just as worthless, would be made once again. Only the heart of depraved humanity could worship gods like that! The theme of *lex talionis* (i.e., of eye for eye) is sounded for the second time. It will be heard many times more in this book.

2. Judgment on Judah (1:8-16)

8　Therefore I will weep and wail;
　　　I will go about stripped and naked.
　I will make lament like the jackal's,
　　　and [I will make] mourning like the eagle owl's.
9　Because the wound inflicted by Yah is incurable;
　　　for it falls upon Judah.
　He reaches the gate of my people,
　　　even Jerusalem.
10　In Gath tell it not,
　　　weep not at all [there]!
　In Beth-le-aphrah, roll yourselves in dust!
11　Pass on, inhabitants of Shaphir, in shameful nakedness!
　　　The inhabitants of Zaanan do not come forth.
　Beth-ha-ezel is in mourning,
　　　its place to take a stand is taken from you.
12　Surely, the inhabitants of Maroth
　　　wait anxiously for good.
　But no! Calamity comes down from *I AM*
　　　to the gate of Jerusalem.
13　Harness the race horses to the chariots,
　　　inhabitants of Lachish —

    she is the beginning of sin to Daughter Zion —
        because in you were found Israel's transgressions!
14   Therefore you will give parting gifts to Moresheth Gath;
        the workshops of Achzib will prove deceptive to Israel's kings.
15   Also, the conqueror will come upon you, inhabitants of Mareshah;
        to Adullam will come Israel's glory.
16   Make yourself bald and shave
        for the children in whom you delight;
    enlarge your baldness like the vulture's,
        for they will go away from you into exile.

EXEGESIS

The text of vv 8-16 fares badly in the hands of both the ancient translators and modern critics. Instead of discussing all variant readings and conjectures, economically it is better to validate four principles of textual criticism pertinent to this passage and then discuss the text on that base.

Principle 1: MT is to be preferred to LXX. LXX differs so considerably from MT in these verses that one must decide whether they stem from a common original, and, if so, whether to refine MT by the Greek or vice versa.

M. Collin[1] sought to prove that LXX presupposes a Hebrew text very different from MT and that on the level of meaning it is unified in continuing the threat against Samaria (1:2-7). Micah's virulent attack in 1:10-15 in its primitive form, according to Collin, was against the cities and lands that bordered on that capital and that had rejoiced and mocked its fall in 722-721 B.C. MT, by contrast, according to him, was prepared in Babylon so as to relate the text to Jerusalem's fall. Renaud[2] with more probability argued that LXX simply misunderstood the Hebrew text and tried to make sense of it as best it could. Against Collin he wrote:

> In front of this translation one does not escape the impression that the Greek text remains heavy and far-fetched [*alambiqué*]. In the background one perceives a Hebrew text that is hardly intelligible for the translator, who strove to give an interpretative translation of it. Is it so sure that the Hebrew text, presupposed by the Greek, is more intelligible than MT? Here the delicate problem of reconstructing the Hebrew poses itself. When looked at

1. M. Collin, "Récherches sur l'Historie Textuelle du Prophète Michée," *VT* 21 (1971) 281-97.

2. *La Formation,* 19.

more closely, the Greek text seems to be overloaded with facilitating readings. In effect, LXX seems to have lost sight totally of plays on words in connection with the names of the cities. . . . LXX obfuscated some city names by taking them purely and simply as common nouns. By contrast, it is highly unlikely that [an editor] restored names of cities from common nouns. . . . Moreover, it seems that LXX, like many modern critics, stumbled on the apparent hiatus between vv 6-7, where it is a question of Samaria, and vv 8-16, which list cities of Judah. It attempted to erase the change by making Samaria the singer of the lament. . . .

Similarly, Schwantes drew the conclusion "that the Vorlage of LXX must have been quite illegible."

W. C. Graham,[3] along different lines from LXX, rewrote the text. According to him, Micah sarcastically and scornfully depicts the destruction of the fertility rites practiced at the local sanctuaries. In this perspective, *yôšebet* (vv 11, 12, 13, etc.) does not mean "inhabitants" but "mother-goddess" of the local cult, and the verbs should be interpreted in terms of cultic practices; for example, the dance refers to a cultic dance. Renaud[4] rightly objected: "One must give to many terms meanings that are exceptional or non-existent in the Bible and end up revising the text with the net result that not less than a third of it has to be sacrificed. . . ."

Principle 2: The text of MT is relatively well preserved. K. Elliger[5] and Schwantes,[6] followed by *BHK* and *BHS*, argued that the primitive text was materially damaged at its extreme right edge, necessitating the text critic to conjecture reconstructions at the beginning of each line. Renaud[7] cogently objected:

This hypothesis leads K. Elliger to propose corrections where MT is perfectly clear; for example, in 1:10A. Then, too, it presupposes that the text in its primitive form was displayed in stichs so that the new verse began on a new line. This remains without proof. The most ancient manuscripts that we possess, such as the scroll of the Twelve Minor Prophets found in the cave of Wadi Murabba'at, attest that the diverse stichs are placed one after the other without bothering to make a new verse to coincide with a new line. . . . Indeed, the text has been damaged, but these corruptions, less nu-

---

3. W. C. Graham, "Some Suggestions towards the Interpretation of Micah 1:10-16," *AJSL* 47 (1930-31) 237-58.

4. *La Formation*, 17.

5. K. Elliger, "Die Heimat des Propheten Micha," *ZDPV* 57 (1934) 81-152; repr. in *Kleine Schriften* (Munich: Kaiser, 1966), 9-71 (hereafter *KS*).

6. S. Schwantes, "Critical Notes on Micah 1:10-16," 38.

7. *La Formation*, 17-18.

merous than has been believed for a long time, are found as well at the beginning, middle, and end of the verse.

Principle 3: No a priori restraint that each binary verset must contain a pun may be placed on the text. I reject K. Elliger's other theory in the same article, followed by many, that each binary verset of vv 10-15 contains a town name, and just one, and that the play on words is displayed in those versets. D. R. Hillers[8] accurately objected:

> Although wordplay occurs here in abundance, yet fairly obvious puns occur in only about half of the sayings in the text as we have it, without emendation. Are we to compose some for the other lines, or is the situation perhaps like that in the "Testament of Jacob" (Genesis 49), where the sayings about Judah, Dan, and Gad contain obvious plays on the names, while other sayings about the tribes, including some that are intelligible, lack paronomasia? Isaiah's poem on the Assyrian advance seems to have just one pun (10:30), *'ănîyâ 'ănātôt.* Genesis 49 and the similar portions of Judges 5 and Deuteronomy 33 also display lack of uniformity in the length of sayings about the tribes, and it seems unwarranted to posit that in Micah 1 there was originally a neat uniformity.

Principle 4: MT, the traditional text, should be emended only where necessary. By Occam's razor all unnecessary emendations of a reliable tradition should be ruled out.[9]

8 B. Renaud,[10] seconded by H. Wolff,[11] by comparing *'al-zō't (therefore)* in such passages as Jer 4:8; Amos 7:3, 6; 8:8; Ps 32:6 showed that this prepositional phrase always functions as a logical conjunction linking what follows as being a consequence of what precedes. In the editing of the book of Micah, the prophet Micah, or a later redactor, bound an originally independent prophecy against the cities of Judah (vv 8-16) as a logical consequence of the sentence against Samaria (vv 6-7). The judicial sentence against Samaria, fulfilled in 722/721 B.C., certifies the doom of idolatrous Judah, predicted in connection with Sennacherib's invasion of the Shephelah in 701 B.C. The sentence against Samaria in vv 6-7 is based exclusively on the accusation in v 5; the sentence against Judah, approximately a quarter of a century later, is based explicitly on the accusation in v 5 and implicitly on the sentence against Samaria in vv 6-7.

---

8. Hillers, *Micah,* 24-25.
9. Cf. E. Würthwein, *The Text of the Old Testament* (Grand Rapids: Eerdmans, 1979), 111-16.
10. *La Formation,* 39-40.
11. Wolff, *Micha,* 17.

LXX reads *'espĕdâ (I will weep)* as "she," and so with all verbs in v 8, the pronoun referring back to Samaria, a *lectio facilior* to couple v 8 with vv 6-7. Tg reads third masculine plural; Syr agrees with MT. *spd* is the principal word to denote the mourning ritual, signifying wailing cries of anguish (cf. Amos 5:16), perhaps accompanied with the beating of the breast (Isa 32:12). All three verbs — *'espĕdâ (weep)*, *wĕ'êlîlâ (wail)*, and *'ĕlĕkâ (go about)* — are cohortatives of resolve.[12] Micah consciously and deliberately resolves on his ominous lamenting behavior. "Weep and wail," though representing the two verbs in 1:8Aa, captures the assonance of the next two Hebrew verbs, *wĕ'êlîlâ 'êlĕkâ*, in vv 8Aa and 8Ab. *'êlîlâ (I will wail)* in the hiphil means "to howl."

P. Haupt[13] explained the spelling *'êlĕkâ (I will go about)* as influenced by *wĕ'êlîlâ*. In the *Kethib (šîlāl)/Qere (šôlāl)* reading, with no difference in meaning *(stripped)*, *Qere* is preferred because *Kethib* is otherwise unattested and because in cursive Aramaic script *y* and *w* are readily confused. H. Bauer and P. Leander[14] consider the form a qal-passive (i.e., *qûtāl*) or a shortened pual participle whose full form would be *mĕšôlāl*. TNIV and NRSV render the same adjective by "stripped" in Job 12:17, 19 but "barefoot" here; RSV consistently uses "stripped." One should not appeal to Isa 10:6 for the meaning "barefoot" because *ḥānēp* is used there. The adjective may be derived either from I *šll* "to draw out" or from II *šll* "to plunder," though some lexicographers, such as F. Buhl,[15] treat it as one root. If the former be correct, it may have the added notion of "to strip off clothing" (= "stripped"), or "to strip off a shoe" (= "barefoot"). BDB, assuming root I, noted that its three occurrences are with the verb *hlk* and so thought it meant "stripped with regard to walking" (i.e., "barefoot"). If that be its meaning, it could still be part of a mourning ritual (cf. 2 Sam 15:30; Ezek 24:17, 23). Its coupling with *wĕʿārôm (and naked)*, whether *šôlāl* means "barefoot" or "stripped," shows, however, that Micah, in addition to being the first to see the impending catastrophe and so the first to suffer, is not merely performing a lament ritual, but supplements and completes it by symbolizing Judah as going into exile. H. Wolff[16] noted that mourners do not go about naked but wear sackcloth (Gen 37:34; 1 Kgs 21:27; Joel 1:8) and cover their heads (2 Sam 15:30, etc.):

---

12. *IBHS* §34.5.1.

13. P. Haupt, "The Book of Micah," *AJSL* 26 (1909-10) 216.

14. H. Bauer and P. Leander, *Historische Grammatik der hebräischen Sprache des Alten Testaments* (Halle/Saale: Max Niemeyer, 1922), 1:287, 475.

15. F. Buhl, ed., *Wilhelm Gesenius' hebräisches und aramäisches Handwörterbuch über das Alte Testament* (Berlin/Göttingen/Heidelberg: Springer, 1962; repr. of 1915 ed.); hereafter GB.

16. Wolff, *Micha*, 27.

Only one other time is it said in the OT that "one went barefoot and naked," and that of Isaiah (20:2-4). There it is unquestionably a symbolic act, signifying a threatening captivity (cf. also Amos 2:16). Exactly the same thing is met with here in Micah, for at the end of Micah's proclamation of lament stands the announcement of captivity (16Bb). Therefore the prophetic, symbolic act is added to the lament of weeping. Indeed, one can now see the weeping ritual as part of the symbolic action.

The mourning ritual is used both for lamenting the death of a loved one and/or lamenting the destruction of a city or land (Isa 15:3; Jer 48:37; Lam 2:10).

'e'ĕśeh (I will make), probably another cohortative, with *mispēd* and *'ēbel*, points to further gestures of mourning (Gen 50:10; cf. Jer 6:16; Ezek 24:17). These doleful cries and actions expressed either contrition (Isa 22:12; Joel 2:12; Zech 12:11) or lamentation for the dead (Gen 50:10; Zech 12:10) or for calamity (Jer 6:26; 48:38; Ezek 27:31; Amos 5:16-17; Mic 1:11). Here it signifies the latter, with the additional connotation of going into exile. The repetition of *spd* in vv 8Aa and 8Ba suggests that the text should not be read linearly; rather, v 8Ba parallels v 8Aa and, accordingly, v 8Bb matches v 8Ab. *kattannîm (jackals)*, masculine plural of *tan*, was mistakenly thought by older versions (LXX, Vg, KJV) to mean "dragon" through a confusion with *tannîn*, "sea monster." Jackals howl mournfully in waste places (Job 30:29, where it is also parallel with *bĕnôt ya'ănâ;* Isa 13:22), deserts (Isa 43:20, also parallel with *bĕnôt ya'ănâ*), and deserted sites (Jer 9:9[10]; 10:22; 49:33). The similes evoke a picture of howling in a deserted land; Micah pictures himself not in the company of desert inhabitants but in the company of Judeans in their wasted land.

'ēbel (mourning) is the object of the gapped *'e'ĕśeh*. LXX, probably confusing *bĕnôt ya'ănâ (eagle owl's)* with *'nh* "to sing," rendered the compound expression by "sirens." GB, BDB, and KB, following the ancients, give the meaning "ostrich," but Aharoni corrected this to "eagle owl." G. R. Driver[17] explains:

> The literal meaning of *bat ya'ănâ* . . . is either 'daughter of greed' (Gesenius) or 'the daughter of the wilderness' (Wetzstein), and it has consequently been always explained as the ostrich (LXX, Vulg., Targ., Pesh.); for this bird is noted for its voracious appetite and is found only in the wilderness. Not all, however, that is said of this bird in the O.T. is applicable to the ostrich. This indeed inhabits the open wilderness but requires water (Is. xliii 20; cp. xxxiv 13), but it does not haunt deserted or ruined cities (Is. xiii 21; Jer. i 39); it certainly does not wail (Mic. i 8) but booms; nor is it raptorial. These are all habits of owls, so that the *bat ya'ănâ* may well be the

17. G. R. Driver, "Birds in the Old Testament," *PEQ* 87 (1955) 12-13.

eagle owl (Aharoni), a large owl which is found in semi-desert areas covered with scrub, where it rests on bushes during the day and hunts partridges, hares and rodents by night. . . . The Syr. *ba(r)t yarora* (Pesh.) "daughter of the vomiter" (Mic. i 8) agrees with the explanation of the word; for all owls bring up the indigestible parts of their food in the form of pellets, which can always be found in large quantities beneath their nests.

Bat with *ya'ănâ* represents the nature of the creature; it belongs to the wilderness.

9 The logical particle *kî (because)* introduces the explicit basis for his mourning, namely, the wound inflicted by *I AM* upon Judah. The fall of Samaria led Micah to lament (cf. "therefore" introducing v 8) because *I AM* will also fatally afflict Judah (v 9). *'ănûšâ (incurable),* a predicate adjective, describes an incurable wound or pain (Isa 17:11; Jer 15:18; 17:9; 30:12; Job 34:6). The tense is contemporaneous with Micah's present wailing. Instead of the plural *makkôtêhā* "her blows," in which the pronominal suffix functions as an objective genitive (i.e., "blows inflicted on her"), the ancient versions probably read singular *makkātāh* "her blow/wound." K. Elliger,[18] followed by many, plausibly conjectures reading *makkat yāh* (wound inflicted by Yah). He should be followed because (1) the short form for *I AM* was often confounded into a suffix in Hebrew; (2) the feminine singular *makkat* finds support in the versions and agrees with complements *'ănûšâ* (feminine singular adjective) and *bā'â* "fall" (third feminine singular perfective); (3) the resulting *I AM* complements *nāga'* (reach) (third masculine singular perfective), which gender is otherwise difficult; and (4) it explains the insertion of *w,* making the form plural (i.e., once *yāh* was interpreted as a suffix, *mkt* had to be understood as feminine plural afformative, requiring *ô*). Parallels involving *makkâ (wound)* with *'ănûšâ* in Jer 15:18; 30:12 favor the meaning "wound(s)." Derived from the root *nkh* "to strike," it can have a causative sense, namely, a scouring, chastising "blow/beating/lashing" (Deut 25:3; Prov 20:30), or a resultative notion, namely, "wound" (1 Kgs 22:35; Isa 1:6; Jer 6:7). It can also mean collectively either "slaughter" in war (1 Sam 4:10; 14:30) or "plague," especially disease (Deut 28:59; 1 Sam 4:8). Here it signifies not the beating of an individual but, as v 9B clarifies, the "slaughter" and "wasting" of the entire land through the onslaught of war (cf. 1 Kgs 20:21). Since the effect is beyond remedy, it denotes the "wound" resulting from the slaughter (Jer 19:8; 50:13). *yāh* is a genitive of agent.[19] Behind the Assyrian juggernaut, the immediate cause, Micah saw *I AM,* the Ultimate Cause (cf. vv 3-4, 12).

18. *KS* 14.
19. *IBHS* §9.5.1.

The logical particle *kî (for)* introducing v 9B connects v 9B to v 9A and not to v 8 because the subject of *bā'â* is *makkôt* in v 9A. Were the former connection in view, *kî* would better be rendered "indeed." One should not make too sharp a distinction, however; all of v 9 gives the reason for Micah's symbolic lament in v 8. The wound is beyond healing *because I AM* has afflicted Judah right up to Jerusalem; nothing survives. The *pašṭā'* accent on *bā'â (will have fallen)* denotes the form as third feminine perfective, a persistent (future) perfective in harmony with the rest of this oracle prophesying the future doom of Judah.[20] With the preposition *'ad (upon), bô'* means "fall or light upon."[21] Micah mentions *yĕhûdâ (Judah)*, the state, before its capital, Jerusalem, both here and in 1:5, for, in contrast to vv 6-7, where *I AM*'s sentence falls first upon the Northern capital, entailing the fall of that kingdom, in the South it falls upon the state while excluding its capital. Vv 10-16 epexegete Judah's wound by depicting the fate of its key cities.

nāga' (he reaches) means "reach, extend to"; its subject, as argued, must be *I AM*; and the perfective tense is again a future perfect. In sum, *I AM* afflicts his wound right up to the gate of Jerusalem. A. Alt,[22] followed by H. Wolff,[23] thinks that *ša'ar (gate)* refers to Jerusalem because Jerusalem is called "gate" in v 12 and its fall would open the way to the conquest of the rest of Judah. Alt should not be followed, however, because had Micah intended the fall of Jerusalem, the most important city in the theocracy, he would not have expressed its fall by the weak verb "reach" (cf. 3:12). Furthermore, this interpretation entails reconstructing the historical background of the prophecy as one in which an Assyrian invasion from the North led to the fall of Jerusalem or as a reference to its fall in 587 B.C. If the latter, then Micah is not addressing his contemporaries, which seems unlikely. If the Assyrian invasion be in view (see v 1), as both Alt and Wolff assume, Micah was either mistaken or our sources are deficient; either explanation is unacceptable. "Gate" in vv 9Bb and 12Bb is not a figurative synecdoche for Jerusalem (cf. Isa 14:31; Obad 13); the Assyrian army factually arrived at its gate (cf. 2 Kgs 18:27).

H. Wolff[24] for his own reasons argues that in the book of Micah *'ammî (of my people)* means consistently the harassed people of the land for whom Micah has taken it upon himself to be the responsible spokesman. In 2:8, 9, however, the same expression designates the oppressors and the oppressed re-

---

20. *IBHS* §30.5.1.

21. See BDB 98, §2b.

22. A. Alt, "Micah 2,1-5," in *Kleine Schriften zur Geschichte des Volkes Israel,* ed. M. Noth (3 vols.; Munich: C. H. Beck, 1959), 3:373.

23. Wolff, *Micha,* 29.

24. Wolff, *Micha,* 29.

spectively. It is also used of the guilty in 2:4; 6:3, and in these passages God, not Micah, is the antecedent of the pronoun "I." One ought not distinguish too radically between "my people" with reference to God and/or the prophet because they are closely identified; the prophet is *I AM*'s spokesman, and, as such, the distinction becomes attenuated. Whereas the oppressors of "my people" in 2:9 and 3:3 are the rich and powerful within Judah, in 1:9 and 2:4 their oppressor is Assyria, the rod in *I AM*'s hand (cf. Isaiah 10). The use of *'ammî* for all the people corresponds with the use of *'am* in 2:11 and 6:2. Note that in 2:2 "his people" and "Israel" are used interchangeably. In sum, the precise identification of *'ammî* in each use must be decided not by unnaturally forcing one interpretation upon all its uses but by paying close attention to each context. In 1:9 it designates not even all the Judeans but the remnant shut up in Jerusalem (cf. 2:12-13). This interpretation is validated by (1) the parallel, *'ad-yĕrûšālayim (even Jerusalem),* in apposition with "to the gate of my people," (2) the rest of the oracle depicting the overthrow of Judah's Shephelah, and (3) the historical fulfillment of this oracle (see v 1). By mentioning Jerusalem last in this introduction, Micah gives it a fine climactic effect (cf. 6:2).

10 I will discuss the text of the adverbial phrase *bĕgat (in Gath)* in connection with the verb. The identification of Gath is disputed. According to A. Rainey,[25] recent excavations have ruled out sites such as Tell Sheikh Aḥmed el-ʿAreinī near ʿAraq el-Menshīyeh,[26] once identified with Philistine Gath, leaving Tell eṣ-Ṣâfī (Tel Zafit), nine and a half miles north of Lachish, as "the only reasonable candidate for identification with Gath." For *'al-taggîdû (tell it not)* LXX reads *mē megalynesthe,* representing either *'al-tāgdîlû* (cf. Job 19:5, but cf. Obad 12) or *'al-hitgadĕlû* (cf. Ezek 38:23, but cf. Isa 10:15). Syr reads *l' tḥdwn* "do not rejoice," perhaps reflecting Heb *'al-tāgîlû,* but Sebök[27] suggests that originally Syr read *l'-tḥwwn* "do not make it known," which would equal MT. 1QpMic reads either *bgwd lw* ("tell him") or, as J. Carmignac[28] prefers, *bgwdly* ("in the greatness of"); the former confirms MT, the latter, LXX. D. Hillers[29] and H. Wolff,[30] preferring LXX, read "Exult not in Gath." The sense is close to that of MT (i.e., do not let the enemy know of our losses), but the change from MT loses the reference to David's elegy in 2 Sam 1:20 and a fine inclusio with v 15B. Using Syr *tḥdwn* as a starting point, many replace *gat* with *gilgal* "Gilgal,"

25. A. Rainey, "Gath," *IDBSup* 353.

26. *Contra* P. Welten, *Die Königs-Stempel,* Abhandlungen des Deutschen Palästinavereins (Wiesbaden: Harrassowitz, 1969), 68-81, followed by Wolff, *Micha,* 29.

27. Cited by Hillers, *Micah,* 25.

28. J. Carmignac, "Notes sur les Pesharim," *Revue de Qumram* 3 (1963) 517.

29. Hillers, *Micah,* 25.

30. Wolff, *Micha,* 12.

giving the sense "in Gilgal do not rejoice." K. Budde[31] sees in the uncertainty of the versions evidence of a text originally illegible, which some redactor emended on the basis of 2 Sam 1:20. S. Schwantes,[32] following K. Elliger,[33] regards *tgylw,* supported by Pesh and forming the best contrast with the parallel *bākô,* as original and reconstructs *běgannôt-giloh,* yielding the sense "in the gardens of Giloh [i.e., Rejoicing Town] do not rejoice" (so also *BHS*).

The combined arguments for those adopting this and similar readings involving the verb *gyl* and place names with the same consonants are: (1) The command to weep seems inapposite with the prophet's weeping in vv 8-9. (2) Gath, a Philistine city, is out of context in the list of Judean towns that follow. (3) Sargon annihilated Gath in 711 B.C., ten years before Sennacherib's invasion of the Shephelah. (4) 2 Sam 10:20 is not quoted exactly. In defense of MT, however, note: (1) Micah's command not to weep in the presence of Gath, Judah's ancient enemy, is no more absurd than the public actions of David, who, on the death of Saul, rent his clothes, mourned, wept, and fasted with his men (2 Sam 1:11-12), yet taught the people in his elegy, ". . . tell it not in Gath" (vv 17-20). (2) The mention of Gath with the Judean towns is not improper because the assonance here functions differently; namely, not as an omen of the city's doom but as a means of linking Micah's lament over the serious defeat of the House of David with David's lament over the death of the House of Saul, Israel's first dynasty. Adullam (v 15B), at the end of this pericope, functions in the same way; other references to royalty in this lament include 1:14B, 15B. D. K. Innes[34] thinks "tell it not in Gath" was a common proverbial saying, but his thesis lacks decisive support and misses the connection with royalty.[35] (3) If Micah is quoting David for a literary allusion, then it does not matter whether or not Gath was in existence. (4) It may be that Micah altered David's elegy, putting *běgat* before the verb, for the sake of assonance. The initial consonants of the words in MT in both v 10Aa and v 10Ab follow the sequence *bêt, 'ayin, tāw,* and the vowel pattern with the verbs is *a, i, u.* Note, too, the alliteration of *gat/tag* in v 10Aa and of *bāk/bk* in v 10Ab. (5) The proposed alterations in v 10Aa also often presuppose dubiously changing *bākô* into *bě'akkô* "in Akko" in v 10Ab. Moreover, these same critics must also emend v 10Ab, without warrant in any MS or version, by either omitting *'al* or changing it to *'ap* (cf. *BHS*) or emphatic *l,* both yielding the sense "surely weep."[36] If, however, v 10Aa reads, "Tell it not in

---

31. K. Budde, "Das Rätsel von Micha 1," *ZAW* 37 (1917-18) 77-108.
32. S. Schwantes, "Critical Notes on Micah 1:1-16," *VT* 14 (1964) 455.
33. *KS* 16.
34. D. K. Innes, "Some Notes on Micah, Chapter 1," *EvQ* 39 (1967) 126.
35. Cf. *La Formation,* 22.
36. Cf. Schwantes, "Critical Notes on Micah 1:1-16," 455; Wolff, *Micha,* 12.

Gath," the parallel, "surely do not weep," is most apposite. In sum, MT, though on the surface a more difficult reading because it lacks *nomen est omen,* the dominant feature of vv 10-15, makes perfectly good sense in this context.

běgat 'al-taggîdû initiates the paronomasia that characterizes Micah's lament. The plural is indefinite. By adding *bākô 'al-tibkû* Micah intensifies David's elegy; a greater than Saul is about to fall. For the infinitive absolute *bākô* ("surely") LXX reads *en Akim* (according to Swete, Rahlfs, and Ziegler), or *enak(e)im* (according to Cyril of Alexander, Theodoret, and Theophilus of Antioch, followed by Tischendorf), or *en bacheim* (according to Eusebius,[37] LXX^Q [margin of Codex Marchalianus], Syro-Hexapla, four miniscules of the Catena group, and Jerome).[38] LXX should be reconstructed, according to Ziegler et al., because (1) *enak(e)im* never occurs elsewhere; (2) the parallel expectation to *en Geth* is *en Akim;* and (3) the variant reading *enak(e)im* suggests that the LXX original was a place name in keeping with the nature of the passage. On the basis of *en bacheim* various place names have been reconstructed: Bokim,[39] Baka, a valley probably near Jerusalem (cf. Ps 84:6[5]),[40] and *běkabbôn* "in Cabbon" (cf. Josh 15:40).[41]

Though some of these readings recover a pun in connection with a town in the Shephelah, they are rejected because (1) the external evidence is very weak; (2) elsewhere *bōkîm* is rendered by *klauthmōn;* and (3) they cannot explain the alternate readings in LXX. John Taylor[42] noted: "If *Bacheim* had stood in our text, the most careless transcriber would hardly have missed the reference to the place mentioned in Judges." By contrast, *bacheim* can be explained as due to a reviser of LXX who sought to improve the meaningless *enak(e)im* by adding *bě,* or, to his thinking, *bě* was not already expressed by *en.*[43] Most critics (cf. NIV note; omitted in TNIV) who opt for *en Ak(e)im* follow Hadrianai Relandi,[44] who thinks it refers to Akko. They explain the Greek text thus: final

37. Cf. Paul de Lagarde, *Onomastica Sacra* (Göttingen: D. L. Horstmann, 1887), 257.

38. Jerome, *Patrologia Latina* 25:1218.

39. J. Wellhausen, *Die kleinen Propheten* (Berlin: Reimer, 1898; repr. Berlin: de Gruyter, 1963), 136, who reads *bbkym bkw bkw,* "in Bokim surely weep."

40. D. W. Thomas, "The Root *ṣn'* in Hebrew, and the Meaning of *qdrnyt* in Malachi 3:14," *JJS* 1 (1948-49) 182-88.

41. J. W. Bewer and Zeev Vilnay, "The Topography of Israel in the Book of the Prophet Micah [Hebrew]," *BJPES* 19 (1939) 1-19.

42. J. Taylor, *The Massoretic Text and Ancient Versions of the Book of Micah* (London: Williams & Norgate, 2d ed. 1891), 20.

43. Cf. V. Ryssel, *Untersuchungen über die Textgestalt und die Echtheit des Buches Micha* (Leipzig: Hirzel, 1887), 23.

44. H. Relandi, *Palestina ex Monumentis Veteribus Illustrata* (Trajecti Batavorum: Ex libraria Guilielmi Broedelet, 1714), 535.

mêm is due to dittography from the following *mē* "not," leaving the reading *Akei* or *Ake* (since *ei* and *e* are constantly interchanged). According to Strabo,[45] *Ake* is Akko. (In Judg 1:31, however, LXX has *Akchō* for ʿakkô.) These scholars also overhaul MT's *bākô*, transforming it from an infinitive absolute into the proper name ʿakkô "Acco," arguing that *bākô* is softened out of *bĕ*ʿakkô and that ʿ can be elided (cf. Josh 15:29; 19:3; Amos 8:8; Ps 28:8). The text for them reads: "Tell it not in Gath; in Acco do not weep," which Relandi congratulates with the words: "elegans est paronomasia." Nevertheless, accepting MT, which has the support of Vg, Tg, and Syr, requires neither textual sophistry nor accepting an exceptional allusion to a city far to the north of the other towns in this pericope. Besides, if Micah wanted a parallel to Gath, it would have been much simpler and more natural to keep David's parallel, the Philistine city of Ashdod. LXX's *anoikodomeite* reflects a misreading of *tibkû* as *tbnw*.

Instead of *bĕbêt lĕ*ʿaprâ *(in Beth-le-aphrah)*, LXX reads *ex oikou kata gelōta*, confounding, according to S. Schwantes,[46] ʿprh with ḥprh "derision" (?) (cf. Mic 3:7) and *bĕ* with *m[in]*. LXX also confounds ʿayin and ḥêt in Mic 1:11A, where it renders ʿibrî by *kata gelōta*. On the theory of a damaged right margin Elliger,[47] followed by BHS, adds *bĕkarmê* "in the vineyards of Beth . . . ," and Schwantes,[48] followed by J. L. Mays,[49] adds *bĕḥūṣōt* "in the streets of Beth. . . ." Both conjectures are unnecessary. Syr and Tg read "houses" (pl.) of Ophrah, instead of singular *bêt*, not understanding that *bêt* "house" (i.e., "temple") in proper names stems from Old Canaanite names involving the temple of the pagan deity worshipped by the town before the Israelite Conquest.[50] Both the *lĕ* and the pointing of ʿprh are problematic. Syr and Theod, according to V. Ryssel,[51] thought of Ophrah of Josh 18:23, a Benjamite town on the Judean border, and therefore do not take *lĕ* as part of the town but revocalize the text to ʿoprâ. K. Budde,[52] with the help of LXX, reads *mbyt-ʾl lĕ*ʿoprâ. Ophrah of Benjamin, however, is out of place in this oracle of doom against Judah. ʿoprâ is the more difficult reading in light of the two Ophrahs, one in Benjamin and one in Manasseh, and, as Elliger[53] noted,

---

45. Strabo, *Geography* 16.2.25.

46. Schwantes, "A Critical Study of the Text of Micah," 38.

47. *KS* 17.

48. Schwantes, "Critical Notes on Micah 1:10-16," 456.

49. Mays, *Micah*, 49, 56.

50. Cf. Y. Aharoni, *The Land of the Bible: A Historical Geography* (Philadelphia: Westminster, 1967), 97.

51. Ryssel, *Micha*, 26.

52. Budde, "Das Rätsel von Micha 1," 77-78.

53. *KS* 16.

lĕ with *bêt* in a place name is otherwise unattested. Is *lĕ* due to dittography from *lĕ* in the next verset? H. Wolff[54] plausibly suggests, however, that *lĕ* was inserted at the outset to characterize it as "House for Dust." D. Hillers[55] calls attention to Robinson's suggestion that the place name Aphrah may be related to the Ophrah in Caleb's genealogy (1 Chr 4:14). The place name is both unparalleled in form and unidentified. K. Elliger[56] supposes that it is *ettaijibe* on the way from *bêt-gibrin* to Hebron.

ʿāpār (in dust) is an accusative of place[57] and sounds like *lĕʿaprâ:* "In Dust Town roll yourself in dust." *Qere* reads *hitpallāšî (roll yourself)*, but *Kethib* reads *hitpallāštî* "I rolled myself," and LXX's *katapasasthe* and Vg's *vos conspergite* render *hitpallĕšû (roll yourselves;* cf. Jer 6:26). Mur 88 reads with either *Qere* or LXX. *Kethib* is a late corruption, perhaps to harmonize with vv 8-9. Since cities and their inhabitants are usually addressed by the feminine,[58] there is no need to correct it by the versions. Their masculine plural forms may be due to the masculine plural pronouns in vv 10A and 11A. The implied subject of *Qere's* feminine singular imperative is *yôšebet* (cf. vv 11, 12, 13, 15). Most ancients translated *plš* by "sprinkle." The meaning "roll" is supported by the cognate languages: Syriac *pls* "to dig, break through," Assyrian *palasu* "dig a hole," and Ugaritic *plt* "to wallow." G. S. Glanzman called to Schwantes's[59] attention an identical phrase in the *Anat Epic,*[60] *ʿpr plṭt* "the dust of wallowing." Rolling in dust symbolized an abject and humiliating defeat (cf. Gen 3:14; Ps 44:26[25]). The strong command to avoid adverse publicity by refraining from weeping among the enemy in v 10A is matched in v 10B by the command to ventilate among one's friends in the most cathartic way the bitter lament over destruction and defeat (cf. Jer 6:26; 25:34; Ezek 27:30).

11 Adopting and adapting the suggestion of B. Duhm,[61] most commentators emend *ʿibrî lākem (Pass on)* in v 11A to read *šôpār yāʿăbi(y)rû lāk,* thereby discovering an assonance with *šāpîr.* In this emendation *ʿbr* means "send abroad" (i.e., "sound") (cf. Lev 25:9) so that v 11A reads: "Sound (for you) the ram's horn . . ." (i.e., "summon the people to a solemn convocation of mourning . . ."). Others read "at the ram's horn they depart far away," but this stretches

54. Wolff, *Micha,* 12.
55. Hillers, *Micah,* 25.
56. *KS* 47.
57. *IBHS* §10.2.2.
58. Cf. *IBHS* §6.4.1.
59. Schwantes, "Critical Notes on Micah 1:10-16," 456.
60. *Anat Epic,* 67.6.15.
61. B. Duhm, "Anmerkungen zu den zwölf Propheten, III: Das Buch Micha," *ZAW* 31 (1911) 183.

too far the use of *'br*. A. S. van der Woude[62] for metrical reasons detaches *t* from the preceding word and reads *t'bry*, and, appealing to Lev 25:9, obtains the same sense without adding *šôpār*. But these conjectures by definition lack textual support. Furthermore, they are unnecessary because the play on assonance in v 11A involves *yôšebet* and *bōšet* and on sense between *šāpîr* (i.e., "Beauty Town") and "passing on in shameful nudity." The feminine singular imperative *'ibrî* agrees with the feminine singular vocative *yôšebet*. The preposition *lĕ* with the pronoun *lākem* marks the action as being of interest to the performer.[63] Because of the gender disagreement between *'ibrî* and *lākem* some MSS, Syr, S. Schwantes,[64] and J. Mays[65] favor singular, reading *lāk*, whereas Vg, Tg, Aquila, and Sym make the verb plural. LXX inexplicably omits both words and adds *kathelo* "I will take down" between *šāpîr* and *'eryâ*. B. Renaud[66] changes *lākem* into *lĕkā* so that the verset reads: "Pass on, go, inhabitant of Shapir." These changes are unnecessary because grammatical discord both in gender and number is acceptable Hebrew style, as I. Willi-Plein[67] points out. Similar phenomena occur in ancient Semitic inscriptions that disallow an extended period of scribal transmission. J. M. Lindenberger of Vancouver School of Theology pointed out to the author changes from third to first person in the inscription (ca. 9th cent.?) from Tell Fekheriyeh.[68] Lindenberger adds, "An index of the stylistic freedom with which such shifts are made is the fact that the first change of persons in the Fekheriyeh text does not take place at exactly the same point in the Akkadian and Aramaic versions." The switch from feminine singular imperative to masculine plural is due to the priority of the masculine gender in Hebrew grammar[69] and serves to break the group down into individuals. In the construct chain, *yôšebet šāpîr* (*inhabitants of Shapir*), *yôšebet* is a feminine collective[70] and *šāpîr* is a locative genitive (i.e., "those who inhabit Shaphir"). *šāpîr* is an adjectival form of the root *špr*, which is not attested in Hebrew but is in Aramaic with the meaning "to shine, to be pleasing or beautiful, to glitter."

62. A. S. van der Woude, "Micah I,10-16," in *Hommages à André Dupont-Sommer* (Paris, 1971), 349, cited in *La Formation*, 23.

63. *IBHS* §11.2.10.

64. Schwantes, "Critical Notes on Micah 1:10-16," 456.

65. Mays, *Micah*, 49.

66. B. Renaud, *Michée, Sophonie, Nahum* (Paris: Gabalda, 1987), 32.

67. I. Willi-Plein, *Vorformen der Schriftexegese innerhalb des Alten Testaments*, BZAW 123 (Berlin and New York: de Gruyter, 1971), 79.

68. A. Abou-Assaf, P. Bordreuil, and A. R. Millard, *La Statue de Tell Fekherye et Son Inscription Bilingue Assyro-Araméenne*, Recherche sur les Civilisations, Cahier 7 (Paris: ADPF, 1982).

69. *IBHS* §6.5.3.

70. GKC §122s; *IBHS* §6.4.2.

The play is sharpened by putting "Beauty Town" back to back with ʿeryâ "nakedness." Its location is uncertain. H. Graetz[71] compares it with šāmîr of Josh 15:48, for which Eusebius gives *Sapheir*.[72] W. Dever,[73] on the basis of archaeological evidence, proposed Khirbet el-Kôm or Tell ʿEitun. LXX reads *tas poleis* "the cities," taking ʿāreyhā instead of ʿeryâ and dropping bōšet "shame." Those who favor adding initial šôpār to the verset also, basing themselves on LXX, often add *min* to ʿeryâ, read either tēšēb for bōšet or drop it, and connect ʿeryâ with yāṣʾâ, so that v 11B reads: "The inhabitants of Zaanan do not come forth from its city," or ". . . do not come forth but stay in its city." If šôpār is not added, the construct ʿeryâ-bōšet (in shameful nakedness) consists of an adverbial accusative, ʿeryâ, modifying ʿibrî, and an attribute genitive, bōšet. Whereas ʿārôm (v 8) is an adjective derived from ʿwr "be exposed, bare," ʿeryâ is a noun derived from ʿārâ "be naked, bare." The two expressions of nakedness occur as a compound in Ezek 16:7, 22, 39; 23:29. Nakedness, an exposure that brings shame, is a marked feature of judgment on evildoers (cf. Deut 28:48; Isa 47:3; Lam 4:21). This common OT motif favors joining bōšet with ʿeryâ. As noted in connection with Micah's going about naked (v 8A), there is also here the added connotation of deportation. V 11A contains two plays involving sound and/or sense: bōšet sounds like yôšebet, and ʿeryâ sounds something like ʿibrî. As they go into captivity, they who once prided themselves on their splendor will be stripped and put to shame. H. Wolff[74] achieves a nice paronomasia in German: "Die Shoene wird geschaendet."

In the construct yôšebet ṣaʾănān (the inhabitants of Zaanan), yôšebet functions in the same way as in the parallel, yôšebet šāpîr. ṣaʾănān is possibly ṣěnān "Zenan" (Josh 15:37). Some Greek MSS and versions substituted *Senaar* (= šinʿār; Gen 10:10) for unknown Zaanan. Syr omits ʿ, which was probably added for the sake of paronomasia with yṣʿ. Theodotion renders the proper name by *euthenousa* "flourishing," presumably equating the name with ṣʿnn. L. Reinke[75] suggested either a play on sound or a paronomasia. In the former, ṣaʾănān is related to ṣōʾn "flocks"; that is, "the inhabitants of 'Flock Town' will no longer go forth in pastoral gladness with their flocks." If the latter, ṣaʾănān is related to lōʾ-yāṣěʾâ (do not come forth) (i.e., to battle as in 1:3): "The inhabitants of 'Going Forth Town' do not go out to battle because, from fear before the en-

71. H. Graetz, *Emendations in plerosque Sacrae Scripturae Veteris Testamenti libros* (Breslau: Schlesische Buchdruckerei, 1895).

72. Cited by Hillers, *Micah*, 26.

73. W. C. Dever, "Iron Age Epigraphic Material from the Area of Khirbet el-Kôm," *HUCA* 40-41 (1969-70) 189.

74. Wolff, *Micha*, 29.

75. L. Reinke, *Der Prophet Micha* (Giessen: Roth, 1874), 95.

emy, they cower behind their walls." The imperative *'ibrî* suggests that the perfective *yāṣĕ'â* is best construed as a persistent future perfective, which represents a single situation extending from the present into the future.[76]

J. Lindblom[77] did not exaggerate when he said that v. 11Bb is the most uncertain of all. No version agrees with MT or with another. The problem is caused by a combination of variables: (1) syntactic disagreement in forms; (2) *'emdâ* "standing place" is a *hapax legomenon;* (3) other words have rare values (e.g., *lqḥ* "to take away"); and (4) versions seem to have had a different Hebrew text. *BHK* reflects a common reconstruction, *mîsōdô bêt hā'ēṣel yuqqaḥ mimmᵉkôn 'emdātô* "Beth-ezel is rent from its foundation wall, from the place on which it lies." Lindblom similarly proposed *yissāpeh bêt hā'ēṣel yuqqaḥ mimma'ĕmadô* "Beth-ezel is uprooted; it is taken from its place." These conjectures and their equivalents dismiss *mispad* "mourning," though it is attested in all the versions — LXX *kopsasthai* misread *mispad* as an Aramaic peal infinitive — build on the unlikely assumption that *'ēṣel* has the meaning "root," and either replace *mikkem* by *mimkôn* without textual evidence or drop it. B. Renaud,[78] retaining *mispad,* reads: "Mourning at Beth-Ha-ezel; your place is taken from you." He adds *bĕ* to *bêt,* with S. Schwantes[79] regards *mikkem* a metathesis of *mimak,* reads *'mdtk* for *'emdātô,* and repoints *yiqqaḥ* as passive *yuqqaḥ.* Schwantes, assuming the damage of the right margin, reads [*'ăśêh*] *mspd byt h'ṣl yqḥ mimmāk 'emdātĕkā* "Make lamentation, Beth-ezel. He takes from you your standing place." In addition to the objections against B. Renaud regarding *mimak* and *'emdātĕkā,* Schwantes's proposal rests on the fallacious damaged margin hypothesis. D. Hillers,[80] who rejects that hypothesis, nevertheless emends the text even more extensively: [*sipdî*] *mispēd bêt hā'ēṣel yiqqaḥ mimmāk ḥemdātēk* "Mourn greatly, Beth-Ezel; he takes away your treasures."

All these conjectures are unnecessary. *mispad (in mourning)* (see v 8) is an adverbial accusative and *bêt hā'ēṣel (Beth-ha-ezel)* is the subject, though conceivably *mispad* could be the subject and *bêt hā'ēṣel* an adverbial accusative, "the mourning at Beth-ha-esel." The name is probably Old Canaanite (see v 10), and the article, though rare in proper names, is acceptable Hebrew.[81] The expression is elliptical: "The wailing at Beth-Ezel shows that the city is destroyed, and therefore it shall. . . ." The location of this town, which is mentioned nowhere else, is unknown. *'ēṣel* may be derived from a verb meaning "take away"

76. *IBHS* §30.5.1.
77. J. Lindblom, *Micha literarisch untersucht* (Åbo: Åbo Akademi, 1929), 47.
78. Renaud, *Michée,* 32.
79. Schwantes, "Critical Notes on Micah 1:10-16," 457.
80. Hillers, *Micah,* 26.
81. *IBHS* §13.5.1.

(cf. Num 11:17, 25). The synonym *yiqqaḥ (is taken),* here as in Prov 27:13 "to take away," explains the *omen* in the *nomen.* The subject is impersonal, "one takes," which is rendered here by the passive. Because the antecedent of *mikkem* is ambiguous, many want to emend it, but all versions attest it. Like *lākem* in v 11A, it refers to the inhabitants of Shapir and, in addition, possibly Zaanan. LXX's *plēgēn odynēs* "blow of pain" (cf. Syr *mḥotāh* "her stroke") for *ʿemdātô (its place to take a stand)* is puzzling. On the basis of LXX, J. Wellhausen[82] reconstructs *makkat dĕmāʿôt* "blow of tears," but both conjectures are far from the Hebrew text and unlikely in light of *mārôt* in v 12. The *hapax legomenon, ʿemdātô,* derived from *ʿmd,* may mean either "its standing ground" (so BDB, KB), or "the steadfastness of its residents" (GB). The former pertains to the destruction of the city, the latter to the deportation of its inhabitants. The theme of exile in this prophecy favors the latter. Beth-ha-ezel probably stands in contrast with Zaanan. Whereas the inhabitants of Zaanan did not come forth to help the inhabitants of Shaphir, Beth-ha-ezel offers no defense either because its mourning inhabitants have been deported.

    12 *kî (surely)* can mean either "because" (NRSV) or "surely." The following interpretation of *ḥālâ (wait anxiously)* favors the asseverative force. Having attached *kāp* of initial *kî* to the preceding verse, B. Renaud[83] is left with its *yôd* as a prefix to *ḥlh* and interprets the resulting *yḥlh* as interrogative, "Will/Can the inhabitant of Maroth hope for good?" He finds support in LXX's *tis.* Not only does his argument rest on his unnecessary conjectured emendations of the preceding line, but he must further suppose that the interrogative mood was given by the tone of voice. S. Schwantes,[84] on the hypothesis of a damaged margin, reconstructs *ʾêk,* "How the inhabitants of Maroth hoped for good." *mî,* which stood behind LXX, can also be an interjection, "How!"[85] If it means interrogative "who," *yôšebet* is vocative. Probably *mêm* and *kāp* became confused in paleo-Hebrew script. MT offers a pungent irony without adding, redistributing, or changing consonants or changing punctuation. The *mêrĕkâ* accentuation of *ḥālâ* identifies the qal third masculine singular as perfective, a persistent future perfective as in v 11, presumably of *ḥûl* "writhe." But Syr presumes the piel of the root *yḥl* "hope"; probably initial *y* of original third feminine singular *yḥlh* was lost through haplography with *kî.* The suggestion finds some support in LXX's *hērxato,* apparently reading *yāḥēl,* the hiphil of *ḥll* "to begin." The original could also have been *hôḥîlâ,* hiphil third feminine singular perfective

82. J. Wellhausen, *Die kleinen Propheten* (Berlin: Reimer, 1898), 136.
83. *La Formation,* 24.
84. Schwantes, "Critical Notes on Micah 1:10-16," 457.
85. *HALOT* 545.

of *yḥl*. One cannot appeal to Judg 3:25 for a bi-form *ḥlh* "to hope" because the form there is hiphil. Others, such as Ibn Ezra, Qimḥi, R. Gordis,[86] and G. R. Driver,[87] invest *ḥûl* with the meaning "to be in anguish for" or "to tremble" (cf. Jer 15:11; Hos 10:1; Jonah 4:4-9); that is, "it trembles for its goods (or its happiness)." These suggestions stumble over *lĕṭôb* *(for good)*. R. Gordis relates *ṭôb* to the Aramaic root *twb'* (Syr *tab*), giving it the meaning "very, much" (i.e., "it trembles greatly . . ."). But why should one replace good Hebrew with Aramaic? Possibly MT can be defended by interpreting *lĕ* as a pregnant preposition, implying another verb:[88] "writhed and waited for good." For the grammar of *yôšebet* see v 11. *mārôt* means "Bitter Town." Its plural form is not uncommon with abstract nouns.[89] Phonemically Maroth can be related to Maarath of Josh 15:59, which is located by K. Elliger[90] somewhere between Gedor (5 km. north of Beth Zur, not far west of the road leading from Jerusalem to Hebron) and Beth-Anoth, which lies close to Hebron. The play in sense between "bitter" and "good" is more subtle than the other plays on place names but just as devastating, especially if *ṭôb* means or connotes "sweet," as D. Hillers[91] thinks on the basis of Song 1:23 and Ugaritic and Akkadian cognates. *Mārâ* is a known opposite of *ṭôb* (Job 21:25). As "Beauty Town" stood in opposition to "shameful nakedness" in v 11A, so now "Bitter Town" stands in opposition to "sweetness." *ṭôb* is a metonymy for military aid, probably from Jerusalem; instead the Assyrian army marched right up to the gates of Jerusalem.

In v 12B *kî (But no!)* can mean either "because" (RSV; corrected in NRSV to "yet") or "but no."[92] For *yārad (comes down)*, another qal persistent perfective, see Mic 1:3. There is no difference in meaning between the gender doublets *rāʿ* (masculine) *(evil)* and *rāʿâ* (feminine). This masculine noun subject can mean either "moral evil" or, as here and in Isa 45:7, "physical disaster." Micah makes a pun on these two meanings in 2:1 and 2:3. *mēʾēt (from)*, in contrast to *mēʿim*, is used almost always with persons.[93] Here it expresses origination: the calamity[94] came ultimately from God. The statement, *yhwh lĕšaʿar yĕrûšālāyim* (I AM to the gate of Jerusalem) helps confirm the emendation proposed in Mic 1:9 of converting *makôte(y)â* to *makkat yāh*. The immediate cause, Sennacherib's

---

86. R. Gordis, "A Note on *ṭôb*," *JTS* 35 (1934) 186-88.
87. G. R. Driver, "Linguistic and Textual Problems: Minor Prophets," *JTS* 39 (1938) 265.
88. GKC §119ee.
89. *IBHS* §7.4.2.
90. *KS* 50.
91. Hillers, *Micah*, 26.
92. BDB 474.
93. BDB 86, §4; for compound prepositions see GKC §119d.
94. Cf. BDB 948, §II.

army, is not mentioned to evoke cosmic truth (see vv 3-5, 9). LXX, Tg, and Syr (*contra* Vg) read *ša'ar* as plural. Favoring MT is the singular *ša'ar* in v 9. Nevertheless, it is easier to see the *yôd* as dropping out rather than being added by dittography from *yĕrûšālāyim*. Jerusalem, the expected source of strength, will prove impotent because God's wrath will fall upon it. V 12B contains both sound and sense plays. Note the alliteration of *yĕrûšālāyim* with *yārad* and of *ša'ar* with *rā'*. *yĕrûšālāyim* is based on the root *šlm* "peace," the antonym of *rā'*, and *rā'* is also a known antonym of *ṭôb* (Isa 5:20).

13 The search for a more certain verb than *rĕtōm* (harness) led K. Elliger[95] to conjecture *'irkî* "prepare for war," and S. Schwantes[96] *'āsart* (second feminine singular qal perfective), "you bound." These conjectures are more uncertain than MT's *hapax legomenon*. BHS, following K. Marti,[97] repoints MT's masculine singular imperative as infinitive absolute to alleviate discrepancy with the feminine singular vocative, *yôšebet lākîš* (*O inhabitants of Lachish*); the disagreement is acceptable in Biblical Hebrew (cf. *lākem* in Mic 1:11). Although the etymology of *rĕtōm* is uncertain, Syr and Tg plausibly give the meaning "harness." BDB relates the word to Arabic *ratima* "to bind thread to a finger as a reminder" and GB, citing P. Haupt, points to Akkadian *ratamu* "to bind," "enclose." The singular distributes action to each one. *hammerkābâ* (*chariots*), probably a collective, refers especially to war chariots, sometimes used in flight (1 Kgs 12:18). The Hebrew strangely commands that the chariot be harnessed *lārekeš* (*to the race horses*). H. Donner,[98] to make better sense, reverses the words to *rekeš lammerkābâ* but thereby destroys the play on sound, *lārekeš lākîš*. W. Rudolph[99] (*contra* Donner) compares MT to classical Latin "currum jungere equis." The author rendered acceptable Hebrew, "harness the chariot to the race horses," by acceptable English. The articles prefixed to the collectives, *hammerkābâ* and *lārekeš*, signify that which is vivid to the imagination.[100] *rekeš* "a team of race horses" are swift-riding steeds (cf. Esth 8:10, 14, "swift horses" [NIV] for courier service) in contrast to *sûs* "chariot horses," with which *merkābâ* normally occurs (Isa 2:7; Mic 5:9). The two kinds of horses are contrasted in 1 Kgs 4:28. Note the pungent irony: harness your war chariots to your race horses (for the fastest evacuation possible). Observing the pictures in *The*

95. *KS* 20.

96. Schwantes, "Critical Notes on Micah 1:10-16," 458.

97. K. Marti, *Das Dodekapropheton*, Kurzer Hand-Commentar zum Alten Testament 13 (Tübingen: Mohr, 1904) (hereafter KHC), 271.

98. H. Donner, *Israel unter den Völkern*, VTSup 11 (Leiden: Brill, 1964), 95.

99. W. Rudolph, *Micha, Nahum, Habakuk, Zephanja*, KAT 13/3 (Gütersloh: Mohn, 1975), 36.

100. *IBHS* §13.5.1.

Ancient Near East in Pictures Relating to the Old Testament,[101] H. Weippert[102] notes that by means of neck-harnesses two or four horses abreast were bound to a chariot.

The construct *yôšebet lākâš (inhabitants of Lachish)* grammatically resembles *yôšebet šāpîr* in v 11. In both instances the *constructio ad sensum,* in which priority is given to the masculine gender, accounts for the masculine singular imperative.[103] Although *lākîš* is almost universally identified with Tell ed-Duweir, G. Ahlström[104] identifies it as Libnah and S. Mittman thinks Tell ʿĒṭūn is Lachish.[105] G. I. Davies[106] defended the consensus:

> The significance of Lachish is clearly indicated in its portrayal on Sennacherib's palace reliefs from Nineveh, whose size and prominence mark out its capture as the major military success of Sennacherib's Judaean campaign. . . . Tell ed-Duweir demands identification with a city of the magnitude of Lachish and there is really no other name that comes seriously into the reckoning.

Lachish is one of the chariot cities built by Solomon (1 Kgs 9:19; 10:26) and fortified by Rehoboam (2 Chr 11:9). Judah's military buildup at the time of the Assyrian menace began with Uzziah (2 Chr 26:9, 11-15), was exacerbated by the tribute demanded by the Assyrian from the Judean kings beginning with Ahaz, and was enlarged by Hezekiah (2 Chr 32:1-9). Judah's defense budget placed an onerous financial burden on the poor. Excavations confirm that the city was strongly fortified in the Iron Age.[107] As soon as Sennacherib captured it, he made it his headquarters (2 Kgs 18:14, 17; 19:8).

S. Schwantes,[108] with neither textual nor historical warrant, emends *rēʾšît*

---

101. J. B. Pritchard, ed., *The Ancient Near East in Pictures Relating to the Old Testament* (Princeton: Princeton University Press, 2d ed. 1969) (hereafter *ANEP*), 11, 166, 184, 190.

102. H. Weippert, "Pferde und Streitwagen," in *Biblisches Reallexikon,* ed. K. Galling (Tübingen: J. C. B. Mohr [Paul Siebeck], 1977), 253.

103. Cf. GKC §145.

104. G. Ahlström, "Is Tell ed-Duweir Ancient Lachish?" *PEQ* 112 (1980) 7-9; idem, "Tell ed-Duweir: Lachish or Libnah?" *PEQ* 115 (1983) 103-4.

105. Cited approvingly by D. Kellermann, "Überlieferungsprobleme alttestamentlicher Ortsnamen," *VT* 28 (1978) 428.

106. G. I. Davies, "Tell Ed-Duweir = Ancient Lachish," *PEQ* 113 (1982) 25-28.

107. D. Ussishkin, "Lachish," in M. Avi-Yonah and E. Stern, ed., *Encyclopedia of Archaeological Excavations in the Holy Land* (Jerusalem: Israel Exploration Society and Massada Press, and Englewood Cliffs, N.J.: Prentice-Hall, 1977), 3:735-53; idem, "Excavations at Tel Lachish, 1973-1977," *Tel Aviv* 5 (1978) 1-97; M. and Y. Aharoni, "The Stratification of Judahite Sites in the 8th and 7th Centuries B.C.E.," *BASOR* 224 (1976) 73-90.

108. Schwantes, "Critical Notes on Micah 1:10-16," 458.

(beginning), a predicate nominative whose subject *hî* ("it") is *bĕʾēr šebaʿ* (cf. Amos 5:5; 8:14). It can mean either "chief" or "beginning," but the latter is preferred because the sense of the former is unclear. The immediate context and the historical military importance of Lachish strongly argue that *ḥaṭṭāʾt (of sin)*, a genitive of measure,[109] is a metonymy for its reliance on military might (cf. Deut 17:16; Isa 2:7; 31:1-2; Hos 10:13-15; 14:4[3]; Mic 5:9-10[10-11]). As Micah implies in 5:9-15, dependence on military might destroys covenantal faith as much as do witchcraft and idolatry (cf. 2 Sam 24:1-10). The first city to introduce the sin of secularism into Judean society will be among the first to suffer the punishment. The switch from second masculine singular imperative *rĕtōm* "harness" in v 13A to third feminine singular *hî* "it" in v 13B to second feminine singular *bāk (in you)* in v 13Bb suggests that v 13Ba is parenthetical. Throughout the passage, however, Micah has changed the genders of his addressees. *lĕbat-ṣiyôn (Daughter Zion)*, in which adverbial phrase *ṣiyôn* is in apposition to *bat,* reflects the poetic inclination to personify cities according to the feminine gender because *ʿîr* "city" is feminine.[110] The reversion to second feminine singular, *bāk* "in you" links v 10Bb with v 10A — only Lachish is singled out for judgment in this verse — and the substantiating particle *kî (because)* connects the judgment announced in v 10A with the cause explained in v 10Bb. Niphal *nimṣĕʾû (were found)* is an incomplete passive.[111] For the meaning of *pišʿê (transgression)* see 1:5; its plural form suggests that all the accusations leveled by Micah against Jerusalem apply as well to Lachish. The connection of v 13Bb with v 13Ba suggests that secularism spawned Israel's other sins. *yiśrāʾēl (Israel's)*, a genitive of agency,[112] refers to the Southern Kingdom (cf. 1:5, 14, 15). In addition to the alliteration of *la.kš (lārekeš lākîš)* there is also that of *rk (hammerkābâ-lārekeš)*.

14 *lākēn (Therefore)* couples the fall of Lachish with the fall of Moresheth Gath, Micah's hometown (see 1:1). *tittĕnî (you will give)*, second feminine singular, presumably an address to Daughter Zion, seems objectionable since *šillûḥîm (parting gifts)* means "dowry," a gift from a father to his daughter. Many reconstruct *yittēn* from LXX *dōsei,* though some Greek MSS read *dōseis* with MT, or Vg's *dabit,* or *yittĕnû,* or its equivalent and so interpret the verb as impersonal (i.e., "one will give"). Similarly, W. Rudolph[113] changes *tittĕnî* to *tittĕnnû,* second masculine plural, "you [impersonal] will give." In keeping with the damaged right hand hypothesis, S. Schwantes[114] conjectures

---

109. *IBHS* §9.5.3.
110. *IBHS* §6.4.2. See Follis, "The Holy City as Daughter."
111. *IBHS* §23.2.2.
112. *IBHS* §9.5.1.
113. Rudolph, *Micha,* 46.
114. Schwantes, "Critical Notes on Micah 1:10-16," 459.

rō'škem yittēn "your chief will give," and Mays[115] vocalizes MT's consonants *lknttny* as *lāk nittěnū* "to you [i.e., Moresheth Gath] they give." "Daughter Zion," however, by metonymy stands for its leaders, and *ad sensum* the notion of "dowry" is acceptable. Also, without second feminine singular here one is unprepared for the reference to Daughter Zion in v 16. Finally, the parallel in v 14B shows that the rulers of Israel are the subjects. *šillûḥîm* means either "dismissal [of the wife to her father's house]" (i.e., "divorce") (Exod 18:12) or "dismissal gift [of the father of the bride to the groom]" (i.e., "dowry") (1 Kgs 9:16; cf. Ugaritic *tlh* "dowry"). The latter meaning finds support in 1 Kgs 9:16, where it is recorded that Pharaoh gave a city as a dowry. "Dowry" is a metaphor for "tribute." *'al (to)* need not be emended because it may govern an indirect object after *ntn*.[116]

môrešet (Moresheth) may be auricularly related to *mě'ōrāśâ* "bride." All versions derived *môrešet (Moresheth)* from *yrš* and interpreted it as a common noun, "inheritance" or "property." The style of the pericope, however, strongly favors taking it as the name of Micah's hometown as in 1:1. P. Haupt[117] by soundplay connects *môrešet* with *mě'ōrāśâ*, pual feminine participle of *'āraś* "to be betrothed" (Exod 22:15[16]; Deut 22:23, 25, 27), and W. Rudolph[118] refines the form to its philological equivalent, *mě'ōrešet*. In paronomasia etymological equivalency is irrelevant. The senseplay is now clear: the rulers of Jerusalem will have to give a dowry (i.e., a tribute), along with the bride (i.e., the loss of Moresheth Gath). A. Saarisalo[119] thinks that Moresheth, which he derives from *ḥarita* "to enclose," was added to *gat (Gath)* to distinguish this Gath from the well-known Gath of the Philistines. The reference to Moresheth in 1:1, however, suggests that Gath qualifies Moresheth to indicate the proximity of Micah's hometown to Gath or some special relation between the cities. Most scholars identify Moresheth Gath with Tell ej-Judeideh,[120] but Zechariah Kallai-Kleinmann[121] thinks that the biblical and traditional data are inconclusive.

A. Demsky[122] argues persuasively that *bottê (workshops)* means "workshops" (cf. also Jer 18:2, *bêt hayyôṣēr* "the house of the potter"). J. L. Mays,[123]

115. Mays, *Micah*, 49.

116. See BDB 757, §7c(a)(b).

117. Haupt, "The Book of Micah," 19.

118. Rudolph, *Micha*, 48.

119. A. Saarisalo, "Topographical Researches in the Shephelah," *JPOS* 11 (1931) 98-99.

120. J. Jeremias, "Moreseth-Gath, die Heimat des Propheten Micha," *PJ* 29 (1933) 42-53; O. Procksch, "Gath," *ZDPV* 66 (1943) 174-91.

121. Cited approvingly by Hillers, *Micah*, 27.

122. A. Demsky, "The Houses of Achzib: A Critical Note on Micah 1:14b," *IEJ* 16 (1966) 211-15.

123. Mays, *Micah*, 49.

following Elliger and ignoring Demsky, destroys the pun by emending to *yôšebet* "community." *'akzîb (of Achzib)*, a possessive genitive,[124] means "deceptive" (i.e., "Deception Town"). Since it is apparently to be located at Tell el-Beida, Demsky identifies Achzib with *kĕzîb* in Gen 38:5 and *kōzēbā'* in 1 Chr 4:22, where it occurs, as in Josh 15:44 and Mic 1:14-15, in conjunction with Mareshah. Y. Aharoni[125] reports an ambiguous reading, *lbyt 'kzy[b]*, on an ostracon. In the nominal clause *lĕ'akzāb (will prove deceptive)*, *lĕ* has the meaning "to become," and the noun *'akzāb (deceptive)* provides the basis for paronomasia with the proper name. This noun occurs elsewhere only in an illuminating complaint by Jeremiah: "The blow inflicted on me is incurable [cf. Mic 1:9]. . . . Will you become to me like a *deceptive* brook?" (Jer 15:18). As a dried-up brook disappoints one expecting a drink, so Achzib will betray the expectations of Israel's rulers of financial gain from the workshops at Achzib, brought about by its fall and the deportation of its productive inhabitants. In both v 14A and v 14B Israel's leaders suffer financial reversal; in the former they had to give tribute, in the latter they lose tribute. *BHS* with many supposes the difficult plural *malkê (kings)* as due to dittography with *yiśrā'ēl*. The versions, however, also read plural, and a reference to the king (singular) would be unique in this book. The plural may signify the loss of revenue to Israel's future rulers as well. At Lachish, Moresheth, and other places, excavations have yielded handles on clay pitchers bearing the inscription *lmlk* "belonging to the king." Achzib, like those sites, also supplied the king with revenue. Consistent with his point of view (cf. 1:5; 3:1, 8, 9), Micah names the rulers in Jerusalem as "kings of *yiśrā'ēl (Israel)*," a genitive of relation.[126]

15 *'ōd (Also)* can mean "beside," or "again" (NRSV). The latter, however, diffuses the threat by raising the question, "When previously did God bring a conqueror against Mareshah?" "Besides" fits the context well. The fall of the other cities and their inhabitants assumes a conqueror. K. Elliger,[127] assuming a damaged margin, unnecessarily conjectures an interrogative *hê* with *'ōd* (Will also . . . ?). His proposal, followed by many, makes sense if *hayyōrēš* means an innocent "heir." But the root *yrš*, behind the qal participle *hayyōrēš (the conqueror)*, can mean either "to dispossess peacefully" or more frequently "to dispossess through hostility," and so with the participle "heir" (2 Sam 14:7; Jer 49:1) or "dispossessor" (i.e., conqueror) (Jer 8:2) respectively. In this judgment oracle, the latter is more probable. A new heir will dispossess by conquest Judah's

---

124. *IBHS* §9.5.1.

125. Y. Aharoni, "Trial Excavation in the 'Solar Shrine' at Lachish: Preliminary Report," *IEJ* 18 (1968) 168-69.

126. *IBHS* §9.5.1.

127. *KS* 22.

old heritage. The article shows that the conqueror is vivid in Micah's imagination.[128] This is the only time in the chapter that Micah mentions the human agent behind the invasion. Most critics (cf. *BHS*) plausibly emend by a simple metathesis the unexpected *'ābî*, a *scriptio defectiva* for *'ābî'* (attested in some MSS), into *yābô' (he will come)*. The use of first person with reference to *I AM* is customary in Micah when switching from accusation to judicial sentence (cf. vv 6-7), but that is not the case here. A use of first person here would be confusing because in vv 8-9 it referred to Micah and in v 12 it referred to *I AM* in the third person. Finally, this *scriptio defectiva* is unparalleled with this very common verb. All versions, with the exception of some Greek MSS, confirm MT, suggesting that metathesis occurred early in the text's tradition. B. Renaud[129] ingeniously conjectures *y'bylk*, hiphil, "he will cause you to wear mourning" (cf. Ezek 31:15; Lam 2:8). His conjecture, however, destroys the play on *bô'* between v 15A and v 15B, which are also connected by *'d. bô'* with Mareshah's enemy as subject and with the preposition *lě* in *lāk (upon you)* has a hostile sense, "to come upon, fall or light upon, attack" (cf. Job 3:25[130]), and does not have the sense, as many critics emend and interpret the clause, "Will an heir still come to you?" The feminine suffix refers to *yôšebet* (see 1:9, 11, 12, 13).

    yôšebet mārēšâ (inhabitants of Mareshah) sounds like *yōrēš* because of vowel patterns and the repetition of *rêš* and *šîn*. A play on sense may also be intended. By popular etymologizing the town name may have been equated with *yōrēš* "a new owner." In Josh 15:44, however, an apparently quiescent *'alep*, not represented in Micah, appears. In that form the name is connected with *rō'š* "head" without a play on sense. Mareshah, Tell Sandahanne,[131] belonged to the Judean system of defense (cf. 2 Chr 11:7). It lay about four miles (7 km.) southwest of Achzib and three miles (5 km.) south of Moresheth.

    Most critics, jumping on Syr *'dammā l'ālam* "forever," instead of reading *'ad-'ădullām (to Adullam)* read *'ad-'ôlām* (forever), explaining the *d* in *'ădullām* as due to dittography from the preceding *'ad*. This *lectio facilior,* however, depletes the verset atypically of a place name and loses the subtle literary allusion to David's exile in Adullam at the close of Micah's lament. V. Ryssel[132] retains Adullam but interprets it as *'ad 'ullām* "to their yoke," so that the verset means "to Adullam [i.e., to their yoke] shall go the nobility of Israel." The play on the name by itself, however, would be unique in this oracle. Also, it misses the probable literary allusion from Israel's nostalgic, national lore of David's life, the

128. *IBHS* §13.5.1.
129. *La Formation*, 27.
130. See BDB 98, §2b.
131. *KS* 25-27; *IDBSup* 566-67.
132. Ryssel, *Micha*, 37.

glory of Israel par excellence. David fled to the cave at Adullam as a fugitive during the darkest days when Saul pursued him (1 Sam 22:1; 2 Sam 23:13). So now his descendants must flee there as fugitives to escape Sennacherib, who hounds them to death. Adullam may be a metaphor for Jerusalem; it has become like that cave into which they must hide themselves for shelter. Adullam is identified as Khirbet esh-Sheik Madkur,[133] also a defense city in the Shephelah (2 Chr 11:7). Critics who emend *'ad-'ădullām* into *'ad-'ôlām* must also emend *yābô' (will come);* K. Elliger[134] prefers *yō'bad* "will perish" (cf. *BHK* and *BHS*).

kĕbôd (glory) is a collective metonymy for "men of rank" (cf. "nobles"; Isa 5:13 NRSV), and *yiśrā'ēl (Israel)* is a genitive of relation[135] with reference to the Southern Kingdom (cf. 1:5). Many of Israel's military leaders and officials had David's blood in their veins. This epithet for royalty poignantly recalls once again David's lament over the disaster that befell the house of Saul, also called "the glory" (*haṣṣĕbî*) of Israel. B. Renaud[136] comments: "Thus the lament ends as it started with an allusion to David and his brave ones. This cannot be accidental."

16 Taking his cue both from *tēs thygatros Israēl* at the end of v 15 in LXX — and supposing that it, having found what appeared to be an inverted *yiśrā'ēl bat,* corrected it to *bat yiśrā'ēl* — and from the lack of an antecedent for the second feminine singular imperative, K. Elliger[137] reconstructs, with an appeal "to the gloss" in v 13Ba, *bat ṣiyyôn* at the beginning of the line. Whether or not he be right — and he must assume the right edge is no longer damaged here — "Daughter Zion" should be taken as the vocative antecedent as in v 14, though possibly the feminine form implies "O City of [Jerusalem]" (cf. Jer 7:29, 34). The root of the qal feminine singular imperative, *qorḥi* "make bald [the head]" *(make yourself bald)* always refers to removing hair from the head to make oneself either partially or entirely bald. Making oneself bald was part of the mourning ritual (Jer 47:5). This extreme measure to comport one's outer countenance with one's true inner disposition by removing one's natural splendor was frequently taken in the face of the destruction of a city and/or land (Isa 3:24; 15:2; 22:12; Jer 47:5; 48:37; Ezek 7:18; 27:31; cf. Job 1:20). The proscription for laity against making oneself bald between the eyes (i.e., a partial tonsure of the forehead) in Deut 14:1 probably refers to a heathen ritual in contradistinction to that of making oneself entirely bald (cf. Isa 22:12). Only priests were prohibited from the latter practice (Lev 21:5). The threefold repetition of the command

133. Wolff, *Micha,* 33.
134. *KS* 22.
135. *IBHS* §9.5.1.
136. *La Formation,* 27.
137. *KS* 24.

along with the comparison to the bald vulture indicates that Micah does not have a partial tonsure in view. *wāgōzzî (and shave)*, the second synonymous command, is used frequently of shearing sheep (Gen 31:19; 38:12; Isa 53:7). The action included removing hair from the top of the head and the cheeks.

ʿal-běnê taʿănûgāyik *(for the children in whom you delight)* designates the reason for the extreme funerary measure; they mourn because the children in whom they delighted, their future nobles, go into exile. *taʿănûg* is an abstract subjective genitive denoting a verbal action affecting the construct *běnê*,[138] and its pronominal suffix, second feminine singular, referring to the Daughter Zion, is a subjective genitive. ʿng points to "delight, pleasure, refreshment, merriment, and joy," and *taʿănûg* means "luxury" (Prov 19:10), "delight" (Eccl 2:8), and "charms" (Song 7:7[6]).

Micah's third synonymous command in v 16Ba, also addressed to the Daughter Zion, *harěhibî qorhātēk (enlarge your baldness)* parallels v 6Aa even as v 16Ab parallels 16Ab and emphasizes the extreme baldness, and so despair, felt by the Daughter Zion. J. Ziegler[139] explains that LXX's *emplatynon tēn chēreian sou* "increase your widowhood" extends the normal sense of *chēreian*. "Widowhood" here means "being bereft of hair," since *chēreian* is often "to be empty, desolate." *nešer*, in the adverbial phrase *kanněšer (like the vulture's)*, can mean either "eagle" or "vulture." W. Nowack[140] prefers the bald vulture *(Gyps fulvus)*, which was common in Egypt and in Palestine. Its bald head and neck make it strikingly noticeable.

kî (for) introducing v 16Bb clarifies v 16Ab. The qal third masculine plural perfective of *gālâ* "to go into exile" *(they will go away)* is another persistent perfective after the imperative (cf. the same grammatical construction in v 11) and *mimměk (from you)* with reference to the city of Jerusalem. Micah symbolized going into captivity by his mourning ritual in vv 8-9 and made it more or less clear in his commands with reference to Shaphir (v 11A), Beth-ha-ezel (v 12B), Lachish (v 13), and Moresheth (v 14). Now he uses the clearest verb of all to express the notion. The land is stripped of its population, even to its children, leaving no hope for the future.

---

138. *IBHS* §9.5.1.

139. J. Ziegler, "Beiträge zum griechischen Dodekapropheton," in *Nachrichten der Akademie der Wissenschaften in Göttingen* (1943), 345-412; repr. in *Sylloge: Gesammelte Aufsätze zur Septuaginta*, Mitteilungen des Septuaginta-Unternehmens der Akademie der Wissenschaften in Göttingen 10 (Göttingen: Vandenhoeck & Ruprecht, 1971), 112.

140. Nowack, "Micha," in *Die kleinen Propheten* (Göttingen: Vandenhoeck & Ruprecht, 1922), 213.

EXPOSITION

Micah 1:8-16, exhibiting its own integrity, was an independent oracle in its preliterary stage but was later linked editorially with vv 2-7 by the logical particle "therefore." The editor prepared his readers for this judicial sentence against Judah by adding in v 5Ab/Bb an accusation against that state in an oracle originally addressed to Samaria. The sentence against Judah is intensified over that against Samaria in three ways: (1) its fall is certified by the fall of Samaria; (2) the judicial sentence is extended from two verses (vv 6-7) to nine; and (3) it comes climactically at the end. Moreover, the radical acts of mourning, first by Micah and then by Jerusalem, which introduce and conclude the sentence respectively, fill it with doleful pathos.

The prophecy against Samaria (1:2-7) found its fulfillment in 721 B.C., and this one, against Judah, in 701 B.C. (see v 1). Both would have been most telling if their messages were still ringing in the ears of their original audiences at the time of their fulfillment. They are edited together, probably after their fulfillment, as authenticating Micah's prophetic gift and as a sober warning to the book's future audiences (cf. v 2).

This judicial sentence takes the more specific form of a funeral dirge, which can be analyzed as follows:

I. Introduction: Micah resolves to engage in a mourning ritual symbolizing captivity (v 8) because *I AM*'s incurable wound afflicted Judah right up to Jerusalem (v 9).
II. Body: After exhorting the nations not to rejoice but to weep over Judah's misfortune (v 10A), Micah predicts by a series of puns on place names the fall of Judah and the exile of its inhabitants (vv 10B-15).
III. Conclusion: The Daughter of Zion is called to engage in mourning rites because her sons go into exile (v 16).

The introduction is linked with the conclusion by the motif of funerary rites, including comparisons between mourners and animals in both, and by following the descriptions of these rites with substantiation for them introduced by *kî* (vv 9, 16B). The introduction is bonded with the body by the motif of wailing (vv 8, 10), by breaking down Judah (v 9) into its cities (vv 10-15), and by the verbal link "to the gate of . . . Jerusalem" (vv 9, 12). The body is tied to the conclusion through the address to Daughter Zion (vv 14, 16). The body is unified by a literary allusion to the house of David in its first and last versets (vv 10A, 15B) and by pivoting on Lachish, the principal city that falls, at its center, to which an entire verse is uniquely given (v 13). The mention that *I AM*'s blow comes up to the gate of Jerusalem caps the first section (vv 10B-12), and the last section pertains to loss for the kings of Israel and for Daughter Zion (vv 14-15). The whole is linked together by the theme of exile: it is symbolized in vv 8-9, more or less implied in vv 10-15 (esp. vv 11A, 13A, 14A), and stated explicitly in v 16.

The striking feature of the body is its extended play between the name of the town and its predicted doom; its finds a parallel in Isa 10:28-32, where Micah's contemporary uses the same style to lament the fall of Judean towns north of Jerusalem. Regarding this style L. Alonso-Schökel[141] wrote:

> Popular etymologies and alliteration with proper names are a very frequent thing in the Bible; the infrequent thing is to take this method as a stylistic base for the whole poem, a thing which Isaiah and his contemporary Micah have done at the apogee of Hebrew literature. Other isolated prophetic passages employing this form include Isa 11:14; 15:9; Jer 6:1; 48:2, 13; Ezek 21:5 (20:49), 16 (11); Amos 5:5; Zeph 2:4.

I. M. Casanowicz[142] analyzed the play on names into three forms: assonance (play on sound alone), senseplay (play on meaning alone), and paronomasia (play on both sound and sense). Alonso-Schökel[143] called this form a "dynamically descriptive arrangement." Casonwicz explained its dramatic effect on an audience: "In a more softened and developed condition of language, and to a more advanced and refined aesthetic feeling, regularly occurring alliteration would have the same effect as the frequent pounding or stamping of the popular speaker." The rapid shift from one locality to another, juxtaposed in opposition to one another within the verses, achieves a very dynamic and dramatic effect. The Judean cities fall and their inhabitants go into exile one after another and in conjunction with one another. The fall of Judah reaches a climax with the threat against the House of David (v 15). The use of imperatives and parallelism further heightens the dynamism.

As a poet Micah aims to ventilate both his own pathos and that of his audiences. Above all, as a prophet he aims to warn them of *I AM*'s coming judgment for sin and to bring them to their knees in repentance. The Hebrews valued names not as identifying labels but for their significance. On Micah's lips *nomen est omen* "the name portends its doom." Bear in mind, however, that Micah is not a linguist; his *jeux de mots* depend on sound, not on precise etymologies and/or phonemic equivalence.

---

141. L. Alonso-Schökel, "Is. 10:28-32: Análisis estilístico," *Bib* 70 (1959) 233.

142. I. M. Casanowicz, *Paronomasia in the Old Testament* (Boston: Cushing, 1894), 8.

143. Alonso-Schökel, "Is. 10:28-32," 233.

Introduction (vv 8-9). *I AM*'s wrath must fall upon the Southern Kingdom just as it had upon the North because they are spiritual twins. Micah goes about wailing and naked both to ventilate his grief and to portray the humiliating exile. He does not shrink from his disagreeable calling but resolves to identify with his people's grief and humiliation.

Behind the incurable overthrow of Judah, Micah saw the wrathful hand of God. But Jerusalem will be spared. As he will make clear, a remnant will survive to constitute the basis of a new age; the God of justice is also the God of faithfulness to his covenant promises and of mercy to his people.

Body (vv 10-15). Micah picks up David's charge from the time when the House of Saul fell, "Tell it not in Gath," and applies it to the fall of Judah, the sphere of David's scions. Unbelievers are warned not to gloat over God's discipline of his own people (cf. Obad 12-13; Pss 25:2; 42:11[10]; 89:51-52[50-51]) because such rejoicing contradicts the essential obligations of the covenant and misinterprets history. The covenant demands that God's creatures love him and his image; gazing at Israel's misfortunes with satisfaction derogates God while exalting the tyrant, and betrays humans' sadism. Moreover, such rejoicing reflects spiritual blindness, for universal salvation flows through Israel. When Israel, God's light to the nations, is itself darkened, the nations are left without light and salvation. Likewise, when God disciplines a carnal church, it confuses, limits, and postpones its witness.

The nine strongholds of Judah, besides Jerusalem, whose names are omens, comprise a circle 14 km. in radius around Micah's hometown of Moresheth Gath and are visible from there.[144] Below is a list of the nine cities, plus Gath and Adullam, both of which function as literary allusions to the life of David and not as destroyed cities, and their modern identifications. The order in which they appear is purely literary, not according to the order of Sennacherib's march; it makes no sense topographically, according to A. Rainey.[145]

City	Identification
Gath	Tell eṣ-Ṣâfî
Beth-le-aphrah	?
Shapir	Khirbet el-Kôm/ Tell 'Eitun?
Zaanan	?
Beth-ha-ezel	Deir el-Asalû
Maroth	?

144. Cf. *KS*.

145. Rainey, "The Biblical Shephelah of Judah," 16.

City	Identification
Lachish	Tell ed-Duweir
Moresheth Gath	Tell ej-Judeideh
Achzib	Tell el-Beida
Mareshah	Tell Sandahanna
Adullam	Khirbet esh-Sheikh Madkur

I AM had graciously offered the people of Beth-le-aphrah ("Dust Town"; v 10B) along with the rest of the covenant nation opportunity to align themselves with the Seed of the woman, who, though bruised for a season, will finally crush Satan and cause him to eat dust (Gen 3:15). Regrettably, unlike Moses (cf. Heb 11:24-26) and like most, they chose the riches of the present world instead of suffering with Christ and ended up forever eating the dust of death.

Jesus warned people like those at Shaphir ("Beauty Town"; cf. v 11A), who celebrate their beauty in this world, that they should not lay up for themselves ephemeral treasures on earth, but rather that they should lay up for themselves imperishable treasures in heaven (Matt 6:19-21). He also cautioned that one should rid oneself of the most valuable assets in this world if they threaten one's eternal salvation in the next (Matt 18:9).

People like those of Zaanan ("Going Forth Town"; v 11B), who, instead of going forth boldly on behalf of the Kingdom of God, establish flimsy walls of their own security, in the time of judgment will cower vainly behind their imaginary walls (cf. Prov 18:11). Human supports not founded on the Rock Christ Jesus, like those at Beth-ezel ("Take-Away Town"; v 11Bb), will also prove worthless when the kingdoms of this world are finally defeated at Christ's parousia (cf. 2 Thess 1:5-10).

People like those at Maroth ("Bitter Town"; v 12A), who look to the powerful rulers of this world for sweet relief from the tyrannies of this life and for peace and prosperity, will experience a bitter end (cf. 1 Thess 5:1-11) because God alone stands beyond the dim unknown, keeping watch to reward the righteous and to punish the guilty (v 12B).

People like those at Lachish (v 13), who trust the latest technology instead of God, will fall into all kinds of sins that spring from man's autonomous, rebellious spirit. Their technology will prove worthless in the time of God's judgment against sin. The fall of the most technologically advanced city guaranteed the fall of the rest of the nation as well (cf. v 14A). Unless the leaven of idolatry in any form is purged immediately, it quickly sours the entire community. As Lachish introduced trust in military hardware, so modern cities like Hollywood promote adultery, and like Reno or Las Vegas give impetus to easy divorce and gambling, and like San Francisco give status to homosexuals.

Rulers like those at Jerusalem, who fleeced their flocks, will themselves one day be fleeced by others under the providential rule of God. Be not deceived: whatever a person sows, he reaps. People like them think they will accrue wealth from their Mareshah ("Bride Town"; v 14A), but instead they will lose their "bride" to the enemy and add a dowry with her. These same rulers falsely place their confidence in Achzib ("Deception Town"; v 14B).

Rulers like those at Mareshah ("Possession Town"; v 15A), who look to possessions gotten by conquest, will themselves be conquered.

Conclusion (v 16). The prophet draws his sermon to a close by denouncing the leaders of the theocracy, who had a unique opportunity to establish the golden Kingdom of God on earth, to mourn and make themselves bald as the vulture, for they brought about the plundering of their land and the deportation of their subjects by foreign tyrants, and left the plundered and stripped kingdom without offspring on whom they could base their hope for a future. Only God's untiring grace can salvage this sorry state. His implicit call for repentance (cf. Jer 18:5-10) should be heeded by all those within the professing church who make their bellies their gods, empty their pews by having a form of godliness without power, and leaven the church without youth willing to be baptized in the place of those who died for the faith (cf. 1 Cor 15:29). As a result of their perfidy, peoples that once belonged to families who worshipped the Lord Jesus Christ now bow their knees to Technology, Mammon, Sex, and Drugs.

B. Greedy Land Barons Accused and Sent into Exile (2:1-11)

1. Woe to the Greedy Land Barons (2:1-5)

1   Woe to you who plan to get rich by violence,
        who plot evil on your beds!
    Who at morning's light carry it out
        because it is in your power to do it.

2   [Woe] to you who, when you covet fields, seize [them];
        when [you desire] houses, [you] take them;
    when you defraud a man, you [take] his house;
        a fellowman, and his inheritance.

3   Therefore, thus *I AM* says:
    I am planning disaster against this clan,
        a [yoke] from which you will not withdraw your necks;
            you will not walk haughtily, for it is a time of disaster.

4   In that day they will take up a taunt against you;

> they will mock you with a most mournful dirge.
> They will say: "We are utterly ruined!"
>> They take away my people's possession.
>> How they take away [what] belongs to me!
>> They assign our fields to the obstinate.
> 5 Therefore you will have no one to divide the land by lot
>> in the assembly of *I AM*.

EXEGESIS

1 LXX reads *egenonto*, a misreading of *hôy (woe)* as *hyh*. The interjection *hôy (Woe to you)* is found only in the mouth of prophets. R. J. Clifford,[1] J. G. Williams,[2] and W. Janzen[3] interpret the interjection here as "alas," the cry of a funeral lament. Clifford, tracing the interjection's meaning diachronically, argued that it meant "alas" in the pre-Jeremianic era, came to mean "woe to" with biting scorn in Jeremiah, and "ho," a cry to get attention, in the postexilic period (Isa 55:1; Zeph 2:10, 11). His thesis is invalid. He himself admits that it means "woe" in Isa 29:15; 33:1. Moreover, of the eight clear cases of "alas" (1 Kgs 13:30; Jer 22:18 [4 times]; 34:5; Amos 5:16 [2 times]) over half occur in Jeremiah! In Amos 5:16 the form is *hô* and, unlike the other occurrences, it is not syntactically connected with a vocative of address. Finally, where it means "alas," it clearly occurs at funerary rites and the vocative address is a term of endearment or honor, "brother," "sister," "lord," "excellence." By contrast, "woe to" occurs in contexts of accusation and threat, and the mood is that of scorn and criticism. Measured by these criteria, it means that here (as recognized by all versions [cf. Matthew 23 and Luke 11]). In sum, the meaning of the interjection must be decided by context, not by chronology. On that basis it can also signify "Ah!" a cry of relief (Isa 1:24). Whether the word corresponds to the series of maledictions threatened in Deut 27:15-26 is uncertain.

D. R. Hillers.[4] on the basis of Classical Arabic and Hebrew, argued persuasively that the second-person elements that come in sooner or later in oracles introduced by *hôy* (cf. 2:3B) are not secondary but suppose a vocative element right after *hôy*. English idiom requires that "to you" be supplied, to which

---

1. R. J. Clifford, "The Use of *hôy* in the Prophets," *CBQ* 28 (1966) 458-64.
2. J. G. Williams, "The Alas-Oracles of the Eighth Century Prophets," *HUCA* 38 (1967) 75-91.
3. W. Janzen, *Mourning Cry and Woe Oracle*, BZAW 125 (Berlin: de Gruyter, 1972).
4. D. R. Hillers, "*Hôy* and *Hôy*-Oracles: A Neglected Syntactic Aspect," in *The Word of the Lord Shall Go Forth* (Winona Lake: Eisenbrauns, 1983), 185-88.

the participles, as the equivalents of relative clauses, *ḥōšĕbê . . . ûpōʿălê (you who plan . . . who plot),* stand in apposition. The expected article and/or the relative use of the participle[5] are omitted for reasons of poetry. Both participles are in construct with objective genitives, *'āwen* and *rāʿ* respectively. The noun *'āwen (to get rich by violence)* signifies negative power against persons. Its parallels include "violence," "oppression," "destruction," and "bloodthirsty men." The word also connotes deception and lying. K. H. Bernhardt[6] said: "The majority of these examples have in mind 'deception' actively practiced by evildoers with the purpose of hurting others." These two notions, power and deception, fit the context of Micah 2 and 3 admirably, which accuse and sentence the powerful rich for taking advantage of the defenseless by illegal means. Micah frequently uses puns in connection with judgment. Note the play between the land barons' *ḥōšĕbê* "planning" and doing *rāʿ* (moral evil) and *I AM*'s *ḥōšēb* "planning" *rāʿâ* (physical evil) in v 3. *pʿl* must mean "do" (i.e., execute [the evil]).

But how can they carry out their machinations on their beds? Many commentators explain *pōʿălê rāʿ* as a prosaic gloss on the double bases that the night's plans cannot be executed until the day (v 1B), and that it recovers the qinah (i.e., 3/2) rhythm of the passage. The second basis must be rejected because our knowledge of rhythm is insecure. *BHS* offers the option of transposing the disputed phrase to v 1B. J. Halévy,[7] followed by H. Wolff[8] and *BHS*, retains the text by repointing *ûpōʿălê* from a participle to a noun, *ûpāʿălê,* so that the word is not parallel to *ḥōšĕbê* but is added to *'āwen* as a second objective genitive of *ḥōšĕbê.* W. Rudolph,[9] followed by D. Hillers,[10] unconvincingly citing Isa 1:31 and Jer 22:13, achieves the same reading without changing the vocalization: "who plan iniquity and evil deeds." All these suggestions, however, run counter to the ancient versions and leave one wondering how the texts and versions came up with their difficult reading if it were not original. J. T. Willis[11] proposed that "bed" be associated with "dreams" (as in Job 7:13-14; 33:15; Song 3:1; Isa 56:10; Dan 2:28-29; 4:6-7[9-10], 10[13]; 7:1) so that the expression means "they do evil in their dreams." While admittedly "bed" and "dream" are naturally associated, nowhere is the verb ever used of executing something in a dream. Renaud's[12] explanation is best:

5. *IBHS* §13.7.
6. K. H. Bernhardt, "*'āven.*" *TDOT* 1:141.
7. J. Halévy, "Le Livre de Michée," *RevSém* 12 (1904) 110.
8. Wolff, *Micha,* 39.
9. Rudolph, *Micha,* 52-53.
10. Hillers, *Micah,* 31.
11. J. T. Willis, "On the Text of Micah 2:1Aαβ," *Bib* 48 (1967) 534-41.
12. *La Formation,* 66.

One must return to the classical meaning and appeal to Semitic anthropology, where the distinction between project and act is fairly attenuated: to project is to act. In Ps 58:3(2) the verb *p'l* is employed with *blb* "in the heart": "even in the heart, you forge iniquity," and the following stich states precisely: "in your hands, on earth, you think over arbitrariness," so establishing between the inward decision and the outward action the same parallelism as in Mic 2:1. Perhaps at the risk of forcing the meaning, one could think that *ḥšb* has in view the elaboration of projects and goals, and *p'l* the putting into action of the necessary means for the success of the enterprise.

'al-miškĕbôtām (on their beds) modifies both participles. As noted at 1:2, Hebrew (and also Classical Arabic) syntax regularly employs the third person in modifying clauses after the vocative (see 2:3 for the alternation between second and third persons in the terse prophetic style).

Verset A speaks of activity of the venal land barons at night; verset B, of their activity at daybreak. *bĕ'ôr (at light)* is an adverbial temporal phrase, and *habbōqer (morning's)* is a genitive of inalienable possession (i.e., the light is intrinsically proper to the morning).[13] Unlike the English word "morning," which means forenoon, *bōqer* denotes the coming of sunrise, from the time when the stars presaging the new day are still visible (Job 38:7) and people and things are scarcely visible (Gen 29:25; 1 Kgs 3:21; Ruth 3:14) to the breaking of the sun over the horizon (Judg 9:33; 2 Sam 23:4; 2 Kgs 3:22), as here. The light of the new day should have brought with it hope for the exposure of the wicked and their condemnation (see Exposition, 106). *ya'ăśûâ (who carry it out)* is also in apposition to the implied vocative. *'ăšer* (who), expected in prose, is not necessary in poetry, and the vocative continues to be modified by clauses using the third person. The second person will not appear until v 3B. The feminine accusative suffix cannot have either *'āwen* or *rā'* as its antecedent because both are masculine; rather, it refers to the situation in general.[14]

kî (because) explains the reason for their vile practice: *yeš-lĕ'ēl yādām (it is in their power)*. LXX reads *dioti ouk ēiran pros ton theon tas cheiras autōn* "for they have not lifted their hands to God." The translator either did not understand the Hebrew expression and/or his eye fell on *nś'w* in the next line. Syr also adopts this reading. *l'l* was then read as *lō'* "not" to make sense of the passage. Vg also misunderstood the Hebrew idiom: *quoniam contra deum est manus eorum* "because their hand is against God." The received text finds confirmation from the same phrase in Gen 31:29; Deut 28:32 and its equivalents in Prov

13. *IBHS* §9.5.1.
14. *IBHS* §6.6.

3:27; Neh 5:5. Literally, the expression means "there is with reference to *'ēl* in their hand"; *'ēl* may mean either "power" or "God." If the former, it has this meaning only in this expression. If the latter, it may mean that the rich exploiters stand up as rivals to God. Although the idiom's exact derivation is uncertain, it clearly means "it is in the power of their hand." H. Wolff[15] explains, "their success is guaranteed."

2 V 2 does not chronologically follow v 1 but epexegetes the character and corrupt practice of the rapacious land barons by concrete examples. "Covet" of v 2A approximates "plot" of v 1A, and "defraud" of v 2B approximates "carry out" of v 1B. As in v 1, the third-person form continues to modify the second-person vocative (*[Woe] to you who*). In the syntax of *wĕḥāmĕdû . . . wĕgāzālû*, both protasis and apodosis are introduced by *waw*.[16] *ḥmd (covet)* refers to the emotional appreciation of finding something desirable or precious on account of its form and splendor. Coveting strikes right at the heart of man's spiritual malady and unethical behavior toward another person's property (Exod 20:17; Deut 5:21). *śādôt (fields)* represent a man's livelihood and so freedom. Deprived of them, a man is forced into servitude. The perfective conjugations in v 2 represent the situation as complete. *gzl (seize)* means "to snatch away violently an object from its owner or its place by a stronger party." More specifically it denotes an illegal action that manifests power and so overcomes a person or thing as to tear it away forcefully. Syr rightly translates: "and take for themselves by force." In Micah's terse poetic style *śādôt* is the gapped object of the apodosis. LXX adds *orphanous* "orphans," perhaps from Job 24:9. That translator, failing to understand the unusual syntax of *waw* protasis and *waw* apodosis, construed *waw* as a conjunctive and so had to add an object to *gzl*.

The syntax of v 2Ab is identical to that of v 2Aa. *Waw* is a protasis *waw* with a gapped *ḥāmĕdû*, and *bāttîm* is an object *(when [you desire] houses)*. *wĕnāśā'û* consists of an apodosis *waw* with the gapped object *bāttîm (you take them)*. Once again, LXX fails to understand the unusual, terse poetic syntax. Taking *waw* as conjunctive, it interprets *bāttîm* as the object of *nāśā'û*. J. M. P. Smith[17] remarks that the Greek seems to have inverted *nāśā'û* and *'āšqû*, "for *nś'* is nowhere else rendered by *katadynasteuein*, nor is *'šq* elsewhere represented by *diarpazein*; whereas *katadynasteuein* is a common rendering of *'šq*, and *diarpazein*, though not elsewhere used for *nś'*, well conveys the idea of violence that *nś'* must carry in this context." But B. Renaud[18] notes, "The LXX

15. Wolff, *Micha*, 47.
16. *IBHS* §32.2.3.
17. J. M. P. Smith, *A Critical and Exegetical Commentary on the Books of Micah, Nahum, and Zephaniah*, ICC (Edinburgh: T&T Clark, 1911), 54.
18. *La Formation*, 67.

without doubt wanted to avoid two *diarpazein*s in a row; this word had already served to translate *gzlw* of v 2A. It is a simple stylistic variation; the inversion is not to be retained."

As v 2 epexegetes v 1, so v 2B epexegetes v 2A. The *waw* with *wĕʿāšĕqû (and they defraud)* is a hendiadys *waw*, which represents two aspects of a complex situation.[19] *ʿšq* represents a situation where the stronger takes away, either directly or indirectly, the produce and labor of the weaker, giving nothing in exchange. It may be by dishonest scales (Hos 12:8[7]), extortion, outright show of force (Isa 52:4; Jer 50:33), or through the court system. The parallel in Amos 5:7, 10-17 suggests that the latter is in view here. D. Hillers[20] specifies: "We are probably meant to think of their making loans and foreclosing." Whereas v 2A has a person's property in view, v 2B has his own self in view. *geber (man)* depicts man in his strength, at his most competent and capable level (cf. 2:8-9). Whereas *bāttîm* in v 2A, in conformity with its parallel *śādôt*, referred to buildings, the singular, *bāyit (house)*, in v 2B, in accord with its linkage with *geber*, refers to family (cf. 2:9).

ʾîš (a fellowman) emphatically individualizes *geber* and underscores that he is a fully enfranchised citizen. *BHS* rightly corrects L *wĕʾîš* to *ʾîš* by many Hebrew manuscripts, LXX, Vg, Tg, and Arabic. The editors omit *waw* in the lacuna of Mur 88. The conjunction is due to dittography from *ûbêtô*. H. Wolff[21] tries to defend MT by appealing to the syntax of 2Ab, but that syntax is different. L. J. Coppes[22] said that *nḥlh*, found in the possessive genitive construction *naḥălātô (his inheritance)*, "basically connotes that which is or may be passed on as an inheritance (e.g., Gen 31:14), that which is one's by virtue of ancient right, and that which is one's permanently." (See his article for an excellent bibliography on the laws governing the partition and inheritance of the land.) "Inheritance" combines the notions of family and property with permanence.

3   The logical particle *lākēn (therefore)* connects the accusation with the judicial sentence, even as *kol-zōʾt* in 1:5 linked the accusation in 1:5 with the punitive epiphany in 1:3-4, and *ʿal-zōʾt* in 1:8 linked the sin and judgment of Samaria with the sin and judgment of Judea. *kōh (thus)* refers to the sentence in vv 3B-5; *ʾāmar (says)* is a *verba dicendi* to be translated by present tense;[23] *I AM* hands down the sentence himself as in 1:6-7.

hinĕnî (behold, I) and the participle have the same force as the interjection followed by the participle in 1:3. The full idea is that *I AM* is about to effect

---

19. *IBHS* §32.3.
20. Hillers, *Micah*, 33.
21. Wolff, *Micha*, 39.
22. L. J. Coppes, "*nahalâ*," *TWOT* 2:569.
23. *IBHS* §30.5.1.

the judgment he has planned. The qal participle *ḥōšēb (am planning)*, though now functioning as a predicate and not as a relative, is deliberately parallel to *ḥšb* in 2:1. The play on words emphasizes the notion of *lex talionis*: the judicial sentence matches the crime. For metrical and syntactic reasons J. M. P. Smith[24] and the like strike out *ʿal-hammišpāḥâ hazzōʾt (against this clan)* as a late gloss; T. Robinson[25] *BHS*, and others also note the allegedly too abrupt change to second person in v 3B. H. Wolff,[26] in addition, notes a parallel in Amos 3:1B and Jer 8:3 and so thinks that the style is not that of Micah but of a Deuteronomistic redactor. As noted above, our knowledge of meter and of Micah's style is too insecure for text-critical purposes, and an abrupt shift between persons is acceptable Hebrew. S. Schwantes retains it as necessary to identify the object of the sentence, but without good reason places it after *rāʿâ*. D. Hillers[27] rightly retains MT, suggesting that the unusual word order is for emphasis. It is found in all texts and versions and should be retained as original. For *ʿal* (against) see 5:5.

mišpāḥâ signifies "species, kind of" animals in Gen 8:19 and Jer 15:3. That use is doubtful here. More probably, as in the close parallel of Jer 8:3, it refers to the nation. Many translators try to alleviate the incongruity between the accusation against the venal land barons and the apparent sentence against the whole nation by rendering *mišpāḥâ* "brood" or another pejorative equivalent such as "gang" or "crowd,"[28] without lexical warrant. B. Renaud[29] and others, in addition to their difficulties with the problems cited above with this phrase, are bothered by the fact that it makes the judicial sentence apply inappositely to the whole nation instead of just the grasping land barons. They suggest that a tradent who lived through the Babylonian captivity added the term so that the text would resonate the condemnation of the entire community at that time. The reasoning is not cogent. Why would a redactor have chosen an unusual word order? Creative wording is far more likely to be the work of the prophet himself than of a redactor. Also, they do not take into account the doctrine of corporate solidarity. In biblical theology the whole "family," bound together by blood and history, suffers for the sins of individuals within it, especially its leaders (cf. Joshua 7). David himself wondered why the whole nation should be judged for his sin (2 Sam 24:17). When the leadership rejected Jesus the Christ, God rejected the nation. The word "family," also translated "clan" or "tribe,"

24. Smith, *Micah*, 58.

25. T. Robinson, "Micha," in *Die zwölf kleinen Propheten*, HAT 14 (Tübingen: J. C. B. Mohr, 1938), 132.

26. Wolff, *Micha*, 39.

27. Hillers, *Micah*, 31.

28. Cf. Hillers, *Micah*, 33.

29. *La Formation*, 73.

points precisely to this economy. The individual within the group, while having individual responsibility, did not regard himself as a tree but as a leaf on the tree. When God laid the ax to its roots, the whole tree fell. Even saints who were not guilty of a certain sin identified themselves with the sins of the people and confessed national sins as their own (cf. Dan 9:5; Neh 9:33). Finally, note that when Samaria fell in 722/721 and Jerusalem fell in 586 the righteous suffered with the wicked. *rāʿâ (disaster)*, a feminine equivalent to *rāʿ* (moral evil) in v 1,[30] is a generic abstract for the specific judgment pronounced in 2:3B-5, namely, humiliating exile (vv 3B-4) and permanent loss of land. This play upon nouns again suggests a precise connection between the crime and the punishment.

The clause *ʾăšer . . . miššām (from which)* begins to explicate the *rāʿâ*. J. M. P. Smith[31] sees *miššām* as dittography from *tāmîšû* "you will withdraw" and conjectures reading the line *ʾăšer lōʾ-tāmîšû miṣṣawwĕʾrōtêkem* "which you will not withdraw from your neck." I. Willi-Plein[32] calls his solution "brilliant," and B. Renaud[33] goes along with it. His restoration, however, is unnecessary, as H. Wolff[34] has shown. *miššām* has an assumed *ʿōl* "yoke" as its antecedent (cf. Isa 10:27). J. L. Mays[35] explains the metaphor: "Yoke on . . . necks is employed to describe how the powerful end up in the control of others. The metaphor is generally used as an image of servitude to a conquering enemy (Isa 9:4[5]; 10:27; 47:6; Jer 27:8; 28:14; Ezek 34:27)." Although the form of *tāmîšû (you will . . . withdraw)* could be qal, the required transitive notion shows that it is hiphil. The second plural shows that this oracle of doom was addressed directly to the venal land barons, whose identity will be unmasked in the next oracle, 2:6-11. The nonperfective form signifies capability.[36] *ṣawwĕʾrōtêkem (your necks)* means especially "back of the neck." The masculine plural of this noun is often a plural of extension,[37] but here the one feminine plural is a countable plural because the verbs are plural.

wĕlōʾ . . . rômâ (and you will not walk about haughtily) is sequential to v 3Ba, but the adverb *lōʾ* demands the nonperfective construction. The nonperfective *tēlĕkû (walk about)* denotes a contingent future;[38] because of the

---

30. *IBHS* §6.4.3.
31. Smith, *Micah,* 54.
32. I. Willi-Plein, *Vorformen der Schriftexegese innerhalb des Alten Testaments,* BZAW 123 (Berlin: de Gruyter, 1971), 75.
33. *La Formation,* 67.
34. Wolff, *Micah,* 39.
35. Mays, *Micah,* 64.
36. *IBHS* §31.4.
37. *IBHS* §7.4.1.
38. *IBHS* §31.6.2.

yoke they will not walk haughtily. *rômâ (haughtily)* is an adverbial accusative of state modifying the subject.[39] Walking haughtily entails an outstretched, arrogant neck (cf. Isa 3:16); by putting a yoke upon them, one takes their haughtiness away. LXX's insertion, *exaiphnēs* "suddenly," after *orthoi* "upright" is unexplained. The logical particle *kî (because)* is explanatory. *'ēt (time)* points to an appointed season (cf. Eccl 3:1-9). *rā'â (disaster)*, an attributive genitive,[40] provides a parallel in v 3B to *rā'â* in v 3A. The literate may have caught a wordplay here with Amos 5:13. Whereas Micah used it in the judicial sentence with the meaning "disaster," Amos a century earlier used it in an accusation with the meaning "evil." If it is deliberate, here is another example of wordplay for expressing *lex talionis*. The difference should instruct us not to force prophets into a common mold. As in v 2, the poet uses the feminine dummy pronoun *hî' (it)* to refer to a situation. By placing the predicate nominative first, Micah classifies the nature of the situation, what it is like, rather than its identification, what it is.[41]

4   *bayyôm hahû' (in that day)* refers back to *'ēt rā'â* in v 3, the time I AM executes his sentence and introduces a new section of the judicial sentence. The shift from *I AM* as speaker in v 3 to Micah in v 5 probably occurs at v 4. A. Lefèvre[42] found that in Isaiah "almost half of the uses of *bayyôm hahû'* date back to Isaiah himself. These are often found at the beginning or the end of an oracle." In Mic 4:6 and 5:9 it also introduces the oracle. Here it introduces a new starting point within the judicial sentence. Perhaps two originally independent oracles of judgment were later combined. In addition to personal servitude (v 3), the criminals will lose their sacred land (v 4). The root of *yiśśā' (will take up)* often occurs with verbs of saying, usually *'mr*, as here, of formal and solemn utterance.[43] The third masculine singular form is impersonal *(they)*.[44] The prepositional phrase *'ălêkem (against you)* has a hostile sense, and the second masculine plural pronominal suffix refers back to the second masculine plural with verbs in v 3, namely, the clan, especially the venal land barons. The prophet sustains his oracle of doom in direct address against the accused. *māšāl (a taunt)* in parallel with *nĕhî* has its specific sense here of "mocking verse," "taunt." W. McKane[45] says that the effectiveness of a proverb over ordinary

39. *IBHS* §10.2.2.

40. *IBHS* §9.5.3.

41. *IBHS* §8.4.2.

42. A. Lefèvre, "L'Expression 'en ce jour-là' dans le Livre d'Isaïe," in *Mélanges Bibliques Rédigés en l'Honneur d'André Robert* (Paris: Bloud & Gay, [1957]), 174-79.

43. BDB 670d, §1,b,(7).

44. *IBHS* §4.5.2.

45. W. McKane, *Proverbs: A New Approach*, OTL (Philadelphia: Westminster, 1970), 28.

speech derives from its concreteness and from its ability to get attention and stimulate the imagination. Since "taunts" frequently contain metaphor and enigma (cf. Prov 1:6; Hab 2:6), one should hesitate in emending their texts on the basis of unparalleled usage.

Many do hesitate, however, to alter the obviously rhetorical sequence *wĕnāhâ nĕhî nihyâ (and they will mock with a most mournful dirge)*. The third masculine singular subject of *wĕnāhâ* is impersonal of the enemy, and the *waw* with the suffix conjugation is a *waw* relative, subordinating the clause to the preceding clause, which uses nonperfective *yiśśā'*.[46] *nĕhî* is an accusative expressing an effected object: "one groans a groaning" = "one makes a groan."[57] *nihyâ* is problematic. D. Hillers[48] deletes it as arising from dittography. F. Hitzig[49] and H. Wolff[50] interpret *nihyâ* as niphal, "it has happened!" According to Wolff,[51] it is an original error interrupting the text and understood by a later redactor as confirmation of the loss of land that in the interim had come true. He supports himself on the basis of the niphal of *hyh* in 1 Kgs 12:24; Joel 2:2. On the other hand, as B. Renaud[52] recognizes, it is unnecessary to accept such an unlikely interruption of the text. *nihyâ* may be a feminine doublet of *nĕhî*[53] (cf. *rā'* and *rā'â* in vv 1, 3), in which case *nĕhî nihyâ* is a superlative genitive: "a groan of groaning" = "one makes the most awful groan."[54] This interpretation does not depend on a debatable text in Q[55] but was proposed by BDB before the discovery of Q and is defended by W. Rudolph[56] not only on the basis of Q but also of LXX, Syr, Tg, and, in its own way, Vg. Such a play would be expected in a *māšāl*. The enemy exaggerates their groaning to mock the disenfranchised barons.

As noted above, *'āmar*, an expected perfective with *verba dicendi*,[57] occurs frequently with *nś'*; it is represented in the versions. The third masculine singular impersonal subject matches the other two verbs *(they say)*. Several MSS and Syr plausibly read syndectic *wĕ'āmar*, and LXX may have read *l'mr*. The mock-

---

46. Cf. *IBHS* §33.2.1.

47. *IBHS* §10.2.1.

48. Hillers, *Micah*, 32.

49. F. Hitzig, *Die zwölf kleinen Propheten* (Leipzig: Weidmann, 1852), 187.

50. Wolff, *Micha*, 39.

51. H. W. Wolff, *Dodekapropheten 2: Joel, Amos*, BKAT 14/2 (Neukirchen-Vluyn: Neukirchener, 1969), 293-94.

52. *La Formation*, 75.

53. *IBHS* §6.4.3; BDB 624.

54. Cf. *IBHS* §9.5.3 and GKC §133i for examples of superlatives involving two sing. nouns.

55. Cf. Hillers, *Micah*, 32.

56. Rudolph, *Micha*, 52.

57. *IBHS* §30.5.1.

ing enemy taunts the defeated land barons by quoting their despairing lament. Niphal *nĕsaddūnû (we are . . . ruined)*, instead of *nĕsaddônû*,[58] may be either dialectical or deliberate for the sake of assonance.[59] First-person plural has the venal land grabbers as its antecedents. They represent themselves as a group by the plural "we are ruined" and "our fields," and in this chiastic parallelism as individuals by the singular *'ammî* "my people" and *lî* "to me." The perfective of this fientive verb denotes the present perfect tense.[60] They are in a state of ruin as a result of their fields having been taken from them. The enemy's taunts, though future in history, are represented as said after Israel's defeat and at the time of its exile. The niphal denotes an incomplete passive.[61] *šdd* means "deal violently with, despoil, ravage, devastate, ruin." V. P. Hamilton[62] noted: "The ferocity of *shādad* is indicated by its coupling with the activities of a wolf (Jer 5:6), who pursues, attacks, and mauls its victim." H. Wolff[63] says: "*šdd* describes not only the general devastation of the land, but especially the plundering and wasting of it (Amos 3:10; Hos 7:13; 9:6; 10:2; Obad 5; Joel 1:15), and also the tearing down of the strongholds (Hos 10:14)." This strong word is further emphasized by the infinitive absolute *šādôd (utterly)*, emphasizing the factual mood: "we are ruined."[64] It is not unusual to augment niphal with qal.[65]

"Possession" inadequately represents the quasi-technical term *ḥēleq (possession)*. Its root essentially means "(give or receive) the portion coming to one by law and custom" and has social overtones. M. Tsevat[66] explained: "Its concrete reference, the 'portion,' is something in which giver and receiver, the individual or small group and the community, have an equal interest. The portion (defined in economic or other terms) maintains the individual or small group, and society is based on the totality of all portions." According to him, in contrast to common pastureland (Heb. *migrāš*), *ḥēleq* refers to the arable fertile land essential for life. In addition, D. J. Wiseman[67] said:

> Early in the OT the word is used with a technical nuance of share of land given to all the tribes when they entered the land. In this use the term is

---

58. Cf. GKC §67u.

59. Cf. H. Bauer and P. Leander, *Historische Grammatik der hebräischen Sprache des Alten Testamentes* (Halle: Niemeyer, 1918-22; repr. Hildesheim: Olms, 1962), 439.

60. *IBHS* §30.5.1.

61. *IBHS* §23.2.2.

62. V. P. Hamilton, "*shādad*," *TWOT* 2:906.

63. Wolff, *Micha*, 50.

64. *IBHS* §35.3.1.

65. *IBHS* §35.2.

66. M. Tsevat, "*chālaq*," *TDOT* 4:448.

67. D. J. Wiseman, "*ḥeleq*," *TWOT* 1:293.

parallel with "inheritance" *(nahălâ)* [see Mic 2:2]. On the principle that "the land is the LORD's inheritance," the land share came to be regarded as synonymous with "share of land" *(ḥebel)* given out by lot to the tribes [cf. 2:5].

The pronominal suffix of *ʿammî,* a possessive genitive *(my people's),* probably refers to *I AM.* The venal dispossessed rich, falsely identifying themselves as *I AM's* community to whom he had given the holy land to sustain covenantal life, find the loss of that land insufferable and wail together. For the meaning of *ʿamîm* see 1:2. Tg renders *yāmîr (they take away)* as "taking"/"removing" and Vg as "exchange," both following MT, but LXX's *katemetrēthē* "has been measured," followed by Syr, reads *yimmad* and supplies *en schoiniō* "with a line," undoubtedly from v 5. Most critics favor *yimmad* because of the alleged parallel *yĕḥallēq* in the next verset. *yāmîr* in the chiastic parallelism of the versets involved matches *yāmîš,* not *yĕḥallēq.* In addition, B. Renaud[68] notes: "The assonance *yamîr/yamîš* favors the reading of MT"; so does their sense. The almost identical use of *mûr* in Ezek 48:14 for "exchanging" (i.e., as its parallels show, "the sale of") the holy land into other hands confirms MT. The subject once again is impersonal. The nonperfective conjugation unpacks the perfective *nĕšaddūnû.*[69]

Instead of *ʾêk yāmîš lî (How they take away [what] belongs to me!)* LXX reads *kai ouk ēn ho kōlysōn auton tou apostrepsai* "and there was none to hinder him so as to turn him back," confounding consonants and vocalizing *lšwbb* as the pilpel infinitive of *šûb.* On this basis B. Stade,[70] followed by many, restored *wĕʾên mēšîb,* "There is no one to restore," assuming *lĕšôbēb* as due to dittography. To be sure, *ouch* reflects *ʾên,* but *kōlysōn* reflects *mnʿ,* not *šûb* or its equivalents, and *apostrepsai* probably represents *lĕšôbēb,* so that the proposal has little textual support. By linking *lšwbb* to the preceding clause and interpreting it as a pilpel infinitive, LXX loses the nice chiasm of MT: "to me" versus "to the obstinate." B. Renaud,[71] though wanting to show later revisions to the text, says: "MT offers an acceptable meaning." *ʾêk* is an exclamation of lamentation and, although the use of *mûš (take away)* for removal from land is unparalleled, it is an apt metaphor and parallel to *mûr.* Again, the subject is impersonal and the nonperfective conjugation continues to unpack the situation signified by the *nĕšaddunû.* There is no need to correct *lî (to me)* by LXX to *lô,* if either *ḥlq* or *śdh* be understood as the gapped object of *yāmîš* and *lĕ* be taken as signifying possession. The shift from plural ("we are ruined") to singular "to me" is acceptable in Hebrew (cf. 1:11).

68. *La Formation,* 68.
69. *IBHS* §31.3.
70. B. Stade, "Miszellen: Mich 2,4," *ZAW* 6 (1886) 122-23.
71. *La Formation,* 68.

lĕšôbēb (to the obstinate), an adjectival form of *šûb* used substantively, means "treacherous, backslider." Although it often refers to "treacherous and willful apostates" within Israel, it also refers to willful and refractory peoples outside the covenant, as in Jer 49:4 (of the Ammonites) and here (of the Assyrians). *śādênû (our fields)* sounds like *nĕśaddūnû* in this chiastic parallelism. The reference to "fields" links the accusation (v 2) with the threat in strict *lex talionis*. As the oppressive land barons took fields from defenseless citizens, so tyrants will take their fields. *yĕhallēq (they assign)* is another third masculine singular impersonal nonperfective. LXX's *diemeristhēsan*, a passive, does not necessarily represent *yĕhullaq (contra BHS)* but may be the equivalent of MT. Again the root *ḥlq* is used. What unthinkable judgment! The sacred fields of life are apportioned to the tyrannical Assyrians. The chiastic form of the taunt with subtlety underscores the reversal of the land barons' fortunes. With the people removed from their land and yokes around their necks, their lands are exchanged and redistributed.

5 *lākēn (therefore)* links the land barons' loss of land (v 4) with their additional loss of eternal life, the severest judgment of all. The nonperfective *lō'-yihyeh* "will not be," designating a contingent future,[72] also reflects the connection between cause, exile and annexation of land, and consequence, no future hope in the land for the greedy land barons; they will not be represented in the future assembly of *I AM* when he redistributes the land. Since v 5 has a redistribution of the sacred land in view, the nonperfective must denote a future tense beyond the dispossessed's loss of the land (v 4). It is unnecessary to change the singular *lĕkā (to you)* to the plural *lākem*, supposing that final *mêm* dropped out by haplography due to *maślîk*. The singular form matches those of v 4. The *lāmed* of possession with the second masculine singular is a pronominal suffix, and *lō'-yihyeh* is best rendered "you will not have" in English. Micah concludes his oracles by returning to the direct address form.

maślîk ḥebel bĕgôrāl (one to divide the land by lot) means literally, "one who extends the line by lot." It has in view the agent, probably a priest, who redistributes the land and his means, the lot. This vocabulary looks back, on the one hand, to the time when *I AM*, the Owner of the land, originally indicated his will for the distribution of the land among the elect through his priests who cast lots (Num 26:55-56; 33:54; 34:13; 36:2; Josh 14:2; 18:11 and, above all, 19:51), and, on the other hand, to a future when new agents would redistribute the land. Because *I AM* had promised Abraham the land as an eternal inheritance, Micah knew that it must be given back after the Assyrian conquest (cf. 7:20). Those who were removed from land for their moral turpitude, however, will

72. *IBHS* §31.6.3.

have no share in it. Prophets represent the new age by the vocabulary of the old dispensation (see Exposition, 206-7).

qhl in the adverbial phrase *biqěhal (in the assembly)*, means "to gather," and its noun form can refer to a convocation for some purpose, usually a religious purpose, as when Israel was assembled at Horeb for receiving the Law. Often *I AM* spoke or acted when Israel assembled (cf. Deut 5:22; 9:10). Micah later clarifies (cf. 2:13; 4:6-7) that the assembly of Israel in view here is the restored remnant after the exile. The genitive (of *I AM*), a genitive of relationship, describes restored Israel as socially organized once again in covenant with *I AM*. From Jeremiah one learns that it will be a new covenant community (cf. Jer 31:31-34). No unclean outsider could be a part of this assembly (Deut 23:2, 3, 4, 9). This conclusion to the sentence at the same time contains the severest punishment for the venal land barons but also his glimmer of hope for the covenant community. The hard-fisted land barons are consigned to eternal death; the righteous remnant have a future hope. The theme of hope reaches a grand finale in the book's climax.

EXPOSITION

Saint Augustine, in his monumental classic *City of God*,[73] divided mankind into two cities. Those who belong to the City of God are united by their love of God and of one another in God. Those who belong to the earthly city love themselves and so are not united in any real sense but live in wars, persecutions, and all the other evils that make the history of empires so terrible to read. "Two cities," he wrote, "have been formed by two loves: the earthly by the love of self, even to the contempt of God; the heavenly by the love of God, even to the contempt of self." The earthly city glories in its own power, the heavenly city in the power of God. The damned city is built on cupidity; the eternal city is built on disinterested love. The earthly city, built on human depravity and weakness, is doomed to conflict and everlasting death; the heavenly, built on love and faith in a righteous and omnipotent God, lives in peace and can never pass away. God called Israel to become citizens of the heavenly; its majority chose the earthly. In the oracle of doom Micah announces that those who had "succeeded" in the earthly city are about to lose their share in the heavenly.

Until this oracle the prophet spoke abstractly of "rebellion" and "sin" (1:5). Now he specifies the crime, which has both social and theological dimen-

---

73. Augustine, *City of God* 14.28.

sions. Socially powerful, rich landlords in Israel behave unethically by seizing the land and destroying the homes of fellow Israelites who are unable to defend their rightful possessions. Theologically, they erred egregiously in thinking that the land belonged to the powerful instead of believing that it belonged to God and the covenant community to whom he gave it in order to serve him. In sum, they had broken both the spirit and letter of the Law, which instructed Israel both theologically and ethically about property rights. Instead of loving God and their fellowman, they loved only themselves.

The oracle falls into three parts:

I. Accusation: the venal landlords unethically seize sacred property and destroy their persons (vv 1-2).
II. Judicial sentence:
   A. By *I AM*: *I AM* sentences them to a galling and humiliating exile (v 3).
   B. By Micah: they will lose their sacred property to invaders (v 4).
III. Conclusion: the land grabbers are consigned to an eternal death, but Micah implies a hope for a future remnant (v 5).

The prophetic accusation and the divine sentence are linked together by two expressions, which J. T. Willis[74] referred to as a, a' and b, b'; a "those who are planning evil" (v 1), a' "I am planning evil" (v 3); and b "fields" (v 2), b' "our fields" (v 4). Accusation and conclusion are also pulled together by not using second person, implied with *hôy* "woe to" (2:1), until vv 3b-4. *I AM*'s sentence and Micah's elaboration of it are bound by "it is an evil time" (v 3) and "in that day" (v 4). An *inclusio* involving the doleful interjections *hôy* (v 1) and *'êk* (v 4) bind the unit together before the conclusion, which contains a note of hope. The sentence and the conclusion are joined by the particle "therefore" and by technical, sacerdotal vocabulary for land: *ḥēleq* (v 4) and its imagery "one who casts the cord by lot" (v 5).

The lexical connections between vv 1-2 and vv 3-5 are but one more instance in which the principle of *lex talionis* is reflected in wordplay. Other examples include 1:7, 10-15; 2:9-10; 3:5-6, 10-12; 6:10-15; 7:4, 9. Concerning 2:1-3, J. T. Willis[75] concluded by citing P. Kleinert:[76] "The phrase *ḥšb r'* is emphatically repeated from ver. 1, to set clearly before our eyes the *jus talionis* prevalent in God's providence." Regarding vv 2 and 4 Willis noted: "The rich had wrested

74. Willis, "On the Text of Micah 2:1Aαβ," 535-38.
75. Willis, "The Structure, Setting, and Interrelationships," 144.
76. P. Kleinert, *Micah* (New York: Scribner, Armstrong, 1874), 19.

fields from the poor (v 2); therefore Yahweh will send an enemy army to wrest the Promised Land from them (vv 4-5)."

Micah introduces his oracle against the hard-fisted land grabbers with prophetic thunder: "Woe to." Upon their beds at night they plan their turpitude; at morning's light they carry it out. The "legal sharks" against whom Micah inveighed performed their perfidious acts at dawn, when the court met, by perverting the legal system, which aimed to protect every individual of the covenant community against tyranny. In the ancient Near East the light of the new day was the time for justice, after thieves had covered their black deeds with night's darkness. In Egypt the sun-god was thought to dispel all evil.[77] The psalmist notes that when the sun rises, the prowling, rapacious beasts of the forest steal away (Ps 104:20-22). *I AM* challenges Job's intrepid questioning of his administration: "Have you ever given order to the morning, or shown the dawn its place, that it might take the earth by the edges and shake the wicked out of it?" (Job 38:12-13). This expectation of divine help and justice at morning (cf. 2 Sam 15:2; Jer 21:12; Hos 6:3, 5; Zeph 3:5; Pss 37:6; 73:14; 90:14; 101:8; 143:8; Job 7:18) probably had to do in part with the king's practice of administering justice in the morning (Ps 101:8).[78] In this historical context Micah's accusation is honed with irony. Instead of finding the hoped-for justice in Jerusalem's morning court, Jerusalem's stalwart citizens found injustice in their administrators. In modern society many lawyers also teach criminals how to circumvent the law and make a mockery of it. Perpetrators go free and witnesses rot in jail.

The causal clause "because they have the power" strikes at the heart of the problem: misplaced confidence. Instead of trusting God, the vile denizens of the earthly city stand up as rivals to him and behave as despots. Their absolute power gave unbridled expression to their depravity and covetousness. Motivated by greed and armed with the ethical principle that might is right, they rationally, yet unconscionably, schemed to plunder and defraud Israel's stalwart men of their fields and homes. Micah is not a champion of the poor but of the oppressed, in this case the middle class (cf. Mic 2:9-10). In that agrarian economy a person's life depended on his fields, and for that reason his inheritance was carefully safeguarded by the Law. It was a sacred trust, not just another piece of real estate. If a person lost his fields, at best he might become a day laborer; at worst, he might become a slave. In either case he lost his independence, his freedom before God, and became a dependent of the land barons.

Micah bases his accusation on the Law. H. Wolff[79] notes, "Do not covet" is

---

77. Cf. O. Keel, *The Symbolism of the Biblical World* (New York: Seabury, 1978), 288-90.
78. Cf. Keel, *Symbolism of the Biblical World*, 288, and S. Aalen, "'ôr," *TDOT* 1:163.
79. Wolff, *Micha*, 48.

the one commandment of the Ten that is repeated (cf. Exod 20:17; 34:24; Josh 7:21; Prov 12:12A). It motivates the other avaricious acts. The Law also forbade cheating one's neighbor (Lev 5:21, 23[6:2, 4]; 19:3; Deut 24:14; 28:33) and plundering him (Lev 19:13). As the Law distinguished between violence against a person's property (i.e., plundering) and against his own self (i.e., defrauding), so also Micah distinguishes them. The rape, which in v 2A first was directed against the property, "fields" and "houses," of Israel's free and strong men, is seen more specifically in v 2B as against their persons ("house"). Isaiah elaborates upon the exploitation of property in Isa 5:8-10, and Micah comments further on the exploitation of the family in 2:9. *I AM* provided for the lives of his covenant families by distributing their inheritances through Moses (Num 26:52-57; 27:7), and his Law safeguarded that inheritance forever (Lev 25:10; Num 36:1-12). D. Hillers[80] comments: "The economic and social ideal of ancient Israel was of a nation of free landholders — not debt-slaves, sharecroppers, or hired workers — secure in possession, as a grant from Yahweh, of enough land to keep their families."

I AM himself, the avenging Judge, now hands down his sentence (v 3; cf. Mic 1:6-7) on the principle of *lex talionis*. The Masoretic chant casts the statements of authorship as only a portion of the A verset. The poetry of the verse becomes clearer, however, if "Therefore, *I AM* says" be treated as an anacrusis. As elsewhere it functions as a transition from the accusation to the sentence (cf. 1 Kgs 21:17-19; 2 Kgs 1:3-4; Amos 5:16 and 7:19; Mic 1:6-7, 15). As the land barons plotted evil against innocent victims, both with respect to their property (v 2A) and their persons (v 2B), so now *I AM* plots evil against them, both with respect to their persons (v 3) and their property (v 4). The expression "Behold, I am about to do so and so" aims to awaken them from their moral stupor. According to P. Humbert,[81] in 118 of 125 instances this reveille is said of *I AM*. As a master irresistibly enslaves and humbles an animal by a yoke, so Israel's new masters will enslave and humble them, and they shall not escape. Subjugation for this clan came from the hand of the crack troops of the Assyrians, who, like the venal land barons, coveted their lands and so plundered them. The Assyrians, however, are not mentioned because this sentence against criminals focuses on the Judge himself and serves as a paradigmatic warning against all greedy folk living in the earthly city. Their destiny, too, is an irresistible, galling, and enduring bondage.

The wages of sin is death (Rom 6:23). Were people given a second chance, this life would lose its significance and become little more than a trial run. Mi-

---

80. Hillers, *Micah*, 33.
81. Cited by Wolff, *Micha*, 49.

cah now elaborates the divine sentence (v 4). They will lose the land that promised eternal life. The punishment is phrased as a satirical dirge in the mouth of enemies just as heartless as they. "We are utterly ruined," *šādôd nĕšaddūnû*, sounds like *šādēnû* "our fields," another instance of *lex talionis* by wordplay. As the strong and mighty in Israel ravaged others by taking their fields, now others stronger than they will take theirs. "All who draw the sword will die by the sword" (Matt 26:52).

I AM had distributed the land to the tribes and families by casting the lot according to his good pleasure (Joshua 12–22). Without this distribution of the land the priestly nation could not exist. The Owner gave it as a usufruct (cf. Lev. 25:23). Israel could enjoy the land freely and fully as long as they served the interests of the covenant, but should the nation abuse its gift by using it apart from the covenant's designs, *I AM* retained the right to take it away from the traitors and give it to their enemies (Lev 26:33; Deut 28:49-68). Casting the people off the land and redistributing it to others constituted the final act of judgment and decisively established the triumph of the City of God over the Earthly City. The same *I AM* still divides up the nations according to his own good pleasure and justice (Acts 17:26), directing the building of his church by taking away spiritual advantage from those who apostatize and giving it to the faithful (cf. Rom 11:17-21; Rev 2:16; 3:16), and by giving spiritual gifts to his people (Rom 12:3-8; 1 Corinthians 12; Eph 4:7-13).

Micah brings the sentence to its awesome climax in v 5: eternal spiritual death in exile (cf. 1:8-16). In addition to being afflicted with galling and humiliating bondage in exile and the loss of their fields, they will not participate in any future redistribution of the land, the very basis of their life with God.

Nevertheless, the sentence also implies a flicker of promise; *I AM* will redistribute his land among the elect. This prophetic hope is firmly based on *I AM's* covenantal promises (cf. Gen 17:8; Deut 30:1-10; 2 Sam 7:16; Mic 7:20). The faint flicker of hope in Mic 2:5 becomes brighter throughout the rest of the book and is brought into the full light of day with the advent of Jesus Christ. Prophets portray the new dispensation ushered in by Jesus Christ under the imagery of the old dispensation. Now that the heavenly reality has been lowered from heaven in Christ, the earthly imagery is done away, leaving only the reality that was always present in these prophecies. Today the Lord Jesus Christ gives eternal life to the elect of all nations (John 17:2). He gathers the seed of Abraham, all those who believe in him (Gal 3:26-29), into the rest that only he can provide (Heb 4:1-11), and sovereignly apportions them in his church (1 Corinthians 12). The realized promise will find its consummation in the final triumph of the eternal City of God (Heb 11:39-40) in the new heaven and earth (Rev 21:27; 22:15).

2. False Prophets Support the Greedy Land Barons (2:6-11)

6   "Stop prophesying,"
    they prophesy.
They will not prophesy about such things;
    [so their] shame will not depart.

7   Should it be said, O house of Jacob:
    "Does *I AM* become impatient?
      Or are these his deeds?"
Do not my words prosper
    [him who] walks uprightly?

8   But lately "my people" rise up as an "enemy":
    you strip off the rich robes from the tunics
from those who pass by without a care,
    men being returned from battle;

9   you drive the women of my people from their luxurious homes;
    you take away my splendor from her children forever.

10   Get up, go away!
    For this is not a resting place!
Because it is defiled, [the resting place] will bring destruction
      beyond all remedy."

11   If a man comes with windy words
    and lies deceptively:
    "I will prophesy to you of wine and beer,"
he would be just the prophet for this people!

EXEGESIS

The interpretation of this judgment oracle in the form of controversy is difficult because of textual problems — the versions disagree radically with MT and with one another — and because of its "dialogical" character. Instead of attempting to arrange and critically appraise the maze of opinions about its interpretation, I will formulate a few rules to guide the research.

Rule I: The MT should be adhered to as much as possible. Renaud[1] made the point: "The basic option must remain the MT. The versions manifestly came up against the same difficulties as modern criticism and found a way out by formulating a largely interpretative translation. . . . This opinion requires, we

1. *La Formation*, 84-85.

109

believe, that we preserve as much as possible the data of the MT and bring to it only the minimum of necessary corrections."

Rule II: Hebrew expressions should receive their usual meanings as much as possible. One should resort to rare meanings only if other factors in the context put the case beyond reasonable doubt.

Rule III: The first-person pronoun from v 7B through v 9 has the same referent. Since *I AM* most probably is the implied antecedent in the case of "my splendor" in v 9, he should be identified as the referent.

Rule IV: This judgment oracle takes the more precise form of drama, including controversial dialogue within scenes. In vv 7-10 *I AM* addresses, indicts, and judicially sentences the rulers and venal land barons of the House of Jacob directly, using the second person. In vv 6 and 11 Micah employs apostrophe in the third person to accuse and sentence the false prophets, who, instead of distancing themselves from these venal persons, give them theological credibility. Both Micah and *I AM* introduce their speeches in vv 6 and 7 by quoting the prophets and profiteers, who are obviously in cahoots. This theatrical effect is achieved not so much by rubrics indicating the change of speakers as by the content of the speeches themselves. Renaud insists that Micah is the speaker from beginning to end and that we grasp the movement of the dialogue only through the words of Micah. Nevertheless, he must still suppose that Micah's opponents are quoting him within his quotations, though there are no formal markers. Renaud does not dispute the theatrical character of the piece involving plays on scenes and audiences.

6 *'al-taṭṭīpû (stop prophesying)* is a hiphil second masculine plural jussive of the root *nṭp*. A hiphil with this root, which occurs five times in this pericope (vv 6, 11), may be either a two-place hiphil with the object of the causative notion "words" elided (i.e., "stop causing words to drop") or an intransitive, internal hiphil meaning "stop causing yourselves to drip/prophesy."[2] The unexpected plural, equivalent to "you all stop prophesying," probably reflects that an earlier pericope has been roughly edited into the final book. Since the verb *nṭp* hiphil in v 6A means "to prophesy," the speakers and addressees are presumably prophets. It is best to assume that the false prophets opposed to Micah (cf. 3:5-8) are addressing him and his peers, the true prophets. Since Micah has been prophesying, and since the false prophets assume their social superiority, the negative imperative has the force of an urgent command to stop prophesying. *nṭp* literally means "to fall drop by drop" (of clouds [Judg 5:4], of the beloved's fingers dripping with myrrh [Song 5:5], and of her lips with honey [Song 4:11]), and in the hiphil stem functions as a synonym for "to prophesy"

2. Cf. *IBHS* §27.2.

(*nibbā'*). The metaphor approximates Prov 5:3, where the lips of the adulteress drip the honey of her words. It could carry a pejorative connotation in Mic 2:6, 11, especially since in Amos 7:16 the verb is also put in the mouth of a prophet's adversaries. (The LXX uniquely renders *taṭṭîp* in Amos 7:16 by *ochlagōgēsēs* "to attract the crowds," "to stir them up," "to stir them to sedition"). A possible pejorative nuance is neutralized by its good connotation in Ezek 21:2, 7. The evidence is too slim to argue that the word developed from a disparaging sense in Amos/Micah to a favorable sense in Ezekiel.[3] Though the word becomes a technical term for prophetic activity, no text associates the etymological meaning, "to drip" words out of the mouth, with ecstatic behavior. The use of the word for smooth speaking in Song 4:11 and 5:3 calls into serious question the popular notion that the verb, as J. L. Mays[4] suggested, "may have developed from the frenzy which came over the early charismatic prophets in a state of ecstasy." H. Wolff's[5] suggestion that the word means to shower the addressee with drops and that it be rendered "to drivel," "to prattle," is based on questionable etymology and not on usage.

yaṭṭîpûn (*they prophesy*) is a hiphil third masculine plural nonperfective of the same root, *nṭp*, with a paragogic *nûn*. What is the unexpressed antecedent of "they"? Many commentators[6] with good reasons think that they are the venal persons of power whom Micah just excoriated. First, they fit the description of v 6. Second, the preceding accusation and threat were addressed to them, and one expects them to want the prophesying to cease. Third, the rest of the oracle is addressed to them (cf. "O House of Jacob" [v 7], "my people" [v 8], "you" [vv 9-10]) and continues the accusation against them begun in v 2. Fourth, they are looking for false prophets to preach to them (v 11). On the other hand, the verb refers to prophetic speech, and false prophets are clearly in view in v 11, which forms a nice *inclusio* with the introductory verse.[7] Probably the two groups should be combined: the *vox populi* finds expression through its spokesmen, the official theologians of the time.[8] A. S. van der Woude[9] rightly explained that "pseudo-prophets" represent the political-religious establishment (cf. Jer 18:18; Amos 7:14, 17; Mic 3:4-7). The nonperfective in present time denotes the indicative mood and an imperfective aspect, either progressive (they keep on prophe-

---

3. *Contra* Wolff, *Micha*, 51.
4. Mays, *Micah*, 69; *contra La Formation*, 89.
5. Wolff, *Micha*, 51.
6. Cf. Wolff, *Micha*, 50-51.
7. Cf. H. Donat, "Mich. 2:6-9," *BZ* 9 (1911) 350-66.
8. Cf. *La Formation*, 83-84, 88, 116.
9. A. S. van der Woude, "Micah in Dispute with the Pseudo-Prophets," *VT* 19 (1969) 247-48.

sying) or ingressive (they begin to prophesy).[10] Paragogic *nun* in prose signifies contrastivity,[11] which would fit well here, but in poetry it may denote the certainty of the situation,[12] its probable force here. Micah's audience, to whom he quotes his adversaries, is unidentified.

Rendering *lo'-yaṭṭīpû (they will not prophesy)*, another hiphil third masculine plural nonperfective of *nṭp*, by "'Do not prophesy,'" TNIV erroneously suggests that the Hebrew is masculine plural imperative. NRSV's "one should not preach" represents accurately enough the third-person impersonal plural[13] but inaccurately adopts the volitional mood of the first verb. In fact, however, the form is exactly the same as that of the preceding verb, nonperfective, and the negative particle is indicative *lo'* and not jussive *'al*.[14] L. Allen[15] rightly comments that "the subject is naturally to be taken as the same as that of the immediately preceding verb." He colors this nonperfective form, however, with a new meaning, "they should not preach," instead of retaining the more natural indicative mood and progressive aspect of the identical preceding word. Correlatively, those who take it as volitional must also questionably emend v 6B to read, "humility will not overwhelm us" (see below). In the adverbial prepositional phrase *lā'ēlleh (about such things)*, *lĕ* could mean either "to," introducing the so-called indirect object of the verb of speaking, or "about,"[16] and the antecedent of the demonstrative pronoun could be personal, "these people," or impersonal, "these things," respectively. The issue is best decided from v 11. The first *lāmed* after *nṭp* shows that a personal pronoun would be used were that sense intended, and the second *lāmed* shows that the impersonal sense is likely. The use of *'ēlleh* in v 7 confirms the impersonal sense and suggests that its more specific antecedent is not the accusations in vv 1-2 but the judicial sentences in vv 3-5. The use of *lĕ* in v 11 also shows that the emendation to *kā'ēlleh* (cf. *BHS*) is unnecessary. The emendation to *kĕ'ālâ* "about a curse" is inappropriate, for, as W. Rudolph[17] notes, Micah has not used curse words.

Many interpreters, following GB, emend *lō' yissag (will not depart)* to *lō' yassīgēnû (will not overtake us)* (so *BHS*, NRSV, TNIV). Hillers[18] stated the case for this emendation:

10. Cf. *IBHS* §31.3.
11. *IBHS* §31.7.1.
12. *IBHS* §31.7.1.
13. Cf. *IBHS* §4.5.2.
14. Cf. *IBHS* §34.2.1.
15. Allen, *Micah*, 292.
16. Cf. *IBHS* §11.2.10.
17. Rudolph, *Micha*, 56.
18. Hillers, *Micah*, 34.

The niphal of *swg* ("will withdraw") seems inappropriate here, and the masculine singular form lacks a noun subject. Perhaps read *tassîggēnû* equals *taśśîggēnû* (cf. similar exchange of these verbs in Job 24:23 and Mic 6:14); this would be hiphil imperfect of *nśg* with *s* for *ś*; cf. *a' katalēpsē* ("you will overtake"), which equals *taśîg/taśśîg*. The subject would be *kĕlimmôt* ("reproaches"). Cf. Isa 59:9, *wĕlō' taśśîgēnû ṣĕdāqâ*. The object ("us") need not be expressed; cf. 1 Sam 30:8; Exod 15:9; and Ps 7:6 (EV 5).

Against the emendation, however, note that it also demands a rereading of *lō'-yaṭṭipû* (see above). MT, the more difficult reading, has the support of LXX (*apósetai* "he will remove"), and the vocalization of MT is normally to be preferred. According to most scholars, this emendation keeps Micah's critics the speakers throughout the verse, apart from *yaṭṭipûn (they prophesy)*, but the writer's interpretation of MT keeps Micah the consistent speaker throughout the verse and does not demand the ad hoc explanation that *sûg* and *nsg* have been confused. The niphal of *sûg* denotes the middle voice,[19] and the non-perfective has a contingent future force.[20] The full thought is: "They will not prophesy about these things, (so) shame will not depart." Note that the Masoretes linked these two clauses beginning with *lō' (not)* by placing them in the B verset. *kĕlimmôt (shame),* an abstract plural referring to the future humiliating state or condition of the land grabbers and their false prophets,[21] is the subject of the verb; for grammatical disagreement between feminine plural *kĕlimmôt* and masculine singular *yisag* cf. Deut 32:35; 1 Kgs 11:3; Isa 8:8.[22] Jer 23:40, also using *kĕlimmôt,* offers an excellent parallel to MT. According to J. N. Oswalt,[23] *kālam* denotes: "the sense of disgrace which attends public humiliation. In thirty cases the root is used parallel with *bôsh* 'to be ashamed.'" Here it is a parallel to "these things" (i.e., the judgment of the preceding oracle).

  7 As v 6A, 6Ba, and 6Bb began with negative particles (*'al* and *lō'*), so v 7Aaα, 7Aaβ, 7Ab, and 7B begin with interrogative particles (*hă* and *'im*). Who is speaking? TNIV rightly identifies *I AM* as the speaker in v 7B (see Rule IV). The thought of v 7B is apposite only on the lips of *I AM*, and it is linked with v 8 by the adversative "but." Syntactically the interrogatives link v 7A and v 7B, suggesting that *I AM* speaks from the beginning to the end of the verse, and there are no contrary indications. The lack of introductory formulas to the verse may reflect the insertion of material from earlier pericopes. E. A. Neider-

---

19. *IBHS* §23.2.1.
20. *IBHS* §31.6.2.
21. *IBHS* §7.4.2.
22. See GKC §145o.
23. J. N. Oswalt, *"kālam,"* TWOT 1:443.

hiser[24] succinctly summarized the several major attempts to emend *he'āmûr* (*Should it be said*):

(1) *he'āmōr*, reading infinitive absolute instead of the participle — "Shall the house of Jacob say?";[25] (2) *he'emîr*, reading the hiphil with reference to Deut 26:17-18 — "The house of Jacob affirmed," or "He affirmed the house of Jacob";[26] (3) *hamū'ār*, reading a metathesis and altering the root from *'mr* (to say) to *'rr* (to curse);[27] (4) *hᵉ'ārūr*, emending the root as in number 3 and reading a meaning of "to curse."[28] The suggestions of both G. R. Driver and Mays are also interesting in light of a revocalization proposed by Sellin in verse 6.[29] He reads *le'ālāh*, "about a curse." This would provide a certain unity to the passage, but does require piling emendation on emendation.

A. Ehrman[30] achieved the meaning "curse" by unwarrantedly investing *'mr* with this meaning from Job 3:3. His method violates Rule III. Renaud[31] took up these conjectures and others and eruditely criticized them. With Neiderhiser, who also rejected all these emendations, I take MT as it is and understand the passive participle as reflecting a popular saying, a view confirmed by the interrogative *hê*.[32] The interrogative serves to express the conviction that the contents of the statement are well known to the hearer and are unconditionally admitted by him.[33] It may be a technical expression for covenant-making (cf. Deut 26:17, 18).[34] *bêt-ya'ăqōb* (*O house of Jacob*), a vocative, ideally designates all Israel but in historical fact particularly the Southern Kingdom as in 3:1, 9-10, not the North as in 1:5. The parallels show that more specifically the leadership of the South is in view; they began to be addressed in 1:8.

hăqāṣar rûaḥ yhwh (Does I AM become impatient?) consists of a construct chain, "spirit of *I AM*," in which *I AM* is a possessive genitive, and a syntagmatic

24. E. A. Neiderhiser, "Micah 2:6-11: Considerations on the Nature of the Discourse," *BTB* 11 (1981) 105.

25. G. R. Driver, "Linguistic and Textual Problems," *JTS* 39 (1938) 263.

26. van der Woude, "Micah in Dispute with the Pseudo-Prophets," 389-91, and idem, *Micha* (Nijkerk: Callenbach, 1976), 65-70.

27. G. R. Driver, "Linguistic and Textual Problems," 266.

28. Mays, *Micah*, following Klostermann.

29. Noted by Mays, *Micah*, 66.

30. A. Ehrman, "A Note on Micah II,7," *VT* 20 (1970) 86-87.

31. *La Formation*, 91-92.

32. Cf. GKC §100n.

33. GKC §150e. For the use of the passive participle in the sense of "should it be said" see E. König, *Historisch-Comparative Syntax* (Leipzig: Hinrichs, 1897), §323eβ.

34. See A. S. van der Woude, "Micha II,7A und der Bund Yahwe mit Israel," *VT* 18 (1968) 388-91.

compound of the subject, *rûaḥ,* and the verb, *qṣr,* meaning "to become impatient" (cf. Judg 16:16; Prov 14:29). This question and the next in v 7Ab appear to be proverbial sayings, which, according to R. Gordis,[35] are a form of unmarked quotation. *I AM* puts into the mouth of the false teachers proverbial sayings about his patience and goodness. The renderings "Is the spirit of the LORD angry [TNIV]/impatient [RSV]?" fail because they translate *rûaḥ* twice, not understanding the meaning of the compound *qṣr rûaḥ.* R. D. Haak[36] argued that the expression can mean either "impatient" or "impotent" and opted for the latter here. Although Haak offers many helpful insights into the term, his analysis of this passage is superficial. If the false prophets are censuring Micah's judgment oracle in vv 3-5, only the meaning "impatient" fits here. B. Renaud[37] unnecessarily revocalized the text to read with Prov 14:29 because "spirit," the subject, is feminine, and the verb is masculine; nevertheless, with the compound expression "spirit of *I AM*" one expects a masculine verb. The perfective with the stative verb, "be short," has an ingressive aspect (become short).[38]

'im (or are), carrying on the interrogative *hê,* introduces their second question. Their first question pertains to *I AM's* character, their second to his acts. The near demonstrative *(these)* has his judgments, vv 3-5, in view and implies the unity of the chapter. *ma'ălālāyw (his deeds)* is a predicate nominative with a subjective genitive referring to *I AM,* as its parallel in v 7Aaβ shows. Both questions expect a negative answer.

According to M. L. Brown,[39] *hălô' (do not)* could be an interjection meaning "indeed" or an interrogative particle. The parallels in v 7A support the second meaning. Many commentators think that the false teachers are still speaking in v 7B because there is no formal indication of a new speaker and that vv 7A and b are linked both by the interrogative particle *hă*[40] and by the similar-sounding *'im/ 'im* in 7Ab/7Bb.[41] If this be the correct understanding of the text, the false prophets not only put on an armor of orthodoxy but also cloak themselves in the hypocrisy of "self-righteousness" by claiming to themselves the epithet "who walks uprightly." This interpretation, however, often entails emending both *děbāray (my words)* to *děbārāyw* "his words" (though Neiderhiser sees it as part of the pro-

35. R. Gordis, "Quotations as a Literary Usage in Biblical, Oriental, and Rabbinic Literature," *HUCA* 22 (1949) 196.

36. R. D. Haak, "A Study and New Interpretation of *qṣr npš*," *JBL* 101 (1982) 165.

37. *La Formation,* 92.

38. *IBHS* §30.5.3.

39. M. L. Brown, "'Is it Not?' or 'Indeed!': *HL* in Northwest Semitic," *Maarav* 4 (1987) 201-19.

40. See J. T. Willis, "Micah 2:6-8 and the 'People of God' in Micah," *BZ* 14 (1970) 72-87.

41. See Neiderhiser, "Micah 2:6-11," 105.

verbial saying and so retains MT), and *wĕ'etmûl* "formerly" in v 8A to *wĕ'attem* "but you." The first emendation supposes only a common haplography of a *waw* between three *yôds*, with which it is readily confused, and has the support of LXX (but see below). The second is less defensible (see below). Moreover, though the lines are linked by negatives in v 6, no one denies their dialogical character. Why deny the same dialogical character with the interrogatives in v 7? Finally, the emendation and interpretation leave the false prophets unanswered. The proposed interpretation requires no textual emendation, appropriately distinguishes the crimes of the "house of Jacob" from the false preaching of the prophets, and gives an excellent symmetry to the oracle as a whole. The question, like the two in v 7A, again assumes something well known; but unlike those positive questions that expect a negative answer, this negative question expects a positive answer. The pronoun in *dĕbāray*, a genitive of authorship[42] with a plural noun, refers to *I AM*, who is speaking. LXX's *hoi logoi autou* "his words," reading *dĕbārāyw*, could be either an accidental error confounding *yôd* with *wāw*, a frequent error made more likely by three *yodhs* occurring in succession, or more probably in this interpretative version, a facilitating reading to conform v 7B to *I AM* in v 7Aαβ. In either case, H. Wolff[43] rightly rejects LXX in favor of MT and the other versions. (Mur 88 has a lacuna here.) For the meaning, grammar, and theology of *dābār* see 1:1. *yêṭîbû (do good)* is rendered "prosper" (TNIV) in Gen 32:10(9), 13(12). The nonperfective tense denotes a contingent future or a persistent present.[44]

The causative notion of hiphil is extended to the undersubject, "him who walks uprightly," by the preposition *'im* in the phrase *'im hayyāšār hôlēk (with the one walking uprightly)*. Most critics emend the text to read *'im 'ammōh yiśrā'ēl* "with his people Israel," involving extended correction of the text both here and at the beginning of v 8. The emendation violates Rule I. L. C. Allen arrives at the translation "Do we not keep company with one who keeps his word?" by interpreting initial *hălô'* as extending over both clauses, by repointing *hwlk* as an infinitive absolute and interpreting it to mean "to keep company with" (cf. 6:8), and by supplying "we." His conjectures, however, violate our Rule I. More probably the article is a relative, equivalent to *'ăšer*,[45] and *yāšār*, as E. König[46] suggests, is an adverbial accusative of state modifying the subject. The construction is most unusual, however, because such accusatives are indefinite, though a relative article is not unthinkable.[47]

42. *IBHS* §9.5.1.
43. Wolff, *Micah*, 40.
44. *IBHS* §§31.3; 31.6.2.
45. *IBHS* §13.5.2.
46. König, *Historisch-Comparative Syntax der hebräischen Sprache*, 332i, 388.
47. Cf. *IBHS* §10.2.2.

8 Many critics (cf. *BHS*) emend *wĕ'etmûl 'ammî (But lately "my people")* into *wĕ'attem ['a]l-'ammî* "But you against my people." They think that *mûl* is a dittography from *mimmûl* in v 8Abα, and that *'ammî* cannot be the offending subject but the unfortunate victim of the verb *qûm* "to rise up" in v 8Aaβ. The emendation, however, is mere conjecture[48] and involves emending *yĕqômēm* to a participle, *qāmîm*, or to *tāqûmû*. J. T. Willis[49] proposes less alteration by reading *wĕ'ûlām* (cf. 3:8). But his conjecture is unnecessary because similar, though not identical, forms of *'etmûl*, meaning "recently," "formerly," are found in 2 Sam 15:20; Isa 30:3, and it was so understood by LXX. The similarity to the following *mûl* is the result of Micah's love of assonance. In the phrase *'ammî ("my people"), I AM* is the antecedent of the pronoun (cf. v 7) in this genitive of relationship.[50] The precise identification of *'am* must be decided by contextual considerations (cf. 1:9). T. E. McComiskey[51] rightly rejects the emendation: "*'ammî* is used flexibly by Micah to refer to the oppressed classes (3:3) as well as the nation as a whole (1:9; 2:4; 3:5; 6:3, 5). The abrupt change of persons is quite typical of Micah's style (1:2; 2:3, 12; 3:9-10; cf. v. 11, et al.)." More specifically, *'ammî* is used here ironically of the wicked even as they used it of themselves in 2:4. These sinners audaciously claim a covenantal relationship with God (cf. 2:7). In the phrase *lĕ'ôyēb (as an "enemy") lĕ* has a comparative sense as in Deut 9:21.[52] The rulers who should shepherd Israel attack their defenseless subjects like an enemy. In 3:1-4 Micah will liken them to butchers. The pattern CôCēC in *lĕ'ôyēb*, according to Kedar-Kopfstein,[53] "denotes a permanent feature of the subject in character or behavior." *yĕqômēm (rise up)* is a polel third masculine singular nonperfective of *qûm*. The subject is *'ammî*; the nonperfective with *'etmûl* probably has an incipient progressive force, "begin to rise up,"[54] and the polel with this verb of body movement probably has a frequentative aspect.[55]

mimmûl (off) consists of the preposition *min* with an ablative sense[56] and the frozen preposition *mûl* "front of"; the compound means "off." It governs the object *śalmâ (the tunic)*, the basic garment. L. C. Allen[57] unnecessarily spec-

48. *La Formation*, 95.

49. Willis, "Micah 2:6-8 and the 'People of God' in Micah," 81.

50. *IBHS* §9.5.1.

51. T. E. McComiskey, "Micah," in *Expositor's Bible Commentary* (Grand Rapids: Zondervan, 1985), 7:414.

52. *IBHS* §11.2.10.

53. Cited in *IBHS* §5.2.

54. *IBHS* §31.3b.

55. *IBHS* §24.5.

56. *IBHS* §11.2.11.

57. Allen, *Micah*, 293.

ulates that it replaced *šālēm* "peaceful." *'eder* (mantle), meaning "splendor," could be a metonymy for a splendid garment worn over the tunic, but more probably, due to haplography caused by following *tapšīṭûn,* final *t* was dropped from the original *'adderet* "mantle." Many interpreters emend the text to fit the general sense that the rich take the garments of the poor. But Micah does not represent the people as economically poor. He represents the men as stalwart landowners (2:2), their homes as delightful (2:9A), and their children as displaying a glory (2:9B). *tapšīṭûn (you strip off)* is a hiphil second masculine plural of *pšṭ* with paragogic *nun.* The personal object of the hiphil's causative notion, "their victims," is elided (cf. following *mēʿōbĕrîm*), leaving only the impersonal object of the action, "the mantle."[58] The nonprogressive describes a persistent present situation,[59] and the paragogic *nun* in poetry signifies frequency.[60] The root *pšṭ* is frequently used of violently stripping off garments (cf. Gen 37:23) and, as T. E. McComiskey[61] notes, of martial "raids" (Judg 9:33; 1 Sam 23:27). Micah uses the same word in his figure of the enemy as a butcher stripping off skin (see 3:3). The literal reality, the illegal practices of the court, is spelled out in 2:1-2. Our poet often shifts persons (cf., e.g., 1:11; 2:4), here from third, "my people rise up," to second, "you strip off." The second person refers to the wicked leaders, in parallel to the third person, "my people."

mēʿōbĕrîm (from those who pass by) is an adverbial phrase modifying *tapšīṭûn.* This qal active participle functions as an equivalent of a relative clause *(from those who pass by)*[62] and as a genitive after the preposition. It is an antemeria, an adjective for a noun,[63] for the unsuspecting victims of the tyrannical leaders. *beṭaḥ (without a care),* meaning "to feel secure," is an adverbial accusative modifying the state of the passers-by.

The next phrase explains why they feel secure. *šûbê milḥāmâ (men being returned from battle),* in apposition to *ʿōbĕrîm,* consists of a masculine plural qal passive participle, an antemeria parallel to *ʿōbĕrîm* for the same referent, in construct with *milḥāmâ,* a genitive after the participle in place of a preposition.[64] It cannot mean "returned to battle" because, were that the case, they would not feel secure; rather, they are returned from battle (cf. Isa 59:20, where *šûb* with the genitive also means "return from," i.e., "repent of"). The qal pas-

---

58. Cf. *IBHS* §27.3.
59. *IBHS* §31.3.
60. *IBHS* §31.7.
61. McComiskey, "Micah," in *Expositor's Bible Commentary,* 7:413.
62. *IBHS* §37.5.
63. Cf. E. W. Bullinger, *Figures of Speech* (Grand Rapids: Baker, 1968), 495.
64. P. Joüon, *Grammaire de l'Hebreu Biblique* (Rome: Pontifical Biblical Institute, 1923), 344, §121n.

sive participle *šûbê* is a *hapax legomenon*. BDB[65] thinks it means "averse," but this is an overly extended meaning of "return." The passive, "returned," indicates that the subject has been acted upon, though, as often, the agent is unnamed and impersonal. Our poet uses military imagery throughout the verse. Many scholars want to add "like," but he began the metaphor when he called the powerful "enemies."

9 LXX, by adding initial *dia touto* "therefore" and reading *nĕśî'ê* (= *hēgoumenoi* "leaders"), for MT's *nĕšê*, destroys the progress in Micah's accusation from the spoiling of Israel's men (v 8), to women (v 9A), to children (v 9B). In the construct chain *nĕšê 'ammî (women of my people)*, a genitive of relationship,[66] I AM ceases to use *'ammî* sarcastically of the wicked (vv 4, 8). *'iššâ*, in distinction to *'almâ*, usually refers to married women, as here, where it is parallel to children. The word order emphasizes the women as objects of the pillaging. *tĕgoršûn (you drive out)*, a piel second masculine plural nonperfective with the paragogic *nun* of *grš*, is a present persistent nonperfective emphasized with frequentative paragogic *nun*.[67] The piel is resultative (i.e., "you make driven out"),[68] and the second masculine plural refers to the addressed tyrants. The verb *grš* "drive out" continues the martial figure begun in v 8 (cf. Exod 23:28-31; Num 22:6, 11; Pss 78:55; 80:9[8]). *mibbêt ta'ănūgêâ (from their luxurious homes)* brings the martial figure close to the reality of Israel's courts (2:2). *bayit* "house" is not an unconventional collective singular[69] but illustrates the poet's quick shift of number — note also the pronominal suffix — from singular to plural (as in 2:4), moving the attention from the group to the individual (cf. 1:11; 2:4). The attributive genitive with possessive suffix, *ta'ănūgêâ (luxurious)*, is a plural collective with an abstract noun.[70] The root *'ng* refers to taking exquisite delight (cf. 1:16); its *t* prefix denotes action.[71]

mē'al 'ōlāleyâ (from her children), a compound of the ablative prepositions *min* and *'al*, moves the martial figure to the children of the women in the B verset. *'ôlĕlîm* refer to dependent children, from an unborn child (Job 3:16) to a child asking for bread (Lam 2:19; 4:4). The countable plural, with the singular suffix denoting a genitive of relationship, may imply that Israel's mothers had many children. *tiqhû (you take)*, qal second masculine plural nonperfective, has the same antecedent and force of the nonperfective as *tĕgoršûn* and continues

---

65. BDB 997, §5f.
66. *IBHS* §9.5.1.
67. *IBHS* §31.3.3, 7.
68. *IBHS* §24.3.2.
69. *IBHS* §7.2.1.
70. *IBHS* §7.4.1.
71. *IBHS* §5.6.

the military metaphor. *hădārî (my splendor)* is a metonymy for the rich physical benefits that *I AM* gave his children in the sworn land. *hādār* denotes the majesty and dignity that come from wealth; the possessive genitive shows that the wealth was *I AM's* to give. Some interpreters, not having understood that the divine speech began with v 7, want to drop the pronominal suffix or emend to *hĕdrô*. H. Wolff[72] conjectures reading *ḥeder* "bed chamber," which matches "houses" in v 9A and fits the theme of rest in v 10. However, it misses the parallel with "luxury" in v 9A and "splendid mantle" in v 8. B. Renaud[73] restricts the metonymy "my splendor" to "inheritance" because of the parallelism between "houses" and "inheritance" in 2:2, but, although it undoubtedly included the land, rich robes are also not mentioned in 2:2 and a parallel in Ezek 16:9-14 suggests that we should allow the figure its full scope. *lĕʿôlām (forever)*, an adverbial phrase modifying *tiqḥû*, shows that the rulers determined perpetual servitude of the people even as Pharaoh had prior to the exodus. See v 2 regarding Israel's perpetual possession of land.

10 *qûmû ûlĕqû (Get up, go away!)*. Who is speaking? Commentators are once again divided about the speakers. Some think that Micah is quoting the extortioners as they address their victims. B. Duhm[74] and A. Weiser[75] attempted to prove that the rich are driving the women from their houses under the pretext of sanitary measures against contagious sickness. H. Wolff[76] believes that this was the text before it was reworked in the exile. More plausibly, having accused the despots in vv 7-9, *I AM* is now handing down the divine sentence against them. This view requires no textual emendation, no dubious reworking of the text, and fits the typical form of a judgment oracle: a divine sentence matching the crime. Perhaps in a *lex talionis I AM* is using the very vocabulary the extortioners used to oust their victims. The mood shifts from indicative to imperative with *qûmû (arise)*, a qal masculine plural imperative, because of the shift from accusation to sentence. *qûm* means "to start," "to make a move," "to go somewhere," and in connection with another imperative has an adverbial force, "quickly," so that the principal idea is introduced only by the second matching imperative, *lĕkû (go)*.[77]

kî (because) introduces the reason for the hasty departure. *lōʾ (not)* modifies the near demonstrative *zōʾt (this)*, which functions as a neutrum pronoun

72. Wolff, *Micha*, 53.

73. *La Formation*, 96.

74. B. Duhm, *Die zwölf Propheten* (Tübingen: Mohr, 1910), 86.

75. A. Weiser, "Micha," in *Das Buch der zwölf kleinen Propheten*, Das Alte Testament Deutsch 24 (Göttingen: Vandenhoeck & Ruprecht, 4th ed. 1963), 248-50.

76. Wolff, *Micha*, 54.

77. Cf. GKC §120d, g.

for a vague circumstance.[78] The combination, in poetry, expresses pointedly an antithesis or negation, "the sworn land is in no respect the resting place."[79] *hammĕnûḥâ (resting place)* carries the spiritual notion of well-being with it. It is not just an external political reality, but the whole sphere of salvation procured by God.

ba'ăbûr (= compounding of preposition *ba* plus a frozen preposition, *'ăbûr* [*on account of*]) governs *ṭom'â (cultic uncleanness)*; the form may be a qal infinitive construct of *ṭāmē'* with a nominal function.[80] Although Micah uniquely uses a priestly term to stigmatize social injustices — of its thirty-seven uses twenty are in Leviticus–Numbers and eight are in Ezekiel[81] — analogies (see Exposition, 129) show that it is not so unique that one must side with B. Renaud[82] and H. Wolff[83] in suspecting a redactional intervention or that we must emend the text to read *mĕ'ûmâ* "for a mere nothing" (cf. *BHS*). This old emendation harmonizes with an interpretation of v 10B in which *tĕhabbēl* is derived from II *ṭbl* "to take in pledge" and *ḥābōl taḥbĕlû* is read for *tĕhabbēl wĕḥebel* "for a mere nothing you seize in pledge a ruinous pledge." This conjecture, which Renaud dubs "jejune," leaves the pericope uniquely with only accusation and without the expected oracle of judgment. H. Wolff[84] thinks that at a later stage of reinterpretation it was repointed as pual and derived from III *ḥbl* "to ruin, devastate": "you will be ruined, and the ruin will be grievous." Although this is probably the correct root, restores the verse as a judicial sentence, and has the support of LXX, it is unnecessary to postulate a late reinterpretation or repointing of the text. MT, without emendation, appears to be the primitive text. *I AM* declares the whole land unclean in the same way that a spot on the skin or in the house rendered the whole man or thing defiled. It may be inferred from Num 35:34; Deut 21:23 that the unethical exploitation of defenseless victims by the powerful rendered the land unclean.

tĕhabbēl (will bring destruction) is feminine singular in agreement with its subject, *hammĕnûḥâ* "resting place." NRSV makes "uncleanness" (also feminine singular) subject, but it must supply a relative pronoun. There is no need to emend *tĕhabbēl* with LXX and *BHS* to second masculine plural to agree with the plural imperatives of v 10A. MT can be interpreted to mean that the resting place (i.e., the land) brings ruin, inviting a comparison to Lev 18:25, where the

---

78. *IBHS* §17.4.2.
79. Cf. BDB 519, §2d.
80. *IBHS* §§36.1.1; 36.2.1.
81. Cf. F. Maas, *THAT* 1:664-67.
82. *La Formation*, 98-100.
83. Wolff, *Micha*, 41.
84. Wolff, *Micha*, 41.

iniquities of the Canaanites caused the land to spit them out. The same verb is used absolutely in Isa 54:16, where TNIV renders it by "to work havoc." According to S. Ryder II,[85] piel with this verb is an idiomatic use derived from an original "destroy." In *wĕhebel nimrāṣ (even a grievous destruction) wāw* is epexegetical *(even)* and *hebel* is a cognate internal accusative with a gapped *tĕhabbēl*[86] or the direct object of a gapped verb meaning "to do." For the meaning of *nimrāṣ (beyond all remedy)* cf. 1 Kgs 2:8. *mrṣ* means "to be sick." The niphal participle has a gerundive force, "sickening," that is, grievous.

11 A change of speaker from *I AM* to Micah may be suggested by the change from addressing "house of Jacob" in the second person to the third person (see p. 110). Instead of the wish particle *lû* (if), LXX *(oudenos)* and Vg read negative *lō'*. Mur 88 also reads *lō'*, but cf. *lu'* in 2 Sam 18:12, which form may account for the more common, though here less sensible, reading of LXX and Vg. By the unreal conditional protasis, Micah sarcastically makes the point that they would ordain as their prophet any liar who was willing to tailor his message to their greed. Such deliberate liars are even worse, if that be possible, than their presently gifted, but deluded, prophets who theologically justified their crimes (cf. 3:5). The particle with a participle, as here, represents a condition as a real possibility, not as contrary to fact (cf. 2 Sam 18:12; Ps 81:14[13]). *'îš (a man)* (cf. 2:2) is indefinite, "anyone," and subject of *hōlēk, kizzēb,* and *hāyâ*. There is no need to emend the qal active participle *hōlēk (goes about)* into a finite verb *(contra BHS)* because the construction *lû* plus participle plus perfective is acceptable Hebrew.[87] The meaning "goes about" is also used with animals.[88] The predicate participle signifies the durative aspect.[89] *rûah (with windy [words])* is an adverbial accusative of state modifying *'îš*.[90] H. Wolff[91] says that *rûah* here means "windy," that is, "vain, empty, windy words"; windy words are empty words (Job 6:26; 16:3); windy prophets are prophets who say nothing (Isa 14:29; Jer 5:13; Hos 4:9). L. C. Allen[92] suggests a pun on Hos 9:7: "What should have been inspiration was nothing more than wind."

šeqer (lies), possibly a singular expressing kind,[93] signifies a distortion of

---

85. S. A. Ryder II, *The D-Stem in Western Semitic* (The Hague/Paris: Mouton, 1974), 110.

86. *IBHS* §10.2.1.

87. Joüon, *Grammaire,* §121j; cf. 2 Sam 18:21; 2 Kgs 3:14; Ps 81:14(13).

88. Cf. BDB 232, §2.

89. *IBHS* §37.6.

90. *IBHS* §10.2.2; cf. Isa 33:15; Jer 23:14; Prov 6:12.

91. Wolff, *Micha,* 54.

92. Allen, *Micah,* 299.

93. *IBHS* §6.13.4.

facts. It is an effected accusative[94] with the factitive piel *kizzēb;* it was probably chosen for its assonance with *šēkār* in v 11Ab. In chiastic parallelism with *rûaḥ,* *kizzēb* explains it. Many commentators regard *wāšeqer* as a hendiadys with *rûaḥ,* but they differ in their understanding of its syntax. J. M. P. Smith[95] thinks it modifies *hōlēk,* but W. Rudolph[96] believes it modifies *kizzēb.* Rudolph argues that MT intends this by pointing *wāšeqer* instead of *wěšeqer.* This is unlikely; the conjunction is typically pointed *wā* before the accent; also the conjunctive accent *mêrěkā* with *hōlēk* and the disjunctive *paštā* with *rûaḥ* provide the necessary parallelism between v 11Aaα and 11Aaβ. *kizzēb (lies)* is a factitive piel third masculine singular present persistent nonperfective of the root *kzb* (cf. 1:15). As elsewhere in this pericope, no formula introduces the quotation in v 11Abα/β, in this case by the lying "prophet."

In the direct discourse *'aṭṭīp (I will prophesy)* the pronoun refers to *'îš,* who is now the speaker, and the nonperfective denotes a specific future[97] of *nāṭap* hiphil (see 2:6). Commentators agree that the first *lāmed* introduces the indirect object *lěkā (to you),* though some, who seem unaware that the shift of number is perfectly acceptable in Hebrew syntax, read *lākem* to agree with *qûmû* in v 10. They differ about the second *lāmed,* however. B. Renaud[98] wrote:

> In 2:11 the verb *ntp* is construed with two *l*s: the first "for you" designates the addressee of the oracle; the second, its conditions: "by means of wine and of strong drink." Indeed, whether the verb be qal (Judg 5:4; Joel 4:18[3:18]; Prov 5:3; Song 4:11; 5:5, 13) or hiphil (Amos 9:13), the direct object complement is always put in the accusative and is never introduced by the preposition *l.* . . . The fundamental idea clearly stands out from this analysis: The rich desire prophets devoted to them and are completely prepared to listen to anybody who announces to them predictions which they expect and desire, without being surprised by the cupidity and the venality of these so-called men of spirit.

His analysis, however, overlooks the obvious parallel construction in v 6, which constitutes an *inclusio* with v 11. The singular *lěkā (to you)* individualizes the people included in the parallel *'ām. šeker* in all but two of its twenty-three uses in the OT occurs together with *yayin. šeker* denotes not just barley beer but any alcoholic beverage. The article with "wine and beer" marks them out as belong-

94. *IBHS* §10.2.1.
95. Smith, *Micah,* 63.
96. Rudolph, *Micha,* 59.
97. *IBHS* §31.6.2.
98. *La Formation,* 102.

ing to a class unique and determined in themselves.[99] Both are light intoxicants, about 7-10 percent alcoholic content, by comparison with modern liquors and strong drinks (i.e., concentrated alcohol).[100] Wine and beer are favorite themes of carnal rulers and evoke a sense of security (see Exposition, 130).

In *wĕhāyâ (he would be) waw* introduces the apodosis of v 11B, after the protasis introduced by *lû* in v 11A. *hāyâ* has a stative force. *maṭṭîp (who prophesies)* is a hiphil participle of *nṭp* (see 2:6) with a relative use[101] in the predicate nominative slot. In *hāʿām hazzeh* (to this) *hāʿām* is an objective genitive and the demonstrative pronoun is attributive. *ʿām* here designates the same people as in 2:8Aaα.

EXPOSITION

This judgment oracle, accusing and sentencing the perversely obstinate House of Jacob, including both its false prophets and rapacious racketeers, is marked off by: (1) the rare word *nṭp*, a synonym for prophesying in vv 6 and 11; (2) its dialogical and theatrical character; and (3) its formal and thematic coherence in contrast to 2:1-5 and 2:12-13. Yet the oracle has these links with 2:1-5: (1) the accusation that the powerful by oppression take the houses and fields of the weak (vv 2B, 9); (2) the fields are assigned to foreigners (v. 4) and the land vomits them out (v 10); and (3) "these things" (vv 6 and 7) lacks an antecedent without the connection to 2:1-5. J. T. Willis linked this oracle to the same setting as the preceding one. Whether the "dispute" took place immediately after that sermon or sometime later cannot be decided, but one can say that because of the verbal and thematic links that the redactor, perhaps Micah himself, linked the two sermons together.

The oracle can be analyzed as follows:

I. Introduction: Micah, in an apostrophe, identifies, accuses, and sentences the false prophets (v 6).
  A. Address: Micah paints the false prophets as adversaries of the true (v 6A).
  B. Accusation: Micah implicitly accuses the false prophets of failing to preach judgment (v 6Ba).
  C. Judgment: Micah predicts inevitable shame for the impenitent (v 6Bb).

---

99. *IBHS* §13.5.1.
100. Cf. R. L. Harris, *"yayin,"* *TWOT* 1:376.
101. *IBHS* §37.5.

II. Body: *I AM,* addressing the House of Jacob, indicts it for approving the
   faulty theology that leads to social injustices and sentences it to banish-
   ment from the pleasant land (vv 7-10).
   A. Accusation: *I AM* accuses the powerful of adopting a false theology
      and unethical practices (vv 7-9).
      1. *I AM* states and refutes their false theology (v 7).
         a. They teach that *I AM* never becomes impatient (v 7Aa) or
            judges sin (v 7Ab).
         b. *I AM* promises to reward only the righteous (v 7B).
      2. *I AM* exposes the "war" of the powerful against the defenseless
         (vv 8-9).
         a. They strip the mantles off Israel's men (v 8).
         b. They drive out Israel's mothers from their homes (v 9A)
            and plunder their children forever (v 9B).
   B. Judgment: *I AM* sentences them to exile (v 10A) because they made
      the sworn land unclean (v 10B).
III. Conclusion: Micah rakes the powerful as desiring for a prophet any
   windy liar who will support their crimes (v 11).

This oracle, partially an apologia for true prophecy and a polemic against
false, adds to the accusation against the great and powerful their unwillingness
to repent when confronted with judgment; it also makes more explicit their oppression of the defenseless, and accuses them of listening to any liar who cod-
dles them instead of to God's moral law. It adds to the judicial sentence that the
land will vomit them out because of their uncleanness.

In his introduction to this judgment oracle (v 6) Micah makes clear that
false prophets not only oppose true ones but try to silence them, that false
prophets do not preach judgment, and that, though they hate to hear of judgment, they will be put to everlasting shame.

The *vox populi* finds expression through false prophets, the official theologians of the time. A. S. van der Woude[102] explained that the "pseudo-
prophets" represent the political-religious establishment. The self-appointed
theologians defending the entrenched leaders would have included priests, such
as Amaziah, who commanded Amos not to prophesy (cf. Amos 7:14, 17), false
prophets (Mic 3:4-7), and counselors (cf. Jer 18:18). They will not prophesy
judgment. Blinded by Satan, the world system by nature both opposes the message of grace that teaches the heart first to fear and then to believe, and perse-
cutes God's witnesses to the truth (cf. John 15:18–16:4A).

---

102. Van der Woude, "Micah in Dispute with the Pseudo-Prophets," 247.

The plural verb, "You all stop preaching," suggests that the prohibition against judgment oracles was not directed against Micah alone. The plural slightly brightens the dim light in v 5 that a righteous remnant would redistribute the land. The plural may include Hosea (cf. Hos 1:1), Isaiah (cf. 1:1), Micah, their disciples (cf. Isa 8:16), and anonymous prophets (cf. Jer 26:20) — and indirectly the thousands they represent, who had not bowed the knee to Baal. *I AM* has and will always preserve a faithful witness who will not bow the knee to Baal, even as he said to Elijah a century earlier (1 Kgs 19:18; cf. 2 Tim 1:8-14; 2:1-7).

Prophetic conflict appears frequently in ancient Israel (cf. 1 Kgs 22:24; Jer 2:8; 6:13; 8:10; 14:14; 23:9, 17, 22, 25-26, 32; 26:7, 8, 11, 16, 28; 29:1, 8; Ezek 13:1-9, 17-19; Mic 3:8; Zeph 3:4). A badge of false teachers is their distorted preaching on only God's love and never on his wrath and judgment. Preaching half-truths, they lead the populace to death. True prophets must preach the whole counsel of God, for from now on *I AM* of Hosts will not raise up military geniuses like Joshua and David to establish an external kingdom, but prophets, who, through the doubled-edged sword of preaching, cut out spiritual rot and convert the hearts of men, thereby establishing an everlasting spiritual kingdom. Beginning with the classical prophets, *I AM* no longer establishes his kingdom through the military might of Israel arrayed against foreign armies, but through the prophets, whom he has called into his service to take up the Sword even to death against those who want to disarm and destroy them. The "eggshells" of the carnal form of the kingdom pass away completely with Jesus, who took the carnal sword away from his disciples. In the face of opposition the faithful persevere in speaking truth. Peter and John serve as exemplary models who followed the Lord Jesus' good witness (Acts 4:1-21).

God's judgment upon the false theologians and the racketeers whom they represent will be eternal "disgrace." For the false prophets the disgrace, a metonymy for judgment, entails in part a loss of their gifts (cf. 3:6-7), and for the powerful the loss of land and eternal death threatened in 2:3-5. As the glory of that generation departs (cf. 1:15-16), its disgrace will never depart. Had all prophets been true to their gifts and calling, and had the people repented before the ignominy that was threatened by true prophets had come to pass, the humiliating defeat would have been averted. Without repentance, however, it would not turn aside (cf. Jer 23:40).

Micah now accuses the powerful of swallowing a popular, but false, theology that in turn hardened them in unethical social practices. One's worldview, which is always religious, inevitably determines one's social behavior. Along with everyone else they embraced a false view of God's character, one that led to a false view of his actions. The flag of a false theology is its warped view of covenant. As C. J. Labuschagne[103] said: "[False theologians are] entrenched in the spiritual bulwark of election and covenant; with Yahweh watching over their interests and existence, the people feeling secure, and Yahweh backing their cause, they lived complacently, knowing no disquietude." In Amos, where there is found "ease in Zion," *I AM* "roars from Zion as a lion" (Amos 1:2; 3:4, 8, 12; 5:19). These false prophets presumed upon the covenant; they claimed to be *I AM*'s people ("my people," Mic 2:4, 8), through blood and history, denying that the true covenant is spiritual, based on faith and obedience. H. Wolff[104] said: "In Israel solidarity is decided neither through political affiliation nor through a creed of the lips but through brotherliness" (cf. Rom 9:6-7).

The half-baked theologians, focusing exclusively on God's patience and acts of salvation, either ignored or explained away those texts that taught that God's long-suffering is not eternal and that he will not express his wrath in judgment against sin. The House of Jacob was culpable for not removing the leaven of false prophecy from their midst (cf. Deut 13:1-5). The popular theology was probably built on Israel's famous confession in Exod 34:6, "*I AM, I AM*, the compassionate and gracious God, slow to anger, abounding in love and faithfulness" (cf. Num 14:18; Joel 2:13; Jonah 4:2; Nah 1:3; Pss 86:5; 103:8; 145:8; Neh 9:17). Putting on the armor of "orthodoxy," they stood secure and unthreatened in their sinful ways. That theology founders on two rocks. First, it was built on a half-truth, for it left out Exod 34:7: "yet he does not leave the guilty unpunished." Second, it misapplied the text to the wrong situation, just as Satan misapplied Ps 91:11-12 when he tempted the Lord (Luke 4:10-11). The whole truth is that, on the one hand, because of God's benevolent attributes, his covenantal purposes for his people collectively cannot be revoked, and that, on the other hand, individual rewards and punishments are contingent on ethical behavior. When Micah's generation rejected *I AM* and their covenantal obligations, they became God's enemies and lost their privileged position. The popular saying was "like a thornbush in a drunkard's hand" (cf. Prov 26:9). Just as dangerous today are false teachers who apply the doctrine of the believer's security to those who disown their Lord in their lifestyles and who do not bring forth the fruit of repentance from sin (cf. Matt 7:24-37; 12:50; 1 Cor 6:9-11; Gal 5:21; 2 Tim 2:12).

I AM answers their two punchy questions (v 7A) with one long, deliberate one (v 7B). Does he not prosper the person who walks uprightly? Those who walk uprightly in this case include those whom the powerful have oppressed.

---

103. C. J. Labuschagne, "Amos' Conception of God and the Popular Theology of His Time," in *Proceedings of Die Ou-Testamentiese Werkgemeenskap in Suid-Afrika* (1966), 123.
104. Wolff, *Micha,* 53.

Some of the defenseless whom they oppressed will experience his saving acts, including the punishment of their oppressors.

True prophets are distinguished from counterfeits by their message. First, in contrast to false prophets, they insist on a loyalty to *I AM* that issues in keeping his commands (Deut 13:2-6[1-5]), and, second, what they predict comes to pass (Deut 18:21-22). Micah courageously pinned the first badge on himself. With the words of *I AM* in his mouth he calls his audience back to the original covenant: the promises of God are not for sinners but for saints. Later generations pinned the second badge on him when his prophecies came to pass by recognizing the canonical status of his book.

An epexegesis of the accusation in 2:2 is now given in vv 8-9. Instead of walking uprightly the covenant people, identified in corporate solidarity with their leaders, attack innocent victims. Like an enemy army, the powerful and rich plunder the trusting men of Israel (v 8) and drive the women and the children from their homes and off their splendid land.

In typical Semitic style Micah characterizes in a general way Israel's tyrants as an "enemy" and then develops the theme by looking at their victims (cf. 3:5). Israel's leaders might just as well have been the Assyrians or later the Babylonians in despoiling Israel. In v 8 he epexegetes the wrong against the capable and competent men in Israel: the powerful strip off their "rich robes." As Jacob's sons stripped off the cloak from their brother Joseph, so now the advantaged strip the disadvantaged. Divine providence guided both Joseph's and Micah's generations, at the beginning and end of Israel's history, out of the blessed land into bondage in order to make a new beginning. "Rich robes" derives from a root meaning "wide, great." From that it came to mean "high, noble, glory, magnificence" and by metonymy it could designate the wide mantle. The emended word, *'ăderet* "mantle," is used of a prophet's mantle, with the qualifier "hairy" of a royal robe (Jonah 3:6) and of the "robe" Achan coveted, with the qualifiers "goodly Babylonian" (Josh 7:21, 24). Commentators often mistakenly cross-reference this pillaging with the law that aimed to protect the poor by obliging a creditor to give back the coat taken in pledge before sunset (Exod 22:27[28]; Deut 24:13; cf. Amos 2:8; Job 22:6). The garment in view in Mic 2:8, however, is not this basic tunic, but the robe placed over it that displayed the dignity of Israel's men.

Whereas v 8Ab looks at the attackers, v 8B looks at the offended. Israel's stalwart men felt secure within their own borders, as secure as a soldier feels when returning home from battle. The last place they expected the enemy was in their own capitals. But as it turned out, the ignoble men leading them, like many contemporary politicians and church leaders, did not see their offices as positions from which to serve but as prizes they had won in order to pillage those who had been given to their trust.

In a crescendo, Micah moves from pillaging the men's rich robes, to seizing the women's luxurious houses, to taking the children's splendor forever (v 9). The accusation shifts quickly from men, to women, to children, and from rich robes, to luxurious houses, to splendid wealth in general. The qualifying words give an inside view of the prosperity of the nation at the time of its fall. Once again Micah epexegetes 2:2, this time "houses" and "inheritance." *I AM's* splendor, *hădārî*, refers to the riches he conferred on Israel, making her beautiful among the nations (cf. Ezek 16:9-14, esp. v 14, where the word is used). Throughout the accusation the focus has been on the pillaging of the wealth that God had given his people. Like victims of war, the formerly richly endowed children are left without wealth or security forever. *I AM's* enormous wealth distributed across the length and breadth of Israel has now become concentrated in the hands of the few corrupt leaders. Today 35 percent of the wealth of the United States is concentrated in the hands of less than 1 percent of the people, many of whom function as patrons to the supposed representatives of the people. When a person becomes impoverished through his own lack of character or prudent action, he needs the Savior to change him. When poverty comes through a hostile environment, such as drought, he needs the Creator's intervention to restore life. When tyrants spoil him, he needs the Judge to punish them and deliver him. The latter situation is in view here. God will judge these tyrants in the same way that they tyrannized their subjects.

I AM hands down the sentence in v 10A, probably using the same words with which the avaricious drove the oppressed from their lands, and then gives the brief for the sentence in v 10B. As in 2:3-5, *I AM* sentences them to exile from their *mĕnûḥâ* (v 10A). "Resting place" carries the notion of spiritual well-being with it. In Ruth 3:1 its bi-form *mānôaḥ* means "a home," with all the richness of that term. As Naomi sought a "home" for Ruth, so *I AM* procured a "resting place" for Israel when he gave them the land (cf. Exod 33:14; Deut 3:20; 12:10; 25:19; Josh 1:13, 15; 21:44; 22:4; 23:1; Isa 63:14; esp. Deut 12:9; Ps 95:11). Through conquest over Israel's enemies he had procured this home with all its security and wealth (cf. 2 Sam 7:1, 11; 1 Kgs 5:18[4]; 1 Chr 22:9, 18; 23:25; 2 Chr 14:4[5], 5[6]; 15:15; 20:30; esp. Ps 132:14). At the temple the soul should find rest in the presence of God (Pss 23:2; 116:7). In brief, the resting place is not just an external political reality, but the whole sphere of salvation procured by God.

But now God declared the land "defiled." Persons and objects become ritually unclean through birth, menstruation, bodily emissions, "leprosy," sexual relations and misdeeds, and contact with death. Idolatry defiled the temple and the land. Once an object was declared unclean it had to be discarded or at least removed from the presence of *I AM*. The prophets used this primarily priestly term as a metaphor for moral defilement and social wickedness.[105] Micah figuratively applies the cultic term to stigmatize the social injustices of the profiteers and to explain why they must be exiled out of the holy land. Instead of being a "resting place," the land now spits them out (cf. Lev 18:25) to their ruin. The verse ends with "even a sickening (i.e., grievous) ruin."

One is reminded of the Lord Jesus, who later brought judgment on the impenitent churches of Asia Minor. He too spit them out of his mouth (Revelation 2–3; esp. 3:16). A person enters into the "holy land," a type of the Christian's position in Jesus Christ (cf. Hebrews 4), only by faith, as Israel learned at Kadesh-barnea (Numbers 13–14) and Ai (Joshua 7), and he stays in that land only through persevering faith (Leviticus 26; Deut 7:1-5; 28). Those bearing merely the external marks of faith, such as circumcision or baptism, in contrast to the inward mark of a circumcised heart and baptism of spirit, will be banished to eternal judgment, even as Israel was in Micah's time.

Whereas in vv 6-7 Micah accused the powerful of listening to false prophets who neglected to mention *I AM*'s wrath against sin and eternal damnation, in v 11 he scathingly and sarcastically rakes them in conclusion for being too willing to ordain anyone who will deliberately lie and join them in their cupidity. The false preachers they would choose are not merely deluded but deliberate liars. They are prepared to listen to anybody who gives them credibility and are not at all surprised by the turpitude of these so-called "prophets" (cf. Isa 28:7; Amos 2:12).

Wine and beer are favorite themes of these carnal rulers who indulge their swollen appetites, a lust censored by the preexilic prophets (Isa 5:11-12, 22; 28:7-8; 56:12; Amos 4:1; 6:4-6) and warned against by the sages (Prov 20:1; 21:17; 23:20-21, 29-35; 31:4-7). It may also evoke a sense of security and of divine blessing on them in the sworn land (Lev 26:5; Deut 28:4, 11; Joel 2:24; 4:18[3:18]; Amos 9:13). T. E. McComiskey[106] said: "The people of this time had an intense desire for the fruits of their affluent society, expressed in terms of 'wine' and 'beer.' So if someone were to preach to them of great affluence and prosperity, they would listen to him; and he would readily find acceptance among them." Unfortunately the evangelical church today is often associated with the business establishment, usually motivated by serving self not others, and not with the social concerns of the oppressed and needy, in spite of the clear teaching of the NT on this subject (Matt 24:31-46; Mark 12:31; Acts 4:32-37; 1 Thess 4:9-10; 1 John 1:6; 2:10; 3:16-18). Like the venal men of Micah's day they swallow greedily the spiritually lethal message of wealth and prosperity.

105. Cf. E. Yamauchi, "*ṭāme*'," *TWOT* 1:350.
106. McComiskey, "Micah," 7:413.

C. God Preserves a Remnant in Zion (2:12-13)

12   I will surely gather all of you, O Jacob;
        I will surely assemble the remnant of Israel;
          I will bring them together like sheep into a pen.
    Like a drove in its pasture
      they shall be thrown into confusion
       with no man [to care for them].

13   The One Who Breaks Forth will march out to battle before them;
      they will break forth and pass
        through the gate and go out.
    Their King will pass through before them,
      I AM at their head.

EXEGESIS

12 The infinitive absolute *'āsōp (surely)* emphasizes the certainty of the qal first common singular nonperfective designating future time, *'e'ĕsōp (I will . . . gather)*.[1] The first person, though lacking an introductory formula — probably because vv 12-13 are excerpted from a larger pericope — must have *I AM* as its antecedent, for who else sovereignly shepherds Israel? The nonperfective future indicates a contingency; Israel's salvation depends on God's character. *ya'ăqōb (O Jacob)*, a vocative before the following second masculine singular pronoun, and its parallel *yiśrā'ēl* (Israel), are honorific epithets for the eponymous patriarch's descendants. In Micah these terms refer to the ideal nation without political divisions (cf. 1:1, 5). The objective accusative *kullāk (all of you)* underscores the entirety of the nation, that is, as the parallel shows, of the remnant that survived the Assyrian invasion. Many scholars (cf. *BHS*) emend without warrant in any text or version from *kullāk* to *kullô*. As noted in 1:11, however, the grammatical disagreement is acceptable Hebrew. LXX's *syn pasin* points to a different text. The word order, "Jacob, all of you," reflects an old style (cf. Isa 14:29, 31; Jer 13:19).

The piel *(surely)* infinitive absolute with piel first common singular future nonperfective of *qbṣ (will . . . assemble)* again emphasizes the certainty of the promise. Piel has a resultative force (i.e., "make gathered").[2] J. T. Willis[3] says

1. *IBHS* §31.6.2.
2. *IBHS* §24.3.2.
3. J. T. Willis, "Structure, Setting, and Interrelationships," 198-202.

that in addition to the notion of a divine shepherd gathering sheep, the two verbs *'sp* and *qbṣ* are often used in military contexts in the sense of mustering troops for battle and so here connote the action of a "duly authorized leader gathering the people to him to fight." According to him, "Mic 2:12-13 reflects the David tradition as fully as does 5:1ff.," and "the affinities between the Davidic tradition and Mic. 2:12-13 are too numerous to be accidental," so that "2:12-13 . . . envision a revitalization of the Davidic age, one of the characteristics of which was the unity of the twelve tribes."[4] While I agree with Willis, the evidence is extrinsic and inconclusive. J. Lindenberger,[5] though admitting that the two verbs may be used of restoration (Isa 40:11; Mic 4:6-7), argues that this is a judgment oracle and so looks to passages where they appear in threatening contexts (1 Sam 15:6; Ezek 16:37; 34:29; Mic 4:12; Zeph 1:2). But note that Mic 4:6 is in an oracle of salvation, not of doom, and in Mic 4:12 they pertain to the gathering of the nations, not Israel, for judgment. Intrinsically, Willis also has the better argument, for, as the rest of the exegesis will show, this is a salvation oracle; also, the martial language of v 13 is better read back into v 12 than ignored. In *šě'ērît yiśrā'ēl (the remnant of Israel) šě'ērît* is a direct accusative, and *yiśrā'ēl* is a genitive of relationship.[6] In contexts of restoration "remnant" designates the fortunate survivors beyond disaster (cf. Jer 23:3), and in contexts of destruction the few survivors in it (cf. Amos 1:8; 5:15). The former meaning is in view elsewhere in Micah (4:7; 5:6[7], 7[8]; 7:18); the latter here. Only a remnant in Jerusalem find salvation, while the Assyrians demolish Judah.

The emblematic parallel in v 12Ab, *yaḥad 'ăśîmennû kěṣō'n bōṣrāh (I will bring them together like sheep into a pen)* explicates, emphasizes, and adds to the notion of gathering the remnant of Israel. *yaḥad (together)* is an adverbial accusative modifying the state of the remnant as a unity (cf. 2 Sam 10:15; Isa 11:11; Pss 2:2; 31:15[14]; 88:19[18]; 133:1), a parallel to *kullāk*. By the third use in v 12A of the first common singular nonperfective verb *I AM* emphasizes his role as Israel's sovereign Shepherd-King; the root *śîm* carries his work beyond gathering the remnant to that of setting them in security. According to A. F. Rainey,[7] the third masculine singular "energic-*nun*" suffix, *-ennû* shows that the prefix conjugation is a true nonperfective; it has Jacob/Israel as its antecedent. *kěṣō'n (like sheep)* symbolizes *I AM's* protection of the remnant and validates that this is a salvation oracle. As Israel's Shepherd-King, *I AM* protects (cf. Pss 23:1-4; 80:2[1]) the people of his pasture (Ezek 34:31; Pss 95:7; 100:3). False shepherds

---

4. Willis, "Structure, Setting, and Interrelationships," 200, 202, 203.

5. J. Lindenberger, "Micah 2:12-13: A Promise or a Threat."

6. *IBHS* §9.5.1.

7. A. F. Rainey, "The Ancient Hebrew Prefix Conjugation in the Light of Amarnah Canaanite," *Hebrew Studies* 27/1 (1986) 4; cited in *IBHS* §31.1.1.

scatter sheep (Isa 56:11-12; Jer 23:1-13; 50:6) and feed themselves, not the flock (Ezek 34:2-3). The people feel like sheep led to slaughter when, in distress, they feel abandoned by God (Ps 44:12[11], 23[22]; cf. Isa 53:7; Jer 12:3). The simile is often used for God's care for exiled Israel and his intent to return them home (Isa 40:11; Jer 23:3-4; 31:10; Ezek 34:11-16). J. Lindenberger[8] argues from 1 Kgs 22:17; Isa 7:21; 13:4; Jer 50:17, 44-45; 51:40; Ezek 25:5; Amos 3:12; Zech 10:2; 13:7) that it can also refer to violent death. 2 Kgs 22:17; Isa 13:14; Jer 50:17; and Zech 10:2; 13:7 actually argue the other way; they speak of the destruction of a flock for the lack of a shepherd to protect them. Amos 3:12 speaks of the best care the shepherd can give under the circumstances. Jer 50:44-45 has in view Babylon's unsuccessful shepherd in contending with *I AM*, who is likened to a lion, but even here the shepherds are trying to protect the sheep. Jer 50:40 cannot be cross-referenced to Mic 2:12, for in that passage *I AM* presents himself as Defender of his people while bringing Babylon, who has acted like lions against Israel, as sheep to slaughter. Isa 7:21 and Ezek 25:5 in my opinion are not apposite to the argument. As Lindenberger admits, most commentators see here a reference to salvation, not to damnation.

boṣrâ (into a pen), as vocalized by the Masoretes elsewhere, refers to the Edomite northern fort-city (Gen 36:33 = 1 Chr 1:44; Isa 34:6; 63:1; Jer 49:13, 22; Amos 1:12) and Moabite Bozrah (Jer 48:24). Accordingly, J. M. P. Smith[9] interpreted the noun as a genitive of location, "sheep in Bozrah"; in v 12B he also revocalized *mēʾādām* to read "from Edom," envisioning Israel going into captivity in Edom, the home of its ancient enemy (cf. Isa 63:1-6; Obadiah). His view is rejected because his revocalization lacks textual warrant and his historical reference is unattested. Renaud[10] interprets it as a genitive of possession, "sheep of Bozrah," and revocalizes *ʾdm* in "the primitive text" as "Edom." Not only does his conjecture regarding Edom lack support, but why the sheep of Edom? D. J. Innes[11] noted: "Although rams and lambs are mentioned in connection with Bozrah in Edom in Isaiah 34:6, so are wild oxen in the following verse, and there is no adequate evidence that Bozrah was specially famed for its sheep." BDB questionably interpreted *boṣrâ* as uniquely meaning "enclosure," "encampment" here, and the genitive as locative. It may be that Vg *(in ovili)* and Tg *(ḥutrāʾ)* so read it, but more probably, like LXX (*en thlipsei* "in distress"), they read *bĕ* as a preposition. Rashi also related *boṣrâ* to *bāṣar* "to fortify,"[12] as did, independently,

8. Lindenberger, "Micah 2:12-13."

9. J. M. P. Smith, "Some Textual Suggestions," *AJSL* 37 (1920-21) 238-39; *contra* his commentary, *Micah*, 238-39.

10. Renaud, *Michée*, 52.

11. D. K. Innes, "Some Notes on Micah," *EvQ* 41 (1969) 13.

12. Cf. also Sym and Theod *en ochyrōmati* "in a fortress."

F. Hitzig.[13] Many scholars[14] suppose that Vg and Tg read *bĕ* as a preposition, "in," in parallel with *bĕtôk*, and *ṣrh* as an Arabizing form[15] of *ṣîrâ* "enclosure for livestock," vocalizing the word as *baṣṣirâ*. G. Hylmo[16] believes that it is a bi-form of the better-attested *ṭîrâ* "a tent protected by a stone wall" (Gen 25:16; Num 31:10; Ezek 25:4; Ps 69:26[25]; 1 Chr 6:39). J. Lindenberger[17] validates this view by noting that the *ṣ*/*ṭ* correspondence, though unusual, is not unparalleled: "Cognate Arabic words with both *ṭ* and *ṣ* occur already in the Sabaean inscriptions; see J. C. Biella, *Dictionary of Old South Arabic: Sabaean Dialects* (HSS 25; Chico, Calif.: Scholars, 1982), pp. 217 . . . 422-23)." *ṭ*/*ṣ*/*ṣyrh* could be a deeply rooted lexical doublet. In any case, there are no philological grounds for objecting to the identification of *bṣrh* as a cognate of Arabic *ṣīra*. B. Renaud[18] objects to this identification, however, because *ṭîrâ* "never designates the enclosure of sheep, but always 'encampments' for men . . . or a rampart (Song 8:9 and perhaps Ezek 46:23)." The selection of the term may have been idiosyncratic to suggest the human defenses of Jerusalem. Whether one follows Rashi and some moderns without repointing the text or most moderns in repointing it, the word is best interpreted as meaning a secure "enclosure." Many commentators see the metaphor as a reference to Babylon; more probably it refers to the remnant that sought refuge in Jerusalem during Sennacherib's siege in 701 B.C. (see 7, 140).

The figure of the remnant as a united flock is reinforced by the second simile, *kĕʿēder (like a drove)*, but modifies *tĕhîmenâ* instead of *ʾăśîmennû* so that the remnant, instead of being compared to sheep in a protected pen, are represented as a confused herd without a human shepherd-king to protect them. *bĕtôk*, a compound preposition of *bĕ* and *tôk* (in the midst of) governs *haddābĕrô* and introduces the second prepositional phrase modifying *tĕhîmenâ*. In spite of the grammatical "barbarism," *haddābĕrô (in its pasture)*, which prefixes an article and suffixes a pronoun, it is best not to emend the word by prefixing the final *w* as a conjunction with the following verb and, with ancient versions, revocalizing as *haddōber* "pasture," for this would make the prepositional phrases modify *ʾăśîmennû*, creating the inelegant combination, "I will set them as a flock in a pen, as a drove in a pasture." A. van Hoonacker[19] repoints the

13. F. Hitzig, *Die zwölf kleinen Propheten* (Leipzig: Weidmann, 1852), 191.

14. Cf. Willis, "Structure, Setting, and Interrelationships," 196 n. 1.

15. Cf. E. W. Lane, *Arabic Lexicon*, I/4 (London and Edinburgh: Williams and Norgate, 1872), 2754c.

16. Cited by Willis, "Structure, Setting, and Interrelationships," 196.

17. Lindenberger, "Micah 2:12-13."

18. *La Formation*, 104-5.

19. A. van Hoonacker, *Les Douze Petits Prophètes*, Études Bibliques (Paris: Gabalda, 1908), 375.

noun as *deber* "plague" and interprets it as "calamity." Qimḥi, however, considered MT acceptable Hebrew, citing Josh 7:21 (cf. Josh 8:33 and 2 Kgs 15:16), though GKC[20] regards all of them as scribal errors.[21]

tĕhîmenâ (they shall be thrown into confusion) is an internal hiphil, perhaps with a tolerative nuance, "allow themselves to be thrown in confusion/disquietude,"[22] of the root *hûm*. Although this rare form is attested in Mur 88 and used in Ps 55:4(3), many revocalize the verb to the more common *tehĕmeh*, qal third feminine singular of *hāmâ* "to murmur, moan, be noisy" (cf. Isa 59:11; Ezek 7:16; Ps 59:7[6], 15[14]) (cf. "to resound"; NRSV). R. Tournay[23] appeals to Ezek 34:31 (to which B. Renaud[24] adds Ezek 36:38), commenting, "the enormous herds of the vast Edomite plateau raise an immense noise of confusion." There is no reason, however, why the rare word *hûm* could not be used of animals. D. Hillers[25] gratuitously introduces the possibility of the root *hmm* "to be noisy," and suggests that it could be construed as a third feminine singular absolute energic (i.e., without a pronominal suffix). With more radical surgery, H. Wolff[26] speculates that the last two words are a gloss and compares Ezek 36:21: "So will the ruined cities be filled with flocks of people." The feminine form calls for the feminine collective *ṣō'n* as subject, and a collective "may readily be construed with the plural of the predicate."[27] Van Hoonacker[28] emends the text to read *wytmhw ndw m'dm* "they are terrified; they flee far from their disaster (*'ēdām*)." He loosely follows LXX's *exalountai* "they flee," but the rest is conjecture. L. C. Allen,[29] staying with MT, paraphrases: "bleating in fear."

The meaning of *mē'ādām (with no man [to care for them])* is ambiguous. If the *mîn* be causal,[30] the sense is that the confusion is due to the multitude of men (cf. NRSV); if it be privative, it means the opposite: it is due to the lack of a man. The latter meaning comports better with the singular and forms a better contrast with *I AM* as King (cf. v 13) and the lack of a human shepherd to save the remnant. J. Lindenberger[31] cites Zech 10:2B as a particularly close parallel, if it be translated, "Therefore the people wander like sheep, bleating for want of a

20. GKC §127i.
21. Cf. *IBHS* §13.6.
22. *IBHS* §27.2, 5.
23. R. Tournay, "Bulletin," *RB* 72 (1965) 303.
24. *La Formation*, 105.
25. Hillers, *Micah*, ad loc.
26. Wolff, *Micha*, 42.
27. GKC §145b.
28. Van Hoonacker, *Les Douze Petits Prophètes*, 375.
29. Allen, *Micah*, 300.
30. Cf. *IBHS* §11.2.11.
31. Lindenberger, "Micah 2:12-13."

shepherd." (He defends the meaning "bleating" for *ya'ănû* in that passage from Deir 'Alla 1:8.)[32]

13   The LXX badly divides the Hebrew text and reads as the end of v 12 *'al happereṣ* (*dia tēs diakopēs* "through the breach"), entailing dropping final *h* of MT's *'ālâ*, probably through haplography. LXX is an obviously facilitating reading that entails many other modifications for the more difficult MT; besides, MT has the support of Mur 88. *'ālâ (will march out to battle)* is a qal third masculine singular perfective of the root *'lh*. The unexpected perfective is confirmed by Mur 88. *'lh*, according to G. Wehmeier,[33] may have the technical meaning "to march out into battle," "to attack," not only with the prepositions *'al* (Judg 6:3; 1 Kgs 14:25; Isa 36:1), *'el* (Num 13:31; Josh 15:15; Judg 1:1), and *bĕ* (Isa 7:6) and the expressions *'lh bammilḥāmâ* and its equivalents (1 Sam 14:2; 29:9) but even absolutely (Judg 20:28 parallel to *yṣ' lammilḥāmâ;* 1 Sam 17:23, 25; 1 Kgs 12:24 = 2 Chr 11:4 parallel to the niphal of *lḥm;* Isa 21:2; Jer 6:4, 5). The meaning is further validated by the verbs *prṣ* "break out" and the parallel, "*I AM* at their head." Whether or not this is a salvation oracle, the accidental perfective vividly and dramatically represents the future as a single independent situation.[34]

Its subject, *pōrēṣ (the one who breaks out),* is a qal active participle used as an independent relative.[35] The identity behind the antemeria[36] is debated. J. T. Willis[37] cites the following opinions: Cyrus (Binns), a portion of an army or a leader (Driver, Cheyne, Marty), a group of Israelite workmen (Halévy), Sennacherib (Lee and Haupt), Messiah (Horton, Ridderbos, et al.), and Yahweh (Willis and most). Willis[38] plausibly defends the last view as best. According to him,[39] the term harks back to the Davidic tradition (cf. 2 Sam 5:2, 20 = 1 Chr 14:11): "Apparently, the *happōrēṣ* of Mic 2:13 is carefully chosen in order to refer explicitly to the Davidic tradition." Also, the parallel verset identifies the one going before them as a King (v 13Ba), and, more specifically, *I AM* at their head (v 13Bb). J. Lindenberger, arguing that this is a judgment oracle, thinks that the enemy is the one breaching Israel's walls, but he has to adopt an unusual sense for *lipnêhem* "against them" and in mid-sentence change the subject of *wayyēṣĕ'û* to the Israelites. A number of commentators continue the flock meta-

---

32. See J. A. Hackett, *The Balaam Text from Deir 'Allā,* HSM 31 (Chico, Calif.: Scholars Press, 1984) 25, 29, 46.

33. G. Wehmeier, *THAT* 2:277.

34. *IBHS* §30.5.1.

35. *IBHS* §37.5.

36. E. W. Bullinger, *Figures of Speech* (Grand Rapids: Baker, 1968), 495.

37. Willis, "Structure, Setting, and Interrelationships," 197 n. 1.

38. Willis, "Structure, Setting, and Interrelationships," 205 n. 2.

39. Willis, "Structure, Setting, and Interrelationships," 204.

phor of v 12 and see *I AM* as the lead ram, a "divine bellwether" battering
through the wall of the sheepfold (or leaping over it), so that the flock can follow him out. D. Hillers[40] rightly notes that "this departs from the picture of the
shepherd-king, and offers an unparalleled and downright bizarre conception."
J. Lindenberger supports his thesis that this is a judgment oracle by claiming
that *prṣ* is virtually always used of a destructive act, never of a salvific one. But
when *I AM* broke out against the Philistines in 2 Sam 5:20, did it not entail Israel's salvation? So also here, by breaking out violently against the besieging
Assyrians, he saved Israel. The verb can mean either "break forth, burst out,"
from an enclosure (cf. Gen 38:29) or "break through, down" from without. The
verb *wayyēṣĕʾû* "they will go out" shows that the former is in view. The adverbial
phrase *lipnêhem (before them)* has its normal sense, a sense parallel to "*I AM* at
their head" in the B verset. It modifies "march out to battle," and the third masculine plural suffix refers back *ad sensum* to the remnant army that stood behind the flock metaphor of v 12. The martial image in v 12Aa is elaborated upon
in v 12Ab.

pārĕṣû (they will break forth), a qal perfective third masculine plural of
prṣ, has the same tense value as *ʿlh* and the same meaning of the root as in
happōrēṣ. The plural subject has as its antecedent "before them," the army *I AM*
leads into battle. B. Renaud[41] validates his suggestion that the final *waw* in
pārĕṣû (they break) is due to dittography with the next word by the singular in
Vg *(ascendet)* and Syr *(trʾ . . . twrʾtʾ* "he has broken a breach"). Unfortunately
Mur 88 has a lacuna here. The plural form of all Hebrew MSS and LXX
(diekopsan "they break through") is preferred because it makes a better parallel.
As "their King passes through before them" and "they pass through the gate," so
also "*I AM* breaks forth before them" and "they break forth." The scene is similar to the first exodus: *I AM* brought the waters of the sea back over the Egyptians and the armed men passed through on dry ground (Exod 14:29-31). The
waw-relative, *wayyaʿăbōrû (and they pass through)* represents a sequential situation to *pārĕṣû* with the same force as the perfective.[42] The TIV, by collapsing
pārĕṣû and *wayyaʿăbōrû* as a hendiadys, "they will break through the gate," loses
the parallel between *I AM*'s and Israel's twofold activity of bursting forth and
passing through.

šaʿar (through the gate), an adverbial accusative of place,[43] most probably
refers to Jerusalem's gate, the only gate mentioned in this book (cf. 1:9, 12). J. L.

---

40. Hillers, *Micah*, 39.
41. *La Formation*, 106.
42. GKC §111w; *IBHS* §33.3.1; cf. Isa 9:5.
43. *IBHS* §10.2.2.

Mays[44] agrees: "The otherwise obscure mention of 'the gate' must presuppose and allude to the two gates of Jerusalem as the focus of YHWH's assault on Jerusalem in 1:9, 12." The sequential situation, *wayyēṣĕ'û (and they will go out through it)*, clarifies that the previous action was not by the enemy breaking into the city through its gate but by *I AM* and his army breaking out of the enclosed city. The remarkably diverse preposition *bĕ* may mean "through" with verbs of movement in space.[45]

The *wāw*-relative with *ya'ăbōr (for he will pass through [the gate])* must have an epexegetical function,[46] not sequential, for how could the army pass through first, followed by *I AM* at their head? The explanatory parallel B verset aims to keep the focus on *I AM* as Israel's Shepherd-King. *malkām lipnêhem (their King)* should be equated with the parallel, *happōrēṣ lipnêhem*, "the Breaker before them."

Our poet holds his audience's suspense about the identity of the Shepherd-King, who spoke in first person in v 12 and of whom he speaks in v 13 until the climactic parallel: *wayhwh bĕrō'šām* (I AM *at their head*). The *waw* is ascensive, not a copula, because the prophecy nowhere distinguishes between *I AM* and a human king. Rather, the consistent focus has been on Israel's Shepherd-King in contrast to any human ruler. J. Lindenberger,[47] retaining his thesis that 2:12-13 threatens doom, interprets the B verset as irony. He himself has to admit, however, that such an interpretation almost makes Micah guilty of blasphemy.

EXPOSITION

J. Lindenberger[48] notes that the following distinguished commentators interpreted 2:12-13 as a prophecy of disaster: Ephraem Syrus (d. 373?), Theodoret (393?-458?), David Qimḥi (1160-1235), John Calvin (1559), Hugo Grotius (1583-1645), Tarnovius (1626), and the early twentieth-century Belgian scholar A. van Hoonacker. My own exegesis of the words and phrases, however, bore out the traditional interpretation that it is a prophecy of hope and salvation. B. Renaud[49] says of A. van Hoonacker's view: "It leads to torturing the text in order to adapt it to a hypothesis . . . which is not confirmed." While LXX and Syr have

---

44. Mays, *Micah*, 75-76.
45. *IBHS* §11.2.5b.
46. *IBHS* §33.2.2.
47. Lindenberger, "Micah 2:12-13."
48. Lindenberger, "Micah 2:12-13."
49. *La Formation*, 110.

no consistent interpretative viewpoint, Tg clearly interpreted it as a promise of restoration out of the exile. It reads: "12In the end, I will surely gather you who belong to the house of Jacob, all of you. I will surely bring near your exiles, the remnant of Israel. . . . 13Saviors shall arise as in past times, and a royal leader will arise at their head; and he shall break the enemy who oppresses them, he will conquer mighty fortresses."

A major problem with this interpretation is the sudden shift of form from prophecies of reproach and doom to this one of hope. But the same breathtaking shift takes place between chapters 3 and 4 and, in the opposite direction, between chapters 5 and 6. J. T. Willis discerned a pattern of long and short sections of prophecies of judgment and of salvation (see the Introduction, pp. 14-15). Micah intimated a future hope at the end of 2:1-5 and of a remnant at the beginning of 2:6-11. Those two notions are now exploited. Although 2:12-13 is essentially an oracle of salvation, it implies that *I AM* saves the remnant in the midst of an enemy's siege.

What is the historical situation? As we have seen, J. M. P. Smith envisions Israel going into captivity in Edom and coming out again, but his view, besides raising historical questions, required emending the text. B. Renaud regarded this as the original oracle but has to admit that the text was reworked before any of the versions. Several authors, regarding these verses as a continuation of the preceding oracle, place them in the mouths of the false prophets. B. Renaud[50] summarizes the arguments of A. van Hoonacker and R. Vuilleumier against this view: The oracle against the false prophets finds its normal conclusion in 2:11. What place does Mic 2:12-13 play in their argument? When Micah quotes his adversaries, he clearly hints at it (cf. vv 6, 7, 11). It closely resembles Mic 4:6-8, which does not stem from the false prophets. Finally, restoration after the exile does not harmonize with the message of the false prophets who denied that there would be an exile. D. Hillers[51] cites M. Margolis: "It is not likely that the false prophets concerned themselves with the events following the downfall of the nation, which contingency they were most emphatic in denying."

Since B. Stade,[52] most scholars contend that the prophecy is exilic or postexilic. In their view the sheepfolds/city walls symbolize captivity in Babylonia, and Yahweh will break open a way for the exiles and will lead them in a new exodus back to Judah. (As noted, Tg held a similar view, though it probably assumed it to be a true prophecy from the mouth of Micah.) Below I answer B. Renaud's linguistic arguments for this date. Recent scholarship is

---

50. *La Formation*, 111-12.
51. Hillers, *Micah*, 40.
52. B. Stade, "Bemerkungen über das Buch Micha," *ZAW* 1 (1881) 161-72.

now calling the consensus, which in fact is based on historical criticism, into question.

H. Schmidt[53] and E. Sellin[54] read it as an exact description of the events of 701, when the population of Israel fled for protection from the Assyrian invaders into Jerusalem, where, when the Assyrians blockaded it, *I AM* wonderfully saved them by decimating the Assyrian army. L. C. Allen[55] recently buttressed this view with two compelling arguments: from the parallels *šĕ'ērît* "remnant" (v 12) and *yṣ'* "go out" (v 13), and Isaiah (2 Kgs 19:4, 31 = Isa 37:4, 32) and Mic 4:8; 7:14 (cf. Isa 1:8). From the first parallel he draws the conclusion: "Accordingly it is possible not only to find a historical setting for this oracle within the period of Micah's prophetic ministry but also, in the light of Isaiah's explicitness, to identify the venue of salvation as Jerusalem." In the light of the second set of parallels, for which he cites J. T. Willis,[56] Allen says that it is "likely that 'fold' [or 'fortified encampment' in v 12] here refers to Zion or Jerusalem." Other arguments can be added. (3) As noted, the verbs *'sp* "gather," *qbṣ* "assemble," and *prṣ* "break forth" occur as military terms when used with David. J. T. Willis[57] thinks that "the affinities between David and Mic 2:12-13 are too numerous to be accidental." (4) The imagery of being brought together as a flock into "a fortified encampment" (v 12) betters suits a blockade of Jerusalem than exile in Babylon. (5) V 13 envisions some walled place, apparently a city. J. L. Mays[58] envisions the Babylonian siege of Jerusalem. Although he apparently restricts the prophetic gift and dates prophecies of salvation after the time of Micah instead of accepting the book's own attribution of A/authorship (see v 1), his work is of abiding value for the following two arguments that the siege is of Jerusalem. (6) The verb *prṣ* in v 13 fits this venue because it is used elsewhere with *I AM* as subject breaking down the walls of Jerusalem (Pss 80:13[12]; 89:41[40]; cf. Isa 5:5; Ps 60:2[1]). Here, however, he breaks down the fortified gate and leads them out. (7) "The gate" is Jerusalem's. (8) Finally, this venue provides a link with the preceding oracles of doom. As they stressed the doom of Judah and implied a hope for the remnant, this prophecy stresses the remnant's salvation but implies the destruction of Judah.

B. Renaud[59] fails to prove by linguistic typology that the prophecy was

53. H. Schmidt, "Micha," in *Die grossen Propheten* (Göttingen: Vandenhoeck & Ruprecht, 1923).

54. E. Sellin, "Micha," in *Das Zwölfprophetenbuch* (Leipzig: Deichert, 1911), 276.

55. Allen, *Micah*, 242.

56. J. T. Willis, "The Structure of the Book of Micah," *SEÅ* 34 (1969) 26 n. 49.

57. Willis, "Structure, Setting, and Interrelationships," 202.

58. Mays, *Micah*, 75-76.

59. *La Formation*, 112.

composed after the time of Micah. For example, he says that šĕʾērît "remnant" is almost never used before Zephaniah and Jeremiah as a technical term designating the small group of the faithful to *I AM* who are rescued from the catastrophe of the exile. He rules out Amos 5:15, "the remnant of Joseph," by arguing that "the term still remains particularized," and 2 Kgs 19:31 = Isa 37:32; 2 Kgs 19:4 = Isa 37:4, as "of doubtful authenticity." The venue he posits, however, is not in view here, and he begs the issue. Moreover, we know that Jeremiah depended on Micah (cf. Jer 26:18), so it is presumptuous to say that a word common to both was first used by Jeremiah. This objection also applies to his claim that ʿēder "drove" in a metaphorical sense is not found before Jer 31:10. Also, that word occurs in its plain sense in Judg 5:16, one of the oldest pieces of literature in the OT. Appealing to A. Deissler, Renaud claims that the three concepts of gathering, of herds, and of remnant link this passage to the time of the exile (cf. Isa 40:11; Jer 31:8-10; Ezek 34:13-16; 37:21; Ps 78:52). He aims to strengthen his argument by noting that the Shepherd King, using first-person language for gathering his sheep, is unique in Jeremiah (23:1-6) and Micah. But he must concede that Micaiah ben Imlah, who lived a century before Micah of Moresheth, used the imagery of a shepherd-king with sheep (cf. 1 Kgs 22:17). We already noted that Jeremiah more probably depended on Micah than vice versa. Also, the references cited for gathering the flock pertain to gathering out of exile, not into it (cf. Isa 40:11; Jer 23:1-6). Moreover, *I AM*'s deliverance of a remnant from Jerusalem gave a foretaste of Israel's deliverance from Babylon (cf. Mic 4:9-10), so one should not be surprised if Micah is the first to bring these three themes together. His argument that the oracle echoes the motif of a "new exodus," an exilic theme, presumes that Micah could not have originated new ideas. Why could Micah not have associated Israel's miraculous deliverance from besieged Jerusalem with the miraculous exodus from Egypt, which was celebrated annually at the temple? His arguments are not convincing. D. Hillers,[60] though rejecting the specific venue of 701, says: "There is nothing decisive against thinking it is early, or even by Micah, if one allows for positive, visionary elements in his thought." J. T. Willis[61] asserts cogently that the lack of links to the immediate literary context is not in itself relevant to the question of dating. Instead of looking to exilic writings, one ought to look to Exod 13:21; 14:19; 15:13, 16-18; Deut 33:5.

C. Westermann[62] distinguishes three forms of salvation prophecies: "the promise of salvation, the proclamation of salvation, and the description of sal-

---

60. Hillers, *Micah*, 39-40.
61. Willis, "Structure, Setting, and Interrelationships," 316.
62. C. Westermann, *The Old Testament and Jesus Christ,* tr. O. Kaste (Minneapolis: Augsburg, 1970), 27-35.

vation." The first is of a very general kind, delivering with authority the promise of full salvation in a time of hopeless trouble and defeat. The second "concerned a single event through which God turned away trouble, freed from distress, or broke into a succession of events." The third does not announce an event but depicts another future reality, a period of salvation located beyond the present epoch and where everything is different. Micah 2:12-13 is of the second type. Westermann[63] helpfully shows the function of "the proclamation of salvation": "Their purpose was to tell those paralyzed by anxiety and exasperation not to give up hope, to assure them that God's saving acts could make a future possible, in spite of the disasters which threatened." In this oracle Micah contrasts the true prophet's message of salvation with that of the false. False prophets promised no judgment; true prophets threatened judgment but promised salvation through it for the righteous remnant.

The infinitive absolutes and the repetition of synonyms with *I AM* as speaker underscore the certainty of this salvation. He underscores the salvation of all the elect by the collective, honorific terms Jacob/Israel, by the adverb "together," and by the adverbial phrase "all of you," and comforts them by using the "I-Thou" form of address. None of them will be missing (cf. Luke 15:1-32; John 10:27-30).

This proclamation of salvation, so decisively distinct from the proclamations of judgment in 2:6-11 and 3:1-4, has two parts:

I.   *I AM* gathers the remnant of his people within Jerusalem to protect them from the enemy (v 12).
II. *I AM* delivers his people out of besieged Jerusalem (v 13).

In v 12 *I AM* himself is speaking, whereas in v 13 he is spoken about in the third person, a stylistic feature shared with the similar prophecy in 4:6-7. Whereas in v 12 *I AM* presents himself under the image of a Shepherd, that imagery is replaced in v 13 with literal military language and *I AM* is called King. In spite of these differences, however, the two verses are linked by the imagery of "enclosed encampment" and gate and by assuming that those delivered, the "them," are the remnant of v 12. Above all, they are linked with the notion that *I AM*, not man, is Israel's Shepherd-King. His leadership is underscored in v 12B by the notice that the remnant lacks human leadership and in v 13 by the *inclusio:* "The Breaker will march into battle before them," and "Their King will pass through before them, *I AM* at their head." In both verses language is taken from the Davidic tradition, *'sp* and *qbṣ* "gather" and "assemble" in v 12, and *prṣ*

---

63. Westermann, *The Old Testament and Jesus Christ,* 30.

"break forth" in v 13, to link *I AM* with the ideal shepherd-king David, who reigned through the anointing of the Holy Spirit.

I AM alone is true Israel's leader and worthy of their trust. J. T. Willis[64] states the theological point:

> As in the doom sections, Yahweh is represented as the God who acts. This activity is described by the use of verbs in the first person singular with Yahweh as the subject, by the passive voice with Yahweh as the assumed subject . . . According to the hope sections, there is one major task which Yahweh will perform — that of *leading* his people. The purpose of this leadership is to accomplish two main objectives: (1) that of giving Israel victory over her enemies, and (2) that of restoring Israel to her former status as Yahweh's covenant people. It is at this point that the overall purpose of the book of Micah comes sharply into focus. The doom sections depict Israel's plight under human leadership — princes, prophets, priests, rich landowners. Because of (3:12) these incompetent leaders and the people's willingness to follow them, the future holds nothing but disaster. But there is yet one ray of hope which stands open even in this disaster — complete trust in Yahweh as the only leader worthy of Israel's full allegiance.

In the NT the Second Person of the Trinity is the One who shepherds his church.

II. Second Cycle: God Restores Jerusalem's Former Dominion to the Purified Remnant (3:1–5:14 [EV 3:1–5:15])

A. Old Jerusalem and Its Corrupt Leaders Fall (3:1-12)

1. Shepherds Turned Cannibals (3:1-4)

1   Then I said:
    "Listen, you leaders of Jacob,
        even you rulers of the house of Israel.
        Should you not know justice? —
2   "[you] who hate good
        and love evil,
    who tear their skin off them,
        and their flesh off their bones?

---

64. Willis, "Structure, Setting, and Interrelationships," 193-94.

3   "[you] who eat my people's flesh?"
           They strip off their skin
               and break their bones in pieces;
           and they chop them up like meat for the pan
               and like flesh for the pot."
4   Then they will cry out to *I AM*,
           but he will not answer them.
       Indeed, he will hide his face from them
           because of the evil they have done.

EXEGESIS

1   MT accents *wā'ōmar* (*Then I said*) as part of the verse because it so treats introductory editorial notices of fewer than three words (cf. Ps 12:2[1] and 13:2[1]). For poetic analysis, however, it is better treated as an anacrusis. Vg *(dixi)* and Tg *(w'mryt)* support MT, but LXX *(kai erei* "and he will say") and Syr *(w'mr* "and he said") vocalize it as a third masculine singular, LXX interpreting it as *wāw*-consecutive *wayy'ōmer,* Syr as *wāw*-copulative, *wĕ'āmar.*[1] MT, which is more difficult because an anacrusis in the first person is rare (cf. Isa 54:14), is preferred because it retains a tradition, whereas LXX interprets his unvocalized text as best he can.[2] Moderns differ in their interpretation of the word.[3]

(1) E. Rupprecht, J. Steinmann, and E. Kraeling[4] delete the word as a later addition. B. Renaud[5] defended this view from Isa 57:14. He argued that in both passages *w'mr* overloads the rhythm of the text and functions as a liaison between a late addition (namely, Mic 2:12-13; Isa 57:13c) brought to a preceding oracle (namely, 2:6-11; Isa 57:3-13b) and a new pericope (namely, Mic 3:1-4; Isa 57:14-19). His argument, however, is based on the faulty assumption that Micah did not author 2:12-13 and that 3:1-4 originally linked with 2:6-11.

(2) A. Bruno conjectures that this unique term represents the remnant of the messenger formula, *kōh āmar yhwh* "Thus says *I AM*," a conjecture that clashes with the preferred MT.

(3) J. M. P. Smith, W. Nowack, A. Weiser, et al.[6] suspect here the remnant

---

1. Cf. *IBHS* §32.1.1.

2. Cf. J. Barr, *Comparative Semitic Philology and the Text of the Old Testament* (Oxford: Clarendon, 1968), 209.

3. Cf. J. T. Willis, "A Note on *w'mr* in Micah 3:1," *ZAW* 80 (1968) 50-54.

4. Cited by Willis, "A Note on *w'mr* in Micah 3:1," 50.

5. *La Formation*, 121.

6. Cited by Willis, "A Note on *w'mr* in Micah 3:1," 50.

of an autobiographical account. But T. Robinson[7] objects that it seems excessive to draw such a far-reaching and precise conclusion from a single word. And B. Renaud[8] asks: "How is it that the tradition preserved from the account only one single term, and then just the word of introduction! To what motive would the tradition have responded?"

(4) K. Budde[9] held the same view but provided the motivation for dropping the autobiographical narrative; namely, that in an extensive redaction of the prophets, a group of editors in preparing them for canonization removed the words of those opposed to *I AM*. This view stumbles over the same objections, and J. T. Willis notes that if Budde's view be correct, "The redactor would have removed the 'narrative background' of 2:8-11 in 2:6-7 or of 6:8 in 6:6-7!"

(5) C. von Orelli, R. Moulton,[10] and A. S. van der Woude,[11] having put 2:12-13 into the mouths of false prophets and regarding 3:1-4 as Micah's rebuttal, render *wā'ōmar* "But I said." Their interpretation fails because it rests on their faulty interpretation of 2:12-13 (see above) and, as D. Hillers says, "3:1-4 is scarcely a reply to 2:12-13."

(6) B. Duhm, G. A. Smith, J. Lindblom, et al.[12] also render it, "But I said," and link it with 2:11. This view does an injustice to 2:12-13.

(7) J. Beck, J. Halévy, and K. Marti consider *wā'ōmar* as a continuation between 2:11 or 2:3 and 3:1 and translate, "Again I said," or its equivalent. But since pericopes are linked informally throughout the book, why did Micah (see Exposition, 152) uniquely link these? D. Hillers[13] objects to J. L. Mays,[14] who defends this view by suggesting that the notice was added to show that 3:1-4 was spoken to the same addressees as 2:6-11, because it "is not strictly true, since there is no reason to think that chapter 2 is addressed to judges and magistrates" (see Exposition, 153).

(8) J. T. Willis agreed substantially with M. L. Margolis and S. Goldman[15] that *wā'ōmar* functions as the redactor's way of indicating the arrangement of the book; namely, that it introduces a new section so that chapters 3–5 should be separated from chapters 1–2. D. Hillers[16] weakly calls this view "improbable."

---

7. T. Robinson, "Micha," in *Die zwolf kleinen Propheten* (Tübingen: Mohr, 1954), 137.
8. *La Formation,* 120.
9. Cited by Willis, "A Note on *w'mr* in Micah 3:1," 50-51.
10. Cited by Willis, "A Note on *w'mr* in Micah 3:1," 52.
11. Cited by Hillers, *Micah,* 41.
12. Cited by Willis, "A Note on *w'mr* in Micah 3:1," 52.
13. Hillers, *Micah,* 41.
14. Mays, *Micah,* 78.
15. Cited by Willis, "A Note on *w'mr* in Micah 3:1," 54.
16. Hillers, *Micah,* 41.

Willis[17] defends his view from Amos 1:2, where a similar anacrusis, "and he said," introduces Amos's prophecies or a major section of his book (1:2–2:16). B. Renaud[18] objected arbitrarily that Isa 57:14 offers a "better" parallel. In fact, however, Amos 1:2 offers the better parallel because it too is an uncommon expression involving a personal pronoun with reference to the prophet mentioned in the superscription and using the past tense, whereas Isa 57:14 is a more common expression involving an impersonal pronoun with reference to a future event (cf. Isa 65:8). There is no reason why an author should not use first person in editing his own work, and an editor use third person in editing the work of someone else.

šim'û (Listen; see 1:2) begins the first section. Although *nā'* is best left untranslated, it is a logical particle of entreaty denoting that this reproach oracle is a logical consequence of the general situation in the preceding ones.[19] LXX, looking to *zō't* of 3:9, adds *tauta* "these things." The vocative *rā'šê (leaders)* refers principally to the appointed judges of the nation (see Exposition, 153-54). For *ya'ăqōb (of Jacob),* a genitive of relation,[20] refers to the nation viewed ideally as a unity; in fact, however, the leaders in Jerusalem are in view, for Jerusalem is explicitly mentioned in 3:12. Some text critics favor LXX and Syr "leaders of the house of Jacob" because of the parallel in 3:1A and the repetition of *bêt* in 3:9, but Mur 88 supports MT. Perhaps it was omitted because of *wā'ōmar* in 3:1A and was added in the versions precisely because of the cited parallels. There is a deliberate contrast between the faithful *I AM* as true Jacob's/Israel's head in 2:13 and these unfaithful leaders of nominal Jacob/Israel.

For *ûqĕṣînê (even you rulers)* LXX has *kai hoi kataloipoi* "the remnant" (so also v 9) because, according to H. Wolff,[21] *qāṣin* sounded like *qēṣ, qāṣâ,* or *qāṣeh,* all meaning "end." According to J. P. M. van der Ploeg,[22] *qāṣin* is connected to the Arabic root *qaḍa* "he sanctioned," "he judged," and the corresponding Hebrew root *qṣh* "to cut." In Arabic the *qaḍi* is the judge; in Hebrew the *qāṣin* is the man who ought to decide, to cut/cut off/settle a question. In some texts (Josh 10:24; Judg 11:6, 11; Dan 11:18) *qāṣin* clearly designates the military chief, the commander, but even here the basic sense of "chief" does not disappear. In Prov 25:15 it simply signifies "chief," and so also here. The initial *waw* of the second stich of a *parallelismus membrorum* probably replaces the repetition of the

---

17. Willis, "A Note on *w'mr* in Micah 3:1," 54.
18. *La Formation,* 121.
19. Cf. *IBHS* §34.7.
20. *IBHS* §9.5.1.
21. Wolff, *Micha,* 60.
22. J. P. M. van der Ploeg, "Les Chefs du Peuple d'Israël et Leurs Titres," *RB* 57 (1950) 52.

verb *šimʿû*.[23] While *rōʾš(îm)* and *qěṣîn(îm)* occur often in isolation, Micah idiosyncratically connects them (cf. v 9). H. Wolff[24] notes that in Judg 11:11 the two terms are connected; following the battle with the Ammonites, at which time Jephthah served as their *qāṣîn* "commander," he will become their "head" (cf. Judg 11:8, 9, 11), that is, the chief guardian of the law and so one of "the judges" (cf. 12:7). He draws the conclusion that this civil function as upholder of the law prevails in the terms *rōʾš* and *qāṣîn* in Micah's time. Micah parallels these synonymous terms to emphasize the judicial responsibility of Israel's astute magistrates (see Exposition, 152-57). For *bêt yiśrāʾēl (of the house of Israel)*, another genitive of relation, see 1:5.

The rhetorical negative question *hălôʾ lākem lādaʿat (Should you not know?)* expresses the conviction that "the contents of the statement are well known to the magistrates, and are unconditionally admitted by them."[25] In *lākem* (you) *lĕ* expresses interest/advantage, explicitly marking the leaders as the ones who should know justice.[26] In a question *lādaʿat (to know)* marks the topic of the nominal clause;[27] the infinitive construct frequently functions as both a noun, here as the subject, and as a verb, here taking the direct object *ʾet-hammišpāṭ*.[28] The root *ydʿ* designates both intellectual and emotional appreciation of the law and the power to formulate fair laws (see Exposition, 155). In *hammišpāṭ (justice)* the article is generic,[29] marking out "justice" as unique and determined in itself; for the meaning of the word see the Exposition, 154.

2 *śōnʾê ([you] who hate)*, a masculine plural qal stative participle, functions as a relative[30] modifying the leaders of Israel (v 1). As a stative verb, in contrast to a fientive verb, *śnʾ* captures the subjects in a state of being.[31] It signifies an intense feeling of dislike coupled with a strong desire to rid oneself of the disliked object (cf. Judg 11:7). Sometimes the object of one's hatred is metaphorically described as "to stink" (1 Sam 13:4; 2 Sam 10:6; 16:21). Parallels of this for strong emotional revulsion include *tʿb* piel "to detest" (Amos 5:10; Ps 119:163), *qûṭ* hithpael "to become nauseous" (Ps 139:21), *nqʿ* "to turn away from in disgust" (Ezek 23:28), *mʾs* "to reject" (Amos 5:21), and *nʾṣ* "to spurn" (Prov

---

23. Cf. H. A. Brongers, "Alternative Interpretationen des sogennanten *Waw Copulativum*," *ZAW* 90 (1978) 273-77.
24. Wolff, *Micha*, 67.
25. GKC §150e; cf. 2:6B.
26. *IBHS* §11.2.10.
27. *IBHS* §36.2.3.
28. *IBHS* §36.1.2.
29. *IBHS* §13.5.1.
30. *IBHS* §37.5.
31. *IBHS* §30.2.3.

5:12). The objective genitive *ṭôb (good)*, especially in antithesis with *rāʿ* "evil," denotes "moral good." Here it is a metonymy for righteous and compassionate decisions.

wĕʿōhăbê (and love), another qal stative masculine plural participle, modifying the leaders, presents the antithesis of their moral taste. LXX, against all other witnesses, including Mur 88, reads *zētountes* "seeking," though elsewhere in the Minor Prophets that translator uses *agapan* for *ʾhb*. LXX probably represents the more common, and therefore less likely, reading *mbqš* "to seek wrong" (i.e., to harm someone). *ʾhb* signifies a spontaneous affection one feels in various relationships, between the sexes (Gen 24:67), father and son (Gen 22:1-2a[2-3]), or friends (1 Sam 16:21). Here it is used of the bonding of morally perverse men to the objective genitive *rāʿ (evil)*. H. Wolff[32] says that "Q *(rāʿ)*, alongside of *ṭôb*, is to be preferred to K *(rāʿâ)*; cf. 2:1; Isa 5:20; Amos 5:14." There is no difference in meaning (cf. 2:1, 3). *rāʿ* conveys the factual judgment that something is bad, whether it be a physical state (e.g., "ugly" cows [Gen 41:3] or "poor/bad" figs [Jer 24:2]), or, as here, moral behavior. This value judgment depends on the taste of the one making the evaluation; "in one's eyes" is often added.

The qal masculine plural active participle *gōzlê (who tear)*, a fientive verb, describes the activity of the leaders. B. Renaud[33] noted that *gzl* signifies at the same time "to rob" (with juridical and moral nuances; cf. Lev 19:13; Judg 9:25; Pss 35:10; 69:5[4]) and "to remove the skin" (Job 24:9, where it means "to snatch"). The ambiguity facilitates the transition from the figure (i.e., "to strip off") to its significance (see Exposition, 156). The objective genitive *ʿôrām (their skin)* consists of the root *ʿôr* "skin" and the third masculine plural pronominal suffix. The lack of an antecedent for the pronouns causes some to put v 2B after v 3 or v 5, making "my people" the antecedent in *ad sensum* agreement,[34] but this entails emending the text by conjecturing a finite verb. D. Hillers[35] finds the antecedent in "Israel" and "Judah," but it is questionable whether the synonymous parallels can be divided in this way. It is unlikely that the antecedent may be found in the context of a live situation, in which case the prophet may have pointed with his finger to the victims around him on Mount Zion as he spoke. H. Wolff[36] offers the best solution: "In the redaction in hand, which joins the text with 2:1-11 [*sic!*] by *wʾmr* in 3:1Aaα, the suffixes are to be related to the oppressed in 2:2, 8f., whom Micah there as here calls 'my people.'" I independently came to the same conclusions and note that v 4 assumes the judgment prophe-

32. Wolff, *Micha*, 60.
33. *La Formation*, 122.
34. *IBHS* §145b.
35. Hillers, *Micah*, 42.
36. Wolff, *Micha*, 40.

sied in that chapter. For the compound adverbial prepositional phrase *mēʿălêhem (off them)* see 2:9.

The parallel to v 2Ba, *ûšĕʾērām mēʿal ʿaṣmôtām (and their flesh off their bones)* has the emphatic force of, "and what is more." The verb *gzl* is gapped in v 2Bb. On the grammatical level the clauses are paratactic, but on the semantic level they are consecutive: first their skin off their bodies, then their flesh off their bones. The fourfold repetition of the pronoun in v 2B keeps the focus on the plight of the victims. What the gluttonous rulers will do with the flayed flesh, which is full of blood, is developed in v 3. All that is left of their victims is unpalatable skin and bones.

3 LXX reads *waʾăšer (and who)* as *kaʾăšer (hon tropon)*, probably under the influence of vv 3Ba and 4Bb. The change of the syntactic construction modifying the head word, "leaders/rulers," of v 1, from relative participles (v 2) modifying vocatives with the second person to the indeclinable relative pronoun *ʾăšer* with the third person finite verb, may signal a change of speakers.[37] *ʾăšer* here appears to function as the subject of the attributive clause[38] modifying in third person the second plural vocatives of v 1 (see 1:2 and 3:9). The qal third masculine plural perfective of *ʾākĕlû (they eat)* is a constative, persistent (present) perfective[39] and plural because the head word, "leaders/rulers," behind the indeclinable *ʾăšer* is plural. The direct object *šĕʾēr (flesh)* designates the inner meat full of blood, next to the bones. *ʿammî (of my people;* for the meaning of *ʿam* see 45-46) consists of *ʿam*, a genitive of inalienable possession,[40] and the first common singular pronominal suffix, a genitive of relationship. Elsewhere *ʿammî* refers back to *I AM* and has the same sense here as in 2:9. The first-person pronoun plus the change of syntax suggests that *I AM* is accusing in v 3. The situations presented in the two clauses in v 3Ab, "they strip off their skin" and "break their bones in pieces," though presented paratactically with v 3Aa, in fact must occur prior to eating the flesh. Probably the three clauses in v 3A should be interpreted as a hendiadys, representing three aspects of the one situation. The repetition of their skin and bones, first in the prophet's mouth (v 2) and then in *I AM*'s (v 3), emphasizes and confirms the cannibalism of the culprits.

wĕʿôrām mēʿălêhem (their skin off them) repeats v 2A exactly. The hiphil third masculine plural perfective of *pšṭ (they strip)* is another constative persistent (present) perfective. *pšṭ* hiphil links the oracle with v 8. The stylistic change to the more common form *ʿaṣmôtêhem (their bones),* from *ʿaṣmôtām* in v 2, may

37. For this stylistic form see Hillers, *Micah,* 42.
38. *IBHS* §19.3.
39. *IBHS* §30.2.1.
40. *IBHS* §9.1.1.

149

also indicate a change of speaker. The piel third common plural perfective of *pšḥ (they tear to pieces)* is another constative persistent perfective. Piel has a resultative force, "they make their bones torn to pieces."[41] II *pšḥ*[42] is a *hapax legomenon;* it is translated *synethlasan* "they broke" in LXX, *confregerunt* "they broke in pieces" in Vg, and *taberu* "they ground" in Syr, meanings that find support in Arabic and Ethiopic.

ûpārĕśû (and they spread out) is a *waw*-copulative with another constative persistent (present) perfective.[43] The *waw*-copulative with *ûpārĕśû (and who chop [them] up)* does not function as a hendiadys but serves to link the metaphor in v 3A with the simile in v 3B. The scene is emphatically repeated for the third time (cf. v 2B and v 3A). The qal third masculine plural perfective is another persistent (present) perfective, with the gapped *ʾăšer* from v 3A as its subject. The root *prś*, which normally means "to spread out," is usually considered a bi-form of *prs* "break in two," "to divide." LXX has *emelisan* "they dismembered," and Vg *conciderunt* "they cut up." On this basis NRSV renders it "chop up." D. Hillers[44] complains that "divide" does not seem especially characteristic of what is done to meat inside a pot, and so proposes "serve up" since *prs/ś* is used of doling out food in Isa 58:7 and Lam 4:4. The idea of "serving up" in these passages is probably metonymy added to the primary notion of "dividing up" food. More probably the preposition *bĕ* in *bassîr (into the pot)* implies a verb of motion;[45] so it was understood by Syr, which reads, "and they put into the pot." The full idea is "they chop them up and throw them into the pot." The object *ʿammî (my people)* of the A verset is gapped in the B verset and must be supplied after the transitive verb.

In spite of the support of Syr and Vg *(velut)*, MT's *ka'ăšer* makes hardly any sense. Read instead *kišĕ'ēr (like flesh)* with LXX *(hōs sarkas* "as flesh") and Tg *(śᵊrhwn)* and assume a metathesis of the *ʿayin* and *rêš* in MT, probably under the influence of *ka'ăšer* in v 4. *sâr (pot)* is the cooking pot par excellence.[46] The *waw* introducing the emphatic parallel in v 3Bb probably indicates that *prś* is gapped (as *ûqĕṣînê* is gapped in v 1B). The gruesome figure is repeated yet again. *ûkĕbāśār (like flesh)* functions as an emphatic parallel to *kišĕ'ēr*. *bāśār* indicates living flesh. The compound *šĕ'ēr* and *bāśār* underscore the total consumption of *I AM*'s people. The adverbial phrase *bĕtôk qallāḥat (in the cauldron)*, along

41. *IBHS* §24.3.2.
42. Cf. GB, KB, Lis.
43. *IBHS* §32.3.
44. Hillers, *Micah*, 42.
45. Cf. GKC §119ee, ff.
46. Cf. A. M. Honeyman, "The Pottery Vessels of the Old Testament," *PEQ* 71 (1939) 85, pl. xx, fig. 14.

with its parallel *bassîr,* modifies *pārĕśû* and assumes a verb of motion *(and throw them).* For *bĕtôk* see 2:12. Sufficient data are lacking to specify *qallāḥat (the pan).*

4 The adverb *'āz (then)* signifies chronological sequence, for its parallel is *bā'ēt hahî'* "at that time" in v 4B, but it probably also contains a nuance of logical consequence (cf. Ps 56:10[9]). The oracle presumes the judgments predicted in chapters 1-2 (cf. 2:4). The qal third masculine plural nonperfective of *z'q (they will cry out)* refers to that future time; the subject continues to be the heartless, greedy leaders. The root is a bi-form of *ṣ'q,* as also in Arabic, Aramaic, and Samaritan, and always designates a loud, emotional cry for help prompted by extreme distress, which can be either articulate (cf. Exod 5:8, 15) or inarticulate (Isa 26:17).[47] It distinguishes itself from other verbs for crying out that merely express pain by seeking to reach someone else who could give immediate assistance and turn away the distress; it is sometimes parallel to *šw'* piel "to cry out for help" (Hab 1:2; Job 19:7; Lam 3:8). It is sometimes used in contexts of injustice and takes on the specialized sense of crying against injustice and for justice. When God is the one who is appealed to, as here, it becomes an important word for prayer, one that is colored with the strongest emotions and, in contrast to other words for prayer, is used exclusively for a cry for help and deliverance from a situation of acute distress. *'el (to)* particularly emphasizes that the cry is for help. The use of the third-person *yhwh* (I AM) shows that Micah is again the speaker and that *z'q* is used for prayer.

In *wĕlō' ya'ăneh (but he will not answer) wĕ* is antithetical. The qal third masculine singular nonperfective continues the future tense with *I AM* as subject, and the root *'nh* means "to respond" to a cry.[48] Heaven will turn to brass against their prayers as *I AM* refuses to sustain his perverse rulers any longer. *'ôtām (them)* refers back to the leaders.

In *wĕyastēr* the *waw (indeed)* is probably emphatic (cf. v 1) and *yastēr pānāyw mēhem (he will hide his face)* is an emphatic, emblematic way of saying, "he will not answer them." The form *yastēr* could be either jussive or nonperfective,[49] but the parallel in v 4A shows that another future is intended. With *pānîm (face) str* hiphil means "to wrap, cover." The literal sense of the compound is found in Exod 3:6 and Isa 50:6. Its theological and metaphorical sense occurs when God covers his face. G. Wehmeier[50] says, "As the turning of the face is a sign of friendship and favor, so the turning away or the covering of

---

47. Cf. R. Albertz, *THAT* 2:569.
48. Cf. C. J. Labuschagne, *THAT* 2:668.
49. Cf. GKC §109k.
50. G. Wehmeier, *THAT* 2:175.

the countenance is sign of no mercy." It is a very concrete act of his anger and wrath. The worst form of judgment for Israel is not the affliction itself but the absence of God in it (see Exposition, 157). *bāʿēt hahîʾ (at that time)* consists of the preposition *bě* with a temporal sense,[51] the noun *ʿēt*, signifying appointed time whether it be regular, such as rains, harvest, or seasons, or nonrecurring incidents, such as death and as here judgment, and the far quasi-demonstrative pronoun *hahîʾ*.[52]

kaʾăšer (because), literally "according as," has a causal force[53] (cf. Num 27:14; Judg 6:27; 1 Sam 28:18; 2 Kgs 17:26). The conjunction may have been chosen for its assonance with *kišʾēr* in v 3. With *hērēʿû (they make evil)*, hiphil third masculine plural perfective of the root *rʿʿ*, the hiphil is a one-place hiphil with an impersonal object emphasizing the process of making their deeds evil.[54] The perfective is another persistent (present) perfective, a single situation that started in the past and persists into the present. Micah begins and ends his indictment by accusing them of *rāʿ* (see v 2). In the direct object of the causative notion, *maʿalĕlêhem (their deeds)*, the pronominal suffix is a genitive of agency with the verbal noun *maʿălāl*, which is always plural and means "practices." It consists of the root *ʿll* poel "to act severely" and the abstract *mem* prefix[55] (see 2:7). LXX adds *ep' autous* "upon them," a redoubling of the last consonants of *maʿalĕlêhem* with the pointing *mēʿalêhem*.

EXPOSITION

The following three oracles, 3:1-4, 5-8, 9-12, are related by their common addressees, the ruling classes of Israel, their common form, reproach oracles, their common length of four verses each, and above all by their common theme, the miscarriage of justice for personal advantage. In each oracle Micah grafts onto the addressees an accusation by means of a relative participle followed by an announcement of judgment. The accusation and the judicial sentence are linked together by appropriate particles, *ʾāz* "then" (v 4), and *lākēn* "therefore" (vv 6, 12). Since the last is attributed in Jer 26:18 to Micah, one has no reason to question the authorship of the others. The "I" of v 8 clearly refers to Micah, and there is no reason to think otherwise in v 1 (cf. 3:1, and see the exegesis of v 1). These prophecies have clear thematic and verbal links with those of chapter 2.

51. *IBHS* §11.2.5.
52. *IBHS* §17.2.
53. Cf. BDB 455, §2.
54. *IBHS* §27.2.
55. *IBHS* §5.6.

They are addressed to similar groups, powerful persons who are exploiting the defenseless (cf. 2:1-5; 3:1-4), and to prophets (cf. 2:6-11; 3:5-8). But whereas chapter 2 condemns the venal land barons, chapter 3 condemns the magistrates. Each in their own way *gzl* "rip off" (2:2; 3:2) and *pšṭ* "strip" (2:8; 3:3) the helpless. This prophecy against the magistrates assumes that the victims have been identified (v 2) and that judgment has been announced (v 4). As the prophecies of judgment in chapter 2 moved into a salvation oracle where *I AM* is featured as Israel's savior, so these three give way to the salvation oracles of chapters 4–5, where *I AM*'s anointed Messiah, who rules in the name of *I AM*, is featured as its savior and contrasted with these wicked magistrates. 2:13 and 3:1 are hooked together by the verbal link *rō'šām* "their head" and *ro'šê* "leaders." This coupling not only links the prophecies but contrasts the noble divine leadership of Israel's true Shepherd-King with Israel's ignoble, savage-like magistrates.

After an introductory anacrusis, "And I said," this doom oracle has three parts:

I. Address: an appeal to Israel's magistrates to listen (v 1A).
II. Accusation: they debauch their charge to maintain justice (vv 1B-3).
    A. Their charge: to know the law (v 1B).
    B. Their character: their hearts are evil (v 2A).
    C. Their conduct: they behave like cannibals (vv 2B-3).
        1. Micah describes them as cannibals (v 2B).
        2. *I AM* describes them as cannibals (v 3).
            a. by a metaphor (v 3A).
            b. by a simile (v 3B).
III. Sentence: *I AM* will not relent his judgment (v 4).

šim'û "listen" characteristically begins a prophecy (3:9) or a section of prophecies (1:2; 3:1; 6:1), but these are particularly addressed to Israel's talented magistrates. In early usage *rō'š*, literally "heads," was used in a tribal context of men exercising leadership in military and judicial matters. The latter function is in view here, for Micah accuses them of derelict ignorance of the law, of perverting justice, and of accepting bribes (3:1, 9). J. R. Bartlett[56] noted, "The word 'head' . . . has a clear association with the courts of ancient Israel." The title was applied to judges of the tribe, of the city, and of the nation. R. de Vaux[57] argued that, besides the local judges and village "elders," the king instituted professional

---

56. J. R. Bartlett, "The Use of the Word *rō'š* as a Title in the Old Testament," *VT* 19 (1969) 5.
57. R. de Vaux, *Ancient Israel: Its Life and Institutions*, tr. J. McHugh (New York: McGraw-Hill, 1961), 152-53.

judges over the nation even as Moses had appointed competent laymen to dispense justice (Exod 18:13-26; Deut 1:15-18). Alongside of these "elders" and appointed judges stood the priests. The final court of appeal was located at Jerusalem and consisted of priests and the officiating judge (cf. Deut 17:8-13). Jehoshaphat appointed the High (Heb. *rō'š*) Priest for all matters touching *I AM*, and a chief of the house of Judah for the king's matters. The identification of those addressed is underscored by the parallel, *qĕṣînê* "rulers." Isaiah holds the *qāṣîn* responsible to uphold the law and accountable to encourage the oppressed and to defend the cause of the widows and fatherless (cf. v 17). D. Hillers,[58] uncertain about Micah's attitude toward the king, commented:

> Though . . . the king is not mentioned here . . . , this does not . . . permit any conclusion as to the prophet's attitude toward Hezekiah. . . . Isaiah (1:10-20, 21-23; 3:14) and Amos (2:6-7; 5:7, 10-13) also delivered severe indictments addressed to "judges" in the plural, not singling out the king, but this does not . . . define their relation to an Ahaz or Jeroboam II, which we know of only on the basis of other passages. It is fairly common, in protests by peasants or other lower orders, for the deprived and oppressed to believe the king to be innocent, ignorant of their plight and surrounded by evil ministers.

But a prophet differs from common people; Hosea censures *bêt hammelek* "the royal house." Undoubtedly the magistrates, though not restricted by any means to the royal house, include it (cf. v 12), and Hezekiah repents in response to Micah's sermon (Jer 26:18).

These gifted and privileged magistrates, who are probably congregated in the temple court in one of Israel's annual festivals when Micah addresses them, should have known the disposition of the law. *mišpāṭ* designates the act of judging a matter. Its root, *špṭ*, implies the interaction of three parties: the oppressor(s), the oppressed, and a "judge" who has the sanction to condemn and punish the former and to clear and reward the latter. Here it refers to the decisions, which had that aim in view, collected in the sacred law (cf., e.g., Exod 21:1–23:19) and to other verdicts of the court (cf. Deut 17:8-11), as well as to the ability to decide cases fairly (cf. 1 Kgs 3:28; 7:7). In 2 Chr 19:8 Jehoshaphat appointed some of the Levites, priests, and heads of Israelite families to administer *mišpāṭ yhwh* "the law of *I AM*" and to settle disputes. When righteous magistrates delight in God's just laws (cf. Pss 1:2; 19:8-12[7-11]; 119:1 passim) and in giving righteous decisions, justice benefits the land as living, flowing water (Amos 5:24). But the leaders of Micah's epoch despised it and ruined the pleasant land (cf. Isa 1:17,

58. Hillers, *Micah*, 42-43.

21-23, 26; 5:7, 23). Jer 22:15-16 equates "knowing *I AM*" with doing what is right and just. *daʿat mišpāṭ* "knowledge of the law" entails moral taste as well as intellectual prowess. B. Renaud[59] said:

> Knowledge of the law is not understood as only an intellectual appreciation of the principles of justice or of legal exigencies. It is not limited to exact and precise information of the judicial rules. It also implies a power of discerning and of making judgment, even a sympathy for the outcasts of fortune, because, in the biblical mentality, to judge is to reestablish in their rights the poor who have been unrighteously plundered and exploited. In short, "to know the law" is to let reign inside the community in a climate of justice and of brotherhood, which climate is called by the institution of the covenant.

Isaiah also complains that his generation perverted Israel's traditional values: "Woe to those who call evil *(rāʿ)* good *(ṭôb)* and good evil, who put darkness for light and light for darkness, who put bitter for sweet and sweet for bitter" (Isa 5:20). Pathetically, nations that once had the heritage of Israel's law like prodigals have squandered it. In the United States, for example, the Supreme Court in its secularism allows the unborn to be murdered and allows blasphemy and smut to foul society. And in today's world the entertainment media give glory to fools and celebrate vice (cf. Prov 26:9).

The need for moral taste by these magistrates, who should have delivered the covenant families from the tyranny of oppressive land barons, is borne out in the accusation condemning their character. Micah points first to their hearts, their character, by using characterizing participles, stative verb forms, and the highly visceral words "love" and "hate." As the newly appointed judge who is filled with the spirit of justice (3:8), he looks straight into their perverse hearts and puts his finger on the root of Israel's social ills. Its leaders are members of God's outward kingdom, "my people," but they are not part of its inward spiritual kingdom. Nothing short of new birth, a participation in the provisions of the New Covenant (Jer 31:31-34), will save the nation. Micah is filled with the Spirit of Christ, who also will not judge by superficial appearances but by his spiritual perception of the heart and so by truth (Isa 11:1-5; John 5:19-30; Rom 2:5-8).

The magistrates, who should have known "good and evil," the giving of righteous and compassionate decisions based on *I AM*'s law, stood justice on its head. With no taste or passion to preserve the brotherly community, they perversely destroyed it. They took advantage of their position and power to disadvantage the weak, whose only recourse against the venal and powerful men ad-

---

59. *La Formation,* 123-24.

dressed in chapter 2 were the magistrates (cf. Isa 5:20; 61:8; Amos 5:10; Pss 45:8[7]; 97:10; Prov 5:12; 8:13; Job 34:17). Israel's safety net against injustice broke.

Those who should have been shepherds tending the flock instead transform themselves into wolves who fatten themselves on them. If fact, they are worse than wolves; they are cannibals. They, who were most highly endowed with the dignity of humanness, made themselves less than animals. By accepting bribes from the rich (cf. 3:9) they enriched themselves, but in effect the rich food on their banqueting tables came directly from the flesh of God's people. In the most gruesome figure, showing both their brutality and their venality, Micah portrays them as tearing the skin off their victims, tearing their flesh off their bones, and eating their flesh, leaving only unpalatable skin and bones. But as if that were not bad enough, they break even the bones in pieces, chop up the flesh, and throw it into cooking pots before eating it. H. Wolff[60] notes that Amos 2:7 accuses the judges of trampling on the heads of the poor as on the dust of the ground and Isa 3:15 of grinding their faces in the dust, but that no other prophet spoke so crudely as Micah. Our vitriolic prophet does not back off from his macabre figure. He repeats it again and again, detail by detail. Four times he mentions the victims' skin and bones, and four times their flesh. H. Wolff[61] notes that Micah does not arrange the proceedings chronologically — they eat the flesh before chopping it up — but presents the gruesome events individually, each one of which proves that they love evil. The justness and truthfulness of his accusation are underscored by quoting *I AM* himself, who uses the figure in even greater detail than he. By this grotesque figure *I AM* and his prophet not only condemn the reprobate magistrates but aim to awaken their soured consciences.

Unless they repent before the judgment predicted against the nation in chapters 1–2 (cf. Jer 18:7-10), God will not relent at the time of judgment. Israel's beginning as a nation was grounded in their cry for help for deliverance from the social misery of Egyptian oppression (Exod 2:23-24; 3:7, 9; Deut 26:7). Their pleading cry of lament came before their merciful and faithful God, who remembered his self-imposed obligation of covenant with the patriarchs (cf. Gen 15:7-18; 17:8; Exod 6:4-5; Ps 105:8-11; Neh 9:6-8) and so intervened to deliver Israel. The history of the nation depended on his willingness to respond to their cry and his remembrance of his commitment to the fathers. They celebrated this history in their confessions of faith (Num 20:16; Deut 26:7; Josh 24:7; 1 Sam 12:8; Pss 22:6[5]; 34:18[17]; 107:6, 13, 19, 28; Neh 9:4, 9; cf. Isa 19:20). But when God judges these heartless magistrates, he will be as heartless as they had been

---

60. Wolff, *Micha*, 69.
61. Wolff, *Micha*, 69.

toward the oppressed who had called out to them for help. Here is another example of *lex talionis:* as they turned a deaf ear to the plea of others, so God will turn a deaf ear to them, and as they preyed on the helplessness of the weak, so they will experience the terror of conquerors preying on them. "If a man shuts his ears to the cry of the poor, he too will cry out and not be answered" (Prov 21:13; cf. Gal 6:7). Once the time of grace has passed, it is a fearful thing to fall into the hands of an angry God (cf. Prov 1:26; Matt 25:11-13; Luke 16:26; 2 Cor 6:2; Heb 10:31; 12:17).

2. Venal Prophets (3:5-8)

5   Thus says *I AM*
      against the prophets
        who lead my people astray,
    who [when they] bite with their teeth,
        they proclaim, "Peace";
      and whoever does not give what they demand,
        they consecrate against him war.
6   "Therefore night will be to you, instead of vision,
        and darkness will be to you, instead of divination."
    And so the sun will set upon the prophets,
        and the day will become dark upon them.
7   And the seers will become ashamed,
        and the diviners become disgraced;
    and they will cover their mustaches,
        because there is no answer from God.
8   But indeed I am full of power,
        namely, of the spirit of *I AM,*
      and of justice, and of valiant might,
    to declare to Jacob his transgression,
        and to Israel his sin.

EXEGESIS

5 The messenger formula, *kōh 'āmar yhwh (Thus says* I AM*)* (see 2:3), is not an anacrusis (*contra* TNIV) but integrated into the Hebrew verse. A. Weiser[1]

---

1. A. Weiser, "Micha," in *Das Buch der zwölf kleinen Propheten,* 228.

notes: "The introductory formula is closely and organically bound with the participial style of the words of reproach." D. Hillers[2] conjectures *hôy 'al* "woe to you" because the first-person pronoun in *'ammî* "my people" assumes that *I AM* is speaking and MT implausibly introduces *I AM*'s speech with *lākēn* "therefore" in v 6 where for the first time direct address is used. If *I AM* begins speaking after the messenger formula, then one expects *hôy* (cf. 2:1) or an imperative such as *šim'û* (cf. 3:1). He supposes that a haplography of *hôy* was due to its similarity with the preceding *yhwh*. The conjecture, by definition lacking any textual support, is unnecessary: the distinction between the words of *I AM* and the words of his messenger is attenuated. B. Renaud[3] explains: "God invests totally the personality of his envoy: the words of the prophet become then the words of YHWH. . . . The divine message goes through the human experience and the sensibility of the prophet."

'al may mean "as for" (cf. NRSV's "concerning"), but as P. Joüon[4] noted, "The pejorative sense ['against'] is very developed [for this preposition]; a hostile sense fits this pronouncement of doom." Whereas Micah designated the inspired prophets who gave theological justification for the corrupt land barons by the root *ntp*, here he calls them *hannĕbî'îm. nāb'î (prophet)* designates a person authorized to speak for another. As Aaron was authorized to speak for Moses (Exod 7:1), these prophets were regarded as authorized to speak for *I AM* (see Exposition, 169). The article marks out the prophets as the particular and unique group to whom this prophecy is addressed.

hammat'îm (who lead astray) is a definite hiphil masculine plural participle of the root *t'h*. Once again (cf. v 2) Micah characterizes the accused by relative participial clauses, *hammat'îm (who lead astray)* and *hannōšĕkîm (who bite)*, which in this attributive slot require an article.[5] The root is used of the wanderings of a lost person (e.g., of Hagar in the wilderness; Gen 21:14) or of staggering in drunken stupor (e.g., of priests and prophets reeling with wine; Isa 28:7). Here it is used metaphorically of going astray mentally and morally in sins and transgressions (cf. 3:8). The one-place hiphil signifies that the prophets cause the undersubject, the object of the causative idea, to participate in the sinful acts.[6] The prophet's sin is similar to that of the adulterer, who, by putting her away, causes her to become an adulteress (Matt 5:32). They both commit crimes and injustices and promote them.

The pronominal suffix with *'ammî*, which is attested in all the ancient

2. Hillers, *Micah*, 44.
3. *La Formation*, 13.
4. Joüon, *Grammaire*, 407, §133e.
5. *IBHS* §14.3.1.
6. *IBHS* §27:2.

versions and Mur 88, need be seen neither as a corrupted abbreviation of the sacred tetragrammaton *'m y[h]* (cf. *makkôteyhā* in 1:9) and so read *'am yh* "the people of *I AM*" (so *BHS*), nor as an easily corrupted form of *w* and read as *'ammô* "his people,"[7] nor as a form so attenuated that it refers to both God and his prophet.[8] It could refer to Micah himself (cf. 1:9 and his use of the first-person pronoun in 3:1ΑΑα and his autobiographical account in 3:8) or to *I AM*; it is so used elsewhere in this book, but placed in the mouth of Micah to show that he is *I AM*'s true prophet (see Exposition, 174-75). J. T. Willis[9] says that *'ammî* here is a comprehensive term for all Israel in contrast to 2:8, where it designates the oppressors, and to 2:9 and 3:3, where it designates the oppressed. E. Speiser,[10] in differentiating the terms *gôy* "nation" and *'am* "people," argued that the former term is used objectively and impersonally and applies primarily to a loosely knit superorganization by which people are bound together externally, whereas the latter term is used subjectively and personally and is usually associated with strong feelings of kinship. J. T. Willis[11] also notes that "it is significant that *gôy* occurs only in the hope sections of the book of Micah . . . (4:2, 3 [3 times], 7, 11; 5:7, 14; 7:16) and it refers to Israel only once . . . in 4:7." This term for Israel adds pathos to the rebuke.

The second characterizing relative participial phrase *hannōšĕkîm bĕšinnêhem (who bite with their teeth)* begins to supply the motive for the misguided teachings of the false prophets. Syntactically the phrase functions as the protasis before the apodosis introduced by *waw* in *wĕqārĕ'û*. *bĕ* in the adverbial phrase *bĕšinnêhem (with their teeth)* governs the instruments of the circumstance.[12] The combined phrase is a synecdoche for *'kl* "to eat" (cf. 3:3). The prophet crassly illustrates their motives by concentrating on their biting teeth as they eat. *nšk* in ten of its other eleven uses has to do with snakes, and in that one instance (Hab 2:7) it is a denominative from *nešek* "interest"; therefore, D. K. Innes[13] supposes that this intentionally harsh expression metaphorically infers "the deadly effect of these prophets on the community." If so, like malevolent serpents they kill their victims to feed themselves. Certainly, Micah is not thinking of the legitimate food needed for the prophet's livelihood (see Exposition, 172).

wĕqārĕ'û (they proclaim): waw introduces the apodosis after the condi-

---

7. So A. Deissler in A. Deissler and M. Delcor, *La Sainte Bible*, Vol. 8: *Les Petits Prophètes* (Paris: Letouzy & Ane, 1964), 316.

8. So *La Formation*, 130.

9. J. T. Willis, "Micah 2:6-8 and the 'People of God' in Micah," *BZ* 14 (1970) 85-86.

10. E. Speiser, "'People' and 'Nation' of Israel," *JBL* 79 (1960) 160.

11. Willis, "Micah 2:6-8 and the 'People of God,'" 86.

12. *IBHS* §11.5.

13. D. K. Innes, "Some Notes on Micah," *EvQ* 41 (1969) 109.

tional participial construction,[14] and *qr'* means "to cry out loud." C. J. Labu-schagne[15] says, "In prophetic literature *qr'* becomes the technical term for 'making an announcement.'" Instead of proclaiming peace, they declare *milḥāmâ* "war."[16] It is noteworthy, as E. Kutzsch[17] remarks, that *qr'* and *qdš* piel stand in *parallelismus membrorum* (Joel 1:14; 2:15; cf. Mic 3:5); indeed, these verbs can be interchanged and therefore used as synonyms (cf. 2 Kgs 10:20 with Joel 1:14; 2:15; Jer 36:9; Jonah 3:5; Ezra 8:21; 2 Chr 20:3 with Joel 1:14; 2:15; and finally Lev 23:2, 4, 37; Lam 1:15 with Ezra 3:5). This synonymity suggests that *qr'* with a prophet as subject means a sacred proclamation. The accusative *šālôm (peace)*, modifying the dynamic verb *qr'*, means the absence of strife — note its antithetical parallel *milḥāmâ* "war" (cf. Eccl 3:8). Unimpaired in any way and without any limit in one's relationships and activities with others, including God and all mankind, as well as with creation, one experiences physical, economic, and social well-being, the meaning of the root *šlm* with strong emphasis on the material side, and so it can be translated "health," "prosperity," and "peace" (see Exposition, 172). The word sums up and epitomizes the bitter debate between true and false prophets (see Exposition, 170). LXX paraphrases by adding *ep' auton* "upon him." It may be that *'ālāyw* of v 5Bbβ is gapped in v 5Bab, but the syntax of the two versets differs. In the antithetical parallel in v 5Bb to v 5Ba Micah makes the same point, that the false prophets trim their message to fit their own material interests.

Once again in v 5Bbα Micah states the condition in terms of a relative clause, this time introduced by the independent, indefinite relative *wa'ăšer (whoever)*,[18] resolved by an apodosis *waw* construction in v 5Bbβ. The clause in v 5Ba is the subject, the topic, in a *casus pendens* construction with v 5Bb, which has the resumptive pronoun *'ālāyw* "against him"; literally, "as for him who . . . , they consecrate against him war."[19] In *lō'-yittēn (does not give)*, qal third masculine singular nonperfective of the root *ntn* with the adverb *lō'*, the nonperfective functions in a marked contingent clause,[20] the singular personalizes to an individual who must confront a group of prophets, the root has its usual meaning "give" with the implied object "whatever," not "put,"[21] with the implied object "food," and the adverb forms the antithetical parallelism. *'al-pîhem (what*

---

14. *IBHS* §32.2.5.
15. C. J. Labuschagne, *THAT* 2:669.
16. Cf. M. Dahood, "Hebrew-Ugaritic Lexicography IX," *Bib* 52 (1971) 348-49.
17. E. Kutzsch, *"miqrā',"* *ZAW* 65 (1953) 249-50 n. 2.
18. *IBHS* §19.3.
19. *IBHS* §4.4.8.
20. *IBHS* §31.6.1.
21. *Contra* BDB 680, §2b.

they demand; lit. "according to their mouth [= word]") does not mean "into their mouths"[22] but "according to their command." According to H. Wolff,[23] who expresses his indebtedness to A. S. van der Woude,[24] "to put something into the mouth" must be expressed by either *śym běpeh* (Exod 4:15; Num 22:38; Deut 31:19) or *ntn bph* (Deut 18:18; Jer 1:9; 5:14). On the other hand, he argues that *[ntn] ʿal-peh* always means "*to give* on the strength of a word, by order of, according to the wish of" (cf. Gen 45:21; Num 3:51; 2 Kgs 23:35).[25] Wolff says: "*ph* here does not designate the organ, but — as often — its function." Accordingly, the false prophets are not merely accepting bribes but announcing their own determined wishes or even commands. The masculine plural suffix "their," genitive of inalienable possession,[26] represents the prophets as a group against the individual.

In *wěqidděšû (they consecrate)* the *waw*-relative with the suffix conjugation introduces the apodosis, the third masculine plural has "those who bite with their teeth" as its subject, and the piel is factitive,[27] that is, they transfer *milḥāmâ* to the sphere of the holy (cf. Jer 6:4; Joel 4:9[3:9]). As the parallel *wěqārěʾû* shows, they consecrate the battle by their proclamation. Elijah's prophecies were so powerful that, though his power was invisible, he was called "My father, my father, the horsemen of Israel and its chariots" (2 Kgs 2:12; 13:14). Holy war was initiated and carried through by charismatic individuals, such as these prophets claim to be. Since, however, they are concerned not with what the holy *I AM* will gain in victory but with their own unholy, selfish gain, Micah represents their pretensions sarcastically. *ʿālāyw (against him)* shows that they are not concerned with battle in general but with personal animosity against an individual who defies them. As in holy war the LORD hands over the enemy to his servant, so these false prophets hope to exact their will over those who refuse to comply in their defeat. They are not the servants of *I AM*, but lords themselves over the covenant people. *milḥāmâ (war)* is the opposite of "peace"; with *qdš* it becomes the equivalent of "holy war." Not only do the false prophets contend against the poor, who cannot meet their demands, and the righteous who refuse to comply with them, but they hope by their proclamations to bring doom upon their enemy.

6 The logical particle *lākēn (therefore)* shows that the sentence (vv 6-7)

---

22. *Contra* LXX *(eis to stoma autōn)*, Vg *(in ore eorum)*, and so most moderns (cf. NRSV).

23. Wolff, *Micha,* 73.

24. A. S. van der Woude, *Micha,* De Prediking van het Oude Testament (Nijkerk: G. F. Callenbach, 1976), 109-10.

25. Cf. GB 635.

26. *IBHS* §9.5.1.

27. *IBHS* §24.2.

will fit the crime (v 5). Judging by the connection elsewhere of visions with dreams (cf. Num 12:6; Deut 13:1[2]; Joel 3:1[2:28]) and by explicit references to visions coming at night (Dan 2:9; 7:1; Zech 1:8), *laylâ (night)* and *ḥāšĕkâ (plunged into darkness)* would have their normal, concrete meaning here. The preposition *min* and the parallel in v 6B, however, suggest a figurative sense. The shift to the second-person pronoun *lākem (to you)* from the third-person pronoun with reference to the false prophets suggests that the sentence is handed down once again by *I AM* in an "I-Thou" encounter (cf. 1:6-7; 2:3-4). The putative verb *ḥāšĕkâ (plunged into darkness)* in v 6Ab could be gapped in v 6Aa, but more likely this is a nominal clause. The preposition *lĕ* expresses disadvantage *(to you)*.[28] LXX and Syr interpreted *min* in *mēḥāzôn (instead of vision)* and *miqqĕsōm* as denoting source so that they think that the night and darkness came from the visions and divinations. But vv 6B-7 suggest rather that the prophets will be ashamed because no visions came to them. The *min* could be privative "apart from," "without,"[29] in which case "night" is purely literal; that is, the false prophets will experience black nights that will not be illuminated by dreams and visions. It could also be substitutive,[30] as in Hos 6:6; Ps 52:7(5).[31] In this view "night" is figurative, "night/darkness instead of visions/divination." H. Wolff[32] does not decide the matter, and B. Renaud[33] suitably attenuates the two meanings since visions came mostly at night. The parallel in v 6B underscores a figurative sense of *laylâ* and a substitutive sense of *min*. For the meaning of *ḥzh* see 1:1.

Many critics emend the verb *wĕḥāšĕkâ (plunged into darkness)* into a noun, *waḥāšēkâ* "and darkness," with LXX and Vg, because it makes a "better parallel" with *laylâ,* but LXX[R] reads *[ka]i skotast[ēsetai hym]ein*, reflecting the more difficult but traditional vocalization of MT and Syr. D. Hillers explains the third feminine singular as "idiomatic in this expression." Strictly speaking the form is not a qal third feminine singular perfective but a qal infinitive construct[34] with a feminine shape;[35] it functions as the subject as usual in a nominal clause,[36] and the *waw* is not relative but conjunctive. The repetition of *lākem* is emphatic, as is v 6Ab to v 6Aa. In *miqqĕsōm (instead of divination) min*

28. *IBHS* §11.2.10.

29. *IBHS* §11.2.11.

30. Cf. Vg *propterea nox vobis pro visione.*

31. Cf. A. H. Edelkoort, "Prophet and Prophet (Micah 2:6-11; 3:5-8)," *OTS* 5 (1948) 185, and GKC §119w.

32. Wolff, *Micha*, 61.

33. *La Formation*, 131.

34. Cf. GKC §45c.

35. *IBHS* §36.1.1.

36. *IBHS* §36.2.1.

is again substitutive and *qĕsōm* is another qal infinitive construct used nominally as the object of the preposition. Against those who emend to *miqqesem* for the sake of parallelism with *ḥāzôn*, J. M. P. Smith[37] notes, "The rhyme supports MT." *qsm* denotes some form of occult activity in seeking an omen. R. L. Alden[38] notes that "the account in Ezk 21:21-22 [H 27-28] is the only clue to exactly how *qesem* may have been practiced. Shaking or flinging down arrows, consulting teraphim, and hepatoscopy (looking at the liver) may be subcategories of *qesem*." The foreign practice, though forbidden among the covenant people (Deut 18:10; cf. 1 Sam 15:23), was imported into Israel. Since the sentence is addressed to Israel's prophets (v 5), one assumes that *ḥzh* and *qsm* are two forms by which the divine revelation came to the prophets (see Exposition, 170); this is corroborated by the parallel to both in v 6B, *nĕbî'îm*. Because *qsm* in the prophets is presumably always pejorative (cf. Josh 13:22; *contra* Prov 16:10), B. Renaud[39] rightly says that "Micah speaks with a certain contempt for the prophets who are his adversaries." Micah, however, has not accused them of illegitimate activity but of base motives. On the basis of *I AM*'s sentence, Micah draws the conclusion in metaphorical terms that the false prophets will lose their gift of divining, the authoritative basis of their office.

bā'â is qal third masculine singular perfective of the root *bô'*, which means "to enter" = "*to set*" with the subject *haššemeš (the sun)*,[40] inherently definite because of its uniqueness.[41] The language is metaphorical because the sun sets upon everyone daily. From the parallel in v 6A, clearly Micah means that the sun of *ḥāzôn* and of *qĕsōm*, that is, prophetic illumination, will set forever. In *'al-hannĕbî'îm (upon the prophets)* the preposition *'al*, like *lĕ*, expresses disadvantage, perhaps with an added notion of the pathos felt "upon" them.[42] In *hannĕbî'îm* the article is anaphoric, referring to the false prophets singled out in v 6. Because v 6Ba is parallel to v 6Aa and v 6Bb is parallel to v 6Ab, the *waw*-relative with *bā'â* is consequent to v 6Aa and with *wĕqādar* to v 6Ab.

The stative verb *qādar* "to be dark" is ingressive. By repeating the preposition *'al* with the pronominal third masculine plural suffix *(upon them)*, referring back to the *nĕbî'îm*, in this emphatic synonymous parallel, Micah emphasizes the disadvantage and the pathos felt by the prophets. *hayyôm (the day)* is the opposite of *laylâ (night)* with the definite article marking it out as a class of things characterized by light over against darkness, and possibly of moral and

37. Smith, *Micah*, 72.
38. R. L. Alden, "*qesem*," *TWOT* 2:805.
39. *La Formation*, 138.
40. KB 112, §10.
41. *IBHS* §13.4.
42. *IBHS* §11.2.13.

physical goodness over against moral and physical evil (cf. Prov 4:18).[43] "Night," "darkness," "sun going down," and "day becoming black" elsewhere depict calamity and distress (see Exposition, 173).

7   The *waw*-relative in *ûbōšû (and will become ashamed)* signifies that v 7 is (con)sequential to v 6: the false prophets' loss of their gift will lead to their being ashamed. The root *bôš* in this third masculine plural perfective, referring back to the *něbî'îm* of v 6B, implies that one has risked his fortune on someone or something, hoping that the power on which one depended would advance his honor, but as it turned out it proved false and so brought the person to ruin and ridicule. H. Seebass[44] says: ". . . *bosh* expresses the idea that someone . . . underwent an experience in which his . . . former respected position and importance were overthrown. Someone risked something to a power . . . and thus undertook a daring venture. Now he receives the consequence of that venture so that he must suffer the opposite of what he sought, viz., dishonor. . . ." Prophets had social weight because God gave them supernatural revelations; when they failed to answer their quest for such revelations, social disgrace ensued. In *haḥōzîm (the seers)* the article is anaphoric, referring to the false prophets of vv 5-6, and the qal masculine plural active participle functions as *nomen agentis*.[45] The root *ḥzh* links v 7A with v 6A. LXX explicates it by "those who see dreams," and Syr and Vg by "those who see visions."

In *wěḥāpěrû (and will be disgraced) waw* is a consequent not to v 7Aaα but to v 6, and the root *ḥpr* as often elsewhere is an emphatic synonymous parallel with *bôš*. Once again, since the subjects *haqqōsěmîm (the diviners),* a complementary parallel to *haḥōzîm,* are coming into a state, the form is ingressive, though in fact it functions as a nonperfective.[46] These verbs of public disgrace are also used in contexts of calamity (cf. Isa 1:29; 33:9; Jer 15:9; and especially Mic 1:11).

The *waw*-relative with the qal third masculine plural perfective of the root *'ṭh, wě'āṭû (and they will cover),* introduces the further (con)sequence, and the pronouns refer back to both subcategories of prophets, *ḥōzîm* "seers" and *qōsěmîm* "diviners." *'ṭh* with *'al* means to "cover," "wrap" (Lev 13:45). One covers the *śāpām ([the] mustache)* as a sign of mourning (cf. Ezek 24:17-22). The meaning "mustache" is based on 2 Sam 19:25.[47] There may be an association with the unclean lepers, who had to engage in the same rite because in Lam 4:13-15 sinful prophets are treated as lepers by the people. Micah could have

43. *IBHS* §13.5.1.
44. H. Seebass, *"bosh," TDOT* 2:52.
45. *IBHS* §37.2.
46. *IBHS* §32.1.3.
47. *Contra* P. Haupt, "The Book of Micah," *AJSL* 26 (1910) 215.

used other rites of mourning and bereavement (cf. 1:9; 7:16). L. C. Allen[48] notes: "Ironically it will also be a fitting sign that they have nothing to say." According to J. M. P. Smith,[49] LXX's *kai katalalēsousi kat' autōn* "they will scoff all of them" is "a mere guess." *kullām (all of them)* is determinate and therefore indicates the aggregate, the entirety, none excepted.[50]

kî (because) introduces the reason why each of the false prophets covers his mustache. The substantive *'ên* signifies nonexistence *(there is no)*. *ma'ănēh (answer)* consists of the prefix *mem*, forming an abstract noun in the construct state from the root I *'nh (answer)* (see v 4). Some MSS and versions read *ma'ăneh*, probably as a hiphil masculine singular participle of I *'nh* (see below). The root links the judgment of the prophets with that of the magistrates: no answer from God. But whereas the magistrates cried out for salvation from conquerors, the false prophets seek an answer through their material techniques to gain a revelation. *'ĕlōhîm (from God)* is a genitive of agent.[51] A. H. Edelkoort[52] thinks that *'ĕlōhîm* is used rather than *yhwh* "because those prophets sought their oracles not only from the God of Israel but also from other gods." The evidence, however, is too slim for such a far-reaching conclusion. *'ĕlōhîm* occurs eight other times in Micah, but either as a parallel to *yhwh* (4:2; 6:6, 8; 7:2) or in addition to *yhwh* (5:4[3]; 7:10, 17) or in connection with a conversion from the gods to *yhwh* (4:5), so that its use alone here is unique, one that requires explanation. H. Wolff,[53] comparing it with *da'at 'ĕlōhîm* in Hos 4:1; 6:6, thinks that Micah may have picked up a term coined in the prophetic circles, or possibly Micah is making a point of not associating the actions of these unholy prophets with the sacred Name, though they themselves may claim to speak in the name of *I AM* (cf. 1 Kgs 22:11, 24). LXX's *dioti ouk estai ho eisakouōn autōn* "because no one listens to them" represents *kî 'ên ma'ăneh* [hiphil participle of *'nh*] *'ălêhem* in v 7Bb, a modification resembling its blunder at the end of v 4.

8 Micah distinguishes himself from the false prophets by the strong adversative adverb, usually with *wě, wě'ûlām (but indeed),*[54] and the emphatic pronoun *(I).*[55] LXX's *ean mē* "unless" probably represents *'ûlay.*[56] MT finds a striking parallel in Job 5:6-8, where the speaker, in first person, contrasts him-

---

48. Allen, *Micah*, 313.
49. Smith, *Micah*, 72.
50. GKC §127b.
51. *IBHS* §9.1.1.
52. Edelkoort, "Prophet and Prophet," 188.
53. Wolff, *Micha*, 74.
54. BDB 19.
55. *IBHS* §16.3.1.
56. Cf. Smith, *Micah*, 72.

self as a seeker of God to humankind in general (cf. Mic 7:6-7). As in Mic 3:1, Micah is the only suitable candidate as the antecedent. Instead of interpreting the qal first common singular perfective of *ml'* *(I am full of)* as a present stative with a root that denotes an adjectival quality,[57] LXX interpreted it as a future fientive verb, *emplēsō* "I will fill up [myself]." *ml'* is a standard term for indicating that a person has been endowed with a particular ability (cf. Exod 31:3; 35:31, 35). Micah, in contrast to his deflated opponents, has been outfitted for his task. The accusative *kōah* *(power)* complements *ml'*,[58] which is linked with *rûah yhwh* and so expresses vital force and could be translated by "energy, vigor." B. Renaud[59] says: "It expresses here the dynamism of the prophetic action." H. Wolff[60] defines *kōah* thus: "*kōah* means both physical and psychic strength, also to endure in opposition and discouragement (cf. Isa 40:29, 31; it is primarily the power of God himself; 40:26)."

'*et* *(namely)* may mean "with" or be a sign of specification (i.e., Micah's energy is the Spirit of *I AM*).[61] BDB[62] construes it as a preposition and gives it the exceptional, though not unique, sense of "with the help of." More probably Micah attributes his strength entirely to *I AM* himself. Syr and Vg also make *rûah yhwh* a complement of *kōah*, and *mišpāt ûgĕbûrâ* complements *mālē'tî*. LXX's *en pneumati kyriou kai krimatos kai dynasteias* "with the Spirit of the Lord and of judgment and of power" interpreted it as a preposition governing *rûah* and *yhwh ûmišpāt ûgĕbûrâ* as its modifying genitives. The linking of *I AM* as merely another complement condemns the translation. Syr ("I am full of power by the spirit of *I AM*") and Vg *(ego repletus sum fortitudine spiritus Domini iudicio et virtute)* better represent MT by making spirit of *I AM* a complement of *kōah*. *rûah yhwh* *(the spirit of* I AM*)*, a genitive of inalienable relationship,[63] is, as R. Rendtorff[64] says, "the presupposition of a proper oracle." Although many critics emend the text by omitting this specifying modifier because it both overloads the line and breaks up the three complements of *mālē'tî*, it is better retained because our knowledge of Hebrew rhythm is insecure, because all MSS, including Mur 88, and versions represent it, and because it connotes a highly theological value. The spirit of *I AM* gives Micah the supernatural courage to stand up, at the peril of his very life, to address wrongdoers.

57. *IBHS* §30.5.3.
58. *IBHS* §10.2.1.
59. *La Formation,* 136.
60. Wolff, *Micha,* 73.
61. Cf. *IBHS* §10.3.
62. BDB 86, §1a.
63. *IBHS* §9.1.1.
64. R. Rendtorff, *"prophētēs," TDNT* 6:799.

For the meaning of *ûmišpāt (justice)*, the second accusative complement-ing *mālē'tî*, see 3:2. *ûgĕbûrâ (and of might)*, the third complementary accusative, in addition to the general sense of strength, of power, connotes "valor," accord-ing to B. Renaud.[65] He says that it comes from the language of war and repre-sents the prophet as brave, as capable of confronting redoubtable adversaries. It also connotes, particularly in the Deuteronomistic history, capability. H. Kos-mala[66] notes: "In case of a war, it is not mere words, but planning and military power that decide the outcome (2 Kgs 18:20; Isa 36:5)." It connotes power and cunning in executing a triumphant, victorious battle. Since Micah is engaged here in an acerbic battle with false prophets, who undoubtedly consecrated war against him, it is proper to look to this meaning in war. The word is often asso-ciated, as here, with *I AM*'s victory on behalf of justice (Isa 42:1-4; Ps 89:15-16[14-15]). God's *gĕbûrâ* is celebrated in song (Pss 21:14[13]; 71:18; 145:4). The juxtaposition of these three complementary accusatives refers, as H. Wolff[67] says, "to one total concept, a hendiatreis. We may paraphrase: Micah is gifted with courageous readiness to get involved in the cause of justice."

The *lāmed* of purpose with the hiphil infinitive construct *lĕhaggîd (to de-clare)* explains why *I AM* gifted his plenipotentiary with this capacity. The root *ngd* fundamentally means "to place a matter high, conspicuous before a per-son" (KBL). The function of the hiphil can be stated precisely because the verb occurs only in this stem, though it seems to function as an internal hiphil, "to make transgression to be conspicuous."[68] For the indirect object *lĕya'ăqōb* and its parallel *lĕyiśrā'ēl* see 1:5, 15; 2:12; 3:1, and for the accusative object *piš'ô* and its parallel *ḥaṭṭā'tô* see 1:5. The pronominal suffixes on these two forms are geni-tives of agency.[69] The synonymous parallelism of v 8Bb and v 8Ba, with *lĕhaggîd* gapped in the latter, functions as emphatic. The stereophonic message is that the whole nation is corporately identified by its sin. The two words for sin sig-nify that they broke off their relationship with their *I AM* in every kind of wrongdoing.

EXPOSITION

As in chapter 2, where an oracle reproaching the prophets (2:6-11) follows an oracle sentencing the land barons to exile (2:1-5), so also in chapter 3 a judg-

65. *La Formation*, 136.
66. H. Kosmala, *"gābhar,"* TDOT 2:369.
67. H. W. Wolff, *Micah the Prophet* (Philadelphia: Fortress, 1981), 150.
68. *IBHS* §27.4.
69. *IBHS* §9.1.1.

ment oracle against the gluttonous prophets (3:5-8) follows one against greedy magistrates (3:1-4). Both reproach oracles against the prophets imply a collusion between themselves and the tyrants based on their common greed. Instead of barking against the avaricious land barons and the rapacious magistrates, thereby protecting the covenant, these venal prophets, who should have been the moral watchdogs of the theocracy, wagged their tails and joined the cannibals to gratify their own swollen appetites.

In chapter 3 both the magistrates and the false prophets are accused of turning the moral order on its head: the magistrates of loving evil and hating good, and the prophets of misleading the people for money. Micah epitomizes the greed of both groups with figures of eating. Both accusations are presented first by means of characterizing participles (3:2, 5Abβ-Ba) developed by a relative clause with *wa'ăšer* (3:3, 5Bb). In both, the accusation and the sentence are linked by logical particles: *'āz* (3:4) and *lākēn* (v 4). The sentence against the prophets is similar to that against the magistrates: silence from God when they call upon him (cf. 3:4, 7). The magistrates vainly cry out to God for deliverance from sword and exile; the prophets vainly cry out for a revelation from God in order to retain their social status. In both oracles *I AM* hands down the sentence in the first person (3:3, 6), and Micah elaborates on it (3:4, 7). In addition to these stylistic and thematic links pertaining to accusation and sentence, 3:1-4 and 5:8 are also bound verbally: *'ammî* (3:3, 5), *ya'ăneh/ma'ăneh* (3:4, 8), *mišpāṭ* (3:1, 8), and above all the *inclusio ya'ăqōb/yiśrā'ēl* and the first common singular pronoun (3:1, 8).

The authenticity of this piece as coming from the mouth of Micah is, as B. Renaud[70] said, "neither debated nor debatable."

Its structure is:

I. Messenger formula with grafted-on addressees (v 5A).
   A. The messenger formula: "Thus says *I AM*" (v 5Aa).
   B. The addressees: against the prophets (5Abα).
II. The accusation (in third person, grafted onto the addressees) (v 5Abβ-B).
   A. The indictment: "who lead my people astray" (v 5Abβ).
   B. Development of indictment: who preach for hire (v 5B).
III. Judicial sentence, introduced by "therefore" (vv 6-7).
   A. Sentence in second person: no more revelations (v 6).
   B. Development in third person: public disgrace because of their loss
      of their gift and exposed uncleanness (v 7).
IV. The contrasting example of Micah in the first person (v 8).

70. *La Formation*, 137.

A. The basis and capability of his ministry: Spirit-filled power, justice, and valor (v 8A).

B. The purpose of his ministry: to declare to Israel its sin (v 8B).

Apart from v 8 the prophecy exhibits the normal motifs of a prophecy of doom: address, accusation, and sentence, and v 8 forms an *inclusio* with v 5 by stressing that the source of Micah's authority is *I AM*. In the sentence the initial statement and its development are linked verbally: *ḥzh* and *qsm*.

In 2:3 the messenger formula introduces the sentence; in 3:5 it introduces the whole prophecy, including accusation, in order to stress that the source of Micah's authority lies not in himself but in *I AM*, a necessary reminder when reproving prophets who, if one may judge from parallels (1 Kgs 22:11, 24; Jer 28:1-17; Ezek 13:7), claim to represent *I AM*. In an *inclusio* Micah elaborates this truth (v 8).

Micah's addressees, "false prophets," are part of a standing confrontation spanning centuries, from Micaiah ben Imlah to Ezekiel, mostly between lone individuals (true prophets), and the majority (false prophets). All prophets share common features. As is well known, true prophets anoint kings, have ready access to them, and sometimes originate from the priestly caste; false ones are often mentioned with other national leaders, the priests and magistrates (Jer 2:26; 4:9; 8:1; 13:13; 18:18; Ezek 22:25-28; Mic 3:11; Zeph 3:3-4). The connection of prophets with the cultus is uncertain. They discharged certain cultic functions, such as seeking decisions from *I AM* (1 Sam 28:6; 1 Kgs 14:2; 22:5, 7; 2 Kgs 3:11; 22:13; Mic 3:7), and were under the charge of a priest at least in Jeremiah's days (Jer 29:26-27), but the quality and quantity of that connection are uncertain. It is also uncertain whether the prophets were bound together in a profession in the full and exclusive sense of that term. Both groups prophesy in the name of *I AM*, and both claim to prophesy through the spirit of *I AM*. Finally, both proclaim "peace" and "doom" (cf. Isa 7:1-16; Mic 3:5). R. Rendtorff[71] says: "We . . . find . . . salvation sayings in the writing prophets whose authenticity there is no obvious reason to contest. On the other hand Mi. 3:5 shows that the proclamation of catastrophe is possible among the *něbî'îm* too."

How do they differ? When one studies the characteristics of the acerbic adversaries of the true prophets, no single clearly delineated profile emerges; here we draw the profile of those Micah braved both from his own prophecies and from those of others that match, and occasionally we put it in relief by contrasting it with features of other kinds of false prophets.

A. Edelkoort's opinion that Micah's adversaries represented pagan gods

---

71. R. Rendtorff, *"prophētēs," TDNT* 6:807.

was already discounted on exegetical grounds. In addition, though Elijah confronted the prophets of Baal and Jeremiah explicitly stated that the derelict prophets in Samaria who led Israel astray prophesied by Baal, Micah does not castigate the prophets in Jerusalem who preach for hire in the same way (cf. Jer 23:13-14, 32). Finally, Micah would not have attributed genuine revelations to pagan deities (cf. v 7 and Isa 41:21-24).

Sometimes the false prophets are charlatans (cf. Jer 14:14 and Ezek 13:17). Jeremiah says in his polemic that *I AM* has not sent them (14:14-15; 23:21, 32; 27:15; 28:15; 29:9, 31) and that their words come from their own hearts (14:14; 23:16, 26). Ezekiel's charges are similar (Ezek 13:2-23). But this is not always so, as in the cases of Balaam, of Micaiah ben Imlah, and of those whom Micah of Moresheth confronted. Balaam, though a pagan seer, received his revelations from *I AM*, and the false prophets who contested with Micaiah ben Imlah are said by that true prophet to have received the spirit of *I AM*, albeit a lying spirit (1 Kgs 22:19-23). *I AM* and Micah sentence his adversaries with the loss of revelations, a sentence that makes no sense unless it be granted that *I AM* had gifted them with the ability to seek and find visions in the first place. As B. Renaud[72] said: "If they were forgers, one does not see how the silence of YHWH could punish them." Those Micah faced either misrepresented what they received in a vision or, as in the case of Balaam and of those whom Micaiah ben Imlah confronted, they were deluded by *I AM*; it is uncertain which is the case in the book of Micah. Jeremiah was sifted out as the true prophet when his predictions came true (Jer 28:9; cf. Deut 18:21-22). Micah was distinguished as the true prophet when his gift prevailed even in the time of judgment, while those of his adversaries failed and they were disgraced.

All false prophets have a false theology. Micah accuses his adversaries of leading people astray with a theology contrary to the covenant (Deut 12:32; 13:1-4[12:32–13:3]; Mic 2:7, 11; 3:5). The issue between the two contesting groups that spanned the centuries hinged on the catchword *šālôm* "well-being." In OT theology *šālôm* is a gift from *I AM* and may be mediated to those in a covenant of peace with him through the word of his prophets (cf. Ps 85:9-14[8-13]); both groups claimed the power to mediate it (cf. Jer 28:9). G. von Rad[73] says: "*šālôm* seems to have been the culminating point of the theology of some prophetic circles, and therefore the term became the center of bitter controversy between two parties." The false prophets confronted by Micah misrepresented the judicial activity of *I AM*. Like those whom Jeremiah braved, they had tradition on their side. Did not Israel celebrate in song *I AM*'s faithfulness to his covenant in giving

72. *La Formation*, 138.
73. G. von Rad, *"eirēnē,"* *TDNT* 2:404.

Israel *šālôm* in the face of their enemies? The preexilic writing prophets, how-ever, saw for the first time that unless Israel repented the curses of the covenant would be enacted, and that *šālôm* belonged only to the godly remnant who sur-vived the judgment. These true prophets saw the will of *I AM* in the approaching debacle, while their antagonists clung to a message of *šālôm* regardless. As Ezekiel complained, they "whitewashed" the true situation. The message of the writing prophets broke with the popular misunderstanding of Israel's tradition.

But the difference is more than a matter of message; it is also a matter of motivation, method, and manner. The false prophets confronted by Micah were motivated by personal gain, whereas he was motivated by a zeal for justice inspired by the spirit of *I AM*. True prophets had insight into Israel's history from a sympathy with God's kingdom perspective; false ones could not discern the hand of God in their history because they saw it through vested interests. True prophets conditioned the nation's well-being on its fidelity to *I AM*, whereas false prophets arrogantly conditioned it on fidelity to themselves. True prophets seek *I AM*'s gain, false ones their own. Only as long as it is of profit to them do they proclaim peace, says Micah.

In addition to the false motivation, the diabolical enemy used false meth-ods. As noted in the Exegesis (163), they were not only *ḥōzîm* "seers," an accept-able form of revelation but also *qōsĕmîm*, a proscribed method. Micah kept the people in direct contact with the words of their covenantal God; his opponents distanced them from him by their mantic methods. True prophets preached with a burning luminosity, while false ones were merely windbags (cf. Jer 5:13-14; Mic 2:11; 3:7). The decisive feature of true prophets is the living Word.

Finally, true prophets mostly stand alone against a majority, as in the cases of Elijah (1 Kings 19), Micaiah ben Imlah (1 Kings 22), Amos (7:10-17), Mi-cah of Moresheth, Jeremiah, and Ezekiel. The false prophets seem to have re-sponded mostly to the requests of those who consulted them to determine *I AM*'s will; true prophets, though uninvited, unasked, and unwelcome, boldly stepped forward to condemn injustices and crimes. As *I AM* stepped forth from heaven to right the wrongs on earth in a punitive epiphany (cf. 1:4-5), so also Micah steps on stage to redress Israel's breach of covenant. Isaiah lamented that all Israel like sheep went astray (Isa 53:6), and Micah indicts the prophets for causing them to stray. The verb *tʿh* "to go astray" can refer to staggering because of drunkenness. To judge from Isa 28:7 and Hos 4:5, the figure for their moral staggering may have been suggested by their swaying and stumbling as drunk-ards in their vomit. Jeremiah spells out the specifics of the metaphor in the case of the prophets of Baal, who led Israel astray: "they commit adultery, walk in lies, strengthen the hands of evil-doers, so that no one turns from his wicked-ness" (Jer 23:13-14; cf. 23:32).

Whereas the prophets' words should have restored the covenant relationship that had been broken by the sin of greedy land barons and corrupt magistrates, the wicked prophets accused by Micah so abused their gift as to make it an instrument in exacerbating the fracture (cf. Lam 2:14). If the people wanted prophets who would predict inebriating drinks, they certainly had ones who made them stray like drunkards. The land barons' grapes of materialism were fermented by the yeast of corrupt magistrates, sped up by the sugar and heat of the false prophets' perverse messages (cf. Lam 2:14). As noted, Micah also pejoratively accuses them of using proscribed divination, but climactically and most extensively he accuses them of preaching for personal gain. They gave priority to their sensual appetite to feed their mouths over their spiritual responsibility to speak the truth boldly and vigorously attack sin. As H. Wolff[74] said: "What came out of the mouth of those prophets depended on what was put into it." They were not lacking in the gift; they were lacking in moral conviction and strength. For them, as J. L. Mays[75] put it, "Money spoke louder than God," and so they either misrepresented the truthful revelations *I AM* gave them, or *I AM* deluded them.

In either case the effects of their "biting" (see *nšk*) were deadly to the covenant community; they rewarded corrupt and greedy individuals with the blessing of "peace" (see *šālôm*), and against the powerless person who either out of his penury could not afford to give them what they wanted or out of his commitment to righteousness refused to comply and bribe them, they sanctified war. To be sure, a prophet should be given a livelihood (1 Sam 9:6-8; 1 Kgs 14:3; 2 Kgs 8:8; Luke 10:7; 1 Cor 9:4, 7-12), but a true prophet must also know when to refuse it (cf. 2 Kgs 5:15-16). *šālôm,* according to J. I. Durham,[76] "[describes] a comprehensive kind of fulfillment or completion, indeed of a perfection in life and spirit which quite transcends any success which man alone, even under the best of circumstances, is able to attain." The powerful and corrupt landowners and magistrates enjoyed their material plunder while basking in the blessing of the potent religious establishment. The arrogant and corrupt audiences and the proud and dissolute preachers both received what they wanted, but neither of them wanted the will of God, a brotherly community based on mercy and justice. The powerful members of nominal Israel were in back-scratching cahoots against true Israel. Micah singles out their use of money for food to connect their sanguine behavior with that of their cannibal-

---

74. Wolff, *Micha,* 72.
75. Mays, *Micah,* 83.
76. J. I. Durham, "*Šālôm* and the Presence of God," in *Proclamation and Presence,* ed. J. I. Durham and J. R. Porter (Richmond, Va.: John Knox, 1970), 280.

istic patrons (vv 2-3). The prophets cheered the cannibals on so long as they got their fair share of the chopped-up bones. The religious system joined the judicial system in protecting the criminal and left the actual or potential victims at their mercy. It was an open secret, as they say.

Regrettably many church leaders, who should be the moral and spiritual eyes of the church, are willfully ignorant of God's word regarding marriage, charity, and property; they cheerfully welcome vow breakers who withhold love from their spouses; they show a callousness against the homeless; and though they profess to follow the compassionate comforter, they encourage a Lockean materialism.

"It is exceptional," says H. Wolff,[77] "how extensively the sentence [against the prophets] is worked out in comparison with the other sentences in Micah; otherwise the accusation is given more scope." *I AM* directly addresses the prophets in handing down his sentence. The logical particle "therefore" shows that the sentence will fit the crime; it hits them on their own ground. In no fewer than eight clauses *I AM* and his true spokesman forecast that they would lose *I AM*'s gracious gift to them, the source of their pretensions and illicit gain. Like Samson, who lost his gift for abusing it and was plunged into darkness, so also these prophets who should have been the moral eyes of the nation would lose their gifted insight. They would no longer be able to look through the wall of darkness to the bright mystery of divine things. The night (in the literal sense), when they rendered their oracles, would become for them veritable night (in the figurative sense), that is to say, thick darkness, total mystery (cf. Pss 82:5; 69:24[23]). Their "crystal balls" would become utterly black, and their "open eyes" (Num 24:3, 15) would be shut forever. The "light" that gave hope to the corrupt and powerful would become black in eternal night.

Micah develops *I AM*'s sentence in noting that the loss of their gift will bring them public disgrace and public disclosure of their falsity and uncleanness. Their gesture of covering their mustaches may have a threefold symbolism: their mourning (cf. Ezek 24:17, 22), their uncleanness like that of a leper barred from the worshipping community (Lev 13:45), and that they have nothing more to say. When a prophet was exposed as a fraud, he was regarded as unclean. The people cried out to such frauds: "Go away! You are unclean! . . . Away! Away! Don't touch us." J. L. Mays[78] says: "Their profession will become as empty of reality as the oracles they gave." The loss of God's word is elsewhere associated with God's judgment (cf. Isa 29:9-14; Hos 5:6; Amos 8:11-12).

In sharp contrast to these deflated windbags, Micah presents himself in

---

77. Wolff, *Micha*, 73.
78. Mays, *Micah*, 84.

v 8 as so full of the spirit of *I AM* that he contends valiantly and victoriously in the cause of justice by denouncing Israel's sins. An autobiographical element is extremely rare, if not unique, in an oracle of judgment. Micah took advantage of *I AM*'s sentence to convict still further the unfaithful prophets who misled the favored people into sin and death and who sought to discredit him and prepared holy war against him. L. Allen[79] comments: "He speaks not to bolster his own ego but to convince his contemporaries of the truth" (cf. Eph 3:7-8). B. Renaud[80] noted: "It is . . . in the context of controversies that the prophets are led to raise the chaste veil that covered their personal experience" (cf. Amos 7:14-15 and 1 Cor 11:16-32). There are times when fools must be answered according to their folly (Prov 26:5). Micah may also have included this self-portrait to justify his harsh message against his colleagues: he begins and ends his oracles by asserting that his word and power are from *I AM*.

His autobiography consists of his spiritual capacity and his moral message, each of which implicitly contrasts with that of the perfidious prophets. He had the capacity to prophesy because he was full of *kōaḥ* "unvacillating power," even "the spirit of *I AM* himself," and full of a taste for *mišpāṭ* "justice" and of *gĕbûrâ* "valiant might" (see Exegesis, 167). By contrast, his opponents were demoralized by their dependence on monetary rewards; in the time of testing their weakness would be exposed, and they would be put to shame. The sign of the Spirit's presence was not ecstasy but the ability to persevere vigorously, valiantly, and victoriously on the side of justice in the face of uncommon hostility. "When the courts and counting houses of the nation fail in justice," says J. L. Mays,[81] "the prophets must speak for the heavenly court and represent its justice." The prophets by and large failed. Micah stands in their place endowed with a strength and courage from God that does not flinch from the lonely role of standing against the entire power structure of Jerusalem. Later on *I AM* holds every person accountable for justice (Mic 6:8). To justice he adds military, victorious power (see *gĕbûrâ*).

As noted in the Exegesis (167), these three virtues, equipping Micah for ministry, are a hendiatreis; they refer to one total concept: a spirit-energized power that victoriously establishes justice. H. Wolff[82] appropriately quotes Pascal:[83] "Justice without power is powerless. Power without justice is tyrannical. . . . Justice and power must therefore be connected so that what is just is also powerful and what is powerful is also just."

---

79. Allen, *Micah*, 313.
80. *La Formation*, 133.
81. Mays, *Micah*, 85.
82. Wolff, *Micah the Prophet*, 151-52.
83. Pascal, *Pensées*, 298.

The presence of the spirit of *I AM* is the *sine qua non* for effective ministry. TNIV translates "man of the Spirit" in Hos 9:7 as "anyone who is inspired"; it is instructive to note that such a prophet will be considered a maniac by his enemies. Ezekiel also associated the Spirit with force, more specifically, with lifting him up to perform his prophetic tasks (cf. Ezek 2:2; 3:12, 14, 24; 8:3; 11:1, 24; 37:1; 43:5). The Spirit also gifted people with a sense of justice, as with the messianic King (Isa 11:2-9), the redeemed people (32:15), and the anonymous Suffering Servant who brings salvation (Isa 42:1; 61:1). The Spirit does not come from within the human soul, but as an extension of *I AM* himself. The true prophet does not so much carry the Word of God to the people as the spirit of God carries him to them. The spirit of God is also associated with valor. Micah did not flinch before the power structure at Jerusalem because he was filled with the Spirit of Christ, who also withstood the religious and political structures of his day. Paul also pleased God rather than men (1 Thess 2:2-6). "For God did not give a spirit of timidity, but a spirit of power, of love and of self-discipline" (2 Tim 1:7). Micah is a precursor of Jesus Christ, who brought the ministry on behalf of justice to maturity. H. Wolff[84] remarks, "In Jesus justice has come to maturity, not only in the authority of his words but in the fact that he suffered injustice and overcame it. By suffering injustice in place of the unjust, he put justice in force with final authority."

Micah was filled with the Spirit in order to preach against sin. J. L. Mays[85] concludes, "Micah focuses on the sin in Israel, not its gross national product, because it is only in seeing themselves under the judgment of God that the guilty can grasp the reality of what is happening to them in history." The Word of *I AM* came to Micah (1:1), and the spirit of *I AM* enabled him to preach it with effective power (3:8).

3. *Jerusalem to Be Leveled (3:9-12)*

9   Listen, you leaders of Jacob,
        even you rulers of the house of Israel,
    you who detest justice
        and pervert all that is upright;
10   you who build Zion with bloodshed,
        and Jerusalem with injustice —
11   Its leaders judge for bribes,
        and its priests teach for hire,

84. Wolff, *Micah the Prophet*, 151.
85. Mays, *Micah*, 86.

and its prophets divine for money;
and yet they lean upon *I AM*, saying:
"Is not *I AM* among us?
No harm shall come upon us" —
12   Therefore, on account of you,
Zion will be plowed as a field,
and Jerusalem will become a heap of rubble,
and the temple mount will become a great high place in a forest.

EXEGESIS

9   In an *inclusio* Micah introduces his third and climactic oracle of doom by addressing the magistrates with almost the same words as in 3:1: *šim'û-nā'* . . . *ro'šê* . . . *ya'ăqōb* . . . *ûqĕṣînê bêt yiśrā'ēl (Listen, you leaders of Jacob, even you rulers of the house of Israel).* However, it adds *zō't (this)* after *šim'û-nā* and *bêt* before *ya'ăqōb*. Some, who are under the delusion that a gifted poet may not vary his style, against all MSS and versions conform v 9A precisely to v 1A. B. Duhm[1] and J. Lindblom[2] justify eliminating *zō't* "under the pretext that it disturbs the rhythm," as B. Renaud[3] says. He continues: "Besides, whereas some critics want to withdraw the words from 3:9A, others by contrast add it in 3:1A, the two groups having the same goal, namely, to align the two formulas upon each other. One measures the role subjectivity plays in such considerations." The LXX also varies its style in preferring for *rā'šê hai archai* in 3:1A and *hoi hēgoumenoi* here, and Jerome renders *ûqĕṣînê* in 3:1A by *duces* and in 3:9A by *iudicies*. *zō't*, a neutrum, anaphoric, demonstrative pronoun, is weakly emphatic.[4]

The magistrates are again, as in 3:2, characterized and condemned by a relative masculine plural participle, typically with the article, *hamăta'ăbîm (you who detest).* Piel with the root *t'b* has an estimative nuance, literally, "who regard as detestable."[5] The pointing of *mă* is exceptional. B. Renaud[6] renders: "who hold the right in horror." W. F. Albright[7] suggests that the root of *t'b* is

---

1. B. Duhm, "Anmerkungen zu den zwölf Propheten, III: Das Buch Micha," *ZAW* 31 (1911) 187.

2. J. Lindblom, *Micha literarisch untersucht* (Åbo: Åbo Akademi, 1929), 77.

3. *La Formation*, 139.

4. *IBHS* §17.4.2.

5. *IBHS* §24.2f-g.

6. *La Formation*, 140.

7. W. F. Albright, *From the Stone Age to Christianity* (Baltimore: Johns Hopkins University Press, 1940), 176.

w'b, which originally denoted the concept of inviolability or untouchability. Experiencing polar development in the Semitic languages, it came to denote either "holiness" or "abomination." In Hebrew usage *t'b* denotes having one's sensibilities offended by someone or something. That which is "abominable" is relative to the character, values, and/or culture of the individual. The direct accusative *mišpāṭ (justice)* is the *leitwort* linking the pericopes of chapter 3 (3:1, 8).

In the chiastic parallelism of v 9BB the definite object of the verb *yĕʿaqqēšû* is signaled by the emphatic particle *'ēt*:[8] the conjunctive *waw* in *wĕ'ēt* combines their taste and character as depicted in 3:9A with their conduct and actions related in 3:9B. *kol (all)* is in the construct case and with the article denotes "the *entirety*, i.e., *all, the whole*."[9] In *kol-hayĕšārâ (all that is upright)*, *yĕšārâ* is a genitive of measure,[10] and, as in all Semitic languages, the feminine marks it as an abstract noun from the adjective *yāšār*.[11] The ancient versions represented this collective singular by the plural. The root *yšr* originally had the graphic meaning "to be straight" (in contrast to crooked), for example, of a "straight leg" (Ezek 1:7), but it occurs predominantly in the metaphorical sense "to be right." The moral and religious meaning of "uprightness" becomes more precise in specific activities. L. Alonso-Schökel[12] notes that legal terminology uses *yšr* of lawsuits, of judgments, and of (divine or human) judges. Its derivative forms, especially *mêšārîm*, are frequently in parallel with *špṭ*, and it may specifically pertain to executive or administrative activity, as in Mic 3:9-11 (cf. Job 33:27 and Ps 45:7-8[6-7]). G. Liedke[13] points to its parallels with *ṣaddîq* and *tām* and draws the conclusion that *yāšār* also belongs to the notions of relationship that give expression to a unified covenantal relationship.

The factitive piel[14] *yĕʿaqqēšû (they pervert)* means literally "they make twisted," an antonym of *yšr*, and like that word is used metaphorically with reference to executive and administrative activity: "you who twist all that is straight in legal matters." As in 3:1, 6B, Micah shifts from a relative participle to a relative clause with a finite verb, but here he omits the sign of the relative, *'ăšer (who)*. LXX renders both by participles, but Vg shifts from *quia abominamini* to *pervertitis*. The second-person plural is certainly correct for this relative, modifying the antecedent second masculine plural of the vocative in 3:9A. As noted

8. *IBHS* §10.3.1.
9. GKC §127b.
10. *IBHS* §9.5.3.
11. *IBHS* §6.3.2.
12. L. Alonso-Schökel, *TWAT* 3:1063.
13. G. Liedke, *THAT* 1:793.
14. Cf. S. A. Ryder II, *The D-Stem in Western Semitic* (The Hague/Paris: Mouton, 1974), 114.

in 1:2, in good Hebrew syntax, modifying clauses regularly use the third person after a vocative (as in Classical Arabic) (cf. 3:3).

10   *bōneh (you who build)* is a qal active singular participle of *bnh*, but all versions have a plural, suggesting either an original *bōnê* or *bōni[y]m*, which agrees much better with the plural forms in v 9. The versions, however, are indecisive because they are compelled to render by plurals in harmony with v 9, and Mur 88 is not helpful because it has a lacuna here. Any participial form, however, is unlikely if not impossible because one would expect the article with a continuing relative participle. S. Schwantes[15] and B. Renaud[16] think that the singular form in the parallel text of Hab 2:12 contaminated MT. D. Hillers[17] rejects P. Kleinert's[18] and A. B. Ehrlich's[19] proposal to repoint the form as an infinitive absolute, *bānôh*, as being "stylistically most improbable." But why? The infinitive absolute often functions to epexegete preceding verb forms of various constructions.[20] I. Willi-Plein[21] uniquely regards Zion as the subject and conjectures a passive form, either *nibnh* or *bnyyh*. *ṣiyôn (Zion)* may refer specifically to the ancient Jebusite city (2 Sam 5:7 = 1 Chr 11:5; 1 Kgs 8:1 = 2 Chr 5:2)[22] or to the temple mount where *I AM* dwells (Ps 2:6; 110:2),[23] or be a synonym for the whole city of Jerusalem (Isa 2:3; 4:3).[24] The parallelism of the two terms suggests the latter sense here; the title "Zion" invests the capital of the Southern Kingdom with a theological quality: it is the cultic center of the world. Here it is a metonymy for the splendid religious and political edifices built in it. In *bĕdāmîm (with bloodshed)* the preposition *bĕ* is instrumental,[25] the plural represents composition (i.e., broken-apart collectivity), "shed blood,"[26] and the root *dām* "blood" is a synecdoche for the life of the defenseless victims who, having been "murdered" in villainous courts, lost their property. The rich used their plundered wealth to build temples on what they called *I AM*'s holy hill (Ps 2:6)!

---

15. Schwantes, "A Critical Study of the Text of Micah," 95.

16. *La Formation*, 140.

17. Hillers, *Micah*, 47.

18. P. Kleinert, *Micah*, ed. P. Schaff (New York: Scribner, Armstrong, 1874).

19. A. B. Ehrlich, *Randglossen zur hebräischen Bibel*, 8 vols. (Leipzig: Hinrichs, 1912), 5:5.

20. *IBHS* §35.5.1.

21. I. Willi-Plein, *Vorformen der Schriftexegese innerhalb des Alten Testaments*, BZAW 123 (Berlin: de Gruyter, 1971), 81-82.

22. Cf. K. M. Kenyon, *Jerusalem* (New York: McGraw-Hill/London: Thames and Hudson, 1967), 19-53.

23. Kenyon, *Jerusalem*, 54-62.

24. Kenyon, *Jerusalem*, 63-77.

25. *IBHS* §11.2.5.

26. *IBHS* §7.4.1; cf. Tg's *bdm 'syd* "by blood shed."

In the parallel *bānôh* (?) is gapped, Zion is expanded to included all *Jerusalem*, and the agent for building is *bĕ'awlâ* "wrongdoing" *(injustice)*. G. Livingston notes: "[*'wlh*] often refers to violent deeds, such as murder (2 Sam 3:34; [7:24; Hab 2:12])," the probable reference here according to the parallel. Micah has in mind not violence in general leading to a fatal outcome, but in view of v 3:9, which refers to the magistrates' abuse of "justice," and of 3:11, which refers to taking bribes to pervert justice, more particularly the mishandling of justice that resulted ultimately in the death of innocent victims.

11 With *rā'šê* *(its leaders)* the subject of the clause, Micah shifts from the vocative address to the *ro'šîm* (3:9) to elaboration about them in the third person. The third feminine singular pronominal suffix, a genitive of relation,[27] refers to Zion/Jerusalem, which are treated as feminine because *'îr* "city" is beheaded.[28] Whereas in 3:10 Zion/Jerusalem are literal, here it is a metonymy for its inhabitants. In *bĕšōḥad (for bribes) bĕ*, as in all three instances in 3:11A, is *bêt pretii* ([in exchange] for),[29] and *šōḥad (bribes)*, which modifies *yišpōṭû* "they judge," has its usual sense to take a bribe to pervert justice. This conventional collective singular noun[30] is rendered in all versions, except Syr, by the plural. *yišpōṭû (they judge)* is qal third masculine plural of *špṭ* (see 3:1, 9). The three third masculine plural nonperfectives in 3:9A denote the persistent (present) imperfective aspect.[31]

The third feminine singular pronominal suffix in *wĕkōhăneyâ (its priests)* functions in the same way as with *rā'šê*. Normally *kōhēn* reflects the more restricted concept of a minister for sacred things. In *bimĕḥîr (for hire) mĕḥîr* (price) means "reward/hire." The root of *yôrû (they teach)* is unclear. BDB[32] groups all uses under one root whose basic meaning is "to shoot, throw"; KBL,[33] GB,[34] and F. Zorell[35] give three roots for *yrh*, interpreting I *yrh*, always qal/niphal, to mean "shoot" and III *yrh*, always hiphil, to mean "direct, teach." G. Liedke and C. Petersen[36] succinctly present the three main resolutions of the relationship of these two roots. J. Wellhausen's thesis that III *yrh* "to teach" developed from I *yrh* "to throw" by its unique use in Josh 18:6, "to throw lots," is

27. *IBHS* §9.1.1.
28. *IBHS* §6.4.1.
29. *IBHS* §11.2.5.
30. *IBHS* §7.2.1.
31. *IBHS* §31.3.
32. BDB 434-35.
33. KBL 402-3.
34. GB 317-18.
35. F. Zorell, *Lexicon hebraicum et aramaicum Veteris Testamenti* (Rome, 1968), 329.
36. G. Liedke and C. Petersen, *THAT* 2:1031.

today generally abandoned.[37] W. Gesenius related the two roots through the notion "to stretch out the hand, the finger in order to point the way."[38] G. Oestborn[39] agrees. The third possibility is to separate them fully and normally to suggest that III *yrh* derives from Akkadian *(w)aru* "to lead."[40] Delitzsch thinks that *tôrâ* is a loanword from Akkadian *(tertu)* and *yrh* hiphil is then a denominative from *tôrâ*.[41] G. Liedke and C. Petersen draw the conclusion: "the question can only be advanced through the discovery of new materials." The use of the hiphil depends on that answer. III *yrh* hiphil may be used with the accusative, or, as here, absolutely. LXX paraphrases with *apekrinonto* "answered." B. Renaud[42] comments: "LXX 'answered,' apparently a little free, corresponds in fact to the exact function of the priest, who, consulted on a precise point of the law, had 'to give an answer.'" Presumably the *tôrâ* with its apodictic and casuistic laws is the understood object. Among their duties as ministers of sacred things the priests were custodians and administrators of the Law and had responsibility to keep the received Law available and alive for legal matters as they arose in the ongoing life of Israel (Deut 17:8-10; 33:10; Hos 4:6). Vg and Syr render literally by verbs meaning "to teach," but Aquila and Theod have *ephōtizon*, probably connecting it falsely with *'ôr* "light."

For *ûnĕbî'eyâ . . . yiqsōmû (and its prophets divine)* see 3:5-6. *kesep (money)* means "silver," not in its native state but as mined and smelted, and was the usual standard for trade. The conjunctive *waw* in *wĕ'al (and yet)* combines in a hendiadys the paradoxical activities of Israel's magistrates, priests, and prophets; *'al* is commonly used with the niphal of the root *š'n (lean upon),* a figure for "trust"[43] as the preposition through which that verb governs its object.[44] The object, *yhwh (I AM),* in its other uses results in salvation (cf. 2 Chr 13:18; 14:11[10]; 16:7, 8; Isa 10:20; cf. Isa 50:10). The subjects of the third masculine plural are the three subjects cited in 3:11A; the nonperfective denotes the persistent (present) aspect as in 3:11A; and the niphal is used as a double-status construction, "they lean themselves," with a benefactive nuance.[45] In the con-

---

37. J. Begrich, "Die priesterliche Tora," in *Werden und Wesen des Alten Testaments,* BZAW 66 (Berlin: Töpelmann, 1936), 68-69; G. Oestborn, *Tora in the Old Testament* (Lund: Ohlssons, 1945), 95-97.

38. GB 318a; cf. Gen 46:28; Ps 45:6(5); Prov 6:13.

39. Oestborn, *Tora in the Old Testament,* 4, 33, 169.

40. *The Assyrian Dictionary of the University of Chicago* (Chicago: University of Chicago Press, 1956), A/II, 313-16.

41. Cf. I. Engnell, *Israel and the Law* (Uppsala: Wretmans, 1946), 1-3.

42. *La Formation,* 140.

43. BDB 1043; cf. Isa 50:10.

44. *IBHS* §10.2.1.

45. *IBHS* §23.4.

struction *lēʾmōr (saying) lĕ* with the infinitive is epexegetical; 3:11Bb explains the circumstance or nature of the preceding action in 3:11Ba. The explanation is necessary, for Micah is not saying that these feckless leaders trust in *I AM* but that they profess to trust him.

hălôʾ (Is not) functions as in 2:7B, and the question expects a resounding affirmative answer. All versions interpret it as a question, except Syr, which, probably influenced by the meaning of *hlw/ʿalu* in Aramaic, opts for its other homographic variant *halu,* meaning "behold/indeed." *yhwh* (I AM) in the mouths of these sinners must be understood as an example of taking God's name to *šāwĕʾ* "vanity" (cf. Exod 20:7; Ps 139:20). In *bĕqirbēnû (among us) bĕqereb* is a frozen prepositional compound,[46] and the first common plural suffix in this direct discourse refers to the subjects of *yiśśāʿēnû.*

The adverb *lōʾ* links 3:11Bbα and 3:11Bbβ. The two clauses in these two versets on the surface structure are presented asyndetically and in parataxis, but in the deep structure 3:11Bbβ is in hypotaxis, namely, it expresses the result of their conviction that *I AM* is among them. The qal third feminine singular future nonperfective of the root *bôʾ* has *rāʿâ (evil)* as its subject (see 2:1, 3) and is transitive by means of the preposition *ʿālênû (upon us),* with the first common plural object referring to the blaspheming apostates. 3:11Ba and 3:11Bb are linked by "*I AM*" and "upon"; as they lean upon *I AM, I AM* will not allow evil to come upon them.

12   The logical particle *lākēn (therefore)* (cf. 3:6) links the sentence to the accusation and indicates that the former matches the latter. Israel's unholy magistrates built Zion/Jerusalem through injustice and, along with its debased spiritual leaders, substituted a professed faith in *I AM* for a living faith that seeks justice; therefore, the profaned city would be leveled. *biglalkem (on account of you),* a frozen prepositional compound consisting of inseparable *bĕ* and the noun *gālāl* and the second masculine plural pronominal suffix, attributes the fall of the city not to the impotence of *I AM* but to the *rāʾšê/qĕṣînê* "the magistrates," the antecedents to whom this prophecy is addressed in the second person in an *inclusio* of 3:9, 12. S. Schwantes[47] notes that the rest of v 12 "enjoys the distinction of being the only verse of the OT quoted *verbatim* by another OT writer, namely Jeremiah (Jer 26:18)." But that quotation adds here *kōh-ʾāmar yhwh ṣĕbāʾôt* "Thus says *I AM* of hosts," with *ṣĕbāʾôt* omitted in the shorter Greek version, and omits "therefore, on account of you." K. Budde, against all MSS and versions, conforms Mic 3:12 to the shorter Greek, but more probably the supporters of Jeremiah formally added what was always understood, namely, that *I AM* himself

---

46. Cf. *IBHS* §11.3.1.

47. Schwantes, "A Critical Study," 96.

stood behind the divine sentence, to underscore its authority and truth. B. Renaud[48] explains the additions and omissions of Jer 26:18:

> By this addition one is reminded that God himself expressed himself through the prophet's word, a fact that gave the prophet an incontestable authority. And it is on this very point that the controversy bore, because in Jer 26:18 "the chiefs and all the people told the priests and the prophets: this man is not liable to be put to death, because *it is in the name of YHWH our God that he spoke to us.* Likewise, Jeremiah retorts proudly in v 12: "It is YHWH who sent me to prophesy to this house and to this city all the words which you have heard" (cf. again v 15). Reporting only the sentence . . . and omitting the accusation that justified it, their citation avoids in a completely normal way taking up the words that link the accusation and the judicial sentence, "therefore, because of you." Thus all the peculiarities of Jer 26:18 with regard to Mic 3:12 are explained.

For *ṣîyôn (Zion)* see 3:10. GKC[49] interprets *śādeh (as a field)* as an accusative of result, which would be translated "into a field."[50] More probably it is an accusative of state specifying that Zion will be in the state of being a field.[51] Micah probably chose the adverbial accusative construction over a prepositional for the striking effect: "Zion a field . . . Jerusalem a heap of rubble." *śādeh*, as *tēḥārēš*, the verb it modifies, shows, has its sense of a cultivated field in contrast to pastureland. *tēḥārēš (will be plowed)* is an incomplete passive niphal[52] third feminine singular (see 3:11 for explanation of gender) future nonperfective.[53]

The conjunctive *waw* in *wîrûšālayim (and Jerusalem)* functions as a hendiadys. The three clauses in 3:12 present three aspects of Jerusalem's complex situation. As in 3:10 Jerusalem is not a distinct section of the city in contrast with Zion. *'îyîn (a heap of rubble)* is an Aramaic plural form of *'î* (cf. 1:6 and *'îyîm* in Jer 26:18; cf. Ps 79:1), a plural of extension looking at the rubble in all its complexity,[54] and from the root *'āwâ* "to twist, distort." Differences in style elsewhere in this book (cf. 3:9 versus 3:1) suggest that the form ought not to be made to conform to either 1:6 or Jer 26:18. Commenting on LXX's *opōrophylakion* for *'î*, B. Renaud[55] says: "This unfaithful translation perhaps wants to attenuate the

---

48. *La Formation*, 143.
49. GKC §121d.
50. Cf. *IBHS* §10.2.1.
51. *IBHS* §10.2.2.
52. *IBHS* §23.2.2.
53. *IBHS* §31.6.2.
54. *IBHS* §7.4.1.
55. *La Formation*, 141.

catastrophic effect of this sentence: Jerusalem remains at least a hut (cf. Isa 1:8, where *opōrophylakion* renders *mĕlûnâ*)." The qal third feminine singular future nonperfective of *hāyāh (will become)* probably has its active notion "become," as suggested by *lĕ* in the parallel *lĕbāmôt* with gapped *hyh. lĕ* is omitted from *ʿiyîn*, it was suggested, for the striking juxtaposition with *wîrûšālayim*.

The conjunctive *waw (and)* in *wĕhar* introduces yet another aspect of Jerusalem's plight. *har habbayit (the temple mount),* an attributive genitive,[56] is the cultic/theological center of the city. B. Renaud[57] says: "The prophet envisages the city as an essentially religious unit, finding its center in the sanctuary at the summit of the mountain." In contrast to 4:2, *yhwh* is omitted. Doubtless *har habbayit* refers to the temple (normally *bêt-yhwh "house of* I AM*"*), as Vg *(templi)* and Tg *(mqdš)* understood it. But their imprecision misses the subtle point of the original text, which omits *yhwh* not merely as a matter of style but to "desacralize it." B. Renaud[58] happily notes, "[The omission of *yhwh*] 'desacralizes' this holy place . . . : the temple, sanctuary of the divine presence, becomes a simple residence with regard to which God keeps all his freedom." In *lĕbāmôt (become a great high place)* the *lĕ* with gapped *hyh* means "become."[59] There is no need to emend *bāmôt* to the expected *bĕmôtê* "high places of" because, though the MT form could be a haplography from *y* falling out before *yāʿar*, Jer 26:18 confirms MT. A. Ehrlich,[60] followed by D. Hillers[61] and S. Schwantes,[62] mistakenly gives priority to Mic 5:8(7) and one MS over against the clear parallel in 1:6 and all other MSS and versions, and reads *bĕhāmôt yāʿar* "beasts of the field." The form in MT could be a plural construct as in Num 24:41, but more probably *yāʿar* is an accusative of location *(in a forest),* as is *haśśādeh* in 1:6, especially since the two sentences against Samaria and Jerusalem are so similar. For the meaning and form of *bāmôt* see 1:3 and 5. J. M. P. Smith[63] renders it by a countable plural, "mounds in a jungle," but that seems an unlikely predicate for the geographical singular subject "mountain." LXX *alsos* means "grove," but it may carry the nuances of "sacred wood" or "sacred enclosure." Sym and Theod allowed only a geographical sense, *hypsos* "height" and *bounon* "hill" respectively. The singular of these Greek versions does not confirm an original singular; they may represent a translator's choice. Vg re-

56. *IBHS* §9.5.3.
57. *La Formation,* 141.
58. *La Formation,* 141.
59. BDB 226, §II.2.d.
60. Ehrlich, *Randglossen zur hebräischen Bibel,* 5.
61. Hillers, *Micah,* 47.
62. Schwantes, "A Critical Study," 97-98.
63. Smith, *Micah,* 397.

tains the plural of MT. B. Renaud[64] says: "It seems scandalous that Jerusalem was transformed into a pagan high place. But it is difficult to give the exact interpretation of the thought of Micah." For the significance of *ya'ar (in a forest)* see the Exposition (189-90).

EXPOSITION

This judgment oracle has a classic form: addresses with an invitation to listen, accusation with development, and judicial sentence. The prophecy is addressed directly to the transgressors, with the exception that the accusation is developed in the third person (v 11). It is analyzed as follows:

I. Address in the second person: command to magistrates to listen (v 9A; cf. v 1A).
II. Accusation grafted onto address (vv 9B-10) and developed in the third person (v 11).
  A. Initial indictment of magistrates in the second person (vv 9B-10).
    1. General: they dislike and distort justice (v 9B).
    2. Specific: they build Jerusalem through deadly injustice (v 10).
  B. Explication of indictment in the third person against three groups of leaders: magistrates, priests, and prophets (v 11).
    1. First explication: they prostitute their offices for money (v 11A).
    2. Second explication: they justify themselves by substituting profession of faith for real faith (v 11B).
      a. their profession of faith in *I AM* in general (v 11Ba).
      b. a citation of their profession moving from cause, "Is not *I AM* in our midst?" to consequence, "No harm will happen to us" (v 11Bb).
III. Judicial sentence delivered in the second person to magistrates and introduced by "therefore": Zion to become desolate (v 12).

The primary indictment and its elaboration are linked by the repetition of *rā'šeyhā* "magistrates" (3:9A, 11A) and by the pronoun "its," referring back to Jerusalem/Zion. In addition to the logical particle "therefore," the accusation and sentence are linked by the second-person address, by the logical phrase "on account of you," and by the repetition of "Jerusalem/Zion" (3:10, 12). The accusation and sentence are also linked thematically: the corrupt leaders support

64. *La Formation,* 141.

themselves by the notion that the presence of *I AM* is in their midst. Micah retorts that *I AM* himself will destroy the concrete site of his presence, which gives them their false security.

This oracle of judgment shares many links with the preceding two in style and substance. With regard to style they share a similar length (four verses), a similar form consisting of address (3:1, 5, 9), accusation grafted onto address by relative participles (3:2, 5Ab-B, 9A) and developed by another form (*'ǎšer* in 3:3; 3:6Bb; and possibly infinitive absolute in 3:10), judicial sentence introduced by logical particles (3:4, 6, 12) and embellishing citations: by *I AM* (3:3, 6A) and by the corrupt leaders (3:11Bb). Only this oracle, however, shifts from second person to third person (v 11) and back to second. With regard to substance, all three are addressed to leaders in Jerusalem and indict them for corrupting justice for material gain. The three accusations convey an atmosphere of superficial security and calm, allowing, yes, even encouraging, people the freedom to pursue their base selfish interests and moneymaking. Their security is blasted by the judicial sentences.

Though independent, the three prophecies constitute a unity in which, as B. Renaud[65] has shown, there is a movement toward a climax in this third and final oracle: at the levels of address, of accusation, and of judicial sentence.

At the level of address, the first has in view the judicial magistrates, the second the prophets, and while the third is again principally against the magistrates, it adds prophets and priests so as to gather together for indictment the three principal institutions governing the theocracy.

At the level of accusation, Renaud[66] explains:

The first oracle denounces the shameless exploitation of the poor. The second the bribe required by the prophets. The third takes up the first accusation in v 10 and the second accusation in v 11, while widening it to all those responsible. But in addition, the third oracle brings in another motif that aggravates the guilt of these three responsible groups: the theological justification of such guilty behavior, a justification that leads to making one feel secure and to a closing of the heart before any appeal for conversion. Yet, it is this accusation that provokes the ultimate punishment: by destroying the temple, God will pull out from under the leaders of the people any pretext to justify themselves and to make themselves feel secure.

With regard to the level of judicial sentence, B. Renaud[67] continues:

65. *La Formation*, 141.
66. *La Formation*, 148.
67. *La Formation*, 148.

Ultimate punishment, we just said, because all along the development, the judicial sentence will become more and more severe: in the first oracle God contents himself with being silent; in the second, this silence becomes darkness. In the third, it becomes absence: by destroying the temple, God seems to abandon his people.

Such a grouping of what were probably originally at the preliterary level independent messages into a unified mosaic on the literary level intensifies and enriches the meaning of each oracle, and must have been the work of an editor. The anacrusis in 3:1 suggests that it is the work of Micah himself.

All agree that Micah authored these oracles. One cannot say, however, whether they were pronounced in the same situation and/or for the same occasion. The announcement of the fall of Jerusalem must be credited to a time in Hezekiah's reign before he initiated his reforms (cf. 2 Kings 18–20; Jer 26:18; 2 Chronicles 29–31) and before the prophetic promises to the repentant monarch that the Assyrian tyrant would not lay Jerusalem waste (cf. 1:8-16; Isaiah 36–37). Hezekiah's repentance and the turning aside of the threat serve as a classic illustration that if a nation that *I AM* had warned repented of its evil, then he would relent and not inflict on it the disaster he had planned (cf. Jer 18:8-10). On account of this implication, all judicial sentences are in effect threats (cf. Isa 1:18-19).

C. Westermann[68] noted that judgment oracles of the eighth and seventh centuries were directed to Israel or, as here, to organic groups within it. In Micah's language "Israel" refers to "all Israel" (see 1:5). Here Micah returns to the magistrates, the judicial leaders, but in the development of his accusation gathers together with them priests and prophets, the ecclesiastical leaders of the nation. L. Allen[69] noted that Isaiah specifies these men of influence: "hero and warrior, judge and prophet, soothsayer and elder, captain of fifty and man of rank, counselor, skilled craftsman and clever enchanter (Isa 3:2); to these Micah adds priests" (3:10). These men at the top echelon of Israel constituted the "corporate personality" of the nation, as the parallel in Jer 26:18 shows: "Micah . . . told all the people of Judah." What amazing grace prompts God to appeal to vile sinners to listen. This oracle of reproach extends hope to the sinful people that they can avert God's final and decisive judgment by repentance.

As in the first oracle Micah addresses the magistrates and rulers, but instead of beginning the accusation by noting their responsibility to know justice, he directly accuses them of detesting it, once again tracing the source of the problem

68. C. Westermann, *Basic Forms of Prophetic Speech* (Philadelphia: Westminster, repr. 1991), 169.

69. Allen, *Micah*, 317.

back to the magistrates' moral appetites (see 3:2; Isa 5:20; Matt 15:8-9). As Amos said: "You hate the one who reproves in court and despise him who tells the truth" (Amos 5:10). From their darkened hearts and deformed characters came distorted actions and detestable conduct: they twisted their upright laws (Exod 23:1-3, 6-8; Lev 19:13, 15; Deut 16:19; Amos 5:7, 10, 14-15; 6:12). Instead of being a covenant community bound in love to God and to one another and a theocracy under God's law, Israel had become an oligarchy under criminal tyrants.

As in other oracles of doom, Micah elaborates the general indictment (3:9B) with the specific charge that they built Jerusalem with deadly injustice (3:10). The Chronicler records the unusual building projects achieved under Hezekiah (2 Chr 32:27-29), who tried to model himself after Solomon and his renaissance. The Siloam tunnel, which brought water into the city and whose inscription commemorates this feat of engineering, still exists to corroborate Micah and the Chronicler. Under the protective umbrella of the temple, Jerusalem's "skyline" reached upward and its building projects flourished. Micah, however, instead of being caught up in the proud capital's élan and praising its businessmen for their bravery in adventuring capital and its architects for their brilliant engineering and sophisticated tastes, saw beneath the sham to the economic base: the exploitation of the weak. His condemnation, "building Zion with bloodshed and Jerusalem with injustice," recalls both 2:2, 9, where Micah accused the big landowners of appropriating the houses of defenseless people by unscrupulous actions, and 3:2-3, where he accused the magistrates of behaving like cannibals. Instead of upholding the sixth commandment, "you shall not take innocent life," those responsible to bestow the right to life on others took it from them. "Bloodshed" would have triggered in Micah's audience the truth that God requires payment in kind for shedding innocent blood (Gen 4:10; 9:6; Num 35:33; Deut 19:13; 21:9; 2 Sam 1:16; 4:11; 1 Kgs 2:32; 2 Kgs 9:7; Hab 2:12; 2 Chr 19:10). D. Hillers[70] rightly noted:

> Building the holy city, its fortifications, palaces, and temple, is a divine prerogative (Ps 51:20[EV 18] and 102:17[EV 16]), transferred in the visible kingdom to the ruler. As such, the action is potentially holy and right, as is judging, giving of priestly instruction, or prophecy. Abuse of the sacred is, however, the worst of transgressions.

More than a century earlier Elijah confronted Ahab for taking Naboth's vineyard through bloodshed (1 Kings 21), and about a century after Micah, Jeremiah lodged a similar accusation against Shallum son of Josiah (Jer 22:13-17). To se-

---

70. Hillers, *Micah*, 48.

cure bribes from Israel's greedy land barons, its venal magistrates perverted the legal system, which was designed to protect the innocent.

Micah now explicates his accusation in the third person, grouping magistrates, priests, and prophets together in accusing them of prostituting their sacred talents and offices for money. First he indicts the political rulers who were not oriented toward justice but toward money; they did not mete out the law according to its measure of justice but according to the measure of the bribe, and so perverted justice (Exod 23:8; Deut 10:17; 16:19; Prov 17:23; 21:14). The Law pronounced a curse on the man who accepted a bribe to kill an innocent person (Deut 27:25). These laws are unique. V. P. Hamilton[71] cites J. J. Finkelstein:[72] "'There is no known cuneiform law outlawing bribery specifically. . . . it (i.e., bribery) was not only a common practice, but was recognized as a legal transaction.'" Next Micah charges the religious leaders, priests, and prophets. *I AM* used three instruments in mediating his word to his theocracy (cf. Jer 18:18; Ezek 7:26): sages, who were members of Israel's ruling class and who gave counsel, priests, who taught the law (cf. Deut 17:10; 33:10; 2 Kgs 12:2[1]; Hos 4:6; Mal 2:7), and prophets, to whom he gave visions of divine mysteries. In Micah's day all three had been corrupted by the love of money, the root of all kinds of evil (1 Tim 6:10). Bribes blinded the officials to justice (cf. Isa 1:23; 5:23; 33:15); "honoraria and royalties," as we would say today, dictated where and what was taught by the priests, who evidently wanted to enrich themselves beyond their tithes; and money, a tempting danger to prophets (cf. Num 22:18; 1 Kgs 13:7; 2 Kgs 5:1-2; Neh 6:12-13), deluded the visions of prophets. Like some modern politicians, this unholy trinity regarded both their talents as opportunities to advantage themselves and disadvantage their trust, and their offices as prizes they had won rather than as positions from which to serve God and their fellowmen.

Micah brings his accusation to a climax by accusing all three hacks mentioned in 3:11A of audaciously justifying themselves by professing to trust *I AM*. Micah's citation of their professed faith and false security is important, for it shows that Micah is not saying that they lean upon *I AM* — were that true they would indeed be saved (see Exegesis, 180) — but rather that they claim to lean upon *I AM*. They had deluded themselves into a false faith. Like many in the church today, they think that by professing faith in Jesus Christ they have gained eternal life, but in fact they make empty professions and are headed for eternal damnation (cf. Matt 7:15-27). "What good is it," asks James, "if a man claims to have faith but has no deeds? Can such faith save him? . . . Faith by it-

---

71. V. P. Hamilton, *"shoḥad,"* TWOT 2:914.
72. J. J. Finkelstein, "Middle Assyrian *šulmānu* Texts," *JAOS* 72 (1952) 77-80.

self, if it is not accompanied by action, is dead. Show me your faith without deeds, and I will show you my faith by what I do" (Jas 2:14-18).

"Faith," says L. Allen,[73] "was perverted into a presumptuous, cocksure leaning upon God." They held their immunity from the true prophet's messages of reproach as unanswerable: "Is not *I AM* among us?" The temple on Mount Zion silently but incontestably seemed to support them. As a result they felt no contradiction and no pangs of conscience between their commitment to profit-making and their verbal commitment to *I AM*. They had immured themselves against repentance. Their half-baked and partisan theology was seemingly reinforced to later generations by history. When God spared the temple during Sennacherib's siege of Jerusalem, their false theology seemed vindicated (cf. Jeremiah 7). They justified themselves in the eyes of men, but God knew their hearts (Luke 16:15). L. Allen[74] comments: "If the most sacred institution was not serving its purpose but in the hands of religious perverts was acting as a barrier to God, of what further use could it be to him?"

Micah tries to blast them out of their complacency by predicting, once again in direct address, the destruction of the site that gave them their false sense of security. C. Westermann[75] notes that the announcement of judgment usually included both a statement about God's intervention and the results of the intervention; in 3:12 the LORD's intervention is assumed, only the result is stated. As in 3:6, "therefore" entails that the sentence will fit the crime. Their fine buildings in Jerusalem/Zion will become rubble, and the temple, which had once represented holiness and justice but now, "on account of you," had been profaned and represented injustice and had given them a false sense of security, will become an unholy forest. Their secret crimes, so covertly concealed in the courts under the ruse of justice, and their whitewashed preaching would be exposed for what they really were.

Space in the OT was divided into degrees of holiness. At the lowest level of holiness was the Holy Land itself in contrast to pagan lands. Within the Holy Land the forest was most unholy because there deadly and/or unclean wildlife ruled (cf. Isa 13:19-22; Jer 50:39; Zeph 2:13-15). The arable, tilled land, the source of life, was much more holy, and the city of Jerusalem, where God lived, was more holy still. At the summit of the city, symbolically closest to God, was Mount Zion, which was still more holy (cf. Psalms 15, 24), and on top of it stood the holy temple consisting of a series of courts representing even further gradations of holiness. The building itself with its holy place, where only elect priests

73. Allen, *Micah*, 255.
74. Allen, *Micah*, 255.
75. Westermann, *Basic Forms of Prophetic Speech*, 169.

could enter, was most holy, and finally the Most Holy Place, where only the High Priest could enter, and then only once a year and not without atoning blood, was the most holy of all. But when the Holy One forsook his temple, he reduced it to a pagan shrine in an unholy forest. The forest probably served as a metonymy for wild animals and death. D. Hillers,[76] though wrongly making an association with animals on textual rather than figurative grounds, rightly commented:

> That wild animals should live in the deserted city is a frequent theme of biblical literature. Thus, Isa 13:10-22; 34:11-17; Jer 50:39; Zeph 2:13-15 and also in other ancient Near Eastern literature. A passage from the first Sefire treaty (Sf IA 32-33, from ca. 750 B.C.) illustrates the use of this threat, and also the sequence: the city becomes a ruin-heap . . . , and then is infested by wild animals: "And may Arpad become a mound to [house the desert animal and] a gazelle and the fox and the hare and the wild-cat and the owl and the [] and the magpie."

A similar sort of judgment can be observed in closed churches that once housed the holy Word of God and the holy sacraments; on account of apostasy they now house profane theaters, or museums, or even false religions.

The sentence against Jerusalem resembles that against Samaria: all signs of worship — the idols in 1:6, the temple in 3:12 — will disappear, and in their place will be a "heap of rubble" and "fields." The Lord Jesus likewise threatened the fall of the temple (Luke 24) after denouncing priests who for self-advantage taught the Law in such a way that it prevented people from entering the kingdom of God (Luke 23; cf. also Jer 7:1-15). L. Allen[77] wrote:

> Micah's words, remembered for their shocking severity a hundred years later, deserve to be taken to heart by each generation of God's people. They challenge every attempt to misuse the service of God for one's own glory and profit. They are a dire warning against the complacency that can take God's love and reject his lordship. They are a passionate plea for consistency between creed and conduct. The Lord is content with nothing else.

76. Hillers, *Micah*, 48.
77. Allen, *Micah*, 321.

B. New Jerusalem and the Remnant Exalted over the Nations (4:1-8)

1. Jerusalem Exalted over the Converted Nations (4:1-5)

1   And it shall come to pass in the latter days
that the mountain of the house of *I AM*
        will remain established as the highest mountain,
    and it will remain lifted up above the hills,
and nations will flow [to it and walk] upon it.

2   And many nations will come
        and say, "Come and let us go up to the mountain of *I AM*,
            and to the house of the God of Jacob,
        that he may teach us from his ways,
            so that we may walk in his ordained paths."
    For the Law will go forth from Zion,
        and the word of *I AM* from Jerusalem.

3   And he will judge among many nations,
        and he will reprove powerful [and] far-off nations.
    And they will beat their swords into hoes,
        and their spears into pruning knives.
    Nation will not lift up sword against nation,
        and they will no longer learn to wage war.

4   And each man will sit under his own vine
            and under his own fig tree
        with none terrifying him.
    For the mouth of *I AM* of hosts has spoken.

5   Although all peoples walk,
        each one, in the name of his god,
    we will walk in the name of *I AM* our God forever and ever.

EXEGESIS

Instead of treating in isolation the textual differences between the synoptic passages of Mic 4:1-3 and Isa 2:2-4, I am collecting them here, citing Micah first, and considering their differences throughout. (1) *nākôn* "established" occurs at the end of Mic 4:1Aαβ and at the beginning of Isa 2:2A; (2) *hû'* in Mic 4:1Ab is deleted in Isaiah. (3) *'ālāyw* "upon it" is found in Mic 4:1B but *'ēlāyw* in Isa 2:2B; (4) *kol* is deleted in Mic 4:1 *contra* Isa 2:2B; (5) *'ammîm . . . gôyîm* in Mic 4:1-2 and in 4:3A are reversed in Isa 2:2-3 and in 2:4A; (6) *wĕ'el-bêt* occurs in Mic 4:2A but *'el-bêt* in Isa 2:3A; (7) *wĕyôrēnû* is found in Mic 4:2A but *wĕyōrēnû* in Isa 2:3A; (8) *'ammîm rabbîm . . . lĕgôyim 'ăṣūmîm* appears in Mic 4:3A but *hagôyim . . . lĕ'ammîm rabbîm* in Isa 2:4A; (9) *'ad-rāḥôq* in Mic 4:3A is deleted in Isa 2:4A; (10) *harĕbôtêhem* occurs in Mic 4:3A but *harĕbôtām* in Isa 2:4A; (11) *yiś'û* is found in Mic 4:3A but *yiśśā'* in Isa 2:4A; (12) *yilmĕdûn* appears in Mic 4:3A but *yilmĕdû* in Isa 2:4A; (13) Mic 4:4 is deleted in Isaiah. (14) Mic 2:5 and Isa 4:5 resemble one another but differ in their formulation and intention.

These versions represent differing final texts both in style and in substance and for the most part should not be harmonized or used to reconstruct an original text from which both derived.[1]

1   *wĕhâyâ (It shall come to pass)* has a deictic temporal function,[2] and *hāyâ* has its active sense "to happen." It is specified by the temporal adverbial prepositional phrase *bĕ'ahărît hayyāmîm* "in the latter days" — an unusual word order; normally *bĕ'ahărît* stands at the end of a sentence, not as the initial formula of a prophecy. *hāyâ*, to judge from the rest of the oracle, has its active sense "come to pass." The syntagma *bĕ'ahărît hayyāmîm (in the latter days)* consists of the temporal *bêt* marking an actual time "at/in";[3] and of the abstract feminine noun *'ahărît*, which means "end," "outcome," or the continuance of a family or people, "children," "descendants," "remnant"; and of the partitive genitive *yāmîm* "of days." The syntagma, which occurs fourteen times, is "a prophetic phrase denoting the final period of history so far as the speaker's perspective reaches."[4] It is not a technical expression for the end of history, the last days of historical time. Rather, the content of the envisioned future varies: for example, of Israel's breaking covenant and acting corruptly (Deut 31:29), of their return to I AM afterward (Deut 4:30; Hos 3:5), of hardship followed by prosperity for Israel, Moab, or Elam (Jer 48:47; 49:39; Ezek 38:16), of Israel's enemies overcome (Num 24:14), and of the tribes established in the sworn land (Gen 49:1). There is a certain thickness to the expression; for example, in Daniel (cf. 10:14) it includes the activities of three kings of Persia, Alexander and his successors, their various struggles, and then the "vile person" of 11:21. R. L. Harris[5] says: "It denotes 'latter days' in comparison to the present. . . . The phrase seems to mean 'the future.' All eschatology of course is future. But all of the prophets' future was not eschatology." E. Lipiński[6] said:

1. See B. K. Waltke, "Aims of OT Textual Criticism," *WTJ* 51 (1989) 102-7.
2. *IBHS* §32.26.
3. *IBHS* §10.2.5.
4. BDB 31.
5. R. L. Harris, "The Last Days in the Bible and Qumran," in *Jesus of Nazareth: Saviour and Lord,* ed. C. F. H. Henry (Grand Rapids: Eerdmans, 1966), 75-76.
6. E. Lipiński, "*B'hryt hymym* dans les Textes Preéxiliques," *VT* 20 (1970) 445.

"Today it is admitted that its primary sense is: 'in days to come' and not 'in the last days.'" G. W. Buchanan[7] explains LXX's rendering, *ep' eschatōn tōn hēmerōn*, thus:

> Because *eschatos* seemed the most suitable translation of *b'ḥryt* in the majority of cases, the translators mechanically employed *eschatos* in the same capacity when translating *bĕ'aḥărît hayyāmîm*. Modern Bible students should not be misled by the word *eschatos* in this expression and should not read eschatological meanings into contexts which do not anticipate any kind of an end, but only future time.

The syntagma designates a future that is not presently discernible, the hiddenness of the future things, more clearly than *hinnēh yāmîm bā'îm* "behold, days are about to happen," and it points to a new epoch, which, though it lies in the hidden future, comprehensively alters time and is the goal or outcome toward which an event is striving.

LXX reads Mic 4:1ΑαΒ: *emphanes to oros tou kyriou, hetoimon epi tas koryphas tōn oreōn* "the mountain of the Lord will be manifest, prepared on the tops of the mountains." Scholars differ in explaining LXX. T. J. Meek[8] suggests that it read, instead of *yihyeh*, a form of *yḥzh* "shall be seen." H. Wildberger[9] thinks that LXX rendered *nākôn* twice, at first by *hetoimon* at the place where it is found in Micah and then by *emphanes* at the place where it is found in Isaiah. In that case *yihyeh* would have been missing in LXX of Micah. B. Renaud[10] rejects the solution because "if *nkwn* is rendered several times *hetoimon* . . . it is never rendered by *emphanes*." Renaud suggested that LXX wanted to vary the style between *wĕhāyâ* and *yihyeh*. In sum, LXX is too debatable to reconstruct a differing Hebrew *Vorlage*. Besides, *yihyeh* is attested in Mur 88 and in 1QIsa. K. Marti,[11] H. Wildberger,[12] and D. Hillers[13] omit *bêt-yhwh* from the construct chain, *har bêt-yhwh (the mountain of* I AM's *house)*. H. Wildberger alleges that MT presents a *hapax legomenon,* and D. Hillers points to LXX's reading of Isa 2:2, *to oros kyriou kai ho oikos tou theou,* as a conflate reading that points to early variants of the introductory line. It is also argued that in the following verses it

7. G. W. Buchanan, "Eschatology and the 'End of Days,'" *JNES* 20 (1961) 190-91.

8. T. J. Meek, "Some Emendations in the Old Testament," *JBL* 48 (1929) 162-73.

9. H. Wildberger, "Die Völkerwallfahrt zum Zion: Jes. 2:1-5," *VT* 7 (1957) 63 n. 2; cf. also Hillers, *Micah*, 49.

10. *La Formation*, 152.

11. K. Marti, *Jesaja*, KHC 13 (Tübingen: Mohr, 1900), 25.

12. H. Wildberger, "Die Völkerwallfahrt zum Zion," 63 n. 2.

13. Hillers, *Micah*, 49.

is not a question of the height of the temple but of the mountain. Renaud,[14] however, defends MT:

> In fact, the expression "the mountain of the temple of YHWH" is attested again in 2 Chr 33:15. By disassociating house and mountain, the Greek text of Isaiah appears to be a facilitating reading of a somewhat heavy expression. Moreover, it is not precise to say that in what follows there is no mention again of the temple hill, because Mic 4:2B gives us the parallel: "let us go up to the mountain of YHWH, to the house of the God of Jacob." . . . The Greek text of Micah could have come from a simplification of the Greek text of Isaiah. In any case, the term *byt* is attested by the MT of Isaiah and of Micah, Syr, Vg, as well as the Tg. . . . Mur 88 is laconic here. One must therefore preserve the reading of Mic 4:1A at least as *lectio difficilior*.

1QIsa also supports MT. *bêt* may be a genitive of inalienable possession (i.e., "mountain" is intrinsically proper to the "temple"), and *yhwh* is a genitive of possession.[15] *nākôn (will remain established)*, a niphal masculine singular participle of *kûn*, is a predicate adjective with *yihyeh*, a construction signifying durative aspect.[16] The periphrasis underscores the concrete meaning of *kûn*: "to be firm, fixed, established." In the adverbial phrase *bĕrōʾš hehārîm (as the highest mountain)* the *bêt* is *essentiae* (i.e., in the role/capacity of),[17] and the masculine singular *rōʾš* "head, top, chief" is in construct with the definite masculine plural noun *hehārîm*, a superlative genitive.[18] D. Hillers[19] objects to construing *bĕ* as *bêt essentiae* because "the common *rōʾš* (singular or plural) *hāhār* (singular or plural) seems everywhere to mean 'mountaintop(s).'" But his analysis fails to distinguish between the singular construct and a plural of similar meaning and to take into account that the subject is . . . *har . . . yhwh*.

The thought that Mount Zion will be on the top of the mountains seems unnatural. Rather, the point seems to be that *I AM's* mountain will be established as the chief mountain by its height, as the parallel clarifies. This geological upheaval, making Mount Zion the center of the earth, has the symbolic significance that it, and the God worshipped there, will be established as the true place of worship in contrast to pagan temple-mountains that rival it. H. Wolff[20]

14. *La Formation*, 151.
15. *IBHS* §9.5.1.
16. *IBHS* §37.7.1; Joüon, *Grammaire* §121e.
17. *IBHS* §11.2.5.
18. *IBHS* §9.5.3.
19. Hillers, *Micah*, 49.
20. Wolff, *Micha*, 91.

says: "It expresses an indirect polemic against other divine mountains, as they are known to us from Ugarit to Mesopotamia."

The temple mountain in ancient Near Eastern religions symbolized several theological notions.[21] First, it symbolized a god's victory over chaos. Sometimes it was associated with the primordial hill that emerged out of the chaotic waters. The god who vanquished the powers of Chaos built a temple on a mountain to secure his victory. In Egypt the possession of the primeval hill substantiated a temple's claim to antedate all other holy places. In Mesopotamia the construction of the Esagila, the principal temple of Babylon, was associated with Marduk's conquest of the powers of Chaos, namely, Tiamat and Kingu. Second, the divine mountain, which was sometimes invisible above the clouds, claimed to provide access into heaven itself. Some temples (e.g., the step pyramids in Egypt and the ziggurats in Mesopotamia) took the shape of a huge stairway leading into the heavens. The ziggurat of Larsa bore the name "House of the Bond between Heaven and Earth," the temple at Sidon was called "Heaven on Earth," and the one at Heliopolis "Heaven of Egypt." Third, it symbolized the god's presence with his people; his presence became a reality by placing his house on an earthly mountain. R. E. Clements[22] thinks that in these religions the universe was "a gigantic world-mountain, stretching from the entrance of the subterranean abyss to the highest point of heaven, and embracing all the inhabited world. In this way it linked on a vertical axis the three components of the cosmos, the underworld below, the earth above it, and the heavens above the earth. A real mountain was therefore a fitting symbol for such a god, and expressed the belief that his power extended across all the territory where men dwelt." But R. J. Clifford[23] counters that the imposing peaks of the mountains led people to think of them as the focal point of only the surrounding lowlands.

Whether the divine mountain in pagan religions symbolized universal or local dominion, in OT theology Zion, the divine mountain of the sovereign Creator of all the universe, symbolized his universal kingdom (cf. Ps 68:15-18). In this text its summit is higher than any other mountain, showing that *I AM's* rule extends throughout the whole earth. When the pagan nations in the names of their gods subjugated Mount Zion, however, *I AM* appeared in their eyes impotent and their gods were validated by them as the true cosmic deities ruling the forces of Chaos. In the latter days toward which history is striving, Israel's

---

21. Cf. O. Keel, *The Symbolism of the Biblical World: Ancient Near Eastern Iconography and the Book of Psalms* (New York: Seabury, 1978), 113.

22. R. E. Clements, *God and Temple* (Philadelphia: Fortress, 1965).

23. R. J. Clifford, *The Cosmic Mountain in Canaan and the Old Testament*, HSM 4 (Cambridge, Mass.: Harvard University Press, 1972), 9-11.

religion will be established as the true and universal religion in their eyes as its temple mountain soars high above all its rivals.

wĕniśśāʾ (and it will remain lifted up), which introduces 4:1Ab, could be either a *waw*-conjunctive with a niphal masculine singular participle of *nśʾ* with a gapped *yihyeh*, or a *waw*-relative with a niphal third masculine singular perfect, "and so it will be lifted up," as in LXX *(kai meteōristhēsetai)*. The parallel in 4:1B, *wĕnāhǎrû*, supports the latter, but the closer parallel with *nākôn* in v 4Aa favors the former. The conjunctive has an emphatic notion, which is the function of the parallel in 4:1B. The pronoun *hûʾ*, with the head word *har bêt-yhwh* in 4:1A, is pleonastic and so also emphatic. The *mem* in *miggĕbāʿôt (above the hills)* is comparative, validating that *rōʾš hehārîm* is a comparative superlative. *gbʿ* "hill," according to V. P. Hamilton,[24] is smaller than a mountain and most often refers to a place of illicit worship.

The *waw* in *wĕnāhǎrû (and . . . will flow)* is a *waw*-relative: as a result of Mount Zion's gravitational height peoples will "flow/stream" to it. Worshippers "flowed" by boats on the Euphrates to worship at Babylon, the rival of Jerusalem (Jer 51:44), the only other place where the verb occurs. Probably as a polemic against that pagan practice, Micah employs the verb figuratively to describe the pilgrimages of the nations to Mount Zion. The ancients, not understanding the polemical intention of the figure, were bothered by it. LXX dissolves the figure with *speusousi* "they will hasten" in Micah and *hēxousin* "they will move forward" in Isaiah, followed by the Syr "will turn around," a more neutral reading. Vg faithfully reads *fluent*. Whereas in Isaiah the nations are seen simply as coming *ʾēlāyw*, in Micah the pregnant preposition *ʿālāyw ([and walk] upon it)*[25] demands adding the verb of movement *hlk* "to walk." In contrast to *gôy* "nation," which denotes a territorial and political affinity of people, *ʿam* "people" is used more frequently to denote consanguinity and common racial parentage. Isaiah and Micah, who reverse these terms, probably intend no sharp differentiation between them. Isaiah underscores the universality of worship by adding *kōl* (cf. 4:5Aa).

2 The *waw*-relative with the qal third masculine plural suffix conjugation in *wĕhālûkû (and . . . will come)* represents a situation not (con)sequential to *wĕnāhǎrû* in 4:1B but to that of 4:1A. 4:2 epexegetes the situation in 4:1A, for they must be motivated to go to the heavenly mountain before they will stream and walk upon it. The dischronologization between 4:1A and 4:2A argues against the opinion that they are parallels. The important verb *hlk* occurs three times in this verse, the first two concretely, the last metaphorically. The move-

24. V. P. Hamilton, *"gibʿâ,"* TWOT 1:147.
25. Cf. GKC §119ee.

ment in space from their pagan environs to the Mount of *I AM* matches their movement from their pagan religious "ways" to the religion and ethics of the "ways" of *I AM*. The masculine plural attributive adjective *rabbîm* in *gôyîm rabbîm (great nations)* can mean "many" (a crowd, as in Exod 23:2) or "great" (vast in extent and quantity). If it precedes the noun it must mean "many," but not necessarily so when it follows.[26] The parallel, *'ăṣûmîm*, in 4:3Ab favors "great," and the use of *rabbîm* with *špṭ* in 4:3Aa suggests that great nations are afflicting weak ones. Instructively Micah reproves "powerful nations" in 4:3Ab. Isaiah achieves the notion of extensiveness by inserting *kol* "all." Probably, the use of the synonyms *'ammîm* and *gôyîm* in 4:1A and 4:2A, and especially in 4:3A, also underscores the inclusiveness of the vision: a mighty throng will make pilgrimage to Mount Zion.

wĕ'āmĕrû (and they will say), which is represented as a successive situation, discloses the hearts of the nations as being regenerate and holy, and so they can walk upon the divine mountain. Micah frequently uses dramatic quotations to bring home the truth vividly and with immediacy. The qal masculine plural imperative *lĕkû (come)* shows that the next form is volitional, not nonperfective, and emphasizes it: *wĕna'ăleh (let us go up)*, a qal cohortative first common plural of *'lh*. The geographical movement from the surrounding lowlands up the mountain symbolizes the movement toward God and heaven. H. Wolff[27] says that *'lh* is a technical term for making a pilgrimage to Jerusalem as in Jer 31:6; Zech 14:17; Ps 122:4. He also notes that the expression "God of Jacob" in the parallel verset occurs nowhere else in the prophet, but it does appear frequently in the psalms of Zion (46:8[7], 12[11]; 76:7[6]; 84:9[8]) and other songs involving the cult (Pss 20:2[1]; 75:10[9]; 81:2[1], 5[4]; 94:7; cf. further 114:7; 146:5; also Exod 3:6, 15-16; 4:5; 2 Sam 23:1). He concludes: "We find ourselves in a cultic tradition." The preposition *'el (to)* marks their direction. In the construct *har-yhwh (the mountain of I AM)* the genitive is either a genitive of possession or more specifically a genitive of inalienable relationship[28] (see 4:1). Due to haplography the first phrase, *'el-har-yhwh*, suffers dittography in 1QIsa.

The *wāw* with *wĕ'el (and to)* is either emphatic "even" or, more probably, a hendiadys introducing another aspect of the situation. The two prepositional phrases unpack the compound chain "mountain of the house of *I AM*" in 4:1. In the construct chain *bêt 'ĕlōhê ya'ăqōb (the house of the God of Jacob) 'ĕlōhê* is a genitive of possession and *ya'ăqōb* is a genitive of relationship. Both phrases make perfectly clear that the nations have access to *I AM*, the true and living

---

26. *IBHS* §12.3.1.1.
27. Wolff, *Micha*, 92.
28. *IBHS* §9.5.1.

God, through Israel, his priestly nation (cf. Exod 19:6). The nations' confession of faith implies that true Israel is now on the scene. The *wāw* with the hiphil third masculine singular nonperfective of the root *yrh* with the verbal suffix first common plural indicates purpose.[29] For the meaning of *yrh* see 3:11. The third masculine singular has *yhwh/ʾĕlōhê yaʿăqōb* as its subject. LXX has the plural *deixousin* ("they will show" = *wyrwnw* with a transposition of *wāw* and *rêš* as in 1QIsa), either with an impersonal sense equivalent to "one," or with "mountain" and "house" as subjects. LXX in Isaiah rightly has *anangelai* with clear reference to *I AM*. The action should probably be understood as being mediated through his priests (cf. 3:11).

The *mêm* in *middĕrākāyw (from his ways)* is not partitive (= "some of his ways"),[30] but ablative, designating that their learning originates and derives from "his ways." *Mêm* should not be ignored, as in LXX, or emended to *bĕ*, as by F. Delitzsch.[31] The third masculine singular pronominal suffix with reference to *I AM* is a genitive of possession. "Ways" is a metaphor for the conduct of Israel's merciful King, and the countable plural sums up his behavior as known in the *torah* and the prophetic insights based on it, as suggested by the parallel in 4:2B. His ways include his gracious acts in history and his requirements (cf. Pss 18:22-23[21-22]; 25:4), both of which are summed up in 6:3-8. *wĕnēlĕkâ (so that we may walk)*, a conjunctive *wāw* with qal first common plural cohortative, expresses purpose.[32] The great nations resolve to go up to Jerusalem so that *I AM* might teach them his ways and they might walk in them. In *bĕʾōrĕḥōtāyw (in his paths)* *bĕ* indicates the sphere in which they walk, a metaphor for conduct. B. Renaud[33] complains that MT in both Isaiah and Micah is "doubtless badly punctuated" because he thinks that the form in MT must mean "caravans/conducted tours" and therefore must be repointed *ʾōrĕḥōtayw*. He overlooks, however, the use of *ʾōrĕḥōt* for "paths" in Isa 3:12; Pss 25:4; 119:15; Prov 3:6; 22:25). Apparently, *ʾōrĕḥōt* is a bi-form of *ʾorḥōt*. *tribois* is omitted in LXX of Isa 2:3. According to K. Koch,[34] *ʾōrĕḥōtāyw* is not a precise synonym with *dĕrākāyw*, for "the OT can speak of Yahweh's own *derekh*, while apparently it can speak of Yahweh's *ʾorach* only when it means an *ʾorach* which God has ordained for man (Ps 44:19[18])." If that be so, the genitive is a genitive of authorship. "They expect from Yahweh's instruction," says H. Wolff,[35] "not general information but a concrete 'going in his paths.'"

---

29. T. O. Lambdin, *Introduction to Biblical Hebrew* (New York: Scribner, 1971), 107.
30. So S. J. Schwantes, "A Critical Study of the Text of Micah," 104.
31. Cited by Schwantes, "A Critical Study," 104.
32. *IBHS* §34.5.2.
33. *La Formation*, 152.
34. K. Koch, *"derekh,"* TDOT 3:281.
35. Wolff, *Micha*, 92.

The direct address ends at 4:2A because the first person is lost at 4:2B. The logical particle *kî (for)* introduces the reason for the nations' resolve to make pilgrimage: they can count on the fact that *the Law will go forth from* exalted *Zion*, giving them assurance that it will lead them out of their perplexity and war. In *miṣṣîyôn (from Zion)* the parallel *mêm* is again ablative, and Zion is parallel to "mountain of Yahweh" and "house of the God of Jacob."

Qal third feminine singular future nonperfective *tēṣēʾ (will go forth)* develops further the parallels "he may teach us . . . so that we may walk." The movement, however, is reversed. As the nations first went *(hlk)* and made pilgrimage up to the mountain of *I AM (ʾel-har-yhwh),* now, bearing his Law *(tôrâ),* they move out from Mount Zion *(miṣṣîyôn tēṣēʾ).* The *tôrâ (Law),* the parallel to "his ways" and "his paths," revealed both *I AM'*s gracious acts and his requirements for the elect, who worship him.

In *ûdĕbar-yhwh (and the word of* I AM*)* the *wāw* is conjunctive. As noted in 3:11, priests preserved and interpreted the Law; "the word of *I AM*" refers to the activity of prophets (cf. 1:1; Jer 18:18; Ezek 33:30; Amos 3:1), who interpreted and molded history through divine insights from the perspective of the covenant. For *mîrûšālāyim (from Jerusalem)* see 3:10, where "Zion" and "Jerusalem" are also parallel.

3 In *wĕšāpaṭ (and he will judge),* the *wāw* is a consequential relative; the qal third masculine singular, like the third masculine singular suffixes in 4:2, has "*I AM*" as the antecedent (see 4:2) of the root *špṭ* (see 3:1, 8, 9). Syr takes *tôrâ* as the subject, perhaps to avoid anthropomorphism, but Tg, which has a more pronounced tendency in this direction, clearly reads *ydyn. špṭ* entails contending nations, in which an oppressor is disadvantaging another by its strength. By his word, which gives insight into his Law, as announced in 4:2A, *I AM* adjusts grievances among the nations. *bên (among)* is a manifold locative.[36] For *ʿammîm* see 4:1A, and for *rabbîm* see 4:2A.

wĕhôkîaḥ (and he will reprove) is a *wāw*-relative signifying the results of the judging, third masculine singular with *I AM* as subject, and an unclassified hiphil of the root *ykḥ,* which means "to establish what is right" and which is often in parallel with *špṭ* (cf. Isa 11:3, 4; Hab 1:12; Job 22:4; 23:4). The *lĕ* with *lĕgôyim* after *ykḥ* is either ethical,[37] "on behalf of" (= decide for), as in Isa 11:4, or, more probably, with "strong nations" the object, "against," as in Prov 9:7, 8; 15:12; 19:25; Job 32:12 (= reprove, correct). The attributive adjective *ʿaṣûmîm* can denote "numerous masses," and in that sense may be parallel to a possible meaning of *rabbîm.* It can also suggest "might," "strength," which is probably

36. *IBHS* §11.2.6.
37. *IBHS* §11.2.10.

the case here, both because its parallel *rabbîm* in 4:3Aa probably has this sense and because as a result of *I AM*'s judging and reproving in 4:3A the military powers transform their weapons of war into instruments of peace. Micah also probably has in mind the power of God's Law/word, which can resolve conflicts. *'ad-rāḥôq (far-off)*, literally, "to a distance," though missing in Isa 2:24, and allegedly overloading the verset, is attested in all MSS and versions, including R, which uses a vocabulary much closer to the parallel text in Isaiah than to the Greek text of Micah, and underscores that *I AM*'s word effects peace universally. Nevertheless, D. Hillers[38] proposes that MT reflects a conflation of two alternatives: *gôyim 'ăṣumîm* "mighty nations" and *gôyim 'ad-rāḥôq (far-off nations)* (cf. *gôy rāḥôq* in Joel 4:8[3:8] and *gôy mimmerḥoq* in Jer 5:15; cf. Jer 31:10 and the adjectival use of the prepositions in Isa 5:26 and Jer 23:23). His discussion is helpful in showing that the prepositional phrase is adjectival. Even as *gôyim rabbîm* in 4:2A is an advance on simple *'ammîm* in 4:1A, so also *lĕgôyim 'ăṣūmîm 'ad-rāḥôq* is an advance on *'ammîm rabbîm*.

The *wāw*-relative in *wĕkittĕtû (and they will beat)* introduces the consequences in 4:3B from the situation in 4:3A. *kittĕtû* is a resultative piel[39] third masculine plural with *'ammîm rabbîm/gôyim 'ăṣūmîm* as its subject; it is of the root *ktt* "to beat/hammer." Its definite object is the feminine plural *ḥarbōtêhem* with the masculine plural possessive genitive suffix. In *lĕ'ittîm (into hoes) lĕ* is quasi-allative, stating the goal of the action, and *'ittîm* is the masculine plural of the root *'ēt*. S. T. Byington[40] interprets this root to mean "hoe," not "plowshare," because: "first, it could be made into a sword [cf. Joel 4:10(3:10)] with less change of shape than the plowshare; secondly, it might offer the more appropriate quantity of metal for a sword." Byington also argues that primitive Israel lacked plowshares and that a later tradition interpreted *'ēt* as plowshare because in the course of time it replaced the hoe.

waḥănîtōtêhem lĕmazmērôt (and their spears into pruning knives) is another concrete synecdoche for the same transformation. *ḥănîtōtêhem* is a feminine plural of *ḥănît*, a spear, a short lethal weapon capable of being thrown (1 Sam 18:11; 20:33) and whose butt could also be lethal (2 Sam 2:23). V. P. Hamilton[41] notes: "Most frequently, this weapon is mentioned as being Saul's personal weapon. . . . Possibly this signifies authority. Thus, in Ugaritic text 125:47 the son of King Krt on an important mission carries his spear, presumably as a mark of royal status." Goliath also had his spear (1 Sam 17:7; 21:9[8]; 1 Chr 20:5). "Sword and spear" rep-

---

38. Hillers, *Micah*, 50.
39. *IBHS* §24.3.2.
40. S. T. Byington, "Plow and Pick," *JBL* 68 (1949) 52.
41. V. P. Hamilton, "*ḥānît*," *TWOT* 1:300.

resent the entire military arsenal (1 Sam 17:47). *mazmērâ* is a pruning knife (Isa 18:5). The two concrete images, which are taken from blacksmith shops where swords were forged into hoes and spears into pruning knives, serve as comprehensive synecdoches for the transition from war to peace.

lō'-yiśś 'û (will not lift up) is a qal third masculine plural nonperfective of the root *nś'* (see 4:1), with the singular subject *gôy (nation)*. All the versions and Isaiah have a singular verb, which is grammatically "correct." MT of Micah, however, reflects an *ad sensum* agreement that is also acceptable Hebrew (cf. *wĕyāšĕbû* with *'îš* in 4:4).[42] MT is validated in 4:3Abβ. LXX renders Isaiah by *ou lēpsetai* "will not take," and Micah by *ouketi mē antarē* "will not lift up anymore." Since 4:3Ab does not advance the situation in 4:3Aa but emphasizes it by a negative complement, the tense reverts to the nonperfective. *gôyim* "nations" in 4:3A is broken down distributively in 4:3B. In the prepositional phrase *'el-gôy (against nation)* ethical *'el* has a sense of disadvantage.[43] The negative complement in 4:3Ab parallels the plural *ḥarbōt* "swords" with the singular *ḥereb (sword)*.

The conjunctive *wĕlō' (and . . . not)* introduces another negative complement. The *paragogic nun* with qal third masculine plural of the root *lmd (they will . . . learn)*, which is missing in Isaiah, may denote the certainty of the vision.[44] Isaiah also has a plural here, validating the *ad sensum* plural in 4:3Abα. The negative adverb *lō'* modifies the adverb *'ôd*,[45] the combination meaning "no more" as in Gen 17:5; 32:29; etc. *milḥāmâ (to wage war)* is rendered by an infinitive for good English style as in LXX *(polemein)* and Vg *(belligerare)*; Syr and Tg reflect Hebrew idiom and retain the noun.

4 The *wāw*-relative *wĕyāšĕbû (and they will sit)* with the qal third masculine plural of *yšb* introduces a consequence flowing from transforming the implements of war into instruments of peace and its negative complement that war, yes, even learning how to wage war, will cease. The verb *yšb* "sit" shifts the scene from one of movement in 4:2-3 to one of settled peace in 4:4. Again (cf. *yiśś 'û* in 4:3Abα) the verb is in *ad sensum* agreement with the singular subject. As *gôy . . . gôy* in 4:3Abα broke down *gôyim* of 4:2A and 4:3A into individuals, so *'îš (man)* (cf. 2:11) breaks down *gôy* even further to each of its individuals. The pronominal suffix in the prepositional phrase *taḥat gapnô (under his own vine)* is possessive. The *gepen* "vine" (always grape-bearing except in 2 Kgs 4:39)[46] figures prominently in Israel as a symbol of God's blessing (Deut 8:8; Hos 2:14[12], 17[15]) and as a major source of income (1 Kgs 21:1-4). Assyrian reliefs symbolize Israel by the vine.

42. GKC §145c.
43. *IBHS* §11.2.2.
44. *IBHS* §31.7.1.
45. *IBHS* §39.3.2.
46. BDB 172.

The *wāw* in *wĕtahat*, the parallel prepositional phrase *(under his own fig tree)*, is conjunctive. Judging from modern times and Luke 13:6, fig trees were often planted in vineyards, and sometimes vines grew among fig trees so that one could sit under both at the same time. "More often than not," says R. F. Youngblood,[47] "the fig is mentioned together with the grapevine in the OT." According to H. Wolff:[48] "Grapes and figs are the most costly fruits of the land." The concrete synecdoche depicts every person enjoying God's blessing of lasting peace and prosperity in security, without the fear of danger (2 Kgs 18:31; Isa 36:16; Joel 2:22).

In the phrase *wĕ'ên mahărîd (with none terrifying [him])* the disjunctive *wāw* is circumstantial,[49] with *'ên* as a clausal adverb in the construct state in a verbless clause; as often, it is followed by a participle.[50] *mahărîd* is hiphil masculine singular participle of *hrd* "to shake," mostly in fear. The hiphil is a two-place hiphil with the object elided,[51] "to cause [him] to tremble" (= "to frighten/terrorize [him]"), and the participle, functioning in the predicate slot, emphasizes a durative situation.[52]

The logical particle *kî (for)* introduces the substantiating clause for the entire vision; Micah's prophecies are nothing less than the word of *I AM*. As D. Hillers[53] put it, it is "a kind of divine 'Amen.'" In *pî yhwh (the mouth of I AM) pî* is a metonymy of instrument for the words of the prophecy, and *yhwh* is a genitive of inalienable possession.[54] *şĕbā'ôt (of hosts)* is God's military title: he rules the armies of earth. His sovereign rule over all creation and creatures guarantees the prophecy's fulfillment. *dibbēr (has spoken)* is a piel third masculine singular perfective of *dbr* (see 1:1). There is no noticeable distinction between piel and qal with this root; both, which stand in complementary distribution with each other, are probably denominatives of *dābār*.[55] The perfective signifies the recent past.[56]

5 *kî (Although)* may be causal, as in 4:4, or concessive, as in Isa 54:10; Prov 6:35.[57] If the former, it introduces the second substantiation that hope will

47. R. F. Youngblood, "*tᵉ'ēnā,*" *TWOT* 2:963.
48. Wolff, *Micha*, 94.
49. *IBHS* §39.2.3.
50. *IBHS* §39.3.3.
51. *IBHS* §27.2.
52. *IBHS* §37.6.
53. Hillers, *Micah*, 52.
54. *IBHS* §9.5.1.
55. *IBHS* §24 n. 39.
56. *IBHS* §30.5.1.
57. Holladay, 156, §12.

not be made ashamed: the faithfulness of God to his word (4:4A) and the faithfulness of the remnant to their covenantal obligations (4:5). The connection seems forced, however, and the concessive idea is more probable: "even if the nations do walk . . . we will walk. . . ." The *kol-hā'ammîm (all the peoples)* in view are not those of the future age who resolve to walk in the name of *I AM* (cf. 4:2) but of the present who are now walking in the names of their gods. *yēlĕkû (walk)* is qal persistent present nonperfective[58] third masculine plural of the root *hlk* with its figurative moral use (cf. 4:2).

'îš (each one) functions as an individualizing element of *kol-hā'ammîm.* In *bĕšēm 'ĕlōhāyw (in the name of his god)*, "name" stands as a surrogate for the character and behavior of a person, and *'ĕlōhāyw* is a masculine intensive plural.[59] Instead of *bĕšēm 'ĕlōhāyw (in the name of his god)*, LXX reads *tēn hodon autou* "on his way," probably to remove the objectionable polytheistic formulation in this hope oracle. LXX[R] resembles MT. Tg avoids applying the rabbinical surrogate for God, "The Name," and paraphrases: "became guilty because they worshipped an abomination." This liturgical conclusion, however, returns the audience to the sober realities of the present.

In *wa'ănaḥnû (we)*, the *wāw* introduces the apodosis and is better left untranslated. The emphatic pleonastic pronoun *'ănaḥnû* must refer to Micah and Israel because it contrasts with "all nations," more particularly the believing, persecuted remnant within Israel, for Micah would not put these stirring words of faith into the mouths of the craven. The abrupt introduction of the pronoun suggests that 4:5 was originally an independent liturgical formula in a context where the antecedent would have been more transparent. In *nēlēk (we will walk)*, a qal first common plural nonperfective of *hlk*, the plural pronoun, representing the unity of the remnant, stands in contrast to the individualizing *'îš*, stressing the discontinuity of the nations as each follows its own god. The nonperfective designates the future, as the adverbial phrase "forever and ever" shows. Until all nations join them (see v 2), the believing remnant perseveres in conducting itself appropriately to its profession in its God and so walks in the path that will not come to a dead end or into a cul-de-sac but continues on forever. *bĕšēm-yhwh 'ĕlōhênû (in the name of our God)* in the B verset stands in striking opposition to *bĕšēm 'ĕlōhāyw* in the A verset. The adverbial phrase *lĕ'ôlām wā'ed (for ever and ever)* consists of terminative *lĕ*,[60] the noun *'ôlām* (see Mic 2:9), which, according to E. Jenni,[61] means "the most distant time," *wā'ed*, a

---

58. *IBHS* §31.3.
59. *IBHS* §7.4.3; cf. BDB 43, §2.
60. *IBHS* §11.2.20.
61. E. Jenni, *THAT* 2:230.

conjunctive *waw*, and *'ed*, which also means "perpetuity." Because it points to the extremely remote time, *'ôlām*, whose derivation is uncertain, always occurs with prepositions of direction, or as an adverbial accusative of direction, or finally as a genitive that serves as a prepositional expression. Its meaning of "unlimited and unforseeable duration" is heightened to "unending perpetuity" by the addition of *wā'ed*. It seems to be the language of a solemn liturgical conclusion (Pss 45:18[17]; 145:21).

EXPOSITION

In a breathtaking turn, Micah shifts from the judicial sentence reducing Jerusalem into a heap of rubble and its temple into a pagan high place in a deadly forest to a vision of a hidden future in which Jerusalem and its temple will become the center of global justice and righteousness and of international peace and prosperity. The oracle is marked off from 3:9-12 by an abrupt change in form from an oracle of doom to one of salvation, and from what follows by contrasting themes, namely, the pilgrimage of the nations to Mount Zion to learn to walk in God's Law (4:1-5) versus a pilgrimage of the exiles back to Zion (4:6-8).

Mic 4:1-5 is artistically linked with 3:9-12 by striking verbal contrasts. J. T. Willis[62] noted five: (1) the role of "Zion" (3:10, 12; 4:2); (2) the diminution of the "mountain of [the house] of *I AM*" (3:12) versus its exaltation (4:1); (3) the wicked "heads" *(rō'š)* of Jacob (3:9, 11) versus Zion at the "head" *(rō'š)* of the mountains (4:1); (4) "Jacob" building Zion with bloodshed and injustice (3:10) versus the God of "Jacob" establishing Zion as the center for *I AM's* teaching (4:1-2); (5) the self-serving and malevolent "judging" and "teaching" by Jerusalem's avaricious leaders (3:11) versus *I AM's* loving and beatific "judging" and "teaching" (4:2-3). Their connection is more than an external and superficial contrast of words; rather, as W. Brueggemann[63] noted, "The juxtaposition in the present form of the tradition concerns the end and the new beginning of Israel." By the juxtaposition Micah again shows that *I AM* is Israel's only worthy and faithful Ruler (cf. 2:12-13). Messages that dismantle the old, followed by those that build up the new age, characterize the preexilic prophetic literature. According to R. E. Clements,[64] the prophetic literature is organized around "a

---

62. J. T. Willis, "The Structure of Micah 3–5," *ZAW* 81 (1969) 196.

63. W. Brueggemann, "'Vine and Fig Tree': A Case Study in Imagination and Criticism," *CBQ* 43 (1981) 188.

64. R. E. Clements, "Patterns in the Prophetic Canon," in *Canon and Authority*, ed. G. W. Coats and B. O. Long (Philadelphia: Fortress, 1977) 48.

single theme of Israel's destruction and renewal . . ." (cf. Jer 1:10). Its overall thrust is that God's gracious salvation of man has the last word, not his judgment on man's defeats. In this prophecy, more precisely, Jerusalem, which fell darkly under the rule of lawless judges and ecclesiastics, will not end as a heap of rubble, despised and trampled under the feet of uncircumcised armies, but will in the latter days be esteemed universally and eternally as the place of God's throne and the source of just laws that issue into peace.

The oracle can be analyzed as follows:

I. Introduction: the setting in future days (v 1Aaα, an anacrusis).
II. Body: Micah's vision and reflections (vv 1Aaβ-4A).
   A. His vision of exalted Mount Zion (vv 1Aaβ-2).
      1. Mount Zion firmly exalted above rival divine mountains and nations "flowing" to it (v 1Aaβ-B).
      2. Micah sees the nations going to Zion (v 2Aaα).
      3. Micah overhears the nations exhorting one another to the pilgrimage (v 2Aaβ-Ab).
         a. To learn from God's ways (v 2Aaβ).
         b. To walk in them (v 2Ab).
      4. Micah predicts that the Law will go forth from Mount Zion (v 2B).
   B. Micah's reflections (vv 3-4A).
      1. *I AM* arbitrates among the nations (v 3A).
      2. Nations transform instruments of war to peace (v 3B).
         a. Stated positively (v 3Ba).
         b. Stated negatively (v 3Bb).
      3. Individuals enjoy lasting peace and prosperity (v 4A).
III. Conclusion (vv 4B-5).
   A. A saying formula: *I AM* promises to fulfill the vision and its cogent reflections (v 4B).
   B. A liturgical response by the faithful remnant: they will walk in the name of *I AM* forever (v 5).

L. Alonso-Schökel[65] laid out the movement of the piece by an aesthetic analysis. The centrality of Mount Zion over the world is shown first of all by parallel word pairs, which express totality: mountains and hills, peoples and nations, ways and paths, swords and spears. This centrality is further helped by

---

65. L. Alonso-Schökel, *Estudios de Poética Hebrea* (Barcelona: J. Flors, 1963), 299; repr. in *Das Alte Testament als literarisches Kunstwerk* (Köln: J. P. Bachem, 1971), 350-52.

centripetal and centrifugal movements suggested by a play of sounds and verbal associations. Regarding the centripetal movement he wrote:

> It is the mountain *(har)* where the peoples flow *(nāhar).* It is solidly founded *(nākôn)* and serves as a point of attraction for the movements *(hālak)* of crowds. It is the center of many ways *(derek)* and paths *('ōraḥ).* But it is also the starting point of a centrifugal movement, that of the *tôrâ,* which is compared to a path *('ōraḥ),* that of the word *(dābār),* which is compared to a way *(derek).* From it also depart sovereignty and justice, an efficacious power that creates peace.

If the streaming toward the mountain is described in flowing lines that are astonishingly rich in NHRL sounds, and impoverished, by contrast, in sibilants and explosives, the centrifugal movement is characterized by the opposite. Alonso-Schökel noted:

> The opposed movement toward the exterior is introduced by a half-line: *kî miṣṣiyyôn tēṣē' tôrah,* clearly marked by two *s* and two *t* sounds. Its extends itself later to a line in which the number of its explosive sounds increases and issues finally into a third line where seven *t* and two *h* sounds create an onomatopoeia.

Before expositing the prophecy in more detail, I will lay down a few rules for interpreting prophecies describing Israel's, and as a result the world's, blessed future in contrast to its ignominious past. I reached these conclusions after years of research and teaching; nevertheless, they are not incontrovertible.

First, according to the NT these prophecies about Israel's golden future find fulfillment, though not consummation, in Christ and his church (Luke 24:44; Acts 3:24; 1 Pet 1:10). No *clear* NT teaching, which excludes symbolic apocalyptic literature and questions by uninspired Jews (cf. Acts 1:7), teaches a future national restoration of Israel. Romans 11 teaches the restoration of Israel to the kingdom, not of the kingdom to Israel.

Second, prophets represent the New Age under the symbols of the Old. As P. Fairbairn[66] said, prophecy takes "its hue and aspect from the occasion and circumstances that gave rise to it," and so becomes symbolic of what is to come. This is especially true of prophecy that finds its fulfillment after Pentecost. As I argued elsewhere,[67] prophecies about events prior to Pentecost find a material

---

66. P. Fairbairn, *Prophecy Viewed in Respect to Its Distinctive Nature, Its Special Function, and Proper Interpretation* (Edinburgh: T&T Clark, 1865; repr. Grand Rapids: Baker, 1976), 88.

67. B. K. Waltke, "Kingdom Promises as Spiritual," in *Continuity and Discontinuity: Per-*

fulfillment, for example, in Israel's return from exile and in the life of our Lord, his birth, ministry, death, and resurrection. With Christ's ascension from earth to heaven and the outpouring of his Holy Spirit from heaven to earth, and with the transformation of his body from an earthly physical body to a heavenly spiritual body, the earthly material symbols were done away and the spiritual reality portrayed by the symbols superseded the earthly shadows. Micah does not have in view a universal carnal kingdom but a spiritual kingdom that originates in heaven, is directed by the law of heaven, and is journeying heavenward.

Third, the plain, normal meaning of OT worship had, from its beginning, primarily in view the eternal heavenly realities behind the symbols. For example, the tabernacle was a pattern of the heavenly (Exod 25:9; Heb 8:5), and through the pattern the priestly nation participated in the heavenly. As noted in the Exegesis (195), in the ancient Near East divine mountains symbolized heaven, the presence of the deity, and his victory over chaos. The divine mountain and temple in Mic 4:1 symbolize heaven, and the pilgrimage of the nations to Jerusalem symbolizes their coming to Mount Zion, the heavenly Jerusalem (Heb 12:22). L. Allen[68] noted: "In light of such NT passages as John 4:21-24, the Christian will set little value on the geography of the piece and regard it as a cultural adornment to a deeper and universal truth."

Fourth, when Christ lowered heaven to earth, first at his advent and then at Pentecost, the otiose symbols were forever done away, leaving unveiled the reality, which was so much greater than the symbol (Heb 8:13; 9:26; 10:9). We are not to expect a geological upheaval making Mount Zion physically higher than any other mountain on earth.

Fifth, to show the exceeding greatness of the future the prophets supercharged the old symbols with hyperbole. As E. P. Clowney[69] said: "The outward symbols of the old covenant are so intensified with the fullness of the glory of the new covenant that they are transfigured and transformed. . . . So holy will the city of God become that the inscription on the high priest's diadem will be found on the bells of the horses, and the very wash pots of the town will be as the holy vessels of the temple (Zech. 14:20; cf. Jer. 31:38ff., where the boundaries of the New Jerusalem include all the unclean areas as holy places)." Likewise, *I AM*'s rule will be so extensive that his divine mountain will be, as it were, lifted up above Mount Everest, visibly dominating the entire earth.

Sixth, there is a temporal thickness to these prophecies; they embrace a be-

---

spectives on the Relationship between the Old and New Testament: Essays in Honor of S. Lewis Johnson, ed. J. Feinberg (Westchester, Ill.: Crossway, 1988), 282.

68. Allen, *Micah*, 327.

69. E. P. Clowney, "Israel and the Church: The New Israel," in *Dreams, Visions, and Oracles*, ed. C. E. Armerding and W. W. Gasque (Grand Rapids: Baker, 1977), 214-15.

ginning of fulfillment in Israel's restoration from the exile, a victorious fulfillment in the church age stretching from Christ's first advent to his parousia, and
a consummation in the eschatological new heaven and earth when the spiritual
kingdom is coextensive with creation. Though they represent the future hope in
the garb of its consummation, they are in the process of being fulfilled. Their
glorious consummation rests on Christ's past, present, and future victories. The
future is unfolding, and the completion of that which already exists in Christ
and the Holy Spirit will be carried through triumphantly in spite of sin, suffering, and death. We do not yet see the kingdom of God coextensive with creation,
but our hope for its future is based both on its past victory and its present lack.
Furthermore, while the church presses on to establish justice in the earth, it
looks expectantly to its Lord's parousia, when he will establish justice (2 Thess
1:5-10). Buoyed by these visions and promises of its Lord's triumph, saints in all
ages are nerved to fidelity in testings and succored in sorrows.

Let us now turn to the introduction, where the prophet sets the stage for
his vision "in the latter days," days that lie beyond the possibilities of the present into a future when God will intervene decisively to bring history toward his
intended goal. The "latter days" in Micah 4–5 include the remnant's restoration
from Babylon (4:9-10), the birth of the Messiah (5:1[2]), and his universal rule
and everlasting peace (4:1-4; 5:3[4]). As stated in the Exegesis (192), *bĕ'aḥărît
hayyāmîm* "in the latter days" is not a technical expression for the last stretch of
historical time but denotes in varying contexts a remote future that paradoxically reverses the present situation and at the same time brings to a fitting outcome that toward which it is striving. In the NT the expression is used five
times in two ways: with reference to the glorious age begun with the advent of
Christ (Heb 1:1) and Pentecost (Acts 2:17), and more narrowly with reference to
the dark days just prior to Christ's return in power and great glory at the end of
the present age (2 Tim 3:1; Jas 5:3; 2 Pet 3:3 [= Jude 18]). Whereas the former usages comport well with its use in Mic 4:1, the latter use does not. In the first sermon preached after Pentecost (Acts 2:17), Peter seems to go out of his way to
identify the new age of the church with *ep' eschatōn tōn hēmerōn* "upon the last
days." Pentecost, he says, is what Joel was prophesying, but he curiously and
interpretively transforms *'aḥărê-kēn = meta tauta* in Joel 3:1 (2:28) into *en tais
eschatais hēmerais* "in the last days," apparently linking the church age with
such passages as Mic 4:1. The author of Hebrews considered himself to be living
ep' eschatou tōn hēmerōn toutōn "in these last days," a period of time he radically
contrasts with the time of Moses and the prophets. One would do an injustice
to the NT not to equate Micah's vision of "the latter days" with the advent of Jesus Christ and of Pentecost. To be sure, the NT looked beyond this age to the
resurrection of the body, the judgment of the wicked, and the glorious appear-

ing of Jesus Christ, and beyond that to a new heaven and new earth, but it does not apply the expression "the last days" to that hoped-for future beyond the present age.

Micah first sees Mount Zion exalted above all other mountains (4:1). As noted in the Exegesis (195), a temple mountain in the ancient Near East symbolized: (1) a deity's presence with his people, (2) his abiding victory over chaos, (3) a gateway into heaven, and (4) the mountain deity's rule over the territory it dominates. Micah's superlative for Zion, "the highest mountain," and his comparative "than" *(min)* suggest that he contrasts Mount Zion to pagan divine mountains. Says H. Wolff:[70] "Zion's greatness is Yahweh's greatness. The height of the temple mountain has made him visible as the center of the world, so that he draws the people." Whereas the pagan deities were bound by nature to certain mountains, *I AM*, who becomes incarnate in the language and symbols of a given historical context, sovereignly elected Zion to symbolize his conquest of chaos, in both creation and history, to represent his saving presence with his people and his offering to all who believe in him unique access into his heavenly presence. His temple residence also made his presence a reality, but he retained the liberty to evacuate it on moral grounds. Mount Zion is also implicitly contrasted with Mount Sinai. Whereas God protected his holiness on Sinai by palpable fire so that no one, neither man nor beast, could even touch it, on Mount Zion the Gentiles walk (Heb 12:18-24)! This is so not because God has compromised his holiness, for "our God is a consuming fire" (Heb 12:29), but because he has extended his holiness to all through the perfect and priestly ministry of Jesus Christ. Mount Zion became shrouded under the imperial Assyrian army and became totally hidden under the cloud of the Babylonian army, but its heavenly identity began to emerge when it arose phoenix-like in Israel's postexilic restoration; it became decisively visible and victorious when Jesus was lifted up on the cross to attract all people to himself (John 11:32), and when, having triumphed over Satan and death by his resurrection, he ascended to his heavenly throne in the eternal sanctuary from where he exercises authority over all nations by giving eternal life to as many as the Father has given him (Matt 28:13-20; John 17:2), even to those to whom he is pleased to reveal himself (Matt 11:25-30). Today his church, which is composed of nations and tribes all over the earth, assembles in the heavenly sanctuary when it worships (Heb 9:24; 12:22). Zion's final and consummate vindication will come when the new Jerusalem is lowered from heaven to the regenerated earth (Revelation 21–22).

As a result of Mount Zion's exaltation the nations will "flow" to it; more particularly they will encourage one another to climb its lofty summit to learn

70. Wolff, *Micha*, 91.

from *I AM*'s ways, ways of love and justice (4:2). This vision of the nations' pilgrimage to Zion also entails a dual contrast between pilgrimages in the pagan religions and in the old dispensation. As noted in the Exegesis (196), the nations literally "flowed" by boats to Babylon for the licentious worship of its patron deity, Marduk. In the new age, however, they will "flow" to Mount Zion. Babylon was to the ancient Near East what Rome was to the Middle Ages, and what Mecca is to Islam today. Brueggemann[71] comments: "The enthronement of Yahweh here celebrated carries with it a dethronement of all other gods."

And, whereas formerly only Israel made pilgrimage to Mount Zion, and for some only by external compulsion, in the day of Christ's exaltation in true Mount Zion, all nations will make pilgrimage to it from an inner spiritual compulsion. The pilgrims are not reluctant and in need of a command from an outside source (*contra* Isa 49:22), but encourage one another out of their astonishment at Zion's greatness, as in Zech 8:20-22. This reversal of history, a reversal beyond human engineering and manipulation, is portrayed dramatically by allowing the audience to overhear the conversation of the nations in their liturgical procession to Mount Zion to learn and to live according to God's Law. They will join the "true Israel" (cf. Gal 3:26-29), which enjoys the provisions of the New Covenant (Isa 42:6; Jer 31:31-34; Ezek 36:24-31) through its Mediator, Jesus Christ (Heb 8:6), and whose strength is God, and "who have set their hearts on pilgrimage" (Ps 84:6[5]; cf. Isa 19:23-25; 56:6-8; Zech 8:21:23).

Today, Israel's international anthems, the so-called Songs of Zion, are fulfilled. Commenting on Ps 87:3[4], A. F. Kirkpatrick[72] said: "The poet sees the most inveterate foes of the kingdom of God acknowledging His sovereignty; he sees the nations, the most bitterly antagonistic to Israel, the most diametrically opposed in character to the true spirit of Israel, the most remote from the influence of Israel, brought into harmony with Israel, and adopted into its commonwealth" (cf. Eph 2:19-22). Whereas Isaiah saw the nations coming to Jerusalem to pray (Isa 56:8; cf. Zech 8:20-23), to bring gifts (60:5-18), and to see God's glory (66:18-20), Micah saw them coming "because the Law will go forth from Zion and the word of *I AM* from Jerusalem."

The pilgrims have but one goal: the anticipated teaching from Yahweh's ways. As a result they depart from Zion, walking in his ways and bringing his ways to the ends of the earth. Through all peoples, who have their citizenship in heaven and who have the Law of the Lord written in their hearts, God's ways touch every aspect of culture: education leads mankind into proper social relationships, that is, the worship of God and the love of one another; music and

---

71. Brueggemann, "'Vine and Fig Tree,'" 191.
72. A. F. Kirkpatrick, *The Book of Psalms* (Cambridge: Cambridge University Press, 1902).

art are inspired not by earth's confusion and cacophony but by his order and beauty; politics are motivated not by a love for power but by a desire to serve; and economics is directed not by greed but by justice. More specifically, in the present age his word goes forth authoritatively and interpretively from heavenly Zion through gifted individuals (Matt 28:16-20; Rom 12:3-8; 1 Cor 12:1-30; Eph 4:1-13). How far Micah has progressed from his opening vision in 1:2-7! There he saw *I AM* treading the high places of earth and reducing them in wrath (1:2-7); here he sees *I AM*'s Mount Zion dominating the earth and destroying the pagan mountains by its gracious spiritual attraction.

The prophet now reflects upon and relates in detail the life of this pacified world, the fruit of their conversion (4:3-4). First, God now arbitrates among the nations through his Word and his Spirit-endowed communicators (4:3A). Following V. Herntrick,[73] A. Feuillet[74] contrasted this heightening of Zion with the construction of the Tower of Babel: "Jerusalem is the great antithesis of Babylon. The city of confusion, the creation of a titanic effort by man, is opposed to the city of peace where God alone is master. The nations stir up one another to build the tower (Gen 11:4) and to go up to the Jerusalem in the same way." The result of building the Tower was war; the result of the elect's streaming to Jerusalem is peace. In many respects the United Nations building in New York City is a long shadow of the Tower of Babel, whereas the church is united with the Prince of Peace and shows the way to lasting peace. The new Mount Zion stands in both continuity and discontinuity with the old. Some psalms celebrated the decisions that emanated from the house of David for Israel (Ps 122:1-9); from the true Mount Zion, however, the Greater than David arbitrates among all nations in perfect righteousness. Micah will introduce this Messiah in 5:1-6 (cf. Isa 9:5-7[6-8]; 11:1-5; 42:1-4).

As a result of God's arbitration, war has no usefulness, arms are transformed into agricultural implements, and peace takes up its abode among the elect (4:3A). Once again there is both continuity and discontinuity between the old Jerusalem and the new. In the old, the Lord broke the nations' weapons of war, as when Sennacherib invaded Jerusalem (2 Kgs 19:35-36; cf. Psalms 46–48). In the new arrangement, out of changed hearts, the peoples themselves break the weapons of war and tear down their military academies, guaranteeing a universal and lasting peace among men of goodwill. Within the church the scarce and valuable materials of earth are used to feed the homeless and to

73. V. Herntrick, *Der Prophet Jesaja, kap. 1–12*, Das Alte Testament Deutsch (Göttingen: Vandenhoeck & Ruprecht, 1950), 28-29.

74. A. Feuillet, "Un Sommet Religieux de l'Ancien Testament: l'Oracle d'Isaïe XIX (v 16-25) sur la Conversion de l'Egypte," *RechScRel* 39 (1951) (*Mélanges Lebreton* I) 63-87.

clothe the naked. Micah's vision, however, does not provide an agenda for states composed of unregenerate men to engage in unilateral disarmament. Political states are God's instruments to uphold justice by the sword (Rom 13:1-6). Joel reverses our text and challenges the nations to beat their plowshares into swords to fight against God (Joel 4:10[3:10]). If one does not accept peace through Jesus Christ, then one must be broken according to the former order.

As a result of disarmament, every individual enjoys the fruit of his own labor in security (4:4). The rewards of righteousness on the international level work themselves out to peace for everyone. Instead of having to flee to the narrow confines of fortified cities as in times of war, in the new era of peace everyone can sit peacefully "under his own vine and under his own fig tree." The concrete image depicts the full enjoyment of God's abiding peace and prosperity without fear of danger. The new age will re-experience the joy and happiness of Solomon's golden days (1 Kgs 4:20; 5:5[4:25]; 1 Macc 14:11-12). Zech 3:10 speaks of neighborly fellowship. In fact, there is a flip side to Micah's vision: by sitting under their own vines and fig trees they show that they have also disciplined their swollen appetites. The dreams of disarmament and of agrarian well-being are inseparable. Those who live by war will die in war (Matt 26:52), and those with "swollen appetites" cannot anticipate peace. W. Brueggemann[75] wrote: "[The prophecy] anticipates lowered economic expectations. It anticipates a modest life-style of not having more than one's produce and therefore a respect for the produce of others. . . . Thus this radical vision understands that a dismantling of the military machine carries with it a break with consumeristic values."

The addition "none terrifying him" links the oracle with one of Israel's ancient cherished dreams (Lev 26:6). The imagery of unthreatened people enjoying the fruits of their own labor is also used to describe intervals of peace in the old order (1 Kgs 4:22-25). But here Micah envisions an uninterrupted state. J. L. Mays[76] noted: "The phrase 'with none to terrify' . . . is a feature of descriptions of the restoration of life that YHWH brings about after judgment" (Lev 26:6; Jer 30:10; Ezek 34:28; 39:26; Zeph 3:13). In Leviticus 26 and Ezek 39:26 the security is heightened with the promise that the wild beasts will be removed. Isaiah heightened it even further by picturing the domestic and wild animals grazing and sleeping together (Isa 11:6-9). Those who trust Christ know a peace "which transcends all understanding" (Phil 4:7).

In a prophetic concluding formula (4:4A) Micah guarantees the vision. The same *I AM* who destroyed ancient kingdoms and preserved Abraham and his seed stands behind the vision's fulfillment. The guarantee of the vision pro-

---

75. Brueggemann, "'Vine and Fig Tree,'" 194.
76. Mays, *Micah*, 98.

vides comfort to the faithful in sorrow, restrains them from temptation, and nerves them to fidelity in testing. The focus is not so much on the events of the prediction as on the One who promised them, for the prediction is only as good as his word. The believer's hope is in him, not in some notion that the prophetic word magically bends history to the divine plan.

In a second conclusion the faithful remnant answer with a liturgical response: they will walk in the name of *I AM* (v 5). Once again Micah by quotation represents dramatically, vividly, and immediately the faith of the remnant. They live in the sober realization that at present the confusion and conflict of pagan religions still deny the earth justice and lasting peace and prosperity and that the future still awaits its final consummation. Until then they pledge themselves out of faith in God's word that they will walk in the name of *I AM*. They have already begun in the eternal way (4:2), a way that God watches over and promises to bring to fulfillment (Ps 1:6). If Micah's generation, not having seen even a portion of the vision fulfilled, pledged themselves to fidelity, how much more should the church, which in the course of history has seen many parts of the vision fulfilled, hold on to the end (cf. 2 Pet 3:11-12; 1 John 3:3).

I take this opportunity to append a detailed discussion on the authorship and date of this piece as an instructive exercise in deciding the date and authorship of the book of Micah. Most critics think that it is postexilic; if Micah authored this piece, he probably authored the whole book.

The date and authorship of Mic 4:1-5 are partially related to the question of its connection with Isa 2:2-4. Four explanations have been offered: (1) Micah is the author and Isaiah borrowed it; (2) Isaiah is the author and Micah borrowed it; (3) both of them used the same source; (4) the passage was inserted into both books at a later time. Since the rise of modern criticism, a few interpreters, such as C. Nägelsbach,[77] defended Mican authorship on the grounds that the text in Micah is better and evinces closer contextual links with the rest of the book. More recently, J. T. Willis[78] vigorously defended the latter argument by asking: "One cannot help but wonder how many links like this are necessary to support the view that the passages involved come from the same speaker or writer." E. Nielsen[79] went so far as to say: "The thought forces itself upon us that these passages [3:9-12 and 4:1-5] . . . cannot even have originated independently of each other." L. C. Allen,[80] however, disallows without argumentation the evidence of dovetailing. I will return to this question.

77. C. Nägelsbach, *Der Prophet Jesaja* (Bielefeld: Velhagen & Klasing, 1877), 27-28.
78. J. T. Willis, "Thoughts on a Redactional Analysis of the Book of Micah," in *SBL Seminar Papers 1978* (Missoula, Mont.: Scholars Press, 1978), 99.
79. E. Nielsen, *Oral Tradition* (Naperville: Allenson, 1961), 92-93.
80. Allen, *Micah*, 244 n. 16.

The notice in Isa 2:1 suggests that Isaiah authored the piece. As the teacher of Proverbs adapted the thirty sayings of the wise and made them his own (Prov 22:17), so Micah may have adapted Isaiah's vision as his. Many critics[81] defended Isaianic authorship by an appeal to the affinity of form, including style and vocabulary, and of content between Micah and Isaiah. G. von Rad[82] brashly wrote: "It fits perfectly into the overall pattern of Isaianic thought, but one cannot say the same of the occurrence in Micah." M. Noth[83] does not pronounce himself clearly whether it be Isaianic or Mican, but in any case he argues for the eighth century B.C.

Formerly Hitzig and Ewald[84] argued that both Isaiah and Micah took up an earlier prophecy, and R. Vuilleumier[85] has recently defended the view on the grounds of its liturgical character. B. Renaud[86] objects that although its liturgical character is indisputable, we must also take note that the Jerusalemite liturgy was reconstructed in the postexilic period. Nevertheless, the onus is on Renaud to debunk the preexilic liturgy.

L. Allen,[87] who holds that both are quoting parts of an existing piece, said: "It is likely that this oracle builds upon sacred traditions already established in the period of Isaiah and Micah." A. S. Kapelrud[88] thought the piece derived from an old cultic oracle formulated in the context of the great Enthronement Festival celebrated at the New Year in the fall. Even Renaud[89] has to concede that the piece has incontestable links with the psalms of Zion. But, following G. Wanke,[90] Renaud calls their preexilic origin into question. Wanke, however, holds a very minority opinion here, and it is extremely fragile to build one's case on such a shaky foundation.

H. Wildberger[91] rigorously defended their origin in the preexilic liturgy earlier than both prophets for essentially two reasons. First, they offer close points of contact with the psalms of Zion and a certain number of passages of Isaiah (14:25; 17:12-14; 29:5-8) that move in the same circle of thought as these psalms. These, Wildberger argues, are earlier than Isaiah and come from a

81. Cited in *La Formation*, 161 n. 37.

82. G. von Rad, "Die Stadt auf dem Berge," *Evangelische Theologie* (1948) 439-47.

83. M. Noth, "Jerusalem und die israelitische Tradition," *OTS* 8 (1950) 28-46.

84. Cf. *La Formation*, 160.

85. R. Vuilleumier, "Michée," in R. Vuilleumier and C.-A. Keller, *Michée*, CAT 11b (Neuchâtel: Delachaux, 1971), 47.

86. *La Formation*, 161.

87. Allen, *Micah*, 243.

88. A. S. Kapelrud, "Eschatology in the Book of Micah," *VT* 11 (1961) 392-405, esp. 395-96.

89. *La Formation*, 161.

90. G. Wanke, *Die Zionstheologie der Korachiten*, BZAW (Berlin: Töpelmann, 1966).

91. H. Wildberger, *Jesaja*, BKAT 10 (Neukirchen-Vluyn: Neukirchener, 1966).

Jerusalemite tradition as ancient as the construction of Solomon's temple and the installation of the ark on Mount Zion. In fact, along with many scholars, he believes that this tradition even borrows some of its materials from the pre-Israelite liturgical tradition of Jebus, a Canaanite city before David captured it. Second, he exposed the links that united Isa 2:2-5 and Mic 4:1-5 with the tradition of the psalms of Zion. B. Renaud objects to Wildberger's second argument because he claimed that Wildberger did not show a literary dependence of Isa 2:2-5 on the psalms of Zion. Renaud objects to Wildberger's first reason by arguing that the motif could be earlier and later than the piece being considered. Here, however, Renaud undermines his earlier objection by granting the antiquity of the Zion tradition. He[92] admits: "The tradition of Zion is undoubtedly earlier than that of Isaiah, who has taken it up and even 'theologized' it."

On the other hand, against the view that both prophets borrowed from an earlier liturgical tradition, the themes of the piece in question are theologically more advanced than the songs of Zion. Since the themes of those songs represent the theology appropriate for old Jerusalem and since this piece develops them in a way appropriate for the new Zion, after the fall of the old, it probably does not represent an older liturgy.

B. Renaud now takes the offensive to champion the view that locates the oracle at the time of the return and that it was later inserted into both Isaiah and Micah. He argues his case first on a typology of theological themes and then on the typology of vocabulary.

Before proceeding, I need to lay down some ground rules about the dating of biblical literature. For the sake of argument, in contrast to picking arbitrarily a scholar who supports a prejudice, I will work with the "scholarly consensus" regarding the dates of the following biblical literature: First Isaiah (chs. 1–39), preexilic; Second Isaiah (chs. 40–55), late exilic; Trito-Isaiah (chs. 56–66), postexilic; the Deuteronomist (Deuteronomy–2 Kings), early exilic; psalms of Zion, preexilic.

Renaud argues that the text's three theological themes — the pilgrimage of the peoples to Zion, the elevation of Zion, and universal peace — belong to Israel's theology in the postexilic period. E. Cannawurf[93] cites other motifs, namely, (1) "a warlike hostile march against God" and (2) "*nhr* reminds one of the stream in paradise (Ps. 46:5[4])," and "Jerusalem did not have such a significance as a place of pilgrimage." Renaud[94] gives pride of place to the argument that the pilgrimage of the peoples to Zion (Mic 4:1A, 2A) admirably fits several

---

92. *La Formation*, 164.
93. E. Cannawurf, "The Authenticity of Micah IV 1-4," *VT* 13 (1963) 33.
94. *La Formation*, 156-70.

exilic and postexilic texts (Isa 51:4; 56:3, 6-8; 60:1-22; 66:18-21; Hag 2:7-9; Zech 8:21-23). Moreover, he argues effectively that there are literary contacts between Mic 4:2 and Zech 8:21 and between Mic 4:2 and Isa 51:4. By contrast, he seeks to demolish any contacts between this theme and allegedly earlier texts, especially in First Isaiah. Wildberger had linked the theme in question with the fight of the peoples in their assault against Jerusalem (Isa 17:12-14; 29:5-8) and with the fact that Isaiah's hope clung to Zion. Renaud rightly questions whether one can extrapolate the theme of the pilgrimage of the nations to Zion by combining these two themes. H. Junker[95] with more probability appealed to the same theme in 1 Kgs 8:41-43, where the king prays that *I AM* will answer the prayer "of the stranger who comes from a remote land." Whatever one may say about the final Deuteronomistic form of the book, most scholars recognize that the text contains kernels of ancient traditions, which should not be brushed aside. Renaud, however, justly contrasted its individualistic tone with the nationalistic tone of Isa 2:2-4 and Mic 4:1-3.

More trenchant, however, are Isa 19:23-25 and Psalm 87, cited above. Jeremiah 31 also speaks of the peoples going up to Zion and contains literary contacts with Micah; for example, they (Isa 2:2; Jer 31:12; Mic 4:1) speak of a "flowing" *(nāhar)* to *I AM's* benediction. Renaud[96] notes: "But the verb *nhr* 'to flow' makes the contact particularly significant. It is extremely rare in the Bible, found only in Mic 4:1 (= Isa 2:2), Jer 31:12, and Jer 51:44." He presumed, however, that Mic 4:1 and Isa 2:2 depended on Jeremiah. Even granting his erroneous prejudice, it is now established that the theme is late preexilic or at the latest early exilic, not late exilic or postexilic. But why should one presume that Micah depended on Jeremiah? Since Jer 26:18 clearly quotes Mic 3:12, it seems more likely that Jer 31:12 depends on Mic 4:1 and not vice versa. Also, Renaud fails to recall Alonso-Schökel's analysis that *nāhar* phonetically resembles *har*, an assonance missing in Jeremiah; the resemblance suggests creative originality in Micah. If one wishes to argue that Micah's theology has a more advanced universalistic tone than Jeremiah's more nationalistic one, it should also be noted that it is no more advanced than Isa 19:23-25 and is "more advanced" than the nationalism of Hag 2:7-9 and of Isaiah 60, traditionally dated later than the return.

Moreover, the theme of the preexilic prophets, both early and late, is double-focused, as noted: destruction and renewal. Micah developed aspects of

95. H. Junker, "Sancta Civitas, Jerusalem Nova: Eine formkritische und überlieferungsgeschichtliche Studie zu Is 2," in *EKKLESIA: Festschrift für Bischof Dr. Matthias Wehr*, TThSt 15 (Trier: Paulinus, 1962), 17-23.
96. *La Formation*, 169.

the new from motifs associated with the fallen temple, as argued above, and we should expect those motifs to be picked up by the postexilic prophets. It is wrongheaded to isolate the "renewal" motif from the earlier double focus, and, by comparing it with postexilic prophets, who would naturally use it, re-date the motif by them.

Renaud[97] now takes up the theologoumena regarding the heightening of Zion as the center of the world. If we grant that the psalms of Zion are preexilic, this theme is perfectly consistent with eighth-century prophecy, as Renaud[98] himself would grant (cf. Pss 46:5[4]; 48:2, 3[1, 2]; 87:1, 4-6). Some scholars[99] date Psalms 46 and 48 to Sennacherib's assault against Jerusalem or even as early as the establishment of David's royal cult in Jerusalem.[100] No cogent reasons exist for denying their use in the First Temple.[101] B. Renaud builds his case for the late date of this theologoumena by first denying its presence in First Isaiah, then calling into question the preexilic date of the psalms of Zion, and then by finding the theme in exilic literature (cf. Ezek 5:3; 17:22; 20:40; 38:12) and the postexilic prophets (Zech 14:10-11, 16-19). However, he begs the issue by alleging that Isa 19:24 is a postexilic addition and by overly minimizing the evidence and consensus regarding the dates of the songs of Zion.

Renaud[102] now turns to the theological theme: the universal, eschatological peace (Mic 4:3). For the moment, I do not challenge the terms "eschatological" except to say that it would be better to speak more precisely of "all nations" and of "future" (see above). Two complementary motifs cooperate within this theme: the arbitration of disputes and the destruction of the arms of war. Renaud grants that both motifs are relatively ancient. As noted above, Isaiah associates them in his picture of the messianic future (Isa 9:5[6]; 11:1-5). Renaud counters, however, that, in the first place, the recipients of Isaiah 9 and 11 and Micah 4 differ: whereas in Isaiah 9 only the elect of the people and in Isaiah 11 the "poor of the land" are the recipients of the messianic peace, in Micah 4 the peace is extended universally to many nations. But Isaiah also had in view a "universal" peace (Isa 9:6[7]; 11:1-5). To be sure, Isaiah uses different literary expressions, but the theologoumenon is the same as in Mic 4:1-3. In the second place, Renaud argues against the correspondence between Mic 4:3 and these passages in Isaiah because Micah attributed the establishment of justice to *I AM*, whereas Isaiah linked it with the Messiah. Since Micah will later identify *I*

97. *La Formation*, 170-73.

98. *La Formation*, 172.

99. Cf. L. Krinetzki, "Zur Poetik und Exegese von Ps. 48," *BZ* 4 (1960) 70-92, esp. 82.

100. Cf. P. C. Craigie, *Psalms 1-50*, WBC 19 (Waco, Tex.: Word, 1983), 343.

101. Cf. A. Weiser, *The Psalms*, OTL (Philadelphia: Westminster, 1962), 381.

102. *La Formation*, 173-74.

AM's agent as the Messiah who trusts solely in *I AM*, his argument smacks of hair-splitting.

Renaud[103] has to concede that the psalms of Zion, especially 46 and 76, offer very close parallels to Mic 4:3. They differ, however, he notes, in that in these psalms *I AM* breaks the weapons of war and crushes the peoples. What he fails to note, however, is that the theme is missing in the exilic and postexilic prophets. Let me take the offensive here. Joel (4:9-16[3:9-16]), postexilic according to the scholarly consensus, actually presents an opposite picture: he calls upon the nations to beat their hoes into swords and their pruning knives into spears in order to rally in war against *I AM*, who is about to trample them. This theme actually proves the relative antiquity of our piece.

With regard to these three theological motifs within the theme of renewal, drawn by contrasting old Jerusalem with the new, I conclude: (1) Since Jeremiah probably depended on Micah 4 regarding the "flowing" of the nations to Jerusalem, Micah predates him. (2) The use of this motif in the postexilic prophets reflects an expected dependence on Mic 4:1-3 and ought not be used to date that oracle by them. (3) The songs of Zion, celebrating Jerusalem as the center of the world, belong to the preexilic epoch, giving evidence that that theme is not uniquely exilic or postexilic. (4) Since the theme of "universal" peace is found in First Isaiah and Psalm 46, and not in exilic and postexilic literature, it also supports an eighth-century provenience.

Renaud[104] now turns to vocabulary in his attempt to date Mic 4:1-3 to the time of the return. By way of introduction, he grants that Mic 4:1-3 exhibits a "certain Isaianic or 'Zionistic' vocabulary," but explains that it could easily have drawn upon the treasure of words exploited by earlier texts. He wants to know only if there is a trace of late vocabulary. He prejudices the data in his favor, however, by disallowing the songs of Zion as part of the evidence. In spite of his cavalier assumption, I will work with it anyway. Renaud builds his case on five expressions.

Regarding *bĕ'aḥărît hayyāmîm* "in days to come," he[105] argues: "The majority of attestations is located in the exilic or postexilic texts and is linked either to a certain end of history (Deut 31:29; Jer 23:20 = Jer 30:24; Ezek 38:18) or to a new beginning (Deut 4:30; Jer 48:47; 49:39; Hos 3:5)." He explains away some of these by claiming: "A certain number of those mentioned occur in redactional additions (Hos 3:5; Jer 30:24 = Jer 23:20; Jer 48:47; 49:39)." He resorts to the same expedient to explain away its occurrence in Gen 49:1 and Num

---

103. *La Formation*, 176.
104. *La Formation*, 174-78.
105. *La Formation*, 175-77.

24:14. His argument, however, is patently circular and not convincing. E. Lipiński,[106] using the same data, drew the conclusion that the expression is preexilic!

Renaud[107] discounts "the mountain of the house of *I AM*," his second piece of evidence, in the songs of Zion and pointed away from Isa 30:29 and "my mountain" in Isa 11:9; 14:25 in favor of the one parallel in 2 Chr 33:15. The expression is too rare to decide the issue.

Renaud[108] finds support in *nhr* because he presumes that Micah borrowed from Jeremiah. Since the opposite is clearly the case with regard to Mic 3:12, and since Micah's use is more creative than Jeremiah's, the expression actually favors an early, not a late date, for Micah.

Renaud's[109] fourth word is "powerful nations" in 4:3. "Great peoples" is universally used, he notes, but "powerful nations" without other determination is never attested in the preexilic prophetic texts, does not appear before Deut 9:14; 26:5, and is found in Isa 60:22, a piece very close to Mic 4:1-3. The fact is, however, that the singular is used in Mic 4:7. The data tend to favor a late date, by his presuppositions, but are even then too shaky to date the piece. I already noted that "great peoples and powerful nations" in Zech 8:22 is probably based on Mic 4:1-2.

"They will learn to make war" is, according to Renaud,[110] "uniquely post-exilic: Pss 18:35[34]; 144:1; Song 3:8 and a gloss of Judg 3:2." His own data are obviously less than convincing! He points especially to 1 Chr 5:18, which with Mic 4:3 links the expression "they will raise the sword." The analogy is less than precise, as an examination of the texts will show.

In sum, according to Renaud[111] "five or six expressions are attested only at the exilic or post-exilic epochs." In my judgment only one, "powerful nations," favors this date, and "flow" points in the opposite direction. The rest have been neutralized by contrary data. Even granting the five or six, Renaud wisely concludes: "None of these observations taken in isolation remains decisive by itself, for the absence of such a formula in the Bible before a given date does not mean that it was not used at an earlier period."

I draw the conclusion that since all scholars grant that Micah authored Mic 3:9-12 and since Mic 4:1-3 creatively dovetails with it, Micah probably authored the disputed passage. If the disputed passage is older than Mic 3:9-12,

---

106. E. Lipiński, "*B'hryt hymym* dans les Textes Preéxiliques," 445-50.
107. *La Formation*, 177.
108. *La Formation*, 177.
109. *La Formation*, 177-78.
110. *La Formation*, 178.
111. *La Formation*, 178.

then Micah composed 3:9-12 to fit it, but it is unlikely that the piece, with a more advanced theology than the songs of Zion, is older than Micah. No sound reasons establish that a later writer authored a piece to dovetail with Mic 3:9-12. It may be that Isaiah adopted and adapted the oracle to make it his own (cf. Prov 22:17), but in any case, Isa 2:2-5 is best treated as its own final text.

2. The Lame Remnant Becomes Strong (4:6-7)

6   "In that day" — the utterance of *I AM* —
      "I will gather the lame,
          and the scattered I will assemble,
      even those whom I have afflicted;
7   and I will make the lame into a remnant,
          and those driven away into a powerful nation."
    And *I AM* will reign over them on Mount Zion
      from now and forevermore.

EXEGESIS

6   The adverbial phrase modifying *ʾōsĕpâ, bayyôm hahûʾ (in that day)*, consists of temporal *bĕ*,[1] the definite masculine singular noun *yôm*, and the quasi-demonstrative pronoun *hahûʾ* with a deictic force for the remote. See the Exposition (225), for the meaning of the syntagma *bayyôm hahûʾ* "in that day" in the preliterary stage of this pericope. Here its literary context is taken into consideration. The demonstrative is anaphoric, referring back to *bĕʾaḥărît hayyāmîm* "in the latter days" (4:1), so that the singular *yôm* is a collective.[2] *nĕʾum-yhwh (the utterance of* I AM*)* consists of a noun patterned after the qal passive participle always written *defectiva*[3] of the root *nʾm* and of the genitive of authorship *yhwh*.[4] *nʾm* always occurs in construct with a genitive of authorship, and in all but two of its 360 uses it occurs in prophetic contexts. Its one denominative use in Jer 23:31 designates prophetic speech. *nĕʾum* in itself designates the origin and the authority of the message.[5] The heavenly origin and supreme authority of this prophecy are underscored by the fact that it comes from *I AM*; there is

1. *IBHS* §11.2.5.
2. *IBHS* §7.2.1.
3. GKC §50a n. 1.
4. *IBHS* §9.5.1.
5. Cf. L. J. Coppes, "*nᵉʾūm*," *TWOT* 2:542.

none above him. The Lord Jesus Christ interpreted this formula to mean an utterance inspired by the Spirit (cf. Ps 110:1 with Matt 22:43-44).

The cohortative of the qal first common singular of the root *'sp (I will gather)* (see 2:12) signifies the resolve of God to accomplish his intention.[6] Its object, *haṣṣōlēʿâ (the lame)*, is a definite qal feminine singular participle. The feminine singular participle is a collective,[7] and the verbal adjective, an antemeria, probably stands for "sheep." The rare root *ṣlʿ*, found only in Mic 4:6-7; Zeph 3:19; and Gen 32:32, is translated in LXX by *tēn syntetrimmenēn* "the broken one" and in Syr by "the remote [absent/alienated] one." Its use in Gen 32:32 is decisive; Vg rightly has *claudicantem* "limping, lame."

In *wĕhanniddāḥâ (and the scattered)*, a *wāw* conjunctive with a niphal feminine singular participle of the root I *ndḥ*, the *wāw* adds another characteristic of the implied "sheep." The feminine singular participle functions in grammar and in figure like *haṣṣōlēʿâ*. *ndḥ*, to judge from Arabic and Ethiopic cognates, means "push away." The niphal could be tolerative "let themselves be led away, enticed," as in Deut 4:19, or an incomplete passive, "be scattered." The third modification of the sheep, "whom I have afflicted," supports the versions that interpreted the disputed word according to the latter sense: LXX's *tēn exōsmenēn* "the evicted one," Syr "the dispersed ones," Vg *quam ejeceram* "whom I had cast out." The cohortative *'ăqabbēṣâ (I will assemble)* (cf. 2:12), whose object is *hanniddāḥâ*, functions like its parallel, *'ōsĕpâ*.

The conjunctive *waw* in *wĕ'ăšer (even those whom)* introduces the third modification of those whom *I AM* gathers, but in place of the relative participle Micah resorts to the indeclinable relative pronoun construction with finite verb even as in 3:2, 3. Because 4:6a is a relative clause without a new subject and predicate, the *wāw* is best taken as an ascensive *wāw*; it explains why the "sheep" are limping and scattered. Indeclinable *'ăšer*, the object of *hărēʿōtî*, must agree with the other singular collectives and so be rendered in English by the plural (cf. LXX's *hous*). Both LXX and Syr shifted here from feminine to masculine, probably to move from the figure of the implied sheep to the reality of captive Israel. The hiphil of the first common singular perfective of the root *rʿʿ* (see 2:1, 3), *hărēʿōtî (I have afflicted)*, is a one-place hiphil;[8] *I AM* caused "the sheep" to experience the event of being afflicted. For the meaning of the root see Mic 2:1, 3. Syr and Vg accurately represent the Hebrew with "I afflicted," but LXX inaccurately renders it *apōsmenēn* "I rejected." If Micah is the author of this prophecy, and there is no reason to think otherwise, the perfective is either future per-

6. *IBHS* §34.5.1.
7. *IBHS* §§6.4.2; 7.2.1.
8. *IBHS* §27.2.

fect because Israel's painful exile in Babylon is still future to him (cf. 4:10) or present perfect because Micah presumes the afflicted is in a present state as a result of the event.[9] The temporal adverbial phrase *mēʿattâ* "from now" in 4:7 shows decisively that the latter is Micah's standpoint. For the meaning of the root see 2:3.

7 The *wāw*-relative with the qal suffix conjunction first common singular of the root *śîm* in *wěśamtî (and I will make)* represents a chronological consequent situation to the gathering of the exiles.[10] For the meaning of *śîm* with *lě* "make into/transform into" see 1:6 (cf. Gen 21:13; Exod 14:21; Isa 42:15). Syr curiously reverses the meaning of 4:7Aa, rendering "I will make an end of the dispersed." For the meaning of the definite direct object marked off by *ʾet, haṣṣōlēʿâ (the lame)*, see 4:6. For the meaning of *lišʾērît (into a remnant)*, consisting of the preposition *lě* with a terminative notion[11] and the root *šěʾērît*, see 2:12.

wěhannahălāʾâ (and those driven away) consists both of the conjunctive *waw* introducing yet a fourth modification for the recipients of God's salvation and of the definite niphal feminine singular participle of a disputed root. The feminine singular participle functions in the same way as the three other feminine singular participles in 4:6-7Aa. This *hapax legomenon* is interpreted here with BDB and GB as niphal denominative[12] of *hlʾh* "to be there." KBL and Holladay posit the root *hlʾ* and derive the similar sense "to stray far." The versions hesitate: LXX's *tēn apōsmenēn* "the rejected one," which corresponds to its rendering of *hanniddāḥâ* "the cast away"; Syr's "the remote one," which adjective rendered *haṣṣōlēʿâ* in 4:6; Vg's *eam quae laboraverat* "her that labored/strove." J. Wellhausen proposed the feminine singular participle *hannahălâ* "the sick one" (cf. Ezek 34:21). V. Klosterman thought MT was a conflation of *hallōʾâ* and *hannilʾâ*, but, as S. Schwantes[13] observes: "The first one is attested only in Rabbinic Hebrew." A. van Hoonacker proposed *hannilʾâ* "the exhausted one, the crushed one," from the root *lʾh*. This reading, which supposes that medial *h* of MT is due to dittography, has the advantage of facilitating a contrast: "the exhausted one into a powerful nation." For the form and meaning of *lěgôy ʿāṣûm (into a powerful nation)* see 4:3. It differs from that expression in several ways: the *lě* is terminative, the verb *ʿāṣûm* is gapped, and the form is singular. In contrast to the "powerful nations," the remnant itself will be a power to be reckoned with.

9. *IBHS* §30.5.4.
10. *IBHS* §32.2.2.
11. *IBHS* §11.2.10.
12. *IBHS* §23.5.
13. Schwantes, "A Critical Study of the Text of Micah," 111.

In *ûmālak yhwh (and* I AM *will reign)* the *waw* introduces a third, ulti-mate, consequent situation. The tense, however, is simple future, not cohorta-tive, because the style shifted with reference to *I AM* from first person to third masculine singular. *mālak* may be a qal stative denominative[14] from the root *melek,* which designates "chief magistrate." Human kings were responsible both to uphold statutory law and to decree new laws. *I AM* is the Supreme Majesty who decrees all righteous laws, including those expressed in Holy Scripture (cf. Prov 8:15-16). As King, *I AM* not only demands obedience but in return gives help and protection. Scholars dispute whether *mālak* in the liturgical formula *mālak yhwh* has an ingressive stative force, "has become king," or a constative stative force, "reign." I will not attempt to decide the issue here; it is clear from the *wāw*-relative that *I AM* is inaugurating a new reign and from the adverbial phrase "forever and ever," an enduring reign, so that both notions are present. The shift from first person to third person resembles the similar shift with simi-lar themes in 2:12-13. Whereas, however, 2:12-13 proclaimed a future deliverance from besieged Jerusalem, this verse describes the new and golden era of the rem-nant. The first adverbial phrase signifying the subjects of *I AM's* reign, *`ălêhem (over them),* consisting of the preposition *`al* with the metaphorical sense of be-ing over as a rank[15] and the third masculine plural pronominal suffix, shifts the metaphorical collective feminine of 4:6-7A, which implicitly compares the rem-nant to sheep, to the literal masculine with reference to the people.

The second adverbial phrase, which signifies the center of *I AM's* reign, *bĕhar ṣîyôn (on Mount Zion),* consists of locative *bĕ*[16] and its object, *har,* in con-struct with the genitive of association, *ṣîyôn.*[17] The grammatical structure of this prepositional phrase may be deliberately ambiguous.[18] Micah may be re-stricting *I AM's* reign to Mount Zion and also viewing the restored remnant as concentrated in "heavenly" Mount Zion (cf. 2:12 and 4:1). It is hard to imagine, however, a strong nation restricted exclusively to Mount Zion. More probably there is an ellipsis here: "*I AM,* [who will sit as king] in Mount Zion, will rule over them." The ambiguous phrase pertains to both God and the saved rem-nant. While *de jure I AM* always reigns (cf. Exod 15:18; 1 Sam 12:12; Ps 145:11-13), *de facto* Israel does not always experience it.

The third adverbial phrase, which signifies the duration of *I AM's* reign, *mē`attâ wĕ`ad-`ôlām (from now and forevermore),* consists of the ablative prepo-sition *min* with the temporal adverb *`attâ,* the conjunctive *wāw* with the prepo-

14. *IBHS* §22.5.
15. *IBHS* §11.2.13.
16. *IBHS* §11.2.5.
17. *IBHS* §9.5.3.
18. *IBHS* §11.4.3.

sition *ʿad*, and its object *ʿôlām* (see 4:5). The *ʿattâ* is proleptic (= *then* from our point of view). Concerning the prepositional phrase *ʿad-ʿôlām*, E. Jenni[19] says that the syntagma, the preposition *ʿad* "up to" with *ʿôlām*, is a synonym of Hebrew *dôr wādôr*, *nēṣaḥ*, and *ʿădê ʿōbed*, all of which mean "forever," and of the Northwest Semitic inscription *ʿd ʿlm*, which also means "forever." He renders it "forever," "until in eternity," and adds: "in which case 'eternity' ought not to mean anything other than the unrestricted future."

EXPOSITION

Verses 6-7, a second oracle of salvation, links with the first, 4:1-5, by belonging to the same future "in that day," by the themes of "Mount Zion" (4:1-2, 6), of the coming/gathering to it (4:2, 6-7), of mighty nation(s) (4:3, 7A), of *I AM*'s eternal rulership over his people (4:5, 7A), and of his authoritative speech ("the mouth of *I AM* has spoken" in 4:5; "the utterance of *I AM*" in 4:6). It is marked off from 4:1-5 both by the liturgical concluding formula in 4:5 versus the introductory formulas in 4:6, "in that day" and "the utterance of *I AM*," and by different themes: the strong nations of the world versus the strong nation of Israel; the coming of the nations to Zion versus the coming of ravaged Israel to Zion; universal peace and justice among the nations versus *I AM*'s rule over the remnant. Its terminus is marked off by the characteristic conclusion, "from now and forevermore" (Isa 9:6[7]; Pss 115:18; 121:8), by the climactic formula "*I AM* reigns," and by the distinctive form of 4:8 (see below).

These vocabulary links between the successive oracles serve to unite their messages. They are something like the edges of pieces in a jigsaw puzzle fitting the sections and their pieces together into a comprehensive picture. These sections and pieces, called pericopes, once existed in isolation, which accounts for the obvious seams between them (e.g., the disconcerting change of speakers and addressees), and were brought together later by Micah in his book. L. Allen[20] noted: "It is characteristic of many OT oracles of promise that they do not merely record hope for the future, but lay a realistic trail from the hopelessness of the present to prospects of coming glory." The vision of Mic 4:1-5 is like the frame of a puzzle, and the missing sections and pieces are now fitted in. The first section, Mic 4:6-7, presents the picture of *I AM* restoring scattered Israel and making them into a strong nation with the ultimate goal of ruling over them in Mount Zion. The section is built up of three pieces, three motifs, re-

19. E. Jenni, *THAT* 2:232-33.
20. Allen, *Micah*, 329.

flexes of Mic 2:12-13 based on the verbs *'sp/qbṣ, śîm,* and *mlk.* But whereas in 2:12-13 *I AM* proclaims that he will bring the remnant into besieged Jerusalem, and as king delivers them, in 4:6-7 he gathers them into the new Jerusalem, makes them into a strong remnant, and rules over them on Mount Zion. It presumes the doom oracles of chapters 1–3. It can be outlined as follows:

  I. Introduction to prophecy (v 6ΑaΑ, an anacrusis).
   A. Its setting, "in that day."
   B. Its origin and authority: "the utterance by *I AM.*"
 II. Body (in first person): *I AM* will save scattered and afflicted Israel (vv 6Αaβ-7Α).
   A. *I AM* regathers the dispersed of Israel (vv 6Αaβ-6Β).
   B. *I AM* transforms the remnant into a strong nation (v 7Α).
III. Conclusion (in third person): *I AM* reigns over them on Mount Zion forever (v 7Β).

"In that day — the utterance of *I AM* —" is best treated as an anacrusis introducing the new prophecy. In the preliterary stage "in that day" had a life of its own. S. J. DeVries[21] defines it as: ". . . a summarizing characterization concerning a particular day in which Israel's God was in some way seen to be active in crucial confrontation with his people." Moreover, "that day" refers to a more remote future. De Vries[22] contrasted it with *māḥār* "tomorrow":

> [Tomorrow] designates a today that is stretched out past the coming night into the day that is to follow. The person who announces it can envisage it as though it were today. It lies just over the horizon of time. But, when that horizon gets extended, deferred beyond immediate expectation, it becomes . . . "that day," a day out there, beyond man's immediate reach and in the hand of God.

On the literary level it refers back to "in the latter days" and relates the fulfillment of this oracle as contemporary with the epoch-changing time mentioned in 4:1. With regard to political redemption that future began to be fulfilled with the restoration from Babylon (cf. 4:9-10), but with regard to Israel's spiritual redemption it was fulfilled in the work of Jesus Christ.

Also by way of introduction, the audience is assured that this is a divine revelation. *ně'um-yhwh* signifies that it originates in heaven with all of its authority and contrasts a true salvation prophecy, which implies that Israel must

21. S. J. DeVries, *Yesterday, Today, and Tomorrow* (Grand Rapids: Eerdmans, 1975), 136.
22. DeVries, *Yesterday,* 283-84.

first be disciplined — note the characterizing words "lame," "scattered," and "afflicted" — with a false prophecy that offered salvation without demanding moral rectitude. Also, the prophetic formula that stands back-to-back with the concluding formula, "the mouth of *I AM* has spoken," shows that this revelation, in contrast to the former, will be delivered in the first person.

In the future golden era of spiritual Israel *I AM* will not only incline the nations to go to Mount Zion but he will also assemble redeemed Israel there. This new revelation picks up the same verbs and themes mentioned in 2:12-13, *'sp* "gather," *qbṣ* "assemble," I *śîm* "make/bring into," and *mlk* "king/reign," but whereas in 2:12-13 these verbs proclaim an immediate salvation in 701 B.C., here they refer to a remote salvation. The deliverance in 701 B.C. serves as a type of the more remotely future salvation. As noted in 2:12, *'sp* "gather" and *qbṣ* "assemble" may hark back to the time when David assembled *I AM's* armies to expand the kingdom, but whereas in 2:12 the certainty of the event was underscored by infinitive absolutes, *'āsōp* and *qabēṣ*, rendered "surely," here it is underscored by the mood of resolve with *I AM* speaking, "I *will* gather . . . I *will* assemble."

The repetition of synonymous verbs further emphasizes the resolve and its sure fulfillment. The similar verbs suggest that the same imagery of the Shepherd tending his sheep is employed here, though there it is explicit, whereas here it is implicit. The word choice, *qbṣ* (Ezek 34:13), *hanniddāḥâ* "that which is scattered" (Ezek 34:4), and *haṣṣōlēâ* "that which is lame" (cf. Ezek 34:4) fit that imagery. The transparent imagery for the community as a flock is removed in 4:7A by the personal pronoun "them." In the ancient Near East the ideal king is represented as a Shepherd-King (*contra* Ezekiel 34) and evokes feelings of tenderness and personal concern. Here too, the only true King, *I AM*, is contrasted to Israel's faithless kings who destroyed the flock and its fold. The rarity of *haṣṣōlēâ* suggested to B. Renaud[23] that there might be an allusion to the laming of Jacob, the only personal use of the term, and his renaming to Israel. This allusion ought not be ruled out, especially since the eponymous ancestor represents the corporate destiny of the nation (cf. Hos 12:2-5[1-4]). R. Martin-Achard[24] said, "[The Yahwist] suggests that this [adventure of Jacob at Penuel] is an example for the children of Israel. The episode at the ford of the Jabbok prefigures what will be the destiny of the children of the patriarch." Having exiled and lamed "Jacob," God now triumphantly blesses and restores "Israel." R. de Vaux[25] remarked, "The patriarch clings to God and forces from

23. *La Formation*, 187-88.

24. R. Martin-Achard, "An Exegete before Gen 32,23-33," in *Structural Analysis and Biblical Exegesis: Interpretational Essays* (Pittsburgh: Pickwick, 1974), 55.

25. R. de Vaux, *Jerusalem Bible* (Garden City, N.Y.: Doubleday, 1966), 53.

him a blessing; henceforth all who bear Israel's name will have a claim on God." Scattered Israel began to be regathered politically to earthly Mount Zion from its affliction, namely, the exile, in the restoration at the end of the exile (Jer 23:3; Neh 1:9), but its spiritual restoration occurs today in the church of the Lord Jesus Christ.

Consequential to the regathering of lamed Israel *I AM* will transform them into a "remnant," even a strong nation. G. F. Hasel[26] showed that the notion of remnant, that which remains of any entity after most of it is used or destroyed, is deeply rooted in the religious literature of the ancient Near East, since the Sumerian texts already knew it. It is found in the accounts of the flood in the Akkadian, Ugaritic, and Egyptian recensions. J. L. Mays[27] succinctly noted its various uses in prophetic literature: "The term is used in threats (catastrophe will leave *only* a remnant, Amos 5:3; Isa. 7:3 [*sic*]), promises (a remnant *will* survive judgment, Isa. 37:31f.), and as a designation of the surviving community as the object of God's saving activity (Isa. 11:11, 16; 46:3)." Although the idea of judgment is implied in v 6 in the expression, "those I have afflicted," the term has the last sense here.

H. Wolff[28] says that *šĕʾērît* here means that "the new, remaining posterity" (cf. Gen 45:7),[29] "the people of the survivors, begins something new with God." G. F. Hasel's[30] comment on the Akkadian use of the term is appropriate here: "No remnant means no life and existence; a remnant means life and existence for the individual, community, tribe, city or people." Thus the remnant becomes the goal of history, as Mays continued: "'Remnant' has become the name for the eschatological goal of YHWH's ways with Israel. The remnant is by character a mighty nation; by reason of their nature they are a supernatural and invincible reality within world history (see 5:7-9)." Philistia did not survive the test of history because God did not make it a remnant (Amos 1:8), but Israel has and will survive that test because God has made it such. In this remnant the promise to Abraham (Gen 12:2; 17:5; 18:18) will be fulfilled. Isaiah commented: "The least of you will become a thousand, the smallest a mighty nation" (60:22). As the "strong nations" in 4:3 are spiritual nations (cf. Rom 4:16), which have been regenerated from heaven and are making pilgrimage to the heavenly sanctuary, so also the remnant that becomes a strong nation is a spiritual remnant. The vision finds its fulfillment at the present time in the "remnant of Is-

---

26. G. F. Hasel, *The Remnant: The History and Theology of the Remnant Idea from Genesis to Isaiah* (Berrien Springs, Mich.: Andrews University Press, 1974), 186.

27. Mays, *Micah*, 101.

28. Wolff, *Micha*, 95.

29. H. Wildberger, *THAT* 2:847.

30. Hasel, *Remnant*, 100.

rael chosen by grace" (Rom 11:5). What was not as clearly revealed in the OT as in the NT was that Jew and Gentile on equal footing would together make up the strong nation, the church (Eph 3:2-6; 1 Pet 3:9).

The prophecy now reaches its goal and climax in Micah's commentary on *I AM's* words, namely, *I AM* will rule over them on Mount Zion from that day and forever (4:7A). The mention of Mount Zion in the conclusion of this prophecy forms an *inclusio* with 4:1. The climactic liturgical formula "*I AM* reigns" brings the audience to the same historical point as that oracle. *I AM's* reign is often celebrated (cf. Isa 33:22; 41:21; 43:15; 44:6; Zeph 3:15; Zech 14:9) and linked with Jerusalem/Zion (Isa 24:23; 52:7; Obad 21; Ps 146:7-10). *De facto* saved Israel will experience *I AM's* reign in his heavenly sanctuary, a reign that *de jure* was, and is, and will be.

This liturgical formula is now linked with another liturgical formula, "forever and ever" (Pss 115:18; 121:8; 131:3; cf. Isa 9:6[7]; 59:21). Micah expands the summit to include *I AM's* reign over restored Israel as a strong nation and extends it into the eternal future. The eternal future for which suffering and faithful Israel hoped has now arrived. Israel is regathered and restored not to its corrupt state of the preexilic period or of even the postexilic era but to its ideal future state. J. L. Mays[31] said it well: "The dispersion will not be transformed into a mighty nation in order to resume a political career that is the expression of their own power and will. Instead, they will become the social unit whose existence and character is a manifestation of YHWH's reign over them." As stated, this vision finds its fulfillment within history in Christ and his church; its consummation lies in the eschaton. As Geerhardus Vos[32] wrote: "The age to come was perceived to bear in its womb another age to come." And L. Allen[33] noted: "The prophet brings the divine message to the people where they are. With such psychological preparation there is even more likelihood that the word of promise will take root in weary hearts and engender a positive, vigorous attitude to life's ills."

This salvation oracle's consistent note of hope for exiled Israel, including giving "remnant" a positive notion of strength, causes most critics to date it to the exilic or postexilic period. This broad consensus, however, rests on a shallow basis. The picture of a limping, scattered flock is not anachronistic in Micah's own time, as seen in 2:12-13. Then, too, one must not restrict prophecy by the assumptions of historical criticism. D. Hillers,[34] a scholarly iconoclast here, defends the authenticity of this prophecy. He wrote: "The term 'remnant,' or

---

31. Mays, *Micah*, 101.
32. G. Vos, *The Pauline Eschatology* (Princeton: Princeton University Press, 1930), 36.
33. Allen, *Micah*, 329-30.
34. Hillers, *Micah*, 55.

'survivors,' is an old one; to turn it to a positive sense, almost a title of honor, could be the work of a very brief time."

B. Renaud[35] tries to date the passage by vocabulary tests, claiming, among other arguments, that although terms like *qbṣ/'sp, ndḥ, rʿʿ, gôy ʿāṣûm*, and *mlk yhwh* are not all "exclusively late . . . , they are largely used in the exilic or postexilic epochs in contexts extremely similar to those of Micah." His argument, however, is not cogent because: (1) he discounts demonstrably preexilic usages; (2) he redates literature in a circular way (e.g., according to him Isa 11:12 is exilic); (3) he ignores the fact that Micah himself may have initiated some usages and that one might expect later oracles of salvation to have picked them up; and (4), as he earlier admitted, negative evidence in vocabulary is extremely weak. The weakness of his argument can be seen in his handling of the expression "from now and forevermore," which, he says, "appears only in postexilic pieces (Isa 59:21; Pss 113:2; 115:18; 121:8; 125:2; 131:3) and the rereading at the end of Isa 9:6[7]." Elsewhere, however, he complained that the Psalms are difficult to date, and his explanation of Isa 9:6(7) is circular. He notes that *šěʾērît* takes a positive value only with Zephaniah and Jeremiah. For that statement to hold he has to deny the authenticity of Isa 37:32 and 2 Kgs 19:4 (= Isa 37:4), and he must assert that Micah follows Jeremiah (cf. 23:3; 24:8). Renaud seems to make the point that Isaiah prefers the masculine form *šěʾār* whereas later writers prefer the feminine (but see Amos 1:8; 9:12; and especially 5:15). From a scientific viewpoint there is no reason to deny the oracle to Micah.

3. Jerusalem's Dominion Restored (4:8)

8 "As for you, tower for the flock,
        'Ophel,' Daughter Zion,
            unto you [the former kingdom] will come."
    And so the former kingdom will come,
        namely, a kingdom belonging to Daughter Jerusalem.

EXEGESIS

Micah introduces a third prophecy about Zion with *waw*-disjunctive and the vocative form, "As for you." Here initial *waw* introduces a new oracle.[1] The di-

---

35. *La Formation*, 185-86.
1. Cf. Lambdin, *Introduction to Biblical Hebrew*, 132.

rect address to the city itself is used again in 5:1 with reference to Bethlehem. 4:8Aa *wĕ'attâ . . . ṣîyôn* is a *casus pendens* construction with the resumptive pronoun *'ādêkâ* "to you" in the main clause.[2] This nominative absolute construction serves to highlight and clarify the topic "Zion," a stress already present in the literary form of direct address to the city. The masculine singular pronoun, *'attâ* for city, especially with *bat-ṣîyôn* "Daughter Zion," is a bit surprising, but it is acceptable Hebrew.[3] The topic is further emphasized by the vocative *migdal-'ēder 'ōpel bat-ṣîyôn*.[4] *migdal-'ēder (tower for the flock)* consists of the masculine singular construct *migdal*, a locative *mem* with the root *gdl* "to be great, powerful," and of the masculine singular absolute *'ēder* "herd, flock" of sheep or cattle. *'ēder* is best taken as a genitive of advantage,[5] that is, the flock is the recipient of the advantages offered by the *migdal* "tower." Probably a flock of sheep is in view (see 4:7).

B. Renaud[6] painstakingly devastated H. Cazelles's[7] novel suggestion that "Migdal-Eder, Ophel of the Daughter of Zion," represents, if not a city totally independent, at least a large village very close to Jerusalem to which Israelites fled after the fall of Samaria in 722/721 B.C. According to Cazelles,[8] the village lay "between Jerusalem and the present Tell El-Ful, the ancient Geba of Saul, to which an allusion would be found in the expression 'the chief sovereignty.' . . ." Renaud rightly complains that Cazelles's argumentation piles hypothesis upon hypothesis, none of which is compelling. Suffice it to note that "Ophel" can only designate the city of David, that nowhere else does the Bible equate "Daughter Zion" with a city depending on Jerusalem, and that no mention is made of the Northern Kingdom.

E. Sellin[9] also rejects the widely held interpretation that *migdal-'ēder* "tower of the flock" refers to Zion and, following instead the Mishnah,[10] thinks that it is a place name of a small town in the vicinity of Jerusalem (cf. Gen 35:21, where it is on the highway from Ramah to Hebron; Jerome located it one mile east of Bethlehem). But this understanding, also embraced by BDB, does not mesh as well with the rest of the nominative absolute as taking it as an epithet

---

2. *IBHS* §4.7b.

3. GKC §144a.

4. *IBHS* §4.7d.

5. *IBHS* §9.5.2.

6. *La Formation*, 191.

7. H. Cazelles, "La Fille de Sion et Théologie Mariale dans la Bible," *Bulletin de la Société Francaise Études Mariales* 1 (1965) 51-71.

8. Cazelles, "La Fille," 57.

9. Sellin, "Micha," 286.

10. *m. Šeqalim* 7.4.

for Jerusalem in apposition with "Ophel" and "Daughter Zion." GB rightly says that Mic 4:8 can hardly be equated with Gen 35:21.

ōpel (Ophel) confounded the ancient translators. All of them confused it with *ʾōpel* "darkness," and some made it an attributive genitive with *migdal-ʿēder:* LXX "dark/squalid tower of the flock"; Vg "cloudy tower of the flock." Syr and Sym give *ōpel* its metaphorical meaning "hidden" (cf. Ps 11:2) and relate it to the hidden rule of the future ruler. In Tg this prophecy is paraphrased "And thou the Messiah of Israel hidden because of the iniquity of the congregation of Zion." S. Schwantes[11] draws the conclusion that they all missed "its reference to 'fortified hills' in general (Mesha Inscr. 1.22), and specifically to the southern end of the hill Moriah, formerly occupied by the Jebusites (cf. II Chr 27,3; 33,14; Neh 3,26.27; 11,21)." *ōpel* may mean a geological swelling in general or a hill that served as a stronghold, or it may denote specifically the original Jebusite hill. NRSV and TNIV take *ōpel* as an appellative, "hill/stronghold," in construct with "of the daughter of Zion." But the vocative, "stronghold of the daughter of Zion," in direct address to Jerusalem seems inapposite since Jerusalem is not Zion's stronghold.

Rather, it is better to follow MT, which has the disjunctive accent *tĕbîr* here, and to take Ophel, like "tower for the flock" and "Daughter Zion," as an epithet for Jerusalem and therefore as another vocative. This ancient proper name for the original city of David functions as a byword that evokes the strength of David's ancient kingdom and stands in parallel with "tower" (see Isa 32:9-14). (See the Exposition, 234-35.) P. Bordreuil[12] derived the title *bat-ṣiyôn (Daughter Zion)* from the Ugaritic texts where the goddess Anat is called a "virgin." For its more probable derivation and meaning see 1:3. This third vocative is accented in MT by the disjunctive *ṭiphâ.*

The adverbial phrase *ʿādêkā (unto you),* which modifies *tēʾteh,* consists of the older form of the frozen preposition *ʿădê,* related to *ʿad* (see 4:7), with a terminative sense[13] and the second masculine singular resumptive pronominal suffix referring back to *ʾattâ* in the nominative absolute. The topic of 4:8, Jerusalem, is further emphasized by the phrase's emphatic position. *tēʾteh (will come)* is a qal third feminine singular of the root *ʾth*[14] with an unexpected *dāgēš* after the suffix *kā* to signal that the punctuation was uncertain, according to E. A. Knauf.[15] Even more anomalously, according to MT accentuation

---

11. Schwantes, "A Critical Study of the Text of Micah," 112.

12. P. Bordreuil, "Michée 4:10-13 et Ses Paralleles Ougaritiques," *RevSém* 21 (1971) 21-38.

13. *IBHS* §11.2.12.

14. GKC §68f.

15. E. A. Knauf, "Dagesh Agrammaticum im Codex Leningradensis," *Biblische Notizen* 10 (1979) 23-35.

— note *'atnāḥ* dividing 4:8A from 4:8B — it has no subject, whereas 4:8B has two feminine subjects, *hammemšālâ hāri'šōnâ* "the former dominion" and *mamleket* "kingdom." Besides, for many text critics the back-to-back synonyms *'th* and *bô'* create an intolerable pleonasm. V. Ryssel,[16] after giving a brilliant interpretation of the versions, thinks that *tē'teh* belongs to a later stage of the language and that it was added as a gloss to show that *bā'â* was future, and that still later, for the same reason, *waw*-consecutive was added to *bā'â*. *'th*, however, is not used only in late texts (cf. Deut 33:21 and Ps 68:32[31]) and is found in Ugaritic and Arabic as well as in Aramaic. B. Duhm[17] omits *ûbā'â*. BHS thinks that they are variant readings and conjectures *tābō'*, qal third feminine singular perfective of *bô'*, as the possible original reading. S. Schwantes[18] transposes *ûbā'â* before *mamleket*. Syr makes *'ādeykā* the subject: "your time has arrived. He has come, the prince of God"; it either heard *'ādeykā* as *'iteykā* "your time" or equated *'ad* with its meaning "eternity" or with *'ôd* "duration," "lifetime." Possibly Micah gapped the subject "the former kingdom" in v 8Ab. Whereas in 4:8Aa the topic, Jerusalem, is emphasized by being addressed in the vocative, by the nominative absolute construction, and by the word order, adverbial phrase plus verb in 4:8ab, in 4:8A Jerusalem is spoken of in the third person and its dominion is emphasized by placing as an adverbial modifier to the subject "the former dominion," "a kingdom belonging to the Daughter of Jerusalem." After the nominative absolute in 4:8Aa, the structures of 4:8Ab and 4:8B are chiastically matched: prepositional phrase plus [subject] plus verb: verb plus subject plus prepositional phrase. Admittedly it is rare to have an incomplete A verset completed by a B verset, especially in the case of a noun, but the construction, though lacking a precise parallel, is not totally impossible.[19] The prepositional phrases are not exactly parallel because whereas *'ādêkā* is adverbial, *lĕbat-yĕrûšālāim* is adjectival (see below). The anomalies of this verse may be due to the process of editing; in other words, 4:8A, an incomplete pericope addressed by *I AM* to the Daughter of Zion, is commented upon by Micah in 4:8B.

The *waw*-relative with the qal third feminine singular perfective of *bô'* (*and so . . . will come*) indicates a logical result. Having proclaimed in direct address to Jerusalem that her kingdom will come, the prophet reflects upon the announcement: "and so it will come." The repetition serves to emphasize the promise. *hammemšālâ (the kingdom),* the subject of the verb, consists of the defi-

---

16. Ryssel, *Micha*, 77.

17. B. Duhm, "Anmerkungen zu den zwölf Propheten, III: Das Buch Micha," 88.

18. S. J. Schwantes, "A Critical Study of the Text of Micah," 100.

19. Cf. J. L. Kugel, *The Idea of Biblical Poetry* (New Haven and London: Yale, 1981), 54; M. P. O'Connor, *Hebrew Verse Structure* (Winona Lake, Ind.: Eisenbrauns, 1980), 122-27.

nite article, an abstract *mem* prefix,[20] a feminine suffix, and the root III *mšl* "to rule, have dominion, to reign." The combined form, an abstract feminine noun,[21] means "rule, realm, dominion, kingdom." *hāri'šōnâ (the former)* is a definite feminine singular attributive adjective of *ri'šôn*, which means "former" in time, and refers to Jerusalem's zenith of extended authoritative rule under David and Solomon; it must modify the preceding noun. The combined expression admirably matches the parallel "Ophel." LXX erroneously adds "from Babylon," an expanding gloss taken from 4:10; the catena group of MSS omits it.

mamleket (namely, a kingdom) is another abstract feminine noun that is constructed similarly to *memšālâ*; but it is anarthrous and of the root *mlk* (see 4:7A). LXX and Vg understood *mamleket* and *lĕbat-yĕrûšālāim* as a terminative direct object, "kingdom to Daughter Jerusalem," but Syr and S. Schwantes[22] rightly identify it as the construct form with a genitive introduced by the preposition *lĕ*.[23] The parallel *'ādêkā* favors the former interpretation, but the latter makes a better complement with "the former kingdom." The singular verb and the lack of conjunctive *waw* show that *hammemšālâ* is the subject. *mamleket* cannot be in apposition, for in that case it would have to be definite.[24] Rather, the anarthrous construction reveals it to be an accusative of specification indicating "the former kingdom," namely, as a kingdom belonging to Daughter Jerusalem. *lĕbat-yĕrûšālāim (of Daughter Jerusalem)* is best taken as a possessive genitive with the heightening, periphrastic preposition *lĕ*[25] and emphasizing the anarthrous nature of *mamleket*. There is no difference in form or meaning between *bat-ṣîyôn* and *bat-yĕrûšālāim*. For the significance of "daughter" see Exposition, 235.

EXPOSITION

The prophecy in 4:8 fills in with more detail the restoration of Zion/Jerusalem to its former greatness. It is marked off from the preceding prophecy, 4:6-7, by the liturgical conclusion "forever and ever" in 4:7, by its change of themes from the restoration of the remnant to the restoration of Jerusalem, and by its own form. C. Westermann recognized in Mic 4:8 and 5:1(2) the re-use of a very old form of "tribal saying" such as one can still detect in Genesis 49 and Deuteron-

20. *IBHS* §5.6.
21. *IBHS* §6.4.2.
22. Schwantes, "A Critical Study," 113.
23. GKC §130a.
24. *IBHS* §12.1.
25. *IBHS* §9.7.

omy 33. Note these similarities with 5:1(2): the prophecy starts with "and you"; is followed by the name of the addressed city; is followed by the promise of sovereignty to come; and evokes days of old. 4:8 stands apart from 4:9-14(5:1) by *ʿattâ* "Now" (see 4:9, 11, 14[5:1]) and the well-structured form with that, as will be seen, and by the chronological change from prophesying an exclusively future salvation in 4:8 to prophesying a movement from present distress to future salvation in 4:9-14(5:1).

4:8 serves as a hinge between 4:6-7 and 4:9-14(5:1). With the former it shares the symbolism of the flock and *I AM*'s kingship, but it advances the argument by predicting that Mount Zion, to which the flock has been regathered, will become a tower guaranteeing its security and survival as it did in David's epoch. The picture of the flock in 4:6-7A fades into that of the tower, Mount Zion, in 4:7A-8. From his watchtower a shepherd overlooked his flock and protected it against violent animals and vile thieves. The theme of kingship takes on a slightly different coloring, however, for whereas 4:7 refers exclusively to *I AM*'s kingship, 4:8, as will be shown shortly, has the hue of David's kingship.

At the same time 4:8 shares affinities with 4:9-14(5:1): the theme in both is Jerusalem, and both are linked verbally by *mlk* (*mamleket* [4:8] and *melek* [4:9]) and by *bat-ṣîyôn* (4:8, 10, 13). The inference of Davidic kingship becomes explicit in 5:1, which shares the same form. The hint that the House of David will resume its reign in the last days, in the midst of prophecies centered on *I AM*'s victory and reign over the nations, prepares the audience for what will become the main focus of chapters 4–5, the rule of the Messiah. In sum, the verse serves a double function: it is a hinge between 4:6-7 and 4:9-14(5:1), and it prepares the way for 5:1(2).

The oracle falls into two parts: a direct address, probably by *I AM*, to Daughter Zion (4:8A), and a promise that Zion's/Jerusalem's former kingdom will be restored. Three epithets in apposition with "you" evoke Zion's former and future greatness: "tower for the flock," "Ophel," and "Daughter Zion." For some critics[26] the epithet "tower of the flock" evokes the distress of Jerusalem. All that is left of Zion, they suggest, is a watchtower standing alone in the middle of the rubble (cf. Isa 1:8; Mic 3:12). In the words of J. Lindblom, it would represent "a mysterious designation for the ruin of the ancient royal palace in Zion." B. Renaud,[27] however, rightly notes: "The tone is not that of a lament but really that of enthusiasm." A tower is a far cry from the shanty Isa 1:8 pictures, and the lament oracle in 3:9-12 is altogether different from the salvation oracles in chapters 4–5. The glory of Jerusalem will match the coming of powerful na-

---

26. See *La Formation*, 190 n. 132.
27. *La Formation*, 190.

tions to it and will correspond to the glory of the powerful nation that comes to dwell in it (cf. 4:7). The crippled flock that was exiled from Jerusalem will return forever to its protection and security.

That "tower for the flock" aims to glorify Zion/Jerusalem, and not to denigrate it, is validated from the next epithet, "Ophel." NRSV and TNIV pick up the quality of strength associated with this word, an appropriate complement to "tower for the flock," but by not rendering it as a proper name they miss the association of the fortified hill south of the temple, the Jebus where Canaanites lived and which David conquered (2 Chr 27:3; 33:14), with antiquity and glory, notions that will be made explicit in 4:8A. As the name Bethlehem in 5:1(2) evokes David's historical origins, so Ophel conjures up feelings of Jerusalem's ancient past, its glory during the Golden Age inaugurated by David and perfected by Solomon. Jerusalem's future glory is not discontinuous with the past but brings to eternal fruition its ancient splendor and *I AM*'s promise to David in his grant to him of a throne and kingdom that will endure forever (2 Sam 7:13, 16), themes celebrated in the songs of Zion (Psalms 46, 48, 76, 84, 87, 122).

The third title, "Daughter Zion," evokes the feminine notions of a stable, nurturing community. E. R. Follis[28] wrote: "Sons commonly are thought to represent the adventuresome spirit of a society, constantly pressing beyond established boundaries, at the outermost part, the circumference, of the community. Daughters, on the other hand, have been associated with stability, with the building up of society, with nurturing the community at its very heart and center." Follis builds her case on three observations: (1) the same understanding for Athena, patroness of the city of Athens; (2) in half of the twenty-six settings in which *bat-ṣîyôn* occurs it represents Jerusalem's dignity, joy, favor, and exaltation; (3) in the other half the term is used ironically in connection with Jerusalem's defeat. She[29] draws the conclusion: "It is an image of the unity between place and people within which divine favor and civilization create a setting of stability, of home, of fixedness."

These evocations of the vocatives in 4:8Aa become explicit in 4:8B: sovereignty and dominion will once again be centered in the Daughter, Jerusalem, as in the ancient times of David and Solomon. Two points are made about the coming kingdom: it will be connected to and similar to the former kingdom, and it will be the kingdom of Jerusalem. The future Golden Age is not without government, as Marxists think, but finds its government centered in Jerusalem. Government and hierarchy are a positive good, not a necessary evil, and they

28. E. R. Follis, "The Holy City as Daughter," in *Directions in Biblical Hebrew Poetry*, ed. E. R. Follis, JSOTSup 40 (Sheffield: JSOT Press, 1987), 176-77.

29. Follis, "The Holy City," 178.

derive from the City of God. Today this oracle is fulfilled in the role of heavenly Mount Zion over the nations (cf. Mic 4:1-5 and Heb 12:22).

C. The Divine Program of Restoration (4:9–5:14 [EV 15])

1. Zion's Present Pangs Will Give Birth to a New Age, I (4:9-10)

9   Now why do you utter cries?
       Is there not a King among you?
           or did your Counselor perish?
              that anguish grasps you as a woman in labor.

10   Writhe and bring forth,
         Daughter Zion,
            as a woman in labor,
       for now you will go forth from the city
         and you will camp in the field,
            and you will enter into Babylon —
       There you will be delivered!
         There *I AM* will redeem you
           from the hand of your enemies.

EXEGESIS

9 The temporal adverb *ʿattâ (now)* links 4:9 with 4:8, but whereas "now" in 4:8 modifies the clause in itself this "now" functions as a coordinator.[1] Like the "now" in 4:7, it too designates a future time regarded as ideally present ("then" from Micah's perspective). But whereas the "now" in 4:7 refers to a remote future, "in that day," a future beyond the affliction of the Babylonian exile, in 4:9 the temporal adverbs refer to a more immediate, an impending future,[2] for in this prophecy the temporal adverb "now" is wide enough to encompass both Israel's future affliction in Babylon and its redemption from there (see Exposition, 246). LXX and a few Hebrew and Tg MSS add "and now," perhaps under the influence of "and now" in 4:11. Like "in that day" in 4:7, initial "now" is, as B. Renaud[3] comments, "a stereotyped expression that

---

1. *IBHS* §39.3.4.
2. See BDB 774.
3. *La Formation*, 195.

often marks the beginning of a new stage of development." This is especially true when it functions as an initial, stative temporal, deictic, clausal adverb.[4] *lāmmâ (why)* means "for what reason" and introduces a rhetorical question that vents Micah's amazement and indignation;[5] he is not expecting an answer but repentance. For *tārî'î rēa' (do you utter cries)* LXX has *egnōs kaka* "have you known evil things," having read *tdy'y r'* by the common error of confusing *r* with *d*. Syr "Why did you commit the crime?" may have followed LXX or have read II *r'* "to do evil." Vg *mœrore contraheris* "Do you draw together with grief?" probably freely interpreted MT's verb as intransitive hiphil of II *r'*, against its otherwise transitive use (cf. Mic 3:4 and 4:6), and invested *rēa'* with the meaning "grief." *tārî'î* is best taken as a hiphil second feminine singular of the root *rûa'*. There is no reason to follow L. Kopf[6] in connecting *rûa'*, not with Arabic *rg'* "to utter a grumbling cry," but with *rw'* "to terrify, overwhelm, arouse pleasure or admiration." The head word of the second feminine singular is better taken from the same pericope, that is, "Daughter Babylon" in 4:10, though on the literary level it also looks back to "Daughter Jerusalem" in 4:8. The rare verbal noun *rēa'* "shout, roar, cry" (cf. Exod 32:17; Job 36:33) can be construed as an effected object accusative, "to cry out a cry,"[7] or as an internal accusative, "to cry with a cry (i.e., mournfully)."[8] The "now" shows that the nonperfective denotes a progressive (present) imperfective situation.[9]

hămelek (is . . . a King) consists of the polar interrogative *hă*, which in this case expects a negative answer[10] to the negative question, and the noun *melek*. But which K/king is in view? Opinions are divided between *I AM* and a scion of David. The latter interpretation requires that one introduce into the text the figure of sarcasm, for it asks where Israel's king is while at the same time assuming that he is reigning in Jerusalem.[11] Transforming Micah's rhetorical question into a statement, Micah's meaning according to this interpretation is: "Come on, you should not cry like this because the king in whom you trust is present with you!" However, Micah actually means that in this desperate situation the king is of no more help than a wooden puppet, which is incapable of formulating solutions.

---

4. *IBHS* §39.3.1.
5. *IBHS* §18.3.
6. L. Kopf, "Arabische Etymologien und Parallelen zum Bibelwörterbuch," *VT* 8 (1958) 203-4.
7. *IBHS* §10.2.1.
8. GKC §117q.
9. *IBHS* §31.3.
10. *IBHS* §40.3.
11. Cf. Mays, *Micah*, 105.

H. Wolff[12] and B. Renaud,[13] on the other hand, identify the referent as *I AM*. The answer depends in part on the form of the oracle: if reproach, then a human king is in view; if promise, then probably *I AM*. Those who make it reproach tend to disassociate v 9 from v 10, but the "now," which has a thickness to refer to both affliction and salvation in both verses, links them as a unified prophecy of salvation. They are also unified by the figure of childbearing, a figure that entails moving from pain to joy (see Exposition, 246). Renaud wrote:

> If there is a reproach it rather bears on the despair of the Daughter of Zion, and the latter is vigorously invited to put her confidence in the true King, who is God, as the rest of the text shows well. There is an obvious connection between this reproach of her despair and this promise of salvation: you do not have the right to cry this way, because there is somebody to save you and to buy you back.

Three lines of evidence support this interpretation. First, and most indirectly, in the close parallel of Jer 8:19 *I AM* is named: "Listen to the cry of my people from a land far away: 'Is *I AM* not in Zion? Is her King no longer there?'" Renaud analyzes the similarities between these two texts:

> . . . the cry of Israel, the similitude of the formula Daughter of Zion/ Daughter of my peoples, and especially the complete identity of the way in which they are formulated . . . : the same redoubling of the question with the two adverbs of *h* . . . *'m*, the identity of the second interrogation of Jeremiah with that of Mic 4:9 ["Is there not a/her King in you/her?"], the presence of the king in *Zion*. The only difference, the formulation in the second person in Micah, is explained by the fact that the Daughter of Zion is here addressed.

Another difference is that Mic 4:9 employs the epithet "Counselor." One ought not think, however, that "king" and "counselor" are different persons (cf. 2 Sam 15:12; Isa 3:2-3), for in the parallel versets of 4:9Aaα and 4:9Aaβ they are the same (cf. Isa 9:6) (see below and Exposition, 247). Mays notes the parallel in Jer 8:19 but unsuccessfully tries to parry it by gratuitously assuming without argument that "counselor" must be scornful. Second, and more directly, the prophecies of 4:9-10 and 4:11-13 are linked closely together not only in their common form (see Exposition of 4:11-13) but, as suggested by H. Wolff,[14] also

12. Wolff, *Micha*, 111.
13. *La Formation*, 205.
14. Wolff, *Micha*, 111.

in their themes of "counsel" and "plan." In 4:12A it is clear that *I AM* is the One who drew up the plans and counsel, so that there is more reason to think that the Counselor in 4:9 is *I AM* than someone else.

Third, and most directly, in 4:10 of this unified pericope *I AM* is named as the One who will save Daughter Zion from her cry of pain, which has now been likened to the pain of childbearing.

'ên (. . . there not) is the negative for verbless clauses and is usually in the construct form.[15] *bāk (among you)* consists of the second feminine singular pronominal suffix with reference to Daughter Zion under the government of the preposition *bě*, not in a locative sense as though Daughter Zion were pregnant with a king, but in the sense of "amid" a domain,[16] as the parallel in 4:9Aαβ and the arguments pertaining to the identification of the king show. Bethlehem, not the Daughter of Zion, will give birth to the messianic king (cf. Mic 5:1).

The polar interrogative *'im (or)* introduces the second parallel question, which also expects a negative answer (cf. 2:7). Both questions are rhetorical in that they ask for assent rather than a reply.[17] In the qal masculine singular participle with the second feminine singular pronominal suffix *yô'ăṣēk (. . . your Counselor)* the participle functions as a *nomen agentis*[18] and the pronominal suffix is a genitive of relation.[19] The referent is the same as for "King," namely, *I AM*. For the meaning of "Counselor" see Exposition 247. LXX has *hē boulē* "council," a confusion also found in Prov 11:14 and Isa 9:5(6); perhaps it was influenced by *'ṣh* in 4:12. Syr has "counselors," apparently taking form as collective. Though better than LXX, it too destroys the parallelism with *melek* and diffuses the argument. Aquila and Vg rightly have respectively *ho symboulos sou* and *consiliarius tuus*. *'ābād (Did . . . perish)* is qal third masculine singular preterite perfective[20] of the root I *'bd*, which inherently denotes a telic situation.[21] The original meaning of I *'bd* seems to have been "to run away," and this meaning was expanded to mean "to perish" with the nuances of "by becoming lost" (cf. Lev 26:38), or "by going astray" (Ps 2:12), or simply "to die" (Esth 4:16). The verb is common in the expression "and you shall perish away from the land . . ." (Lev 26:38; Deut 4:26; 8:19-20; 11:17; 30:18; Josh 23:13, 16). B. Otzen[22] says: "Other

15. *IBHS* §39.3.
16. *IBHS* §11.2.5.
17. *IBHS* §40.3.
18. *IBHS* §37.2.
19. *IBHS* §9.5.1.
20. *IBHS* §30.5.1.
21. *IBHS* §30.2.1.
22. B. Otzen, "'ābhadh," *TDOT* 1:22.

passages state even more directly that the people shall perish in exile (Jer. 27:10, 15; Ob. 12; cf. Isa. 27:13)." The notions of becoming lost or of going astray are particularly apt, and so perishing is particularly ironic and poignant with reference to a counselor. To judge from 4:10, the exile is also in view here. Micah's full thought is: "Your Counselor did not become lost and so perish in the exile, did he?"

The logical particle *kî (that)* gives the reason why Micah asks the double rhetorical questions: "[I ask this] because. . . ." In *heḥĕzîqēk (grasps you)* the hiphil is a two-place one of the qal intransitive *ḥzq* "to be strong."[23] The specialized meaning "to grasp" is found only in the hiphil, and "[t]he semantic shift from 'make strong' to 'grasp' is not easy to explain," says F. Hesse,[24] though he connects it through the route of appointing someone to office by grasping him by the hand. The perfective is a present perfect,[25] and the second feminine singular verbal pronominal suffix, referring to "Daughter Zion," is the object of the transitive verb. Following J. Strugnell, M. Collin[26] wants to restore here the fragment 3 of 1QpMic that reads *h(ḥz)yqkh*, exhibiting the less common *plene* form of the second masculine singular verbal suffix. This reading, it is alleged, harmonizes better with the masculine suffix *ʿādeykā* in 4:8. On this basis he reconstructs masculine singular suffixes throughout 4:9, but as B. Renaud[27] notes, he reaches an excessive conclusion, "for the feminine is here necessary because it is about Daughter Zion," and so "The MT should be preserved." The subject of the third feminine singular form is the masculine noun *ḥîl (anguish)*, which is derived from the root *ḥûl* "to writhe," "be in labor," and which has the figurative sense of that root, "to fear, tremble." The figurative sense, which derives from a woman's extreme distress, recalls the outward action of a woman in labor. A. Bauman[28] tries to validate the figurative sense by the simile "as a woman in labor," but that argument will not stand because the same figure is used with a literal sense in 4:10. In any case, the noun always has the meaning "anguish" with this simile (Jer 6:24 = 22:23; 48:7; 50:23) except in Exod 15:14. The connection between *ḥîl* and *ḥûl* is disputed (see 4:10). The reference in Jer 50:43 is arresting because the anguish is explicitly caused by the king of Babylon, who is implicitly in view in Mic 4:10 and probably in Jer 6:24 (see Exposition, 247). *kayyôlēdâ (as*

---

23. *IBHS* §27.2a.

24. F. Hesse, "*chāzaq*," *TDOT* 4:304.

25. *IBHS* §30.5.2.

26. M. Collin, "Recherches sur l'Histoire Textuelle du Prophète Michée," *VT* 21 (1971) 286.

27. *La Formation*, 196.

28. A. Bauman, "*ḥyl*," *TDOT* 4:345.

a woman in labor) consists of the preposition *kĕ*, with the sense of correspondence,[29] and the article of class, a use especially common in comparisons,[30] and the qal feminine singular participle as a *nomen agentis*[31] of the root *yld* "to bear children." A. Bauman[32] notes: "The application of this metaphor to males is anything but flattering; it is tantamount to saying that men in panic have become 'like women.'"

10 *ḥûlî (Writhe)* is a second feminine singular imperative of the root *ḥûl* that is here related in meaning to *ḥûl* "writhe," "be in labor," though the exact connection to that root is unclear.[33] In any case, twisting and writhing in childbirth is in view here (cf. Isa 13:8; 23:4-5; 26:17; etc.). LXX's *ōdine kai andrizou* appears to have doubly translated the form, first from *ḥûl* with the meaning "to be in birth pangs" and then as a cry of encouragement, "be manly/valiant," a denominative from *ḥayil* or from II *ḥîl* "to be strong/enduring" (cf. Ps 10:15; Job 20:21). *wāgōḥî (and bring forth)* consists of a conjunctive *waw*, which is typically pointed with *qâmēṣ* before the monosyllable, and of qal second feminine singular imperative of a disputed root.

Numerous corrections have been suggested:[34] *pĕʿî* "cry" (Buhl; cf. Isa 42:14, precisely about a woman who gives birth), *wḥwšy* "hurry up" (Köhler). Most appeal to *hĕgî* "cry out/moan" (Elhorst; cf. Jer 48:31). J. Levy makes *gōhî* derive from *gnḥ* "groan/moan/whimper/whine," but this root, though attested in Syr and Rabbinic Hebrew, is unattested in Biblical Hebrew. Syr "be strong" probably depends on LXX's double reading for *ḥûl, andrizou*, and so is useless. LXX's *kai engize* "draw near" may have read *ngʿy*, which it derived from *ngʿ* "to rest upon." That form could also be interpreted as a qal feminine singular imperative of *gʿh* "to howl/bellow," but this meaning is used only with animals (cf. 1 Sam 6:12; Job 6:5). H. Wolff[35] holds that in this context it is best to think of *gōḥî* as an unusual imperative of *gḥḥ*, which in Ps 22:10(9), where *gōḥî* is a qal active participle with a first common singular suffix, describes the "drawing forth" of a child in delivery. Were the root *gḥḥ*, however, the form would also have been *gĕḥî*. As an unusual imperative of the doubly weak root *gyḥ*, it could mean "to burst forth," as of a breaching brook (Job 38:8; 40:23), with the under-

---

29. *IBHS* §11.2.9.

30. *IBHS* §11.5.1.

31. *IBHS* §37.2.

32. A. Bauman, *TDOT* 4:346.

33. Solomon Mandelkern, *Veteris Testamenti Concordantiae Hebraicae atque Chaldaicae* (Berlin: Margolin, 1923), 1:374, lumps them together under one root, whereas GB 217-18 finds three roots of *ḥûl*.

34. See *La Formation*, 196, and Schwantes, "A Critical Study," 116.

35. Wolff, *Micha*, 130.

standing of either R. Vuilleumier,[36] "to shout forth a yelling," or G. de la Fuente,[37] "to leap, to jump." There are good Semitic parallels of *gyḥ/gwḥ* meaning "to gush" (Arabic), "to burst forth" (Syriac), though admittedly never with childbirth.

Nevertheless, it probably means "to burst forth" into the light in connection with childbirth. Vg's *dole et satage* "be in pain and labor" for the first two verbs probably also had the cries of an excruciatingly painful childbirth in view; so did Syr's *ḥṣnk* "be in labor." H. Wolff suggests that the two imperatives sound like a midwife who challenges Daughter Zion not to despair but to strain every nerve to persist through the pain to the delivery. Similarly, Renaud[38] says: "This image in any case would accord well with the representation which runs through all these verses. Daughter Zion must understand her cry of pain as a cry of deliverance. The suffering of the present moment prepares for the liberation to come." For the vocative *bat-ṣîyôn (Daughter Zion)* see 1:13; 4:8, and for the simile *kayyôlēdâ (as a woman in labor)* see 4:9. But whereas in 4:8 the personification refers to the city, here it refers to its inhabitants.

The logical particle *kî (for)* connects the command employing the simile of child labor in 4:10A to the explanation in 4:10B, also addressed to Daughter Zion, namely, that out of the pain of the exile she will give birth through *I AM*'s redemption to a new situation. Like the "now" introducing 4:9, the temporal deictic adverb *ʿattâ (now)* in 4:10 is wide enough to encompass both the distress of entering into Babylon and of being redeemed from there.[39] *tēṣ'î (you will go forth)*, a qal second feminine singular future nonperfective of *yṣ'*, depicts the first of Daughter Zion's three labor pains. For *yṣ' min* see 1:13 and 4:2. *miqqiryâ (from the city)* consists of the preposition *min* and the feminine noun *qiryâ*, a synonym for *ʿîr* "city." Here, as most frequently elsewhere, the city must be Jerusalem, for Daughter Zion is being addressed. Though the anarthrous construction is common in terse poetic style, the construction here is probably deliberate to contrast the changed situation from dwelling in a city to camping in a field.[40] *qiryâ*, while mostly used in poetry, is also used in prose, especially with reference to a city's excitement and noise (cf. 1 Kgs 1:41, 45) and to its strength (cf. Deut 2:36; 3:4, where, in contrast to *ʿîr*, it designates the highest cities). It probably derives from *qrh* "to gather" and hence has overtones of a meeting place.[41] In sum, the combi-

36. Vuilleumier, "Michée," 54 n. 3.
37. G. de la Fuente, "Notas al Texto de Miqueas (1:4; 2:4; 4:10; 6:1; 6:14)," *Aug Rom* 7 (1967) 145-54.
38. *La Formation*, 196.
39. See BDB 774, §1b.
40. *IBHS* §13.2.
41. See KBL 855.

nation "to go forth from a bustling, strong city" is a reflex upon 2:13, but instead of emerging victorious out of the Jerusalem, as in 701 B.C., now Jerusalem's inhabitants go forth as captives, camp in the field, and finally arrive as exiles in Babylon.

The *wāw*-consecutive qal second feminine singular suffix conjugation *wĕšākant (and you will camp)* refers to a second, subsequent painful situation.[42] *škn* means "to hold up, stop, stay," "to dwell." Other modifiers must determine the duration and character of the "staying." It can be "forever" (Isa 34:17; Ps 37:27, 29) or the circumstances may be those of dwelling in tents (Gen 9:27; Judg 8:11). A temporary dwelling in tents (i.e., "to camp") is suggested by the qualifying prepositional phrase *baśśādeh (in the field)*. The field, vivid in the prophet's imagination,[43] designates the open country, the unfrequented country exposed to violence (Gen 4:8; Deut 21:1; 22:25) and/or wild beasts (Exod 22:30[31]) and/or the sword (Jer 6:25; 14:18; 40:7, 13), between the cities of Jerusalem and Babylon, as the preceding and following clauses show. The reference to Jerusalem being plowed as a field (Mic 3:12) puts beyond reasonable doubt that the situation of camping in the field on the way to captivity in Babylon is a second phase of Daughter Zion's labor pains as she writhes and wails under the hand of her enemy.

The third *wāw*-consecutive with the qal second feminine singular perfective of *bô'* (see 1:9, 15) *(and you will enter)* designates the third and climactic part of Daughter Zion's anguish and weeping. Before the former kingdom returns to Daughter Zion (4:8), she must first enter Babylon. For the spatial meaning of the preposition *'ad (into)* see 1:9 and 4:3. *bābel (Babylon)*, under the government of *'ad*, is among the earliest references to the Babylonian captivity in prophetic literature (cf. Isa 39:1-7). Because of the iron-clad strictures imposed by the canons of historical criticism upon the prophetic gift, scholars usually delete 4:10Aαβ and 4:10Ab as later insertions. Others, such as A. S. Kapelrud[44] and S. Schwantes,[45] more cautiously retain it (see Exposition, 248-49).

šām (there) is a constituent deictic locational adverb showing that Babylon, its antecedent, is a remote place relative to the prophet.[46] In *tinnāṣēlî (you will be delivered)* the niphal is an incomplete passive,[47] though *I AM* is clearly the agent in the parallel, "There *I AM* will redeem you"; the second feminine singular continues the direct address to Daughter Zion; and the nonperfective

42. *IBHS* §32.2.1.
43. *IBHS* §13.5.1.
44. A. S. Kapelrud, "Eschatology in the Book of Micah," *VT* 11 (1961) 399.
45. Schwantes, "A Critical Study," 116.
46. *IBHS* §39.3.1.
47. *IBHS* §23.2.2.

points to the future. LXX makes clear that *I AM* is the agent by transforming the structure from passive to active: *rysetai se* "he will redeem you." In contrast to the future tense up to this point, here it refers to the future beyond the distress, and implicitly announces freedom in association with *I AM*. *nṣl* is one of those mixed verbs in which the active sense is designated by piel and/or hiphil.[48] In the hiphil it means "to take away," "to free from some sort of being held fast." U. Bergmann[49] contrasts it with other verbs belonging to the field of salvation: "While . . . *yš*ʿ hiphil designates the removal of the oppressor and *mlṭ/plṭ* the making escape possible, *nṣl* hiphil designates similarly as *pdh* the departing from the sphere of distress." The word choice aptly suits Israel's restoration from Babylon.

The parallel *šām* emphasizes that Israel's salvation will take place from Babylon, the stronghold of pagan political and religious strength (see Exposition, 247-48). *yigʾālēk (will redeem you)* consists of a qal third masculine singular with *yhwh (I AM)* as subject — LXX adds *ho theos sou* "your God" — a second feminine singular verbal suffix continuing the direct discourse to Daughter Babylon, and the root *gʾl*. *gʾl* in its nontheological uses has the legal notion that the family/tribal leader protect a disadvantaged member by paying off his debt, or freeing him from slavery, or avenging his murder. This legal sense carries over with *I AM* as subject, but in this use the notion of "setting free, liberating," comes to the fore and so forms an apt parallel to *nṣl*.

mikkap ʾōyĕbāyik (from the hand of your enemies) consists of ablative *min*, which specifies that from which Israel will be redeemed, the feminine singular noun *kap*, which is the object of the preposition and is used figuratively here for "power, strength,"[50] and the genitive of inalienable possession[51] *ʾōyĕbāyik*, a masculine plural noun with the second feminine singular pronominal suffix continuing the address to Daughter Babylon, of the root *ʾyb* (see 2:8). The powerful enemies are unidentified, but one may imply that since *I AM*'s redemption takes place in Babylon, fierce people are in view. The singular *kap* may suggest their singularity, and the plural *ʾōyĕbê* may individualize them and emphasize their strength in contrast to the weakness and vulnerability of Daughter Zion.

48. *IBHS* §23.6.2/3.
49. U. Bergmann, *THAT* 2:97.
50. See BDB 496, §2.
51. *IBHS* §9.5.1.

EXPOSITION

The next three prophecies share the common form of initial "Now" (4:9, 11, 14[5:1]) and a situation of distress, namely, Jerusalem's cry of pain (4:9), the gathering of the nations against it (4:11), and the siege of the city and the humiliation of its magistrate (4:14[5:1]), followed by a situation of promise. The initial "now" in each case refers to a temporal present and introduces the prophecies. Each of these three sections is addressed with a vocative, "Daughter Zion" (4:9, 11) and "Daughter of Troops" (4:14[5:1]), following imperatives: "Writhe and bring forth" (4:10), "Arise and thresh" (4:13), and "gather together in troops" (4:14[5:1]). The first two prophecies are particularly similar; they are of the same length, use the vocative "Daughter Zion," have the situation of distress immediately following the temporal/logical adverb "now," and conclude with a promise of salvation introduced by two imperatives followed by *kî*. B. Renaud[52] answers the objection that in 4:13 the two imperatives relate to joyful victory, whereas in 4:10 the two imperatives relate to excruciating pain, by tracing the argument of the passage:

> But one must place these two imperatives [of v 10] within the development of the imagery of vv 9-10: the prophet started with the cry of suffering that Israel shouted — "Why do you cry aloud" — and then he justifies his astonishment. The questions of vv 9-10 imply a positive response: Of course there is a king; of course there is a counselor. Therefore, the imagery of the woman who gives birth will give to this cry of suffering a significance of hope. *Because* [in the original] it is a cry of a woman in childbirth. This cry of suffering will be transformed into a cry of deliverance. . . . The "because" bears on the end of the verse: "There you will be delivered! . . . YHWH will buy you back." . . . Both the coming out of the city and the exile to Babylon constitute the conditions preliminary to salvation. The circumstances preceding this salvation always constitute harbinger signs. The "now" has two faces: a face of suffering (you will come out of the city, you will remain in the fields, you will go up to Babylon), and a face of deliverance (There you will be delivered! . . . There YHWH will redeem you from the hand of your enemies). The promise only unfolds what was pregnant in the imagery of the cry of a woman in childbirth: a cry of pain, but also a cry of deliverance.

Renaud[53] supports his interpretation and analysis by pointing to the grammatical structure undergirding the development of the argument in 4:10:

52. *La Formation*, 200.
53. *La Formation*, 201.

245

One can even state precisely that the distinction of the two stages is stylistically underscored: the first three clauses [leave . . . camp . . . go] are connected by two conjunctive [*sic!*] *wāw*(s); the last two, those that announce deliverance by simple juxtaposition. . . . One could not express better the pause and the contrast between the two stages.

Essentially following Renaud, one can schematize the parallelism of the two passages as follows:

9A	Now	11A
9B	Situation of distress	11B
10A	Appeal to Daughter of Zion with two feminine imperatives	13Aaα
10B	Situation of victory	13Aaβ-B

The "now" and the imagery of "Daughter Zion" writhing in childbirth open the way toward a comprehensive interpretation of the passage. The initial "now" embraces both the situations of distress, the cry of going into exile, and of victory, the cry of deliverance in coming out of exile. So also in 4:10 "now" coincides with the exile to Babylon and at the same time with the deliverance that *I AM* will perform there. The "now" of catastrophe is also the "now" of salvation. So also in so-called Deutero-Isaiah the "now" is not complete but essential for what follows. Neither of the prophets lives in the fullness of the "now" of which they speak. P. Beauchamp[54] put it this way: "It is situated in the intermediate register and is familiar to us in the concept of the already and not yet, of the new which is partially in the now but is germinating." The imagery of Daughter Zion in childbirth expresses precisely this message: the cry of pain, as of a woman in childbirth, gives to the pain a positive significance, the childbirth of a new world, the prelude to the cry of deliverance. Renaud[55] said: "Babylon represents in a way that cannot be disassociated both the place of punishment and of liberation." Out of the darkness of the exile the new age will burst forth into light. The prophecy pivots on Daughter Zion's labor pains: distress and deliverance. This theological truth was anticipated in the protoevangelium that the Seed of the woman in having his heel bruised would crush Satan's head (Gen 3:15), and it finds fulfillment in the death of our Lord, who through the sufferings of the cross brought salvation to the earth. In the same way that the apostles strengthened the disciples and encour-

---

54. P. Beauchamp, *Le Deutero-Isaïe dans le Cadre de l'Alliance* (Lyon: Cours de la Faculté de Théologie de Fourvière, 1970).

55. *La Formation*, 203.

aged them to remain true to the faith, saying, "We must go through many hardships to enter the kingdom of God" (Acts 14:22), Micah strengthened the hands of a coming generation in Jerusalem who were about to go into exile by prophesying that their situation of distress was a necessary preliminary to their future situation of victory.

That this prophecy aims at hope and salvation is underlined immediately by his reproachful rhetorical question: "Why do you cry?" His following two questions, "Is there not a King among you? or did your Counselor perish?" aim to shame them into faith, to assure them that their Sovereign *I AM* has a wonderful plan for them, and to encourage them to persevere through the tribulation until they give birth to the new age. In his sovereign grace their *I AM* will turn their cries into the cry of childbirth. The King and the Counselor designate the same Person as in Isa 9:5(6) where the messianic King is called "Wonderful Counselor." *I AM* is "marvelous in counsel" (Isa 29:29; Jer 32:19), and counsel belongs inherently to him (Dan 2:20; Job 12:13). He is above every counsel (Ps 16:7; cf. Ps 20:6[5]), and he executes infallibly his immutable plans (Isa 5:19; 23:8-9; 25:1; Jer 49:20; cf. Pss 106:13; 107:11; see 4:12). The Counselor not only elaborates plans but brings them to beneficial fruition. P. A. H. de Boer[56] showed that counsel is practically identical with action, an action that has in view the maintenance or the recovery of life and whose effects are security, victory, and salvation. *I AM* designs and wills to bring Israel to a successful end, life from the dead, as it were. The heathen do not know his plan/counsel (Mic 4:12), but he expects his elect to understand it.

Whereas in 4:9 Micah rebuked the elect for crying as a woman in the panic and agony of labor, he now commands them in 4:10A to labor because from their pain will come forth the new salvation. Jeremiah often likens the pain and agony of the people at the time of the captivity to labor pains (cf. Jer 4:31; 6:24; 13:21; 22:23; cf. 49:24). The expanded notion of birth through pain, introduced in 4:9, is unraveled in three historical events: they must leave the security of the old city (cf. 2 Kgs 25:2-7; cf. Jer 52:7), camp in the open and unprotected field (cf. Jer 6:25; 14:18; 40:7, 13), and enter diabolical Babylon (2 Kgs 24:16; 25:7; Jer 34:3). Their deliverance follows these three excruciating, painful events. There, repeated twice for emphasis, in Babylon, the epitome of evil and death, they become the new Israel. They must first die, as it were, to live again (cf. John 12:24).

What Rome was to the Middle Ages, Babylon was to the ancient Near East. It was the "Mecca" of the pagan religions, the very antithesis of Jerusalem. From its very commencement it was the type and symbol of pagan imperial

---

56. P. A. H. de Boer, "The Counsellor," *VTSup* (Leiden: Brill, 1955), 56.

power (cf. Gen 10:10). God gave Israel over to this epitome of evil and redeemed them from there as a type of true Israel's being handed over to the powers of hell and triumphing over them. The Family Avenger of the covenant people will faithfully deliver them from all evil. The prophecy not only explicitly announces the freeing of the elect from the hand of their enemy, but implies the new life of freedom in the hand of *I AM*. "The tone at the end," says H. Wolff,[57] "lies in the fact that Yahweh's will to deliver is mightier than the oppression of the present enemies."

Micah's prophecy that the elect would go to Babylon creates problems for biblical critics committed to the tenets of historical criticism, which restricts the prophetic gift to merely human dimensions and rules out divine predictions beyond what unaided human prescience could guess. To make biblical prophecy fit their procrustean bed, some (e.g., W. Nowack[58] and E. Sellin[59]) explain that portion of the prophecy about going into Babylon in 4:10Ab as a gloss, while others think that the piece was authored during the exile by Jeremiah or one of his or Micah's disciples. B. Renaud[60] rejects the idea that it is a gloss because the style and structure of the piece "forbid one to appeal to such an easy expedient." He also rejects Jeremiah as the author because he asks why the oracle was not incorporated into Jeremiah. He speculates that someone in Jeremiah's school authored it, while H. Wolff[61] posits the later school of Micah in the Babylonian epoch. Renaud fails, however, to answer the question why material from Jeremiah's school is found in Micah and not in Jeremiah. J. T. Willis[62] plausibly located the composition of the oracle in 705 B.C., when the embassy from Merodach-baladan, sovereign of Babylon, came to Hezekiah in his quest for Judah's military assistance in throwing off the Assyrian yoke. Hezekiah responded favorably (2 Kgs 20:12-19 = Isa 39:1-8), but Isaiah denounced it, and in that connection predicted that Hezekiah's house would be ruined, that his wealth would be carried to Babylon, and that his sons would serve the king of Babylon as eunuchs. In sum, he spiritually foresaw that by making an unholy alliance with the very epitome of pagan religion, Judah would sell its soul to a treacherous enemy that in the end would destroy it. Historical critics, such as B. Renaud, do not question the authenticity of the Bible's historical memory regarding the visit by Merodach-baladan's men, but they do reject the prophecy

---

57. Wolff, *Micha*, 112.

58. W. Nowack, "Bemerkungenüber das Buch Micha," *ZAW* 4 (1884) 285.

59. Sellin, "Micha," 284-85.

60. *La Formation*, 207.

61. Wolff, *Micha*, 111.

62. J. T. Willis, "Review of *Structure et Attaches Litteraires de Michée 4–5*, by Bernard Renaud," *VT* 15 (1965) 402-3.

and accuse the editor of Kings, the so-called Deuteronomist, of forgery. Renaud[63] reasons as follows:

> The fact of the embassy of Merodach-baladan seems historically incontestable. One is more reserved about the authenticity of Isaiah's oracle at this point. . . . Isaiah's oracle is composed in prose, which hardly corresponds to the prophet's normal style. Especially, it has so much affinity with the theology of the exilic editor of the book that it leads us to suspect here a work of reinterpretation. It is very possible that this editor profited from this mention of Babylon to attach to it an oracle announcing the Babylonian exile. Is not one of his masterpieces showing that Israel under the conduct of its kings runs to its ruin and that the trial of the captivity constitutes the right punishment of its betrayal? By making Isaiah predict the exile to Babylon beforehand he gave his thesis new weight.

The issue, however, does not proceed from examining the data scientifically — many prose sections are found in Isaiah (cf. Isa 7:1-6, 10-25), and Isaiah, as well as the Deuteronomist, consistently warned against alliances with the pagan world (Isa 30:1-5; 31:1-3) — but from a theological prejudice that contradicts the biblical witness. There is no scientific reason to dispute that these two prophets of the second half of the eighth century predicted Israel's exile in Babylon and their restoration from there. Here we have good evidence that prophets addressed future generations beforehand for their encouragement (cf. Isa 41:21-29; 44:25-26; 48:3-8) and for the edification of their contemporaries.

2. Zion's Present Pangs Will Give Birth to a New Age, II (4:11-13)

11 But now, great nations
        are gathered against you,
    those who are saying, "Let it be desecrated!
        Let our eyes gloat over Zion!"
12 But they do not know *I AM*'s plan,
        and they do not understand his immutable purpose.
    Surely he assembles them together
        as newly cut grain [is gathered] to the threshing floor.
13 Arise and thresh, Daughter Zion! —
        for I will make your horns of iron,
            and your hooves of bronze —

---

63. *La Formation*, 207.

and pulverize great peoples!
and devote their unjust gain to *I AM* by destroying it,
even their wealth to the Lord of all the earth!

EXEGESIS

11 The coordinating *wĕ˓attâ (But now)* introduces a second prophecy, 4:11-13, whose form is almost identical with that of 4:9-10. But whereas that prophecy announces to Daughter Zion her future distress at the hands of the Babylonians and her deliverance from there, this one refers to her distress at the hand of the Assyrians and her deliverance from their siege. Accordingly, whereas *˓attâ* in 4:9 refers to a future conceptualized as present, here it refers to Micah's own time. It too, however, has a thickness, for the "now" includes both the distress inflicted by the Assyrians and Jerusalem's victory over them. *ne˒esĕpû (are gathered)* is niphal third masculine plural perfective, with *gôyîm rabbîm* "many nations" as its subject. The niphal is essentially reflexive with a reciprocal force: the many nations mutually gather themselves.[1] The notion of "gather" inherently denotes an extended situation, though here it is represented as complete; more precisely the suffix conjugation denotes a persistent present single situation.[2] For the root *˒sp* see 2:12 and 4:6. In *˓ālayik (against you)* the preposition has the sense of disadvantage, and the second feminine singular suffix shows that this oracle is also addressed to Daughter Zion. Whereas Daughter Zion in 4:9-10 refers to Jerusalem's inhabitants in 4:11, as in 4:8, it alludes to the city itself. *gôyîm rabbîm (great nations)* (see 4:2) are not identified, but since this prophecy was probably delivered during Sennacherib's siege of Jerusalem in 701 B.C., Assyria and its international army is in view. No source mentions "great nations" as joining Nebuchadnezzar in his siege of Jerusalem — they are all his victims, but in Isa 8:9 and 17:12-14 "great nations" are identified with Assyria in its conquests. J. Lindblom,[3] comparing Isa 22:6; 29:7 (cf. Hos 10:10), refers them to the various national units that made up the imperial Assyrian army. H.-M. Lutz[4] also calls attention to the songs of Zion, which may be dated to the crisis in 701 B.C., and suggests that the roots of this motif dip into the pre-Israelite cultus at Jerusalem. Although B. Renaud[5] dates the oracle to the time of the Babylonian exile,

1. *IBHS* §23.4.
2. *IBHS* §30.5.1.
3. J. Lindblom, *Micha literarisch untersucht* (Helsinki: Åbo, 1929), 91-97.
4. H.-M. Lutz, *Jahwe, Jerusalem und die Völker*, WMANT 27 (Neukirchen-Vluyn: Neukirchener, 1968), 91-97.
5. *La Formation*, 210.

he conceded: "The mysterious preservation of the city at the time of the siege of 701 could provide a good anchorage point [for this motif]." No parallel texts exhibit this motif for the exile, though the motif is taken up again in the exilic and postexilic apocalyptic literature (Ezekiel 38–39; Joel 3; Zech 12:14). To be sure, 2 Kgs 24:3 mentions other nations in connection with Babylonian invaders, but they are not represented as comprising a common army (cf. 25:1-4) but as individual armies that invaded Jerusalem during the reign of Jehoiakim.

The relative participle with the relative article *hā'ōmrîm (who say)* is a reflex contrasting what the great nations will say in the future when *I AM* brings his purpose for his sacred city to fruition with what they are saying when he disciplines his city for following unholy kings instead of himself (see Exposition, 258). *teḥĕnāp (let it be desecrated)* is a qal jussive — note the parallel *wĕtaḥaz* — third feminine singular with reference to Zion of the adjectival stative root *ḥnp*. K. Seybold[6] distinguishes between the meaning of *ḥnp*, which is always used intransitively and for the most part absolutely with reference to "land" and its subsidiary Zion and with reference to individuals. The concept lying behind the former passages, he says, "leads us to the concrete and figurative meaning 'make dirty,' 'pollute,' hence 'desecrate,' which emerges primarily from Isa. 24:5 (*taḥaṯ*); Ps. 106:38; and Nu. 35:33 . . . ; Jer 3:1f., 9 (the same idea is expressed in Dt. 24:4 with *ṭm'*); and possibly Mic. 4:11 (a visible process?)." This accords well with the definition of F. Horst:[7] "act or attitude through which a state of sacral relation to the Godhead is intentionally set aside." The nations have in mind to profane the sacral relationship between *I AM* and his holy city. Did LXX's *epicharoumetha* "we will rejoice (with malicious joy)" read *mśmḥ*? More probably it guessed at its meaning with some plausibility (see below); Vg guessed *lapidetur* "let it be stoned." Some critics suppose that *teḥĕnāp* is unnatural in the mouth of non-Israelites and so make various conjectures:[8] Wellhausen conjectured *tissāḥēp* "let it be prostrated/thrown down"; Sellin proposed *tēḥāśēp* "let her be stripped" (cf. *BHS*), which makes a better parallel with *taḥaz* (cf. Isa 47:2); and J. Lindblom excised the word altogether. G. R. Driver takes the root as II *ḥnp* and repoints the text as niphal, "may she be ruthlessly treated," after an Amarna tablet; and P. Haupt vocalizes it as hophal, "she shall be paganized." All these conjectures are unnecessary, as the next clause shows.

The *waw* with *wĕtaḥaz (and let . . . gloat)*, a qal jussive third feminine singular of the root *ḥzh*, coordinates 4:11Ab with 4:11Aa and clarifies how the holy

---

6. K. Seybold, *"ḥānēp," TDOT* 5:38.

7. F. Horst, *Hiob*, BKAT 16/1 (Neukirchen-Vluyn: Neukirchener, 1968), 132.

8. Cf. S. J. Schwantes, "A Critical Study of the Text of Micah," 117-18.

city will be desecrated. Micah, instead of describing the bare acts of the heathen nations by indicative verbal forms, rhetorically projects the strong volition behind their actions against Daughter Zion by using jussive forms, thereby creating the literary texture of *oratio variata*.[9] By quoting them, Micah dramatically and vividly brings the scene immediately into his audience's imagination (cf. 4:2) and damns them with their own words (see Exposition, 258). H. Wolff[10] thinks that the unexpiated blood that pollutes a land is in view (Num 35:33; Ps 106:38), but it seems unlikely that the pagan states would have had that Israelite law in view. Temples, throughout the ancient Near East, had holy places and most holy places, so that the notion of defiling a temple by exposing its sacred sanctuary is not uniquely Israelite and would have been understood by the pagans. The root *ḥzh* may designate a prophetic form of revelation (cf. Mic 1:1), especially in nocturnal perception of a divine voice (Mic 3:6-7), or, in other contexts, a close inspection. The latter sense is probably in view here, though A. Jepsen[11] hesitates to distinguish its use here from *r'h*. *ḥzh* with "eyes" as subject can govern the direct accusative. Micah intends, however, more than their scrutinizing the sacred precincts of *I AM*'s holy house. The preposition *bě* in the adverbial phrase *běṣîyôn (over Zion)* adds the nuance "to look on maliciously," "to gloat over" (cf. 1 Sam 6:19; Ezek 35:12, 14-15; Obad 12; Mic 7:10; Song 1:7; and LXX). The dual subject with the first common plural suffix, a genitive of inalienable relationship,[12] *'ênênû* "our eyes," "can be considered a collective and the verb put in the feminine singular"[13] so that there is no need, with ancient versions (not LXX), to transform the subject to singular. The heathen nations longed to profane Zion by removing its sacred enclosures, the temple with its sacred precincts and curtain that veiled *I AM*'s holiness, and so open to public inspection with malicious joy the symbolic revelation of God in those sacred areas that were reserved for his consecrated priests alone. Of course, in the process they would have plundered its gold.

12 In *wěhēmmâ (but they)* the disjunctive, adversative *waw* contrasts the strategy of the nations with *I AM*'s plan, and the third masculine plural personal pronoun *hēmmâ*, looking back to "many nations," sets an explicit antithesis between them and *I AM*.[14] In *lō' yādě'û (do not know)* the *lō'* is a clausal negative,[15] and the qal perfective third masculine plural of the stative

---

9. *IBHS* §34.3.
10. Wolff, *Micha*, 112.
11. A. Jepsen, *"chāqāh," TDOT* 4:289.
12. *IBHS* §9.5.1.
13. Joüon, *Grammaire*, §150a; GKC §145n.
14. *IBHS* §16.2.
15. *IBHS* §39.3.2.

verb *yd'*, which entails both intellectual awareness and emotional internalization (see 3:1), becomes quasi-fientive with the direct object *maḥšĕbôt yhwh* (*plan of* I AM). The feminine plural abstract verbal noun *maḥšĕbôt*, which refers to both the action of planning and its results, consists of the prefix *mêm* of abstraction,[16] and the root *ḥšb*, which means here "to plan," "to calculate creatively and rationally," and, more specifically in connection with persons, "with a malevolent intention," as noted by K. Seybold,[17] and an abstract feminine plural suffix, hence rendered by the singular.[18] As in 2:1, 3, the plans of the wicked are contrasted with the plan of *I AM*, a genitive of authorship.[19] His punishment, to destroy them as depicted in 4:13, will creatively and appropriately offset the malevolent schemes of the uncircumcised multitude to desecrate his holy city and house.

The formally and semantically synonymous coordinate clause in 4:12Ab, *wĕlô hēbînû 'ăṣātô (and they do not understand his immutable purpose)*, is an emphatic parallel to that of 4:12Aa. Probably no distinction is intended either between *yādĕ'û* and *hēbînû*, a hiphil third masculine plural of *bîn*, though *bîn* involves the use of the faculties to gain personal knowledge (cf. Prov 1:2), or between the objects *maḥšĕbôt* and *'ăṣātô*, a feminine singular verbal noun of the root *y'ṣ*. The heathen horde have no personal awareness because they are insensitive to right and wrong and lack the moral logic to link sin and hubris against God with punishment from him. The meanings of *'ēṣâ*, from the verbal root *y'ṣ*, range from "counsel" or "advice" to "admonition," "prophecy," or "immutable will," depending on the social relationship between the speaker and his audience and the situation in which he speaks. If the one giving *'ēṣâ* is socially inferior to the one addressed it means "advice" or "counsel," but if he is superior it means "admonition," "immutable plan," or "unchangeable purpose." Contrast its uses in Ps 33:10-11: "*I AM* thwarts the plan (*'ēṣâ*) of the nations . . . but the plan (*'ēṣâ*) of *I AM* stands firm forever." Whereas the plans of the nations are temporary and qualified, *I AM*'s are eternal and unqualified. P. R. Gilchrist[20] reminds us that LXX translates *'ēṣâ* by *boulē*, which occurs in Eph 1:11, "the counsel of his will," that is, the immutable foreordination of God's will, and in Heb 6:17 by the expression "the unchangeableness of his purpose." Elsewhere the two terms, *'ēṣâ* and the feminine abstract plural *maḥšĕbôt*, also occur together, probably to denote *I AM*'s comprehensive plan (cf. Jer 49:20; 50:45; Ps 33:10-11).

16. *IBHS* §5.6.
17. K. Seybold, "*ḥašab*," *TDOT* 5:231, 233.
18. *IBHS* §7.4.2; cf. LXX *ton logismon kyriou*.
19. *IBHS* §9.5.1.
20. P. R. Gilchrist, "*'ēṣâ*," *TWOT* 1:390.

kî (surely) is an emphatic causal adverb modifying the clause that explains the immutable plan *I AM* has designed. *qibbĕṣām (assembles them together)* is piel third masculine singular perfective of the root *qbṣ* with a third masculine plural verbal suffix with reference to the "many nations." The piel denotes the resulting state,[21] and the perfective denotes a persistent present single situation,[22] the same as *'sp* in 2:12. Both verbs are colored with martial tones (see 2:12).

ke'āmîr (as newly cut grain) consists of the preposition *kĕ*, a particle denoting correspondence, more specifically here an evocative agreement in kind,[23] and the collective noun *'āmîr* "newly cut grain,"[24] with a nominal pattern common to words for certain agricultural activity.[25] Stalks were cut off just under the ears, so that the word does not mean "sheath."[26] *gōrĕnâ (is gathered to the threshing floor)* consists of the noun *gōren* "threshing floor" and the unaccented adverbial directional *hê* suffix. The word modifies *ke'āmîr*, not *qibbĕṣām*, so that *qbṣ* must be supplied to the elliptical comparison. With the cut grain (i.e., the hostile soldiers) spread out on *I AM*'s threshing floor at Jerusalem, the stage is set for the climactic scene in 4:13.

13 Micah now unpacks *I AM*'s plan by quoting *I AM*'s address to the Daughter Zion, which expands upon Micah's simile that *I AM* has gathered the international horde to his threshing floor at Jerusalem. For the meaning and adverbial function of the qal imperative feminine singular of *qûm, qûmî (Arise)*, see 2:10. The principal imperative *wādôšî (and thresh)* consists of waw-conjunctive in a hendiadys with another qal feminine singular imperative of the root *dûš (thresh)*. The *ô* sound instead of the expected *û* is unexplained;[27] perhaps it is an intensifying variant after *qûmî*. *I AM* does not have in view the grain that survived the threshing but the pulverizing process that was accomplished by the treading oxen (Deut 25:4; Hos 10:11). In Isa 41:15 and Amos 1:3 the focus is on the threshing sledge, while in Micah's zoomorphism the focus is on the threshing heifer. The figurative imperative makes the promise or prediction more emphatic and vivid than would be the case were the form indicative. For the vocative *bat-ṣiyôn (Daughter Zion)*, see Mic 1:13; 4:8, and for the meaning and function of *kî*, see 4:12. The distinction between the city and its

---

21. Cf. S. A. Ryder II, *The D-Stem in Western Semitic* (The Hague/Paris: Mouton, 1974), 108.

22. *IBHS* §30.5.1.

23. *IBHS* §11.29.

24. Holladay, 276.

25. *IBHS* §5.3.

26. See Holladay, 277.

27. Cf. Joüon, *Grammaire,* §80k.

inhabitants is attenuated; here, in contrast to 4:11 and 4:8, it designates its faithful citizens, as in 4:10. Daughter Zion has nothing to fear in accomplishing the divine command because her *I AM* has supernaturally equipped her for her supernatural task.

qarnēk (your horns), a second feminine singular suffix, a genitive of inalienable possession[28] looking back to "Daughter Zion," with the feminine collective singular noun *qeren* "horn" — translated as plural in LXX and Syr but not in Vg — implicitly likens Daughter Zion to a threshing heifer and symbolizes her power (cf. Deut 33:17; 1 Sam 2:10; 2 Sam 22:3; Jer 48:25; Pss 22:22[21]; 75:11; 132:17; Song 2:3). In ancient Near Eastern literature and iconography horns commonly depict power. *'āśîm (I will make)*, a qal first common singular future nonperfective of the root *śîm* (see 1:6-7; 2:12; 4:7, 14), breaks up *I AM*'s commands to Daughter Zion with his somewhat parenthetical promise in the indicative mood. *I AM* nerves the Daughter of Zion for her supernatural task by transforming her into an Amazon, as it were. The second accusative of material, *barzel (of iron)*, with the first accusative of the thing made, "horn,"[29] symbolizes both hardness and strength (cf. Isa 48:4; Jer 17:1; Pss 2:9; 105:18) and harshness (Deut 28:48; Dan 7:7). A century earlier the prophet Zedekiah made for himself iron horns to symbolize Israel's superiority over Aram (1 Kgs 22:11). The double accusatives depict the Daughter of Zion as having invincible superiority.

ûparsōtayik 'āśîm nĕḥûšâ (and I will make your hooves of bronze) also comes under the government of *kî* and is syntactically synonymous to the preceding clause. *parsōtayik*, a second feminine singular suffix with reference to Daughter Zion and the feminine plural noun of *prs* "hoof," is another synecdoche for the threshing heifer, referring to her might (cf. Isa 5:28; Jer 47:3; Ezek 26:11), and *nĕḥûšâ* "of bronze" also evokes hardness and harshness (cf. Judg 16:21; Jer 52:11; 2 Chr 33:11; 36:6). The two images of the iron horns and of the bronze hooves emphasize Daughter Zion's invincibility, but whereas the former speaks of her power to defend herself as she threshes out the grain, the second reverts back to the aggressive action of grinding her enemies. Tg uniquely refers "your horn" to "the people in you," and "your hooves" to "their remnant."

In *wahădiqqôt (and pulverize)*, a *wāw*-relative with hiphil second feminine singular perfective of the root *dqq* "to crush," "to grind to powder," the *waw*-relative with the second feminine singular form[30] picks up on the first two feminine imperatives, "arise and thresh." This third imperative intensifies the

---

28. *IBHS* §9.5.1.
29. *IBHS* §10.2.3.
30. *IBHS* §32.2.2.

first two: one may cease threshing before totally pulverizing the grain into powder and nothingness (cf. Isa 28:28). So *I AM* commands the supernaturally
equipped Daughter Zion to complete the task by grinding them as fine as dust
(cf. Isa 41:15; Hab 3:12). *dqq* means "to grind fine" both in the qal (cf. Isa 28:28;
41:15) and in the hiphil. The hiphil is probably elliptical, and one should understand a second accusative, "into dust" (cf. 2 Kgs 23:6, 15).[31] For the object of the
verb *'ammîm rabbîm (great peoples)*, see 4:11 and 4:1-3.

 wĕhaḥăramtî (and you will devote . . . by destroying it) consists of a *wāw*-
relative with a hiphil perfective of the root *ḥrm* and either an archaizing second
feminine singular suffix[32] or an erroneous first common singular suffix due to
the twice-repeated *'āśîm*. The latter explanation is unlikely in light of the parallel *hădiqqôt*. The *wāw*-relative denotes a subsequent action to the *hădiqqôt*
"pulverize," and the hiphil forms the denominative of the root *ḥrm*[33] and
means "to consecrate to destruction." Whereas 4:13A speaks of the annihilation
of the enemy in a military defeat, 4:13B vividly predicts the subsequent sacred
destruction of their unholy loot. In this passage, as in Josh 6:17 and in the
Mesha inscription, the two uses of *ḥrm*, for war and for the sacred, overlap.
Daughter Zion will irrevocably give over the filthy loot of the "many peoples"
to *I AM* by totally destroying it. In Leviticus 27 and Numbers 18 *ḥrm* is associated with *qdš* "to be holy" and denotes "consecrate," but in fact it refers to irrevocably consecrating something to the countersphere of holiness and totally
destroying it. *ḥrm* is contrasted with *zebaḥ*, a pleasing "sacrifice," in 1 Sam 15:15-
23, and is something that is abominable and detestable (cf. Deut 7:26; 13:15-16;
20:17-18). Israel consecrated themselves to *I AM* by removing the *ḥērem* from
their midst (Josh 7:13), validating that *ḥērem* belongs to the countersphere of
positive holiness. Israel gave the *ḥērem* over to *I AM* by totally destroying it (Isa
43:28). By consecrating it to unholiness and destruction, not taking anything of
the booty for themselves, Israel bore testimony that the spoils belong to *I AM*
and rid the earth of their illicit gain. This punishment perfectly fits the crime of
the many nations: they intended to rid the earth of God's holiness by profaning
his sacredness; instead, God will rid the earth of their "unholiness" by totally
destroying their pillage. They intended to deconsecrate the temple by destroying it; *I AM* will consecrate their wealth to destruction. *layhwh (to* I AM*)* is an
indirect object of *haḥăramtî*[34] — their gain is consecrated to *I AM* in its destruction — and *biṣ'ām (their unjust gain)* is the direct object.

31. Cf. *IBHS* §27.3.
32. Cf. GKC §44h.
33. *IBHS* §27.4.
34. *IBHS* §11.2.10.

beṣaʿ, from the root *bṣʿ* "to cut off," has the figurative meaning "to take one's cut, profit," and in almost all the OT usages of the noun it refers to "(illegal) profit or gain." Although when it does not refer to material gain *beṣaʿ* may have a neutral sense, "profit," with reference to material gain, which must be the sense here, it has the added negative idea of unjust gain (cf. Exod 18:21; Isa 33:15; 56:9-12; Jer 6:13; 22:13-19; Ezek 22:12-13, 27; 33:31). The word is similar to the English word "cut," as when a racketeer takes his "cut" of that which has been gained through fraud and/or violence. More specifically, their unjust gain is the booty they stripped from the temples of their pagan victims (cf. Mic 1:7). The pronominal suffix with reference to the heathen horde is possessive. Israel preserved its positive holiness by consecrating this detestable loot to *I AM*.

In *wĕḥêlām (even their wealth)*, consisting of emphatic *waw* and the masculine singular noun *ḥayil* with the third masculine plural possessive genitive pronominal suffix with reference to the many nations/people, *ḥayil* can mean either "strength and power," with a strong nuance of military might,[35] or "wealth." The parallel, "their unjust gain," certifies that the latter is in view here.[36] Probably the term is a synonym for "unjust gain," more precisely pillage and booty (cf. Num 31:9; Zech 14:14). In the chiastic, emphatic synonymous parallel in Mic 4:14Ab to Mic 4:14Aa *haḥăramtî* is gapped and *layhwh*, "to *I AM*," is expanded by the indirect object *laʾădôn kol-hāʾāreṣ (to the Lord of the all the earth)*. For the meaning of *ʾādôn*, see 1:3; for *kol*, a genitive of a mediated object (i.e., *I AM* who rules over),[37] see 1:5; 3:9 and 4:5; and for *ʾereṣ*, a genitive of measure,[38] see 1:2. This title evokes the notions that the earth is *I AM*'s and everything in it (Ps 24:1), and that the just Lord will appropriately punish those who in hubris seize it for themselves and will rid the earth of that which they profaned.

EXPOSITION

As noted above, the form of the prophecy in 4:11-13 is the same as that in 4:9-10, but the substance is different. Whereas in the former the distress consists of going into the Babylonian captivity and salvation in being redeemed from there, in the latter the distress takes the form of many nations gathered against Jerusalem and salvation consists in pounding them into submission and devoting their booty to *I AM*, presumably plundered from their victimized states, by to-

---

35. Cf. H. Eising, *"chayil," TDOT* 4:349, LXX *tēn ischyn autōn*, and Vg *fortitudinem*.
36. Cf. Eising, *TDOT* 4:352.
37. *IBHS* §9.5.2.
38. *IBHS* §9.5.3.

tally destroying it. Whereas Babylon is identified as the oppressor in 4:9-10, in 4:11-13 the "many nations" (4:11) (= "the many peoples" [4:13]) are not identified. Though unidentified in the text, "the many nations" in Micah's historical context are best identified with the international horde of mercenaries that comprised Sennacherib's standing army in his invasion of Jerusalem in 701 B.C. (see Exegesis, 250). Micah will mention the Assyrians explicitly in the next prophecy (4:13–5:6, especially v 6). In contrast to the "now" of 4:9-10, which refers proleptically to a time later than Micah's, the "now" of 4:11 pertains to Micah's own age. In 4:9-10 Daughter Zion referred to Jerusalem's inhabitants; in 4:11 it designates the city itself. Finally, they also differ somewhat in style in that in 4:9 Micah expresses the distress in the form of a rhetorical question, whereas in 4:11 he assumes the posture of an observant reporter.

The situation of distress seems hopeless for Daughter Zion. Standing isolated and alone, with no apparent means of help, and with great nations, each under its own proud ensign, gathered against her, she is no match for them. It seems inevitable that the united imperial armies, which are so well disciplined and heretofore so successful (see 1:1), will certainly rape and plunder her along with all their other victims. Micah exposes the spiritual condition of the "great nations" by quoting them, but whereas their speech in the remote future that lies beyond Micah's horizon revealed their new hearts that love *I AM*, here it betrays their old hearts that hate *I AM*. By restricting himself as a reporter to the facts that he sees and hears, he allows the nations to condemn themselves by their own words (cf. Matt 12:33-37; Mark 7:20). Religious zeal informs their concerted military campaign against Daughter Zion. In unison they aim to destroy the city in order to profane it. By destroying the walls protecting the holy city and the temple precincts they gloat over the prospect of gazing malevolently on sites restricted to those who have clean hands and a pure heart (Psalms 15 and 24). More specifically, the malicious eyes of the uncircumcised throng hope to gloat over the Most Holy Place, the very sanctuary of *I AM*, the Lord of all the earth, and so plunder and profane it and rid the world of his sacred presence. In their thinking Israel's God will become but one more deity in their pantheon whom they manipulate magically to serve them. J. L. Mays[39] commented: "When nations see themselves as the centre of history and seek a destiny that fulfills their power, they can tolerate no Zion; they are gripped with a compelling need to destroy whatever stands in judgment and restraint on their pride." Was this not the same motive that moved unrighteous Cain to murder his righteous brother? And did it not find complete expression when the world, Roman and Jew alike, impaled the Son of God on the cursed tree? That same unholy

39. Mays, *Micah*, 109.

zeal accounts for the persecution of the church, Christ's body in this world, throughout its history (cf. John 15:18-25; Col 1:24). Behind every attack on the church, saints hear the deadly hiss of the Serpent.

The scene of distress, the nations fighting against Zion in 4:11, is dramatically reversed in 4:12-13 to a scene of salvation, *I AM* fighting against the nations. The act of salvation takes place in two scenes united by the common Hero, the Lord of all the earth, and the common setting, a threshing floor. In the first scene (4:12) *I AM* is revealed as plotting the destruction of the nations by bringing them to his threshing floor. In the second scene (4:13) he eliminates them by commanding Daughter Zion to pulverize them and burn up their plundered, filthy wealth. Micah puts off his guise as a reporter, quoting the enemy, and once again assumes his role as a prophet, quoting *I AM*. From this vantage point the present distress is seen in an entirely new light; it is part of God's plan! What had seemed to be a setback for the City of God is in fact an opportunity for its advance. The pagan throng do not understand that they are in *I AM*'s hands the unwitting tools of their own destruction. *I AM* turns their animosity against him to bring about their defeat, just as he outwitted Satan in the cross of Jesus Christ. "None of the rulers of this age understood it [God's secret wisdom], for if they had, they would not have crucified the Lord of glory" (1 Cor 2:8). So also, had they understood *I AM*'s immutable plan, they would never have gathered around Jerusalem, for, in fact, it is *I AM* who gathers them to destroy them. "The willfulness of the nations," says H. Wolff,[40] "is only a link in the chain of Yahweh's great planning." What they thought was their own will goes back instead to God's immutable will (cf. Gen 50:20). They willfully conspired to break into the temple precincts, but in *I AM*'s comprehensive will they brought themselves of their own accord to his threshing floor where they are about to be pulverized; they came to Jerusalem to strip its temple, but precisely there they will be stripped; where they conspired to desecrate *I AM*'s name and sanctuary, their filthy loot will be consecrated to *I AM* for destruction; where they hoped to rid the earth of the transcendent and holy God, the Lord of all the earth will rid the earth of them. Their threshing and winnowing as wheat in *I AM*'s hand serves as an earnest that the Son of God will burn up the chaff of the agodly and ungodly with unquenchable fire (cf. Matt 3:7-12).

The prophecy reaches its climax in 4:13. The battle of the nations against God now turns fully to the battle of *I AM* against the great nations. Now that the mulling crowd has been brought to *I AM*'s threshing floor like a multitude of heads of cut-off grain, *I AM* addresses Daughter Zion first with two commands in 4:13Aaα, then with two promises in 4:13Aaβ, and then with two new com-

40. Wolff, *Micha*, 113.

mands in 4:13AB-B. The threshing floor scene is developed by likening Daughter Zion to a threshing heifer that one drives over the grain, as the subsequent mention of iron horns and bronze hooves shows (Deut 25:4; Hos 10:11). In their willfulness the nations vainly exhorted one another; now the triumphant *I AM* commands Daughter Zion to prevail. *I AM*'s first command resonates with Israel's cry in holy war: "Arise!" (Num 10:35-36), but whereas that old command was addressed to *I AM*, now in the new situation it is addressed by *I AM* to Israel. The second command, "to thresh," means to crush them brutally (cf. Isa 21:10; Amos 1:3) and to destroy them (Isa 41:15; Hab 3:12).

I AM interrupts his commands with two promises: he will supernaturally equip Daughter Zion for her supernatural assignment, and he will equip her with both iron horns and bronze hooves. In her own strength the holy heifer is impotent before what appears to be an invincible crowd, and so *I AM* supernaturally equips for the task. With her hard and harsh iron horns she can defend herself by goring her attackers, and with her bronze hooves she can pulverize their heads exceedingly fine (see Mic 1:1 for historical background). Now that she is thoroughly equipped, the third and climactic command related to the imagery of threshing is given: "Pulverize the great peoples into dust!"

This third command shows that the threshing is to be total (*contra* Isa 28:28). Having been pulverized into dust, they will be blown away with the wind and forever removed from the earth (2 Sam 22:43; 2 Kgs 23:6, 15). In this way *I AM* will, as J. L. Mays[41] said, "crush the pretensions of all the peoples who plot the desecration of the city of God."

But what about the unholy plunder, the silver and gold stripped off pagan idols and temples, that is left behind? In 4:13A the final command is given: "Devote the unclean stuff to *I AM* by totally and irrevocably destroying it." Now not only is the land rid of the unclean swarm but also of their filthy wealth. By devoting it to *I AM* Daughter Zion shows clearly that it is *I AM*'s holy war, and she too is a link in his chain. Only *I AM* who performs all this is worthy of the title, "The Lord of all the earth." Israel's sovereign *I AM* has shown that he sovereignly rules not only Israel (Isa 3:11, 13) but even the great nations according to his own immutable counsel (Zech 4:10, 14; 6:5).

The motif of *I AM* fighting for Jerusalem goes back to Israel's ancient memories of holy war. At times *I AM* fought for Israel and almost independently of it, as at the Red Sea (Exod 14:13, 14) and at Jericho (Joshua 6–7), but at other times he fought through it, as at Rephidim (Exod 17:8-13) and at Ai (Joshua 7). In either case Israel must exercise faith to prevail. When Sennacherib besieged Jerusalem, *I AM* fought for Israel, but the people inside had

41. Mays, *Micah*, 110.

to have faith that God would make them invincible and that they would prevail (cf. 2 Kgs 19:20-36; Isa 17:12-14; 29:1-8; cf. Pss 46:6-8[5-7]; 48:7-8[6-7]; 76:4-7[3-6]). Although the situation of distress in 4:11 as a preliterary pericope referred to the crisis in 701, in this canonical book it lacks a clear historical referent so that it functions as encouragement to God's saints in every crisis (Psalms 27, 91, and 46:2[1]). The motif of Israel's triumph over her enemies dips its roots into Israel's most ancient prophecy (Gen 49:8-12; Num 23:24; 24:9, 17-19) and is found again in prophecies associated with the exile (Isa 41:14-16) and with late apocalyptic (cf. Zech 12:6-9). Jeremiah may have had this prophecy in mind when he likened Babylon to a threshing floor (Jer 51:33). It finds fulfillment today in the church's victory over Satan and hell (Matt 16:18). It will find its consummate fulfillment in the new Jerusalem (Revelation 21–22).

3. Birth and Exaltation of the Messiah (4:14–5:5 [EV 5:1-6])

14   Now marshall yourself [as a troop], Troop-like Daughter;
        a siege has been set against us.
    With a scepter they strike on the cheek
        Israel's ruler.

5:1   But as for you, Bethlehem Ephrathah,
        an insignificant [town] to be among the clans of Judah,
        from you on my behalf he will come forth
          to be a ruler over Israel;
    and his origin will be from of old,
        from days long ago.

2   (Therefore, he [*I AM*] will give them up
        until the time [when] she who brings forth will bear [the child],
    and [when] the rest of his brothers
        will return to the sons of Israel.)

3   And he will stand forth and shepherd [his flock]
        in the strength of *I AM*,
          in the majesty of the name of *I AM* his God;
    and they will live securely
        because now he will become great
          to the ends of the earth.

4   And he will be the one of peace.
    As for Asshur, when he penetrates into our country,
        and when he marches through our lands,

> then we will raise up against him seven shepherds,
>> even eight sheiks.
>
> 5   And they will shepherd the land of Asshur with a sword,
>> and the land of Nimrod with a drawn sword.
>
> And so he will deliver [us] from Asshur
>> when he penetrates into our country,
>>> and when he marches through our territory.

EXEGESIS

14   Initial *ʿattâ (Now)* (see 4:11 for function and meaning) marks off the third oracle (see 4:9, 11) that moves from present distress (4:14[5:1]) to future salvation (5:1-5[2-6]). *titgōdĕdî (marshall yourself as a troop)* is a hithpolel second feminine singular nonperfective of a disputed root, a dispute that also involves its congeneric noun *gĕdûd* "troop" in *bat-gĕdûd*. On the one hand, the hithpolel of *gdd* normally means "to cut oneself," as in heathen religious practices. In Jer 5:7 (cf. also Ps 94:21), however, it clearly means "to throng together." If one follows the former meaning because it has statistical priority, then Micah is sarcastically calling upon Zion to engage in heathen mourning rites that involved cutting oneself (cf. 1 Kgs 18:28; Jer 16:6; 41:5), for the Law forbade it (Deut 14:1; cf. Lev 19:28). On the other hand, the congeneric noun *gĕdûd* always means "band, troop," except in Jer 48:37, where it means "cuttings upon the hands as a sign of mourning." If this statistical preference be followed and the verb be regarded as denominative, then Micah is ordering Zion to form herself into a troop. The latter interpretation is preferable because, as in 4:9 where the figure of sarcasm was also disallowed, it better fits an oracle of salvation. The notion of hope is even stronger in this description of distress because in the preceding two oracles the second feminine singular imperative form with *bat* is found in the sections about future salvation (4:10, 13). This interpretation of the root was also adopted by Syr, "you will advance in troops," and by Tg, "assemble together." The hithpael is a direct reflexive; the subject is also the object of the verbal notion[1] of a denominative piel.[2] The second feminine singular form is addressed to "the daughter of troops," and so the nonperfective form is best interpreted as denoting injunction because the speaker is imposing his will on his audience.[3] There is neither evidence nor

---

1. *IBHS* §26.2.
2. *IBHS* §24.4.
3. *IBHS* §31.5.

need to conjecture an imperative form by changing initial *t* to *h;* nonperfectives are frequently found in conjunction with imperatives, suggesting that the injunction is linked with the preceding imperatives "Arise and thresh, Daughter Zion." If so, the interpretation "gather together as a troop" is certified. RSV's "you are walled around with a wall" (cf. the note in NIV, "Strengthen your walls, O walled city" [not in TNIV]) is based on LXX's *emphrachthēsetai thygatēr emphragmō* "daughter Zion shall be completely walled in." LXX confounded *d* with *r* and so read the root as *gdr* "wall" (cf. Mic 7:11) in the hithpael stem. But *gdr* never occurs in this stem, and, as noted, MT is both difficult and satisfying, suggesting that LXX erred in the common confusion of *d* and *r* in both the paleo-Hebrew and Aramaic scripts.

In *bat-gĕdûd (Troop[-like] Daughter)* the *nomen regens bat* functions the same as in the expression *bat-ṣîyôn* (see p. 81, 4:8, 10, 13), and the *nomen rectum* "troop" functions as an attributive genitive. The construction actually means "Troop [feminine]," but the English cannot capture the feminine gender and the verbal links with the earlier references to "Daughter Zion." To facilitate the meaning "as a troop," I paraphrased "troop" as "troop-like" in my translation. The phrase is a metaphor for Zion, to judge from the co-text and the context. Regarding the co-text, note the trilogy of oracles subsequent to 4:8, namely 4:9-10, 11-13; 4:14–5:6(5:1-6), each of which begins with *'attâ*, moves from present distress to future salvation, and is addressed to "Daughter Zion/troop." Regarding the context, note that according to 4:14Ab(5:1Ab) the command is given during a siege, mostly probably Sennacherib's siege of Jerusalem (see Exposition, 298). An article is omitted from the vocative because Jerusalem is pictured in imaginary terms.[4] There is no reason to confer on "troop" its pejorative notion, such as "a raiding band" (Gen 49:19; Jer 18:22; Hos 6:9; 7:1; so Vg *filia latronis*). If the interpretation proposed thus far be correct, it is a synonym for "army" in a neutral sense (cf. Job 25:3; 29:25; passim), but Micah chose "troop" over *ṣb'* "army" to stress the smallness of Zion's army against the hosts of nations besieging it (cf. 2 Kgs 19:23; Job 14:11).

LXX avoids the unique figure both by reading the verb, not as second feminine singular vocative, but as third feminine singular with "daughter" as its subject and by reading *gdr* instead of *gĕdûd*. LXX, followed by NRSV, demands that "wall" be understood as a metaphor of the besieging nations that form "a wall" around the city. That figure, however, is unlikely in a context where Jerusalem's defense is the literal wall protecting her against the siege referred to in 4:14Ab (5:1Ab; cf. 2:12-13). The Jerusalem Bible gets around this problem by rendering, "Look to your fortifications, Fortress" (cf. NIV note [not in TNIV]). The

---

4. *IBHS* §13.5.2.

rendering, though grammatically acceptable, must be rejected because it is based on the insupportable LXX, which read *ttgdr bt-gdr*. In sum, LXX is too difficult with reference to the *gdr* in the hithpael stem, too facilitating with reference to the unique figure "Troop Daughter," and less satisfying co-textually than MT. NRSV, probably following T. Robinson,[5] facilitates the sense even further by textually removing *bat* "daughter" altogether. "Daughter of Troop," though unique, is not too difficult, for, as S. Schwantes[6] noted, *běnê-gědûd* "sons of troop (= troops)," also an attributive genitive, occurs in 2 Chr 25:13.

māṣôr (a siege), consisting of the root *ṣûr* "to shut in/up" and the abstract prefix *mem*, is the object of *śām* in the clause of v 14Ab(5:1Ab), a clause that asyndetically substantiates the command in v 14Aa(5:1Ba). Some critics[7] questionably change *śām (have set)* into either *śmw* "they have set" a siege on the basis of plural forms in Syr, Vg, and Tg or into the passive participle *śwm* on the basis of Sym, "siege is laid." Both bases are faulty because the versions more probably are interpreting the third masculine singular of both MT and LXX as indefinite "one has set a siege" = "a siege is set" or "they set a siege."[8] The former option would have been facilitated by *yakkû* in the next clause. The perfective signifies the perfect tense — the city is in a state of siege as a result of the international armies having gathered against it (4:11). *śûm* with *'al* elsewhere is used for a siege against someone/thing.[9] The preposition *'ālênû (against us)* provides another link between the distress in 4:14(5:1) and that of 4:10, but the change of pronoun alters the perspective. Whereas in 4:10 Micah stands apart from Daughter Zion, a metonymy for its inhabitants, in 4:14(5:1) he personally identifies himself with them by using the first-person plural pronoun. In 3:1 Micah also injected himself into his book by the use of the first-person pronoun.

In *baššēbeṭ (with a scepter) bě* is instrumental,[10] and *šēbeṭ* probably has beyond its neutral meaning "rod," "staff," the additional nuance of a "rod of authority" = "a truncheon," "a scepter." Because the object of the affliction is a *šōpēṭ* "ruler," it seems likely that the agents are also rulers; as the object of *yakkû* it stands in parallel with *māṣôr*. The subject of *yakkû (they strike)*, a hiphil third masculine plural nonperfective of the root *nkh*, could poignantly be "the powerful nations" of 4:10, and by implication their rulers. More probably, however, it is simply a variant form of an indefinite subject because this suits better the

5. T. Robinson, "Micah," in *Die zwölf Propheten,* HAT (Tübingen: C. B. Mohr, 1954), 142.

6. S. J. Schwantes, "A Critical Study of the Text of Micah," 121.

7. Schwantes, "A Critical Study," 123.

8. *IBHS* §4.4.2.

9. BDB 963, §1b.

10. *IBHS* §11.2.5.

immediate parallelism in v 14Ab(5:1Ab) and the singular object "scepter." The hiphil is unclassified, and the nonperfective, in parallel with the perfective *śām*, may denote a present progressive imperfective (= "they keep on striking") or a present incipient imperfective (= "they begin to strike").[11] In *'al-hallĕḥî (on the cheek)* the preposition has its simple sense of location, "upon," which is omitted in Ps 3:8(7) in favor of a simple adverbial accusative of place, and the article with *lĕḥî* designates a particular "jaw," "cheek,"[12] namely, that of the ruler. The clause "they strike upon the jaw/cheek" is not literalistic, as in 1 Kgs 22:24 (= 2 Chr 18:23). Since the ruler is holed up inside his city during the siege, the striking is not to be taken woodenly but as metaphorically to represent the ruler's humiliation, as in Ps 3:8(7); Job 16:10; cf. Isa 50:6. The buffet on his cheek represents a climactic insult that all power of resistance was gone.

The emphatic particle *'ēt* in *'ēt šōpēṭ yiśrā'ēl (the ruler of Israel)* to mark the definite direct object of *yakkû*[13] is highly emphatic because *'ēt* is normally omitted in poetry. The masculine singular construct substantive *šōpēṭ* signifies a *nomen agentis* or actor-noun "judge," and *yiśrā'ēl (of Israel)* is a genitive of relation, "Israel." *šōpēṭ* here designates what others call Israel's *melek* "king." Note, for example, the parallels in Ps 148:11, "kings of the earth and all peoples, officials and all judges of the earth" (cf. 2 Kgs 15:5; Isa 16:5; Ps 2:10). In Amos 2:3 "the judge of Moab" very likely represents the politically responsible person (cf. Amos 1:15, where in the parallel oracle against Ammon the king is expressly mentioned). "The sliding from one term to another," says Renaud,[14] "came about from the fact that the king himself had to render justice (2 Sam 15:2-6; 2 Kgs 15:5; Isa 11:5; Prov 29:14)."[15] Probably the title *šōpēṭ* was chosen instead of *melek* "king" for a couple of reasons. First of all, for its assonance with *šēbeṭ* in v 14Ba(5:1Ba). Second, and more significantly, it diminishes his stature both with reference to God and to another ruler who smites him upon the cheek with his scepter. Micah reserves to *I AM* the title of king (cf. 2:13; 4:9).

5:1 *wĕ'attâ (But as for you)* consists of adversative *wāw* and the second masculine singular personal pronoun. The *wāw* on the literary level of the final text is adversative because in this co-text it contrasts the role of Bethlehem in Israel's future salvation with the present distress. On the "preliterary" level it probably served as an initial *wāw* as in 4:8. The two uses are reflected in the confused versification; it is rightly linked with 4:14 (= 5:1, NRSV) in the English

11. *IBHS* §31.3.
12. *IBHS* §13.5.1.
13. *IBHS* §10.3.
14. *La Formation*, 214.
15. Cf. G. C. Macholz, "Die Stellung des Königs in der israelitischen Gerichtsverfassung," *ZAW* 84 (1972) 157-82.

versification and wrongly separated from it in the Hebrew. For the grammar of this construction see 4:8. The highly emphatic *'attâ* "you" in this *casus pendens* construction is resumed in the main clause by *mimmĕkā* "from you."

In the expression *bêt-lehem 'eprātâ (Bethlehem Ephrathah)* "Bethlehem" stands in apposition to the lead word "you," and "Ephrathah," having the same syntactic function and agreement and comparable reference, is an appositive of "Bethlehem."[16] Each substantival appositive qualifies the preceding pronoun/noun more precisely.[17] On the basis of LXX *Bēthleem oikos tou Ephratha* (= *bêt-lehem bêt-'eprātâ*) many text critics contend that the original text read *bêt-'eprātâ* "House of Ephratha" and that "Bethlehem" was later added as a gloss to identify, correctly according to most, Ephratha with its later location south of Jerusalem (cf. Gen 35:19-20) instead of with its earlier location on the northern border of Benjamin. (The question of a northern Ephratha need not engage one here). Also argued in favor of this is LXX emended by the conjecture that one expects in an address to people, "House of Ephrathah," not a locality. Against this view, however, note that "Bethlehem" is found in all texts and versions (cf. Mur 88, which lets one surmise the final *mêm* of Bethlehem) and that, more precisely, Syr, Vg, and Tg support MT. S. Schwantes[18] plausibly explains the addition of *bêt* with *'eprātâ* in LXX's *Vorlage* due to dittography from *bêt-lehem*. B. Renaud[19] summarizes against the conjecture the use of Ephratha elsewhere in Scripture as a place and not a people, as advanced by T. Lescow:[20]

> The expression Beth-Ephratah would be unique, for the usual gentilic is Ephrathite (*'prty*) attested precisely under the form as "Ephrathite of Beth-lehem" (1 Sam 17:12; Ruth 1:2). Ephrathah is not the name of a people but of a district where Bethlehem was located. Besides, many times the two cities are identified (Gen 35:20; 48:7; Ruth 4:11). In Ps 132:6, especially, Ephrathah is placed in parallel with the "fields of Jaar," where one clearly gets a glimpse of an allusion to Qiryat-Jearim situated to the northwest of Bethlehem. Officially one called the large village "Bethlehem in Judah" (Judg 17:7ff.; 19:1ff.; 1 Sam 17:12; Ruth 1:1, 2) and named its inhabitants Bethlehemites (*byt-hlhmy*) (1 Sam 16:1; 17:58; 2 Sam 21:19). Therefore, it is never a question of a "house of Ephrathah" in the strong sense of the term. The address of Mic 5:1(2), an *ad hoc* formulation, combines in its own way the two classical ex-

16. *IBHS* §12.1.

17. *IBHS* §12.2.

18. Schwantes, "A Critical Study," 126.

19. *La Formation,* 220.

20. T. Lescow, "Das Geburtsmotiv in den messianischen Weissagungen bei Jesaja und Micha," *ZAW* 79 (1967) 172-207, esp. 192-99.

pressions: Ephrathite of Bethlehem and Bethlehem in Judah, because the second stich locates the city in Judah.

Renaud then adds his own arguments from the co-text and from 1 Samuel 16 for retaining Bethlehem in the original text:

> Let us add, for our part, that the very close parallel we have noted between Mic 4:8 and 5:1(2) favors retaining Bethlehem in the original reading. In 4:8 it is, indeed, the city of Jerusalem that is addressed, personified Jerusalem, but designated with the very name of the city where the population resides.... The same sliding of meaning is found in 5:1(2), where the city represents a clan, a collectivity. Because ... Mic 4:8 imitates 5:1(2) closely ... , one can infer that it was really a locality that was addressed and personified. Moreover, with the majority of commentators, it is fitting to see in this phrase an allusion to the choice of David, born in Bethlehem. In particular, it clearly refers to 1 Samuel 16, which recounts the election and anointing of the future king. Yet, this last text mentions explicitly "Jesse the Bethlehemite," father of David. Much more, this account underlines the mysterious character of the divine initiative that chooses its elect from among the small: Jesse, who made his children, the eventual candidates for election, march past, did not even think of mentioning his last born; he was still an adolescent, almost a child. In the eyes of the father, who thought according to views that were too human, such an insignificant person could hardly appear as the beneficiary of the divine choice that entailed his bearing very heavy responsibilities. It is, however, he whom God chose. Likewise, in 5:1(2), the Messiah will come out of the small Bethlehem, without very great numerical importance. It seems insignificant in the eyes of the world. The parallelism that bears upon the city and the personage stemming from this city calls for the mention of the city where the first David is born.

In Matt 2:6 *Bethleem gē Iouda* "Bethlehem in the land of Judah" does not represent a different text but an explanation of the textual tradition. *ṣāʿîr (insignificant)* is a further qualification of the topic: "You, Bethlehem Ephrathah." It is not an attributive adjective, "the least," because it is indefinite.[21] Rather, it is indefinite to emphasize the nature of the one addressed, "weak/little/insignificant," and elliptical with "city/town" elided; with that addition it clearly becomes another appositive. The adjective *ṣāʿîr* occurs twenty-two times, and in all but two or three instances it designates the "younger" of two or more, almost always with the additional coloring of inferiority in strength and/or in social stature.

---

21. *IBHS* §14.3.1.

Occasionally the idea of "young" is lost, leaving only the sense of small in contrast to many/great (cf. Isa 60:22; Dan 8:9; cf. Ps 119:141). Its closest English equivalent is "small," which connotes "littleness" with reference to age, size, and/or strength. Only in Josh 6:26 and 1 Kgs 16:34, where the man who builds Jericho is cursed by losing his *běkôr* "firstborn" and his *ṣā'îr* "youngest" son, is the word used without the additional connotation of insignificance/inferiority. Even in Gen 19:31, 34, 35, 38; 29:26; 43:33; 48:14, where the *běkôr*, who inherits the double portion, is contrasted with the *ṣā'îr*, the nuance of inferiority is felt. Elihu senses his inferiority because of his "youth" in Job 32:6, and the inferior status of youth is clear in Job 30:1, where Job complains that even men younger than he mock him. The notions of "young" in age and "little" in size coalesce with reference to Benjamin in Ps 68:28(27). Parallels to *ṣā'îr*, *dal* "poor" in Judg 6:15, *qāṭôn* "small" in 1 Sam 9:21, and *nibzeh* "despised" in Ps 119:141, make the notion of weakness, in physical and/or social stature, explicit. Other antonyms of *ṣā'îr* are *rab* "many/strong" and *'mṣ* "be strong" in Gen 25:23, *'āṣûm* "powerful" in Isa 60:22, and *gādôl* "great" in Dan 8:9. The "young" are defenseless in Jer 48:4; 49:20; 50:45.

Bethlehem may have been young among the clans of Judah, but was certainly "small" in physical and social stature, and hence insignificant for leadership in government and prowess in war. Although the word is not used in 1 Samuel 16, where David, Jesse's youngest son, is unexpectedly chosen before his elders, the theme is the same. Micah probably intends to note a striking coincidence between David's lowly place of birth and his social position, a coincidence that matches the Messiah's career. Only divine intervention can account for the transformation of David and the Messiah into greatness. The adjective is implicitly, though not formally, comparative: Bethlehem is implicitly being compared with the other clans of Judah, just as *ṣā'îr* elsewhere often implies a contrast with older siblings.

Some want to push the comparative to make it a comparison of capability (= "too little to be among the clans of Judah").[22] *lihyôt (to be)* means "to be," "to exist," as in LXX and Syr, but the comparative of capability would demand comparative *min*, and so the form would have *mihyôt*, as in Isa 49:6. Conscious of the grammatical irregularity, J. A. Fitzmyer[23] appealed to Ugaritic and identified the *lāmed* of *lihyôt* as *lāmed comparativum*. Renaud[24] rightly complained that his appeal seems forced. Why a unique Ugaritic construction here? W. A. van der Weiden[25] discovers a *lāmed comparativum* in Ezek 16:13; Mic 5:1(2); Nah 1:7; Ps

---

22. *IBHS* §14.4.
23. J. A. Fitzmyer, "*Lě* as a Preposition and a Particle in Micah 5:1 (5:2)," *CBQ* 18 (1956) 10-13.
24. *La Formation*, 221.
25. W. A. van der Weiden, *Le Livre des Proverbes* (Rome, 1970), 45.

30:8(7); Song 1:3; Qoh 7:19, but none is compelling. T. Lescow[26] originally understood it as an epexegetical *lāmed* "small with reference to being,"[27] but he later gave it up.[28] Hitzig, Renaud, and others omit *lihyôt* altogether, explaining it as a dittography from the next line. Vg is of little help, for *es* in *"parvulus es in millibus Judah"* may represent either a copula supplied by Jerome or *hāyîtâ* in his *Vorlage.* KJV also omitted it. F. Hitzig,[29] followed by *BHS,* makes the adjective superlative, "the most little," by reading *'eprāt* and joining its final *hê* in MT with *ṣ'yr* (= *hṣ'yr*) because the form *'eprāt* is known from Gen 48:7. But the most usual form is Ephrathah (Gen 35:16, 19; 48:7; Ps 132:6; Ruth 4:11), even of Caleb's wife (1 Chr 2:24, 50; 4:4). One could conjecture that *hê* dropped off *ṣā'îr* by haplography. One cannot, however, appeal to the superlative in LXX's *oligostos* "most little" for either conjecture because it, with the other ancient versions, read *'eprātâ* in its *Vorlage.* It seems best to retain *lihyôt* with the *l* of purpose the same as in 5:1Abα(5:2Abα) so that the text reads "little to be among the clans of Judah" (RSV). But NRSV has, "who are one of the little clans of Judah."

This does not imply a comparison of capability; that would demand *mihyôt* (cf. Isa 49:6) and would deny Bethlehem any standing among the clans of Judah. But what about Matt 2:6, which reads *oudamōs elachistē ei* "you are by no means the least"? His text could have been influenced by several Greek MSS that read *mē* before *oligostos* (= are you then too small to be?)[30] T. Robinson[31] conjectures *ṣ'yr lō' hyyt* "you are not little," approximating Matthew, but, though *hyyt* has the support of Tg and possibly of Vg, no one attests the negative. More probably, as elsewhere in the verse, Matthew's rendering is free and interpretive. B. Renaud[32] noted:

> Matthew's formulation takes the opposite of the MT, but in reality the idea is not very different: it is in virtue of the divine choice that Bethlehem is not the least of the clans of Judah; by its natural importance it would not preserve such preeminence. It is nevertheless true that the primitive theme of the preference of God for smallness is here blurred.

In *bĕ'alpê yĕhûdâ (among the clans of Judah)* the *bĕ* marks a location *amid* a domain[33] governing the masculine plural construct *'alpê* with the absolute

26. Lescow, "Das Geburtsmotiv," 194-95.

27. *IBHS* §36.2.3.

28. Lescow, "Das Geburtsmotiv," 73 n. 100.

29. F. Hitzig, *Die zwölf kleinen Propheten* (Leipzig: Weidmann, 1954), 142.

30. Cf. Schwantes, "A Critical Study," 127.

31. Robinson, "Micha," 142.

32. *La Formation,* 222.

33. *IBHS* §11.2.5.

yĕhûdâ (see 1:1), a genitive of relation.[34] *'elep* means "thousand, a thousand" (cf. Mic 7:1). Originally the thousands referred to a military unit of a thousand men that a clan had to provide when a tribe summoned itself to arms (Num 31:4; Deut 1:15; 1 Sam 8:12; 10:19; Amos 5:3; 1 Chr 13:1; 27:1). In that way it may have the specialized sense of designating the largest basic unit to be governed politically and/or militarily (cf. Exod 18:21; Num 1:16; 31:4; Deut 1:15; Josh 22:14; Amos 5:3; 1 Chr 13:1; 27:1). It designates the united clan itself (Judg 6:15; 1 Sam 10:19, 21) and/or the territory it occupied within the tribes, which can be identified with a city itself (Amos 5:3; Mic 5:1[2]). The clans in the book of Numbers clearly numbered a thousand soldiers, to judge from other numerical notes in that book (cf. Num 31:5), but they varied in power/prestige. Gideon complains that his clan is *haddal* "the weakest/poorest/meanest" of the clans in Manasseh (Judg 6:15) and that he is *haṣṣā'îr* "the least." *'elep* is the opposite extreme of that which is quite small or few in number (Deut 32:30; Josh 23:10; Isa 30:17; 60:22; Job 9:3). The lowly clan at Bethlehem stands in marked contrast with the other noble clans of Judah. Instead of *bĕ'alpê* "among the clans of" Matthew reads *hēgemosin* (= Heb. *b'lwpy*) "among the chiefs," which is found in some Greek MSS (see TNIV footnote) instead of LXX's *en chiliasin*. The difference, however, is not textual but interpretive. By the change the apostle aims to form a better contrast between *hēgemosin* "the chiefs" of the other clans with *hēgoumenos* (= *môšēl*) "ruler" in Mic 5:1Abβ(5:2Abβ; see *hēgoumenos* below).

The text and meaning of *mimmĕkā lî yēṣē'*, literalistically, *"from you to me he will come forth,"* is difficult. What are the pronouns' antecedents? What is the value of *lĕ*? What is the subject of *yēṣē'*? Because of these difficulties various textual emendations have been proposed.

E. Sellin, while granting that in *lî* one must see in the pronoun a reference to God, disallows the text because elsewhere "God is spoken of in the whole prophecy in 3. Pers." He sees the *yôd* dittographical before *yēṣē'* and the *lāmed* as the remains of a *melek* "king"; through haplography, induced by *mimmĕkā*, Sellin argues that initial *mêm* and final *kāp* disappeared. He supports himself from LXXᴬ, which reads here *hēgoumenos* "chief" (cf. Matt 2:6), which in Ezek 43:7 stands for *melek*.

J. A. Fitzmyer[35] agrees that the verb needs a subject, but he objects that the *lāmed* is problematic: "How could the *mem* and *kaph* be dropped on either side of the *lamedh*, without it, too, being lost?" He solves the riddle by inserting *melek* from whole cloth, by explaining with E. Sellin the *yôd* as dittography, and by construing the *lāmed* as a particle of emphasis, "akin to the Arabic *la* and the

---

34. *IBHS* §9.5.1.
35. Fitzmyer, "*Lĕ* as a Preposition and a Particle in Micah 5:1(5:2)," 12.

Accadian *lu*." In sum, he reads *mimměkā* [*melek*] *l'yēṣē* "[but] from you a king shall indeed go forth." He finds support in the facts that he could find no instances of ethical dative preceding a verb, and that Syr omits *lî* entirely. An inseparable emphatic particle, however, before the prefix conjugation would be so exceptional in Hebrew grammar that it would put into serious doubt the rest of the conjecture.

A. Bruno and S. Schwantes see in *lî* the remains of *yeled* "a child," but their proposal faces the same objection that Fitzmyer raised against Sellin. J. Lippl[36] considers the *yôd* of *lî* as an abbreviation of the sacred tetragrammaton, but that resolves only the problem of the unexpected first-person pronoun for *I AM*, and it is doubtful because the abbreviation is usually *yāh* (see 1:9). Moreover, the ancient versions support MT against these conjectures: LXX, *ek sou moi exeleusetai;* Vg *ex te mili egredietur;* Tg "From you the Messiah will come out in front of me," representing the same textual tradition. Syr "from you [feminine] a sovereign will come out who will be over Israel," rearranges the word and omits *lî*, but otherwise matches the tradition. Matt 2:6 also omits it, but his interpretive rendition undercuts any textual value.

B. Renaud[37] rightly draws the conclusion: "Thus each of the proposed corrections does not offer a satisfying solution. Besides, in general, the versions support MT. In these conditions one must have recourse to textual corrections only when the meaning is totally unintelligible." The rough text is more likely due to the process of compilation. As suggested in the Introduction, pp. 13-14, Micah builds up his prophecies on the literary level of the book by employing earlier, probably written, sources. In an earlier source the antecedents would have been clear.

J. T. Willis,[38] while maintaining MT, offers an unusual interpretation: "from you [a city] will come out to me [a person]" means to him that the Messiah will come out of Bethlehem as an inferior king to meet *I AM*, his superior king, in order to submit himself to him. He finds *'el, 'al,* and *lě* interchangeable, and that *yṣ' 'el/'al* elsewhere connotes submission (cf. 1 Sam 11:2, 3, 10; 1 Kgs 20:31, 33; 2 Kgs 18:31-32 [= Isa 36:16, 18]; 2 Kgs 24:12; Jer 38:21, 23).

B. Renaud[39] cogently objects because: (1) *yṣ' 'el/'al* are elsewhere technical expressions, and *yṣ' lě* is found nowhere else in the OT. (2) In what precise way did the Messiah come out to God? Elsewhere the expression has in view the physical action of a person who approaches another (Exod 2:11; 2 Sam. 13:39;

---

36. J. Lippl, *Die zwölf kleinen Propheten* (Bonn, 1937), 207.
37. *La Formation,* 224.
38. J. T. Willis, "*mmk ly yṣ'* in Micah 5,1" *Jewish Quarterly Review* 58 (1967-69) 317-22.
39. *La Formation,* 224.

2 Kgs 4:11), but one conceives only with difficulty a sovereign physically approaching *I AM.* (3) All the invoked parallels are located in a precise context, namely, that of capitulation, which is not the case here. "This cannot be the case in Mic 5:1(2)," Renaud writes, "where the context is rather of victory, in any case of salvation; the sovereign of Mic 5:1(2) does not capitulate before YHWH. One cannot invoke Mic 4:14(5:1) and the atmosphere of defeat which one breathes there, because . . . it is not of Jerusalem but of Bethlehem, the city of David, that the sovereign must 'come out.'" Besides, it is clear that the person represented by *lî* "for me" has nothing to do with the invader of Mic 4:14(5:1).

It is best, then, to return to a more traditional interpretation of the passage. In *mimměkā (from you)* the preposition *min* is ablative and the second masculine singular pronominal suffix looks back to *'attâ,* linking the *casus pendens* with the main clause. The skewed syntax of this clause is due in part to the desire to make "from you" emphatic. The focal point in redemptive history is none other than the insignificant town of Bethlehem, showing that Israel's future greatness does not depend on a great human king but on divine intervention to bring greatness out of nothing. The usual understanding of *lâ (on my behalf)* as dative of advantage to whom the action is directed,[40] and of referring the pronoun to God, as E. Sellin says it must mean in MT, is clear enough. The syntax is further twisted by placing *lî* also in an unusual syntax, again to emphasize that the Messiah comes to serve *I AM* and not himself. B. Renaud[41] paraphrases: "from you, yes, but for me he will come out." This blessed hope probably owes its inspiration to 1 Sam 16:1, "I am sending you [Samuel] to Jesse of Bethlehem because I have seen [= I have chosen] among his sons *for me* a king." As Samuel had hope for a David who would replace Saul, so Micah has hope for a greater than David to replace Israel's feckless leadership.

yēṣē' (he will come forth) is a qal third masculine singular nonperfective of the root *yṣ'.* The subject of *yēṣē'* is at first mysterious in MT and LXX, simply an unidentified "he," holding Micah's audience in suspense as he fills in the Messiah's features one by one in the rest of the oracle. Matthew (2:6) paraphrases this prophecy by supplying the subject, *hēgoumenos,* from Mic 5:1Aβ(5:2Aβ). The nonperfective denotes future time, as the rest of the exegesis and exposition of this oracle will validate. *yṣ'* can mean "to be born" when used for coming out of the womb (Job 1:21) or "to stem from" (Gen 17:6; 35:11), but mostly it has the comprehensive meaning "to come forth" in the sense of "to go forth." The meaning of *yēṣē'* must be drawn in the first place from *môṣā'ōtāyw* "his origins,"

40. Cf. *IBHS* §11.2.10.
41. *La Formation,* 225.

which is built on this verbal root, and so is related to the idea of coming forth in birth. This matches two other instances of *yṣ'* in connection with the Messiah's origins: "a root will come out *(wĕyāṣā')* from the stump of Jesse" (Isa 11:1), and "I will maintain after you the descendants [singular] which will come out *(yēṣē')* of your loins" (2 Sam 7:12). These three passages link the Messiah's origins with David. But the more immediate co-text: "On my behalf he will come forth to be ruler in Israel" points also to the more comprehensive sense, namely, the destiny for which he steps forth; that nuance may also be present in 2 Sam 7:12 and Isa 11:1. B. Renaud[42] raises the question, "If the precision 'Ephratha' brought to Bethlehem does not make reference to the etymological sense of the word, viz., *prh* means 'to be fruitful.' By allusion, one would understand 'Bethlehem the fruitful.'"

lihĕyôt (to be) has the same form and function as its parallel in 5:1Aαβ (5:2Aαβ). Whereas many critics delete the first *lihĕyôt*, they retain this one, even though it would place the missing subject immediately after its verb. However, this *hĕyôt* is supported in the ancient versions and Tg, and provides for critics, who reckon with a regular meter in Hebrew poetry, a better meter, and if there be dittography, it would more likely be in the inverse direction. In any case, it underscores the divine purpose for which the Messiah comes forth.

Furthermore, the text strongly resembles 2 Sam 7:8, *lihĕyôt nāgîd 'al-'ammî 'al-yiśrā'ēl* "to be a leader over my people, over Israel," and once again links the birth of the Messiah with David. It is uncertain, however, why Micah changed *nāgîd 'al-yiśrā'ēl* to *môšēl bĕyiśrā'ēl (a ruler over Israel)*. The *qôṭēl* pattern in *môšēl* denotes *nomen agentis.*[43] The root *mšl* can be used either in a general sense for varying sorts of dominion such as the dominion of man over the creation (Ps 8:7[6]) and of man over his fellowman (e.g., Gen 3:16; 37:8 [parallel *mlk*]; Exod 21:8), or in the more particular sense of "rule" politically, as in Gen 45:8, 26; Josh 12:2, 5. The subject or parallel is sometimes *melek* (Josh 12:5; Isa 19:4; 49:7; Dan 11:3-5), or it may be parallel to "who sits on [David's] throne" or its equivalent (Jer 22:30; Zech 6:13; 1 Chr 9:26; 23:20). *I AM* can also be used as subject or in connection with it (Isa 40:10; 63:19; Ps 22:9[8]), but that cannot be the sense here, for this one rules to serve *I AM*. Sometimes the root *mlk* is apparently consciously suppressed by using *mšl*. It is usually thought that in the Deuteronomistic literature *melek* could not designate kingship in the premonarchic period, for in that theology Israel should be ruled theocratically, and so *môšēl* was used, as in Judg 8:22-23 and 9:2. Subsequently, through the negative experience of the monarchy, *melek* became discredited for Israel's future

42. *La Formation*, 225.
43. *IBHS* §37.2.

ruler at the end of history, and so that term became reserved for *I AM* alone; so in Micah, as noted (p. 265). But *melek* is used of Messiah in Zech 9:5, 9. Ezekiel does not designate the leader of the restoration by *melek* but by *nāśî'*. *môšēl* is best construed as an accusative of state specifying the first feature of the indefinite subject:[44] "he will become a ruler." *hēgoumenos* in Matt 2:6, though it can represent *môšēl* (cf. Ezek 19:11; Hab 1:14; Prov 29:26; 2 Chr 7:18; 9:26), does not derive from Mic 5:1(2), for LXX reads *archonta*. To be sure, Codex Alexandrinus and a few minor MSS read *hēgoumenos* in Mic 5:1(2), but almost certainly their reading is Matthean. Rather, Matthew creatively introduced *hēgoumenos* into the text from the confession by the tribes of Israel in 2 Sam 5:2: "*I AM* told you [David]: you will shepherd my people Israel, and you will be ruler *(hēgoumenos)* over Israel," and from the introduction of *I AM*'s covenant with David: "I took you from the pasture and from following the flock *tou einai se eis hēgoumenon epi ton laon mou epi ton Israēl*" (2 Sam 7:8). By this literary device Matthew associated Jesus with David and *I AM*'s covenant with him. *mšl* is mostly construed with *bĕ*, and so, *bĕyiśrā'ēl (over Israel)*. "Israel" in this book could refer to just the Southern Kingdom (see 1:5 passim), but its significance here is spelled out in 5:2(3). This new beginning involves all of true Israel.

The conjunction *wāw* in *ûmôṣā'ōtāyw*, consisting of the conjunctive *wāw*, the prefix *mêm*, the root *yṣ'*, the feminine plural suffix, and the third masculine singular pronominal suffix with *môšēl* as its antecedent, gives the Messiah's second feature: he is ancient. The prefix *mêm* and the feminine plural form mark the root as an abstract noun.[45] The singular of Syr and Vg (?) do not point to a different text. Tg's paraphrase "and whose name is a name from you," according to Schwantes,[46] "may have been suggested by passages like Num 30:13(14), Deut 23:24(25), and Jer 17:16, in which *mwṣ' śtym* always means that which comes out of one's lips, and therefore 'vow,' or 'mention.'" "Goings forth" is a euphemistic metonymy for latrine in the *Qere* of 2 Kgs 10:27.

E. Sellin[47] thinks that the term predicates a supernatural and prehistoric, and so a divine, origin, because: (1) one would have expected *twldwtyw* to be used; (2) its parallel *mwṣ'* specifically designates the radiant rising of the sun (cf. Pss 19:7[6]; 69:5[4]; 75:7[6]); (3) the ancient kings of Babylon and Egypt were indeed also praised in this way (cf. Num 24:17; Mic 5:2; and *'ăbî'ad* in Isa 9:5[6]; 49:2 [*sic!*]); and (4) *'ôlām* and *qedem* are "obviously" best suited for this sense (cf. Ps 90:3[2]).

44. *IBHS* §10.2.2.
45. *IBHS* §§5.6; 6.4.2.
46. S. Schwantes, "A Critical Study," 129.
47. Sellin, "Micha," 289.

S. Mowinckel[48] also believes that "there is an allusion to the king's 'rising' like the sun," which "seems to suggest that the future king would come into existence in a wonderful way." More specifically, in his view "the ancestor is, as it were, re-created in a wonderful way. He brings to fulfillment what the dynasty was in its origin (in ancient eastern thought anything was seen at its truest and best in its origin). The nation's misfortune . . . will last only until this scion of David is born."

A. Bentzen[49] more explicitly links the Messiah's origins with the first king at the time of creation. "Messiah's epiphany," he says, "is compared with the sunrise," and his enthronement is "a repetition of the first king in the days of the beginning, the primeval age," as celebrated by myth and ritual all over the ancient Near East in connection with their divine or sacral kings. A. Weiser,[50] H. Ringgren,[51] and A. S. Kapelrud[52] all agree. Says Weiser: "The Messiah's origin lies in the Urzeit; . . . the conception of 'Urmensch' is here transferred to the Messiah. Thus the bridge between Urzeit and Endzeit, between creation and redemption, is theologically hit upon, and God's plan of salvation is anchored already in the beginning of the world in the design of creation."

But *tôlĕdôt (generations)* does not specifically mean "origin" and is probably avoided deliberately to link the Messiah exclusively with David's cradle and to eliminate his lineage from his apostate successors. The linkage of "origin" with sunrise is arbitrary, and the patterning of Israel's king after pagan kings is highly questionable. The meaning of *mwṣ'h* in 5:1B(2B) should be connected with *yēṣē'* in 5:1A(2A); both refer to the Messiah's origin. In 5:1A(2A) *yēṣē'* refers to his local origin in Bethlehem; in 5:1B(2B) it refers to his temporal and, by implication, his ancestral origin. His local coming from Bethlehem implies his ancestral origin from Jesse and the house of David. A connection with a mythological Urmensch, while lexically possible, is co-textually arbitrary. The ablative sense of the inseparable preposition *min* in *miqqedem (from of old)* marks the movement away from a specified beginning point, and this sense underlies the designation of origin.[53]

qedem "in front of" can refer to space, "the East" (Gen 2:8), or time, "earlier time, remote antiquity." In contrast to *'ôlām* and *'ad*, which denote "perpetuity," *qedem* denotes an idyllic state. Concerning this important theological term E. Jenni[54] notes:

48. S. Mowinckel, *He That Cometh* (Nashville: Abingdon, 1956), 184-85.
49. A. Bentzen, *King and Messiah* (London: Lutterworth, 1955).
50. Weiser, "Micha," 244.
51. H. Ringgren, "König und Messias," *ZAW* 64 (1952) 136.
52. A. S. Kapelrud, "Eschatology in the Book of Micah," *VT* 11 (1961) 400.
53. *IBHS* §11.2.11.
54. E. Jenni, *THAT* 2:588.

It can have an accompanying connotation that more or less strongly approximates the divine sphere. God himself according to Deut 33:27 is the "'*lhy qdm* the ancient, eternal God" (Deut 33:27), . . . but *qdm* by itself is generally not used as a designation for God. . . . Correspondingly, his creative works also take this qualification: wisdom (Prov 8:22, 23), the mountains (Deut 33:15) and the heavens (Ps 68:34[33]). . . . It can refer to a mythical primeval time (Isa 51:9; cf. Ps 74:12) or to an earlier time of one's own life (Job 29:2). . . . In other passages the word is used with reference to the time of the fathers (Mic 7:20), the beginning of the nation (Ps 44:2[1]; 74:3[2]), or the time of David (Neh 12:46) or of the prophets (Ezek 38:17).

Its mythical connotations are clear in Ps 74:12 and Isa 51:9, in contrast to Mic 5:1(2). A mythical connotation, however, is precluded by the next phrase. Rather, the reference to Bethlehem suggests a use here similar to that in Neh 12:46.

In the next phrase, an apposite construction *mîmê 'ôlām (from days long ago)*, the inseparable *min* is also ablative and *'ôlām* after the masculine plural construct *yĕmê* is a genitive of measure.[55] *'ôlām* normally refers to the most distant time in either the past or the future within some historical framework; it may refer to eternity without a historical horizon only with respect to God who existed before creation. Concerning this important theological word E. Jenni[56] says:

> The German translation *Ewigkeit* (= "eternity") . . . is unsuitable for numerous passages with *'ôlām* in the OT, and even in those passages where it appears appropriate, one must not read into the text a preconceived notion of eternity, which is loaded with all sorts of later philosophical or theological contents. . . . With the exception of a few later passages in Koheleth, *'ôlām* in the OT . . . has the meaning "the most distant time." . . . Typical of the notion of extremity is the circumstance that it does not occur in the language independently (as subject or object), but only in connection with prepositions of direction (*min* "since" . . . *'ad* "unto" and *lĕ* "until" . . . or as an adverbial accusative of direction . . . or finally as the second member of a construct chain, i.e., as genitive, which substitutes for a prepositional expression. . . . In the latter case *'ôlām* by itself can express the meaning of the whole adverbial use "since the/until the most distant time" . . . ; cf. J. Barr, *Biblical Words of Time* (1962), 73, rem. 1: "We might therefore best state the 'basic meaning' as a kind of range between 'remotest time' and 'perpetu-

55. *IBHS* §9.5.3.
56. E. Jenni, *THAT* 2:229-31.

ity.'" . . . The "most distant time" is a relative concept according to the temporal horizon assumed in the context. . . . 'ôlām is connected with the prep. *min* for the designation of the origin out of the distant past (apart from the Bible only the Mesha Inscription, line 10: "and the people of Gad lived from time immemorial in the land of Ataroth") . . . 'ôlām never designates a settled earliest space of time. Even in the translation "from Urtime," it designates the most extreme *terminus a quo* (= "since time immemorial"). Only where, in theological contexts, a beginning of creation, respectively God is supposed as existing before any beginning, can it be translated with "from the Ur-beginning" (Isa 44:7, text em.; 46:98; 63:16; Prov 8:23) or "from eternity on" (Ps 25:6; 90:2 . . .) In other instances adverbial expressions suffice: "of old" (Gen 6:4), "a long time ago" (Isa 42:14), "from early times on" (Jer 28:8), "long ago" (Jer 2:20), "since time immemorial" (Josh 24:2). . . .

Like *qedem*, 'ôlām opens the lexical door to the possibility of a past Urtime, but that door is closed by the construct *yĕmê*. E. Jenni says that 'ôlām can refer to the Urtime "except when the *nomen regens* already contains a definite time ('days,' 'years,' 'generations'; Deut 32:7; Isa 51:9; 61:9, 11; Amos 9:11; Mic 5:1[2]; 7:14; Mal 3:4; Ps 77:6[5] . . .)." The reference to the house of David in Amos 9:11 parallels "the days of long ago" in Mic 5:1(2); both refer to the founding and rebuilding of David's house. Says B. Renaud:[57] "If the mention of Bethlehem refers to the childhood of David, the 'ancient days, the times of old' must correspond to the times of David. . . . Amos 9:11 associates in a completely similar fashion 'the raising up and reparation of the hut of David (the theme of beginning again of Davidic history as in Mic 5:1[2])' with 'the days of old (*kymy 'wlm*).'"

2 The logical particle *lākēn (therefore)*, a combination of the preposition *lĕ* and the adverb *kēn*, which occurs in a medial position in a discourse, introduces a proposed or anticipated response after a statement of certain conditions (i.e., "the foregoing being the case, therefore."[58] The foregoing verses have been preoccupied with time: In 4:14(5:1) "Now" with reference to the present distress, and in 5:1(2) "he will come forth" with reference to Israel's future Savior, whose origin has been in the past, "from long ago." The logical conclusion to be drawn from the promise of a new David is that Israel's deliverance from the Assyrians, and implicitly all her enemies, ultimately awaits the time when the remnant will give birth to the Messiah. Schwantes[59] strangely parrots others when he says that v 2(3) is "most inappropriate after the promise of v. 1(2)." The

---

57. *La Formation*, 244.
58. *IBHS* §39.3.4.
59. Schwantes, "A Critical Study," 130.

logical particle, sewing 5:2(3) tightly with 4:14–5:1(5:1-2), introduces the cogent conclusion. Though the focus in vv 2-5(3-6) is on *môšēl*, Israel's future messianic ruler, he cannot be the subject of *yitĕnēm (he will give them up)*, a qal third masculine singular nonperfective of the root *ntn* with the third masculine plural verbal suffix. The subject could be either the impersonal "one will give them up" (= *ytmsrwn* "they will be given up" of Tg) or *I AM*. The singular is validated by LXX *(dōsei)* and Vg *(dabit)*. Since *I AM* is the speaker in 5:1(2) and unquestionably the antecedent of the first-person pronoun *lî* "for me," in this resolution of the conflicting temporal situations, *I AM* is the antecedent. The literary process of piecing together earlier oracles into a new literary unit best accounts for the rough syntax. The only satisfying meaning of *ntn* here is to "give over, deliver up."[60] H. Wolff[61] says: "*ntn* here is an elliptical expression in the sense of *ntn byd 'wybym* 'to give into the hand of the enemy'; cf. 2 Sam 5:19; 1 Kgs 22:6." The enemy on Micah's historical horizon is Assyria (see Exposition, 296), but after his time it came to include Babylon, Persia, Greece, and Rome. The following temporal phrases show that the nonperfective denotes future time. The antecedent of the third masculine plural object is "Israel" of v 1(2); as noted many times in Micah, the disagreement between a collective singular and plural pronoun is acceptable Hebrew.

The preposition *'ad* with *'ēt* is not allative (movement toward) but terminative (movement up to), because with the Messiah's advent Israel's (mis)fortunes will be decisively reversed. There is no reason to upset a unified textual tradition for Torczyner's[62] undefended suggestion to read the phrase as *lkn ytn mô'ēd 'ēt* "therefore he sets a period, a time. . . ." One will note, however, an assonance between *'attâ* (4:14[5:1]) and *'ad-'ēt*, helping to link these verses not only in substance but in style. *'ēt*, according to L. C. Coppes,[63] "relates to time conceived as an opportunity or a season." The former is in view here; more specifically, it will be qualified by the next two asyndetic relative clauses:[64] the birth of the Messiah and the return of his brothers to him. The identity of the qal third feminine singular active participle of *yld*, *yôlēdâ (she who is in labor)*, is unclear if this oracle be considered in isolation from its literary context.

S. Mowinckel,[65] along with A. Bentzen and A. Weiser, who saw an allusion to the Urmensch in 5:1(2), sees an allusion here to the supernatural world of myth in which goddesses give birth to divine princes; if that be so, the pas-

60. BDB 679, §1s.
61. Wolff, *Micha*, 117.
62. N. H. Torczyner, "Dunkle Bibelstellen," BZAW 41 (1925) 279.
63. L. C. Coppes, "'ēt," *TWOT* 2:680.
64. *IBHS* §19.3.
65. Mowinckel, *He That Cometh*, 185.

sage is stressing the Messiah's miraculous birth as inaugurating the new age. A. S. Kapelrud[66] also discerns an ancient conception and expression behind *yôlēdâ* and cites in particular the Nikkal and Kathirat myth, known from Ras Shamra, in which myth an unnamed woman, a *'almat,* shall bear a son to the moon god, Yarih. He continues:

> No further explanation is given in the Micah oracle. . . . We can see the mythological background, and can guess that the son who is going to be born is the coming ruler, the *môšēl,* but apart from that everything is wrapped in obscurity. Ideas from ancient divine kingship, with the king supposed to be born by the goddess, are here combined with historical features: the rise of a new dominating ruler from the house of David, whose centre was in Bethlehem-Efrathah.

But his presentation is paradoxically both presumptuous and unnecessarily hesitant. Any mythological resonances are to be excluded from this book, which is so zealous for the exaltation of *I AM* as Israel's only King. "Therefore" closely links 5:2(3) with 5:1(2), and since associations with a primeval Urmensch divine king were rejected there, a mythological background should also be excluded here.

On the literary level, the audience has already met *yôlēdâ* in 4:9-10, in the first of the three oracles closely linked in style and substance (4:9-10, 11-13; 4:14–5:6[5:1-7]). The *yôlēdâ* is Zion, the surviving remnant, as commented on in those verses. In both cases *yld* refers to the birth of salvation. According to the first of the three oracles, *I AM* would give Zion new birth by redeeming her from Babylon, but more significantly, according to this oracle, her restoration as a strong and unified nation and her triumph over her enemies must await the birth of the Messiah. B. Renaud[67] rightly says: "The *yôlēdâ,* the woman who gives birth, of 5:2(3) identifies itself with 'Daughter Zion' of Mic 4:9-10, that is to say, with the community of the covenant." He calls this literary contact "incontestable and fundamental." Nevertheless, Renaud, who applauded Lescow for interpreting "origin" in 5:1(2) by the immediate context and not by outside passages, yet now blunders with many critics, hoping to tease out the meaning of 5:2(3) by comparing it with Isa 7:14. Whereas they connect both verses with a mythological background, Renaud regards it as a later midrash on that prophecy. If the verse be compared with Isa 7:14, there would be a double entendre: in addition to Zion, the *yôlēdâ* is also the *'almâ* who gives birth to the Messiah. The two prophecies are allegedly linked by the words *lākēn, ntn,* and *yld,* and by

66. Kapelrud, "Eschatology in the Book of Micah," 400.
67. *La Formation,* 247.

the theme of a time of trial connected with the appearance of a marvelous child. The verbal links, however, are weakened by the facts that *lākēn* functions differently, that *ntn* is used in different senses, and that the key word *ʿalmâ* is not used. Moreover, the trial and deliverance are very different. While Isa 7:14-16 has in view salvation from Ephraim and Aram, which adversaries will be replaced by Assyria, in Micah deliverance from Assyria is in view. By Occam's razor Isaiah 7 should be excluded from the discussion; it is an unnecessary intrusion into the exegesis when the reference to Mic 4:9-10 is an altogether sufficient explanation. *yālādâ (gives birth)* is qal perfective third feminine singular of the root *yld*. The perfective refers to a complete situation, and the root denotes one that is telic; the subject is *yôlēdâ*. The object is elided,[68] but by the co-textual connection of v 2(3) with v 1(2) the birth of the Messiah must be in view. Since in 5:2B(3B) "his" brothers are spoken of, Sellin[69] thinks that an earlier reference is necessary and so restores *yldthw* (gives him birth). It is unclear why he thinks the pronominal suffix needs an antecedent in the B verset but not in the A verset. This is the sense of the passage, but no texts or versions have the verbal suffix.

The conjunctive *waw* with *wĕyeter ʾeḥāyw (and the rest of his brothers)* introduces the second clause modifying the time when God reverses Israel's disaster into deliverance. The third masculine singular pronominal suffix looks back to *môšēl* in 5:1(2), and the masculine plural of *ʾḥ* refers here not to the offspring of his father and/or mother but of his people, his kinsmen. LXX *(hoi epiloipoi)* and Vg *(reliquae)* rightly understand *yeter* as a collective in view of the plural verb *yĕšûbûn*. The Messiah's kinsmen have been variously identified:[70] the authorities dispersed in Babylonia, that is, the elite of the people,[71] the surviving members of the Davidic descendants (Mowinckel), the exiles of the Northern Kingdom (van Hoonacker, Sellin).

As for *yeter*, ever since J. Wellhausen some want to see in it an allusion to the symbolic name of Isaiah's son *Šĕʾār Yāšûb*, that is to say, "a remnant will return" (Isa 7:3). But Renaud rightly notes that *yeter* never has the value of a technical term to designate "the remnant," which is normally represented by *šĕʾār* or *šĕʾērît*. The resolution lies in noting the precise meaning of *yeter*, namely, "what is left over." R. de Vaux[72] noted that the word "'rest' draws attention not to the remnant which subsists, but to the totality (ensemble] to which this remnant was joined; the sense of excess is fundamental in the root." The "remnant of Ja-

---

68. Cf. BDB 408, §1a.

69. Sellin, "Micha," 289.

70. Cited in *La Formation*, 249.

71. F. Nötscher, *Zwölf prophetenbuch oder kleine Propheten* (Würzburg, 2d ed. 1957), 100.

72. R. de Vaux, "Le Reste d'Israël d'après les Prophètes," *RB* (1933) 528 n. 1.

cob/Israel," on the one hand, are Micah's contemporaries who survived the invasion of Jerusalem by Sennacherib (2:12-13), who survived Jerusalem's destruction and the Babylonian Captivity generations after Micah's time, and who were redeemed from there to be replanted in Palestine. The remnant is the kernel of the messianic community, and from them the Messiah will come forth. The "rest," on the other hand, are those from the Northern and Southern Kingdoms who did not return after the diaspora. With the advent of the Messiah's birth, however, they will rejoin themselves to the messianic kernel, the "remnant." B. Renaud[73] says: "Thus in comparison to the oracles of the Exile, the perspective of Mic 5:2(3) has moved: the hope does not rest on the 'Golah' but on the Palestinian community, more specifically, Judean, purified by the trial and transformed by the divine initiative. The sons of Israel represent then the messianic community." At the time when the Messiah appears and restores Israel's fortunes there will no longer be a remnant within Israel, but all Israel will know *I AM*, as Jeremiah foresaw (Jer 31:31-34). The messianic community will no longer consist of nominal members, of merely blood relatives who are not also spiritual relatives. E. Sellin[74] arrives at a different sense by interpreting *yeter* after a cognate Semitic root meaning "distinguished" and by redividing and reconstructing *yĕšûbûn ʿal* into *yšbw nṣl;* according to him, the verse means: "and the preeminent among his brothers shall return, and the sons of Israel shall be saved." His conjecture is unnecessary, loses an important theological dimension regarding the Messiah's community, and finds no support in the versions.

yĕšûbûn (will return) is a qal third masculine plural nonperfective with a paragogic *nun* of the root *šûb*. The subject is the rest of the Messiah's brothers; the nonperfective, as *ʿad-ʿēt* indicates, is future; the paragogic *nun* in poetry signifies certainty.[75] *šûb* here denotes "to be reunited with"[76] and connotes conversion. E. Nielsen,[77] though mistakenly restricting "the rest of the brothers" with the Northern Kingdom, rightly notes: "For an exhortation 'to return,' or a prophecy that so-and-so 'shall return,' must be [*sic!*] directed at the apostates (cf. Amos 4:6ff [= 11]; Hos 6:1; 2:9 [= EV 2:7])." Isa 66:5 also speaks of the conversion of "brothers who hate you [the godly]." The unity and conversion of Israel in the Messianic Age is underscored by the unexpected preposition *ʿal (to)*. Many critics want to emend *ʿal*, literalistically "upon," to *ʾel* "unto," but B. Renaud[78] rightly resisted the emendation, noting the force of MT: "While the

73. *La Formation*, 249.
74. Sellin, "Micha," 336-37.
75. *IBHS* §31.7.2.
76. BDB 994, §3b.
77. E. Nielsen, *Oral Tradition* (London: SCM, 1954).
78. *La Formation*, 277.

preposition '*al* indicates the simple idea of movement toward, it implies the idea of contact and also of complete restoration, of total reintegration. . . . The formula *yšwbwn* '*al* 'to return upon' expresses the idea of coming back to a prior state. . . ."

The object of the preposition *bĕnê yiśrā'ēl (sons of Israel),* consisting of the masculine plural construct *bĕnê* and the genitive of relation *yiśrā'ēl,* represents Israel ideally, faithful to *I AM* and united, and connotes the age of David when Israel measured up to that Mosaic ideal, the state to which all Israel shall be restored. R. de Vaux,[79] while erroneously denying the term before David, says, "The twelve-tribe system, uniting the tribes in the same genealogical or tribal lists, was, during the reign of David, the ideal structure of a 'great Israel.' . . . The same faith in Yahweh, the God of Israel, was, however, shared by Judah, and it was with this religious significance that the word was finally used until the last period described in the Old Testament, and so it has been since." B. Renaud[80] comments: "It is really, indeed, this typically religious sense that one must give to the expression of Mic 5:2(3)."

3 In *wĕ'āmad (and he will stand forth)* the *wāw*-relative with the qal third masculine singular perfective of the root '*md* is best construed as representing the (con)sequential situation[81] not to *yittĕnēm* in v 2(3) but to the future nonperfective *yēṣē'* in v 1(2) because the subject is the same, "he" (i.e., the Messiah), and the sequence "he will come forth and stand forth" is more cogent than "*I AM* will give them up, and he will stand." It now becomes clear that v 2(3) is parenthetical, explaining that the hoped-for salvation in v 3(4) must await the divine intervention effecting the Messiah's birth and Israel's spiritual restoration. Whereas v 1(2) spoke of his identity as coming from Bethlehem, v 3(4) speaks of his function. '*āmad* here probably has its sense of standing forth, of appearing, of coming into being, as in the cases of the creation coming into being and standing forth (Isa 48:13; Pss 33:9; 119:90) and, more poignantly for this context, according to S. Schwantes,[82] of a king assuming his new rulership (Dan 8:23; 11:2, 3). (L. Allen[83] thinks that there is a parallel use in 2 Kgs 11:14, but that allusion is more questionable.) If that special sense be allowed, the first function of the Messiah is said to be that of appearing as *I AM*'s new ruler. This particular notion of '*āmad,* nevertheless, also retains the verb's primitive connotation of being unmovable or firm, or standing still. His rule cannot be shaken (cf. Isa 14:24; Pss 33:11; 102:27[26]; 111:3). The Messiah's "stand-

79. R. de Vaux, *The Early History of Israel* (Philadelphia: Westminster, 1978), 749.
80. *La Formation,* 250.
81. *IBHS* §§32.1.3; 32.2.1.
82. Schwantes, "A Critical Study," 131.
83. Allen, *Micah,* 346.

ing forth" is specified by the consequential *wāw*-relative with the qal third masculine singular perfective of *rā'āh (and he will shepherd)*. In contrast to MT, Syr, and Vg, LXX reads "he will see and he will shepherd," but LXX[R] omits "he will see." The surplus of LXX, also reflected in some Hebrew MSS, arose from its refusal to choose between the variants *r'h* "to see" and *r'h* "to shepherd." LXX also adds "his flock" after "he will shepherd." LXX[R] omits this paraphrastic expansion. This sober expression of the Messiah's function also evokes the government of David (2 Sam 5:2; 7:7). The verb links this promise pertaining to the Messiah's rule with *I AM*'s rule as depicted in 2:12-13 and developed in 4:7. The verb is a common metaphorical cliche from the court style of the ancient Near East to represent ideal kingship, but in David's case it took on a particular felicity because he was a shepherd of a flock before he became by divine choice the shepherd of the flock, Israel. Mic 5:3-5(4-6), like Ezek 34:23-24, exploits this Davidic tradition: as shepherd he leads, defends, and cares for his wards.

The preposition *bĕ* marks the object of a variety of verbs; its meaning in *bĕ'ōz yhwh (in the strength of* I AM*)* after *rā'āh* is similar to its use in the expression *bĕkā ya'ămînû* "he will trust in you"; namely, the Messiah's power derives from his special relation with *I AM*. H. Wolff[84] says: "He emphasizes that the pasturing of the new rulers will take place in their empowering by Yahweh." C. Schultz[85] notes that *'ōz* is used primarily of God: it is one of his essential attributes (Pss 62:12[11]; 63:3[2]), and he bestows it on the king (1 Sam 2:10), on his people (Ps 29:11), and on Zion (Isa 52:1). Schultz writes: "But not only is strength a quality given by God; he himself is that strength." That is the notion here, as indicated by the possessive genitive "of *I AM*." There is no reason to suppress *yhwh*, as T. Robinson[86] and A. Deissler[87] propose. The Messiah will keep covenant by depending on the strength and might of *I AM* his God.

Parallel to the phrase "in the strength of *I AM*" is the second qualification of his rule: *bigĕ'ôn šēm yhwh 'ĕlōhāyw (in the majesty of the name of* I AM *his God)*. The *bĕ* functions similarly to the preceding parallel, showing that not only is the Messiah's power derived from *I AM* but his authority is also delegated from him. The masculine singular construct noun *gĕ'ôn* consists of the root *g'h* and the suffix *-ôn*, which transforms it into an abstract noun.[88] *g'h* means literally "to be high," and it and its congeners are often used for towering over something and of being majestic: of waters too deep to pass through (Ezek 47:5; cf. Pss 46:4[3]; 89:10[9]; Job 38:11), of thunder (Job 8:11; 37:4), or of smoke

84. Wolff, *Micha*, 118.
85. C. Schultz, "'ōz," *TWOT* 2:659-60.
86. Robinson, "Micha," 142.
87. Deissler, *La Sainte Bible*, 8:331-33.
88. *IBHS* §5.7.

(Isa 9:17). His majesty is often associated with his power: *I AM* is "highly exalted" because he threw the horse and rider into the sea (Exod 15:1), and he is clothed with "majesty" because he shows the surging seas their place (Ps 93:1). The glory of his "majesty" disseminates fear (Isa 2:19). In Mic 5:3 that majestic might belongs to *I AM*'s *šēm* "name," another possessive genitive (for its meaning see 4:5).

'ĕlōhāyw, in which the pronominal suffix is a genitive of relationship, is an appositive sortal, specifying *I AM* as belonging to the divine class of beings (cf. 3:7).[89] The pronominal suffix implies a contrast to other gods and expresses a particularly close and personal relationship between the Messiah and the God he worships. R. Ringgren[90] notes that in the Psalms "my God emphasizes that the worshipper is convinced that his God is ready to hear his prayer favorably." So also the phrase "your God," says Ringgren,[91] "emphasizes the special relationship of the person named to God, and it is assumed that the result of this relationship extends out to those who come in contact with them [*sic!*]." In sum, the Messiah rules not as a king in his own right but in the derived authority and majestic power he finds in *I AM* his God. LXX achieves a somewhat different sense by reading/or adding a conjunction with *bigĕ'ôn*, by understanding a third masculine plural pronominal suffix with *'ĕlōhîm*, and by omitting *wāw* with the following *wĕyāšābû*, so that it interprets Mic 5:3B(4B) as "and they shall dwell in the glory of the name of the Lord their God." LXX[R] also reads *wāw* with *gĕ'ôn* but also with *wĕyāšābû* so that it stands much closer to MT. The unique readings of LXX, especially its change of pronominal suffix from singular to plural, suggests that it misinterpreted the verse. Moreover, in cases of this sort, partially involving vocalization, it is best to stay with MT.[92]

LXX, however, comes closer to the meaning of *wĕyāšābû (and they will live securely)*, a *wāw*-relative with qal third masculine plural of *yšb* in pause (*contra* 4:4), with its free rendering *hyparxousin* "they will be, they will exist," than Vg, Syr, and several Hebrew MSS that, probably under the influence of *yĕšûbûn* in v 2, understood it as *wĕyāšûbû* from the verb *šûb* "they will return." That notion was expressed in 5:2, and its repetition here would cause the text to walk backward. The messianic function in 5:3 presumes this conversion. Tg, "they will be gathered," meets the same objection. The *wāw*-relative shows that the situation denoted by "and they will live" is consequent upon the Messiah's appearing and ruling by the authority and power he receives from his unique

89. *IBHS* §12.2.
90. R. Ringgren, "*'ĕlōhîm*," *TDOT* 1:279.
91. Ringgren, *TDOT* 1:280.
92. Cf. *IBHS* §1.6.3.

relationship with *I AM*. The subject of this third masculine plural verb, attested in all versions, must be "the sons of Israel" mentioned in v 2, for it is the only plural antecedent in this context. The root *yšb* "to dwell" in this context means more specifically "to abide, endure,"[93] which the writer paraphrases by "to live securely." J. T. Willis,[94] after rejecting various emendations of the text, retains MT with the note: "The language is pastoral and probably refers to a flock dwelling safely without fear of attack from enemies, because of the capable leadership of the shepherd. Furthermore, the brevity of expression here corresponds to the brevity of expression in the first two words of the verse." B. Renaud[95] comments on the significance that 5:3B echoes 4:4:

> The redactor would then kill two birds with one stone: he would reintroduce here the idea of quiet residence that he seems to have at heart. . . . But, at the same time, he would articulate one upon the other the two forms of the eschatological future: Messianic time would coincide with the universal conversion of the peoples. In our opinion, that is one of the major objectives of this redaction of Micah 4–5 that aims to dispose in a unique tableau the diverse current of the eschatological hope.

The next clause with its focus "to the ends of the earth" validates Renaud's thesis. The logical particle *kî* introduces the clause that substantiates the promised security. For the meaning of *'attâ* "now" with reference to a future conceptualized as present see 4:7. *yigdal (he will become great)* is a qal third masculine singular nonperfective with an ingressive force in future time with the stative, intransitive root *gdl*.[96] Once again a promise made to David is invoked: "I will make your name great" (2 Sam 7:9), a greatness connected with cutting off all his enemies (2 Sam 7:8). The Messiah's greatness stands in parallel with the majesty of the name of *I AM* his God, from whom it is derivative. LXX uniquely reads "and they will be great," a *lectio facilior* to agree in number with the preceding verb. For terminative *'ad* see 5:2(3), but whereas there it was terminative in time, here it is terminative in space.

'apsê (the ends of) is no longer used independently in the OT but always in the stereotyped formula with the genitive of measure *'ereṣ (of the earth)*,[97] and so of the earth's limits. This is more than the hyperbolic language common to the "court style" of the ancient Near East. For Israel to enjoy security all her en-

---

93. BDB 442, §2a; cf. Joel 4:20; Ps 121:1.
94. J. T. Willis, "Structure, Setting, and Interrelationships," 332.
95. *La Formation*, 233.
96. Cf. *IBHS* §30.5.3.
97. *IBHS* §9.5.3.

emies must be crushed. Moreover, since *I AM* is Creator and Overlord of history, omnipotent in all his works both in creation and history, one may presume that his rule is unlimited (1 Sam 2:10; Ps 59:14[13]). The concepts of Mic 5:3(4) are similar to those of Ps 2:8: through prayer the future Davidic king will participate in this omnipotence of God and become great by extending his kingdom to the ends of the earth (cf. Zech 9:10; Ps 72:8; Acts 1:8; 13:47), a concept found as early as the Blessing of Moses (Deut 33:17).

4 Whereas *wĕhāyâ (and he will be)* in 4:1 has a deictic temporal function specified by a temporal adverb, here it introduces a consequent situation to v 3(4). The subject is not impersonal but continues to be the Messiah. Consequent upon his securing the security of the sons of Israel by extending his kingdom to the ends of the earth, the Messiah becomes their source of abiding peace; his universal sovereignty leads to universal peace. MT of Mic 5:4A(5A) can be translated "and this one will be peace." Vg's *et erit iste pax* "and he will be peace" possibly comes closer to this than does LXX's *kai estai hautē eirēnē* "and such will be peace" or Tg's "and there will be peace for us from then on"; Syr omits *zeh*. B. D. Eerdmans advanced the understanding of this clause by interpreting *zeh (the one of)* by Arabic *du* "the one of."[98] J. M. P. Smith[99] rejected this rendering as "necessary nowhere else," but he found it necessary to connect *šālôm* "peace" with what follows by the expedient of conjecturing a haplography of *mêm* prefixed to *'aššûr*, citing Job 21:9 and Zech 8:10 as instances of *šālôm min* in the sense of "protection from." The full sense, according to his guess, is: "And this will be our protection from Assyria." J. M. Allegro[100] independently, however, arrived at the same conclusion as Eerdmans, rendering the expression "Possessor of (Lord of) Peace" on the analogy of *zeh sînay* "Lord of Sinai" (Judg 5:5; Ps 68:9[8]). K. J. Cathcart in 1968[101] validated this interpretation from Ugaritic, drawing the conclusion: "In our text . . . *zeh šālōm* means 'the One of Peace.' The phrase is an excellent link between vv. 1-3 and vv. 4-5." Cathcart reversed himself, however, in 1978[102] and defended Smith's suggestion by appealing to the final *mêm* of *šālôm* as a shared consonant with the following *'aššûr*. D. Hillers[103] agrees with Eerdmans, Allegro, and the earlier Cathcart, and, citing divine titles with *d (*du)* in Ugaritic, says, "This is a royal, quasi-divine title." For the use of *zeh* in so-called independent relative clauses, a true

---

98. In Smith, *Micah*, 109.

99. Smith, *Micah*, 109.

100. J. M. Allegro, "Uses of the Semitic Demonstrative Element in Hebrew," *VT* 5 (1955) 309-12.

101. K. J. Cathcart, "Some Notes on Micah 5:4-5," *Bib* 49 (1968) 511-12.

102. K. J. Cathcart, "Micah 5:4-5 and Semitic Incantations," *Bib* 59 (1978) 39.

103. Hillers, *Micah*, 65.

demonstrative usage, see *IBHS* §19.5. For the meaning of *šālôm (of peace)*, a genitive of quality,[104] see 3:5; here it means specifically "wholeness," "preservation," or "salvation," as in 1 Sam 16:4 and Isa 9:5-6(6-7). E. Sellin[105] notes: "The military capability of the Messiah is here exactly the same as in Isa 9:3[4]."

'aššûr (As for Asshur), a metonymy for Assyria's invading armies,[106] is a nominative absolute, a *casus pendens* construction, focussing attention on the topic of the following clause.[107] BDB[108] notes: "N.B. with *ky* — *when* or *if*, the subject is often prefixed for distinctness and emph.: 1 Ki 8:37 . . . , Is 28:18, Mic 5:4[5]. . . ." Critics are divided as to whether or not to take Asshur at face value. On the one hand, those who take it so attribute the prophecy to Micah[109] or, arbitrarily, his adversaries.[110] But A. Weiser[111] defends Micah's authorship. On the other hand, some interpreters avoid the obvious (see also Mic 5:5[6]) and speak instead of the piece's "mysterious character," its "apocalyptic aspect," its "nationalistic and revengeful tone," and push it down after the exile, to the Persian epoch[112] or the Maccabean period, more precisely into the context of the persecution of Antiochus Epiphanes.[113] According to them, "Assyria" is a sort of coded word symbolically designating Israel's enemies. They argue that the name of Asshur was applied a long time after the disappearance of that empire to the Babylonians (Lam 5:6), or to the Persians (Ezra 6:22; Zech 10:10), or to the Syrians (Isa 19:23; 27:13; perhaps Ps 83:9[8]). None of these passages unquestionably supports their very dubious thesis. The issue is put beyond reasonable doubt by "in the land of Nimrod" in 5:5(6), as will be seen. Micah projects Israel's archenemy of his own time (see 1:1) into the future Messianic Age in accord with the principle that prophets represent the future under the imagery and traits of their own historical situation (see 4:1, Exposition). The *kî (if)* introduces a conditional protasis that is envisioned as more real than one introduced by *'im*.[114]

---

104. *IBHS* §9.5.1.

105. Sellin, "Micha," 290.

106. Cf. BDB 78, §2.

107. *IBHS* §4.7.

108. BDB 473, §2b.

109. Sellin, "Micha," 290; Robinson, "Micha," 143; J. T. Willis, "Micah 4:14–5:5 — A Unit," *VT* (1968) 545.

110. *Jerusalem Bible* (Garden City, N.Y.: Doubleday, 1966), 1503; note Vuilleumier, "Michée," 63-64.

111. Weiser, "Micha," 274.

112. Deissler, *La Sainte Bible*, 8:336, not without hesitancy; Willi-Plein, *Vorformen*, 93-95.

113. Smith, *Micah*, 107; R. E. Wolfe, "Micah: Introduction and Exegesis," IB 6 (Nashville: Abingdon, 1959), 932; T. Lescow, "Redaktionsgeschichtliche Analyse von Micha 6–7," *ZAW* (1972) 287.

114. Cf. Cathcart, "Micah 5:4-5 and Semitic Incantations," 39.

yābô' (he penetrates) is a qal third masculine singular nonperfective in a contingent clause[115] with *'aššûr* the antecedent of the root *bô'* (see 4:10). *bô'* with *bĕ* means "to enter to," "to penetrate," here of an invader and so with hostility. The goal of the penetration is *bĕ'arṣēnû (into our country)*. Whereas heretofore in the book of Micah *'ereṣ* referred to the "earth" (see 5:3[4]), here, as also in 5:5(6), the parallels "our lands" and "our territory" show that it refers to the holy land that *I AM* swore to give his people; the first common plural possessive pronominal suffix validates this meaning. The pronoun refers to the "sons of Israel" in v 2(3). As in 4:14(5:1), Micah again identifies himself with Israel; this time not merely with the persecuted remnant (4:14[5:1]) but with the restored and triumphant messianic community in which he hopes to have a part, a share he denied the avaricious landlords in 2:5. Greek codices and the related version of LXX read *epi tēn gēn hymōn* "upon your country," but Ziegler rightly presumes that this is an inner Greek corruption and so reconstructs *hēmōn* with MT.

In *wĕkî (and when)* the conjunction *wĕ* introduces a coordinate situation to emphasize the devastation wrought by the Assyrian invasion and the second *kî* has the same value as the first. *yidrōk (and treads down)*, a qal third masculine singular nonperfective of the root *drk*, functions grammatically the same as its parallel *yābô'*. The root *drk*, however, intensifies the scene, for it means here, in connection with an invader, "to trample," "to march," as in Judg 5:21; Ps 91:13 (cf. Mic 1:3). In *bĕ'armĕnōtênû (through our lands)* spatial *bĕ* means "through" with verbs of moving through an area.[116] MT's *'armĕnōtênû* "our citadels," followed by Vg and Syr, though possible because prominent strongholds were particularly suspect to attack and plunder,[117] should be rejected in favor of LXX's *chōran hymōn* (= Heb. *'admāntēnû*) "our lands" because it constitutes a better parallel with "into our country" in 5:4Ba(5Ba) and with "through our territory" in 5:5Bb(6Bb). The confusion of *d* and *r* is common (see 4:14). K. Cathcart[118] defends MT by the dubious arguments that LXX rendered *b'rmntynw* with *eis tēn gēn hymōn* in Jer 9:20(21), and so why not here; that the LXX translators were ignorant of the meaning of *'armôn;* and from the parallels in Amos 2:2, 5; 3:9. More probably, however, Jer 9:20(21) represents the same orthographic confusion, and, if so, the translator's ignorance of *'rmn* is irrelevant; the parallels in Amos differ from these in Micah and so are also irrelevant.

The *wāw* with hiphil first common plural perfective in *wahăqēmōnû (then we will raise)* introduces the apodosis.[119] The versions rightly render it as future.

115. *IBHS* §31.6.1.
116. *IBHS* §11.2.5.
117. Cf. BDB 74.
118. Cathcart, "Micah 5:4-5 and Semitic Incantations," 41.
119. *IBHS* §32.2.1.

E. Lipiński[120] wants to translate the verse, "when the Assyrians invaded our land, then we raised up. . . ." This is grammatically possible, but since 5:1-5(2-6) is looking to the future Messiah, it is co-textually impossible. In v 5(6) *wĕrāʿû* and *wĕhiṣṣîl* cannot refer to past time. The hiphil is a two-place one with "we" (i.e., the unified and restored sons of Israel under Messiah's rule) the subject, and the "seven shepherds" the objects who participate in the action.[121] *qûm* basically means "to rise up from a prostate position" and often refers to preparatory activity, especially, as here, in martial contexts (cf. qal in Exod 2:17; Judg 7:15). The verb recalls the cry in holy war calling upon God "to rise up" (Num 10:35; Ps 3:8[7]). Wellhausen[122] and Weiser[123] conjecture *hqym* so as to make *môšēl* of 5:1(2) the subject, while P. Riessler,[124] E. Sellin,[125] and J. Lippl[126] conjecture *hitqummû* "there will rise up." LXX's *epegerthēsontai* "they will be raised up" (= *whuqmû* hophal?), a third masculine plural, is probably a *lectio facilior*, but LXX[R] reads with MT. MT is supported by the first common plural suffix in 5:4Ba(5Ba). W. Nowack[127] contends that this text knows nothing of the *môšēl*. As argued in the Exposition (294-95), it is part of the same pericope, at least on the literary level, as that prophecy and must be interpreted in its light. The spiritual unity of the messianic community, as developed in v 3(4), is now shown by their spiritual unity in contending against their enemies. Recall (see 1:1) that Israel was divided in its response to Assyria, some calling for submission, others for rebellion. In the Messianic Age, confident of the Messiah's salvation, the new Israel will concertedly oppose the uncircumcised invader. In *ʿālāyw (against him) ʿal* has its hostile sense (see 2:1, 3) and the pronominal suffix looks back to Asshur in 5:4Ba(5Ba). E. Lipiński[128] would like to omit the prepositional phrase because it "does not have any correspondent in either the Greek text of the exegetical recension of the C group, or in Theophylacte d'Acride, or in some MSS of the Ethiopic version." His textual evidence is too weak.

šibʿâ . . . ûšĕmōnâ (seven . . . eight), cardinal substantives of "three-ten" group, oppose the grammatical gender of the nouns enumerated.[129] This typi-

120. E. Lipiński, "Nimrod et Assur," *RB* 73 (1966) 90-91.

121. *IBHS* §27.2.

122. Wellhausen, *Die kleinen Propheten*, 146.

123. Weiser, "Micha, " 273.

124. P. Riessler, *Die kleinen Propheten* (Rottenburg: Bader, 1911), 120.

125. Sellin, "Micha," 338.

126. Lippl, *Die zwölf kleinen Propheten*, 208.

127. W. Nowack, "Micha," in *Die kleinen Propheten*, Göttingen Handkommentar zum Alten Testament, 3d ed. (Göttingen: Vandenhoeck & Ruprecht, 1922), 225.

128. Lipiński, "Nimrod et Assur," 90.

129. *IBHS* §15.2.2.

cal heightening of the number, found already in the Ugaritic texts, is an intensifying movement in synonymous parallelism.[130] In these cases the real number is the second, and in this particular case it is one beyond the number signifying perfection. "Seven" symbolizes both sacredness and totality.[131] The point is that there will be more than full cooperation among the holy sons of Israel in contrast to their historic unholy discord and disinterest in furthering the kingdom of God (see Deborah's complaint against Reuben, Gilead, Dan, and Asher in Judg 5:16-17). Micah chooses *rōʿîm (shepherds)* to designate the rulers of the tribes in order to identify them with the *môšēl*, the messianic ruler, who will *rʿh* "shepherd" them (see v 3[4]). Whereas the Messiah takes the initiative in 5:1(2) and 3(4), the way is prepared for his people to take the initiative in 5:4-5(5-6) by the mention of the conversion of the "rest" to the "remnant" in 5:2(3) and so the constituting of the new "sons of Israel." The linkage between the two initiatives is provided by "And he [the Messiah] shall be the One/Lord of peace." Faith in him spiritually unifies and fortifies the people for battle.

E. Sellin,[132] struck by the rather strange language "leaders of man," prefers to read in Mic 5:4Bbβ(5Bbβ) not *nĕsîkê,* but, following LXX's *dēgmata, nšyky* "biters — or persecutors of men," a designation for persecuting demons (cf. 3:5, though Sellin strangely does not cite this text in favor of Gen 49:17; Jer 8:17; Amos 5:19; 9:3). From this he works backward and reads in Mic 5:4Bbα(5Bbα) not *rōʿîm,* but, following P. Riessler, *rāʿîm* "wicked men," reminding him of the seven evil men in the Babylonian incantations texts. But MT is perfectly intelligible, has the support of the versions, and provides an excellent linkage between vv 3(4) and 4(5). LXX (*contra* Aquila's *kateptammenous* "prefects" and Sym's *christous* "anointed one") mistook *šîn* for *sāmek,* a common scribal error. The masculine plural construct *nĕsîkê (sheiks)* of the root *nsk* is found only in the plural and of tribal chiefs (of Midian in Josh 13:21, of the north in Ezek 32:30, and of Israel's enemies, including Assyria, in Ps 83:12[11].) H. Cazelles[133] and F. E. Peiser[134] noted that the term *nsk* is found in Assyrian texts concerning the campaign of 720 into Syro-Palestine. In all these uses it is used of tribes confederated against Israel. Micah may have chosen the term deliberately with reference to the unified sons of Israel as a polemic against the nations confederated in the Assyrian imperial army (see 4:11). D. Hillers,[135] finding MT *ʾādām* "mankind" a genitive lacking cogency and a precise parallel, emends the text to *ʾārām*

---

130. Cf. R. Alter, *The Art of Biblical Poetry* (New York: Basic Books, 1985), 11.

131. See G. G. Cohen, *"shebaʿ," TWOT* 2:898.

132. Sellin, "Micha," 290.

133. H. Cazelles, *EncJud* 11:1, 480-83.

134. F. E. Peiser, "Micha 5," *Orientalistische Literaturzeitung* 10 (1917) 363-67.

135. Hillers, *Micah,* 68.

"Aram," for the Aramean tribes were also led by *nasiku* in neo-Assyrian and neo-Babylonian inscriptions, though some had more than one sheik *(nasiku)*.[136] But "Aram" seems even less cogent in this prophecy pertaining to the Messiah's salvation through renewed Israel and without biblical parallel elsewhere. GKC[137] properly understood it as a genitive of genus (= men of leadership), like *kěsîl 'ādām* "a fool of a man" = "foolish man" and, even more precisely, *'bywny 'ādām* "needy of mankind" = "needy mankind." In Ezek 44:25 *mēt 'ādām* is a "dead person." It is best left untranslated. L. Allen's[138] translation "eight men as generals" is too free. The focus is not on their roles but on their character: they are leaders or fighters by nature.

5   *wěrā'û (and they will shepherd)* consists of a *waw*-relative with the suffix conjugation, introducing the sequential situation to v 4(5), qal third masculine plural with *rō'îm/něsîkê 'ādām* as its antecedents and the root I *r'h* "shepherd" (not II *r''* "to shatter"; so KBL against versions and context), linking this verse tightly with the same root in vv 3(4) and 4(5). The common verb entails that Assyria has been brought within the messianic rule. LXX omits the definite direct object *'et-'ereṣ (the land of)*, but it should not be followed because, even though it may be more likely that *'et-'ereṣ* was introduced from the parallel in v 5Ab(6Ab) than dropped from v 5Aa(6Aa), the sense demands its presence. The verses move from the defensive posture of chiefs defending their homeland against Assyria to the offensive posture in v 4(5) of their ruling Assyria's homeland. Furthermore, *'et-'ereṣ 'aššûr* begins with initial *'*, a textual environment conducive to haplography. *'aššûr (of Asshur)*, a genitive of association,[139] also couples v 5(6) with v 4(5). Whereas in v 4(5) Asshur was a metonymy for Assyria's invaders, here it is a metonymy for its citizens. In *baḥereb (with a sword)* the preposition *bě* denotes instrument,[140] and the article denotes class.[141] O. Kaiser[142] notes that the sword is a military weapon and an instrument of justice and of punishment. Micah may intend to intensify the instruments of subjugation: whereas Assyria smote Israel's king with a rod (Mic 4:14[5:1]), the Messiah's helpers will rule with a sword.

Parallel to "the land of Assyria," entailing the same grammar and as a second object to *wěrā'û*, is *'et-'ereṣ nimrōd (and the land of Nimrod)*. By locating

136. See J. A. Brinkman, *A Political History of Post-Kassite Babylonia, 1158-722 B.C.*, AnOr 43 (Rome: Pontifical Biblical Institute, 1968), 273-75.

137. GKC §128l.

138. Allen, *Micah*, 339.

139. *IBHS* §9.5.3.

140. *IBHS* §11.5.2.

141. *IBHS* §13.5.

142. O. Kaiser, "*ḥereḇ*," *TDOT* 5:157.

"the land of Nimrod (i.e., Babylonia)" second, Micah subordinates it to Assyria. This notice helps to establish Micah as the author of this piece (see Exposition, 296). The reading *bipĕtāḥêhā* "in its entrances" *(with a drawn sword)* in MT is remotely intelligible if one retains *b'rmntynw* "in its citadels." Even then, however, the association is far-fetched because "citadels" in MT pertains to those in Israel while "its entrances" belongs to those in Babylon. LXX renders it "in its trench," probably by confusion with *pḥt* "pit." Syr also gropes for meaning by interpreting "in his anger." Vg's *in lanceis eius* successfully restores the text to the much more rare word, and so more difficult *bappĕtîḥâ* "with a drawn sword" (cf. Ezek 21:33[28]; Ps 55:22[21]), involving an inversion of *yôd* and *ḥêt* and a different punctuation than the more common word of MT. This reading is also attested by Quinta of Hexapla and by the Dodecapropheton found at Murabbaʿat: *en paraxiphisidia autōn* "by their dagger"; cf. also Aquila's *en seiromastais autēs*. Both Ibn Ezra and Qimḥi so understood the text. Obviously, it gives the desired parallel both in grammar and significance with its parallel, *baḥereb*.

With *wĕhiṣṣîl (and he will deliver)* Micah returns again to Messiah's initiative. The *wāw*-relative with the perfective is best construed as consequential *wāw*-relative, more specifically a summarizing epexegetical use *(and so he will deliver)*.[143] This use parallels *wāw*-relative with the prefix conjugation (= "and so," "thus"), as in Gen 2:1's *wayĕkullû haššāmayim wĕhāʾāreṣ* "and so the heavens and the earth were completed." The singular form is confirmed by all the ancient translations. The *wāw*-relative does not introduce a chronologically sequential but a summarizing situation because the subject, a third masculine singular, returns to the Messiah as the deliverer, and the apodosis in Mic 5:5Bb(6Bb) repeats almost word for word the apodosis in Mic 5:4Ba(5Ba), "and he will deliver from Asshur" (Mic 5:5Ba[6Ba]), parallels "and he will be the one of peace" (Mic 5:4A[5B]), and "when he penetrates into our country and when he marches through our territory" (Mic 5:5Bb[6Bb]) matches Mic 5:4Ba(5Ba). *hiṣṣîl* is an unclassified hiphil;[144] it is best construed as a two-place hiphil with the object "us" elided,[145] a common elision.[146] Some[147] emend the text by adding the suffix = *wĕhiṣṣîlānû*, but the textual evidence is slim; LXX by a *lectio facilior* transforms the verb to plural to match 5:5A(6A) and lacks the object. Vg, Syr, and Tg probably supplied it, as I do, from the co-text. The root *nṣl*, another link between this oracle and the earlier promises (cf. *nṣl* niphal in 4:10), designates taking away or freeing from some sort of being held fast: "to snatch away,"

---

143. *IBHS* §32.1.3; cf. §33.2.
144. Lambdin, *Introduction to Biblical Hebrew*, 157e.
145. *IBHS* §27.2.
146. Jouön, *Grammaire*, §146i.
147. Cf. Robinson, "Micha," 142; Vuilleumier, "Michée," 62; *BHS*.

"to take away." Rescuing or releasing the object from the sphere of affliction leads to the meaning "to save." *I AM* does this for the godly because it is right, and so in the background of this word the faithful expect *I AM* to free them from distress when threatened by the godless, either collectively and/or individually, in manifold ways, and so save them when they are threatened by the godless. According to Bergman,[148] it typically (115 times out of 191 times) is construed with *min*, as here with *mē'aššûr (from Asshur)*. "Asshur" is a metonymy for its ruthless invaders, as in 5:4Ba(5Ba). The Messiah will deliver his community from godless "Asshur" by subordinates filled with his spirit and power to execute justice by the sword.

After the apodosis, "he will deliver [us] from Asshur," the temporal/conditional protasis repeats 5:4Ba(5Ba), except that *bigĕbûlēnû (through our territory)* replaces *bĕ'admĕnōtênû*. Tg substitutes: "that he *not* come into our land and that he *not* enter our border." *gĕbûl* is singular in MT, *contra* plural in LXX and Vg. If it be correct, the boundary of the sworn land Canaan is in view, and this becomes a synecdoche for the whole territory (cf. Judg 19:29; 1 Sam 11:3, 7; 27:1) and thus a synonym for *'ereṣ* "land."

EXPOSITION

Like the preceding two oracles of salvation in 4:9-10 and 11-13, the one in 4:14–5:5(5:1-6), the most famous of all on account of its prediction that the Messiah — a theological term for David *redivivus* in his ideal son — would be born in Bethlehem (Matt 2:6), also progresses from a present distressful situation in 4:14(5:1) to a future salvation. Like those oracles it introduces the distress by *'attâ* "now," and includes an injunction *titgōdĕdî* "assemble yourself as a troop" addressed to Jerusalem under the expression of "Daughter" (cf. 4:10, 13). Unlike them, however, (1) this feature is found not in the situation of salvation but in the situation of distress; (2) Jerusalem is not addressed as *bat-ṣiyôn* "Daughter Zion" but as *bat-gĕdûd* "Troop-like Daughter"; (3) only one injunction and not two is given, and (4) that in the form of a nonperfective and not an imperative; and finally, (5) the situation of salvation is not developed by a *kî* "because" clause but by an entirely new form, met in 4:8. As a result the form of the salvation section differs significantly from the earlier ones. Moreover, the salvation section is much more extensive and heavily imbalanced in its direction, in contrast to the preceding oracles where the situations of distress and deliverance were given about equal weight.

148. Bergman, *THAT* 2:97.

With the exception of 5:1(2) Micah speaks throughout. The rough transitions between the verses suggests that on the preliterary level 4:14(5:1), 5:1(2), and 3(4), 5:2(3) and 5:4B-5A(5B-6A), and 5:5B(6B), before their redaction into this literary ensemble, existed in isolation. Whatever may have been its prehistory, the pericope in hand is strongly unified not only by the form of moving from distress to deliverance as in the preceding two oracles but also by the *inclusio* using the first-person pronoun "us" in 4:14(5:1) and 5:5(6) in connection with mention of Assyria's siege and invasion of the holy land (see also 5:4[5]). By the end of the oracles the tables are completely turned from *their attack against us* to *our attack against them*. The distress and deliverance motifs are linked by the assonance of *'attâ* "now" in 4:14(5:1) and *'attâ* "you," and by the adversative *wāw* in 5:1(2) "but," which radically contrasts the defeat of the present epoch with the future glorious victories of Messiah. In addition to these stylistic and thematic links, it is above all unified by contrasting Israel's present humbled *šōpēṭ* "ruler," who depended on his own military hardware (cf. 5:9-10[10-11]), with her future humble *môšēl* "ruler," who will conquer "in the strength of *I AM*, in the majesty of the name of *I AM* his God" (5:3[4]).

The section pertaining to salvation (5:1-5[2-6]) falls into two halves: a focus on the victorious messianic shepherd-ruler in 5:1-3(2-4) and on his triumphant undershepherd-leaders in 5:4-5(5-6). 5:1-3(2-4) is unified and developed by a nonperfective "one will come forth to be a ruler" in 5:1(2) followed by chronological *wāw*-relative forms with the suffix conjugation in 5:3(4), "and he will stand forth and shepherd." 5:1(2) focuses on the Messiah's origins from David's roots, and 5:3(4) on his program of government, namely, in complete subjection to the will of *I AM* and in manner comparable to the shepherding skills of David. 5:2(3) is parenthetical, answering the pressing question as to when the distressful situation will be reversed; in other words, it awaits the Messiah's birth and, in connection with it, the conversion of all Israel. As elsewhere in Micah, the line between *I AM*'s address and Micah's comment upon it is attenuated (cf. Mic 2:3-4 and 5). Each of these verses entails a spiritual kingdom. The Messiah's advent must be the result of supernatural intervention because he originates in insignificant Bethlehem, even as David, who was also the least of his brothers; and when he comes, he rules "for me," says *I AM* (5:1[2]). His advent depends upon God's faithful preservation of a remnant who bring him forth according to the divine calendar, and his advent will effect the conversion of Israelites who theretofore were not numbered among the faithful remnant (v. 2[3]). Finally, the Messiah will stand forth and rule by the power and authority derived from the strength and name of *I AM* (v 3[4]). One notes a movement in these verses from the Messiah in v 1(2), to the remnant and the rest of his brothers, and so all Israel, in v 2(3), to the ends of the earth in v 3(4).

5:4-6(5-7) is developed chiastically:

1a And he will be the one of peace.

1b As for Asshur, when he penetrates into our country,

1c and when he marches through our lands,

> 2a then we will raise up against him seven shepherds,
> even eight sheiks.

> 2b And they will shepherd the land of Asshur with the sword,
> and the land of Nimrod with a drawn sword.

1a′ And so he will deliver [us] from Asshur

1b′ when he penetrates into our country,

1c′ and when he marches through our territory.

1a(2a) and 1a′(2a′) pertain to the Messiah's peace and protection of his *imperium;* 1b, c(2b, c), and 1b′, c′(2b′, c′) to Assyria's threat against Israel's security; and 2b, c(3b, c) to Messiah's subordinate "shepherds" through whom he accomplishes his victory over "Assyria," and who speak dramatically using the first-person plural pronoun. The chiasm functions to subordinate the sheik-shepherds to the Messiah and to attribute victory to him. The introductory statement, "and he will be the one of peace," forms the transition from the focus on the Messiah to the sheik-shepherds who deliver Israel and dominate Assyria. Furthermore, 5:4-6(5-7) is coupled with 5:1-3(2-4) by the subject, "the Messiah," by the root *rʿh* in 5:3(4) and 5:4-5(5-6), by the restored "sons of Israel" in 5:2(3), who are the antecedents to the first-person plural pronouns in 5:4-5(5-6), and finally by the common notion of security within Messiah's *imperium:* "and they will live securely" (5:3[4]) and "he will be the one of peace" (5:4[5]).

4:14–5:5(5:1-6) is distinguished from 5:6-7(7-8) by the introductory formula *wĕhāyâ* in 5:6(7), by the new subject *šěʾērît yaʿăqōb* "the remnant of Jacob" in 5:6-7(7-8), and by the new theme that the remnant will become a savor of both life and death.

The oracle in 4:14–5:5(5:1-6) epexegetes the earlier salvation oracles in 4:1-13. Micah's diverse currents of eschatological hope are here sewn together into a unique tableau. He articulates the vision of the Law going forth from Mount Zion to instruct converted nations that are afar off (4:1-5) with the Messiah's rule over all of true Israel and reaching to the ends of the earth (5:3[4]). This tableau shows clearly that the universal salvation envisioned in 4:1-5 will not transpire until the advent of the Messiah and Israel's restoration in connection with it; and, even more significantly, it will be accomplished through the Messiah, who will become great "to the ends of the earth." The notion of Israel's universal dominion is also prepared for in the closing words of 4:12-13 entitling

I AM, "the Lord of all the earth." The restoration of Jerusalem's former *memšālâ* "dominion" (4:8) finds an echo in the coming *môšēl* "ruler," suggesting that the two may be related. Jerusalem's past and future greatness originates from a cradle in Bethlehem. These two prophecies are also bound by sharing a common, ancient, tribal form (see 4:8). The remnant in Jerusalem, who have been likened to a woman in labor in 4:9, 10, are now said to give birth to the Messiah himself in 5:2(3) and so to renewed Israel. Finally, Jerusalem's triumph over the nations as predicted in 4:11-12 is now seen to be accomplished ultimately by the Messiah and his shepherd-sheiks. 4:14(5:1) is knit tightly with 4:10-11 by four or five verbal links: *'attâ* "now," *'al* "against," *bat* "Daughter" with an injunction, and *yiśrā'ēl* "Israel" at the end of the line in 4:14(5:1); 5:1-2(2-3). This unique tableau, weaving together Israel's disparate hopes, features the Messiah from whom all divine blessings flow.

This prophecy is best construed as having been delivered during Sennacherib's siege of Jerusalem; no other historical setting is more fitting for any of its parts. That setting was validated in the exposition of 2:12-13 and matches the historical notice in 1:1. B. Renaud assigns 4:14(5:1) to the preceding oracle, and insists that 5:2(3) is a later redactor's gloss inserted between 5:1 and 3(2 and 4)[149] and that 5:4B-5(5B-6) once constituted a brief independent oracle;[150] reserves judgment on whether 5:4A(5A) belongs to the primitive oracle of 5:1, 3(2, 4) or whether it is the word of a redactor; and grants that a later redactor put together this anthology of material into an ensemble without burdening himself to smooth out the resulting roughness and unevenness of the text. He dates 5:1, 3(2, 4) to the end of the exile or early return and 5:2(3) to several decades after the return, and reserves judgment on the date of 5:4B-5(5B-6). His arguments tend to be subjective and circular, lacking conviction to overthrow the historical credibility of the superscription. In fact, there is good reason to assign the oracle and its parts to the prophet Micah, who lived during the turbulent time of Assyria's invasions of Judah in the last half of the eighth century B.C. and the first part of the seventh. Renaud himself[151] established that 5:4-5(5-6) with its reference to Assyria and its suggestion that "the land of Nimrod" (= Babylon) was subordinate to it should be dated to the eighth-century prophet. Regarding the reference to Asshur, he argued that apart from very clear contrary indications, "which are missing here," it is more obvious to give "Asshur" its natural meaning. Regarding the subordination of "the land of Nimrod" he wrote:

149. *La Formation*, 230-33.
150. *La Formation*, 234-39.
151. *La Formation*, 252-53.

The mention [of the land of Nimrod] could furnish us with an indication of the date of this passage. The name occurs only three times in the OT: in Mic 5:5(6); Gen 10:8-12, which is echoed in 1 Chr 1:10. Whatever be the debated origin of the term — mythological, geographical, or more probably historical — it is transparent from Gen 10:10 that the land of Nimrod coincides with Babylonia, the land of Shinar. But that passage also tells us that "from this land Asshur came out." In that way the biblical authors "wanted to signify manifestly." E. Lipiński[152] comments "that the Assyrian empire had replaced the Babylonian empire." In its own way, by the bias of the parallelism, Mic 5:4-5(5-6) wants to say the same thing. Let us note that it places Asshur first and the land of Nimrod second. One could understand that while being unified under a sole and unique power, these two lands constitute two distinct entities, especially since Genesis 10 distinguishes them clearly. Is this also a way of expressing a certain subordination of the second in comparison to the first? One would thus be led to date the text from a time when Asshur reigned over Babylonia, which would indeed correspond to the epoch of Isaiah and of Micah [see 1:1].

Furthermore, as noted in the Exegesis (290-91), the rare word *něsîkê* "sheiks" in 5:4(5) also occurs in an Assyrian inscription from 720 B.C., helping to corroborate this date. Micah's use of the first-person plural pronoun in connection with the Assyrian invasion clearly in 5:4-5(5-6) and as an *inclusio* with 4:14(5:1) strongly suggests that the siege of Jerusalem mentioned in 4:14(5:1) is also that of Assyria, and if so, more specifically of Sennacherib (see 1:1; 2:12-13). J. L. Mays[153] inferred that 4:14(5:1) refers to the Babylonian siege on faulty data: "In descriptions of a particular historical occasion the term [*māṣôr* "siege"] is used only of Nebuchadnezzar's sieges of Jerusalem (2 Kgs 24:10; 25:2; Jer 52:5; Ezek 4:3, 7; 5:2)." In fact, however, the Chronicler (2 Chr 32:10) quotes Sennacherib as using this very word for his siege against Jerusalem! In light of this *inclusio* the onus is on critics to prove that 5:1-3(2-4) does not also originate in Micah's mouth, but they offer no firm facts.

Israel cherished this prophecy in the first century A.D., at which time, according to the inspired apostolic interpretation of it, the Lord Jesus Christ fulfilled it (Matt 2:5-6; John 7:42; Eph 2:14). Readers need to remind themselves that Micah clothed this prophecy in the earthly garb of the eighth century but that it finds its fulfillment in the heavenly garb of the Son of God. L. Allen[154] said well:

152. Lipiński, "Nimrod et Assur," 84.
153. Mays, *Micah*, 114.
154. Allen, *Micah*, 350.

Religious truth can never be communicated in a vacuum. It must be giv[e]
firm place within the religious frame of reference held by its hearers, conforming to their own general beliefs and tailored to their mental attitudes.
Otherwise it would be a meaningless conundrum. "The future is presented
as an evolution from the historically existing" (J. Orr, *The Problem of the
Old Testament* [1906], 461).

Because Israel's humiliation is remedial and not penal, temporary and
not permanent, Micah exhorts the faithful remnant, who are holed up within
Jerusalem during Sennacherib's siege of that city, to galvanize themselves as a
troop. The remnant's puniness by comparison with Assyria's greatness is suggested by the contrast between "powerful nations [of the Assyrian imperial
army] are gathered against you [Jerusalem]" (4:11) and "assemble yourself [Je-
rusalem] as a troop." The prophet who wept over the fall of Judah in 1:8-9 now
shares their affliction and humiliation in the besieged capital (see 1:1). The Assyrian imperial army's siege threatens the life of the resolute remnant sheltered
behind Jerusalem's wall, and Assyria's leaders, presumably under Sennacherib
their great king, humiliate Israel's ruler (*šōpēṭ*) by metaphorically and symbolically smiting him on the cheek with their scepters, the symbols of their dominion. By striking him on the jaw they give him the ultimate insult (Job
16:10; Lam 3:30), for it shows that with all resistance gone the victim can no
longer protect himself. One is reminded of the taunt by Sennacherib's supreme commander to Hezekiah: "Come now, make a bargain with my master,
the king of Assyria: I will give you two thousand horses — if you can put rid-
ers on them! How can you repulse one officer of the least of my master's officials?" (2 Kgs 18:23-24).

The *šōpēṭ* "judge" normally wields the scepter in his role to deliver the oppressed and to punish the oppressor, but here the degraded "judge" is himself
oppressed with no one to deliver him. Since historically God raises up "judges"
to right wrong, as in the book of Judges and elsewhere (cf. Ps 72:1-2), the reversed situation with Israel's "judge" cringing like a criminal beneath the repeated blows of the *šēbeṭ* "truncheon" in the hands of impious Assyrian tyrants
implies the collapse of Hezekiah's authority due to his decadence (cf. Isa 10:5-
19). Says L. C. Allen:[155] "The prophet points out the grim incongruity of this
happening with another wordplay, *shēbeṭ* 'rod' and *shōpēṭ* 'judge.' The venerable
judge has become but a whipping boy." By refusing to call Israel's apostate ruler
"king," Micah reminds them that they have but one King, *I AM*. Sometimes the
church is rocked by scandals involving pretentious church leaders who have

155. Allen, *Micah*, 342.

muddied the waters by giving way before Satan's attack. In situations like these, Micah's clarion voice still raises itself above the turmoil, summoning the faithful remnant by its stirring martial language to galvanize itself in hope because the ultimate victory belongs to its Lord. "Do not be afraid of what you have heard — those words with which the underlings of the king of Assyria have blasphemed me" (2 Kgs 19:5), the Lord still says to the repentant and faithful through Isaiah.

In this dark context, Micah now gives the faithful troop bright hope to fight on against insurmountable odds: through them *I AM* will bring his triumphant ruler, the Messiah, into the world. The humble ruler triumphing over Assyria brilliantly stands out in the frame of the humbled ruler under Assyria. As Judah's once proud Jerusalem is besieged and humbled, Micah turns to little Bethlehem as Israel's source of hope. The little town is sublimed with glory as it alone is addressed directly by *I AM* himself. As in Mic 1:10-16, one may presume *nomen est omen* and that *bêt-leḥem* "house of bread" and *'eprātâ* "fruitful" pregnantly portend the Messiah's career. Through the technique of chiaroscuro our poet paints and highlights features of his subject, the Messiah.

In the first place, he accents that the Messiah represents a new commencement, a new beginning in the house of David. God will not frustrate his covenant with David but will gloriously fulfill it with a new David in the last days. This feature of starting afresh in David's lineage is but dimly lit by the ancient literary form, which reaches back to Israel's tribal epoch, in which the prophecy is given (see 4:8). It is illuminated even more by the collocation of terms in 5:1Aa(2Aa), Bethlehem, Ephrathah, and Judah, reminding one familiar with the Davidic tradition of, "Now David was the son of an Ephrathite named Jesse, who was from Bethlehem in Judah." Matthew ties him even closer to the David tradition by calling him *hēgoumenos* rather than *archonta* (LXX of Mic 5:1[2]), taking his term from the Davidic tradition in 2 Sam 5:2; 7:8 (LXX). Amazingly God bypasses Jerusalem, the city he chose and loved above all cities according to the songs of Zion celebrating its greatness (cf. Psalms 46; 48; 76; 84; 87; 122). Rather, as the doorway through which Messiah would step forth onto center stage of salvation history, *I AM* chose the same portal through which David entered to play his role on the stage of sacred history. The common cradle suggests the connection between them and the fact that the Messiah represents a second David and so a fresh start in salvation history through the dynasty to whom God had given an eternal covenant. As out of Saul's death and Israel's humiliation under the Philistine David commenced Israel's former golden age in the sworn land, so out of the humiliation of David's house and Judah's ashes the greater David, originating in the same lowly crib by the same mysteries of divine election and enablement, will inaugurate Israel's future universal and eternal golden age. Isaiah expressed the same thought in his prophecy: "A shoot will come up from the stump of Jesse; from his roots a branch will bear fruit." *I AM*, he implies, will lay his axe to the base of the dead tree of David's failed lineage and from Jesse's stump will raise up the second and greater David. The Messiah's trait as a second David commencing Israel's new and superior golden age in space and time is accented in the brightest tones in 5:1B(2B): his *origin will be from of old, from days of long ago*, presumably, according to the reference to Bethlehem and by inference to Jesse, of the Davidic dynasty. Though David's house failed, God's covenant to David will never fail (2 Samuel 7; Psalm 89; 1 Chronicles 17). On a moral level of interpretation, Bethlehem represents a new start for Christians even as Bethel did for Jacob (cf. Gen 35:1-5).

Bethlehem throws light on yet another feature of the Messiah: he is lowly and despised so that through sovereign grace alone he becomes great. By the emphatic syntax "As for you, Bethlehem Ephrathah . . . *from you* . . . ," our poet-painter highlights that *I AM* is able to draw from smallness the greatest things, the most prestigious men: the first David and the new and greater David. In contrast to the proud and powerful clans of Judah, Bethlehem was *little,* small and insignificant. How like Israel's God to choose the weak and lowly in the eyes of men to shame the proud and clothe himself in glory (cf. 1 Cor 1:26-31). Our poet, without saying so directly, evokes the impression that Bethlehem's "littleness" matches the Messiah's career even as it matched David's (see Exegesis, 268). By supernatural intervention both David's place and David's person are miraculously transformed from lowly meanness to exalted greatness and in that way become a shadow, a type, of the career of David's greater Son. Bethlehem, too little, too despised, and too weak to be mentioned by the cartographer who listed the towns of Judah in the book of Joshua or by Micah in his list of towns that fell to the Assyrians in 1:10-16, fittingly becomes the birthplace of the lowly Jesus, who was born in a stable, whose birth was announced to lowly shepherds, and who was circumcised by parents too poor to offer as their sacrifice at his circumcision anything more than turtledoves that migrated through the land in the spring and fall, or young pigeons that could be had by anyone for the taking during the other two seasons (Luke 2:1-24). Even children could catch the plentiful birds in their hands. The Messiah's success depends on sovereign grace: God's election, intervention, and empowering. He renounces all human pomp and circumstance and power so that it might be evident to all that *I AM* elected him and his strength is in *I AM* (Mic 5:3[4]). His rise to universal and eternal significance defies man's ways and thoughts and can best be accounted for by divine intervention and enablement. Indeed, he triumphs not as the Gentiles by exalting himself and lording it over others and/or by honing his natural resources but rather by committing himself in faith and obedience to his God who elected him and delighted in him. His lowliness with reference to human ambition and standards of strength and majesty, and correlatively his faith in God's choices and strength, prompted him to ride as a lowly king into Jerusalem on a donkey and its colt, about the size of a great dane dog, and led him to the despised cross on the way to his exaltation at God's right hand and his universal sway. History mutely bears witness that human ways to greatness lead finally to humiliating defeat (4:14[5:1]), whereas God's ways lead ultimately to triumph (cf. Isa 55:8-9). As it turned out, and as Matthew interpreted this prophecy in dramatic irony through the mouth of unbelieving scribes: "But you Bethlehem, in the land of Judah, are by no means least among the clans of Judah" (Matt 2:6). Amazingly, today thousands make an annual pilgrimage to Bethlehem, as citizens of Christ's kingdom around the world sing of its greatness in association with the Christ's triumphs.

A third quality of the Messiah, also a reflection of David, is that he serves *for me*, says *I AM*. This blessed hope for a true servant of *I AM* probably owes its inspiration to 1 Sam 16:1, "I am sending you [Samuel] to Jesse of Bethlehem because I have seen [= I have chosen] among his sons *for me* a king." As Samuel had hope for a David that would replace a Saul, so Micah and the remnant hope for a greater than David to replace Israel's feckless leadership. No higher epithet is given to a leader in the OT than that given to Moses and David and his Messiah: "a servant of *I AM*" (e.g., Exod 14:31; 2 Sam 7:8; Isa 42:1 respectively; cf. Matt 25:21, 23).

The fourth and final property of the Messiah, also rooted in the mystery of God's sovereign will, is that he will step forth from Bethlehem to be *a ruler over Israel*. This portion of the prophecy is stimulated by *I AM*'s statement to David that he chose him "to be a leader over my people, over Israel" (2 Sam 7:8). Significantly, in neither case is the leader called "king." That title is reserved for *I AM*, who raises up his elect rulers who subordinate themselves to their God in order to serve him on behalf of his people. That which is in God's interest never competes with the interest of the elect because of God's sublime attributes of mercy, grace, and goodness.

Having challenged Israel's remnant in stirring martial language to fortify itself while the Assyrians besiege Jerusalem and humble their decadent ruler, and having fortified them with the promise of a humble, godly ruler, Micah with a "therefore" draws the conclusion that their deliverance will not occur until the one who gives birth, that is, the remnant (see 4:9-10), gives birth to the new David, the Messiah, at which time they will also be reunited with the rest of converted Israel to become the new Israel. By this chronological notice Micah inserts a certain thickness into the prophecies of 4:9-10, 11-13, both of which pertain to present distress and future salvation. As B. Renaud[156] said: "This time of crisis must prolong itself during an undetermined period; it will end only with the birth of the Messiah." The chronological notice in 5:2(3) keeps Israel's hopes pinned on the advent of the Messiah; it helps focus the tableau of chapters 4–5 on him. Once again, the community is thrown back in faith on *I AM*, who rules history and its times according to his own counsel. With him in whose hands are the times of all people, a thousand years is as a day, and before the remnant gave birth to the Messiah, it had first to endure seven centuries under the continued sway of Assyria, and then of Babylon, Persia, Greece, and Rome respectively. Typically, however, our prophet refers to the future by using language appropriate to his own day and so refers only to the Assyrians. In this way the remnant are kept vigilant as they await the imminent advent of the Messiah. As God in the fullness of time rewarded the childlike faith of people like Joseph and Mary, and Simeon and Anna (Luke 2:25-38), so also he will reward the faith of his elect today who await his imminent second advent. At the time of his coming forth his brothers will also be converted and reunited with him.

Part of Hezekiah's problem was an ever diminished and shrinking kingdom: first the North had been taken away by gradual measures, then Judah's plains and hill country, until only the remnant in Jerusalem were left. "In wartorn Judah," says L. Allen,[157] "lay the sole vestiges of sacred nationhood." The Messianic Age, however, would recover Israel's exiles from the North and the South (cf. Isa 11:12-13; Jer 30:10-11; 31:2-6, 15-20; Ezekiel 37; Hos 2:1-2[1:10-11]; 3:5) and also its former strength, perhaps in a way immeasurably greater than the prophets imagined (cf. Eph 3:20). After Messiah's resurrection and ascension to his heavenly throne, which David's throne symbolized on earth, he began the process of joining the rest of his brothers to the new Israel. At Pentecost 3,000 were added to the 120 of the faithful remnant (Acts 2:41), and "the Lord added daily those were being saved" (Acts 2:47).

Beyond Abraham's direct blood descendants the rest of his brothers also came to include Gentiles, those who historically were not his people but who came to be reckoned as Abraham's seed and fellow heirs of the covenant (cf. John 10:16; Eph 2:12-22; 1 Pet 2:9-10) by their spiritual baptism into the Messiah (cf. Gal 3:29). They too are his brothers, the true Jacob and true Israel (cf. Jer 31:31-34; 2 Cor 3:3; Heb 8:6-13). Jesus Christ prepared the way for this meaning of his "brothers" when he called all those who did his will his brothers (Matt 12:50). Paul (Eph 2:14-18) seems to have interpreted the passage in this way, for

156. *La Formation*, 232.
157. Allen, *Micah*, 345.

he relates the statement in 5:4, "and he will be the one of peace," to Christ's unification of Jew and Gentile into one new man, "thus making peace" between those who were far away and those who were near. Although on the preliterary level perhaps only blood relatives were in view, on the literary level spiritual brothers are probably also in view because the initial oracle envisioned converted Gentile nations making pilgrimage to Mount Zion to hear the word of *I AM*. Whereas in the old dispensation those who were called Israel did not necessarily have the Law written on their hearts and so remained spiritually unconverted, in the new dispensation all his brothers, the true Israel, know the Lord. Today his brothers are found in every corner of this broad earth without regard to race, sex, or social status (Gal 3:26-29).

After weaving into the tapestry of his tableau the chronological notice pointing to the Messiah, Micah returns to fill in more details of his ministry. Like the unshakable stars that appear in the firmament, he will "stand forth" in his role as Israel's new ruler, and he will "shepherd" them through the skill and empowering of his personal relationship with God. From the context of the Assyrian invasion and from the co-text that the Assyrian invaders will both be driven out of the land and themselves "shepherded" by a sword, the metaphor of shepherding pertains not so much to feeding the flock as to guarding them. Its meaning is more fully expressed in Ps 2:9 (LXX), "he will shepherd them with a rod of iron." Micah probably intends his audience to picture the Messiah with the shepherd's formidable oaken club, fit to be a scepter (cf. Gen 49:10).

His shepherding will be magnificent because it will be done in the splendor of the name of *I AM*, his God, with whom he enjoys intimacy. God's name is a surrogate for God himself, and so the Messiah's power and majesty derive from that unique relationship entailing God's election of him, on the one hand, and his faith in God, on the other. In practical terms he shepherds the new Israel by prayerfully seeking, looking, and relying on God (Ps 105:4; Matt 7:9-11), the same ways in which he encourages his followers to prevail and to establish God's kingdom so that his will is done on earth as it is in heaven (cf. Luke 11:1-11).

In this way Messiah's rule will become great, even to the ends of the earth, and so Israel will live securely. Once again a promise made to David, "I will make your name great" (2 Sam 7:9), a greatness connected with cutting off his enemies, is appropriated to the Messiah. Then too there is probably a nostalgic echo of the Davidic covenant: "And I will provide a place for my people Israel and will plant them, so that they can have a home of their own, and no longer be disturbed. Wicked people will not oppress them anymore" (2 Sam 7:10). The future "now" is linked with the "days of long ago," showing unmistakably the grand design of God in history and his faithfulness to his covenant promises.

Even in the section of hope related to Messiah's vice-gerents (5:4-5[5-6]), by the literary device of *inclusio* Micah keeps the spotlight on the Messiah: he is the one of peace . . . and he will deliver from Asshur. Because he reconciles formerly unreconciled brothers in a new Israel (5:2[3]) and because his greatness extends to the earth (5:3[4]), it follows that he will become the one of peace. His career will lead to universal peace partially because he will protect his wards and punish the oppressor. His achievement is depicted by his strategy against the Assyrian invaders, Israel's dreaded nemesis in Micah's day, who repeatedly attacked the holy land and successively lopped off sections of it. The predictions of the Messiah's peace and deliverance in v 4A(5A) and v 5B(6B) frame a central core that sounds like an ancient war-song put into the mouth of Messiah's community. L. Allen[158] notes:

> In origin it is evidently a national war-song, yet not a song of victory but one expressing confident hope of victory such as has fired every generation at war. Like other Hebrew popular war-songs it is marked by a rhyming jingle of first-person plural pronouns [Judg 16:23-24; Jer 21:13]. With nationalist fervor the claim is made that if the enemy sets foot on Judean territory, he will find himself driven back by so vigorous a counterattack that his own country will be invaded.

Without the frame, which assumes corporate solidarity between king and people, the song may sound jingoistic to some. In fact, however, leaders have a sacred responsibility to protect their boundaries. Under the Messiah, against the likes of Assyria, the restored and unified Israel will raise up seven, yes, eight leaders, that is, a more than sufficient supply of holy leaders against them to defend their God-given territory. V. P. Hamilton[159] notes:

> In the ancient Near East there was, at least on paper, a great respect for another's boundaries whether these were national boundaries or individual and private boundaries. To violate them is to violate something God has ordained. He has established the boundaries of all peoples (Deut 32:8). He has arranged the borders of the whole earth (Ps 74:17; 104:9). He has placed the sands as a boundary to the sea (Jer 5:22).
>
> It is little wonder then that the Bible prohibits the moving of a neighbor's ancient landmark *(gĕbûl)* (Deut 19:14). Whoever does this is to be "cursed" (Deut 27:17). The offense, of course, was not violation of tradition, but stealing of real estate — and unalienable real estate at that.

158. Allen, *Micah*, 347.
159. V. P. Hamilton, "*gᵉbûl*," *TWOT* 1:147.

When Assyria violates the boundary of the land promised to God's elect, Messiah's leaders, as the Messiah's vice-gerents, are obliged by *I AM* to protect it and so uphold *I AM*'s order and justice.

The audience is to presume that the Messiah's magnificent, skillful shepherding inspires renewed Israel to raise up men of this quality. Since they are not greater than their master, they do not rise up out of their own self-ambition and celebrate their own strength; rather, from their divine election and faith in the Messiah, they themselves "shepherd" in the strength of *I AM* and in the majesty of the name of their God, whom they too, as the Messiah's brothers, know intimately as their God. These men are leaders by nature.

The prophecy finds its fulfillment in the church: Christ is raising up elders and gifted men to protect it against evil men (cf. Eph 4:7-13; Titus 1:5-9). They are leaders by nature because God called them and equipped them (Rom 12:3-8; 1 Corinthians 12). In light of the Messiah's greatness, how great is the condemnation of church leaders today who are derelict in upholding their sacred trust by not protecting the church against the inroads of materialism, humanism, and secularism.

Israel's new and spiritual leadership will not only protect the Messiah's *imperium* from Assyrian invasions; they will also "shepherd" the land of Assyria, the epitome and symbol of God's enemies in Micah's era, and "the land of Nimrod" (i.e., Babylon), the historic symbol of Jerusalem's enemies. When the Messiah rules, the very gates of hell will not overcome those who confess him as Son of God (Matt 16:18). Again readers need to remind themselves that Micah represents the new by using the traits of the old. Today God's people rule by the living and active sword of God's word, which, because it is sharper than any double-edged sword, penetrates even to dividing soul and spirit, joints and marrow, and judges the thoughts and attitudes of the heart (Heb 4:12; cf. Eph 6:17). In this way, the Messiah will deliver his flock from "Assyria" when it invades the sworn and holy land. This land is God's gift to his elect; it is entered only by faith and continued in by persevering faith that works; it is the one place where the elect experience unique and blessed fellowship with their God.

4. The Remnant Rules the Nations (5:6-8 [EV 7-9])

6   The remnant of Jacob will be among the nations,
        in the midst of great peoples,
      like dew from *I AM*,
        like showers upon plants,

> which do not look expectantly to mankind,
>   and do not count on humans.

7   The remnant of Jacob will be among the nations,
>   in the midst of great peoples,
>   like a lion among the beasts of the forest,
>   like a young lion among the flocks of sheep.
>   Which, when it passes by, tramples and tears;
>   then there is none to deliver.

8   May your hand, [*I AM,*] be raised triumphantly
>   against your adversaries,
>   and may all your enemies be cut off.

EXEGESIS

6   *wĕhāyâ (and it will be),* consisting of a *wāw*-relative with the qal third masculine singular of the root *hyh,* introduces another prophecy in the sequence of prophecies about the last days (cf. 4:1; 5:9[10]); its temporal function is similar to that of *wĕhāyâ* in narrative.[1] Unlike the preceding three prophecies, this one pertains exclusively to Israel's future and is represented by the relative *wāw* as finding fulfillment after the Messiah's advent. Were *wĕhāyâ* merely a temporal indicator, one would expect a qualifying temporal phrase such as is found in 4:1 and 5:9(10) (cf. 4:5).

Whereas *wĕhāyâ* in 5:4(5) has the "ruler who will come forth . . . and stand and shepherd," as its subject, its subject in 5:6(7) is *šĕ'ērît ya'ăqōb (the remnant of Jacob),* consisting of the feminine singular construct of the root *š'r* "to be left over" and the partitive genitive *ya'ăqōb.*[2] "Jacob" is Micah's term for all Israel (see 1:5). Micah does not intend to exclude the brothers who have been joined to Israel, but probably does not mention them because the oracle, which once existed in isolation, was intended to nerve the despised remnant to fidelity with the hope of their glorious future. The mention of "remnant" links the oracle with 4:6-7 and assumes that the formerly lame and scattered remnant has been transformed into a mighty nation.

LXX and Syr add here *among the nations,* which supposes that *baggôyim,* attested in the otherwise precisely parallel Mic 5:7Aaα(8Baα), was originally also found here. Although the expression is repetitious with "in the midst of great peoples" and tautologous and therefore one is tempted to drop it from both

---

1. Cf. Lambdin, *Introduction to Biblical Hebrew,* 123, §110.
2. *IBHS* §9.5.1.

v 6(7) and v 7(8), especially since it seems to disturb an otherwise regular meter, yet Hebrew parallelism demands just this sort of redundancy for emphasis. The same repetition is found in 4:3A (cf. 4:1B and 4:2Aaα). Also, the haplography in MT may be dittographical. Finally, all ancient texts and versions attest *baggôyim* in v 7(8), calling the argument from *metri causa* into serious question.

In the adverbial phrase *bĕqereb ʿammîm rabbîm (in the midst of great peoples)*, which is the emphatic and clarifying parallel to *baggôyim* (LXX, Syr), *bĕqereb*, as in 3:11, is a frozen prepositional phrase governing the object *ʿammîm* (see 4:1) and its attributive adjective *rabbîm* (see 4:3). As *šĕʾērît* links this prophecy with 4:6-7, providing more information about the remnant's future, so *ʿammîm rabbîm* links it with 4:3, and so this prophecy articulates more fully the glorious vision of 4:1-5.

The second adverbial phrase, *kĕṭal (like dew)*, consists of the preposition *kĕ* "like," indicating that the logical outcome of the comparison between the remnant and dew is correspondence,[3] and the masculine singular noun *ṭal* "dew," "light rain," which is thought of as coming from the sky (Gen 27:28, 39; Deut 33:28; Hag 1:10; Zech 8:12; Prov 3:20) and "descending" *(yrd)* upon the earth (Prov 3:20). Some scholars want to interpret the comparison unnaturally as signifying the sudden eruption of Israel against her enemies in such a way as to strike them down. Although this interpretation retains the motif of Israel's military triumph over surrounding nations found in the other oracles of salvation and is consistent with Mic 5:8(9), it contradicts the image's natural and consistent evocation with blessing. Israel cherished the dew from heaven that brought precious water and life, and never death. Against this unlikely interpretation B. Renaud[4] observed: "But it exploits the symbol of dew in the opposite way to its usual meaning in the Old Testament, where it always is a sign of benediction." J. L. Mays[5] thought the simile evokes only the heavenly origin of the remnant's influence: "It is independence of the human realm which the comparison emphasizes. The remnant will be like the dew of mysterious heavenly origin. The existence of the eschatological Jacob will be wholly the work of God, neither dependent upon nor vulnerable to mere human strength." Although the simile emphasizes that the remnant's blessing originates in heaven with God, the association of dew and rain with fertility and life in both Israel's agrarian economy and its literature disallows the evocation of divine blessing. When biblical writers intend merely heavenly activity, they will use some other heavenly phenomenon such as the sun or a hot wind. The imagery of dew and

3. *IBHS* §11.2.9.
4. *La Formation,* 257.
5. Mays, *Micah,* 122-23.

showers may also evoke the notion of the remnant's large numerical numbers over against many peoples; in that sense it would be an equivalent of the stars in the sky and sand on the seashore. The adjectival prepositional phrase modifying "dew," *mēʾēt yhwh* (*from I AM*), consisting of the compound prepositional ablative *min* "from"[6] and comitative *ʾēt* "with,"[7] shows that the figure aims to stress the complex idea[8] that the remnant and their salubrious presence among the nations, like dew, originates from Israel's God, with whom they enjoy intimate fellowship. LXX adds *piptousa* "falling" to explicate the particle *mēʾēt*, which it rendered by *para*. *ʿālê-ʿēśeb* "upon plants" in v 6Aβ(7Aβ) is gapped in 6Abα(7Abα); the full thought is "like dew upon plants."

A second simile, *kirĕbîbîm ʿālê-ʿēśeb (like showers upon plants)*, shares the same syntax as the first, namely, the inseparable preposition *kĕ* with the same value as in the first simile, governing the masculine always plural noun *rĕbîbîm* "showers," possibly from the root *rbb* "to be/become many/much," modified by an adjectival prepositional phrase introduced by a simple locative, *ʿālê* "upon,"[9] governing the object, the masculine singular collective noun *ʿēśeb* "plants." The connection of *rĕbîbîm* "mild rain" with *rbb* is uncertain.[10] An etymology from Akkadian *rababu* "to be weak" cannot be verified. The Ugaritic root *rb/rbb* "rain," also a parallel to *tl* in those texts,[11] does not help decide the issue. T. Hartmann[12] cites several authorities for the meaning "rain similar to dew." This conventional plural in Hebrew is best rendered by the English conventional collective singular "shower,"[13] for the languages differ in their distribution of collectives, and *rĕbîbîm* is a simile for the singular "remnant." Whereas the first simile stresses the notion of *heavenly/divine* origin, without excluding earthly blessing, the second, while not excluding the notion of heavenly origin, evokes primarily the penetrating, pervasive, and beneficent influence of the remnant among the nations on earth.

LXX curiously has *arnes* "lambs" instead of "shower." Does it aim by "lambs upon the grass" to give a better contrast with "like a young lion among flocks of sheep" (7Aβ[8Aβ])? In any case, its simile, altering the sense from the remnant blessing the nations to feeding upon the nations, destroys the parallelism and destructively diffuses the thought. Happily, the other versions and

6. *IBHS* §11.2.11.
7. *IBHS* §11.2.4.
8. Cf. *IBHS* §11.3.
9. *IBHS* §11.2.13.
10. Cf. GB 742B: to II *rbb*.
11. Cf. UT no. 2298.
12. T. Hartmann, *THAT* 2:723.
13. *IBHS* §7.2.1.

Mur 88 follow MT. *'ălê (upon)* has its simple location force,[14] and *'ēśeb* is a conventional Hebrew collective best rendered in English by a countable plural since it is the part of the simile that pertains to the *gôyim/'ammîm* "nations/ plants." As *'ălê-'ēśeb* is gapped in v 6Abα(7Abα), so *mē'ēt yhwh* is gapped in v 6Abβ(7Abβ); the full thought is "as a shower from *I AM* upon plants." By its repetition the synonymous parallelism reinforces, heightens, and intensifies the effect of rain upon plants, and so of the remnant upon the nations. LXX deviates notably from MT by reading ad hoc "like lambs [Heb. *kĕbaśîm*] on the grass." Was it influenced by "flocks of sheep" in v 7(8)?

The indeclinable relative pronoun *'ăšer (which)*, like the parallel in v 7(8), does not modify the nearest antecedent *'ēśeb*[15] but *ṭal* "dew" and *rĕbîbîm* "showers" with their qualifying prepositional phrases, and so also "the remnant," on account of the identity of the rain with the remnant. In fact, the predicates pertaining to not trusting in man, and by implication trusting in God, presume an animate, not an inanimate subject, so that the simile is here personified, allowing the "remnant," the animate subject equated with rain, to shine out from beneath the thin simile. The dependent relative clause does not aim to emphasize the remnant's beneficent efficacy or possibly its multiplicity but rather the divine initiative behind its efficacy and their dependence on him.

LXX changes the sense of v 6B(7B) significantly, reading *hopōs mē synachthē mēdeis, mēde hypostē en huiois anthrōpōn* "so that none may assemble nor resist among the sons of men." It was probably led astray by confusing *yĕqawweh* with II *qāwâ* niphal "to be gathered" (cf. Gen 1:9) and/or by the animate predicates in MT with the inanimate subject *ṭal/rĕbîbîm*.

For *lō' (not)* see Mic 1:11; 4:12. *yĕqawweh (look expectantly)* is a third masculine singular with *'ăšer* functioning in the nominative slot, a persistent nonperfective[16] and a frequentative piel[17] of the root *qāwâ*. The writer resisted the translation "wait for" (TNIV) because it suggests the meaning "linger," "delay," "tarry" (i.e., the rain does not postpone its falling until man arrives on the scene) but, as J. E. Hartley[18] says, it means "to wait"/"to look for with eager expectation." *qāwâ* is related to *qaw* (tense string) and so depicts man's expectation and hope as a tense attitude with reference to a specific goal. The thought is not that rain does not tarry for man (i.e., it falls according to its own schedule), but rather that rain (= remnant) does not look expectantly to man to send it forth (i.e., it does not count on man for its success) but to God, as the parallel

---

14. *IBHS* §11.2.13.
15. *Contra* Smith, *Micah*.
16. *IBHS* §31.3.
17. *IBHS* §24.7.
18. J. E. Hartley, "*qāwâ*," *TWOT* 2:791.

"from *I AM*" supplies. *qāwâ*, moving in the semantic realm of faith, entails that the remnant do not trust man for ministering water and life on an otherwise parched and dreary earth, but God.

The allative *lě* in *lě'îš (to mankind)* marks *'îš* as the object toward which the psychological looking is extended, and *'îš* is used with reference to "mankind." Of the words for "man" *'îš* is carefully chosen, for, as N. P. Bratsiotis[19] says, "it makes a sharp distinction between man and God." The sharp contrast is signified by the antithetical statements that rain (i.e., the remnant) comes from *I AM* and that it does not look to man. In the synonymous parallel *wělō' yěyaḥēl libnê 'ādām (and do not count on the sons of mankind) lō'* matches *lō'*, the piel third masculine singular nonperfective of *yḥl* matches *yěqawweh*, and *libnê 'ādām* matches *lě'îš*. Precise synonymous parallelism of this sort is rare, and the parallels dynamically empower each other. *yḥl* means to be in a state of painful expectation. It seems to be related to the root *ḥûl* "to be in labor." Both *qāwâ* and *ḥûl* have the psychological state of intense/painful waiting in the forefront. Both words belong to and are used with others in the semantic realm of "trust," as C. Westermann[20] notes. P. R. Gilchrist[21] says: "*yāḥal* 'hope' is a close synonym to *bātaḥ* 'trust' and *qāwâ* 'wait for, hope for,' as in Mic 7:7." *libnê 'ādām* is a type of attributive genitive in which the genitive *'ādām* represents the nature, quality, or character of the individuals. *'ādām* "man" denotes mankind as a dependent creature; he cannot determine his own destiny. F. Maass[22] comments: "There is no guarantee that he can determine his own destiny or think that his life will be prosperous by his own efforts and accomplishments." The rain/remnant appropriately do not depend on such a creature.

7 *wěhāyâ šě'ērît ya'ăqōb baggôyim běqereb 'ammîm rabbîm (and the remnant of Jacob will be among the nations, in the midst of great peoples)*, paralleling the same expression in Mic 5:6Aaα(7Aaα) and functioning in the same way, prepares the way for the antithetical parallelism between v 6Ab-B(7Ab-B) and v 7Ab-B(8Ab-B). The contrast between v 6(7) and v 7(8), which is not established grammatically, shows that *wěhāyâ* is not sequential to v 6(7) but functions in the same way as its initial *wěhāyâ*.

Both *kāp*s *(like)* in v 7Ab(8Ab) function in the same way as in v 6Ab (7Ab), that is, they compare and equate the remnant with a lion. Mur 88 reads *b'ryh* instead of *k'ryh* due to the similarity of *bêt* and *kāp* in the Aramaic square script. According to G. J. Botterweck,[23] *'aryēh (a lion)* is one of seven words for lion in

19. N. P. Bratsiotis, "*'ish*," *TDOT* 1:229.
20. C. Westermann, "*yāḥal*," *THAT* 2:624.
21. P. R. Gilchrist, *TWOT* 1:374.
22. F. Maass, "*'ādhām*," *TDOT* 1:86.
23. G. J. Botterweck, "*'ărî*," *TDOT* 1:375-77.

Hebrew. According to L. Köhler, cited by Botterweck, *'ărî* and *'aryēh* designate the African lion, which also inhabited southern Palestine. As *šĕ'ērît ya'ăqōb* is parallel to *kĕ'aryēh*, so *baggôyim* is parallel to *bĕbahămôt ya'ar (among the beasts of the forest)*. In *bĕbahămôt* the preposition *bĕ* has the same value as in *baggôyim*, and the feminine plural noun picks up the plural *'ammîm rabbîm*; *ya'ar* may be construed as a locative genitive (= "in the forest")[24] or as a genitive of inalienable possession referring to the beasts as something intrinsically proper to a forest.[25] The forests in biblical times were dense enough that wild animals roamed at will (2 Kgs 2:24; Isa 56:9; Jer 5:6; 12:8; Ezek 34:25; Amos 3:4; Ps 8:14[13]). Perhaps under the influence of the parallel "among flocks of sheep" Syr corrupts "forest" into "pasture," thereby destroying the merism between v 7Aba(8Aba) and v 7Abβ(8Abβ). In some texts *bĕhēmâ* "animal" is contrasted with *ḥāyâ* "beast," but in others, as in Mic 5:7(8), no distinction is intended. The versions, however, not recognizing that *bĕhēmâ* is a generic term for animal, either domestic or wild, thought that it meant only the former. G. J. Botterweck[26] says that "*bahamoth ya'ar . . .* is equivalent to *chayetho ya'ar* 'the beasts of the forest.'" Since "beasts of the forest" are themselves dangerous and predatory, the simile aims to accent the surpassing pride, prowess, and predatoriness of the lion, and so the exceeding greatness of the singular remnant compared to that of the many great nations.

In *kikĕpîr (like a young lion) kĕpîr*, according to Botterweck, who bases himself on studies by T. Nöldeke and L. Köhler,[27] "originally meant a 'young animal,' but then especially a 'young lion' who goes out on his own in search of prey." This parallel to *'ărî* emphasizes the lionlike character of the remnant and is appropriately used with *bĕ'edrê-ṣō'n (among the flocks of sheep)*. The masculine plural noun *'edrê* because its plural form continues to contrast the singular "remnant" and because the root *'ēder*, meaning "flock," is the opposite of "beasts" and so constitutes a merism. Syr loses this juxtaposition by rendering it as singular. The synecdoche involving exact opposites, in this case wild animals versus domestic ones, represents all animals. The combined similes represent the remnant of Jacob dominating all nations, both great and powerful and weak and small; none is exempted. The absolute feminine collective *ṣō'n* "small cattle," "flock," "sheep," or "goats," after construct *'dr* means "sheep," according to BDB,[28] and is a genitive of material.[29]

24. *IBHS* §9.5.2.
25. *IBHS* §9.5.1.
26. G. J. Botterweck, "*bᵉhēmāh*," *TDOT* 2:7.
27. Botterweck, *TDOT* 1:376.
28. BDB 727, §1a.
29. *IBHS* §9.5.3.

Indeclinable *'ăšer (which)* is parallel to the identical dependent relative introducing v 6b(7b) and functions in the same way, this time modifying "beasts of the forest"/"flocks of sheep." The qualifying relative clause in turn consists of a conditional protasis introduced by the conditional particle *'im* and the apodosis introduced by apodosis *wāw*, probably with *wě'ên*. The condition is not only capable of fulfillment but likely, so that it seems to have a more precise sense of "when." The three verbs *'ābar wěrāmas wěṭārap (it passes by and tramples and tears)* are all qal third masculine singular perfective with conjunctive *wāw*. The perfective has a gnomic force.[30] Exegetes differ regarding the identification of apodosis *wāw*; some locate it with *wěrāmas* (= *when it passes by, then it rends and tears, and there is none to deliver*); others with *wěṭārap* (= *when it passes by and rends, then it tears and there is none . . .*); and still others with *wě'ên* (see Translation, 306). The first has some support in the disjunctive accent *těbîr* with *'ābar;* the second has no support, for the accent *mêrěkā* with *wěrāmas* is conjunctive;[31] and the third has the support of the disjunctive accent *ṭiphā* and presents through three grammatically identical verbs the remarkable lexical crescendo: "pass by, trample, rend." The conjunctive *wāw*s signify not sequence but coordinate actions; that is, "when it passes by, and when it tramples, and when it rends, then there is none. . . ." Here one must distinguish between grammatical sequence, which is missing, and this lexical sequence like English "divide and conquer." Unlike the human predicates "look expectantly" and "count on," which semantically best match "the remnant," here the animal predicates suit the lion simile: *'ābar* "passes by," a verb of movement through the land, *rāmas* "tramples" with reference to some object under foot, more specifically here its victims, and *ṭārap (rends),* whose full thought is "to seize a creature in a predatorial way and tear its flesh violently." *wě'ên maṣṣîl (then there is no deliverer)* consists of apodosis *waw* with the negative for verbless clauses, the construct *'ên*, typically followed by a participle: hiphil masculine singular of the root *nṣl* (see Mic 5:5[6]).

8 *tārōm (let . . . be raised triumphantly, [I AM])* is a qal third feminine singular jussive of the root *rûm*, here of the intransitive root *rûm* with its value not as a stative as in some texts but as a fientive verb of movement "be raised up," with the feminine singular noun *yād* "hand" as its subject. The versions, followed by NRSV and TNIV, read a nonperfective (= *tārûm*), but in this case of textual differences involving vocalization MT, if it cannot be explained as a *lectio facilior* and is sensible, should be preferred.[32] The jussive expresses either

---

30. *IBHS* §30.5.1.
31. *Contra La Formation*, 255.
32. *IBHS* §1.6.3.

a petition to God by Micah and probably the steadfast remnant with him[33] or a benediction upon the remnant by Micah as *I AM*'s plenipotentiary in an *oratio variata,* more specifically an apostrophe.[34] The use of the jussive cannot be discussed apart from the identification of the second masculine singular pronominal suffix, a genitive of inalienable possession,[35] with *yādĕkâ (your hand).* The use of the jussive and the identification of the pronoun depend in part on how one interprets the gesture of a raised hand.

The feminine singular noun *yād* "hand" denotes the forearm, wrist, and hand (e.g., bracelets are worn on it in Gen 24:22) and is often associated with power.[36] The gesture of a raised hand in Ps 89:14(13) and Isa 26:11 clearly symbolizes God's triumphant power in gaining mastery over his enemies, and for that reason I, along with TNIV, interpretatively added "in triumph." In Ps 112:9 "horn," also a symbol of divine power, replaces "hand." The symbolic gesture could have been extended to the remnant of Jacob (cf. Exod 14:8; Deut 32:27). If the remnant's hand be in view, the gesture could also symbolize prayer (cf. Exod 17:11) or rebellion (cf. 1 Kgs 11:26-27), but a command to the remnant to raise its hands in prayer, while possible and somewhat parallel to the liturgical addendum in 4:5, seems more far-fetched in a liturgical addendum than a prayer addressed to *I AM* (see below). A gesture of rebellion would be especially unfitting after the promise that Israel's triumph over their enemies will occur in their eschatological future due to divine initiative and the remnant's faith. Either a gesture of prayer or of rebellion is less apt with the parallel "let your enemies be cut off" than the gesture of a hand raised triumphantly in victory. Moreover, a command to the remnant to raise its hands in prayer would probably have been expressed by *rûm* hiphil.

The issue cannot be decided lexically; rather, one must look to literary form and theology. A liturgical petition in v 7(8) after the prophetic vision of vv 6-7(7-8) not only better suits the liturgical form (cf. Pss 19:15[14]; 20:10[9]; and especially with *rûm* qal, 21:14[13]: 57:6[5], 12[11]; 108:6[5]) and the immediate context, but also rings more true to biblical theology, especially in the prophets, who inveigh against human strength and call for faith in divine intervention. The link between this pericope and the next, Mic 5:9-14(10-15), validates that Micah, and presumably the loyal remnant, is petitioning God to let his hand be raised, for in that pericope it becomes clear that God is the subject of *krt* and that he is the one who will punish the hostile nations (5:14[15]). It also agrees

---

33. *IBHS* §34.3.#9.
34. *IBHS* §34.3.#25.
35. *IBHS* §9.5.1.
36. Cf. P. R. Ackroyd, "*yāḏ*," *TDOT* 5:418-22.

with the promise in the preceding pericope that God would raise up the Messiah to deliver Israel and conquer all their enemies. In sum, after the promise that the remnant will become a savor of life and death among the nations because of the divine initiative and the remnant's faith in him, the faithful, but still small, remnant within besieged Jerusalem petition God to initiate the eschatological victory.

Since the hand of God opposes his enemies, *'al (against)* has its hostile sense (see 2:3; 3:5). *ṣāreykā (your adversaries)* consists of the masculine plural noun *ṣār* of the pattern *ṣarr-* of the root II *ṣrr*, hence *ṣār-*, with a pronominal suffix as an objective genitive (= adversaries against you).[37] Like *'ōyēb* (cf. Mic 2:8; 4:10), *ṣār* is, according to E. Jenni,[38] "a general designation for 'enemy, adversary,' which, with the exception of Est 7:6 . . . , is used not for individuals, but generally or collectively. . . ." This root deals with the harassment and torment engendered by those who oppose *I AM*'s kingdom, both its King and his subject, and supplant it with a rival one.

The parallel *wĕkol-'ōyĕbeykā (and . . . all your enemies)* consists of coordinate *waw*, the construct *kol*, and the genitive of measure *'ōyēb* with the second masculine singular suffix as another objective genitive with reference to *I AM*. This parallel to *ṣāreykā* intensifies and heightens the meaning by adding *kol*; no one is exempt, and so, by implication, *I AM*'s kingdom becomes coextensive with his creation (= "to the ends of the earth") (cf. 5:3[4]). *yikkārētû (may . . . be cut off)* is a niphal third masculine plural jussive of the root *kārat*. In this chiastic parallel one should assume that the ambiguous prefix form, which could be nonperfective or jussive, will have the same value as its parallel *tārōm*. That sense also better suits a liturgical addition. The niphal is an incomplete passive,[39] for the parallel shows that *I AM* is the agent of the earth's purification. For the meaning of *kārat* see 5:9.

EXPOSITION

The change of theme, from the Messiah to the remnant of Jacob, along with indications of the structural unity of 4:14–5:5(5:1-6; see above) versus the striking parallelism between vv 6(7) and 7(8) clearly sets 5:6-7(7-8) off from 4:14–5:5(5:1-6). Few dispute this division. The parallelism between vv 6(7) and 7(8) involves a precise parallelism between vv 6Aa(7Aa) and 7Aa(8Aa), two similes introduced

37. *IBHS* §9.5.2.
38. E. Jenni, *THAT* 2:582.
39. *IBHS* §23.2.2.

by *kĕ* in both vv 6Ab(7Ab) and 7Ab(8Ab), and a further clarification of the similes introduced by *'ăšer* in vv 6B(7B) and 7B(8B). The result in *BHS* is that the initial letter of the first half of each line in these verses is *wāw, kāp,* and *'ālep* and of the second half *bêt, kāp,* and *wāw.* Less clear, however, is the relation of v 8(9) to vv 6-7(7-8) because: (1) the subject is now *I AM*, (2) general "adversaries/enemies" replaces "peoples/nations," and (3) *I AM* is no longer spoken of in the third masculine singular as in v 6(7) but in the second masculine singular of direct address. Moreover, the mood in MT changes from specific future, "and it will be," to "let be." In fact, however, this change of mood gives insight into the relation of v 8(9) to vv 6-7(7-8). Were retroverted *tārûm* "will be raised" of the versions correct, then v 8(9) could be considered a separate prophecy predicting *I AM*'s triumph over his enemies from the prediction in vv 6-7(7-8) that the remnant will triumph over the nations. If, however, the jussive of MT be correct, then v 8(9) functions nicely as a liturgical conclusion to those verses. Having said that the triumphant remnant originate with *I AM*, it would be fitting for the remnant to conclude with a prayer that *I AM* be victorious implicitly through them.

The two introductory formulas in 5:9(10), "And it will happen in that day" and "says *I AM*," distinguish 5:9-14(10-15) from 5:6-7(7-8), and the last word in v 8(9), *krt* with *I AM* as agent, serves as a verbal link with the first word of the new oracle, after the introductory formulas, in v 9(10); see Exposition of 5:9-14(10-15).

Several catchwords sew 5:6-8(7-9) into the broad tableau of 4:1–5:5(5:1-6): initial *wĕhāyâ* "and it will be" (4:1; 5:4, 6, 7[5, 7, 8]); *šĕ'ērît* "remnant" (4:7, 5:6, 7[7, 8]); *'ammîm rabbîm* "great nations" (4:3, 13; 5:6, 7[7, 8]); and *nṣl* "deliver" (5:5, 7[7, 9]). Salvation oracles regarding the hope for the "remnant" in this eschatological depiction of Israel's future glories chiastically frame the piece as second pericopes from the beginning (4:6-7) and from the end (5:6-8[7-9]). The overarching theme of the piece is that God will overturn the tables of history: the victim will become the victor. Like their Messiah, they step forth small and lowly among the nations and become great by the divine initiative. The verb "will be" orients this promise exclusively to the future, beyond the present distress (cf. 4:9-10, 11-13; 4:14–5:5[5:1-6]). In the light of their gathering in 4:6-7, of Israel's redemption from Babylon in 4:10, and of its unification in 5:2(3), the remnant is conceptualized not as scattered in the Diaspora but as a restored nation in the midst of the nations. Under God's leadership Israel, the weak victim, becomes a threshing bull and a mauling lion in the midst of the powerful nations. How great is its God!

The precise grammatical parallelism between vv 6(7) and 7(8) allows the striking thematic antithetical parallelism within that frame to stand out boldly. In v 6(7) the accent falls on the remnant's heavenly origin; in the second, on their effect on the earth. Some interpreters mistakenly want to limit the contrast to only this difference so that in effect the verses are not antithetical but synthetic. H. Wolff[40] says:

> The two comparisons in vv 6 and 7(7 and 8) do not stand antithetically to one another, as if the remnant of Jacob were at one time a blessing for the peoples and then a curse (A. Weiser, T. H. Robinson, T. Lescow 78 with appeal to Prov 19:12), as the quietists speaking one time and then the militant activists (W. Rudolph), one-time pacifists and then militarists (R. E. Wolfe, *IB*), according to Gen 12:3A one time to Israel's friends and then to its enemies (T. H. Robinson). Rather, the parallelism of the verses is to be understood synthetically. V 6(7) says what the remnant of Jacob "out of Yahweh" will be: the divine miracle not explicable from human possibilities (cf. 4:6-7A). And v 7(8) says what the remnant of Jacob will be among the other peoples: the all-surpassing and invincible power (cf. 4:13). According to 5:5B(6B) the Messiah will save Israel from Asshur *(whsyl)*; according to v 7B(8B) no one will be able to save the peoples from the remnant of Jacob.

In spite of these excellent observations on the text, I cannot escape the conclusion that in addition to this synthetic relationship between the verses, there is an even more striking antithesis regarding the effect of the remnant among the nations, which is the topic of both: in v 6(7) it is beneficial; in v 7(8), baneful. Without dispute the lion in v 7(8) (= the remnant of Jacob) is among victimized animals (= the nations), and in v 6(7) the gentle rain (= the remnant of Jacob) falls upon plants (= ?). In the light of the strict parallelism, is it not more likely that *'ēśeb* "the plants" represent the nations than nothing? Moreover, since dew and showers are such exclusively positive figures for blessing, fertility, freshness, and life, Micah would hardly have used them to represent the remnant of Israel among the nations, emphatically repeated in v 6Aaα(7Aaα) but neglected by Wolff, if all he intended was their heavenly origin, to be synthetically developed by figures evoking a very opposite meaning, namely, the veritable carnage that the remnant of Jacob inflicts upon the nations.

J. M. P. Smith[41] says that the plants are "the remnant of Israel among the nations which will rise to power, notwithstanding the absence of all human help." But, although Calvin[42] interprets v 6(7) similarly, it seems unlikely for the stated reasons. J. M. P. Smith rejects interpreting the refreshing influence of the dew as representing "Israel's moral and religious influence among the nations"

40. Wolff, *Micha*, 130.
41. Smith, *Micah*, 111-12.
42. Calvin, *Minor Prophets*, Vol. 3: *Johah, Micah, Nahum*, 313.

because "this . . . yields a sense for v. 6(7) entirely at variance with that of v. 7(8), for Israel, which is here a blessing, is clearly there an agent of destruction."

B. Renaud[43] effectively sets aside this *a priori* assumption by means of other OT texts and by the immediate context of chapters 4–5:

> This antithetical perspective is found in other texts that cannot be disarticulated: Zech 2:10-17[6-13]; Isa 25:6-11; 60:10-12. We will find the same opposition within the structure of Micah 4–5, where the oracles of Mic 4:1-4 and 5:9-14(10-15) are placed in the parallelism of *inclusio*. Besides, 5:14(15) will give the key of the enigma, if enigma there be. YHWH will chastise the nations "which did not obey."

Finally, and conclusively, the prophecy finds fulfillment in the dual roles of the church (2 Cor 2:14-17). In sum, the remnant of Jacob will be at the same time a source of benediction and a fomenter of misfortune; a channel of salvation and a cause of punishment; an instrument of hope and of tragedy. In either case, though only a remnant, it is always triumphant with regard to all the nations.

In 5:6-8(7-9) Micah ripens his theme regarding the role of the remnant of Jacob among the nations in Israel's eschatological figure. He planted the seed in 2:12-13: out of the remnant that God gathered as a flock into Jerusalem during the Assyrian invasion of Judah and siege of its capital, *I AM*, their true King, would lead them forth triumphantly. He watered it in 4:6-7: out of the gathered remnant of Jacob, whom *I AM* had lamed once again before conferring his blessing on them, the King, who miraculously led them out of the city in triumph, promises to make them a great nation under his eternal Kingship. In 5:6-8(7-9) he nourishes it to maturity: that great nation, spiritually unified under their eternal King and having been handed over by *I AM* to his faithful Messiah for his skillful shepherding, will be *I AM*'s instrument both of life among the nations, like a gentle rain falling upon plants, and of death, like a lion mauling its victims. The dew and the gentle shower come from *I AM*. L. Allen[44] remarked: "Man is singularly impotent over water supplies. He can store rainwater and tap underground springs, but his native helplessness before the cruel sun comes to the fore in times of prolonged drought. Ultimately man can neither help nor hinder the supply of so basic a commodity." God's providential, gracious, and faithful blessings on the earth cannot be manipulated by man. As it falls upon the plants, it pervasively and penetratingly fructifies the earth. Therefore, since man cannot manipulate heavenly blessings, the elect remnant

43. *La Formation*, 258.
44. Allen, *Micah*, 353.

looks expectantly not to mankind but to *I AM* to send it forth on its mission and to prosper it. But to those peoples who refuse to acknowledge the remnant as God's mediators of blessing, it becomes a lion that passes by proudly and sovereignly, tramples its victims into subjugation, and tears them fatally with no one to deliver.

The figure also functions as a polemic against the great nations of Micah's day. Egyptian rulers are represented by lions both in their iconography and in their literature. More significantly for the interpretation of Micah, the Assyrian kings liken themselves to lions.[45] Sargon II becomes furious "like a lion," and stalks through the land of his enemies "like a raging lion that strikes terror." Similar comparisons are made concerning Sennacherib, Esarhaddon, and Ashurnasirpal. The majestic lion is also a favorite motif as a decoration in the temples and palaces of Mesopotamia. Tourists to the British Museum can still see Ashurbanipal's stone reliefs portraying him contesting lions. The proud lion, who retreats before no one, is mighty among beasts (Prov 30:30). G. J. Botterweck[46] depicts the lion on attack from poetic texts:

> Roaring and rapacious (Ezek 22:25), he is eager for prey (Prov 17:12). In the thicket (Jer 4:7; 25:38; 49:19), the lion lurks after his victim (Ps 10:9; 17:12) and waits in ambush (Lam 3:10); with his fierce teeth (Joel 1:6; Ps 58:7[Eng. v. 6]; Job 4:10), he tears it in pieces (Ps 7:3[2]; Mic 5:7[8]). He carries off prey (Hos 5:14; Isa 5:29) into his cave; he fills his dens with it (Nah 2:13[12]). Then he devours it and his young lions growl over his victims (Amos 3:4). . . . Even man is not safe from the ravening lion (Isa 15:9; Ezek 19:6) and trembles when he hears his roar (Hos 11:10; Amos 3:8).

On the broad canvas of salvation history the remnant of Jacob, though so small and insignificant among the great nations of the earth, will inherit the ancient benedictory blessings of the patriarchs and prophets. In v 6(7) Micah confers on them Isaac's ancient blessing on Jacob: "May God give you of heaven's dew and of earth's richness. . . . May nations serve you and people bow down to you. . . . May those who curse you be cursed and those who bless you be blessed" (Gen 27:28-29), and in v 7(8) Jacob's ancient tribal blessing on Judah: "You are a lion's cub, O Judah; you return from the prey, my son" (Gen 49:9), and Balaam's, the pagan "donkey" prophet, on Israel: "The people rise like a lioness; they rouse themselves like a lion that does not rest till he devours his prey and drinks the blood of his victims." Whereas Hosea in his oracle of judgment (5:14[15]) against Israel prophesied that *I AM* would

---

45. G. J. Botterweck, *TDOT* 1:380.
46. Botterweck, *TDOT* 1:382.

become a rending lion from whom no one could deliver Israel, Micah in his oracle of blessed salvation reverses the curses, fulfilled in most of Israel, prophesying that the remnant will become the rending lion from whom no one can deliver (cf. Zech 8:13).

The remnant of Jacob's decisive role in history depends entirely upon *I AM*'s initiative: he chose them; he disciplined them; he gathered them; he led them forth; he raised up their Messiah; he converted them; and he sends them forth. Who could have dreamed that out of the remnant within Jerusalem, besieged by an international army, would come forth a church that encompasses the world as it administers eternal life and eternal death? Who could have dreamed that from the Lord Jesus hanging on a cross would have sprung the church like a mighty army? Who could have dreamed that the church within the mighty Roman Empire and throughout history would always be led in triumphal procession so that they became the fragrance of the knowledge of Christ everywhere: "the aroma of Christ among those who are being saved and those who are perishing. To the one . . . the smell of death; to the other, the fragrance of life. And who is equal to such a task (2 Cor 2:15-16)?" Since only the sovereign *I AM* is equal to such a task, the faithful ever respond to his initiative with the prayer that their sovereign *I AM*'s hand be raised in triumph over all and that all his enemies be cut off so that he might reign extensively and entirely and eternally. To the King of kings, and Lord of lords, belongs the praise both now and forever. The prayer entails, as Calvin[47] commented, "not that the church shall be in a quiet state, but victorious, and declares also that there will never be wanting enemies." Their prayer paves the way for the promise in vv 9-14(10-15) that God will vanquish his enemies.

5. I AM *Protects His Purified Kingdom (5:9-14 [EV 10-15])*

9   And it will come to pass in that day,
            says *I AM*,
    I will cut off your horses from among you,
    and I will destroy your chariots;
10   and I will cut off the cities of your land,
    and I will tear down all your strongholds;
11   and I will cut off sorceries from your power,
    and you will not have diviners;
12   and I will cut off your idols

---

47. Calvin, *Minor Prophets*, 3:316.

and your cultic stone pillars,
and you will no longer bow down
to the work of your own hands;

13   and I will uproot your Asherahs from among you,
and I will destroy your cities;

14   and I will avenge my sovereignty
in anger and in wrath
against nations
who do not obey [me].

EXEGESIS

9 Initial *wĕhāyâ (and it will come to pass)* with the adverbial phrase *bayyôm-hahû'* functions the same as in 4:1, and *bayyôm-hahû' (in that day)* functions the same as in 4:6. For *nĕ'um-yhwh (says* I AM) see 4:6. *wĕhikrattî (I will cut off)* is a two-place hiphil of a qal transitive verb with a nonpersonal object so that the full sense is "I will cause to be cut off."[1] The first common singular suffix refers to *I AM,* as the introduction "says *I AM*" makes clear. The *waw*-relative with the suffix conjugation is left untranslated because it typically introduces the clause after *wĕhāyâ* with a temporal modifier.[2] Literalistically: "and it will happen in that day . . . , then I will."

The meaning of the root *kārat* depends on the object and the stem: "cut down" trees (Deut 19:5), "cut off" branches (Num 13:23), "break off" head and hands (1 Sam 5:4), "cut in half" an animal (Jer 34:18), "make" a covenant. In the hiphil it means "to cut off," "to destroy," "to annihilate," usually animate objects. Many scholars recognize that the purifying laws of excommunication in Leviticus color this divine promise. J. L. Mays[3] says: "The verb is a feature of a sacral formula for the removal of persons who have violated the holiness of Israel (e.g., Lev 17:10; 20:3, 5, 6; niphal in Lev 7:20-21, 27; 19:8; 20:18); the removal is not only a judgment upon the persons, but a measure to preserve the corporate people in the face of YHWH's wrath against the unholy." More specifically, as R. Vuilleumier[4] notes: "The root *krt* (with *mqrb*) is used for the cult and designates excommunication by extermination." In the holiness code (Leviticus 17–26), the niphal of *kārat* is frequently found in parallel with *mwt ywmt* [he

---

1. *IBHS* §27.3.
2. Lambdin, *Introduction to Biblical Hebrew,* 123, §110.
3. Mays, *Micah,* 125.
4. Vuilleumier, "Michée," 66.

will surely be put to death]." G. von Rad[5] traces the development of these laws of excommunication to the presentation of *I AM*'s holy wars and in the traditions about the gift of the land, only instead of man executing them, *I AM* himself carries out the purification of the land. D. Vetter[6] also sees the concept of purification connected with holy war related to this passage (see below).

The objects consigned for annihilation are those that threaten Israel's covenantal relationship with *I AM*, which is based on faith in him: military might (vv 9-10[10-11]), sorcery (v 11[12]), and idolatry (vv 12-13[13-14]). *sûseykā (your horses)* consists of the second masculine singular pronominal suffix with the masculine plural noun of the root *sûs* "horse." The suffix functions as a possessive genitive,[7] but who is its antecedent? One cannot infer that it is the "mighty nations" of vv 6-7(7-8) because this pericope is clearly set off from that one by the introductory formula. B. Renaud[8] argues that on the literary level it refers to them: "The purification of Israel has become the purification of the nations." He finds support in Tg, which thought that it referred to nations, for it added "the peoples" in vv 9, 10, 12, 13(10, 11, 13, 14): "the horses of the people . . . the cities of the peoples . . . the statutes of the peoples . . . the plantations of the peoples." More probably apostate Israel is always in view. *I AM* promises to purge from his realm the forbidden objects and practices that, partially because they break covenant, were proscribed in the Law: military guarantees (vv 9-10[10-11]; cf. Deut 17:16-17), divination (v 11[12]; cf. Deut 18:9-13), and idolatrous cults (v 12[13]; cf. Deut 7:5; 12:3; 16:21). In other words, this prophecy assumes that the people *I AM* is addressing had been elected to a covenantal position and that they had broken it by looking to false securities instead of to him.

The interpretation is validated by a parallel prophecy in Isa 2:6-8, which accuses Israel of placing their confidence in the very objects specified here: pagan divination (v 6[7]), financial resources to support their military might (v 7[8]), and idols, "the work of their/your hands" (v 8[9]). Besides, if the nations were in view, one would expect plural suffixes, not singulars, and the plural form *'arṣôt* "lands," not *'ereṣ* "land," in v 10(11). The nonconventional collective pronoun "you" (sing.) is also found frequently in the book of Deuteronomy for all Israel (cf. Deut 5:6). The horses here are not cultic objects, as T. Robinson[9] offers as an alternative, citing 2 Kgs 23:11. Rather, as part of Israel's

5. G. von Rad, *Holy War in Ancient Israel*, tr. M. Dawn (Grand Rapids: Eerdmans, 1991), 13, 19, 68-69.

6. D. Vetter, *THAT* 2:965.

7. *IBHS* §9.5.1.

8. *La Formation*, 270.

9. Robinson, "Micha," 145.

arsenal they tempted the elect nation to redirect its faith away from God to military security. To be sure, "horses" are remotely parallel to idols in v 13, but they are immediately parallel to defensive cities, which were never objects of worship. *miqqirbekā (from among you)* is a frozen prepositional compound (see 3:11; 5:6, 7[7, 8]), consisting here of ablative *min* plus *qereb* and governing the second masculine singular suffix; it is a common adverbial phrase with *kārat* denoting the sphere of cleansing.

wĕha'ăbadtî (and I will destroy) is also a two-place hiphil, but with a qal intransitive verb transforming it into a transitive[10] first common singular with *I AM* as subject, *wāw*-relative with the suffix conjugation of the root *'bd* (see 4:9). The *wāw*-relatives in this section seem to function as part of a longer series of identical forms acting as a semantic unit, that is, representing different aspects of "in that day." Therefore, each is better construed as functioning in the same way as the first *wĕhikrattî* in 5:9Ab(10Ab), then as sequential to one another. Against all texts and versions Syr repeats the translation of *hikrattî* in 5:9B(10B). *markĕbōtêkā (your chariots)* is a feminine plural noun of *merkābâ* (see 1:13) with the second masculine singular possessive pronominal suffix. Since *merkābâ* is the common term for a vehicle drawn by a horse, and since Israel did not possess the modern equivalent of cavalry in the sense that troops are mounted on horseback, one should assume that Micah has broken up a coordinate stereotyped phrase "horses and chariots." M. O'Connor[11] calls this phenomenon the word-level trope of coloration by coordination. The combined expression means "horse-drawn chariots," as also in Ps 20:8(7).

10 Initial *wĕhikrattî* repeats initial *wĕhikrattî* in 5:9Ab(10Ab) and functions in the same way. Such precise repetition is rare and stands at the opposite extreme of the trope of coloration by coordination.[12] In the construction *'ārê 'arṣekā (cities of your land)* *'ereṣ* means "country of Israel" as in 5:4(5) and is a genitive of location.[13] *'ārê* is a masculine plural construct with the feminine noun *'îr*; contrary to its uncertain use in v 13B(14B), in v 10A(11A) it certainly has its normal sense of designating any permanent, usually fortified, settlement without regard to size and claim, though Deut 3:5 mentions "unwalled towns." A. R. Hulst[14] says that "nothing certain can be said about its basic meaning; nevertheless one ought to think in connection with *'îr* of some form of fortification." H. Strathmann[15] agrees: "This is much more comprehensive than the

10. *IBHS* §27.2.
11. M. O'Connor, *Hebrew Verse Structure* (Winona Lake, Ind.: Eisenbrauns, 1980), 112-14.
12. See O'Connor, *Hebrew Verse Structure*, 109.
13. *IBHS* §9.5.3.
14 A. R. Hulst, *THAT* 2:267.
15. H. Strathmann, *"polis,"* *TDNT* 6:522.

word 'town' and embraces any fortified place." C. Schultz[16] says that cities were important for the protection they offered their inhabitants against aggressors. The suggestion of fortification is certainly applicable here, as the parallel in v 10B(11B) shows.

The *wāw*-relative with the suffix conjugation in *wĕhārastî (and I will tear down)*, a qal first common singular with *I AM* as subject, functions in the same way as in *wĕha'ăbadtî* in v 9B(10B). The root *hrs* means "to tear down," and its object is often "cities" (2 Sam 11:25; 2 Kgs 3:25), so it becomes a technical term for warfare (Jer 45:4; Ezek 13:14; Song 2:2). *kol-mibṣāreykā (all your strongholds)* consists of *kol*, meaning the aggregate with no one exempted, and the genitive of measure *mibṣārêkā*, a masculine plural noun with the abstracting prefix *mêm* of the root *bāṣar* and the possessive second masculine singular pronominal suffix. *bāṣar* means "to cut off," "to make inaccessible," "to fence," "to fortify." One need not decide the question of etymology here except to note that, according to J. N. Oswalt,[17] "of the seventy-three occurrences of *bāṣar* and its derivatives, all but eight have to do with fortification (or inaccessibility)." The parallels *'îr* and *mibṣār* are best construed as a breakup of the stereotyped phrase *'ārê hammibṣār* (Num 32:17, 36; Josh 10:20; 19:35; 2 Kgs 3:19; 10:2; 17:9; 18:8; Jer 4:5; 5:17; 6:27; 8:14; 34:7, etc.), like *sûs* and *merkābâ* in v 9(10), but this time as a trope of coloration by combination,[18] for *mibṣār* in these passages functions with *'îr* as an attributive genitive; the combined idea is "your fortified cities."

11 For *wĕhikrattî (and I will cut off)* see 4:9, 10. *kĕšāpîm (sorceries)* occurs elsewhere only in 2 Kgs 9:22; Isa 47:9, 12; Nah 3:4 and is undoubtedly related to Akkadian *kussupu* "to practice sorcery," probably a D denominative. LXX's *ta pharmaka sou* "your sorcery" presumes *kšpyk*, probably due to the confusion of *kāp* and *mêm* and of the frequent second singular pronominal suffix with the other objects of the verbs in this section. *kešep* had something to do with divination — its species within this genre is unknown — because in Deut 18:10 it constitutes a parallel with *qesem* (see 3:6-7) and because in Israel, in contradistinction to pagan cults, the diviners' place was taken by prophets who foretold the future. This sense is validated in Jer 27:9, where, in addition to being listed along with "prophets" and "dreamers," *qōsĕmîm*, Jeremiah cites their prediction. *miyyādekā (from your power)* is rendered by a plural in LXX, probably as a matter of style. *yād* probably means "power" as in 2:1, and *miyyād* elsewhere may mean, as probably here, "out of the hand" = "out of the power of";[19]

16. C. Schultz, "*'îr*," *TWOT* 2:664.
17. J. N. Oswalt, "*bāṣar*," *TWOT* 1:123.
18. Cf. O'Connor, *Hebrew Verse Structure*, 112-15.
19. See BDB 391, §5g.

thus *miyyādekā* means "from your power." This sense is validated by the singular. In *ûmĕ'ônĕnîm* the *wāw* is coordinate and the form is a masculine plural poel participle, a *nomen agentis,* of the root II *'nn.* The word pertains to practicing some form of divination, for along with *kešep* it too occurs in Deut 18:10, 14 and Jer 27:9. Some scholars hold that the *mĕ'ônēn* or *'onen* ("soothsayer"; Deut 18:10, 14; Isa 57:3; Jer 27:9; Mic 5:11[12]) is related to the Arabic *'anna* "to appear," and so they think the *mĕ'ônēn* is one who causes the spirit of the dead to appear.[20] How they differed from other forms of divination, however, is uncertain. For *lō' yihyû-lāk (you will not have)* see Mic 2:5.

12 For *wĕhikrattî* see 5:9, 10(10, 11). *pĕsîlêkā (your idols)* consists of the masculine plural noun of *pesel* with the second masculine singular pronominal suffix (see *sûsêkā* in 5:9[10]); for *pĕsîl* see Mic 1:7. *ûmaṣṣēbôteykā (and your cultic pillars)* consists of a coordinate *wāw,* a prefix *mêm* denoting instrument,[21] a feminine plural suffix with a pronominal suffix, and the root *nṣb* "to hew." Isa 19:19 also assumes that *maṣṣēbôt* were an accepted part of the Judean cult in Micah's day. *maṣṣēbâ* designates an unhewn, upright monumental stone marking a grave (Gen 35:20), serving as a memorial (Gen 31:45; 35:14; 2 Sam 18:18), or functioning in some way within a cult, as memorials with reference to Israel's God (Gen 28:18; Exod 24:4) or as stylized, venerated representations of the god Baal at his shrine. For the "stickwort" *miqqirbekā (from among you)* see Mic 5:9(10).

wĕlō'-tištaḥăweh 'ôd (and you will no longer bow down) consists of coordinate *waw,* the negative clausal adverb *lō',*[22] the adverb *'ôd,* and the second masculine singular nonperfective designating a contingent future of a disputed stem and root used 170 times in the OT. Most moderns, largely on the basis of Ugaritic, identify the root as *ḥwy* "to strike," in the St stem "to throw down striking the earth." A few point to the root *ḥyy* "to live," and in the St stem "to cause oneself to live (by worship)." J. A. Emerton, however, returns to the common view before the Ugaritic evidence, namely, that the root is *šhy* "to bow" and that the stem is hithpalel "to bow oneself/to prostrate oneself." The issue is unresolved.[23] The nonperfective was required when the *wāw*-relative construction was dropped, and, like them, it designates the contingent future. Because *I AM* annihilated the detestable pagan idols and pillars from among the Israelites, they will no longer worship them. For the second masculine singular see Mic 5:9(10). *'ôd,* derived from *'ûd* "to repeat," functions as an adverb here, not as a substantive, and has its usual temporal sense "still," "again," indi-

20. S. Aḥituv, "Divination," *EncJud* 6:114.

21. *IBHS* §5.6.

22. *IBHS* §39.3.

23. *IBHS* §21.2.3.

cating the continuance of a past or present event; with *lō'* it means "not again," "no longer."

lĕma'ăśēh yādeykā (to the work of your own hands) consists of allative *lĕ*[24] with the masculine singular construct *ma'ăśēh*, composed of the abstract prefix *mêm*[25] and construct of the root *'śh* "to do," "to make," and the genitive of agent/instrument[26] *yādeykā*, composed of the masculine plural and the second masculine singular genitive of inalienable possession.[27] R. Vuilleumier[28] thinks that v 12B(13B) was added from the parallel text in Isa 2:8, noting that it is a synonym for idol in Hos 14:4(3); cf. Isa 44:9-20, but B. Renaud[29] notes that "work of your hands" is found in parallel with *pesel* in Deut 27:15 and that the verb "to prostrate oneself" accompanies *pesel* in Exod 20:4. He reasons: "This word *psl* in Mic 5:12A might therefore very easily have led to Mic 5:12B"; in fact, v 12B, according to Renaud, "constitutes the peak of the piece," but he says this on the shaky ground of its disparate meter.

13 *wĕnātaštî (and I will uproot)* consists of a *wāw*-relative with the suffix conjugation, continuing the series of situations initiated by *I AM* to purify his realm in Israel's eschatological future — a qal first common singular of the root *ntš* with *I AM* as speaker (see 5:9A[10A]). He chose this verb because it is most appropriate with the object *'ăšêreykā (your Asherahs)*. H. Wolff,[30] who is usually a cautious text critic, conjectures that *'ăšêreykā* is a corruption of an original *'ôyĕbeykā* "your enemies," because (1) it forms a better parallel with *šryk* "your adversaries," attested in Tg in v 13B(14B); (2) *ntš* almost never has *'ăšērîm* as its object but ordinarily becomes a technical term for the deportation of nations and groups of people (1 Kgs 14:15; Amos 9:15; Ps 9:7[6]); especially instructive is the fact that *ntš* is used in the Jeremianic-Deuteronomic material in the broader context as here (v 14B[15B]!) of "nations who do not listen" (Jer 12:17; 18:7-10) and that *I AM* roots out "in anger and wrath," as here in v 14A(15A) and in Deut 29:27(28); (3) the elimination of the *'ăšērîm* is described with many other verbs; and (4) *'ăšêreykā* could "easily [*sic!*]" have been read instead of *'ôybyk* because of the frequency of the threefold series *pĕsîlîm, maṣṣēbôt, 'ăšērîm* (Deut 7:5; 12:3), and even more so of the twofold series *maṣṣēbôt, 'ăšērîm* (Deut 16:21; 1 Kgs 14:23; 2 Kgs 17:10; 18:4; 2 Chr 31:1), and because in the angular Hebrew script the letters *yôd* and *sāmek* as well as *bêt* and *rêš* are graphically similar. Without attempting

---

24. *IBHS* §11.2.10.
25. *IBHS* §5.6.
26. *IBHS* §9.5.1.
27. *IBHS* §9.5.1.
28. Vuilleumier, "Michée," 66 n. 3.
29. *La Formation*, 266.
30. Wolff, *Micha*, 124, 132-33.

to refute his arguments one by one, suffice it to note Würthwein's[31] first principle of textual criticism, which is applicable here: "When MT and all other witnesses offer a text which is unobjectionable, which makes sense, and has been preserved without a variant . . . we may naturally assume that the original text has been preserved by the tradition, and that it should be accepted implicitly."

In the OT Asherah, who is primarily a fertility goddess, appears as the companion of Baal (Judg 3:7; 1 Kgs 18:19; 2 Kgs 23:4), and her cultic object, from which she is inseparable, was a tree or some other wooden object driven into the ground (Judg 6:26; 1 Kgs 16:32-33; 2 Kgs 17:16; 2 Chr 33:3). Its precise description is unknown (a grove? a stylized/carved tree/pole? a cult image?), possibly because Israel's prophets refused to elaborate upon such a detestable object. A living tree cannot be in view because, as J. C. de Moor[32] notes: "Asherim 'were made' (1 Kgs 14:15; 16:33 . . .), and they stood under green trees (1 Kgs 14:23; 2 Kgs 17:10)." J. C. De Moor[33] thinks that it is possible to assume that the *'ăšērâ* was a stylized tree, for, among other reasons, it appears as such on a clay model of a cultic scene from Cyprus. On the other hand, he notes that since the *pesel hā'ăšērâ* "the graven image of Asherah" in 2 Kgs 21:7 is called simply *hā'ăšērâ* "the Asherah" in 23:6, this favors "the view that it was an image of a god [*sic!*]." For the "stickwort" *miqirbekā* in the excommunication formula see Mic 5:9.

wĕhišmadtî (and I will destroy) is the last *waw*-relative in the series with an unclassified two-place hiphil, probably with the stative force "cause to be destroyed," first common singular of the root *šmd*. D. Vetter[34] says that "*šmd* Hi. means visible elimination," and he validates this from the expressions added to it, such as "from the face of the earth" (Deut 6:15; 1 Kgs 13:34), "from before someone" (Deut 2:21; Josh 24:8), or from the more precise determination "until its extermination." He also urges that "*šmd* Hi. takes the place of *krt* Hi/Ni with separative *min* with reference to excommunication [see above] in an echo of the formula in Deut 4:3 and in a late formulation in Ezek 14:9." In sum, according to Vetter, "it corresponds to the law of excommunication, which ordered from the cultic community the physical elimination (*šmd* Hi.) of the thing banned (*ḥerem*) out of its midst (Josh 7:12; 2 Sam 14:7, 11, 16)." As noted in connection with *kārat*, G. von Rad saw this law of excommunication as standing behind *I AM*'s holy wars and gift of the land. D. Vetter[35] agrees: "From the law of excommunication the use of the verb in connection with the presentation of the LORD's war . . . and gift of the land traditions can be understood: the original

31. Würthwein, *The Text of the Old Testament*, 116.
32. J. C. de Moor, "*ᵃshērāh*," *TDOT* 1:442.
33. de Moor, *TDOT* 1:443.
34. D. Vetter, *THAT* 2:965.
35. Vetter, *THAT* 2:963-64.

sense of the excommunication law is preserved where humans execute the command (Num 33:52; Deut 2:12, 23; 7:24; 33:27; Josh 9:24; 11:14, 20; 2 Sam 22:38; Ps 106:34); it is developed under the influence of that tendency which ascribes to the LORD all activity in the course of warfare, and to the assimilated land traditions, when the LORD himself executes through corporal annihilation the excommunication." Vetter develops this insight into the prophetic literature: "The prophetic use of *šmd* Hi. is connected to the accomplishment of excommunication in the war of Yahweh (hi.: Amos 2:9;[36] 9:8; 1 Kgs 13:34; Mic 5:13[14]; in vv 9-13[10-14] it developed the form of the excommunication formula. . . ." In sum, *šmd* hiphil constitutes an appropriate ending of the series begun with *krt* hiphil.

Though *'āreykā (your cities)* normally means "your cities" (LXX, Vg, followed by NRSV, TNIV), the mention of "cities" here is curious because they have already been mentioned in v 10(11) and form a very bad parallel to the Asherah poles. J. T. Willis[37] presents the variety of solutions proposed until 1969; here I concentrate on the last twenty years. K. Jeppesen[38] defended this interpretation from Jer 2:28; 11:13, "your gods are just as many as your cities, O Judah!" He argues: "Here *'āreykā* is clearly meaningfully combined with *'ĕloheykā* in conjunction with Judah." His argument, though appealing, questionably assumes that Micah's audience would have equated "cities" with "gods." Some critics conjecture other words. Tg, adopted by H. Wolff as noted above, read *ṣryk* "your adversaries"; A. van Hoonacker,[39] *'ṣyk* "your trees"; W. Nowack[40] (cf. *BHS*), *'ăṣabbeykā* "your idols" *(BHS)*; E. Sellin[41] and A. Deissler,[42] *šyryk* or its defective form *šryk* "your images" (cf. Isa 45:16); W. Rudolph,[43] *uzzêkā* "your refuge"; R. Vuilleumier,[44] taking up a proposal advanced in *BHK* but dropped in *BHS*, *bĕ'āleykā* "your Baals."

Others have sought to derive the word from a different root than usual — it occurs 1,092 times, according to A. R. Hulst[45] — for the consensus of the texts and versions, apart from Tg, support the consonants of MT and invite looking for a homonym in the cognate languages. J. P. Michaelis, and many commenta-

---

36. Cf. Wolff, *Micah*, 204-5.

37. J. T. Willis, "The Authenticity and Meaning of Micah 5:9-14," *ZAW* 81 (1969) 353-54.

38. K. Jeppesen, "Micah 5:13 in the Light of a Recent Archaeological Discovery," *VT* 34 (1984) 462-65.

39. van Hoonacker, *Les Douze Petits Prophètes*, 394.

40. Nowack, "Micha," in *Die kleinen Propheten*, 231.

41. Sellin, "Micha," 292-93.

42. Deissler, *La Sainte Bible*, 8:340.

43. Rudolph, *Micha*, 103.

44. Vuilleumier, "Michée," 67-68.

45. A. R. Hulst, *THAT* 2:270.

tors since, understood *'rkyk* as a place of trees. T. Gaster[46] noted that in one of the Ugaritic texts *ǵr* (= *'r* in Hebrew) stands in parallel with *pesel* "carved image," making an excellent parallel here to the Asherah; he also connected the word to Arabic *ǵyr* "bedaubed stone." J. M. Sasson,[47] on the basis of the Ugaritic parallel, translates "forest" or "statues of wood." M. Dahood[48] looks to a Ugaritic root *ǵyr* "to protect," hence *'ārîm* "protectors." He questionably deduces that this is a name for pagan divinities from Mic 5:13(14) and thinks that Jer 2:28 is a pun on "cities" and "gods." J. Gray,[49] commenting on 2 Kgs 10:25 and not mentioning Mic 5:13(14), says that *'yr* is related to *ǵr* in a certain Ugaritic text, meaning "inmost recess, or shrine, of the temple" and that it "may be a cognate of the Arabic *ǵawr* ('a hollow' [cf. *muǵara* ('cave')])." L. R. Fisher[50] does not look to a cognate Ugaritic root but argues that "*'ir* is a flexible term meaning not only village, city or state, but that it can also have the meaning of temple quarter or even of the inner room of the temple." He applies this insight to 2 Kgs 10:25 along with at least three other passages, not citing Mic 5:13(14), but A. S. van der Woude[51] also, without citing either Gray's or Fisher's study, appeals to 2 Kgs 10:25 and applies the meaning "temple recess" to Mic 5:13(14). Because these researches do not dialogue with other views, no consensus has been reached. Of these proposals the two best are those of J. Sasson and L. Fisher: the former because of the parallelism; the latter because it is an adequate parallel and does not call for a new root. Nevertheless, the data from the cognate languages are too weak and too conflicting to overthrow the otherwise unambiguous meaning of *'î* in Hebrew: "village or city."

14 I. Willi-Plein[52] arbitrarily says that *wĕʿāśîtî . . . nāqām (I will avenge myself)* cannot be connected on linguistic grounds, yet *'śh* takes *nāqām* as its object in the conventional idiom "to vindicate oneself" in Judg 11:36; Ezek 25:17; Ps 149:7.[53] The *waw*-relative with the suffix conjugation in *wĕʿāśîtî* "And I will do," a qal first common singular of the root *'śh* with *I AM* as antecedent (cf. Mic 5:9Aa[10Ba]), functions the same as the other initial *waw*-relatives introducing each verse of this pericope, after the anacrusis in Mic 5:9Aa(10Aa).

46. T. Gaster, "Notes on the Minor Prophets, 2: Micah V,13," *JTS* 38 (1937) 163.

47. J. M. Sasson, "Flora, Fauna, and Minerals," in *Ras Shamra Parallels*, ed. L. R. Fisher, AnOr (Rome: Pontifical Biblical Institute, 1972), 1:435-36.

48. M. Dahood, *Psalms 1–50*, AB (Garden City, N.Y.: Doubleday, 1966), 55-56.

49. *I & II Kings: A Commentary*, OTL (Philadelphia: Westminster, 2d ed. 1970).

50. L. R. Fisher, "The Temple Quarter," *JSS* 8 (1963) 34-41.

51. A. S. van der Woude, *Micha*, 187.

52. I. Willi-Plein, *Vorformen*, 97.

53. Cf. BDB 794, §I.1.a(3) *contra* §2, and GB 623, §2, "with abstract object . . . *nqm 't*, Mic 5:14 etc."

In *bĕ'ap ûbĕḥēmâ (in anger and in wrath)* the preposition *bĕ* situates the psychological circumstances of *I AM*'s action[54] and could be rendered by an adverb, "angrily and wrathfully." The masculine singular noun *'ap* from the root *'ānēp* "to be angry," which always has God as its subject and whose etymology is debated, can mean either "nose" or "anger," reflecting its original connection with angry snorting. It appears as the subject of *ḥārâ* "to glow/burn," of *bā'ar* "to burn," and of *'āšan* "to smoke." It is used most frequently in parallel with *ḥēmâ*, thirty-three times according to E. Johnson.[55] "Other words," says Johnson, "used synonymously with *'aph* are *'ebhrah* 'fury' (10 times), *za'am* 'indignation' (8 times), and *qetseph* 'wrath' (4 times). Words meaning 'compassion,' 'grace,' and 'mercy' . . . are used as antonyms of 'anger.' *ḥēmâ* is derived from *yāḥam* 'to be hot.' The noun can also mean 'venom' and possibly 'fiery wine.'" "It is easy to understand," says Johnson,[56] "how bodily 'heat' is brought about by anger as well as by poison or wine." The coordination of the two words brings to a flash point the holy *I AM*'s burning anger against those who rebel against his sovereignty. The masculine singular object of *'āśîtî, nāqām* "defensive vindication," is one of the Bible's legal terms signifying that a ruler secures his sovereignty and keeps his community whole by delivering his wronged subjects and punishing their guilty slayers who do not respect his rule. G. E. Mendenhall[57] draws the conclusion on the basis of the biblical and prebiblical ancient oriental usages of language that the "'vengeance' of Yahweh actually designates those events in human experience that were identified as the exercise of the sovereignty — what the ancient Romans called *imperium*." After studying a number of examples of *nāqām* in the Amarna letters, he[58] draws the conclusion "that the root NQM designates what we have termed 'defensive vindication.' . . . Nowhere does NQM specifically imply anything similar to vengeance. . . ." He then turns to study the use of the root in the Bible, fifty-one instances of which involve situations in which *I AM* himself is either the actor, or an agency to which he has delegated power to act. He writes: "Thus in over two thirds of the total occurrences, the root designates the exercise of the divine *imperium* either directly or indirectly."[59] This exercise of force is directed against enemies of the divine *imperium*, whether it be Israel itself or foreign nations. In the exercise of his sovereign power *I AM* both punishes the aggressor

---

54. *IBHS* §11.2.5.

55. E. Johnson, "'anaph," *TDOT* 1:354.

56. Johnson, *TDOT* 1:352.

57. G. E. Mendenhall, *The Tenth Generation: The Origins of the Biblical Tradition* (Baltimore: Johns Hopkins University Press, 1973), 70.

58. Mendenhall, *The Tenth Generation*, 82.

59. Mendenhall, *The Tenth Generation*, 82-83.

and protects his subjects, and so the word may sometimes be translated by "defeat" or by "rescue." Mendenhall[60] says: "If one views the situation as the hostility between sovereign and enemy, the word must be translated by 'defeat' or 'punish' . . . ; if one views it as the relationship between sovereign and faithful subject, the same act is to 'rescue' or 'deliver.'" Mic 5:14(15) belongs to the category of punitive vindication.

The emphatic particle *'et (against)* is used here with the definite adverbial accusative of limitation "with regard to,"[61] and is translated "against" because *nāqām* signifies defensive vindication with regard to/against rebels, *haggôyim (the nations)* (see Mic 4:3; 5:7[8]). For a rebuttal of conjectures that would remove "nations" see J. T. Willis.[62] The sign of the dependent relative *'ăšer (who)* introduces a nonrestrictive clause. Since *nāqām* presumes that the nations in view are rebellious, the clause is tautologous; nevertheless, this pleonastic construction removes all ambiguity about the nations in view and contrasts these disobedient nations in this closing prophecy of salvation oracles in chapters 4–5 with the converted nations described in the opening oracle of 4:1-2. In *lō' šāmē'û (do not obey) lō'* is a clausal negative adverb with the qal third masculine plural of the root *šm'*, with "nations" as subject. Although *šm'* always means "hear," in most texts it has a more precise meaning, such as "pay attention," "understand," "examine," or "obey," depending on the situation and the social status of the speaker and audience. H. Schult[63] says: "In theologically relevant texts *šm'* plays no other role than usual: it designates (a) God as hearer of human utterances, (b) mankind as hearer of (direct or mediated) divine utterances." He[64] goes on to note that in the latter use it predominantly pertains to mankind as hearing God's commands and means to do what God or his representative said and wanted. Furthermore, of interest to Mic 5:13(14), though he does not cite it, he notes: "the content of what ought to be heard and/or is not heard, cannot be enlarged upon in isolated instances (e.g., Exod 6:12; 16:19-20; Num 14:22-23; Judg 2:2; 1 Kgs 20:35-36; Zeph 3:2; Hag 1:12; Zech 7:7ff.). Occasionally the content (even in context) is not stated, but 'to hear' is used absolutely, so that the one being addressed must either know precisely what is meant or cannot know (1 Sam 15:22 . . . ; Isa 1:19)." In Mic 5:14(15) the expression is used absolutely, but what Schult fails to realize is that this absolute use does not presume an elided object. Rather, the point of this absolute expression is that these nations do not submit to *I AM*'s rule but stand rebelliously against his sovereign lordship.

---

60. Mendenhall, *The Tenth Generation*, 84-85.
61. *IBHS* §10.3.1.
62. Willis, "The Authenticity and Meaning of Micah 5:9-14," 355-56.
63. H. Schult, *THAT* 2:979.
64. Schult, *THAT* 2:980.

EXPOSITION

The prophecy in 5:9-14(10-15) is marked off from the preceding prophecy in 5:6-8(7-9) by the introductory formulas "in that day" and "says *I AM*," and from the following prophecy in 6:1-8 by its introduction: "Hear what *I AM* is saying" (6:1). The concluding prayer in 5:8, "May all your enemies be cut off [Heb. *krt* niphal]" is answered by: "I will cut off [Heb. *krt* hiphil]" all enemies both within and outside the kingdom (see below).

After the introductory anacrusis in 5:9Aa(10Aa), the oracle falls into two unequal parts, vv 9Ab-13(10Ab-14) and v 14(15), distinguished from each other both by structure and by theme. In the first section *I AM* introduces the first verset of each verse, with the exception of v 13A(14A), with the refrain "And I will cut off," and introduces the second versets with a synonymous parallel (e.g., "I will wreck, tear down, destroy"), with the exception of vv 11B(12B) and 12B(13B), and concludes each verset without exception with the second masculine singular suffix "your/you" with reference to the remnant. In v 14(15) the pronominal suffix "you/your" and the direct address to Israel are dropped and in its stead one finds "nations who do not obey" spoken of in the third person. In vv 9-13(10-14) *I AM* promises through the repeated refrain and synonymous parallels to purge his kingdom from those things that fracture its covenantal relation with him: trust in its military power, in divination, and in Canaanite idolatry. The theme of purging Israel from these false securities is underscored by the refrain "from among you" repeated in the first and last verses, vv 9 and 13(10 and 14), forming an *inclusio* around this section. Verse 14(15), on the other hand, presents *I AM* as taking punitive vindication against the nations that do not submit to his rule. The first section limits his empire to within Israel; the second expands it implicitly to the ends of the earth.

On the other hand, the two uneven parts are connected by structure, theme, and situation. Both share the initial first-person pronoun with reference to *I AM* as speaker, "I will . . . ," thereby showing clearly that v 14(15) also belongs with the section introduced by "*I AM* says." Moreover, both pertain to the theme of *I AM* protecting his *imperium* by purifying his realm: in the first section by purging unbelief and attendant unholiness from among nominal Israel and so preserving it from his final wrath, and in the second section, after Israel has been purged, by taking punitive vindication against those nations that rebel against his rightful claim to universal sovereignty through Israel. Calvin noted: "The salvation of God [cf. v 14(15)] could not otherwise come to them than by stripping them of all vain and false confidence [vv 9-13(10-14)]." "To cut off . . . from among you" (vv 9-13[10-14]) and "to avenge sovereignty" (v 14[15]) share the common notion of punishment to preserve a community. The first pertains to enemies within, and the punishment is remedial; the second pertains to enemies outside, and the punishment is penal. In both cases the enemies trust in something other than *I AM*. The oracle aims to sober unbelievers and to strengthen believers. This theme and aim fits the situation in 701 B.C. J. T. Willis[65] says: "5:9-14 is parallel in structure and thought to 4:9-10. An enemy army is attacking Israel, and Israel is retaliating with human power — both military and religious, thereby demonstrating her lack of faith in Yahweh. Yahweh declares that he himself will remove these objects of faith, and will then give Israel the victory over her oppressors." He also argues for the authenticity of the oracle by noting that Jer 26:16-19 indicates that Micah's announcement of the destruction of Jerusalem and the temple (Mic 3:15) motivated Hezekiah to seek the favor of *I AM* and that the precise form of his reform took the shape of the reform predicted here and described in 2 Kgs 18:3-6, which, according to N. H. Snaith,[66] involved "the destruction of sacred pillars and sacred poles generally, and the suppression of heathen or semiheathen cults wherever they happened to be." J. T. Willis draws the conclusion: "The oracle originated with Micah as he attempted to inspire Hezekiah to reform Judean worship by removing those objects which betrayed the influence of Canaanite Baal worship on the Yahweh cult. It declared that in spite of the fact that Israel was constantly threatened by powerful foes, Yahweh would remove the objects of her trust, leaving her with no alternative but to trust in him alone. This trust, intimately connected with the restoration of 'pure' Yahwism, would be vindicated when Yahweh himself delivered Israel from her oppressors."

Within vv 9-13(10-14), vv 9-10(10-11) are linked by the merism of the purging of offensive weapons, horse-drawn chariots, in v 9(10), and of defensive fortifications, fortified cities, in v 10(11). Vv 11-12(12-13) are linked by the reference to "your power." By this motif, Israel's false security in its military power is linked with divination (v 11[12]) and idolatry (v 12[13]), both of which religious practices are expressions of its own power. Vv 12-13(13-14) are linked by changing the refrain from "I will cut off" to "I will uproot" with reference to idolatry, by the refrain "from among you," and by the merism of stone cult objects in v 12(13) and of wooden cult objects in v 13(14), both of which were also employed in divination, providing yet another link between vv 11(12) and 12-13(13-14).

In sum, one can outline the oracle in 5:9-14 (EV 10-15) as follows:

---

65. Willis, "The Authenticity and Meaning of Micah 5:9-14," 356.
66. N. H. Snaith, "The First and Second Books of Kings," *IDB* 3:289.

I. Introductory anacrusis:
   A. "In that day": the oracle is located in Israel's eschatological future (v 9Αаⲁⲁⲁ).
   B. "Says *I AM*": the oracle is invested with heavenly authority (v 9Αаⲁⲃ).
II. *I AM* himself will protect his *imperium:*
   A. *I AM* himself will purge Israel of false securities (vv 9Ab-13).
      1. Of faith in its own military power (vv 9Ab-10).
         a. in its offensive weapons (v 9Ab-B).
         b. in its defensive fortification (v 10).
      2. Of faith in its own religious power (vv 11-13)
         a. in magical and manipulative divination (v 11).
         b. in cult objects of its own making (vv 12-13).
            (1) in stone cult objects (v 12).
            (2) in wooden cult objects (v 13).
   B. *I AM* himself will avenge his sovereignty against disobedient nations (v 14).

This concluding oracle of promise in chapters 4–5 shares many links with the earlier one in that section: the mention of nations in v 14(15) functions as an *inclusio* with "nations" in 4:1-2, but whereas the latter deals with obedient nations, this one has to do with the disobedient. The connection is enhanced by the unique repetition of *wĕhāyâ*, by the motif of the destruction of weapons, and by linking the fortunes of the nations with eschatological Israel. As 5:6-8(7-9), the penultimate oracle, matches 4:6-7, the second oracle, so in an enveloping chiasm the last pericope, 5:9-14(10-15), matches the first, 4:1-5, as observed by B. Renaud.[67] It should also be recalled that in the center 4:9-13 matches 4:14–5:14(5:1-15) by its reference to the remnant as the "one who brings forth" the new age (4:9, 10 and 5:2[3]), by the Assyrian menace and *I AM*'s supernatural deliverance (4:9-13, 4:14–5:5[5:1-6]), and by *I AM* as King (4:9, 12), shepherding his people through the Messiah (5:3[4]). 5:9-14(10-15) also has links with 4:6-7 through the introductory formulas *bayyôm hahû'* and *nĕ'ûm-yhwh*. Finally, it is linked with 4:14–5:5(5:1-6) by *wĕhāyâ* in 5:9(10) and 5:4, 6, 7(5, 7, 8); with the motifs of the spiritual conversion of all Israel in 5:2(3) and 5:9-13(10-14), of the Messiah's supernatural protection of *I AM*'s *imperium* in 5:4-5(5-6), and of *I AM*'s supernatural protection in 5:14(15); and by the explicit promise that *I AM*'s rule will extend to the ends of the earth in 5:3(4), a promise implied in 5:14(15).

Isaiah (2:6-8) accused Israel that at the time of the Assyrian threat Israel

---

67. B. Renaud, *Structure et Attaches Litteraires de Michée IV–V* (Paris: Gabalda, 1964), 13.

was full of horses and chariots, of soothsayers and of magicians, and of vain idols. The striking similarities between this complaint and Micah's promise suggest that the two oracles derive from a common oracle including accusation (Isaiah) and threat, transformed in Micah into promise. The linkage strongly supports the historical credibility of the book's superscription in 1:1.

Nothing is said here about how *I AM* will purge his *imperium* of these false securities that alienated it from its covenantal relationship with him founded on faith alone. Perhaps one should suppose from the oracles of judgment in chapters 1–3 that *I AM* began to purge Israel of its artificial supports through the harsh political rod of Assyria. Under that chastening rod Israel learned the futility of its false securities. After the scourge of 701 B.C. (see 1:1), Israel, as Isaiah foresaw, threw away to the rodents and bats their idols of silver and of gold, which they had venerated (Isa 2:19). The historical books confirm this presentiment. Hezekiah radically reformed the nation by replacing apostasy with faithful adherence to *I AM* and his Law (cf. 2 Kgs 19:14-19; Isa 37:1-4; 2 Chronicles 29–31). Only the miracle of God's intervention in response to these reforms preserved the remnant through that perilous time. But Hezekiah's reform was temporary, whereas Micah foresees a time when these false securities will no longer exist in true Israel. His vision finds fulfillment in the church of Jesus Christ for which he gave himself up, "to make her holy, cleansing her by the washing with water through the word, and to present her to himself as a radiant church, without stain or wrinkle or any other blemish, but holy and blameless" (Eph 5:26-27).

The first introductory deictic temporal clause, "and it will come to pass in that day," deftly fits the oracle in 5:9-14(10-15) into the tableau of salvation prophecies in chapters 4–5 pertaining to eschatological Israel's golden age under the Messiah's rule. J. T. Willis[68] plausibly locates the prophecy in the Assyrian siege of Jerusalem, but wrongly, because he neglects this introduction, which situates the prophecy's fulfillment in eschatological Israel, interprets its fulfillment as occurring at the time of Hezekiah in Israel's loss of military might at the hands of the Assyrians. The apparently hopeless situation to which Assyria reduced Judah, causing Hezekiah and the desperate nation to turn in simple faith to *I AM* and his miraculous deliverance of Jerusalem (cf. 2 Kings 19), functions rather as a harbinger of Israel's blessed future under the Messiah, at which time they will renounce their trust in human resources and find God's miraculous intervention.

The second introductory clause, "says *I AM*," invests it with heavenly authority (see 4:6). The repeated refrain, "and I will . . . ," introduces a series of divine initiatives by Israel's Sovereign to purge his realm of relying on human

---

68. J. T. Willis, "The Structure of Micah 3–5," *ZAW* 81 (1969) 199.

power, both military and religious. Israel's independent spirit both fractured the covenantal relationship, which was based on faith in the God who elected Israel in the first place, and prevented Israel from fulfilling its sacred mission of sanctifying the earth.

"To cut off" means to purge unholiness from the sacred community by excommunication and annihilation in order to protect it against *I AM*'s wrath. The strikingly repeated refrain, "I will cut off," and its synonyms, says J. L. Mays,[69] "sketches a programme of the eradication and removal of things offensive to YHWH's sovereignty." Precise repetition of this sort is rare in any poetry. By this anaphora Micah not only unifies his prophecy but expletively shouts out its promises. *I AM* had commanded Israel in Leviticus to purify and sanctify themselves by annihilating from among them that which offended him, and he further applied that command to annihilating from among them the Canaanites, whom he detested for their unholy practices in relation to holy war and his gift of the land. Israel, however, lacked cultivated religious taste, and instead of being deeply offended by the unholy ways of the Canaanites, they at first tolerated them and then embraced their contagion, bringing the divine wrath against themselves. In Israel's eschatological future *I AM* himself will purge his *imperium* of unbelief and its correlative unholiness, "from among you," and thereby preserve it in the future from his righteous wrath. The text does not specify how *I AM* will do it, but one can be sure that it stems from their converted natures (Mic 5:3[4]). Micah may have given pride of place to the removing of Israel's false military guarantees because they had first place in their unbelieving hearts.

Then too, Lachish, Israel's strongest fortified city, is said to be the beginning of sin in Judah (cf. Mic 1:13). Scriptural notices that the land bristled with military hardware at the time of Sennacherib's invasion (cf. 2 Kgs 18:13, 24; Isa 31:1; 2 Chr 32:1-5) find mute support in Hezekiah's still extant water tunnel. To many moderns, having embraced for non-elect nations a secular point of view, having grown accustomed to overblown defense budgets, and having found security in weapons, the first sin is less obvious than the other two. But the law in Deuteronomy proscribing building up military might aimed to protect the chosen nation against this sin (Deut 17:16-17). Isaiah, Micah's contemporary, accused Israel of putting this screen between themselves and *I AM* (Isa 2:7; 30:16; 31:1), and Hosea, also Micah's contemporary, shared a similar vision for Israel's golden age (Hos 14:4[3]). As noted in Mic 4:1-5, when people obey God's moral laws they can throw away the paraphernalia of war, but when they disobey they arm themselves to the hilt to protect their evil ways.

69. Mays, *Micah*, 125.

One needs to be reminded that this law pertained to ancient and elect Israel, where no distinction was made between church and state, but does not apply to modern democracies where the distinction is usually maintained, and that this promise finds its fulfillment not in nations such as those affiliated with the United Nations, but in the church.

Who are the "you" (masculine singular) to whom this promise is addressed? In this booklet of salvation, the "you," apart from personification for the cities of Jerusalem (4:8) and Bethlehem (5:2[3]), refers to the remnant besieged in Jerusalem. The singular, encountered repeatedly in Israel's covenant with *I AM* (cf. Deut 5:6), represents them as a corporate unity both synchronically and diachronically, but this promise by *I AM* himself to excommunicate unbelievers from their midst entails that the remnant is not yet clean; unbelievers among them must still be sifted out before they become the new Israel of God, destined to extend his kingdom universally.

This verse stands both synthetically and antithetically in relation to v 9(10): synthetically by moving from offensive horse-drawn chariots to defensive fortified cities, but at the same time, as that opposition suggests, antithetically; together as a synecdoche of extremes, similar to "night and day," "summer and winter," they represent all armament. When enemies invaded the land, the populace that worked the fields fell back behind the walls of the fortified cities, with thick walls and special watchtowers, to preserve their lives and their families from slavery in foreign lands. These largest and most important sites within Israel (cf 2 Kgs 17:9) became sinful because they separated Israel from its true Creator and protector (Hos 8:14; 10:14). Although he does not cite Mic 5:10(11), what Oswalt[70] says about fortified cities is noteworthy:

> Such cities were very important strategically since they were almost impregnable until the perfection of siege techniques by the Assyrians (Jer 5:17). . . . Since fortified cities were so strong, it was a great temptation for the Israelites to put their trust in them instead of in their God. Thus the prophets are at pains to show the folly of such trust (Isa 17:3; Lam 2:5; Hos 10:13-14, etc.). God alone is mankind's stronghold (cf. Ps 27:1).

Verse 10B(11B) intensifies v 10A(11A) by the specific and telic word "tear down," by adding "all," and by enlarging on the basic notion of a city, as a fortified settlement, by its parallel "fortifications." G. Münderlein[71] says, "The verb *hāras* becomes a term for Yahweh's act of judgment. When Israel's foes are finally destroyed, the walls of their cities are thrown down (Jer 50:15; cf. Ezek

70. J. N. Oswalt, *"bāṣar," TWOT* 1:123.
71. G. Münderlein, *"hāras," TDOT* 3:462.

26:4, 12) and their foundations torn down (Ezek 30:4)." Here *I AM*, who formerly directed his holy war against pagan nations (cf. Ps 46:10-12[9-11]), now directs it against unbelieving Israel. This technical military term refers to the last of *I AM*'s acts against Israel's trust in its military might: the land vanquished, he tears down its last symbol of a false confidence. Does this mean that ideal Israel will lack any military hardware? On the one hand, the reference to all fortifications in v 10(11) and the stripping of Jerusalem of all military resources in the days of Hezekiah suggests an affirmative answer. On the other hand, other Scriptures calling for complete faith in *I AM* did not exclude immediate means, and so a negative answer seems called for. Deut 17:14-17 hamstrung the king by restricting his military might but did not strip him of all practical sanctions. Instructively the saints in whom God delights have the praise of God in their mouths and a double-edged sword in their hands (Ps 149:6), a posture fleshed out in noble Nehemiah (cf. Neh 4:10[16]). The same David who said "Some trust in chariots and some in horses, but we trust in the name of *I AM* our God" (Ps 20:8[7]) also had troops. These apparently contradictory attitudes are reconciled when one realizes that the Sovereign Lord equips his people without any synergism on their part. The church is a miracle. No earthly means raised Jesus from the dead or sent his Spirit upon the church. But the Holy Spirit, according to the sovereign will of Christ, equips the saints.

After mentioning the military power that separated Israel from faith in its covenant God, Micah now turns to their own religious power in vv 11-13(12-14): manipulated sorcery (v 11[12]) and handcrafted idolatry (vv 12-13[13-14]). The precise species of divination denoted by the terms "diviners" and "soothsayers" is unknown; perhaps, to judge from other parallels in this passage, together they constitute a merism to indicate all forms of divination and magic. H. Wolff[72] suggests that "sorceries" lumps together the charms of all sorts that its practitioners manipulated, citing Nah 3:4 *b'lt kšpym*, the sorceress as "mistress of charms." Isa 2:6 associates divination with the Philistines and apparently with superstitions from the east. As known from Ashurbanipal's library, its practice entered very largely into the religious life of the Babylonians and Assyrians, from the personal religion of individuals to the most important departments of the national religion. Its complex rites were jealously guarded, as elsewhere, and were practiced by a large and organized body of the priesthood. The specific vocabulary for varying classes of augural phenomena and its practitioners bear witness to this complexity, but their differentiations in meaning are unknown to us.

The zeal for divination is explained not only by man's natural curiosity about the future but also by his desire both to advantage himself and disadvan-

---

72. Wolff, *Micha*, 131.

tage others by prescience and through magic to manipulate it. Joseph, by his ability to interpret dreams, saved Egypt and Canaan from starvation; kings seek favorable omens before engaging in battle. The adverbial phrase "from your power" does not aim to clarify the kind of sorcery but to point out that Israel's sin lies in trusting its own power to manipulate the occult. Sorcery was a capital offense in Israel (Exod 22:17[18]), and Malachi (3:5) saw sorcerers being judged along with adulterers, perjurers, those who defraud laborers and oppressors of widows, the fatherless, and aliens; a similar grouping is found in Rev 21:8; 22:15. This judgment shows how seriously *I AM* regarded the attempt by Israel to annex to itself spiritual forces outside of himself, thereby opening itself to demonic and dark forces.

Divination is close to magic, but the latter is distinguished by attempting to influence the future for good or ill. Both are probably in view here because Israel must be purged of manipulating the occult. The verse ends with a promise: when *I AM* purges Israel, they will not have diviners. In place of sorcerers *I AM* gave Israel prophets who mediated his word to the people, a word that demanded faith in the One who rules the future according to ethics. Today, as Joel foresaw (Joel 3:1-5[2:28-32]), all Israel, that is, the entire church, mediates God's message to the world because the Spirit of the Lord empowers them for that task (Acts 1:7-8; 2:14-21).

Finally, *I AM* promises in vv 12-13(13-14) to purge Israel of idols, the incarnate representations of pagan deities. These verses function together as a merism for all kinds of idolatry. V 12(13) refers to the representations in rock of the Canaanite male fertility god Baal, and v 13(14) to the representation in wood of his consort, Asherah. The *mṣbh*, the fertility god's cultic stone pillars (cf. 2 Kgs 10:27), along with the stylized tree or wooden statue of the goddess Asherah, were erected beside the altar and sometimes received sacrificial blood and, as appears from their polished surface, were kissed by the devotees (1 Kgs 14:23; 2 Kgs 3:2). These sexually opposite emblems are often associated in the OT (cf. Judg 2:13; 3:7; 10:6; 1 Sam 7:4; 12:10; 1 Kgs 18:19; 2 Kgs 23:4). The second commandment proscribed making idols (Exod 20:4; Deut 5:8; 7:25), and the Law mandated that Israel tear down Baal's detestable stone pillars (Exod 23:24; Deut 7:5; 16:21-22), which could be adorned (Hos 10:1).

An idol gave concrete expression to two pagan concepts: animism and voodooism. Pagans did not distinguish between the Creator and his creation but confounded spirit with matter and so venerated the innate forces of life within nature with the hope of participating in that life. Furthermore, they thought that through magical voodoo in the cult, including both the magical recitation of myth and magical mimetic ritual, they could manipulate the idols to endow annually their crops and wombs with life.

Unlike Israel's God, who connected the future and life with ethics and sexual purity, these gods did not link moral rectitude with destiny and pandered to the sensual lusts of their devotees. Representing *I AM*'s heavenly presence in his house, in contrast to manmade gods of silver and gold that could be manipulated, were the Ten Commandments expressing his transcendent will. "Do this, and live," *I AM* said, and provided atonement for the sin of the faithful. No wonder these gods that themselves behaved no differently from depraved man and demanded no cross seduced Israel and provoked the prophetic response (e.g., Isa 2:8; 10:10; Hos 3:4; 8:4-6; 10:1-2; 13:2; 14:4[3]). Idolatry and the stone pillars not only seduced Israel into pagan thinking and eroticism, but it also caused them to substitute rocks associated with demonic forces for the true Rock, even the One who made them to serve and glorify himself; they used the works of their own hands to serve themselves (cf. Deut 32:15-17). The reference to idols as the works of man's hands (cf. Deut 4:28; 27:15; 31:29; 2 Kgs 19:18; 22:17; Jer 1:16; 10:3; 25:6; Pss 115:4; 135:15) shows that they belong to the same spiritual stuff of trusting in oneself, not in *I AM*, of trusting in one's military might and manipulated sorcery. L. Allen[73] brightly commented: "The hands of God's people must be emptied of all that smacks of help not derived from God if he is to give victory to their hands when they strike in battle."

Finally, they sought to probe the future through the wind whispering through these stone and wood objects instead of listening to the clear voice of *I AM* through Moses and his prophets (see v 13[14]). These detestable emblems *I AM* promises Israel to purge "from among you," the technical expression for purging through excommunication and annihilation. Hezekiah's reforms involved their destruction (2 Kgs 18:3-6), but his reform was temporary, for Manasseh, his son, restored them (2 Kgs 21:2-9). When *I AM* purges the remnant, however, Israel will no longer bow down to the works of their own hands. When *I AM* frees his people from trusting themselves, then he also creates the spiritual climate in which they can return to their original faith in him.

By changing the initial verb from *krt* to *ntš* Micah indicates that v 13(14) continues the attack against pagan idolatry begun in v 12(13). Lest one think that it stands outside the series of purifying divine acts listed in vv 9-12(10-13), note the threefold repetition of the second masculine singular suffix and the adverbial phrase *miqqirbekā* "from your midst," which modified *hikrattî* in 5:9(10) and 12(13). As noted, the *maṣṣēbôteykā* "your cultic stone pillars" of v 12(13), and *'ăšêreykā* "your Asherahs" of v 13(14), the male and female symbols of fertility respectively, stand as a merism representing all idolatry. The sacred personnel associated with these shrines involved themselves in erotic sex-acts.

73. Allen, *Micah*, 357.

Of interest in Mic 5:9-13(10-14) is the function of stones, Baal's symbol, and trees, Asherah's symbol, in giving oracles: they "murmur" and "whisper," and mantics were associated with Asherah. J. C. de Moor[74] says: "Trees and stones were . . . specifically connected with the oracle at Ugarit. When Hosea says that the people inquire of 'a thing of wood' (4:12), this could refer to the 'asherah, which was later mentioned in connection with the *matstsebhah,* 'pillar,' instead of the tree." He[75] goes on to: "Trees and stones seem to have played a role particularly in the giving of oracles: they 'whisper' or 'murmur' messages. To be sure, they are never used in connection with Atirat, but rather with Ba'al and 'Anat. And yet, the Taanach Letter No. 1, 20f. mentions a mantic of the Asherah." Once again, the formula for purging through excommunication and annihilation is used: "from among you."

Having purged his *imperium* within and thereby protected it against the divine anger against unholiness, *I AM* now promises to protect it against enemies without. V 14(15) is offensive to modern taste both because it speaks of *I AM's* vengeance and of his wrath. "It is too bad," said B. W. Anderson,[76] "that these words ['avenge,' 'vengeance'] are translated from the Hebrew by English words which in our thought world have a negative connotation. No one wants to be regarded as 'vengeful' and therefore it hardly seems right to apply the term to God! However, the Hebrew verb *nāqām* [vindicate] has the basic meaning of 'save' in the Old Testament, as it had in other ancient literature, and therefore can be used in exactly the same sense as the Hebrew verb *yasha'* from which the noun 'salvation' comes." As the exegesis of this word suggests, however, B. W. Anderson has oversimplified the meaning. *wĕ'āśîtî nāqām* "I will avenge my sovereignty" means that *I AM* secures his sovereignty and keeps his community whole by delivering his wronged subjects and punishing their guilty slayers who do not respect his rule. Viewed from the perspective of the Sovereign acting on behalf of his besieged community, a translation such as "deliver" or "rescue" is called for, but where the perspective is between the ruler and the enemy, as in Mic 5:14(15), a translation such as "defeat" or "punishment" is appropriate. Only the Sovereign himself has the legitimate right to use force to protect his *imperium;* the exercise of force by an individual is actually a hostile act. G. E. Mendenhall[77] notes: "With reference to the early usages of NQM, one must conclude that the normative value system of the early biblical society would never tolerate an individual's resorting to force in order to obtain redress for a

---

74. J. C. de Moor, "'ªshērāh," *TDOT* 1:443.

75. de Moor, *TDOT* 1:440.

76. B. W. Anderson, *Out of the Depths: The Psalms Speak for Us Today* (Philadelphia: Westminster, 1974), 64-65.

77. Mendenhall, *The Tenth Generation,* 95.

wrong suffered. . . . Yahweh was the sovereign to whom alone belonged the monopoly of force. Self-help of individuals or even of the society without authorization of Yahweh was an attack upon God himself." To take matters into one's own hand, to avenge oneself, was an act of unbelief, directly challenging the Sovereign's character and power, and brought his rebuff (cf., e.g., Ps 8:3[2]). Only a remnant purified of unbelief would have the faith not to avenge itself but to trust its Lord to protect them. He protects his *imperium* against rebels in fiery anger and wrath.

Today there is widespread neglect, if not denial, of the concept of God's wrath. "Anger in every shape and form is foreign to God Whose mercy is infinite," wrote Nicholas Berdyaev.[78] According to others, divine anger originally belonged to demons, who later became associated with *I AM*;[79] according to Rudolf Otto,[80] the lower "daemonic dread" in primitive relations "has already been long superseded by the time we reach the Prophets and the Psalmists." But the doctrine is found throughout the OT (2 Sam 3:39; Isa 13:9, 16; Amos 3:2; Ps 110:5). Marcion disassociated the angry God of the OT from the loving God of the NT, but R. V. G. Tasker[81] demonstrated the importance and significance of the doctrine in the NT (cf. Rev 6:16).

Some have sought to make God's "strange work" (Isa 28:21) more palatable by restricting the notion of God's wrath to retributive justice. St. Augustine[82] asserted: "The anger of God is not a disturbing emotion of His mind, but a judgment by which punishment is inflicted upon sin." To be sure, retributive justice with its rewards for righteousness and punishment for sin is associated with God's wrath in scores of OT passages, but A. P. Saphir[83] has shown that this notion does not exhaust or explain God's wrath in scores of other passages.

God's wrath against the nations is aroused by their pride (Isa 16:6-7), by their wickedness and brutality (Amos 1:3–2:3), by their oppression of Israel (Obad 10-15), or by the violation of his holiness (Ps 2:12). His anger is also aroused by those who violate his holiness and thumb their noses at him. God extends his holiness in his contact with his property and servants. Those who

78. N. Berdyaev, *Freedom and the Spirit* (New York: Scribner's, 1935), 175.
79. A. Ritschl, *The Christian Doctrine of Justification and Reconciliation*, ed. H. R. Mackintosh and A. B. Macaulay (Edinburgh: T&T Clark, 1900), 3:324.
80. R. Otto, *The Idea of the Holy* (Oxford: Oxford University Press, 1923).
81. R. V. G. Tasker, *The Biblical Doctrine of the Wrath of God* (London: Tyndale, 1956).
82. Augustine, *The City of God* 25:25.
83. A. P. Saphir, "The Mysterious Wrath of Yahweh: An Inquiry into the Old Testament Concept of the Suprarational Factor in Divine Anger" (Ph.D. diss., Princeton Theoloogical Seminary, 1965).

fail to recognize his holiness in these tangible and visible expressions of his presence with mankind violate his very character and incur his awesome wrath, as seen when Uzzah and the men of Beth-shemesh desecrated the ark of the covenant (1 Sam 6:19; 2 Sam 6:7), and when the sons of Korah tried to supplant Moses and Aaron in the handling of the sacred vessels (Numbers 16). David feared to touch *I AM*'s anointed (1 Sam 26:19; cf. 2 Sam 1:14). An affront against God's Person must be met with a wrath that vindicates his honor and his holiness. Saphir[84] comments: "God affirmed and accomplished his absolute claim of lordship and 'otherness' by his wrath which struck back the offenders of his holiness." Ezekiel proclaims judgment to vindicate his honor and holiness (Ezek 20:41; 28:22; 36:21-24). God is not a machine but a person, and some things need to be said and done with passion. His burning wrath and punitive destruction, Micah says, are against nations who do not obey. Nations who disobey him snub his lordship, profane his holiness, and therefore properly incur his wrath and punishment that affirm his very character.

The expression assumes that *I AM*'s legitimate exercise of power extends to the ends of the earth. This study confirms G. E. Mendenhall's[85] thesis, though unfortunately he restricts himself to the Late Bronze Age: "The very many references to Yahweh as the one who acts with legitimate power, which is most characteristic of all usages in the Hebrew Bible, powerfully reinforces the main thesis of these essays, that in the thought of early Israel *I AM* had actually succeeded to and replaced the kings and empires of the Late Bronze Age as far as His community was concerned. *I AM* was the sovereign to whom alone belonged the monopoly of force." That lordship over the nations the Father committed to his Son (Matt 28:18-20; John 17:2; Phil 2:9-11). Paul considered himself as the chief of sinners because he persecuted the church (1 Tim 1:15).

III. THIRD CYCLE: GOD FORGIVES THE REMNANT OF HIS SINFUL PEOPLE (6:1–7:20)

A. Israel Accused of Breaking Covenant (6:1-8)

1   Hear [Micah's audience] what *I AM* says!
        "Arise [Micah]! Make an accusation before the mountains!
           And let the hills hear your voice!"

2   Hear, Mountains, *I AM*'s accusation!

---

84. Saphir, "The Mysterious Wrath of Yahweh," 200.
85. Mendenhall, *Tenth Generation*, 95.

[Hear], Enduring ones: you foundations of the earth!
For *I AM* has an accusation against his people;
    even against Israel he will establish what is right.
3 "My people, what have I done against you?
    and how have I overburdened you?
Testify against me!
4 Surely, I brought you up from the land of Egypt,
    even from a slave house I redeemed you;
and I sent before you
    Moses, Aaron, and Miriam.
5 My people, remember what he plotted,
        that is, Balak king of Moab,
    and how he responded to him,
        that is, Balaam son of Beor.
[Remember the crossing] from Shittim to Gilgal,
    in order to know the saving acts of *I AM*."
6 "How can I come before *I AM*? [— a worshiper asks]?
    Should I bow down to God on high?
Should I come before him with burnt offerings?
    with calves a year old?
7 Would *I AM* be pleased with thousands of rams?
    with myriads of torrents of olive oil?
Should I give my firstborn as my transgression offering?
    the fruit of my body as my sin offering?"
8 It has been told you, Human Being, what is good.
    And what does *I AM* require from you?
[Not these sacrifices!] Rather, [he requires you] to practice justice
        and faithful love
    and walking wisely with *I AM* your God.

EXEGESIS

1   For *šimʿû-nāʾ* (*Hear*), a qal masculine plural imperative of *šmʿ*, see 1:2, 14; 3:1, 9. For the identification of the antecedent see Exposition (373). The *nāʾ* suggests that this section builds on the reproaches and promises of the preceding sections.[1] *ʾēt ʾăšer* (*what*) consists of the emphatic particle *ʾēt*[2] and the so-called

---

1. *IBHS* §34.7.
2. *IBHS* §10.3.

independent relative *'ăšer,* functioning as the object of *šîmû.* The construction is prosaic, showing that this anacrusis is an editorial intrusion, more precisely another introduction, in the book (cf. 1:1; 3:1Aa). On the basis of LXX (*Akousate dē logon Kyrou; Kyrios eipen,* "Hear the word of the Lord. The Lord said"), many interpreters[3] reconstruct *'ēt haddābār 'ăšer.* MT, however, is validated (1) by the same construction in Gen 30:29; 2 Sam 19:36; and (2) by all the other ancient versions and Mur 88, but LXX (1) "made subjects and objects of sentences explicit whereas they were often only implicit in the original text,"[4] (2) has support only in medieval MSS whose "actual value for the recovery of the original text is very small,"[5] and (3) even that is conjecturally emended. *yhwh* (trad. the LORD, *I AM*), the subject of the objective clause to *'ōmer,* invests additional heavenly authority to this section of Micah's book. *'ōmer (says),* a qal masculine singular active participle, functions as a predicate of the verbless objective clause and thus emphasizes the durative circumstance.[6] LXX interpreted this form as typically perfective (cf. 2:3, 4; 3:5; cf. 4:2, 11), but the vocalization of MT is much preferred to that reconstructed by Greek translators.[7]

    qûm (Arise!), a qal masculine singular imperative, is addressed to Micah because no other addressee is mentioned (see also Exposition, 374); the one addressed in turn carries out the instruction of calling the mountains and hills to listen in v 2, and Micah is the one called to mediate God's word in this book (see 1:1). *qûm* "arise" before another imperative means to act quickly (see 2:10) and functions to invest Micah with heavenly authority as *I AM*'s messenger. *rîb (make an accusation)* is a qal masculine singular imperative of the root *ryb.* J. Limburg's[8] form-critical studies confirm the philological studies of E. Würthwein[9] and of J. Harvey[10] that the root *ryb* means "complaint/accusation." Only in Exod 21:18, out of about twenty nontheological uses of its sixty-six occurrences, does it have a reciprocal sense, "quarrel (with one another)"; otherwise, *ryb* denotes an oral complaint made by an aggrieved party against the party held responsible for the grievance. Harvey[11] rightly defines it "to reclaim the right of."

---

3. E.g., Smith, *Micah,* 119; Sellin, "Micha," 294; *BHS.*

4. R. Klein, *Textual Criticism of the Old Testament: The Septuagint after Qumran* (Philadelphia: Fortress, 1974), 75.

5. Würthwein, *The Text of the Old Testament,* 38.

6. *IBHS* §37.6.

7. *IBHS* §1.6.3.

8. J. Limburg, "The Root *ryb* and Prophetic Lawsuit Speeches," *JBL* 88 (1969) 291-97.

9. E. Würthwein, "Der Ursprung der prophetischen Gerichtsrede," *ZTK* 49 (1952) 1-16.

10. J. Harvey. "Le '*Rîb*-Pattern,' Réquisitoire Prophétique sur la Rupture de l'Alliance," *Bib* 43 (1962) 172-96; idem, *Le Plaidoyer Prophétique contre Israël après la Rupture de l'Alliance* (Bruges/Paris: Desclée de Brower; Montreal: Bellarmin, 1967), ch. 1.

11. Harvey, *Le Plaidoyer,* 117.

The preposition *'et (before)* (not to be confused with the emphatic *'ēt* in v 1) after *rîb* elsewhere means "against" (cf. Syr and Vg *adversus*), as do the prepositions *bĕ* (Gen 31:36; Judg 6:32; Hos 2:4[2]) and *'im* (Gen 26:20; Exod 17:2; Mic 6:2). B. Renaud[12] disallows the meaning "before," and, insisting on its usual usages, arrives at[13] the far-reaching conclusion that 6:1b is a gloss reflecting an "eschatological and cosmic re-reading, in perfect agreement with some postexilic prophecies (e.g., Joel 2:10; 4:15-16; Zechariah 14)." But this interpretation must be rejected. (1) It fails to note that *rîb 'et* "to make an accusation against" elsewhere pertains to persons, whereas here the mountains are in view. (2) *'et* means "before" in Gen 20:16 and Isa 30:8[14] and, according to Limburg,[15] "clearly" means that here; LXX has *pros*. (3) *I AM* makes no accusation against the mountains in the rest of the pericope but rather against "my people"; were "against" the meaning, one is left strangely without accusation. (4) The eschatological and cosmic changes in the passages cited have nothing to do with *I AM*'s complaint against the creation; he also made the mountains melt in his punitive epiphany described in Mic 1:3-7. (5) The change of prepositions with *rîb* in 6:1b and 6:2 does not "attest the presence of an intervention into the text," as Renaud[16] thinks, but, more probably, two different meanings. (6) It is wrongheaded to pit Mic 1:1 against 1:2. V 2, reporting Micah's response to *I AM*'s command, shows that Micah understood *'et* in the sense of "before" because he summons the mountains "to hear" *I AM*'s complaint "against his people." (7) The parallel in 6:1bb screens out the usual, but unintended, meaning and brings the text into harmony with 6:2aa, for both share the same subject, "hills/mountains," and the same verb, "hear." S. J. Schwantes[17] changes *'et* to *'al* to get the meaning "before," but fails, because *rîb 'al* also means to "complain against," according to Harvey.[18] For the masculine plural noun *hārîm (the mountains)* see 1:4. The Suzerain summons his messenger to present his lawsuit against his vassal before the mountains probably because, as H. B. Huffmon[19] effectively argued, they functioned as witnesses in validating *I AM*'s case.

In 6:1bb *wětišma'nâ (and let . . . hear)* is a qal jussive, judging from the parallel volitional form in 6:1b of the root *šm'* (see 5:14[15] and 6:1aa) and third feminine plural with *haggĕbā'ōt (the hills)* (see Mic 4:1) as subject. The articles

12. *La Formation*, 291.
13. *La Formation*, 304.
14. BDB 84, §II.1.c.
15. Limburg, "The Root *ryb* and Lawsuit Speeches," 301.
16. Renaud, *La Formation*, 290.
17. Schwantes, "Critical Notes on Micah 1:10-16," 145.
18. Harvey, *Le Plaidoyer*, 117.
19. H. B. Huffmon, "The Covenant Lawsuit in the Prophets," *JBL* 78 (1959) 285-95.

with *hehārîm* and its emphatic parallel *haggĕbāʿôt (the hills)* point to "the mountains/the hills" as the unique referents of the original covenant.[20] In *qôlekā (your voice)* the pronominal suffix presumes that Micah, the prophet in this book, is the antecedent and that this oracle in the preliterary stage was delivered orally. Renaud's suggestion that this is a later gloss inserted into the book tarnishes the text's faithfulness.

2 For *šimʿû (Hear)* see 6:1; but whereas the assumed vocative was Micah's audience for his book, here it is *hārîm (Mountains)* (see 6:1), which perhaps now lacks the article because the "mountains" are more or less imaginary.[21] According to V. Ryssel,[22] Codex Vaticanus, "as also Hab 3:10 *laoi*, stands for *hrym* in all Greek MSS," and the Arabic translation may have substituted "peoples" for *hārîm* under the influence of Mic 1:2. In *ʾet-rîb yhwh (I AM's accusation)* the emphatic particle *ʾet* introduces the definite object of *šimʿû; rîb* is the nominal form of *rîb* in 6:1 with the meaning "accusation/complaint," and *yhwh* is a genitive of authorship.[23] The reader will note the chiasm between 6:1Ba, *rîb ʾet-hehārîm*, and 6:2Aa, *hārîm ʾet-rîb*.

MT's definite masculine plural adjective from the root *ytn*, *hāʾētānîm (Enduring ones)*, is sometimes rendered as an adjective with *mōsĕdîm* (so Aquila, Vg, Sym, Theod) and sometimes interpretively as a substantive (LXX [likewise Arabic] "gorges," Syr "the deep," Tg "the roots"). In spite of the differences among the latter, as Ryssel[24] remarks, "they did not read anything different than the other translations." Nevertheless, most commentators follow Wellhausen's conjecture that the original text was the same as Judg 5:3; Isa 1:2, 10 (cf. Hos 5:1), where *hʾzynw* parallels *šmʿw*. But his conjecture becomes a *lectio facilior*, for why would a scribe substitute *zayin* for *tāw* and double final *mêm* for the conjectured expected parallel, especially when the *uniform tradition* is lexically more rare and grammatically more difficult, and yet provides a helpful explanation as to why the cosmic elements are being summoned in this arraignment? B. Renaud[25] defends this conjecture of "the immense majority of commentators" by arguing that an editor was so shocked by Micah's summoning the foundations of the earth as witnesses to God's trial that he intentionally altered the text to make them present at the birth of Israel. But why should an editor be shocked by Micah's calling the "foundations of the earth to give ear" when twice already the mountains had been summoned? And how does calling

---

20. *IBHS* §13.5.1.
21. *IBHS* §13.5.2.
22. Ryssel, *Micha*, 92.
23. *IBHS* §9.5.1.
24. Ryssel, *Micha*, 92.
25. *La Formation*, 291-92.

the foundations of the earth "enduring" lessen the problem that is addressed in the exposition of v. 1? Does not Renaud support the conjecture because he does not understand the function of these cosmic elements within Israel's worldview? This adjective may mean either "flowing forever, perennial" (cf. Deut 21:4; Amos 5:24; Ps 74:15), or pastures that are always watered (Jer 49:19; 50:44), or "permanent," "enduring" (Exod 14:27; Num 24:21; Jer 5:15; Job 12:19). The latter meaning suits this context best.

The definite article is necessary to show that the word is vocative after the gapped *šim'û;* grammatically, *mōsĕdê 'āreṣ (you foundations of the earth)* stands in apposition to *hā'ētānîm*. What is unusual here, and therefore emphatic, is that the characterizing word comes first.[26] In *mōsĕdê 'āreṣ* "foundations of the earth" *mōsĕdê* consists of the prefix *mem* denoting place,[27] the root *ysd* "to lay a foundation/to establish," and the masculine plural construct ending with *'ereṣ,* an inherently definite noun referring to the unique, what today one calls planet, and a genitive of inalienable possession.[28] O. Keel noted: "The OT postulates pillars (1 Sam 2:8; Ps 75:3; Job 9:6), foundations (Pss 18:8[7]; 82:5), or supports (Ps 104:5) . . . on which the earth disk rests. These conceptions may have an experiential basis in the mighty rock walls, articulated like pillars of the deep-cut wadis. . . ." In Jonah 2:7(6), however, "the roots of the mountains" were at the bottom of the sea. In that light it seems more plausible to suppose that Micah is not introducing other cosmic elements than the one *I AM* commissioned him to invoke and that "foundations of the earth" refers to the roots of the mountains on which the earth is thought to rest. If so, "mountains" and "foundations" represent by a merism: their heights in the clouds, their depths at the earth's foundations (see Exposition, 374-77).

kî (for) substantiates the summons to "hear." *rîb (accusation)* is repeated for the third time in this introduction (see 1:1B and 2Aa). In *layhwh* (I AM *has*) *lĕ* denotes possession in this nominal clause,[29] and the reference to *yhwh* shows clearly that he is the aggrieved party making accusation, with Micah functioning merely as his messenger. For *'im (against)* with *rîb* see 1:1B. Concerning the prepositions *lĕ* and *'im* Renaud[30] comments:

> The construction *ryb lĕ* always designates a trial where the person introduced by the preposition *lĕ* seems to take the initiative. Thus in 2 Sam 15:2, 4, it is a plaintiff who asks for justice from the royal court; in Jer 25:31, the

26. *IBHS* §12.2.
27. *IBHS* §5.6.
28. *IBHS* §9.5.1.
29. BDB 513, §5.b.a.
30. *La Formation*, 292.

formula is in parallel with "to enter into judgment." The preposition *'im* (or *bĕ*), when it is found joined to the formula *ryb lĕ*, introduces the adversaries of the plaintiff, the accused (Hos 4:1; cf. Hos 12:3[2], whereas in Mic 6:2 God starts the trial).

'ammô (his people) consists of the third masculine singular suffix with *yhwh* as its antecedent and of the masculine singular noun *'am (people)* with reference to professing Israel (see 1:9; 2:4, 9, 11), especially the wicked (cf. Ps 50:16), and not the oppressed within it (cf. 2:9; 3:3).

In *wĕ'im (even against)* the *wāw* is ascensive, introducing a specifying and intensifying parallel clause with the preposition *'im*, whose meaning depends on *yitwakkâ*, though the parallel by itself suggests the meaning "against," not "with."[31] *yiśrā'el (Israel)* comes climactically at the end of the introduction and in emphatic parallel with *'ammô (his people)*; in this book "Israel" designates the whole kingdom (see 1:5; cf. Ps 50:7 for the same parallel in a covenant lawsuit). *yitwakkâ (he will establish what is right)*[32] is a hithpael third masculine singular of the root *ykh* (see 4:3), with *yhwh* in the parallel the antecedent. *ykh*, according to G. Liedke,[33] "belongs originally in the sphere of judicial proceedings (cf. 'in the gate' in Isa. 29:21; Amos 5:10)." Following the studies of H. Boecker and F. Horst, he draws the conclusions respectively that its basic meaning in the hiphil is "to establish what is right" and "the legal procedure of setting something right." It is found in connection with *rîb* (in Hos 4:4; Mic 6:2; Job 13:6; 40:2) and with *špṭ* (Isa 2:4 = Mic 4:3; Isa 11:3, 4; Hab 1:12; Job 22:4; 23:4), and with *'nn* (in Job 32:12). It is particularly appropriate in a covenant lawsuit (cf. its use in *rîb* in Isa 1:18; Hos 4:4; Ps 50:8, 21). The notions "to reclaim one's rights" (= *rîb*) and "to establish one's rights" (= *ykh* hiphil) are closely related. M. Dahood[34] translates *ykh* by "accuse" in Ps 50:21. From this basic meaning is derived the meaning "to arbitrate" (Gen 31:7; Mic 4:3), "to justify" (Job 13:3, 15), and sometimes "to reprimand" (Job 13:10, where God would show Job's friends that they are in the wrong). The hithpael is not reciprocal (i.e., "to quarrel"/"argue"),[35] for the form in that case would be plural, a sense that detracts from the force of the root and from *rîb*, which, as stated, does not signify a quarrel between two parties but an accusation of an aggrieved party against the aggrieving party. The double status stem is a benefactive reflexive designating that the action is on the subject's behalf; the full sense is "he will establish what is right

31. *Contra* BDB 407.
32. Cf. GKC §69i for the form.
33. G. Liedke, *THAT* 1:730.
34. M. Dahood, *Psalms 101–150*, AB (Garden City, N.Y.: Doubleday, 1970), 3:305, 310.
35. *Contra* BDB 407.

for himself."[36] That notion also fits *ˁim* with the meaning "against" in both v 6Ba and v 6Bb.

3 The shift from the third masculine singular suffix in *ˁammî (my people)* signals the change from indirect discourse to direct discourse, with *I AM* speaking. By placing this vocative as a *casus pendens*, *I AM* highlights the topic of the verse, his elect people (see v 2). *meh (what)* is the inanimate interrogative pronoun functioning as an accusative.[37] Though exclamatory, this is not a rhetorical question, for *I AM* calls for an answer. *ˁāśîtî (have I done)* is a qal first common singular (with *yhwh* as antecedent) indefinite perfective[38] of the root *ˁśh*. According to J. Vollmer,[39] this root occurs 2,627 times, making it the third most frequent word in the OT; its nuances are exceptionally broad, depending on its many subjects, objects, and prepositions. Its basic meaning in its English equivalents is "to do" or "to make"; here it has its most general sense, "to do" (see Exposition, 378). In 6:3Aa *lĕkā (against you)* the preposition *lĕ*, to judge by the parallel in 6:3Ab, is a *lāmed* of disadvantage,[40] a common use of *lĕ* with *mh*,[41] and the second masculine singular pronominal suffix is a resumptive pronoun in the main clause after the *casus pendens ˁammî (my people)*. For the use of the singular see 5:9-13.

In *ûmâ (and how)* the conjunction *wĕ* introduces another question that adds to and explains the first, and the inanimate interrogative pronoun, taking the pointing of an article, has its exclamatory value, "how," with the adjectival verb *helˀētîkā (have I overburdened you)*.[42] That verb is first common singular, with *I AM* as subject, a two-place hiphil transforming a qal adjectival stative verb "to be overburdened/weary" into a transitive verb (= "to cause to be weary/overburdened") with the second masculine singular suffix, the object of causativity, also a resumptive pronoun with the gapped *ˁammî*. Only elsewhere in Job 16:7 is God used as the subject of *lˀh* hiphil; there Job complains that God's unreasonable demands have worn him out; it is parallel to "devastate." H. Wolff[43] says: "The root *lˀh* expresses overburdening, burdensome, weariness." Syr may witness the presence of the preposition *bĕ* before *mâ*. LXX, in addition to the first question "Wherein have I grieved you?" adds a second that was thought to be more accurate, "What molestation have I given you?"

---

36. *IBHS* §26.2.e.
37. *IBHS* §18.3.
38. *IBHS* §30.5.1.
39. J. Vollmer, *THAT* 2:360.
40. *IBHS* §11.2.10.
41. *IBHS* §18.3.
42. *IBHS* §18.3.
43. Wolff, *Micha*, 147-48.

'ănēh (Testify) is qal masculine singular, addressed to *'ammî*, of the root I *'nh*. This root, according to C. J. Labuschagne,[44] occurs 309 times and does not mean primarily "to answer" but "to respond" (cf. Mic 3:4). Frequently, however, the reaction pertains to words, in which case "answer" is an appropriate translation. In contrast to Mic 3:4, where man takes the initiative in calling upon God for a response, here *I AM* takes the initiative. Labuschagne[45] says: "It is of great theological interest when, even though a human is the subject of *'nh*, not the human but Yahweh, who 'calls,' takes the initiative (*qr'*; Isa 50:2; 65:12; Jer 7:13; 35:17; Job 14:15; further Mic 6:3: 'testify with respect to me'). It is always a matter of a provoking address by Yahweh, eventually expressed by a mediator, leading to a response by man." With *rîb*, signifying a judicial context, one must give the expression *'nh bě* its more precise meaning "to testify/witness against." Says R. B. Alden:[46] "One secondary meaning of this root is 'to testify' with the emphasis on speaking. . . . In many such cases a trial *(rîb)* is in view (1 Sam 12:30). This is especially interesting in passages like Isa 3:9; 59:12; and Jer 14:7 where men are tried and found guilty by God." The meaning "testify against" usually appears with the preposition *bě* as in *bî (against me)*, with the first singular pronominal suffix forming a parallel with the first word of the verse, *'ammî*.

4 *kî (surely)* is a disjunct adverb modifying a clause in relation to the act of speaking, and, in this case, conveys *I AM's* zealous attitude toward the content.[47] The statement in v 4 is also logically connected to v 3; along with v 5 it substantiates with details what *I AM* "did," and it gives the reason why Israel cannot testify against *I AM*: he has done them only good. By substituting the negative *lō'* for *kî*, the Syr seems to have understood the sentence as an interrogative. But were this the intention, one would have expected *hl'*. It is better to stay with the other versions, which understood MT as a declarative clause.

he'ělîtîkā (I brought you up) is first common singular, with reference to *I AM*; past definite perfective,[48] looking back to the Exodus; and a two-place hiphil of the qal intransitive verb *'lh* with the second masculine singular suffix, a reference to *'ammî*, the object of the stem's causativity (= I caused you to come up).[49] Though represented as a preterite situation, in historical fact *I AM's* bringing of Israel up out of Egypt took place over an extended period of time (cf. Exodus 1–15). G. Wehmeier[50] notes that Israel's primeval confession in

44. C. J. Labuschagne, *THAT* 2:336-37.
45. Labuschagne, *THAT* 2:339.
46. R. B. Alden, "*'āna*," *TWOT* 2:680.
47. *IBHS* §39.3.4.
48. *IBHS* §30.5.1.
49. *IBHS* §27.2.
50. G. Wehmeier, *THAT* 2:287.

its relation to *I AM* is that he is the one who brought them up out of Egypt, expressed either by *'lh* hiphil (42 times) or *y'ṣ'* hiphil (76 times). He also says with reference to the former:

> The most important forms are the confession "Yahweh brought us out of the land of Egypt" (Josh 24:17; Judg 6:13; Jer 2:6); the divine speech "I brought you (sing.)": Mic 6:4; Ps 81:11[10] . . . , cf. Gen 46:4; "you (pl.)": Gen 50:24; Exod 3:17; Lev 11:45; Judg 2:1; 6:8; Amos 2:10; "them": 2 Sam 7:6; Amos 3:1, etc.; cf. Exod 3:8, and the expression "Yahweh brought up Israel" (1 Sam 16:6; 2 Kgs 17:7; Jer 16:14; 23:7; Hos 12:14[13]); "you (sing.)": Deut 20:1; "you (pl.)": 2 Kgs 17:36. The introductory formulas show that the formula was used frequently in liturgical situations (cf. the cultic proclamation "Israel, these are . . ." [Exod 32:4, 8; 1 Kgs 12:28]; "this one is . . ." [Neh 9:18]; "where is Yahweh . . . ?" [Jer 2:6]; "has Yahweh not . . . ?" [Judg 6:13; cf. Amos 9:7]; the oath formula "as Yahweh lives . . ." [Jer 16:14; 23:7]; the messenger formula "so says Yahweh" introduces a divine speech in Judg 6:8; 1 Sam 10:18).[51] Usually Yahweh is the subject of the action. It makes no essential difference, however, whether occasionally the angel of Yahweh (Judg 2:1) or Moses (Exod 17:3; 32:1, 7, 23; 33:1, 12; Num 16:13; 20:5) [and Aaron] step in as actors; because through them God himself is at work (cf. Hos 12:14[13], 'through a prophet Yahweh led Israel up out of Egypt'). In Num 21:5 God and Moses are even seen together as subject. Consequently there is no difference between the varying grammatical subjects.

In *mē'ereṣ miṣrayim (from the land of Egypt)* the preposition has its separative sense, "out of," designating movement away from a specified beginning point;[52] *'ereṣ* designates "country" (cf. Mic 5:4, 5[5, 6]); and *miṣrayim* is a genitive of association.[53]

The conjunctive *wāw* in *ûmibbêt 'ăbādîm (even from a slave house)* is ascensive, intensifying in 6:4Ab what was said in 6:4Aa. In this chiastic parallel *min* has the same value as in 6:4Aa, and *bêt 'ăbādîm* functions as a characterizing apposition to "land of Egypt." *bêt* "house" can be used in combinations of structures for varying purposes; in this case it is characterized by *'ăbādîm*, a genitive of species (i.e., a house where slaves live).[54] Only Egypt is likened to a slave house (Exod 13:3, 14; 20:2; Deut 5:6; 6:12; 7:8; 8:14; 13:6[5], 11[10]; Josh 24:17; Judg 6:8; Jer 34:13; Mic 6:4), most instructively in the formula introducing the

---

51. Cf. J. Wijngaards, "*hwṣ'* and *h'lh*: A Twofold Approach to Exodus," *VT* 15 (1965) 99.
52. *IBHS* §11.2.11.
53. *IBHS* §9.5.3.
54. Cf. BDB 109, §1.a.3.9a.

divine speech in connection with the Ten Commandments (Exod 20:2; Deut 5:6). In some contexts, such as that of a servant of a king, *'ebed* can have a very positive sense. Servants of the king are free men; they are not persons deprived of rights; in fact, they could have a high rank and hold high office. In that sense Israel is honored to be called servants of *I AM* (Lev 25:42-43). On the other hand, *'ebed* can just as clearly have a negative sense, as in the texts that speak of Israel in the slave house of Egypt. *pĕdîtîkā (I redeemed you)* is a qal preterite perfective[55] first common singular with the speaking *I AM* as antecedent, with a second masculine singular suffix of the root *pdh* with reference to "my people," whom *I AM* is addressing (see Exposition, 380-81).

wā'ešlaḥ (and I sent) consists of a qal first common singular, with reference to *I AM* as the continuing speaker of the root *šlḥ* "to send," and a *waw*-relative with the short prefix conjugation designating another preterite situation sequential to the perfectives in 6:4A.[56] Though the situations are represented as sequential, in historical fact they overlapped, for Moses, Aaron, and Miriam led Israel out of Egypt. *lĕpāneykā (before you)* is the frozen preposition *lipnê* (cf. 2:13) governing the second masculine singular suffix looking back to "my people" in direct address. The preposition shows that the three persons, marked out by the emphatic particle *'et* before the inherently definite proper names[57] *mōšeh 'ahărōn ûmiryām (Moses, Aaron, and Miriam)*, are singled out for their leadership. All ancient versions smooth the text by adding a conjunction to *'ahărōn*.

5 S. J. Schwantes[58] says of v 5: "Verse 5 has suffered in the hands of the critics more than any other verse in Micah. Marti, Sievers and Gunkel omit it as a historical expansion, while Smith is of the opinion that 'it constitutes an excellent close for this phase of the thought and it conforms to the metric and strophic norm.'" For the repeated vocative in the continued direct discourse, *'ammî (my people)*, see 1:3. Sellin,[59] followed by Lindblom and *BHS*, conjectured transposing *'ammî* to 6:4b and reading it *'immô* "with him" (i.e., Aaron and Miriam with Moses). H. Wolff[60] observes, however, "One can hardly imagine that omission of *'my* at the beginning of v 5 is parallel to the opening of v 3. *zĕkār-nā' (remember)* is a qal masculine singular imperative of the root *zkr* (see Exposition, 383) with the particle *nā'*, which shows that the command is based on the general situation accusing Israel of breaking covenant and calling upon Israel to testify

55. *IBHS* §30.5.1.
56. *IBHS* §§33.2.1; 33.3.1.
57. *IBHS* §10.3.1; GKC §117b.
58. Schwantes, "Critical Notes on Micah 1:10-16," 148.
59. Sellin, "Micha," 295.
60. Wolff, *Micha*, 137.

against *I AM*. The inanimate interrogative *mah (what)* (see 1:3), functioning here as an accusative in an embedded clause in indirect question, approximates in meaning the simple relative *'ăšer*.[61] What he determined is given in Num 22:24: to curse Israel. *yā'aṣ (he plotted/devised)* is a qal third masculine singular preterite perfective[62] of the root *y'ṣ* with reference to Balak. The noun *'ēṣâ* occurs about eighty-five times, and its probable verbal root *y'ṣ* about forty-five times. Its meanings range from "advise/advice," "counsel" to "admonish/admonition," "prophesy/prophecy," "immutable will," depending on the social relationship between the speaker and his audience and the situation in which he speaks. For example, it means "counsel" when his excellency Jethro in Exod 18:19 from the wisdom attained by age and/or experience "counsels" Moses on an organizational plan and how to carry out the administrative responsibilities for ruling and judging Israel; Moses, as chief administrator of the people of God, is not obligated to accept it. On the other hand, in Ps 33:10-11, after using *'ēṣâ* for "the plans" of the nations, which *I AM* thwarts, it is used for *I AM's* "purpose," which stands firm forever. Since Balak is specifically designated a *king*, and the prophet *Balaam* is his hired prophet, the word is better rendered "devised" (NRSV) than "counseled" (NIV [corrected in TNIV to "plotted"]). When the king ordered the prophet according to his own purpose, his will was not open to debate or evaluation. LXX, followed by Syr, paraphrases the text by adding *kata sou (against you)*.

The subject, *bālāq melek mô'āb (Balak king of Moab)*, consists of the proper name *bālāq (Balak)*, which means "lay waste," the sortal appositive *melek* "king,"[63] and the genitive of relation *mô'āb* "Moab." Since Micah reserves the title "king" of Israel to *I AM* (cf. Mic 2:13; 4:9, 14[5:1]; 5:2[3]), the contest recorded in Numbers 22–24 is between the "King of Israel" and the "king of Moab." Although many want to omit the apposition, Schwantes[64] cautions: "Since all the versions support M, one would be particularly wary to delete or add anything to the text. As the verse makes fairly good sense as it reads, and since it may be scanned as a 3:3, 3:3, 2:2, 2:2, we submit that M reproduces substantially the original composition."

In *ûmeh (and how)* the conjunctive *waw* introduces a compound sentence, and *mh* (cf. 6:3 and 6:5Aa), which has a broad repertory of senses,[65] is best rendered in English by "how" because *'ānâ (responded)* is a qal third masculine singular (in agreement with the subject *bil'ām*) preterite perfective[66] of the root

61. *IBHS* §18.3; BDB 552, §1b.
62. *IBHS* §30.5.1.
63. *IBHS* §11.2, 3.
64. Schwantes, "Critical Notes," 149.
65. *IBHS* §18.3.
66. *IBHS* §30.5.1.

ʿnh. The root has its broad meaning "to respond," not just its more precise meaning "to answer," a statement with words, though that too was involved in the encounter between the king and this heathen prophet. The direct object *ʾōtô (to him)* is a personal pronoun; were *ʿānâ* rendered "answer," the direct accusative would be transitive without a preposition, but the English "respond" requires the gloss "to."[67]

bilʿām ben-bĕʿôr (Balaam son of Beor), the subject of the verse *ad sensum,* consists of the proper name *bilʿām (Balaam),* which may derive from *belaʿ ʿām =* "destruction of the people,"[68] of the sortal appositive *ben (son)* and of the genitive of relation *bĕʿôr (of Beor).*[69] The biblical tradition about Balaam son of Beor in Numbers 22–24 and Mic 6:5 finds confirmation in the Balaamite inscription found at Tell Deir ʿAlla, which is generally dated to the time of Micah (i.e., to the late eighth or early seventh century B.C.) on paleographic grounds,[70] though a minority has argued for a mid-eighth-century date.[71] E. Sellin,[72] on the dubious grounds of *metri causa,* wanted to delete both appositives, namely, "king of Moab" and "son of Beor." In that connection A. Weiser,[73] followed by R. Vuilleumier,[74] emends *ben-bĕʿôr* into *bĕʿobrĕkā* "when you crossed over" and places it with the beginning of v 5B, and A. Deissler[75] emends to *b(y)n ʿăbōr* "consider the crossing of." H. Wolff[76] rejects both conjectures because he feels the appositives, attested in all textual witnesses, are original. Instead, he suggests that Deissler's reading dropped out due to haplography. The only difference between the two statements, were *b(y)n* written *defectiva,* would be a metathesis of *bêt* and *ʿayin* in the first and second consonants. In his view some such reading is necessary at the beginning of v 5B because the gapped *zĕkār-nāʾ* needs either an object or a parallel imperative. His proposal merits consideration.

---

67. Cf. *IBHS* §10.2.1.

68. Cf. W. C. Kaiser, *"bilʿam,"* *TWOT* 1:112.

69. *IBHS* §9.5.1.

70. J. Hoftijzer and G. van der Kooij, *Aramaic Texts from Deir ʿAlla* (Leiden: Brill, 1976), 300-302; F. M. Cross, "Ammonite Ostraca from Heshbon: Heshbon Ostraca IV-VIII," *AUSS* 13 (1975) 12; J. A. Hackett, *The Balaam Text from Deir ʿAlla,* HSM 31 (Chico, Calif.: Scholars, 1984), 18.

71. J. Naveh, *Early History of the Alphabet* (Jerusalem: Magnes and Leiden: Brill, 1982), 109; A. Lemaire, "L'Inscription de Balaam Trouvée à Deir ʿAlla: Épigraphie," in *Biblical Archaeology Today: Proceedings of the International Congress on Biblical Archaeology, Jerusalem, April 1984* (Jerusalem: Israel Exploration Society, 1985), 301-12.

72. Sellin, "Micha," 295.

73. Weiser, "Micha."

74. Vuilleumier, "Michée," 72.

75. Deissler, *La Sainte Bible,* 8.

76. Wolff, *Micha,* 138.

One ought not to suppose that by haplography *bĕʿobrĕkā* dropped out of the text, because that proposal would make the clause "when you crossed over from Shittim to Gilgal" merely a temporal circumstantial clause instead of part of Israel's historical credo. B. Renaud rightly objects to Weiser's proposal: "The episode of Balaam . . . represents a central fact of salvation history on the same plain as the coming out from Egypt (Deut 6:21-23; 26:6-9; Josh 24:2-13)." The united textual witness can be maintained by suggesting that, in addition to *zĕkār-nāʾ* being gapped, the preposition *min* with *min-haššiṭṭîm (from Shittim)* is a pregnant preposition implying a word of motion, such as a verbal noun *ʿbwr (crossing over)*.[77] Balaam is mentioned fifty-one times in Numbers 22–24. In the incident recorded there Balak sought propitious omens through the pagan prophet to prosper his attack against Israel, but *I AM* reversed his tactics and instead brought blessing upon Israel through the pagan seer.

The adverbial phrase *min-haššiṭṭîm ʿad-haggilgāl (from Shittim to Gilgal)* does not modify *ʿānâ*, for although Balaam met Israel at Shittim, he did not accompany them to Gilgal. The article with *haššiṭṭîm* elevates a common word *šiṭṭîm* "acacia," trees that grow in dry places, into a proper name.[78] LXX curiously renders *šiṭṭîm* by "rushes." B. Renaud[79] asks whether LXX was thinking of the Sea of Reeds, but notes that this is not the Greek term normally used for that reference. With more probability, Ryssel[80] supposes that *schoinōn* might be an error for *schinon*, the designation of the mastich tree found in Arabia and all over the Near East. The spatial *min*, written fully before the article, designates the location from which the crossing originated,[81] and the spatial *ʿad* looks to the location up to which the movement terminated. The historical scene in view must be Israel's crossing the Jordan, which took place from Shittim to Gilgal (Joshua 3–5). Shittim is to be located at *tell el-hammam*, about 10 km. east of the Jordan rift leading to Jericho, and Gilgal lies on the other side of the Jordan close to Jericho. The conjunction of these prepositions with an implied verb of motion strongly argues against interpretations of the passage that associate Shittim and Gilgal with Israel's sin(s). According to G. J. Botterweck:[82] "In Shittim, which is the last camping site in Transjordan, is the place where Israel broke covenant with Yahweh; in Gilgal, the first camping site in Canaan, the covenant was renewed through circumcision." According to

---

77. Cf. GKC §117ee, ff.
78. *IBHS* §13.6.
79. *La Formation*, 296.
80. Ryssel, *Micha*, 94.
81. *IBHS* §11.2.11.
82. G. J. Botterweck, *"Gott erkennen" im Sprachgebrauch des Alten Testaments* (Bonn: Hanstein, 1951), 47 n. 4.

L. Ligier,[83] Gilgal does not evoke here the first stage of Israel after the Jordan (Josh 4:19), but the high place of that name condemned by Hosea (Hos 4:15). J. Harvey[84] appeals to Hos 9:15, where Gilgal is placed in proximity with Baal-Peor (Hos 9:10). B. Renaud[85] rightly rebuts these interpretations in favor of seeing the reference to God's saving acts in crossing the Jordan:

> In reality Mic 6:5 does not speak at all of Baal-Peor, but of Shittim. However, it is clear that Shittim and Gilgal in Joshua 3–5 frame the crossing of the Jordan, the first as its starting point, the second as its point of arrival, and that text does not envisage at all any sort of covenant renewal. Besides . . . vv 3-5 of Micah 6 re-use an old historical-liturgical credo, which mentions the great facts of the history of salvation: the Exodus and Entrance into the Promised Land. There is usually not present in the credo a reference to Israel's treason. Finally, and above all, Mic 6:3-5 constitutes a justification of God, responding to the reproaches that are not expressed but assumed in the text. The latter supposes that Israel had formulated some grievance against YHWH. God defends himself by reminding them of the great salvific acts of the past. The evocation of Israel's sin has no place here.

lĕmaʿan (in order to) is a frozen preposition consisting of the substantive *maʿan* from the root of either I *ʿnh* "respond"[86] or III *ʿnh* "to be occupied, worried by"[87] and always with preposition *lĕ*. It has two uses: either as a conjunction, in which case it is always with a finite verb, or as a preposition, in which case it precedes either an infinitive or a noun. Normally (but see Mic 6:16) as a preposition it denotes purpose and is best rendered "in order to," but occasionally it indicates result, which is rendered "therefore," "as a consequence." H. A. Brongers[88] says that "the rendering 'in order to' is especially apt, indeed even demanded, when it is a matter of a transitive verb," which is the case here. "Many times," he also notes,[89] "there is no essential difference between *lĕ* and *lmʿn*." Syr's rendering, "because he [Balaam] knew . . . ," cannot be validated by Hebrew grammar. *daʿat (to know)* is a qal infinitive construct of the root *ydʿ* "to know," the most embracive of the Hebrew words for "knowing" (see Exposition, 383). LXX mostly renders the Hebrew construction preposition plus infinitive construction by a finite verb; here, without affecting the sense of the passage, it

83. L. Ligier, *Péché d'Adam, Péché du Monde* (Paris: Aubier, 1960), 1:158 n. 33.
84. Harvey, *Le Plaidoyer*, 44 n. 1.
85. *La Formation*, 295.
86. Cf. BDB 775.
87. Cf. KB 549, 719.
88. H. A. Brongers "*Lĕmaʿan* in der biblisch-hebräischen Sprache," *OTS* 18 (1973) 87.
89. Brongers, "*Lĕmaʿan* in der biblisch-hebräischen Sprache," 84.

chose a passive construction: *hopōs gnōsthē* "so that . . . it might be known." In fact, none of the versions reproduces MT exactly, but none presupposes a different text. The object to be known is *ṣidqôt yhwh* (the saving acts of *I AM*).

ṣidqôt (saving acts) is the feminine plural of *ṣĕdāqâ*, and *yhwh* (*of* I AM) is a genitive of agent.[90] J. Lindblom,[91] T. Robinson,[92] and *BHS* conjecture reading *ṣidqôtāy* "my saving acts," since *I AM* is the speaker. The expression, however, may be stereotyped and the distinction between *I AM* and his prophet is attenuated in this book. B. Renaud,[93] who rejects the emendation, says: "The sliding from God to his messenger is frequent in prophetic literature."[94] The writer opts with NRSV and J. P. Hyatt[95] to render *ṣidqôt* by "saving acts" because it is now established that *ṣedeq/ṣĕdāqâ* denotes satisfying the demands of a covenantal relationship. Concerning *I AM*'s obligation toward Israel, E. Achtemeier[96] says: "Yahweh's righteousness is his fulfillment of the demands of the relationship which exists between him and his people Israel, his fulfillment of the covenant which he has made with his chosen nation." He upholds the right, so that when his covenant people are threatened and afflicted, as in the case of Balak and Balaam, he delivers them. For this reason his righteousness becomes equated with his deliverance. Achtemeier,[97] after citing several passages, says: "In short, Yahweh's righteous judgments are saving judgments. . . . Yahweh's salvation of Israel is his righteousness, his fulfillment of his covenant with her." V 5B appears uniquely to I. Willi-Plein[98] "to be added later as a theological explication of the data of salvation history." Against her conjecture B. Renaud[99] notes that "remember . . . in order that you might know" is found several times in Deuteronomy and forms an indissoluble literary scheme.

6 *bammâ (how)* consists of the preposition *bĕ*, which governs the material with which the act is performed[100] and in this case what one brings with one[101] (= "with what" [NRSV, TNIV]). The compound, however, adds the further nuance of "with what means," "whereby," "how."[102] TNIV elsewhere renders

---

90. *IBHS* §9.5.1.
91. Lindblom, *Micha*, 99.
92. Robinson, "Micha," 144.
93. *La Formation*, 296.
94. For other uses of the plural *ṣidqôt* denoting "righteous acts" see BDB 842, §7a.
95. J. P. Hyatt, "The Translation and Meaning of Amos 5:23-24," *ZAW* 68 (1956) 22.
96. E. Achtemeier, "Righteousness in the Old Testament," *IDB* 82.
97. Achtemeier, *IDB* 83.
98. Willi-Plein, *Vorformen*, 98.
99. *La Formation*, 296.
100. *IBHS* §11.2.5.
101. BDB 89, §1b.
102. Cf. BDB 553, §4a.

BDB's other examples of the compound not in direct discourse by "how" (cf. Gen 15:8; Exod 33:16; 1 Sam 6:2; 2 Sam 21:3; Mal 1:2, 6, 7; 2:17; 3:7, 8), but uniquely here by "with what." That the speaker intended the normal sense is clear from Micah's answer to the question: "And what does *I AM* require of you?" *'ăqaddēm (can I come before)* is a denominative piel[103] first common singular nonperfective of the root *qedem* "front" (= "come or be in front," "meet"). *qdm* piel signifies the meeting between human beings in Deut 23:5; Isa 21:14. It has the same meaning with reference to God, but because of the difference in social status between God and man, it is best rendered in that relationship "to come before." The parallel question in v 7, "Would *I AM* accept . . . ?" and Micah's answer in v 8 show that the nonperfective has the modal nuance of capability (= "can").[104] The antecedent of "I" is a petitioner seeking access to God; more specifically, he seems to be a king, at least to judge from the size of his offering (see v 7) and his representative capacity. Vv 6-7 probably are an adaptation of a liturgy sung in connection with entering the temple, a liturgy that consists of a question about what is required for entering into the temple followed by priestly instruction (cf. Pss 15:1 and 2-5; 24:3 and 4; Isa 33:14B and 15) (see Exposition, 386-87). *yhwh (I AM)* is the direct object, showing that *I AM* who was the speaker in vv 3-5 is no longer the one speaking in vv 6-7.

'ikkap (Should I bow down) is a unique niphal first common singular deliberative nonperfective[105] of the root *kpp*. The root surprisingly is not found elsewhere in cultic language. In qal it designates the posture of one fasting, whose head is bent over like a reed; in Ps 57:7(6) the word appears in the language of the hunt; in Pss 145:14; 146:8 it describes one bowed down under affliction. The niphal is reflexive[106] and describes the deportment of the petitioner, who in deep humiliation humbles himself by bowing down his whole body before "God on high." In *lē'lōhê mārôm (to God on high)* the *lĕ* has its allative nuance (i.e., its spatial sense of marking the object of motion "toward"),[107] and *mārôm* is a genitive of location,[108] a not uncommon reference for heaven as the place of God's throne and his dwelling (Isa 33:5; 57:15; Ps 93:4, etc.). *'ĕlōhîm*, a reference to God in his transcendence, is a fitting parallel to *yhwh* in conjunction with *kpp* and *mārôm* (cf. 3:7; 4:2). LXX interpretively renders the compound by *theou mou hypsistou* "God very high," the usual translation for *'ēl 'elyôn*.

ha'ăqaddĕmennû (should I come before him) consists of interrogative *hă*

---

103. *IBHS* §24.4.
104. *IBHS* §31.4.
105. *IBHS* §31.4.
106. *IBHS* §23.4.
107. *IBHS* §11.2.10.
108. *IBHS* §9.5.2.

asking a polar question demanding a "yes or no" answer,[109] the denominative piel first common singular deliberative imperfective of the root *qdm* (see the parallel in v 6Ab), and the third masculine singular pronominal suffix with so-called energic *nûn*[110] with *yhwh* in the parallel the antecedent. In *bĕʿôlôt (with burnt offerings) bĕ* has the same value as in the parallel, and *ʿôlôt*, a feminine plural of *ʿôlâ*, designating the whole burnt offering, all of which was consumed, except the hide and what could not be cleaned, in flame and smoke on God's altar.

The abstract *bĕʿôlôt*[111] is now specified in the appositive parallel as *baʿăgālîm bĕnê šānâ (with calves a year old)*. *bĕnê šānâ* is itself an appositive to *ʿăgālôm*,[112] consisting of the Hebrew idiom *bēn* and the attributive genitive to represent the nature, quality, or condition of someone/thing, in this case more specifically the age, *šānâ* "a year old."[113] The petitioner begins escalating the value of that which he hopes will win him an encounter with God by offering a valued offering. A year-old calf is esteemed on account of its tenderness as a preferred sacrifice, though it appears only in Lev 9:3 as a burnt offering. From the eighth day of life onward calves, sheep, and goats could be offered (Lev 22:27).

7 *hăyirṣeh (would I AM . . . be pleased)* consists of the polar interrogative *hă* (see v 6) and qal third masculine singular with *yhwh* as subject, and a deliberative (cf. v 6) nonperfective of the root *rṣh* "to accept, be pleased." This further refinement of *qdm* "to come before" specifies the idea of finding acceptance and so granted an audience with God. God's acceptance of the offering also entails his acceptance of the one offering it (cf. Judg 13:23). In Gen 33:10 it is parallel to *māṣāʾtî ḥēn bĕʿênêkā* "I have found favor in your eyes." H. Wolff[114] says, "*rṣh* means the act of (agreeably) accepting the offering in the sense of the cultic-judicial recognizing and crediting that is spoken by the priest in the name of Yahweh on the basis of some special cognizance. If the priest recognizes the offering, then at the same time God himself has accepted the one making the offering (cf. Lev 1:4; 7:18; 19:7; 22:23, 25, 27; Jer 14:10, 12; Ezek 20:40f; Hos 8:13; Amos 5:22; Ps 51:18[16])." The Coptic version caught the sense by adding "me" as direct object of the verb. Many[115] want to omit the subject *yhwh*, but T. Lescow[116]

---

109. *IBHS* §40.3; cf. Mic 2:7.

110. Cf. *IBHS* §31.1.

111. Cf. *IBHS* §6.4.2.

112. *IBHS* §12.3.

113. *IBHS* §9.5.2.

114. Wolff, *Micha*, 151-52.

115. Cf. Schwantes, "A Critical Study," 153; Vuilleumier, "Michée," 72; Willi-Plein, *Vorformen*, 98; *BHS*.

116. T. Lescow, *Micha 6:6-8: Studien zur Sprache, Form, und Auslegung* (Stuttgart: Calwer, 1966).

points out: "Yahweh appears in all three verses [of this liturgy] as the expressly mentioned subject, and must be maintained." In *bĕʾalĕpê ʾêlîm (with thousands of rams)* the preposition *bĕ* functions the same as in v 6, and the masculine plural *ʾalĕpê* "thousands," a vague indicator of great magnitude[117] is followed by the genitive of measure *ʾêlîm* "rams."[118] Here is the second qualitative escalation of the costly objects, but it is the first of an immense addition suggesting that the speaker is a king (see Exposition, 387-88).

bĕribĕbôt naḥălê-šāmen (with myriads of torrents of olive oil) consists of the preposition *bĕ* (see parallel and v 6), the feminine plural construct of *rĕbābâ* "multitude, myriad, ten thousand," designating vaguely a very large number and the normal parallel to *ʾlp* "thousand"; it is followed by the item enumerated *naḥălê-šāmen* ("wadis of oil"), a masculine plural construct of II *nāḥāl*, "a dry river bed or ravine which in the rainy season becomes a raging torrent, and/or the resulting torrent [cf. Ezek 47:5; Amos 5:24; Ps 104:10],"[119] and the genitive of material, "olive oil."[120] Instead of *cheimarron* "torrential," Codex Vaticanus (followed by Syr) reads *chimaron* "goats." It differs only by the addition of an *e* and the doubling of the *r*, a confusion facilitated by "rams" in the parallel. While it is true that *rbbh* is the normal parallel of *ʾlp* (cf. 1 Sam 18:7; Dan 7:10; Ps 91:7), the escalation here is not merely stylistic but intentional, for it is part of the ever-mounting sacrifices deliberated by the petitioner.

haʾettēn (should I give) in parallel with *hăyirṣeh* consists of a polar *hă*, a qal first common singular with reference to the petitioner in direct discourse, and the deliberative nonperfective of the root *ntn* "to give," more specifically "to give an offering,"[121] with "to Yahweh" elided but understood from the parallel. *bĕkôrî (my firstborn),* consisting of *bkwr* and the first common singular pronominal suffix, a genitive of inalienable possession,[122] functions as a direct-object accusative,[123] and the masculine noun *pišʿî (as my transgression offering),* consisting of *pšʿ* ("transgression offering")[124] and the first common singular pronominal suffix, a genitive of possession,[125] functions as an adverbial accusative of state, specifying a feature of the firstborn when it is given.[126] For the

117. *IBHS* §15.2.5.
118. *IBHS* §9.5.3.
119. L. J. Coppes, *"naḥal,"* *TWOT* 2:570.
120. *IBHS* §9.5.3.
121. BDB 679, §1.k.
122. *IBHS* §9.5.1.
123. *IBHS* §10.2.1.
124. BDB 833, §6.
125. *IBHS* §9.5.1.
126. *IBHS* §9.5.2.

meaning of *ḥaṭṭa't* see Mic 1:5; 3:8. While *ḥaṭṭa't* commonly means "sin offering" (cf. Lev 7:37; 2 Kgs 12:17),[127] *pšʿ* is used uniquely with this sense here. T. Robinson,[128] followed by T. Lescow[129] and J. T. Willis,[130] rejects this interpretation. "Rather," he says, "here also occurs an accus. causae." None of these authors, however, validates the interpretation grammatically. A. Deissler,[131] followed by R. Renaud,[132] renders it "for the price of my transgression . . . for the price of my sin," but again without grammatical justification.

The parallel to *běkôrî, pěrî biṭnî (fruit of my body)* consists of the masculine construct *pěrî* "fruit" and the genitive of inalienable possession *bṭn*. *bṭn* can mean either "womb" or "body" in opposition to *nepeš* "soul." From the Hebrew point of view the former is preferred here because "soul" does not occur in opposition to it — the linguistic situation when it means "body" — and it can refer to the father (cf. Ps 132:11, where God says to David: "from the fruit of your womb" *(bṭn)*.[133] From the English point of view, however, that translation is impossible. T. Lescow[134] says that the pronoun qualifies the *nomen regens* and the expression should be rendered "my child." B. Renaud[135] responds: "Grammatically the comment is right, but the translation loses much of its color. The expression 'fruit of my flesh' expresses the carnal attachment of the father to his child and the present context underlines the costly character of the expiation proposed. . . ." The parallel to *pišʿî* is *ḥaṭṭa't napšî (my sin offering)*, consisting of the feminine singular construct *ḥaṭṭa't* and the possessive genitive *napšî. napšî*, which consists of the feminine singular of *npš* and the first common singular suffix, a possessive genitive, functions in the parallel as a surrogate for the pronominal suffix "yet," as I[136] said elsewhere of this use, "its intensive, passionate sense peculiar to the word is always present." V 7вb heightens and explains 7ва, while gapping *ha'ettēn*.

8 *higgîd (It has been told)* is an unclassified hiphil third masculine singular indefinite perfective[137] of the root *ngd*, which means "to be conspicuous" (cf. Mic 1:10). Because the antecedent, the subject, of the third masculine singu-

---

127. See BDB 309, §4.

128. Robinson, "Micha," 146.

129. Lescow, *Micha 6:6-8,* 54 n. 41.

130. J. T. Willis, "Review of *Micah 6:6-8: Studien zu Sprache, Form, und Auslegung,* by Theodor Lescow," *VT* 18 (1968) 274.

131. Deissler, *La Sainte Bible,* 8:343.

132. *La Formation,* 296.

133. BDB 106, §3.

134. Lescow, *Micha 6:6-8,* 53.

135. *La Formation,* 297.

136. B. K. Waltke, "*nepesh*," *TWOT* 2:590.

137. *IBHS* §30.5.

lar is undetermined, Wellhausen,[138] followed by many (cf. *BHS*), reconstructs the hophal, appealing to LXX's *anēngelē*, a second aorist passive. More probably, however, LXX reflects a translator's choice of rendering the indefinite third masculine singular "one," the so-called "impersonal subject," by the passive.[139] The indefinite perfective matches this indefinite subject (see Exposition, 390). In *lĕkâ (to you)* the *lĕ* signifies an indirect object after the verb of speaking,[140] and the second masculine singular refers to the imagined petitioner in vv 6-8, showing that the direct discourse ends with v 7.

'ādām (Human Being) is vocative. B. Renaud[141] draws the conclusion that the term belongs to the covenant people. His discussion is important for lexical, theological, and literary reasons:

> T. Robinson[142] underlined that vv 1-5 deal only with Israel, while the term "man" gives to v 8 a universal import. J. Harvey[143] justly refuted such an argument: vv 6-7 refer to a ritual that is properly Israelite. Let us add, on our part, that the term *mšpṭ* designates the law of the covenant and that *ḥsd* expresses the solidarity that must be manifested in the midst of this same covenant. The eventuality of a sacrifice of the firstborn corresponds perfectly to the mentality of the people at this time because this kind of cultic rite, [though] prohibited by the Law, already appears at the time of Ahaz (2 Kgs 16:3) and therefore of Micah. Especially, "the word *'adam* itself occurs two times in the context of *rîb*, in order to designate the hearer of the requestor, who is always a partner of a covenant (Hos 6:7; Isa 58:5)."[144]
>
> It remains to be said that the use of this term *'ādām* remains difficult to interpret. J. Harvey appeals to a purely lexical phenomenon, namely, the usual designation of man by *'ādām*, in preference to *'îš*, in the Northern Kingdom. That fact is unquestionably accurate with respect to the Phoenician branch of Northwest Semitic,[145] but one has not been able to prove it at the level of Hebrew lexicography because the history of the language is still badly understood. Usually one orients oneself toward a theological explanation for *'ādām* in this text. According to R. Hentschke,[146] the prophet

138. Wellhausen, *Die kleinen Propheten*, 147.
139. *IBHS* §4.4.
140. *IBHS* §11.2.5.
141. *La Formation*, 316-17.
142. Robinson, "Micha," 145.
143. Harvey, *Le Plaidoyer*, 43.
144. Harvey, *Le Plaidoyer*, 43.
145. M. Dahood, "Canaanite-Phoenician Influence in Qohelet," *Bib* 33 (1952) 202-3.
146. R. Hentschke, *Die Stellung der vorexilischen Schriftpropheten zum Kultus*, BZAW 75 (Berlin: Töpelmann, 1957), 106.

wants to underline in that way the character of the creature and the necessity of submission to God. But one can also think that the term "reaches each one in what he has of a universal and of a singular character,"[147] while it addresses the members of the covenant. Should one see in it a discrete reminder that righteous people can exist outside of the covenant? The fact that the expression "to walk with God" is found only concerning Enoch (Gen 5:22, 24) and Noah (Gen 6:9) would support this hypothesis. But one cannot press such a correspondence because the vocabulary differs somewhat: these two texts put the verb "to walk" in the hithpael and not in the qal, and construe it with the preposition 'et instead of 'im. [Moreover, those uses occur before the institution of the covenant relationship between I AM and Israel.] Others want to see in it an echo of Genesis 1–3: "The hearer is in view, less as a member of the community than as encompassed in the general condition of man, such as Genesis defines it."[148] Likewise, T. Lescow[149] draws attention to the fact that the expression *higgîd lĕkā* occurs in Gen 3:11. Each member of the covenant must not try to escape the fundamental condition of every man as man, who is required to search out what is *ṭôb* "good," like Adam in the book of Genesis. It may be, however, that . . . in the final analysis vv 6-8 are addressed to the members of the people of God, just as vv 2-5 had in view the nation itself.

The inanimate interrogative *mah (what)* functions in the indirect discourse the same way as in v 5. The masculine singular predicate nominative of identification[150] *ṭôb (is good)* signifies "moral good" (cf. Mic 3:2) and functions by metonymy for I AM's requirements (see Exposition, 391). *ûmâ (and what)* consists of disjunctive *wāw* in an explanatory or parenthetical use,[151] and the inanimate interrogative functioning as an accusative (cf. v 3). *dôrēš (require)* is a qal masculine singular active participle (in its predicate use of emphasizing a durative circumstance and not an event)[152] of the root *drš*, which means "to seek with care,"[153] a notion that implies movement, action, activity, and energy.[154] With the abstract objects that follow it is used figuratively, and with *yhwh* (I AM) as its subject it is also used anthropomorphically.[155]

147. L. Ligier, *Péché d'Adam*, 159.
148. Ligier, *Péché d'Adam*, 159.
149. Lescow, *Micha 6:6-8*, 649.
150. *IBHS* §8.3.
151. Cf. Lambdin, *Introduction to Biblical Hebrew*, 164, entry (c).
152. *IBHS* §37.6.
153. Cf. L. J. Coppes, *"dārash,"* *TWOT* 1:198.
154. Cf. S. Wagner, *TDOT* 3:294, 295.
155. *Contra* Wagner, *TDOT* 3:298, 304.

kî 'im, "but" *(rather)* is a clausal restrictive adverb intermediate in sense between negative and emphatic adverbs and highlighting the special status of the clause it introduces. Here it entails some elision: the full thought is, "You thought *I AM* requires sacrifice, *but rather* he requires ethical behavior."[156] *'ăśôt (to practice)* is the qal infinitive construct of *'śh* (see v 3). J. Vollmer[157] notes: "The sphere of personal relationships, the responsibility of a person toward another human or toward God, is frequently expressed by the verb *'śh* in manifold ways . . . with a whole series of nouns in the accusative: *mišpāṭ* "justice" (over 50 times). . . ." For *mišpāṭ (justice)* cf. 3:1, Exposition (391-92). *wĕ'ahăbat (and . . . love)* consists of the conjunction *waw* and the qal infinitive construct of the root *'hb* (see Mic 3:2). On the basis of parallels in the *Manual of Discipline*, J. P. Hyatt[158] draws the conclusion that the infinitives *'ahăbat* and *leket* are not parallel to *'ăśôt* but its objects, along with *mšpṭ*. In that case, he further argues that *ḥesed* is not the object of *'ahăbat* but an attributive genitive after the construct, meaning "*ḥesed* love" or "love of the *ḥesed* type." He rejects as grammatically impossible Brownlee's suggestion, based on the same data, that it be translated "loving devotion," but *ḥesed* could be an exepegetical genitive.[159] Nevertheless, the attributive genitive is more usual and more likely if *'ahăbat* is the object of *'ăśôt*. For the meaning of *ḥesed (faithful)* see Exposition (392-93). In sum, the *nomen regens*, *'ahăbat*, and its modifier, *ḥesed*, underscore the covenantal and spiritual nature of what *I AM* requires.

Micah now moves to the horizon of Israel's covenantal responsibilities toward one another, namely, their walk with the Author of the covenant. *haṣnēa' (and . . . wisely)* consists of conjunctive *waw* and the *hapax* hiphil infinitive absolute, which is used adverbially to qualify *leket*,[160] of the root *ṣn'*, also found as a qal passive participle in Prov 11:2. Although traditionally the adverb is rendered "humbly," D. W. Thomas,[161] J. Hyatt,[162] and H. J. Stoebe[163] see this meaning as secondary. Thomas looks to cognate languages for its meaning: in Aramaic, "to guard, hold back, reserve," a meaning reflected in Quinta's *phronizein* "consider, reflect, pay attention," in Vg's *sollicitum* "solicitous," in Sym's *para de tois epimelesi* "with the careful, attentive," and in South Semitic "to strengthen,"

---

156. Cf. *IBHS* §39.3.5.

157. J. Vollmer, "'*śh, machen, tun*," *THAT* 2:362.

158. J. P. Hyatt, "On the Meaning and Origin of Micah 6:8," *ATR* 34 (1952) 232-39.

159. *IBHS* §9.5.3c.

160. *IBHS* §35.3.2.

161. D. W. Thomas, "The Root *ṣn'* in Hebrew, and the Meaning of *qdrnyt* in Malachi 3:14," *JJS* 1 (1949) 182-88.

162. Hyatt, "On the Meaning and Origin of Micah 6:8," 232-39.

163. H. Stoebe, *THAT* 2:565-68.

reflected in Theodotion's *aspalizou* "to forgive, secure, make fast." He brings the two together in suggesting that the basic meaning of *ṣn'* is "to guard, strengthen." He further thinks that the strong, guarded man is in a state of readiness, explaining LXX *hetoimon einai* "to be ready." Stoebe tries to validate the meaning "guard, strengthen" from four passages in Sirach, one of which is a hiphil infinitive absolute, which he renders "with care, circumspection, discretion, moderation." The jump, however, from "to strengthen, to guard," to the semantic domain of "to be discreet" is neither certain nor convincing. J. P. Hyatt and H. J. Stoebe bypass the cognates and begin with the qal passive forms in Sir 34:22 (LXX 31:22) and 42:8 and the hiphil infinitive in 16:25, rendered by the Greek *en akribeia* "with exactness," and 35:3 (LXX 32:3, where Hebrew *hṣn' śkl* is represented in the Greek by *en akribei epistēmē* "with sound understanding"). They also look to its use in the *Manual of Discipline:* 1QS 4:5; 5:4; 8:2 (*hṣn' lkt* as in Mic 6:8). The last is most significant because it also includes both *'ăśôt* and *'ahăbat ḥesed*. Hyatt renders 1QS 8:1-3: "In the council of the Community there shall be twelve laymen and three priests who are blameless in all that has been revealed from the whole torah concerning the doing (*'ăśut*) of truth and righteousness and justice and *'hbt ḥsd* and *hṣn' lkt*, everyone with his neighbor." Stoebe[164] notes "the general affinity to expressions for 'wisdom, prudence' (*ḥokmâ,* Prov 11:2; *śkl,* Sir 35:3; *d'y,* Sir 16:25; *'ormā,* 1QS 4:5-6). Furthermore, against the consensus of the versions that renders *ṣānûa'* in Prov 11:2 by "humility," Stoebe thinks that it can scarcely mean that. "Rather," he says, "it must be understood after the analogously constructed Prov 13:10 (*y'ṣ* niphil 'to allow oneself to be advised') as an expression for discerning behavior, to which *zādôn* 'arrogance' stands in opposition." Stoebe finds that meaning confirmed in Sir 34:22 and 42:8. He concludes: "In the three passages from the Qumran texts the behavior of the members within the community constitutes the focal point, yet even here it is a matter of insight and understanding for the furthering of the community." All three scholars come to the meaning "circumspectly," but Hyatt and Stoebe more specifically see it as a wisdom word for prudence or skill. The hiphil may be denominative, "to cause oneself to behave wisely."[165]

leket (to walk) is a qal infinitive construct of *hlk* "to walk," a common metaphor for behavior in life. Following 1QS 8:3 Hyatt makes it an object of *'ăśôt* (i.e., "to practice . . . living wisely"), but Stoebe[166] seems to take it as a parallel to *'ăśôt*. That is possible because of the disjunctive accent with *ḥesed* and because v 8ʙʙα pertains to one's behavior toward the community, whereas

164. Stoebe, *THAT* 2:567.
165. *IBHS* §27.4.
166. Stoebe, *THAT* 2:567.

v 8Bbβ has to do with behavior toward God. On the other hand, the parallels in the *Manual of Discipline* and in this verse favor Hyatt's interpretation. BDB[167] thinks that the preposition *ʿim (with)* means here dealing with (i.e., *toward*) a person, or the relation in which one stands with/toward another. But that does not tally well with the verb *hlk*. Here it has its more usual meaning of fellowship and companionship. *ʾĕlōheykā (your God)*, the object of the preposition, consists of the second masculine singular pronominal suffix with reference to the elect community and *ʾĕlōhîm* (see Mic 6:6).

EXPOSITION

After the prose anacrusis in 6:1A, calling upon Micah's audience to hear the new and final section of his book, chapters 6–7, and validating its divine source and timelessness, the first oracle, 6:1B-8, follows essentially the form of a *rîb* "a lawsuit speech" (cf. Isa 1:2-3, 18-20; 3:13-15; [5:1-7]; Jer 2:5ff.; 25:31; Hos 2:4-17[2-15]; 4:1-3, 4-6; 12:3-15[2-14]; Mic 6:1-5; Mal 3:5; cf. also C. Westermann[168]). A detailed description of this trial form is given by H. Gunkel.[169] In outline this form essentially is:

I. A description of the judgment scene
II. The speech of the plaintiff
   A. Heaven and earth appointed judges
   B. Summons to the defendant (or judges)
   C. Address in second person to the defendant
      1. Accusation in question form to the defendant
      2. Refutation of the defendant's possible arguments
      3. Specific indictment

Bearing this form in mind, Micah 6:1-8 can be analyzed thus:

I. Judgment Scene (vv 1B-2).
   A. *I AM* summons Micah to make accusation before the mountains (v 1B).

---

167. BDB 767, §d.

168. C. Westermann, *Basic Forms of Prophetic Speech* (Philadelphia: Westminster, 1967), 199.

169. H. Gunkel, *Einleitung in die Psalmen: Die Gattungen der religiösen Lyrik Israels* (Göttingen: Vandenhoeck & Ruprecht, 1933), 364-65; cf. C. Westermann, *Isaiah 40–66*, OTL (Philadelphia: Westminster, 1969), 17-19.

B. Micah summons the enduring mountains to hear the accusation against Israel (v 2).

II. The Covenant Lawsuit (speech of plaintiff in second person): *I AM*'s Case against Israel Based on His Sovereign Grace in Israel's Formative Period (vv 3-5).

A. *I AM* accuses Israel of false charges and implicitly accuses them of unreciprocated fidelity by reciting their exodus from Egypt (vv 3-4).

1. Summary accusation in question form: *I AM* accuses Israel of false charges of wrongdoing (v 3).

2. *I AM* implicitly accuses Israel of unreciprocated fidelity by reciting Israel's miraculous exodus from Egypt (v 4).

   a. He brought them up out of Egypt (v 4A).

   b. He gave them exceptional leaders (v 4B).

B. *I AM* calls upon Israel to renew the covenantal relationship by reciting Israel's miraculous entrance into the sworn land and implicitly accuses them of forgetting his covenant faithfulness (v 5).

1. *I AM* commands Israel to "remember" the safe passage through Moab (v 5A).

2. and across the Jordan that they might know his saving acts (v 5B).

III. A Torah Liturgy (a refutation of wrong response): *I AM* rejects costly gifts as an acceptable means of atonement for sin and access into his presence; rather, he demands justice that proceeds from a spiritual covenant (vv 6-8).

A. *I AM* rejects costly gifts (vv 6-7).

B. *I AM* requires justice and covenantal fidelity (v 8).

1. *I AM* made known what he requires (v 8A).

2. *I AM* requires covenantal solidarity (v 8B).

   a. with one's fellow (v 8Ba).

   b. with God (v 8Bb).

H. J. Boecker[170] introduced the illuminating distinction between discourses of accusation *(Anklagerede)* and discourses of defense *(Verteidigungsrede)*, the latter being subdivided into counterattack, on the one hand, and the demonstration of innocence, on the other. He also noted a distinction between the judicial processes prior to the trial and the unfolding of the trial itself. Mic 6:1-5 would correspond to a discourse of defense. God defends himself as an ac-

---

170. H. J. Boecker, "Anklagereden und Verteidigungsreden im Alten Testament," *Evangelische Theologie* 20 (1960) 398-412.

cused human: "What did I do to you?" and sends back to his adversary his own words in vv 4-5, which in all probability were taken from an ancient confession of faith. To be sure, this study has the merit of putting into new light the pleading aspect of v 3, but it must be rejected as the definitive understanding of its form.

B. Renaud[171] noted that it fails to do justice to the fact that God takes the initiative: *I AM* has a case against Israel (v 2), and he challenges them to formulate precise charges against him (v 3). He says: "It is YHWH who speaks and provokes his people to the debate." Besides, Renaud notes the interrogative style alongside the plea of the defense: "One finds it, for example, in the Mari texts as an introduction to an act of accusation addressed to King Zimri-Lim." T. Lescow, who prefers to speak of Mic 6:1-5 as a discourse of appeal *(Appellationsrede)*, notes several mistakes of Boecker: v 1B does not address the people but the prophet who was summoned to open the debate. By reporting the words that God addressed to him the prophet communicates something of the experience of revelation. More to the point, the affinity of Mic 6:1-4A with Jer 2:5-8 justifies regarding the piece as accusation. With L. Allen[172] we also note that elsewhere in covenant lawsuits after "interrogation of the guilty party (cf. Deut 32:4-67; Ps 50:16-17)" there follows "an accusation of Israel's ingratitude, including a recital of benefits they have received from Yahweh (cf. Deut 32:7-15; Ps 50:7-13, 18-21)," and "a rejection of recourse to sacrifice to Yahweh or other gods (Deut 32:16-18; Ps 50:8-13)."

H. Huffmon,[173] following other studies, especially that of G. E. Mendenhall[174] demonstrated that these covenant lawsuits dip their roots into the Hittite international treaties preserved from the latter part of the second millennium, to which Huffmon adds an Aramean treaty from the eighth century. J. Harvey[175] also came to the conclusion that the *rîb* derives from the sacred international law of the second half of the second millennium. These treaties invoke the cosmic elements and the deities that belong to them to bear witness to the treaties. Huffmon validates this appeal to extrabiblical literature by noting that within biblical literature the appeal to natural phenomena, other than in connection with the lawsuit (cf. Isa 1:2-3; Jer 2:4-13; Mic 6:1-8), are connected with covenant ceremonies (Deut 4:26; 30:19; 31:28). On these two bases he draws

---

171. *La Formation*, 306.

172. Allen, *Micah*, 364.

173. E. Huffmon, "The Covenant Lawsuit," *JBL* 78 (1959).

174. G. E. Mendenhall, *Law and Covenant in Israel and the Ancient Near East*, Pittsburgh Biblical Colloquium, 1955 (repr. from *BA* 17 [1954] 24-46, 49-76).

175. J. Harvey, "The 'Rîb-Pattern,' Réquisitoire Prophètique sur la Rupture d'Alliance," 172-96.

the conclusion: "The natural elements appealed to in the 'lawsuit' oracles . . . are addressed because they are witnesses to the (prior) covenant." Huffmon further supported his thesis by noting the resemblance between the recitations of *I AM*'s saving acts in the prophetic lawsuits with reference to the Exodus, wilderness wanderings, and entrance into the promised land (cf. Deut 32:6B-14; Jer 2:6-7; Mic 6:4-5) and the historical prologues of the international treaties, which celebrate the suzerain's gracious acts toward his vassal. B. Renaud[176] approves this interpretation because, in addition to explaining the appeal to the natural phenomenon, it also explains how *I AM* could play the roles of plaintiff, of accuser, and of judge: "In the breaking of treaties by vassals, the wronged suzerain himself engaged the appropriate procedure. He therefore played at the same time the roles of plaintiff, of accuser, and of judge. This is exactly the situation that we have in Micah 6." J. Limburg[177] found that the *rîb* functions in three settings: in the court at the city gate (e.g., Exod 23:2, 3, 6; 2 Sam 15:2, 4; Prov 18:17), or in the cult where *I AM* functions as advocate for the individual or the people (Mic 7:9; Pss 35:1; 43:1; 74:22; 119:154; Lam 3:58), or in international relationships (Judg 11:12-28; 12:2; and in the eighth-century Aramaic steles), in which case the complaint is lodged through messengers. Turning to the prophetic lawsuit speeches (see above), he learned that the *rîb* is always *I AM*'s complaint/accusation; that *I AM* appears as an aggrieved party with a complaint versus an unfaithful priest (Hos 4:4-6), nations (Jer 25:31), the wicked and godless (Mal 3:5), or his people — only in Isa 3:13-15 does *I AM* appear as an advocate for his people; and that the form originated in international relationships with prophets functioning as his messengers. These three conclusions shed remarkable light on Mic 6:1-5. G. W. Ramsey,[178] enlarging the discussion to include Judg 2:1-5; 6:7-10; 10:10-16 and Psalm 81, divided the "covenant lawsuit" oracles into two divisions: "complaint speech" and "judgment speech." The former, to which Mic 6:1-8 belongs, in contradistinction to the latter, to which Mic 6:9-16 belongs, lacks an emphasis on coming punishment. On this basis Ramsey drew the plausible conclusion that the "complaint speech" aimed to move the Israelites to contrition: "At least in its cultic use," he writes, "the purpose of the 'Complaint Speech' was to facilitate restoration of the covenant relationship."

The oracle in Mic 6:1-8, however, has been seen to employ two forms and so two settings. In addition to the lawsuit, what older scholars called the word

---

176. *La Formation*, 312-13.
177. Limburg, "The Root *ryb* and the Prophetic Lawsuit Speech," 291-97.
178. G. W. Ramsey, "Speech-Forms in Hebrew Law and Prophetic Oracles," *JBL* 96 (1977) 45-58.

of judgment (*Gerichtsrede:* vv 2-5 or 3-5), most scholars recognize since the suggestive study of J. Begrich[179] that what is labeled the "refutation" motif of the "covenant lawsuit"/"complaint speech" can also be categorized as the "torah oracle"/"entrance liturgy" form. K. Koch[180] states the form precisely: the question of the conditions for access into the sanctuary, presumably addressed to the priest who has responsibility in such cultic matters (Isa 33:14; Pss 15:1; 24:3), and of the priestly response formulating the divine requirements (i.e., *torah*) (cf. Isa 33:15-16; Pss 15:2-5; 24:4-5). B. Renaud[181] cites approvingly the objections of N. Lohfink[182] and T. Lescow.[183] They argue that it differs from the *torah* liturgies because it is concerned not with conditions of access to the temple, but with the number of sacrifices to be offered with the intention, according to Lohfink, of atoning for sin, but, according to Lescow, of determining whether one's offering is acceptable.

But their objection misses the points that the petitioner is concerned to determine "how can I meet with *I AM*," who of course dwells in the temple, and that the form employed incontestably shows affinities with the entrance liturgy: the question of what is required for meeting God and securing his favor (vv 6-7) and the reply in the form of *torah* (v 8). J. T. Willis[184] smartly critiques Lescow's conclusions that Mic 6:6-8 is an independent pericope, clearly isolated from its surrounding context, and that it is not a *torah* liturgy but merely a prophetic sermon. One of Lescow's arguments is that vv 6-7 contain rhetorical questions so absurd that they could not have been asked by a sincere worshipper and so must have been put into his mouth by the prophet as a preparation for the reply in v 8. Willis notes, however, that they may be real because of the extreme situation:

> The "exaggerated, extreme, absurd" questions in vv 6-7 are to be explained in light of a very severe crisis threatening the Jewish [*sic!*] community, perhaps Sennacherib's invasion of Jerusalem in 701 B.C. The worshippers may have reasoned that the great destruction which threatened the land was an indication of Yahweh's wrath, which could be appeased only by an abun-

179. J. Begrich, "Die priesterliche Tora," *Werden und Wesen des Alten Testaments,* ed. P. Volz, F. Stummer, and J. Hempel, BZAW (Berlin: Töpelmann, 1936), 79-80.

180. K. Koch, "Tempeleinlassliturgien und Dekaloge," in *Studien zur Theologie der alttestamentlichen Überlieferungen: Festschrift für Gerhard von Rad,* ed. R. Rendtorff and K. Koch (Neukirchen-Vluyn: Neukirchener, 1961), 45-60.

181. *La Formation,* 309.

182. N. Lohfink, *Das Hauptgebot: Eine Untersuchung literarischer Einleitungsfragen zur Dtn 5–11,* AnBib 20 (Rome: Pontifical Biblical Institute, 1963), 220 n. 11.

183. T. Lescow, "Redaktionsgeschichtliche Analyse von Micha 6–7," *ZAW* (1972) 189.

184. Willis, "Review of *Micah 6:6-8,* by Theodor Lescow," 273-78.

dance of sacrifices. . . . This would explain the "breathless" emotional character of these questions, to which Lescow himself calls attention. . . .

B. Renaud[185] objects that the vocabulary, especially *kpp* ("bow down") and *ḥṣnʿ* ("[to walk] wisely"), is not sacerdotal but sapiential. He draws the conclusion, therefore: "One is led to think that the prophet borrowed from the literary genre of the liturgies of entrance. But he modified, retouched, and reexpressed them in his language and in terms of his own objectives. One can therefore speak of prophetical imitation of a cultic genre." That conclusion, however, is too firm in the light of the limited available linguistic data and of the ad hoc nature of the situation, and, as Willis[186] says, "The verbs *qdm* ("come/meet") and *kpp* ("bow down") in v 6 certainly may refer to entering the sanctuary to worship." Moreover, the worshipper cannot have in mind an ordinary situation because the Law defined the required sacrifices precisely for the traditional liturgy. Rather, one supposes an extraordinary situation such as a cataclysmic famine or hostile attack. Renaud[187] also objects that there is no evidence that a prophet performed the sacerdotal function of guarding the temple gate, and the prophet did not deliver *torah* but oracles. But Micah's book supposes an extraordinary situation: derelict priests have corrupted the temple, perhaps Israel's very existence is being threatened by attacking Assrians, and in truth Micah does deliver a *torah* in v 8, showing that he has assumed the sacerdotal function either in a cultic setting and/or in imitating priestly language.

In sum, Mic 6:1-8 comprises two literary forms: a complaint speech lawsuit (vv 1-5) and an entrance *torah* liturgy (vv 6-8), though the *torah* liturgy also functions as a refutation of a wrong response to the lawsuit, but it remains a moot point whether they reflect living situation(s) or merely prophetic literary inventions. If the former, the question must be asked whether these two forms demand two settings, at the gate (6:1-5) and at the sacred hill (6:6-8). J. L. Mays,[188] for one of many, thinks so and thus denies the unity of the piece: "The language and sphere of thought shift from the legal to the cultic." Other scholars unify the piece by supposing that the complaint speech/covenant lawsuit also has a temple setting. T. Lescow[189] says of his arbitrarily truncated pericope, Mic 6:1-4A: "This kind of appellation [to the mountains and foundations of the earth] clearly has its *Sitz im Leben* in the cult," and "the old credo about the coming up out of Egypt [cf. v 4] receives here [in the cult] a critical function."

185. *La Formation,* 309.
186. Willis, "Review of *Micah 6:6-8*," 276.
187. *La Formation,* 310.
188. Mays, *Micah,* 138.
189. T. Lescow, "Micha 6–7," 184.

One can plausibly reconstruct the setting at the temple as follows: besieged worshippers are seeking access to *I AM*'s presence to win his favor and protection against the attacking Assyrians. The King-Priest, however, through his envoy, Micah, judicially accuses them of breaking covenant and invites them to renew it. They blindly and unrepentantly respond by offering costly gifts as their sin offering. *I AM*'s envoy reproves them for their ignorance and reasserts the terms of the covenant: *I AM* requires justice from renewed hearts that understand the nature of the covenant. G. W. Ramsey[190] said: "I myself find more satisfactory the thesis of a cultic setting in which the cries of the Israelites to Yahweh for deliverance from misfortune were answered by the complaint *(ryb)* of Yahweh, citing the unfaithfulness of the vassal people; this was followed by ritual penitence and supplication on the part of the people, which was followed in turn by renewal of the covenant." That Israel renewed the covenant is uncertain, but on the basis of the "complaint speech form" and the explicit appeal "to remember . . . that you may know *I AM*'s saving acts," the oracle certainly aims to renew the spirit and the behavior of the covenant. One may even imagine that Micah delivered this sermon at Passover because he would have chosen such an auspicious occasion, when all Israel flocked to the temple, to lodge the complaint, and, as will be shown, Israel confessed at that feast the two saving acts that Micah calls upon them to remember: the exodus from Egypt and the crossing of the Jordan.

N. Lohfink[191] discerned from certain texts in Deuteronomy 5–11 with traces in Deuteronomy 32; 1 Sam 24:10-23; Jer 26:7-19; Mic 6:3-5, yet a third form, what he called *Beweisführung* "demonstration (of a truth of something)." The complete form appears only in Deut 8:2-6 and 9:4-7. It is composed of three members introduced by the three verbs *zkr* "to remember," *yd'* "to know," and *šmr* "to keep." The first member recalls *I AM*'s saving acts; the second draws conclusions from it on the level of faith; and the third points out the consequences for action and practical behavior. This form, he suggests, derives from the schema of the international treaties: the historical prologue (cf. the first member), the principal commandment to love (the second member), and the particular stipulations (cf. the third member). He limits the form here to the first two, vv 3-5.

B. Renaud,[192] however, is undoubtedly right in pushing the so-called form through to v 8 because that verse corresponds to the motif of concrete behavior. If it be objected that "to keep" is not found in v 8, Renaud responds that it is also explicitly missing elsewhere. He says:

190. Ramsey, "Speech-Forms in Hebrew Law and Prophetic Oracles," 46.
191. Lohfink, *Das Hauptgebot*, esp. 134-35.
192. *La Formation*, 314.

It is the same YHWH who reminds Israel of his kindnesses and of his salvific acts ("remember"), who invites it to draw from the consequences at the level of religious experience ("in order that you know the righteous acts of YHWH"), and who finally traces the behavior from this action of election (v 8). Much more, these salvific acts gave the basis for the law that YHWH claims to lay before Israel as the requirements of the covenant.

Renaud, however, is also certainly right in acknowledging that this is not a form in a strict sense, and that it would be better to speak of a theological motif. Nevertheless, these studies help establish the unity of vv 3-8 and illuminate the thematic connections between v 5A "remember," v 5B "to know the saving acts of *I AM*," and v 8 "to do justice." As will be seen, it is precisely this connection that lies behind the instruction "to walk wisely with the LORD your God." Others[193] arrive at the same unity by comparing the connection of vv 3-5 and 8 with the covenantal formulations in Exod 19:3-6, Joshua 24, and 1 Samuel 12. These formulations consist of a recital of *I AM's* saving deeds and a call to obedience. The thematic unity of Mic 6:1-8 is enhanced by the lively dialogical style employing second person in direct address, by the verbal links of *mâ* (see below), and by the *inclusio ʾsh,* with reference to God in v 3 and with reference to man in v 8.

Having considered the form of Mic 6:1-8 as a whole, let us now consider its parts. Following a unique introduction calling upon the book's audience to hear the book's last and final section (v 1A), the oracle develops as a dramatic and complex legal suit. First *I AM*, the Plaintiff, summons Micah, his messenger, to call the mountains to serve as witnesses at the trial; then Micah summons the mountains to hear *I AM's* complaint/accusation (vv 1B-2). The rest of the passage unfolds dramatically in the form of a dialogue, allowing the audience to participate in the event (cf. Mic 2:6-7; 4:2). The argument develops by the repeated use of *mâ* "what?" *I AM*, now functioning as Prosecutor, addresses accused Israel and asks what fault they find with him (vv 3-5). A worshipper asks with what sacrifice (= "How") *I AM* would be pleased (vv 6-7). *I AM*, now as Judge, has the last word in refuting the worshipper: he has made known what he wants, namely, right attitudes and acts toward one's neighbor and oneself (v 8).

In the prosaic introduction (v 1A), to whom is the invocation "hear/listen" [you all]" in 6:1A addressed? Unlike 1:2; 3:1, 9, where the vocative after the linking imperative *šimʿû* identifies the antecedent, none is found here. Since 6:1A is best construed as an editorial suture, stitching chapters 6–7 with 3–5 (see Introduction, 13), the "you" is the audience to whom the book is addressed, namely, the covenant community in succeeding generations. This interpreta-

193. Cf. Allen, *Micah,* 249.

tion is validated by the prosaic form of this anacrusis (see Exegesis, 344). Two additional points should be noted: *I AM* is the author, investing the prophecy with heavenly authority, and the tense of both verbs, "hear" and "says," is a timeless present. *I AM* still speaks through these chapters.

The keyword, which is repeated in each verset of the judgment scene (vv 1B-2), is *rîb,* a technical term here to accuse the people of having broken the covenant. This accusation, however, differs in two very significant ways from the accusations in "the oracles of reproach" in chapters 2 and 3: Whereas those accusations were addressed to the venal land barons (ch. 2) and Israel's corrupt leadership (ch. 3), this one is addressed against Israel as a nation, "my people" (vv 3, 5); and whereas those oracles aimed to condemn and sentence, this one aims to restore.

In these verses the audience is introduced to the Plaintiff *(I AM),* the accused (Israel), the messenger on behalf of the Plaintiff (Micah), and the witnesses, the cosmic elements represented by the lofty mountains reaching down to the earth's foundations. First, *I AM* summons Micah as his envoy (v 1B). Mays[194] thought that *arise* (sing.) was addressed to Israel, but this cannot be because Israel is the accused, not the prosecutor. No other addressee is mentioned, making Micah, the book's author, the most likely candidate. In addition to stressing the urgency of the situation, the prophet reports his call to "arise" in order to authenticate his prophetic investiture authorizing him to summon witnesses and to arraign the defendant in order to set forth *I AM*'s lawsuit. L. Allen[195] noted that Israel is deliberately not mentioned as the accused until the climactic end of the trial's setting. *I AM* instructs his emissary to set forth his case before the mountains/hills. "Mountains" and "foundations of the earth," a merism, signify the whole earth. H. Wolff[196] says: "As the upper and lower outer limits, the two together point to the whole of the earthly cosmos." Earth's mountains and foundations function in the same way as "heaven and earth" in other contexts (cf. Deut 4:26; 30:19; 31:28; 32:1; Isa 1:2).

But why are inanimate mountains summoned to hear the trial? And in what precise sense can they "hear" a case anyway? The two questions are best answered together. Most moderns, building on the epoch-making study of G. E. Mendenhall,[197] interpret Micah's summons of the mountains and hills as a linguistic heritage from the international suzerainty treaties that summoned gods and cosmic elements such as "mountains, rivers, springs, heaven and

---

194. Mays, *Micah,* 128, 131.
195. Allen, *Micah,* 364-65.
196. Wolff, *Micha,* 147.
197. Mendenhall, *Law and Covenant in Israel and the Ancient Near East.*

earth, winds and clouds" "to listen and to serve as witnesses" to the treaty. G. E. Wright[198] plausibly suggests that the cosmic elements in these treaties are not in addition to the gods "but rather summarizing categories into which all gods . . . would have fallen in polytheistic thought." These gods and their elements were summoned to listen to the terms of the treaty and, according to D. R. Hillers,[199] were expected to wreak vengeance upon the vassal should he break it.

The covenant God mediated through Moses with Israel at Sinai, and later supplemented at Moab, has this kind of treaty form in its background, and, instructively, in that covenant ceremony heaven and earth are called upon to witness that Moses has dutifully warned Israel that if it violates the treaty, *I AM* will invoke the curses of the covenant (cf. Deut 4:26; 30:19; 31:28). So also in his song, recited "from beginning to end in the hearing of the whole assembly of Israel" (Deut 31:30) and which, according to G. E. Wright,[200] has the form and setting of "the divine lawsuit, or *rîb*," Moses summons heaven and earth to hear the words of his song. The mountains served as sober and silent witnesses to the truthfulness of *I AM*'s accusation. They "saw" both his saving acts that demanded as the only reasonable response Israel's heartfelt commitment to *I AM* and also Israel's unfulfilled obligations. At the making of the covenant they also "heard" Israel duly warned with its promise of blessings and threat of curses for obedience and disobedience respectively (cf. Leviticus 26 and Deuteronomy 28). H. B. Huffmon[201] says: "The witnesses serve as an indication or guarantee that an unfulfilled obligation exists, which justifies Yahweh in actually invoking the curses of the covenant."

Without witnesses and/or written contract there could be no case (cf. Deut 19:15-16). But in what precise way can inanimate mountains serve as witnesses? R. B. Y. Scott, as interpreted by H. B. Huffmon,[202] thinks that "heaven and earth" in Isa 1:2 are not cosmic elements but a metonymy for the heavenly hosts and the people on earth. Though it is true that heaven and earth function this way elsewhere in the OT (cf. Mic 1:2; Ps 96:11), this does take into account either the treaty form behind the covenant mediated by Moses or his song in Deuteronomy 32, nor the prophetic lawsuits, which assume that form; furthermore, though "heaven and earth" may function this way, there is no evidence that "mountains/hills" might.

---

198. G. E. Wright, "The Lawsuit of God: A Form-Critical Study of Deuteronomy 32," in *Israel's Prophetic Heritage*, ed. B. W. Anderson and W. Harrelson (New York: Harper, 1962), 46.

199. D. R. Hillers, *Covenant: The History of a Biblical Idea* (Baltimore: Johns Hopkins University Press, 1969), 36-37.

200. Wright, "The Lawsuit of God," 41-42.

201. Huffmon, "The Covenant Lawsuit," 293.

202. Huffmon, "The Covenant Lawsuit," 290.

G. E. Wright[203] thinks that Israel invested the mountains with psychic life, and he seems to equate the mountains with the Divine Assembly when he asks with reference to Micah's command that they hear: "Must we not interpret such passages in the light of the Divine Assembly, the members of which constitute this host of heaven and of earth?" More specifically, he[204] means that "Israel simply took the polytheistic mode of expression poetically as a designation for the 'angels,' that is, for all those divine powers whom God associated with himself as his 'ministers' or assistants in the administration of his universal realm, with duties over both heavenly and earthy spheres." F. M. Cross[205] seems to agree, for he suggests that these addresses to the mountains "contain direct reminiscences of Yahweh's address to the powers of heaven and earth which formed his court."

H. B. Huffmon[206] rightly objects to this interpretation because "there is no direct evidence for it." Furthermore, the suggestion that Israel animated the cosmic elements with psychic life smacks of pagan animism and polytheism, not biblical theism. Huffmon[207] thinks that the natural elements serve as judges in the sense that they can "carry out the curses and blessings." But in the treaties and prophetic lawsuits based on them the cosmic elements are called upon merely as witnesses, not as avengers.

More probably the mountains function in the same way that memorial stones served as witnesses to covenants between peoples (cf. Gen 32:43-50; Josh 22:21-28). In these two passages the contractor(s) erected stone objects, a pillar surrounded by a heap of stones and an altar respectively, as tangible witnesses to an inviolable oral covenant/agreement. In the case of a treaty handed down by tradition they bore witness to the parties and their successors of the binding nature of the covenant/agreement. Likewise, the Creator of the cosmic elements, which outlast generations, appointed the oldest natural phenomena as witnesses to the covenant/agreement between him and Israel, a covenant that was passed on by tradition from generation to generation.

This appeal to inanimate elements as witnesses to a treaty could have carried conviction to the parties entering into treaty and to later generations only if the parties had a psychology of canonicity; that is, the original contractors must have assumed that the covenant would be unchanged and the succeeding generations must have believed that it had been transmitted faithfully. For *I*

---

203. G. E. Wright, *The Old Testament against Its Environment*, SBT 2 (Chicago: Henry Regnery/London: SCM, 1950), 36.

204. Wright, "The Lawsuit of God," 48.

205. F. M. Cross, "The Council of Yahweh in Second Isaiah," *JNES* 12 (1953) 275 n. 3.

206. Huffmon, "The Covenant Lawsuit," 291.

207. Huffmon, "The Covenant Lawsuit," 293.

AM's appeal to the mountains as witness to his covenant with Israel through Moses to have carried weight with Micah's original audience, they must have presumed that their fathers in the intervening generations had not altered it. Here one finds a strong argument for the antiquity and authenticity of the biblical traditions ascribed to Moses. In the same way the church through the centuries has celebrated the Eucharist, confident that it accurately recounts the enactment of the new covenant that *I AM* made with her at the beginning.

In the second judgment scene, in solemn dignity Micah summons the enduring mountains to hear *I AM's* accusation against Israel (v 2); here he introduces the Plaintiff, *I AM* himself, who, as the aggrieved party, *has an accusation* and so initiates the trial, and finally with dramatic suspense names the accused, his people/*Israel!* The roots of the mountains in Micah's cosmology probably were considered the foundations of the earth; they are entitled enduring ones precisely because they existed long before Israel appeared on the stage of history. Micah enhances the solemnity of the judgment scene by piling up descriptive terms of the witnesses: hills, mountains, enduring ones, foundations of the earth. *I AM* initiates the trial not to condemn Israel but to save them; so also he confronts mortals with the gospel of Jesus Christ not to condemn them but to save them. But this is their condemnation: that without reason they reject him and his gifts and unacceptably substitute their own gifts.

The Plaintiff's case is presented in two strophes, each introduced by "my people" (vv 3-4, 5). These two strophes, while they serve somewhat different purposes, are united by being part of the accusation in the lawsuit and by their common theme: *I AM's* saving acts for Israel. This theme becomes even more unified by mentioning *I AM's* saving acts both at the beginning and end of Israel's formative period — its miraculous exodus from Egypt (vv 3-4) and miraculous passage through Moab and entrance into the land (v 5) — and by calling attention to the supernatural godly leadership of Moses, Aaron, and Miriam that led them out of Egypt's slavery and the supernatural ungodly leadership of Balak and Balaam, who intended to curse Israel but in fact blessed them and gave passage to the promised land. B. Renaud[208] objects to T. Lescow's separation of vv 4 and 5: "It is completely arbitrary to disassociate the two motifs of the coming out from Egypt (v 4A) and of the crossing of the Jordan (v 5B). Jer 2:5-8, which Lescow himself cites very appropriately to illuminate Mic 6:1-4, unites the going up from the land of Egypt (Jer 2:6) to the entrance into the Promised Land (Jer 2:6; cf. also Josh 24:2-14; Pss 105:37, 44, etc.)." The implication for Micah's immediate audience and the audience of his book is clear: if *I AM* miraculously saved Israel at its inception from the bondage and

---

208. *La Formation,* 307.

affliction of Egypt and Moab, can he not unshackle it from the ruthless tyranny of Assyria and Satan, whatever other guise Satan may take? The church fails not because *I AM* fails in his covenantal commitment but because the church fails to respond properly in its obligations.

In the first strophe *I AM* begins with summary questions that both accuse Israel of false allegations and defend him against their accusation of wrongdoing (v 3), to which v 4 brings some concrete precision. Furthermore, in v 4 the Plaintiff seizes the initiative in implicitly accusing Israel of unreciprocated fidelity (v 4). These two verses are linked thematically by moving from a general accusation/defense to specific instances, syntactically by the emphatic *kî* ("surely") introducing v 4, and phonologically by the similarity in sound between *hel'ētîkā* "[how] have I overburdened you?" (v 3) and *he'ĕlitîkā* "I brought you up" (v 4). True to the covenant lawsuit form, the Plaintiff initiates his complaint in the form of questions as part of what G. Ramsey[209] calls the "pretrial encounter." With pathos and tenderness aimed straight at Israel's heart both to reprove and to woo them, *I AM* calls them *my people.* His speech is filled with grace and truth. E. B. Pusey[210] says: "This one tender word, twice repeated, contains a whole volume of reproof."

The first question, "What have I done against you?" is both defensive, protecting the Plaintiff's innocence, and accusing, for it implies Israel's distrust in *I AM.* Instead of acting to Israel's disadvantage, as they accuse him, it turns out that he has acted toward their advantage. And what grace that he should stoop to become involved in Israel's history with saving acts! The verb "do" takes on an explicitly theological value because *I AM* is the subject and is speaking of his "acts" either in creation and/or in history.[211] Commenting on this use of *'śh,* T. E. McComiskey[212] says: "When used of God, the word frequently emphasizes God's acts in the sphere of history. These contexts stress one of the most basic concepts of OT theology, i.e., that God is not only transcendent, but he is also immanent in history, effecting his sovereign purpose. Moses could recall God's acts in Egypt, reminding the people of all that God 'did' (Deut 29:1)." If this oracle were given at one of Israel's cultic celebrations, such as Passover, at which times *I AM*'s saving acts were recounted, the question would be especially telling.

The second question, "How have I overburdened you?" implies even more clearly than the first that Israel has been complaining that *I AM* has in-

---

209. Ramsey, "Speech-Forms in Hebrew Law and Prophetic Oracles," 49.
210. E. B. Pusey, "Michah," in *Minor Prophets* (London: Parker, 1860), 2:339.
211. Cf. Vollmer, "'śh, machen, tun," *THAT* 366 §4b.
212. T. E. McComiskey, "'āśâ," *TWOT* 2:701.

flicted intolerable burden(s) upon them. The congeneric noun *tĕlā'â* more specifically designates the hardship that Israel experienced in Egypt and in the later periods of its history (Exod 18:8; Num 20:14; Lam 3:5; Neh 9:32). The question, "How have I overburdened you?" in the light of those data suggests that the people are under duress from foreign oppressors, but H. Wolff[213] curiously draws the conclusion that the question "suits . . . only a time which is *not* [my emphasis] marked by strong external political burdens, but in which nevertheless one is dissatisfied with Yahweh." But why rule out external political affliction, especially since that is a normal usage of a congeneric noun? Wolff himself recognizes that the question presumes the people feel dissatisfied, but, while offering no reason for it, he arbitrarily rules out the most likely candidate in Micah's epoch, namely, the Assyrian invasion.

J. Limburg[214] judiciously remarked: "The people think that they have a complaint against Yahweh, but in reality Yahweh is the one who has the complaint." His discipline through the Assyrian rod (see v 1) is not due to his unfaithfulness, as apostate Israel seems to allege, but precisely the opposite; they are the ones who have been unfaithful. He invites the accused to "testify against me," that is, to formulate precise accusations (cf. Num 35:30; 1 Sam 12:3; 2 Sam 1:16; Isa 3:9) before the Tribunal. Their nonmotivated hostility against God lacks formulation. Quite the contrary; their mouths are silenced by the recounting of God's saving acts in vv 4-5.

So also in the future day of judgment people who thought they had a complaint against God will find out too late that they have no testimony against him. He dealt with them in the grace of the cross of Jesus Christ, but they responded unnaturally in unthankful apathy and neglect, and so their mouths will be silenced, and they will be held accountable before him (cf. Rom 3:19). *I AM's* questions also imply that *I AM* does not want to terminate the covenant.

With an emphatic "surely" *I AM* points concretely to his initial saving act, Israel's redemption out of Egypt (v 4). Presumably after a period of silence, *I AM* advances his case that instead of complaining against him they should have praised him (cf. Psalm 95). The accusation surprisingly does not explicate Israel's sins in terms of overt transgression as in chapters 2 and 3, though the rejoinder in v 8 has those in view, but, by recounting *I AM's* saving acts, points to a guilt more profound, namely, a hardness of heart that did not respond to sovereign grace. This too is the condemnation of the world: in sovereign grace God sent his Son to be its Lord and Savior, but the world rejected his grace and crucified his Son. This cold response to sovereign grace can lead to only one ver-

---

213. Wolff, *Micha*, 148.
214. Limburg, "The Root *ryb* and the Prophetic Lawsuit Speeches," 302.

dict: "Light has come into the world, but men loved darkness instead of light because their deeds were evil" (John 3:19).

I AM initiated his relationship with Israel with two benevolent acts: he brought them out of the land of Egypt and provided them with the superior leadership of Moses, Aaron, and Miriam. There is a play here between *hel'ĕtîkā* "I burdened you" and *he'ĕlītîkā* "I brought you up." This play could be captured in English by either, "How have I overburdened you? . . . I unburdened you," or "How have I ground you down? . . . I brought you up." We also noted that this primeval confession that *I AM* brought them up/or out of the land of Egypt was confessed regularly at important festivals, particularly Passover. L. Allen[215] focuses on "brought up": "God did not only bring Israel out but up: the implication is that it was a prelude to bringing them safe and sound to the promised land."[216] C. Westermann[217] notes that Israel's history begins with coming up from the land of Egypt: "Israel's *national* [my emphasis] history begins with slavery in Egypt (Exod 1:13, 'and the Egyptians made the Israelites into slaves with violence')." Westermann then notes the use of *'ōl* "yoke": "The typical picture for slavery is the yoke (*'ōl*, 40 times in the OT, almost always used figuratively). It brings to expression both sides [of slavery]: working for others and the loss of freedom)." So also saints begin life in the cruel bondage of their wills to sin and receive its wages of death (Rom 6:23) until God in sovereign grace saves them through regenerating faith in his Passover: Jesus Christ (1 Cor 5:7).

pdh ("redeem") signifies "to ransom," that is, to transfer or free someone from another's ownership through the payment of a price. In the legal sphere, especially in marriage laws, it pertains to transferring a slave (woman) from one master to another or to freedom (cf. Exod 21:7-11; Lev 19:20). In the cultic sphere it takes on the more technical meaning to redeem the firstborn of humans and animals by compensation. In Exod 34:19-20 all firstborn mammals (= "who open the womb") belonged to *I AM*, and therefore a ransom had to be paid to him for their survival. This is clarified in Num 18:15-18: the firstborn of human beings and unclean animals were ransomed with a redemption price paid to the priest, but the firstborn of herds and flocks were offered to *I AM*. The practice of ransoming the firstborn took on a special religious significance in connection with the Exodus (Exod 13:2, 12, 13): the redemption of Israel's firstborn sons commemorated that *I AM* paid the Egyptians with their own firstborn to free his son from their harsh ownership.[218] Furthermore, although

---

215. Allen, *Micah*, 366.
216. Cf. J. Wijngaards, "*ḥwṣy'* and *h'lh*: A Twofold Approach to the Exodus," 98-101.
217. C. Westermann, *THAT* 2:190.
218. Cf. W. B. Coker, "*pādâ*," *TWOT* 2:714.

pdh is not used in connection with the Passover lamb, recall that the Passover lamb protected Israel's firstborn when *I AM* passed through the land and struck Egypt's firstborn (Exod 12:12-13), thereby linking the Passover lamb with the redemption of Israel's firstborn.

According to J. Stamm,[219] however, a "religious linguistic use" of *pdh* ("redeem") distinguishes itself from the profane (legal) and cultic literature in that it knows only *I AM* as the subject of the freeing/liberating action and correspondingly never the paying of a compensating price. "In this use," Stamm says,[220] "the specifically legal notion steps to the background and the liberating/freeing notion steps to the foreground." He analyzes this relatively frequent religious use into the salvation of the individual (in the past and present) and of the people (in the past and in the eschatological future). The liberation and salvation of the people in the past pertains mostly, as here, to their liberation from Egypt.

If, however, this oracle was recited at Passover, as seems likely, then the verb *pdh* probably connoted to Micah's audience its cultic significance, namely, the vicarious redemption of its firstborn through *I AM*'s payment of a price and the provision of the Passover lamb. If only a so-called religious notion is in view, the questions in vv 6-7 about what price God demands to extend his favor appear inexcusably obtuse (see below). Moreover, if the cultic connotation is present, then the deliberation whether *I AM* now demands Israel to pay its firstborn appears even more obnoxious (see below).

According to M. Lestienne,[221] wherever the expression "the God who redeemed from the house of slavery" occurs (cf. Deut 5:6; 6:12; 8:14; 13:11[10]; cf. Josh 24:15; Judg 6:8; Jer 34:13; especially Deut 7:8 and 13:6[5]), "The expression seems aimed to support a claim of YHWH or concerning him. It is a title which gives to him the right to speak as master or which supports a claim made with regard to him."

In addition to freeing his son from the ruthless tyranny of Egypt to fulfill his destiny to serve him as priest, *I AM* says, "I sent before you" exceptional leaders (v 4B). The credo that *I AM* sent before them the noble "Moses, Aaron, and Miriam" contrasts strikingly with the magistrates, priests, and prophets who were condemned and sentenced in chapter 3. Moses bore the administrative burdens of all the people and their judicial burdens in particular (cf. Deut 1:12); Aaron, the high priest, removed their religious burdens (cf. Exod 28:12), and Aaron and Miriam were *I AM*'s prophets (Num 12:1-8). The women undoubtedly identified with Miriam, who celebrated in song Israel's release from the burden of Egypt (cf.

219. J. Stamm, *THAT* 2:389.
220. Stamm, *THAT* 2:395.
221. M. Lestienne, "Les 'Dix Paroles' et le Décalogue," *RB* 79 (1972) 484-510, esp. 502.

Exod 15:20-21). The prophet Samuel (1 Sam 12:6-8) centuries earlier shamed Israel for their lack of faith in *I AM* by mentioning the superlative leadership of Moses and Aaron as the human agents by whom the *I AM* miraculously brought Israel out of Egypt (1 Sam 12:6-8). In the cult Israel recalled the gifted Moses and his consecrated brother, who led them out of Egypt (Pss 77:21[20]; 99:6; 105:25-27; 106:16). Instructively, in the ceremony to renew the covenant after the Conquest, Joshua also mentions them (Josh 24:5). To these outstanding brothers, Micah uniquely adds their gifted sister, Miriam (Num 26:59; 1 Chr 5:29). To be sure, her insubordination to Moses and subsequent deadly uncleanness (Num 12:1-15) reminded Israel of the deadly consequences of disobedience (Deut 24:9; cf. Num 19:1–20:1). But this woman, the first bearing the honorific title "prophetess" to describe her as she led the women in music, in dancing, and in singing a hymn of praise to celebrate the crossing of the Red Sea (Exod 15:20-21), is remembered by Micah, and implicitly by Jeremiah (31:4), as one of the triumvirate that saved Israel. As the older sister at the banks of the Nile, she first displayed the astuteness and boldness that would begin the undoing of Egypt (Exod 2:1-8), and as a mature woman, this time at the banks of the Red Sea, she sings, with tamborine and dance, of *I AM*'s consummate victory over Egypt (Exod 15:20-21) through the infant brother she saved. Her exceptional gift may be inferred from the mention of her in the cited genealogies and from her daring with Aaron to rival the leadership of Moses, the founder of the nation (Num 12:1-3)!

The implication for Micah's audience is clear: their poor leadership under corrupt magistrates, venal priests, and extortive prophets (cf. chs. 2 and 3) is not due to a lack of divine power or grace, but to their phlegmatic hearts toward sovereign grace. At the beginning of the twenty-first century, in comparison and contrast to the nineteenth century, the church by and large lacks spiritual leadership. Is this because the church forsook the covenant in the twentieth century?

After "my people," the second strophe continues to implicitly accuse Israel of unrequited fidelity and, in addition, calls upon Israel to renew the covenant: they are to remember his saving acts, particularly with reference to the safe passage through Moab and across the Jordan "so that they might know *I AM*'s saving acts" (vv 5-21). The command to "remember" *(zkr)* God's saving acts serves the manifold purpose of justifying God's innocence, of accusing Israel of ingratitude and unbelief, and of opening the door to them to participate anew in God's saving acts. "To remember" in Hebrew is somewhat different from its English gloss, where to remember may be used for a history examination. "To remember" is not merely recalling (a) past event(s) but of actualizing the past into the present. B. S. Childs[222] comments on this important theological term:

---

222. B. S. Childs, *Memory and Tradition in Israel* (Naperville, Ill.: Allenson, 1962), 56.

Boecker has shown that the appeal to memory is characteristic of a defendant's speech. The accused attempts to demonstrate from the past that he is not guilty of the wrong of which he is charged. Yet it is apparent that in this passage the verb *zkr* has received a meaning in respect to Israel's past tradition which differs greatly from the typical usage within a trial. . . . The acts of remembering serve to *actualize* [my emphasis] the past for a generation removed in time from those former events in order that they themselves can have *an intimate encounter* [my emphasis] with the great acts of redemption. *Remembrance equals participation* [my emphasis]. The present rupture in the relationship of Yahweh with his people stems from Israel's failure to understand the saving acts.

H. Eising,[223] on the basis of parallels with *zkr,* agrees: *zkr* denotes "the presence and *acceptance* [my emphasis] of something in the mind." T. Robinson[224] likewise says: "To speak of the past is to *make it effectual, authoritative* [my emphasis] for today." In sum, memory entails faith and actualizes the past into the present. If Israel remembers God's saving acts, it will entail that by faith they also accept them and participate in them.

The notion that memory functions to make the past effectual is validated by the stated purpose: "to know the saving acts of *I AM*." Without further specification *yd'* "know" denotes both cognitive and effective knowledge of someone/thing. Comprehension entails not only reflection upon the object to be known — a purely thought process — but also an intimate and practical acquaintance with it. The object being perceived is at first external to the knower; through psychological processes, in this case through remembering in faithful and active acceptance, it becomes internalized into one's heart. Had Micah wanted to say "that you may know about the saving acts," he would have said *yd' kî* (contrast Isa 45:3 and 4). Likewise, when the church remembers her Lord in the Eucharist, which replaced the Passover, in obedience to his command "do this in remembrance of me" (Luke 22:19), it actualizes *I AM's* presence and accepts his atoning work.

Moreover, to remember *I AM's* saving acts entails keeping his commands. One obeys his commands out of a sense of debt for what he has done (cf. Deut 6:21-25; 26). Commenting on the role of memory in Deuteronomy, B. Childs[225] says: "Memory plays a central role in making Israel constantly aware of the nature of God's benevolent acts as well as of her own covenantal pledge." The continuity between *I AM's* historical acts and Israel's keeping their covenant obliga-

223. H. Eising, *"zākhar," TDOT* 4:65.
224. Robinson, "Micha," 146.
225. Childs, *Memory and Tradition,* 51.

tions is assumed here, for vv 6-8 discuss how Israel should respond, as pointed out above in connection with covenant formulations. In other words, v 5 continues the accusation against Israel, for it assumes that they have not remembered and so severed their relationship with him, but moves beyond it by implicitly asking Israel to repent and to accept God's past acts and so renew the covenant.

Specifically, Israel is to recall the Balak-Balaam incident: "what he plotted, that is, Balak king of Moab; and how he responded to him, that is, Balaam son of Beor," which occurred at "Shittim" (Num 22:1), and the crossing of the Jordan that began at Shittim and ended at "Gilgal" (Josh 3:1; 4:19). The Balak-Balaam incident is linked with the entrance into the promised land at the end of Israel's formative period, even as Moses, Aaron, and Miriam are linked with the coming up out of Egypt at its beginning. More specifically, the Balak-Balaam incident is coupled with the entrance into the sworn land to bind Israel's miraculous political and spiritual deliverance from Moab with crossing the blockading Jordan, even as at the beginning *I AM* brought them up out of the spiritual and political bondage of Egypt and then led them through the blockading Red Sea. Three times Balak counseled Balaam to curse Israel, and three times, yes four, *I AM* resisted the ungodly king and his hireling prophet, and instead put a word in the pagan prophet's mouth that blessed Israel, just as three times, yes four, the angel of *I AM* resisted Balaam's donkey, and *I AM* put a word in the donkey's mouth (Num 22:2–24:19)!

In the ancient Near East a prophet might practice a form of incantation that, by a combination of a power-charged ritual word and act, it was thought, could persuade the gods to a course of action. According to A. Wolters,[226] the Balaamite inscription found at Tell Deir ʿAlla and dated to the time of Micah (see Exegesis, 353) confirms Israel's memory that Balaam was a pagan prophet from northern Syria centuries before the time of Micah. Furthermore, according to Wolters, the Balaamites who wrote it were a colony of exiles who had been deported there by the Assyrians from one of the Aramean states of northern Syria. The presence of this colony in Trans-jordan would have caused Micah's audience to fear the dreaded Assyrians (cf. 2 Kgs 18:31-35), but *I AM* asks Israel to relive the situation centuries before when he conquered the dreaded Balak and Balaam and instead blessed them so as to prevail over all their enemies.

Whereas in the salvation from Egypt the focus is on God's supernatural intervention through godly, gifted leadership, the focus in the salvation at Shittim is on his supernatural intervention through demonic, gifted leadership. If God saved Israel through jackasses like Balak and Balaam, would he not save re-

---

226. A. Wolters, "The Balaamite of Tell Deir ʿAlla as Aramean Deportees," SBL paper, 1987.

pentant Israel through the likes of Micah (cf. 3:8), in spite of their otherwise wretched leadership? (Will not the God who speaks through a she-donkey do mighty things today for a repentant church?)

Moreover, the deliverances from Egypt and from Shittim to Gilgal oc-curred at the same season, namely, Passover (cf. Exod 12:1-3 and Josh 4:19). Joshua also couples these events when he renews the covenant upon entrance into the sworn land (Josh 24:2-13). Both at the beginning and end of Israel's for-mation, to which the mountains are witnesses, *I AM* defeated spiritual and po-litical enemies in the order of history and then conquered rivers opposing them in the order of creation. He performed these mighty acts in both realms that Is-rael might know that he is both the Creator and the Redeemer and, as such, su-pernaturally does what is right with those whom he sovereignly calls to serve him. But over the following centuries unregenerate and degenerating Israel did not trust him so as to practice justice. But if *I AM* brought Israel safely through Moab and across the surging Jordan to the sworn land, will he not bring his people safely through history's perilous vicissitudes to the destiny to which he has sworn himself (cf. Heb 6:13-20)?

He calls his acts "righteous" ("saving") in the sense that he did what was right; namely, he delivered Israel. Now he expects Israel to do what is right: to fulfill its covenant obligations.

"These things," says Paul with reference to Israel's experiences in the Exo-dus and the wilderness, "occurred as examples to keep us from setting our hearts on evil things . . ." (1 Cor 10:6). The Passover lamb, the baptism in the Sea, the miraculous manna and drink, the victory over potent enemies, and the safe passage into the sworn land are types of Christ and his church's spiritual experience. He is her Passover lamb (1 Cor 5:7), the manna from heaven (John 6:33), the spiritual rock that accompanied her (1 Cor 10:3), and the one into whom she is baptized (cf. 1 Cor 10:2; 12:13), who causes her always to triumph (Matt 16:18; 2 Cor 2:14), and he will bring her to her sworn eschatological land (John 10:27-29; Eph 5:27; Hebrews 4; 11:39-40). The church's only reasonable spiritual response is to offer herself up as a living sacrifice, holy and acceptable to God (Rom 12:1-2).

The "Torah liturgy" (vv 6-8) is tightly linked by its form: question (vv 6-7) and answer (v 8); by the repetition of *I AM* in each verse; and by *kî 'im* "rather," contrasting the questioner's assumptions with *I AM*'s answers. Its question section (vv 6-7) is tightly linked by form — each consists of two vers-ets spoken by a representative worshipper in contrast to the speakers in vv 3-5 and 8, by language — after the introductory interrogative *bammâ* "with what" the versets are begun with interrogatory polar *hê*, and by theme — in a striking crescendo the material and size of the sacrifice are escalated. Micah stirred Israel's sluggish conscience but not to godly repentance. In diverse ways exegetes think that the petitioner aims through his questions to justify himself. H. B. Huffmon[227] says: "It may be an indignant defense by the accused, or it may be a mocking defense put into the mouth of the defendant (vv 6-7)"; in either case, according to him, the proud worshipper refuses to humble himself before God. But his interpretation is based in part on his regarding vv 6-8 as the refutation of the accused's defense in the lawsuit form. As seen, however, the form of vv 6-8 is better construed as a torah liturgy that does not function as a refutation of possible defense but as a rebuttal denying them entrance to the temple: Israel's place of safety. The worshipper condemns himself by his profound unbelief in God's grace; a profound refusal to repent of his sin; and a profound misunderstanding of his covenantal obligations.

R. Hentschke[228] thinks that by its "counter-question" Israel contests God's right to accuse them of disobedience because they are ready to name their sins. What, then, is *I AM* complaining about? What more does he want? T. Lescow[229] also suspects a polemical intention behind the fictitious questions of vv 6-7. L. Allen[230] similarly suggests: "The accusation that Israel was sick and tired of Yahweh was a patent untruth which must be repudiated. How dare God level against them an implicit charge that they have failed to remember or appreciate all he has done for them?" Against A. Weiser's view that the complaint is to be characterized as repentance, I. Willi-Plein[231] also believes that it is self-justification, but she approaches the truth when she says that "it proceeds that . . . from an understanding of the cult as a fulfillment of the covenant which is conducted *ad absurdum*." Micah's response in v 8 does not support the idea that the worshipper is defending himself against the accusation in vv 3-5. He does not condemn the petitioner for either rejecting *I AM*'s accusation and/or for defending himself, but for profound misunderstandings.

Micah rebuffs the worshiper's ignorance with "it has been told you" (v 8A); Micah's concern is "what *I AM* requires" (v 8Ba); and he answers, not gifts in the cult "but *rather*" the practice of justice (v 8Bb). This interpretation also best satisfies the connection noted above between vv 3-5 and 6-8; the former pertains to what was required of *I AM* to meet his obligations to the covenant, the latter to Israel's obligations.

P. Buis[232] notes the similarity between Mic 6:1-8 and Deuteronomy 9–10:

227. Huffmon, "The Covenant Lawsuit," 287.
228. Hentschke, *Die Stellung der vorexilischen Schriftpropheten*, 104-7.
229. Lescow, *Micha 6:6-8*, 21.
230. Allen, *Micah*, 371.
231. Willi-Plein, *Vorformen*, 99.
232. P. Buis, *Le Deuteronome* (Paris: Beauchesne, 1969).

"After the reproaches formulated in Deut 9:6-9, 22-24 [cf. Mic 6:3-5], it is normal to find a reminder of the requirements of the covenant such as Deuteronomy formulates them (Deut 10:12)" (cf. Mic 6:6-8). The accusation of unreciprocated fidelity and the command to "remember" prick Israel's sluggish conscience, but they remain spiritually blind to the nature and obligations of the covenant of grace. The miscreant, probably the king to judge from his ostentatious gifts and representative capacity, realizes his need for a sin offering (v 7B) and feels his alienation from God in heaven (v 6A), but instead of thinking within the frame of the covenant of grace, he thinks resolutely in terms of assuaging gifts. He hopes by costly gifts to "come before God" (v 6) and to "win his pleasure" (v 7A). As Jacob sought to mollify Esau's anger against him by a gift and be accepted favorably by him (cf. Gen 33:10), so the petitioner seeks to pacify *I AM's* anger against him by offering ever more costly objects. "They would offer everything, . . . excepting what alone he asked for, their heart, its love and its obedience," says E. B. Pusey.[233]

Israel's blindness is incredible. Out of sovereign grace and without cost to Israel, *I AM* had saved the nation from Egypt and Moab and brought her to her promised destiny; how could the nation now suppose extravagant gifts were required to save her from Assyria? If, as suggested above, vicarious Passover lambs were being offered that saved Israel's firstborn, and if their children were being instructed that *I AM* killed the firstborn of Egypt to ransom the nation from their ruthless taskmaster, what utter folly for them to think that *I AM* required the petitioner to kill his firstborn to secure Israel's release from the Assyrian yoke. Profound unbelief in God's gracious character and actions induces such spiritual blindness, and as a result it debases the covenant of grace, based on unilateral love, into a non-loving, bargaining contract. Moreover, in those initial acts of salvation *I AM* had graciously shown himself immanent with his people. Why does the obtuse petitioner now think that it would take extraordinary sacrifice on his part to bridge the gap between *I AM* in heaven and himself on earth? Israel ritualistically recited their creeds, but because they refused to live by a faith that risks itself in doing justice, they never comprehended their meaning. Instead of living by faith in God's saving acts, demonstrating *I AM's* grace and immanence with his people, the petitioner hopes instead to meet God and earn his favor by escalating the size and material of his gifts.

Outwardly the worshipper appears very religious as he bows before God with gift in hand, but in truth his insulting questions betray a desperately wicked heart. Blinded to God's gracious character and acts, he reasons within his own depraved frame of reference: he need not change, God must change. In effect, by

---

233. Pusey, "Micah," in *Minor Prophets*, 340.

his refusal to repent of his unbelief and injustice, he suggests that God, like man, can be bought! In the same way countless people spurn God's gift of his Son who gave his life a ransom for many, and what these events typify, and substitute their own gifts. In truth, however, they are unwilling to trust the Lord Jesus Christ, the one who died for their sins and rose from the dead, enough to risk their lives for his kingdom. Instead of accepting spiritual regeneration, they hope to buy God off by their works. Such an approach can neither bridge the gap between God and man, nor give peace to a person's conscience, nor secure assurance of acceptance with God, nor provide salvation from sin and its penalties.

The first question raises the issue: "How can I come before *I AM*?"; that is, as the parallel question in v 7 clarifies, "Would *I AM* be pleased," and so allow the worshipper into his saving presence. His first deliberative question, "Should I bow down to God on high?" betrays the remoteness he feels between himself and God, in contrast to *I AM*'s address that implied his presence with his covenant people in the Exodus, the wilderness, and the crossing of the Jordan. The question, "Should I come before him with burnt offerings?" begins the bargaining and is coupled with the introductory question by echoing *'ăqaddēm*, "Can I come before?"

He escalates the bargaining from holocausts, to "calves a year old" (already more costly), to "thousands of rams," to a "myriad of wadis of oil," and, finally, to the cruel sacrifice of offering his child: "my firstborn." In connection with offering thousands of rams, H. Wolff[234] says: "That an individual offers a thousand [*sic!*] rams is something so exceptionally unusual that it is reported otherwise only of kings like Solomon, and even then only in connection with a one-time event (1 Kgs 3:4; cf. 8:63; 1 Chr 29:21; 2 Chr 29:32)." In venturing myriads of torrents of oil the bargaining becomes so extreme that it becomes apparent even to the densest observer that this absurd approach has no limit and establishes neither covenant relationship with God nor assurance of salvation. H. Wolff[235] adds: "The escalation of the proposed offering advances not only numerically from thousand [*sic!*] to ten thousand [*sic!*] ..., but also in the fact that in the bidding of the olive oil all normal units of measurement in the cult are abandoned and now (as never) the speech is of 'streams of oil.'" Olive oil is indispensable in the preparation of the dough and cakes connected with the meal offering (Lev 2:1, 15; 7:12; Exod 23:40) and likewise in the production of the anointing oil (Exod 30:24). The directions usually call for a quarter, a half, or a whole hin of oil from pressed olives (from less than a pint to a quart; cf. Exod 30:24; Num 15:9; 28:5). In that light H. Wolff says: "'Ten thousand [*sic!*] streams of oil' as a sacrifice by an individual

234. Wolff, *Micha*, 152.
235. Wolff, *Micha*, 152.

points clearly to the absolute superfluity. At least here the question arises whether the teacher, who so formulated the amounts, wants to caricature more and more the nonsense of all sorts of excessive sacrificial performances."

In offering his firstborn as his sin offering, however, he not only betrays his total darkness about divine grace but also falls into the black apostasy of the licentious pagan cult. H. Wolff[236] comments:

> In the last question (v 7B) he overshoots himself in that he pushes now the exaggerated bidding of extravagance even to being obscene. He depicts a clearly desperate design to practice the complete surrender for atonement that is beyond all possible legal choices in Yahweh's cult and tenders the firstborn as an offering. With that he appears to go back beyond the history of Abraham's offering (Gen 22:2ff., 12ff.; cf. Exod 13:2; 22:28[29] with Exod 13:15; 34:20; Lev 18:21; 20:2-5; Deut 12:31; 18:10) and betakes himself into the custom of the licentious cult (2 Kgs 3:27; 16:3; 21:67 and . . . ; the first child which was begotten in the sacred grove was offered to the fertility deity). According to 2 Kgs 23:10, child sacrifice was performed for the shameful Moloch in the Valley of Hinnom. Jeremiah (7:31; 19:5; 32:35) and Ezekiel (16:20f.; 20:26-31) polemicized against it vehemently enough. Whoever thinks he himself is able to resolve the quarrel with God, that one, while questioning, must venture even to that extreme sacrifice, though rejected long ago. With that, however, at the same time a confession is laid down to the extremity of apostasy from Yahweh, which cannot be atoned for, a life misspent. The teacher who formulates the question in 6f. has masterfully carried the possibility of cultic sacrifice to the absurd and indirectly points out that Yahweh did not demand too much of his people in this direction.

In v 8 *I AM*'s prophetic messenger answers authoritatively and "with what seems a studied disdain"[237] what *I AM* requires for his favor and acceptance: covenant fidelity. The most costly rites are worth nothing without faith that establishes a covenant relationship and fidelity to the Torah. In vv 4-5 *I AM* fulfilled his part of the covenant relationship: saving Israel out of distress. In v 8 he now rebukes Israel for ignoring their covenant responsibility, namely, doing acts of brotherly love out of faith in the saving of *I AM*.

Should one see in the response a condemnation of the cult *en toto?* B. Renaud,[238] against those who answer affirmatively, says that the prophet does not explicitly reject the cult:

---

236. Wolff, *Micha*, 152.
237. Mays, *Micah*, 141.
238. *La Formation*, 316.

He simply reminds one that respect for the covenant has priority over cultic practices. The opposition of vv 7 and 8 stems in great part from a rhetorical process. In any case, it is not said that the cult could not recover its place in a religion where the conversion of the heart would take first place. It is better to compare this passage with Hos 6:1ff. From a formal point of view, the two pieces are not without analogy: it is a matter of a dialogue between God and his people, a dialogue that is more literary than historical, and that, at the same time, is an echo of real words. Concerning the theological content itself, God does not appear at all as a pitiless judge, but rather as the friendly partner of a covenant, hurt by treason, yet ready to forgive. In Hos 6:1-6, the tone becomes more severe, but both texts give the same preference to *hesed* over the cult.

L. Allen[239] makes the cross-reference: "First be reconciled to your brother, and then come and offer your gift" (Matt 5:24). Micah first rebuffs the pretentious worshipper for inexcusable ignorance; *I AM* has made known what he requires (v 8A). The insulting questions cannot be chalked up to ignorance. In the same epoch that *I AM* saved Israel, both at the Red Sea and at the Jordan, he had also given them his covenant, first at Sinai (Exodus 19–23) and then in a supplemented form at Moab (Deut 28:69[29:1]). To this the mountains were witnesses. The priests had transmitted these covenant stipulations to succeeding generations, but now the prophet must take up where the priests miscarried. He frames his response indefinitely, "one has told you" (= "it has been told you") to take the focus away from the historical incident and to locate it in the answer. His answer is not new; rather, it needs to be energized by the Spirit of God to penetrate hard hearts.

Micah's nomenclature for the worshipper as "Human Being" denotes a member of the covenant and possibly connotes his identification with all humankind (see Exegesis, 362-63). L. Allen[240] thinks that it aims to pick up the stress on the distance between God and man expressed in v 6A: "Here it is intended to remind the people of their subordination to God and to cut them down to size after their presumptuous retort." Having disallowed ignorance as an excuse, the prophet now sets forth that *I AM* requires covenantal solidarity (v 8B). He expresses it first generally by calling it "what is good." Mays[241] noted: "The prophets spoke of YHWH's requirements under the theme of 'good' (Isa 1:17; 5:20; Amos 5:14-15; Micah 3:2) and on occasion gave brief generalizing summaries of YHWH's will composed of two or three elements (Isa 5:7; Hos

239. Allen, *Micah*, 374.
240. Allen, *Micah*, 371.
241. Mays, *Micah*, 141.

4:1; 6:6; 13:7; Amos 5:24)." That demand cannot be met apart from faith in *I AM* who saves those who put their lives in jeopardy on behalf of his justice. Nevertheless, nominal Israel and all humankind are held accountable to the covenant's standards and will be judged by them. In that sense the Law condemns all unregenerate people. It is one thing to be "in-law" by experiencing through faith a spiritual union with its Author; it is another thing be "under the law" in self-effort; the former posture saves; the latter damns (cf. 1 Tim 1:8-11).

I AM never allowed ritual to replace covenant trust and obligation as a way of establishing a relationship with him, a relationship wherein sin must be atoned for. Before instructing Israel in worship (Exodus 25–40 and the book of Leviticus), he gave the redeemed people the Ten Commandments from his own mouth and finger (Exod 19:1–20:17), and then he mediated through Moses the Book of the Covenant that regulated social behavior (Exod 20:18–24:18). The judicial law was ratified (Exodus 24) before Israel was told about the ceremonial law (Exodus 25–40), and that instruction ceased when the people disobeyed the former (Exodus 32–33). The prophets did not repudiate sacrifice but subordinated it to ethics (1 Sam 15:22-23; Isa 1:12-20; Amos 5:21-27). When *I AM* through the Holy Spirit regenerates a heart to trust him, he both justifies that person through the finished work of Christ on the cross and sanctifies him by the Spirit who effected faith in the first place. Justification and sanctification, though distinct aspects of sovereign grace, are not chronologically separate spiritual experiences but synchronic and unified ministries of the Spirit that accompany his gift of faith: what theologians call the *ordo salutis*. A person who does not practice mercy and justice in covenant solidarity with his fellows (v 8Bbα) has never participated in the covenant of grace.

Micah begins to specify "good" by another generalization: "to practice justice." According to B. Renaud,[242] *mišpāṭ* "justice" denotes all the decisions of the Law and connotes a covenant relationship. He wrote:

> Originally *mšpṭ* signified the decision of justice and the action of judging. In the course of history, however, its semantic field extended itself to encompass the juridical norm, the content of law, and even to religion and grace. In the last resort, it is the law, even casuistic, that is connected to YHWH, Lord and supreme Judge, what in this passage the clause "what YHWH requires from you" expresses well. As an encompassing term (cf. Ps 147:19), *mišpāṭ* designates here then the incarnation of all the *mišpāṭîm*, of all the dispositions of the law, in which the will of YHWH is manifested. In the biblical perspective, however, "to practice justice" is not only to obey

242. *La Formation*, 298.

commandments, it is to establish with a partner a relationship conformed to the ideal of the covenant established by God. It is then a matter of giving back to each one what is due to him. In the book of Micah the term receives a highly moral connotation (cf. Mic 3:1, 8, 9).

Its spiritual connotation becomes explicit in the second expression of what *I AM* requires: the practice of faithful love. "Love" (*'ahăbat*) is the language of ancient Near Eastern international covenants, of covenant obedience, and of covenantal spiritual commitment. W. L. Moran[243] demonstrated that the term "love" in covenant relationship between *I AM* and Israel is the juridical language of international law. It is also the language of obedience, for it can be commanded (Deut 11:13, 22; Mic 6:8). Finally, as D. Hillers[244] has shown, it is the language of emotional/spiritual commitment. *'ahăbat* reinforces the nuance of the internal spiritual aspect that lies behind the practice of justice. It gives to the expression a note of cordiality. B. Renaud[245] says: "To love is to show oneself faithful vis-à-vis the partner, to show oneself concerned with respecting the engagement of the person vis-à-vis with whom one is engaged."

That *I AM* requires behavior that springs from a regenerate heart that loves one's fellow is further heightened by the modifying word *hesed*, "faithful, loyal kindness," a most important term for describing the nature of the covenant and its spiritual obligations. Renaud[246] records the history of the study of this most theologically important, but much debated, term:

> Critics do not agree on the precise meaning of the word *hsd*, and the term remains a *crux* for translators. N. Glueck[247] forcefully insisted on the link which unites *hsd* to the covenant. The latter traces between the partners of the covenant a line of conduct that is conformed to the community's ideal that ought to regulate the life of the people of God. H. J. Stoebe[248] has partly contested this interpretation; he puts the accent, when it is about YHWH, on the unconditional friendship and the generosity with which he gives himself to man. E. Jacob[249] adopts a more nuanced position, and, in

243. W. L. Moran, "The Ancient Near Eastern Background of the Love of God in Deuteronomy," *CBQ* 25 (1963) 77-87.

244. Hillers, *Covenant*, 154.

245. *La Formation*, 299.

246. *La Formation*, 298-99.

247. N. Glueck, *Das Wort hesed im alttestamentlichen Sprachgebrauch*, BZAW (Berlin, 1927).

248. H. J. Stoebe, "Die Bedeutung des Wortes hesed im Alten Testament," *VT* 2 (1952) 244-54; *THAT* 1:600-621.

249. E. Jacob, *Théologie de l'Ancien Testament*, 2d ed. (Neuchâtel, 1968), 82-86.

our opinion, more exact: "It is fitting to bring to the unilateral interpretation of Glueck a few attenuations," for *ḥesed* is sometimes located beyond the covenant, outlives the covenant, and represents something like the basis on which this covenant will be renewed; but the initial point of view of this author must not be abandoned." Explicating the probable etymological sense of the root of *ḥsd* "force," E. Jacob would gladly define it as "the force which guarantees the covenant, which makes it solid and durable." With J. Guillet[250] one could state precisely that *ḥesed* is not a feeling: "It is never a question to feel *ḥesed* toward somebody; the word is almost always associated with the verb 'to do.' It is not a matter, however, of such a precise process, but of a complex behavior made of respect, benevolence, generosity and of faithfulness [*fidélité*].' It is by this last word that we have chosen to translate *ḥesed* in Mic 6:8, without ignoring that this French word does not overlap with all the fullness and nuances of the Hebrew term.

Renaud's study must be updated with the important work by K. D. Sakenfeld,[251] who sees in the word unobligated deliverance by a stronger covenant partner to a weaker member.

Sakenfeld[252] recognizes that *ḥesed* assumes a covenant relationship; she defines the term's sense in many texts as "deliverance or protection as a responsible keeping of faith with another with whom one is in a relationship." *Ḥesed* connotes at one and the same time faithfulness, love, mercy, grace, and kindness. The relationship may be personal or intimate (husband-wife, father-son, brothers, friends) or voluntary and nonintimate (spies–residents of an enemy city [Josh 2:12-14; Judg 1:24], rival kings [1 Kgs 20:31]). The word occurs commonly in a context where one of the parties finds himself in a weaker situation and is utterly dependent upon the stronger party to meet his need. The stronger party accepts freely the responsibility of providing deliverance and protection to the one in need. Abraham, threatened by Abimelech, is dependent on Sarah's *ḥesed* to protect him (Gen 20:13). Hushai, David's "friend" (i.e., "royal counselor") is expected to stand by the exiled king in his hour of trial (2 Sam 16:14), and Abraham's hope for a pure wife for Isaac, who must remain in the land with the polluted Canaanites, depends on Laban's *ḥesed* to let Rebekah come to Canaan and marry Isaac (Gen 24:29). The dying Israel depends on Joseph to see to it that his bones are carried out of Egypt and buried in his father's burial place; he cannot bury himself (Gen 47:29).

---

250. J. Guillet, *Themes bibliques* (Paris, 1950), 43ff.

251. K. D. Sakenfeld, *The Meaning of Ḥesed in the Hebrew Bible*, HSM 17 (Missoula, Mont.: Scholars Press, 1978).

252. Sakenfeld, *The Meaning of Ḥesed*, 233.

ḥesed's notion of "deliverance" comes to the fore in the relationship when one party is totally hopeless and entirely dependent on the other to exhibit the responsibility the stronger party publicly assumed when the relationship was entered. The superior party, however, is absolutely free not to respond to the weaker's appeal, and for that reason the word also connotes "mercy," "grace," and "kindness." Should one fail, however, to bring relief, the honorable badge of proclaiming him as one characterized by *ḥesed* would be stripped from him. It is now apparent that the practice of *ḥesed* is closely related to *mišpāṭ*: both pertain to the deliverance of an oppressed, weaker party by the stronger party, but whereas *mišpāṭ* puts the emphasisis on the action, *ḥesed* puts it on the attitude behind the action. Although *I AM* practices both justice and *ḥesed* toward Israel, Israel failed to respond by extending these virtues to one another (see chs. 2 and 3). Mic 6:8 shows that the *I AM* Jesus in his famous Sermon on the Mount did not abolish *torah* but indicated its true spiritual nature (cf. Matt 5:17-48).

Micah now moves from covenant solidarity on the human, horizontal axis to covenant solidarity with God (v 8Bbβ) on the vertical axis: "to walk wisely with your God." As argued in the Exegesis (365), *ṣn'* (trad. "humbly") means "circumspectly" in the sense of behaving discerningly, wisely, prudently. Applying that meaning to Mic 6:8, Stoebe[253] says: "The expression ought to be understood in connection with vv. 3-5, which names Yahweh's saving acts, and signifies a walk with God which insightfully recognizes God's gifts and accepts the consequences that proceed from that for one's behavior, even toward other human beings." The divine love expressed in Israel's deliverance out of Egypt and her entrance into the promised land showed what was required. Before such love mortals are not free to grab what they can out of life and/or be indifferent to others. The "image of God" knows better.

B. The Covenant Curses Fulfilled on Jerusalem (6:9-16)

9   The voice of *I AM*! He cries out to the city,
        — and whoever fears your name is wholly sound in judgment —
    "Listen, Tribe, and the assembly of the city!
10   Should I forgive in the house of the wicked granaries filled by injustice,
        and the scanty ephah that is accursed?
11   [If I forgive], would I be acquitted of your unjust scales
        and of your pouch full of deceptive weights?

253. H. J. Stoebe, *THAT*, 2:567-68.

12 The city's rich people are full of violence,
      and her inhabitants speak lies.
    Yes, their tongue is totally deceitful when they speak.
13 And so in recompense I am going to strike you sorely,
      bringing horror upon you for your sins.
14 As for you, you will eat, but you will not be satisfied,
      for dysentery will strike you in your inward parts.
    You will press toward birth, but you will not deliver;
      and what you do deliver I will hand over to the sword.
15 You will sow grain, but you will not harvest it;
      you will press olives, but you will not anoint yourself with oil;
      you will tread out the new wine, but you will not drink it.
16 And the city observed the precepts of Omri,
      and all the deeds of the house of Ahab;
    and you [all] went in their counsels.
    So I am going to give you over to horror,
      and its inhabitants to scornful hissing;
      for you [all] will bear the reproach against my people."

EXEGESIS

9 In *qôl yhwh* (*The voice of* I AM!), *qôl,* modified by *yhwh* — a genitive of inalienable possession (lit., "the voice of *I AM* cries out"; cf. Ps 29:3) — is often taken as the subject of the verb,[1] but grammarians differ. GKC[2] takes *qôl* as an independent, exclamatory nominative (= "A voice! ['Hark!'/'Listen!' English glosses] *I AM* cries out"). Joüon[3] takes the whole phrase as an exclamation (= "The voice of *I AM*! He cries . . ."). Although H. Wolff[4] finds the evidence for the exclamatory meaning of *qôl* less than compelling, it seems probable.[5] The parallel imperative *šimʿû* also favors interpreting it as an exclamatory nominative. The MT accents and the other uses of exclamatory *qôl,* all in the construct state, favor Joüon's understanding of the syntax. *qôl yhwh lāʿîr yiqrāʾ* is a unique introductory prophetic formula. *lāʿîr* (*to the city*): the article designates a unique referent because the historical situation allows only one city,[6] probably Jerusalem, "the

---

1. Cf. Hillers, *Micah,* 80.
2. GKC §146.
3. Joüon, *Grammaire,* §162d.
4. Wolff, *Micha,* 191.
5. *IBHS* §40.2.3b.
6. *IBHS* §13.5.1.

usual venue of Micah's oracles."[7] The city is a metonymy for its citizens. *yiqrā*" *(cries out):* the nonperfective signifies an incipient present imperfective situation[8] of the root *qr*" "to make sacred proclamation" (see Mic 3:5).

In *wĕtûšîyâ (and is wholly sound in judgment)*[9] the *wāw* is a clausal conjunctive linking those who regard *I AM*'s name with the message given in his name. *tûšîyâ* functions as a predicate nominative with an independent relative clause as subject (lit., "he who fears *I AM* is sound in judgment"). This use of a substantive as predicate where an adjectival construction is expected gives the attribute a certain emphasis.[10] English is best served by the glosses "wholly," "altogether," or an equivalent (i.e., wholly characterized by the quality indicated by the noun). A parallel found in Isa 41:24 is *tô'ēbâ yibḥar bākem* (lit., "an abomination is he who chooses you,"[11] better glossed: "Whoever chooses you is wholly abominable"). In both Isa 41:24 and Mic 6:9 (cf. 3:5) the independent relative *'ašer* is omitted, and the predicate nominatives function as predicate adjectives: "abomination" = "abominable" and "sound in judgment."[12] *yir'eh (whoever regards):* the nonperfective signifies a habitual imperfective situation,[13] and *rā'â* has its metaphorical sense "to regard" (cf. Deut 33:9). In both contexts *r'h* pertains to an inferior's attitude toward a superior. The ancient versions, confused by the unusual syntax and meaning of *r'h*, read *yr'* "to fear" — LXX *phoboumenous = yir'ê* — and then further altered the clause in various ways to make sense of it. Following the versions, A. Deissler[14] and H. Wolff[15] gratuitously conjecture the infinitive *yireh* (a bi-form of *yirat/yirâ*) of the root *yr'* "to fear," and translate: "It is prudence to fear your name." The shift to the second person with *šĕmekâ (your name)* shows that this is an apostrophe by Micah. Though the oracle is addressed to *I AM*, he implicitly exhorts his audience to pay regard to God's name.

The textual, lexical, and syntactic problems of v 9B are so interrelated that it is best treated as a whole before considering its parts. TNIV retains MT's *sim'û maṭṭeh umî yĕ'ādâ* and glosses it: "Heed the rod and the One who appointed it," but judiciously notes that "the meaning of the Hebrew for this line is uncertain." It takes the interrogative pronoun *mî* as a relative ("the One who"; cf. Josh 24:15) and *maṭṭeh* "rod" as an incomplete metaphor for Assyria (cf. Isa 10:5). Problem-

7. Allen, *Micah*, 377.
8. *IBHS* §31.3.
9. Or "successful," or "resourceful"; see Waltke, *Proverbs*, 2:225.
10. GKC §141c.
11. Cf. GKC §146, 2(b).
12. *IBHS* §8.4.2.
13. *IBHS* §31.3.
14. Deissler, *La Sainte Bible*, 8:346.
15. Wolff, *Micha*, 159.

atic to this understanding, however, is the fact that the feminine verbal suffix of *yě'ādâ* refers back to the masculine *maṭṭeh*. In v 9B LXX reads *kai tis kosmēsei polin*, which can be retroverted as *ûmî ya'ădeh 'îr* ("and who shall order [= marshall?] the city?"). The translation presumes with reference to initial *'ôd* in v 10 the common confusion of *wāw* and *yôd* and of *dālet* and *rêš*. On that basis, assuming *maṭṭeh* has its other meaning, "tribe," J. Wellhausen, followed by most scholars (cf. NRSV), plausibly reconstructed the text to read *šim'û maṭṭeh ûmô'ēd hā'îr (Listen, Tribe, and the assembly of the city)*. This forms a good parallel to *lā'îr* in v 9Aa.

šim'û (Listen) (see 6:1): God is speaking (see v 9A). *maṭṭeh (Tribe)*, vocative after the second person imperative, means "tribe," not "rod," with "and the assembly of the city." "Tribe" refers to a clan led by a chief and his staff. That sense fits well the rest of the prophecy where the ruler and the officials of the city are in view. The reconstructed *ûmô'ed (assembly)* designates coming together at an appointed time (1 Sam 9:24; 13:8, 11; 2 Sam 20:5) or at an appointed place (Josh 8:24), or both (1 Sam 20:35). Here the sacred place, *hā'îr (the city)*, Jerusalem, is in view, a metonymy for the city's leaders (see chs. 2–3).

10 Assuming that v 9B reads *šim'û maṭṭeh ûmô'ed hā'îr*, v 10 begins with *h'š*. The text of v 10A is also disputed and best treated as a whole. MT reads with difficulty: "Are there in the house of the wicked treasures of wickedness?" or "Are there, House of the Wicked, treasures of wickedness?" MT's *ha'iš* ("are there") is best construed as intending the polar interrogative *hă*,[16] demanding a "yes" answer,[17] with a particle of existence (*'iš*).[18] V. Ryssel[19] notes: "The form *'iš*, instead of the customary form *yēš*, is also found in 2 Sam 14:19," and to this should be added Prov 18:24. The ancient versions, aside from the Tg, probably mistook it as having the usual meaning of *'ēš* "fire" (cf. LXX *mē pur* "Is there not fire"?). Although D. K. Innes[20] defended *ha'iš* of MT (and AV), most scholars emend it. J. Wellhausen,[21] looking for a parallel to the interrogative and first person of initial *ha'ezkeh* in v 11, proposed *ha'eššeh*, "shall I forget," from the root II *nšh* "to forget," with interrogative *hă* (cf. NRSV, TNIV), and B. Duhm suggested *ha'eśśā'*, "shall I forgive/or bear," which offers an even better sense. Assuming the emendation, the imperfect is best construed as deliberative (*Should I forgive*).[22] B. Renaud[23] looks for a parallel to the well-preserved v 10B. Accord-

---

16. GKC §100m.
17. *IBHS* §40.3.
18. *HALOT* 1:93, s.v. *'iš*.
19. Ryssel, *Micha*, 105.
20. Innes, "Some Notes on Micah," 217-18.
21. Wellhausen, *Die kleinen Propheten*, 148.
22. *IBHS* §31.4e.
23. *La Formation*, 329-30.

ingly, he attractively emends the frequent *bêt* "house" to the less frequent *bat* and points *rāšâ* as *reša'*, yielding "unjust bath." T. Gaster[24] suggested that when *bat reša'* was corrupted into the pointing of MT, an editor attempted to emend the text by glossing the "absurd" *bêt rāšâ* as *'ōṣĕrôt reša'*; these words must therefore be excised and *reša'* substituted after the *nomen regens bat*. This emendation is highly attractive: the liquid measure not only provides an excellent parallel with the equivalent dry measure in v 10B — *bat (bath)* "the liquid measure = 'ephah of dry measure, each being a tenth of a *ḥōmer*[25] — but the two together, which are also found in Ezek 45:11, nicely balance v 11. The versets, now of equal length (three words), pertain to false measures (v 10) and weights (v 11). Moreover, Ezek 45:10 mentions *mō'zĕnayim* "scales," *'êpah* "ephah," and *bat* "bath," almost exactly the same as Mic 6:10-11. Furthermore, each verse now begins with an interrogative *ha*, and *I AM* as the subject with a nonperfective. Although very attractive, the emendation is unnecessarily too radical. *bêt rāšâ* syntactically can be either an accusative of place *(in the house of the wicked)* or vocative ("you wicked house," TNIV). The reference to Ahab's house in v 16 (cf. 1 Kgs 22:39) suggests that the "wicked house" is the king's and his official's granaries in this nonconventional collective singular (1 Kgs 22:39).

'oṣĕrôt (granaries, traditionally "treasures") denotes either the treasure houses and vaults filled with rich materials and valuable things (1 Kgs 7:51; 14:26) and/or the precious metals, valuable foods, furnishings, spices, and the like themselves (cf. Josh 6:19, 24; Isa 2:7; 39:2; Jer 15:13; 38:11). The parallel and the verses that follow suggest at least granaries and probably storehouses of wine and oil here and in Prov 10:2. The substantive *reša'* ("of wickedness") is a genitive of instrument ("by wickedness," glossed here *filled by injustice*, i.e., "unscrupulous trade practices"), the opposite of *ṣedeq:* "In contrast to the positive root *ṣdq, rš'* expresses negative behavior — evil thoughts, words, and deeds — antisocial behavior that simultaneously betrays a person's inner disharmony and unrest (Isa 57:20)."[26]

Conjunctive *wĕ* adds *'êpat* as a second object of reconstructed *ha'eśśâ'* modified by the attributive genitive *rāzôn (the scanty ephah)*. Elsewhere *rāzôn* refers to leanness of the body, a taking away of fatness (cf. Isa 10:16; Ps 106:15). *zĕ'ûmâ (accursed)*, the qal passive participle of *z'm*, functions as an attributive adjective modifying the construct phrase. *z'm* refers to human damning in Prov 24:24 and to divine cursing in Num 23:7. Ultimately, though it is prayed for by the wronged party, God inflicts the curse. A metonymy connects the curse with

24. T. Gaster, "Notes on the Minor Prophets," 164.
25. BDB 144.
26. C. van Leeuwen, *"rš',"* *TLOT* 3:1262.

the cheating seller. When the social networks (i.e., priests teaching Torah, judges upholding the law, and prophets calling the people to repent) fail (cf. ch. 3), then God as the Ultimate Judge upholds his law by answering the prayer of the innocent victim that he curse the offender.

11 *ha'ezkeh ([If I were to forgive,] would I be acquitted!)*: The root is *zkh*, a bi-form of *zkk* "to be clean/pure." Metaphorically, it means to be "pure of sin," "to be righteous," "to be innocent," either of man (Job 15:14; 25:4) or of God (Ps 51:6[4]). MT *ha'ezkeh* could mean grammatically, "Am I innocent," but that seems unlikely in the mouth of *I AM*. If the MT's qal stem is accurate, then *ha'eśśā'* probably is elided and must be supplied from v 10, and the nonperfective introduces the apodosis of an unreal conditional clause. Most commentators (cf. TNIV) follow the Vg's superficially more easy reading *numquid justificabo stateram impiam* "I shall not justify the wicked balance, shall I?" repointing with Wellhausen the stem as piel *(ha'ăzakkeh)* and investing it with a delocutive/estimative value (i.e., "declare innocent," from which "acquit" derives).[27] Since, however, nowhere else is a preposition used to gloss the object of *zkh* piel,[28] as Vg assumes, and, since, as Wellhausen[29] says, "the object can only be the godless," one must conjecture a third masculine singular suffix, yielding *ha'ăzkkennû* ("Will I justify him"). But the emendation is unnecessary. Jerome probably attempted to make sense of the passage, having failed to reckon with the emendation of *h's* to *h'sh* and its elision in v 11. The LXX, on its part, attempted to make sense of its Hebrew *Vorlage* by supplying *rāsā'*, yielding: "Will the wicked be justified?" Willi-Plein proposes *hā'ōzĕnâ* "the one who weighs," but while the root *wazina* is attested in Arabic, "in Hebrew [it] must be regarded as hypothetical."[30] In sum, it is best to stay with the more enigmatic but not too difficult MT. In *bĕmō'zĕnê (of . . . scales)* the preposition signifies specification[31] and the construct dual, to judge from the absolute *mō'zĕnayim* refers to both pans of the balance. *reša'* (lit., "wicked" [i.e., *unjust*]) is its attributive genitive.

The personal pronoun *(your)* has been elided in the terse poetry. Conjunctive *waw* links the parallel prepositional phrase *bĕkîs (and of your leather pouch)*. *'abnê (weights)* has a more specific sense than "stones" here and is a genitive of material in the sense that the leather bag is filled with weights *(full of)*.[32] *mirmâ*

---

27. *IBHS* §24.2.

28. Cf. *IBHS* §10.2.1.

29. Wellhausen, *Die kleinen Propheten*, 148.

30. I. Willi-Plein, *Vorformen der Schriftexegese innerhalb des Alten Testaments*, BZAW 123 (Berlin: de Gruyter, 1971), 81.

31. *IBHS* §11.2.5.

32. *IBHS* §9.5.3.

is an attributive genitive, as is *reša'* (cf. Hos 12:8[7]; Amos 8:5; Prov 11:1, where it is the opposite of a "full [Heb. *šělēmâ*] weight"; 20:23).

12 The antecedent of the relative *'ăšer (whose)* is the feminine *'îr* "city" (v 9), as indicated by the feminine singular resumptive pronominal suffix[33] in *'ăšîreyhā*. Appealing to Syr, H. Wolff[34] interprets it as a causal conjunction ("because") linking v 12 with v 13, not with vv 9-11. Though not grammatically objectionable, it suffers from not alleviating the problem of the suffixes linking v 12 to v 9, from investing *'ăšer* with its less usual meaning with resumptive pronouns, and from strangely linking the accusation of v 12 with the judicial sentence of vv 13-16, not with the accusations of vv 10-11. Lindblom (cited approvingly by many) thinks that *'ăšer* is a dittography from the following *'šrh*. But *'šr* is attested in all the versions and helps to link v 12 with v 9. Note that in v 16, after the break of vv 13-15, the same suffix also refers back to "city." *'ăšîreyhā (rich people)* is the subject. *mālě'û (are full of)* is a transitive stative perfective[35] complemented by *ḥāmās (violence)*.

wěyôšbêhā (and her inhabitants) is to be distinguished from the "rich people," even as "tribe" was distinguished from "assembly of the city" in v 9B. *dibběrû (speak)* is a persistent present perfective.[36] For the form and function of *šāqer (lies)* see Mic 2:11.

In *ûlěšônām (yes, their tongue)* the *waw* is ascensive because v 12B does not add yet another group to the rich and inhabitants but epexegetes their speech by focusing on their tongues. The tautology "their tongue" and "in their mouth" underlines their deceitful speech. The singular "tongue" is an unconventional collective[37] and a metonymy of subject for their speech. *rěmîyā (is totally deceitful)* is a predicate nominative. Since the physical organ cannot be an abstract quality, it must be a metonymy of adjunct. It should be construed as a noun for an adjective wholly characterizing the subject (cf. *tûšîyā* "wholly sound in judgment"/"unsuccessful," v 9). As in the case of "tongue," tautological and so emphatic *běpîhem* ("in their mouth") is a metonymy of cause: *when they speak*. In other words, the effect of their tongues when they speak is nothing but treachery and deceit. The singular *pî* is also a nonconventional collective. By naming both organs of speech in this short clause ("tongue" and "mouth") *I AM* underscores the utter corruption of their speech.

13 In *wěgam-'ănî (and so I on my part)* the clausal conjunctive links the condemnation (vv 13-15) with the accusation (vv 10-12). The connection is

33. *IBHS* §19.3.
34. Wolff, *Micha*, 187.
35. *IBHS* §30.5.3a, 491.
36. *IBHS* §30.5.
37. *IBHS* §7.2.1.

underscored by the correlative particle *gam*, expressing correspondence: "in recompense,"[38] especially in the matter of *retribution*.[39] The independent personal pronoun *'ănî* is emphatic, contrasting what *I AM* will do with what the rich magistrates and merchants have done.[40] *heḥělêtî (I will strike you)* is hiphil of the root *ḥlh* "to be sick," and the perfective signifies resolve.[41] H. Wolff, however, says that it "cannot be related to the infinitive 'to strike you.'" Following LXX, Syr, Vg, Aquila, and Theod, most critics emend the form to *haḥillôtî* "I have begun." Others, however, retain MT with Sym and Tg because the same two verbs, *ḥlh* "to make sick" and *nkh* hiphil "to strike/ destroy," are juxtaposed. The constructions are often obscure and idomatic: *makkâ naḥlâ*, probably "blow or injury that makes sick" = "incurable injury" (?) (Jer 10:19; 14:17; 30:12; Nah 3:29);[42] *wyhwh hpṣ dkk'w hḥly* "and *I AM* was pleased to strike him, he made him sick" = ". . . to strike him sorely"(?) (Isa 53:10); and *hpl' yhwh 't-mkkt* "and *I AM* will make wonderful the striking of you" = "*I AM* will intensify your plagues"(?) (Deut 28:59). Mic 6:13 reads literally, "I will make the striking of you sick" = *I will strike you sorely*. The texts involving *ḥlh* are uncertain and confounded in the versions. In that light the versions are more easily explained away than MT, whose reading is probably idiomatic. *nkh* in the hiphil "to strike" is used with reference to bodily illness (1 Sam 5:6), the sword (2 Sam 20:10), and fruitless harvests (Amos 4:9), as in vv 14-15. The suffix, an objective genitive, probably refers to the ruler who bears the scepter (cf. v 9).

The hiphil infinitive absolute *hašmēm (devastating you)* functions as an adverbial complement, describing the attendant circumstances of the idiom "to make sore the smiting of you."[43] The "you" of v 13A is gapped. *'al-ḥaṭṭō'tekā (on account of your sins)* functions as a parallel to the correlative *wěgam-'ănî*, linking the crimes of vv 10-12 with the punishment of vv 13-15.

14 The emphatic pronoun *'attâ (As for you)* juxtaposes the "I," the heavenly Judge (v 13), with the "you," Israel's condemned, representative ruler.[44] *tō'kal wělō' tiśbā' (you will eat and not be satisfied)* is the first of the five judgments that share the same syntax: adversative *waw* plus clausal negative adverb *lō'* plus specific future imperfective verb.[45]

---

38. Cf. *IBHS* §39.3.4d.
39. BDB 169.
40. *IBHS* §16.3.2.
41. *IBHS* §30.5.1.
42. Cf. K. Seybold, "*chālāh*," *TDOT* 4:403.
43. *IBHS* §35.3.2.
44. *IBHS* §16.3.1, 2.
45. *IBHS* §39.3.3.

In *wĕyešḥākā (for dysentery will strike you)* the disjunctive *waw* signifies cause.[46] *yšḥ* is a *hapax legomenon,* giving rise to many emendations.[47] Some scholars emend on the basis of a difficult *hapax* in MT, and others on the basis of LXX (*skotasei en soi* "there will be darkness in you," retroverted *wĕye-ḥĕšak*). None is without difficulty, and none has gained a following. A. Ehrman, who wisely stays with MT, proposes two differing etymologies: he related it to the Arabic cognate noun "dirt," "filth," "soil"; whence, "your wastes shall be locked up within you,"[48] and later[49] defended Syr's rendition of *yšḥ* by "dysentery" with four arguments: (1) Its root is *šḥh* "to be bent over." Ehrman asks: "In what physical condition of great anxiety and fear, such as Micah depicts, would a man not be sated with food that he eats? And in which physical condition would he be bent over? (2) The Arabic cognate of *šḥh* means "to urinate" or "to defecate." (3) Tg. Jonathan and Rashi also understood *yšḥ* to refer to a violent disorder of the bowels. (4) It fits the context admirably. Note MT's *ḥlh* "to be sick" in v 13. His solution has lexical, historical, and contextual support. If so, the pronominal suffix is best construed as a genitive of mediated object (i.e., "dysentery [will strike] you."[50] *bĕqirbekā (in your inward parts),* though elsewhere in Micah glossed "amid, in the midst of" (see 3:11; 5:6, 7, 9, 12, 13), here refers to the interior part of the body (cf. Gen 18:12; 41:21).

In *wĕtasseg (and you will press toward birth)* the clausal, conjunctive *wāw* piles on another curse.[51] The verbal root of *tasseg* is disputed.[52] Mention should be made of NRSV's "you shall put away" and of TNIV's "you will store up" (cf. LXX's *ekneusei* "and he shall depart," retroverted *yāsōg*). In spite of their apparent differences, both understood the root to be I *sûg* "to move away." Elsewhere, however, that root in the hiphil means "to displace," always with the object *gĕbûl* "boundary marker." The extension "to remove" an implied object such as goods or articles lacks a parallel. Syr, Vg, Aquila, Sym, and Theod all understood the root to be *nāsag* "to reach, seize." On that basis G. R. Driver[53] offers the best interpretation: "you shall bring (to the birth) but not deliver." The medieval Jewish commentators Ibn Jannach, Ibn Ezra, and Qimḥi and the modern Jewish exe-

---

46. *IBHS* §39.2.3.b.
47. See *La Formation,* 331-34; S. Schwantes, "A Critical Study of the Text of Micah," 166-68.
48. A. Ehrman, "A Note on *yešaḥ* in Mic. 6:14," *JNES* 18 (1959) 156.
49. A. Ehrman, "A Note on Micah 6:14," *VT* 23 (1973) 103-5.
50. *IBHS* §9.52c.
51. *IBHS* §39.2.1c.
52. See *La Formation,* 333, and Schwantes, "A Critical Study," 168.
53. G. R. Driver, "Linguistic and Textual Problems: Minor Prophets," *JTS* 39 (1938).

getes Margolis, Torczyner, and S. Goldman[54] also interpreted the verb in this way. V 14Bb supports this interpretation, for life, not property, is given over to the sword. The jussive form may function as a nonperfective.[55] Finally, as Sellin[56] remarks, in the enumeration of curses one expects mention of barrenness or miscarriage in ancient Near Eastern literature (cf. Deut 28:18; Hos 9:11, 12, and esp. 16). In that light the *wāw* is conjunctive *(but)*. *lō taplîṭ (you will not deliver)*: Although *plṭ* normally means "to deliver" in the sense of bringing into security, in Job 21:10 ("his cow *tĕpallēṭ* 'calves,' it does not miscarry"), it refers to delivering in birth, the sense expected here after *tassēg*. In the case of both verbs the natural object, "offspring," is elided and assumed. The hiphil is causative (as opposed to resultative piel): "you cause the deliverance [of offspring]."[57]

Another *wāw (and)* piles on yet another curse. Indeclinable *'ăšer (what)* syntactically functions as the object of the resultative piel *tĕpallēṭ (you do deliver;* lit., "do make delivered"). The indirect object *laḥereb (to the sword)* before the verb is emphatic and in conjunction with *'ettēn (I will hand over)* means "consign to total annihilation."[58]

15 The emphatic pronoun *'attâ (you)* in this anabasis sustains the focus on the judged (see v 14), but the judgment moves from loss of animals (v 14) to loss of crops (v 15). *tizra' (will sow grain)* refers to many agricultural activities, and *tiqṣôr (you will . . . harvest)* to harvesting all kinds of crops. *lō' (not)* emphatically repeats the *lō'* of v 14 with reference to loss of life. Repeated *'attâ (you)* is emphatic; it also shifts the focus from the loss of grain in the spring harvest (v 15A) to the loss of oil and wine in the fall harvest (v 15B).

zayit (olives, v 15Ba), a collective singular, as the object of *tidrōk (you will press)* is a zeugma; that verb is appropriate only with its second object, *wĕtîrôš (and new wine, v 15Bb)*, a metonymy of effect for "grapes"; grapes were trampled by foot in the wine press, but olives were pressed in other ways. Repetition is a figure for emphasis, as in Martin Luther King's famous "I Have a Dream" speech. Here the Creator of Life, *I AM*, repeats *wĕlō' (and not)* to emphasize frustrated labor; instead of their labor producing life, it is ironically frustrated to bring forth sterility and death.

tāsûk (anoint yourself) is often reflexive; *šemen* (olive oil; see v 7) functions as an accusative of means *(with)*.[59] *tîrôš (new wine)* is the object of the

---

54. S. Goldman, *The Twelve Prophets*, ed. A. Cohen (Bournemouth, Hants: Soncino, 1948), 183.

55. Cf. *IBHS* §34.2.1c.

56. Sellin, "Micha," 345.

57. *IBHS* §21.2.2.

58. O. Kaiser, "*ḥereb*," *TDOT* 5:164.

59. *IBHS* §10.2.3d.

gapped *tišteḥ,* the fresh produce of the field together with the grain and olive oil.[60] *wĕlô' tišteḥ (but you will not drink)* is the climactic fourth repetition of the divine curse upon the judged. The *daghesh* in initial *yôd* of *yāyin (wine)* calls the reader to pay special attention to the quiescent letter housed between the other two.[61]

16 In *wĕyištammēr (and they observe) wĕ* is a clausal conjunctive, adding the concluding indictment (cf. vv 12-13) and sentence (cf. vv 14-15). Many scholars follow Wellhausen and emend MT's third masculine singular imperfect hithpael[62] of *šmr* because the pronoun is unexpected and the versions give other readings. LXX reads *kai aphanisthēsetai nomima laou mou,* retroverted as *wĕyištammēr ḥuqqôt 'ammî* "and the ordinances of my people will be abolished," an obviously facilitating reading. Most interpreters emend the text, therefore, with Syrohexapla, Theod, Syr, and Vg to *tišmōr* "and you kept." MT could easily be explained away as due to the metathesis of *tāw* and *šîm,* but the change from *tāw* to *yôd* is not so readily explained away. Elliger *(BHS)* and Hillers[63] interpret the retroverted prefix *tāw* as third feminine singular, not as second masculine singular, with reference to *'îr* (feminine noun for "city," v 9) because of the feminine suffix of *yōšĕbeyhā* ("its/her inhabitants"). They are on the right track, but there is no need to emend *yôd* once it is recalled that it is the unmarked form and can refer to female beings.[64] Had the text read *tāw,* the reader would presume the intended sense would be second-person singular as in vv 13-15, not the third feminine singular as demanded by *yōšĕbeyhā* in v 16bb. "The city" is a metonymy for its people, especially its leaders. The hithpael functions as a benefactive reflexive, "they observe for themselves."[65] Is *'omrî (Omri)* a play on II *'mr,* which in the hithpael means "to deal tyrannically" (Deut 21:14; 24:7)?[66]

Causal conjunctive *wāw* adds a second object to *yištammēr: kōl ma'ăśēh (and all the deeds). kōl* is absolute, meaning "all the kinds of" and not to be rushed over, and *ma'ăśēh* stands in apposition to it. The collective singular treats the "deeds" as a group.[67] *bêt- (of the house* of Ahab) designates his whole "household," i.e., husband/father, wife/mother, children (sons/daughters), dependent relatives, officials, and slaves. The genitive *'aḥ'āb (of Ahab)* designates him as the "owner," "lord" of the household.

60. See R. L. Harris, *"tîrôsh,"* TWOT 2:969.
61. *IBHS* §1.5.4e.
62. See *IBHS* §26.1b.
63. Hillers, *Micah,* 81.
64. *IBHS* §6.5.3.
65. *IBHS* §26.2e.
66. Cf. *IBHS* §9.5.1c.
67. *IBHS* §7.2.1b.

As for *wĕttēlĕkû*, the *wāw*-consecutive after the prefix conjugation probably refers to a present-time situation and represents an explanatory situation.[68] The second masculine plural, though unanticipated, is perfectly acceptable within Micah's style (see 2:12) and points a finger at all the leaders (see v 9). *hālak*, if not a dead metaphor, implicitly depicts their lives as a journey "in which the spatial element recedes into the background, albeit not its dynamic, purposeful character."[69] The nation purposively directs its course away from God toward paganism. As for *bĕmō'ăṣôtām* (in their counsels), *bĕ* indicates the sphere in which the leaders walk/live, and the pronominal suffix looks back to Omri, Ahab, and his household. Outside of Prov 22:20, *mō'ēṣâ* in its other six uses for "plan, decision" has a negative overtone.

The logical particle *lĕma'an, so that,* demands the infinitive construct *tittî (I will give . . . over).*[70] The pronominal suffix, first common singular, a subjective genitive, refers to *I AM.* The singular pronoun *'ōtĕkā (you)* reverts back to its parallels in vv 13-14. Commentators emend the text to smooth the style, but the discontinuity of pronouns in this book, as attested elsewhere in relevant literature (see 2:11), is too pervasive to make the emendations convincing. In *lĕšammâ (to become an object of horror)* the preposition *lĕ* is allative (i.e., "handed over to")[71] and *šammâ* (see 1:7; 7:13) is a metonymy of effect — that is to say, the city will be so ruined that it will cause astonishment and horror for all who see it, at least to judge from the parallel "to hissing" (*contra* v 13).

Clausal, conjunctive *wĕ* adds a second object to *tittî.* The third feminine singular suffix in *yōšĕbeyhā (its inhabitants)* looks back to the city (v 9; cf. v 12), forming an *inclusio* around the pericope. The distinction between the ruling house and the city's inhabitants runs throughout vv 9, 12, and 16, yet they are united in their sin and in *I AM*'s covenant curses upon them. *lišrēqâ (to scornful hissing)* is a syntactic and lexical parallel to *lĕšammâ,* but whereas the latter in v 16Baβ refers to the inward psychological state, the former refers to the outward response of scornful derision (cf. Jer 19:8; 29:18; 51:37; 2 Chr 29:8).

Conjunctive *wĕ* introduces the second purpose/result clause introduced by the logical particle *lĕma'an. ḥerpat (a reproach)* makes explicit that the horror and hissing of v 16Ba/b is that of the enemy. *ḥerpâ* refers to the indelible disgrace that society heaps on one who sought to break up its foundation and its social coherence; they punish him in this way to denigrate his significance, worth, and potential influence. In that light the more difficult reading *'ammî*

68. *IBHS* §33.3c.
69. F. J. Helfmeyer, "*hālakh,*" *TDOT* 3:391; cf. Waltke, *Proverbs,* 1:193-94.
70. *IBHS* §36.2.2b.
71. *IBHS* §11.2.10b.

(my people) is a more probable reading than LXX's facilitating reading *laōn*, which would be retroverted *'ammîm* ("of [the] peoples; cf. Obad 13; cf. Ezek 36:15). Accepting the reading of MT, *'am* is a genitive of disadvantage *(against)*.[72] The nations want to rid the earth of Israel and her God, but she remains *I AM's* people in contradistinction to the rest of the nations, taking the suffix *î* ("my") as a genitive of relationship.[73] *tiśśā'û (you will bear)* shifts back once again at the end of v 16Bb to the second masculine plural as at the end of v 16Ab. *nāśâ* with *ḥerpâ* as its object can mean "to take up reproach against someone" (cf. Ps 15:3), but here it means to bear upon themselves the enemies' taunts (cf. Gen 4:13). According to MT, the people's leaders bear the brunt of the shame hurled against their subjects (cf. 2 Kgs 18:26-36), whom they have forgotten are God's people. According to LXX, the reproach is directed against the leaders themselves.

EXPOSITION

The oracle of 6:9-16 is demarcated from the preceding by the formal introduction, "*I AM* is calling to the city" (*contra* 6:1), by their addressees, "Israel" (v 2) versus "the city" (v 9), and by its form, a typical judgment prophecy, in contrast to the legal complaint and liturgical entrance oracle in vv 1-8. An *inclusio* referring to the city frames the oracle. The two prophecies of 6:1-8 and 6:9-16 are linked by the contrast between what *I AM* requires and what the people in fact do. Instead of covenantal fidelity, expressed in deeds of justice and loyalty, they broke covenant by their venality and violence. Therefore, according to the covenant curses, *I AM* will hand them over to plagues, death, and wasted harvests. Both prophecies refer to the covenant sanctions: its demands (6:1-8) and its curses (6:12-15) (cf. Hos 4:10; 9:11-12, 16; Amos 5:11; Zeph 1:13; Hag 1:6).

Even if the text is emended as much as critics suggest, its structure is still clear: address (v 9), accusation (vv 10-12), and sentence of condemnation (vv 13-15). V 16 recapitulates the structure: accusation (v 16A) and sentence of condemnation (v 16B).

The accusation, for commercial dishonesty, unfolds itself in two stages: *I AM*, using first person, addresses the inhabitants with the specific accusation that they use false measures (v 10) and weights (v 11), and then, speaking of the city's elite in the third person, he accuses them of false speech in the courts (v 12). Both parts are introduced by questions to show that *I AM* must punish such deeds.

72. *IBHS* §9.5.2e.
73. *IBHS* §9.5.1i.

The sentence of condemnation is introduced by "And I (on my part)." It too develops itself in two stages: using the first person *I AM* sentences them to disease and ruin in general (v 13), and then he specifies the curses (vv 14-15): affliction of the body (v 14A), loss of offspring (v 14B), and fruitless harvests (v 15). First *I AM* frustrates them by denying them the privilege of eating their harvest of grain in the spring (v 15A), and then he frustrates them by denying them the joy of their harvest of the grapes and olive oil in the fall. The Sustainer of the creation will not sustain those who denied sustenance to their neighbor. Nevertheless, as the last stich shows, they remain God's people.

One will note that "the accusation" and "the sentence" both span three verses and within each there is syntactic coherence. The accusation is introduced by two questions (vv 10 and 11) followed by a relative 'ašer clause, modifying the whole. The sentence is introduced by the logical phrase "And so I in recompense" (first word of v 13), as in Jer 13:26; Ezek 5:11; 8:18; 9:10; 16:43; 20:23, 25; Mal 2:9. The transition is followed by futility sentences united by the anabasis "you" and "you will not" (vv 14 and 15). Moreover, both the accusations and the judicial sentence begin explicitly in the first person (vv 10-11, 13), and then implicitly *I AM* remains the speaker (vv 12, 13-14). The many types of symmetry between vv 10-12 and 13-15 that I have noted enrich the aesthetic appeal to pay attention and meditate on the oracle's content and argue against those scholars who want to shift the lines around. In sum, the accusation in vv 10-12 depicts the "rich" as using faked weights and measures to heap up riches in their storehouses, and the sentence condemns them to the loss of the treasures for which they worked and schemed. In poetic justice, the guilty are punished precisely in the area in which they have sinned.

In the recapitulation (v 16), the Southerners are accused of committing the same crimes as their Northern counterparts who brought that kingdom to ruin (v 16A). They can expect the same (v 16B): becoming a psychological, inward horror (16Ba) and an ostensive outward reproach (v 16Bb) that is leveled against God's people. The introduction and conclusion are linked by reference to the "city" (v 10), the antecedent of "its" inhabitants in v 16. The *inclusio* frames the oracle into a unity.

Verse 9 introduces the prophecy: its Author and its addressees. Instead of using the typical messenger formula, "Thus says *I AM*" (cf. 2:3; 3:5), Micah employs a unique and shrill introductory formula that stops the audience in its tracks with God's thunder from heaven: "The voice of *I AM*. He cries out," identifying *I AM* as the author of this prophetic thunder. "The voice of God" may refer to thunder (cf. Ps 29:3-5). "To cry out" means to proclaim with a clear voice and full lungs to be heard far and wide in order to attract attention and to bring the audience into contact with the speaker. Micah, presumably, gives the unseen *I AM* this "voice." After Micah's introduction to the oracle, *I AM* himself speaks, introducing his prophecy with an imperative "Listen!" thereby calling to a decision to obey (cf. Deut 4:36; 5:25-28; 8:20; 13:18[17]; 15:5; 18:16; 26:14; 27:10; 28:1, 2, 15). If *I AM* prophesies judgment and the people repent, *I AM* will relent.[74]

The addressees, the city (presumably, Jerusalem), are introduced in v 9Aa and unpacked in the parallel in v 9B, as a "tribe" (i.e., a clan with a chieftain's staff) and as the "[sacred] assembly of the city." Leaders of Jerusalem and common citizens alike are addressed, as the rest of the prophecy shows. Historically the leaders of Judah and its people were not merely one of the sacred tribes of *I AM*, but the one that bore the "staff/sceptre" to rule all the tribes (i.e., Judah; cf. 1:1).

In an apostrophe addressed to *I AM* (v 9Ab), as indicated by "your Name," but with the intention that he be overheard by his addressees, Micah asserts the sober and sound judgment of those who pay attention to *I AM*, the sacred name in which the prophecy is given. As noted at Mic 4:5, the name of *I AM* signifies his whole self-disclosure with all his sublime attributes, acts, and teachings. "Sound judgment" *(tûšîyâ)* denotes "inner power, not necessarily intellectual, that can help one escape a fix."[75] Vv 13-15 define the "fix" the tribe is in. Implicitly, the judgment oracle calls for the wicked rulers and its citizens to repent of the unjust commercial practices catalogued in the indictment (vv 10-12) and escape the sentence of doom (vv 13-15).

I AM himself provides his own, a second introduction. The shift from third person "voice of *I AM*" to second-person imperative marks the change of speaker from Micah to *I AM*. Since *I AM* is commanding "Give heed!" we should probably assume that this is a temple oracle and the leaders are assembled at that place as *I AM* speaks through his incarnate voice of Micah. The abrupt command underscores the urgency that they pay attention to him and respond properly: it is a matter of life or death.

The accusation that follows also has two parts, marked out by addressing the audience in second person (vv 10-12), followed by speaking of them in third person (v 13). The chiasm from third person to second person and then from second person to third person unifies the indictment.

Using first person ("shall I forgive"), showing that nothing is hid from his eyes, *I AM* accuses Jerusalem's assembly of turpitude and cupidity in the mar-

---

74. See R. L. Pratt Jr., "Historical Contingencies and Biblical Prediction," in *The Way of Wisdom: Essays in Honor of Bruce K. Waltke* (Grand Rapids: Zondervan, 2000), 180-211.

75. See B. K. Waltke, *The Book of Proverbs*, NICOT, 2 vols. (Grand Rapids: Eerdmans, 2004), 1:225.

ketplace. The capital city forgot *I AM*, but he has not forgotten their crimes. Their cheating of one another shows clearly their loss of covenant fidelity both with their heavenly King and with one another. But God does not violate his covenant based on his own righteous character. His question, "Shall I forgive?" demands the negative answer, "No." If *I AM* turned a blind eye to their unscrupulous practices, he would become an accomplice with them and thus guilty. Though the question is addressed to ancient Jerusalem, the answer resounds throughout history: the righteous *I AM* will never overlook commercial crimes, wherever they are committed. One cannot declare "bankruptcy" and simply walk away from stealing from one's neighbor. The truth is that apart from God's grace all mortals are thieves at heart. For tolerating, if not outright practicing, cheating in the marketplace and injustice in the courts, the ruler and his household, including his officials, deserve to wear the shameful ribbon: "Wicked!" The holy *I AM* will not tolerate granaries and storehouses filled with the food he graciously provides for all that is taken by the rich through their unjust, sharp trading practices and their legitimatization in corrupt courts.

The precise size of the "ephah," the dry measure, varied from place to place; it may have equaled 285 pounds. Ancient weights had flat bases, were often inscribed with their weight, and were carved into shapes such as those of turtles, ducks, and lions, making them easy to handle and recognize. Because of restricted technology ancient balances had a margin of error of up to 6 percent,[76] and archaeologists have found very few weights inscribed with the same denomination to be exactly identical according to modern standards. The weights were carried in a leather pouch, and a visitor would have had to check the "weights current among the merchants" at a given place.

Standard weights and measures require the legal sanction of the ruler to enforce their authority. The righteous *I AM* stands behind them (Lev 19:35-36; Deut 25:13-16; Ezek 45:10; Prov 11:1; 16:11; 20:23). "Israel's God is no Olympian, remote from everyday living," says Allen.[77] In practice the magistrates, ultimately the king (2 Sam 14:26), and the priests (Exod 30:13) set the standard under *I AM*'s administration. "[Weights and measures] are not something arbitrary which each king can manufacture to suit his convenience. They are fixed by God and delivered into the king's keeping to administer fairly."[78]

Tragically, *I AM*'s anointed king and his subordinate administrators in cahoots with the land barons (see 2:1-5) did not conform their own lives to *I AM*'s righteous administration (Deut 25:15) but took advantage of the potential for

---

76. D. Diringer, "The Early Hebrew Weights Found at Lachish," *PEQ* 74 (1942) 86.
77. Allen, *Micah*, 378.
78. A. Cohen, *Proverbs* (London: Soncino, 1967), 105.

defrauding their fellowmen because of their position and lack of technical expertise. Their scanty measures, however, were "accursed." "Curse" is the most common word for reviling speech by a wronged, weaker party to elevate himself above his oppressor through threatening the evildoer's life.[79] The person who finds no justice within the court resorts to a curse because he feels that he has no other recourse to defend himself.[80] The curse is justified; otherwise *I AM* would not inflict it (Prov 26:2). If *I AM* does not respond to the oppressed's cry to right the wrongs inflicted upon them that led to their loss of their sacred inheritance in the land, he would be as culpable of wrongdoing as the oppressors themselves for not upholding justice (cf. 2:9).

The notion of "curse" forms a janus as to why God will not acquit the guilty. *I AM's* accusation now turns from unjust measures to unjust scales. "Balances" could be falsified by inaccurate pans, a bent crossbow, or mishandling. Moreover, the Law strictly proscribed having diverse "weights" in one's small leather bag that concealed the weights placed on the balance, that is, a small one to cheat the buyer and a larger one to cheat the seller (Deut 25:13). Instead God's catechetical teaching prescribed accurate balances and honest weights. If *I AM*, whose eyes gaze upon all things, overlooked an inaccurate "balance" with "deceptive weights," he too would be guilty, not "innocent." Because of his sublime character, unjust commercial practices must be judged. Even God's common grace in human conscience teaches that deceptive trade practices are wrong. H. Wolff[81] cites The Code of Hammurabi: "If a merchant lent grain or money at interest and when he lent (it) at interest he paid out the money by the small weight and the grain by the small measure, but when he got (it) back he got the money by the [large] weight (and) the grain by the large measure, [that merchant shall forfeit] whatever he lent."[82] He also cites this hymn to Shamash: "He who handles the scales in falsehood, he who deliberately changes the stone weights (and) lowers [their weight], will make himself life for the profit and then lose [his bag of weights]." Unlike many modern preachers, *I AM* does not mince his words but forthrightly names the sins.

I AM's accusation now turns from condemning Jerusalem's unjust weights and measures to condemning their violent speech whereby the people protect their unjust commercial practices. The "rich" of Jerusalem include the rich land barons (2:1-5), the royal family, the military elite, and the false prophets and unscrupulous priests (ch. 3) (see Amos 6:1-3). While *'ōšer* "wealth" is considered a

---

79. C. A. Keller, "*qll*," *TLOT*, 1:1143.

80. A. Meinhold, *Die Sprüche*, Zürcher Bibelkommentare (Zürich: Theologischer, 1991), 501.

81. Wolff, *Micha*, 194.

82. Law 94, "The Code of Hammurabi," tr. T. J. Meek (*ANET*, 169).

gift of God (cf. Prov 8:18), *'āšîr* "rich people," probably a collective singular, are condemned for trusting themselves, for making their more-than-sufficient material prosperity their source of security and significance, and for wronging a weaker neighbor and not showing kindness to the poor but plundering them in their greed (cf. 1 Sam 21:1[20:42d]; Isa 53:9; Jer 9:11[12]; Ps 49:3[2], 7[6]; Prov 18:11, 23; 28:11; but see Exod 30:15; Ps 45:13[12]). The biblical authors show no sympathy for the rich and always regard them with hostility.[83] "Full of violence," they abuse the poor and powerless by bending the law to their advantage. H. Haag says, "A favorite instrument of *chāmās* ["violence"] is false accusation and unjust judgment"[84] (cf. Pss 25:19; 27:12; 55:11[9], 13[11]; 58:2[1], 3[2]). He adds, "That the accused should experience *chāmās* in court is all the more perverse, because it is in court that they should find protection from *chāmās*." The corruption affects all of Jerusalem's inhabitants; the leaven of the ruling class is leavening the whole lump. All its inhabitants speak lies, and everything they say is deceitful. *šeqer* "lies," a collective singular, designates everything that occurs as fraud and trickery, with and without words, in daily life, especially in commerce. To speak lies alludes, among other things, to the scheming of false witnesses with regard to false weights and to the giving of testimony in court. Both in quantity and in quality, the schemes, the news reports, and the conversations of the people are full of deceit to cover up injustice for profit. Whereas they speak lies, in this indictment the righteous *I AM* speaks the truth.

The oracle now turns to the judicial sentence (vv 13-15). The judgment is not a natural catastrophe but the terrible consequence of an armed invasion, resulting in famine, ruin, and exploitation of the riches of the land by the enemy. The Judge himself hands down his just sentence against the corrupt merchants of the city and its leaders (cf. Mic 1:6-7; 2:3-4). Whereas the accusation was delivered impersonally, in the third person (cf. v 12), with reference to the city, the Judge hands down his sentence in second-person singular, addressed presumably to each person in the city. The distinction between the appointed assembly that rules the city and its subjects is so greatly attenuated that the ruler and ruled can be grouped together under the common singular "you" (cf. v 14B). After all, *I AM*'s anointed (i.e., the king) is the very life breath of the people (Lam 4:20). To make clear that the whole city is under judgment, *I AM* shifts from "you" singular to "you" plural: "you walk" and "you will bear," the terminal verbs of v 16A and v 16B respectively. He also indicates the universal judgment by referring to the city in v 16A and its inhabitants in v 16B.

---

83. R. N. Whybray, *Wealth and Poverty in the Book of Proverbs*, JSOTSup 99 (Sheffield: JSOT Press, 1990), 22.

84. H. Haag, *"chāmās,"* TDOT 4:483.

The correlative, "and so in recompense," underscores that *I AM* will match his punishment to the city's crimes. Each will get his just deserts. As they despoiled others, *I AM* will despoil them. The emphatic "And so even I myself" *(wĕgam-'ănî)* strikingly contrasts the Just Avenger with the "you" (see above) and guarantees that he will carry out his just sentence. The affliction *I AM* will strike on them (assembly and citizens) will be so "sore" and grievous that it will fill them with horror. *šmm* may also be glossed "to be appalled, awestruck," "to grow numb." Its basic meaning reaches from "desolation" (objective) to "to be appalled" (subjective). The horror *I AM* inflicts is so severe that it will fill both the judged and those who observe it (v 16) with horror. The former is in view in the first judgment speech (v 13B) and in the second (v 16B). The city's horror is produced by the appalling scenes unpacked in the rest of the sentence, after this summary introduction. All this is on account of their "sins." Despite Koch's objection, the meaning of the root *ḥṭ'* is "miss (a mark)," "fall short." This basic, nontheological meaning is attested alongside its familiar religious meaning of "sin." *ḥṭ'* is used in all sorts of circumstances for disqualifying error.[85] They will reap what they have sown (Gal 6:7). Ironically, they will "reap" frustrating futility.

In an anaphora, repeating emphatically five times "you will . . . but you will not . . . ," *I AM* catalogues what Hillers[86] calls "futility curses": "the guilty will undertake a course of action and inevitably be frustrated in it." In v 14A, this entails eating without being satisfied, and in v 14B, bringing to birth without producing offspring. The curses *I AM* threatened in the covenant now fall upon them (cf. Lev 26:26; Deut 28:30-31, 38-40; Hos 4:10; 5:6; 8:7; 9:12, 16; Amos 5:11). They had been duly warned beforehand, before the judgment fell. However, instead of setting out the well-attested Deuteronomic triad of affliction — "sword, famine, plague" — in vv 14-15 Micah presents the sequence plagues (v 14A), the sword (v 14B), and loss of food due to war (v 15), not drought. The curses pertain both to the order of creation and to history. *I AM* by his "omnicompetence" is sovereign over both. By omnicompetence I mean *I AM's* inseparable attributes of omniscience and omnipotence. These two attributes, unique to *I AM*, go hand in hand, for knowledge without power is weak and power with knowledge is dangerous. To rule the creation and history, *I AM* must know the situation that thwarts his purpose and have the power to overcome it.

They "will eat" and "not be satisfied" because *I AM* will plague them with sickness, more specifically with "dysentery in [their] inner parts." In addition,

---

85. R. Knierim, "*ḥṭ'*," *TLOT* 1:406-8.
86. Hillers, *Micah*, 82.

he will plague them with miscarriages ("they will press toward birth, but not deliver [their offspring]." To this plague he adds the sword. What "they deliver" he will annihilate in war by handing it over "to the sword." Though the sword may become incarnate in such as the Assyrian military arsenal, the hand wielding it is *I AM*'s (Isa 10:1-19).

Continuing the anaphora in a sustained attack against the representative ruler, "you," *I AM* now adds three more futility maledictions, all pertaining to fruitless harvests from the scourge of war: of the grain harvest in the spring (v 15A), and of the olives that produce the gladdening oil (v 15Ba) and the grapes that produce the elixir of gods and mortals in the fall (v 15Bb). These specific maledictions begin with "you will eat, but . . . not be satisfied" (v 14A) and end with the *inclusio*, "you will not drink."

Seed was scattered by hand in the breaks between the early rainy periods, around November/December, and grain was harvested between April (barley) and May (wheat). Grapes were harvested in September/October, and olives, knocked down from the trees, at the end of the vintage. Grapes were trampled by foot for their prized wine, and olives were normally pressed out for their oil by beating them in a stone mortar or in a bowl-shaped depression in the rock or by their being pressed by means of a heavy cylindrical stone, rolled over them in a rectangular or circular press. Here the best kind of wine is in view. "New wine" *(tîrôš)*, according to F. S. Fitzsimmonds, "represents wine made from the first drippings of the juice before the winepress was trodden. As such it would be particularly potent. . . ."[87] The verse begins with food and ends climactically with the best wine.

The olive tree, on account of its prized oil for food, medicine, fuel for lamps, cosmetics, and anointing, was regarded as king of the trees by both gods and men (Judg 9:8-9). One anointed oneself with olive oil after a bath, for example, for its fragrance and cosmetic effect. Oil symbolized prosperity and joy (Deut 32:13; 33:24; cf. Isa 61:3; Ps 45:8[7]). Oil and wine symbolized the joy from labor. God will deprive his miscreant people of both.

The immediate cause of the loss of their harvest was their enemies (Isa 7:18-25; Jer 5:17) and/or the annihilation and/or exile of the people (cf. Isa 16:9; 24:7; Jer 40:12). Ultimately, fruitless sowing and the failure of harvest due to drought (cf. Deut 11:13, 14; 29:22[23]) or to enemies (Lev 26:16; Judg 6:3) are *I AM*'s punishments.

I AM recapitulates the indictment of vv 10-12 by comparing the degeneracy of the city to the infamous apostasy of Omri and Ahab in v 16A, and recapitulates the horrors of the judgment (of vv 13-15) in v 16B. This is the only

---

87. F. S. Fitzsimmonds, "Wine and Strong Drink," *NBD*, 1254.

verse in the entire corpus of Micah's oracle where kings are mentioned by name.

"The precepts [i.e., legal precepts or ordinances] of Omri" contrast sharply with those of David (1 Kgs 3:3). Whereas David had prophetic sanction because he ruled according to the Law of Moses and listened to *I AM*'s true prophets such as Samuel, who founded the monarchy on Mosaic teachings, Omri usurped the throne without prophetic sanction and ruled independently of God's Law. According to the Deuteronomistic historian, "he sinned more than all before him" (1 Kgs 16:25), but the pagan Assyrians so highly regarded him that they named the Northern Kingdom after him, *Bît-Ḫumria,* "House of Omri."[88] What Omri decreed, his son Ahab carried out. Ahab's household included the likes of Jezebel (1 Kings 21) and Athaliah (2 Kings 11), both of whom were notorious for unethical conduct and bloodshed. In Naboth's vineyard story swindling, violence, and false witnesses play a prominent role (cf. v 12). In short, what Omri decreed, Ahab practiced. How galling it must have been to the house of David to be compared with this house that 150 years before had tried to kill them. *I AM* yokes Samaria and Jerusalem together in wickedness and his righteous judgment (cf. 1:1).

The reference to "all" means "all kinds of" and entails Ahab's heinous betrayal of Israel's covenant with *I AM* by substituting the worship of Baal (1 Kgs 16:29-34). Indeed, their unethical conduct was based on Baal worship, a religion that pandered to the sinful nature and demanded no moral rectitude. *I AM* now shifts to the plural "you," accusing the entire leadership of purposively pursuing the policies of those wicked Northern kings.

As a result of their dereliction, *I AM* will hand over the rulers to "horror" (see v 13). The observer's horror is produced by the appalling scene of pestilence, annihilation of offspring, and wasted crops of vv 13-14 inflicted upon the failed leadership. His inward psychological horror will find expression in his scornful hissing against all the inhabitants of the holy capital that under the righteous David ruled over the lands from the River of Egypt to the Great River — the Euphrates — of Mesopotamia. Nevertheless, though the city must bear the pagan's opprobrium against *I AM* and his people, *I AM* still calls its inhabitants "my people." There is still a future beyond the punishment as long as eternal, omnicompetent *I AM* owns them as his people.

88. *ANET* 283-84.

C. Jerusalem's Social Structures Break Apart (7:1-6)

1   Woe is me!
    For I have become as in the gatherings of summer fruit,
        as in the gleanings of a vintage
    [when] not a cluster remains to be eaten,
        not one ripe fig, such as my soul yearns for.

2   A faithful person has ceased from the land;
        and there is not an upright person in it.
    All of them lie in ambush to shed blood,
        each one hunts for his brother with a net.

3   They set both their hands upon the evil [net to weave it] skillfully —
        officials demand compensation,
        and judges make rulings for repayment;
        and the great one speaks the craving of his soul —
    and so they weave it.

4   The best of them is like a brier hedge;
        the most upright is a hedge.
    The day of your watchmen — of your punishment — is at hand;
        now their panic will come.

5   Do not rely on your friend,
        do not trust your intimate friend!
    From the one who lies in your bosom
        keep the doors of your mouth [sealed]!

6   Surely a son treats his father as a fool;
        a daughter rises up against her mother.
        a daughter-in-law against her mother-in-law.
    A man's enemies are the men of his own household.

EXEGESIS

1   The exact meaning of the exclamation *'alĕlay lî (Woe is me!)* is unknown.[1]
To judge from its only other use in Job 10:15, it could be a woe pronounced
upon one who is found guilty. In both passages, perhaps for the assonance of
lāmed in the original *'ll*, it is followed by *lî (to me)*, a *lāmed* of disadvantage.[2]
    The clausal adverb and conjunctive *kî (for)* melds "surely" and "because."

1. *IBHS* §40.4.5.
2. *IBHS* §11.2.10.

It is the first of three initial palatal stops in 7:1Abα: k–k–q. In *hayîtî (I have become)* the antecedent is gapped but the speaker is probably the prophet, *I AM*'s surrogate, in a vineyard (cf. Isa 5:1-7). *I AM*'s voice becomes incarnate in Micah (see the introductions to the two preceding oracles in this cycle: 6:1-2, 9). The root *hyh* has its active sense of "become," and the suffix conjugation designates the perfect tense. Micah was not always forlorn but has become distraught with his contemporary Isaiah due to the increasing loss of justice in the so-called holy land. *kĕ'ospê qayiṣ (as in the gatherings of summer fruit)*, after the comparative preposition *kĕ*, consists of the masculine plural construct of the nominal use of the qal infinitive construct[3] of the root *'sp* "to gather, remove," and the objective genitive *qayiṣ*[4] "summer fruit (especially figs)."[5] A superficial reading of MT yields "I am like the gleanings of the harvest," an inapposite notion, for it represents the speaker as being like a first fig or cluster of grapes, the very comparison he denies in the B verset. LXX and Vg stumbled over the difficulty. LXX reads *hōs synagōn kalamēn en amētō* "like one who gathers stubble at harvest." Many commentators follow LXX and read a masculine plural participle *'ōsĕpy*, interpreting the final *yôd* as a *hireq compaginis*[6] or as a plural construct ("like those who pick"). But a participle in v 1Aa finds no parallel in v 1Ab, and thus many scholars emend *kĕ'ōlĕlōt* to *kĕ'ōlēl* (like a gleaner of). Others emend *'spy* in 1Aa as a participle and read *kĕ'ōlĕlōt* in v 1Ab as "in the time of gleaning" (= "I have become like some picker of fruit at the time gleanings are left by the vine harvest"). Vg's *sicut qui colligit autumno racemos vindemiae* ("as one who gleans in autumn the grapes of the vintage") interprets *'llt* as a complement accusative of *'ōsēp* and *qayiṣ* as a temporal accusative. These variants and other emendations, however, become unnecessary once it is understood with Sym that the preposition *kĕ* can "absorb" another preposition such as *bĕ*.[7] The same phenomenon occurs in Isa 17:5, where one finds the same words, the same imagery, and the same construction, except that it is singular (cf. also Isa 24:13). This parallel suggests that BDB[8] is wrong in analyzing *'ospê* as the noun *'ōsep* (cf. Isa 32:10). The countable plural indicates that the harvest was gathered several times so as to leave no gleanings whatsoever.

kĕ 'ōlĕlōt bāṣîr (as in the gleanings of a vintage) consists of the comparative *kĕ*, which again "absorbs" *bĕ*, its object *'ōlĕlōt*, a feminine plural construct of the root *'ll*, a poel form, "to act severely" and so "to go over a second time" (i.e.,

---

3. *IBHS* §§36.1.1; 36.2.
4. *IBHS* §9.5.2b.
5. KBL 838.
6. *IBHS* §8.2e.
7. *IBHS* §11.2.9a.
8. BDB 63a.

"gleaning"), and the objective genitive *bāṣîr* "vintage." The countable plural again emphasizes that nothing is left.

The predicator of nonexistence *'ên* (*[there] is not*) stands juxtaposed to the existential verb *hyh* "to be" with the nominative subject *'eškôl* (*a cluster/ bunch of grapes*). Since 7:1B explains the prophet's distressed situation of 7:1A, the English gloss is helped by adding *when*. In *le'ĕkôl* (*[remains] to be eaten*) the *lĕ* with the infinitive construct in a verbless clause has its normal modal significance, here of capability; literally: "there is not a cluster of grapes for the possibility of eating" = "not a cluster of grapes remains to be eaten."

bikkûrâ probably has the restricted sense *first ripe fig* (so Vg) and not the general meaning "first fruits" (so LXX and Syr), a collective singular, and is the parallel subject with gapped *'ên*. The singular is a countable,[9] not a collective, to judge from its value in Isa 28:4 and the plural form in Jer 24:2. If so, there is an escalation from not a bunch of grapes to not a single fig. The denominative piel *'iwwĕtâ* (*which . . . craves*) denotes producing the state indicated by the noun *'awwâ* ("desire"/"longing")[10] as an asyndetic relative clause qualifying *bkwrh* signaled by "which."[11] For *napšî* ("my soul") see 6:7. The genitive denotes inalienable possession.[12]

2 *ḥāsîd* (*a faithful person*) has a pattern that may be active (i.e., "one who practices *ḥesed*") or passive (i.e., "one who receives *ḥesed*") or stative ("one who is *ḥesed*").[13] All three have been argued for. The last is probably best.[14] In *'ābad* (*has ceased*) the suffix conjugation functions similarly to *hayîtî* of v 1. *min-hā'āreṣ* means *from the land*. The preposition is partitive, and the definite article points to a unique referent,[15] the holy land of Israel.

Conjunctive *waw* (*and*) piles on an intensifying parallel clause. For *yāšār* (*an upright person*) see 2:7, and for *'ên* see 1:7B. *bā'ādām* (*among humankind*) is a conventional collective masculine singular noun.[16] "In the land" is gapped.

kullām (*all of them*) indicates totality, and the parallel *'iš* (*a person*) distributes them to each individual. The plural pronominal suffix looks back to the collective *'ādām*. In *lĕdāmîm,* the preposition *lĕ* marks the person against whom the

---

9. *IBHS* §7.2.1.
10. *IBHS* §24.4e.
11. *IBHS* §19.6.
12. *IBHS* §9.5.1h, 145.
13. *IBHS* §5.3.
14. See J. Morgenstern, "The *Ḥᵃsîdîm* — Who Were They?" *HUCA* 38 (1967) 59-73 and K. Sakenfeld, *The Meaning of Ḥesed in the Hebrew Bible,* HSM 17 (Missoula, Mont.: Scholars Press, 1978), 241-45.
15. *IBHS* §13.5.1b.
16. BDB 9, §2; *IBHS* §7.2.1d.

action is directed[17] and *dāmîm* "bloodshed" is a plural of composition or a plural of result,[18] "blood shed by rude violence."[19] "For bloodshed" is better glossed in English *to shed blood*. The plural (in pausal form) *ye'ĕrōbû (lie in wait)* agrees with the subject *kullām;* the prefix conjunction in present time, as indicated by the predicator of nonexistence, represents an iterative situation.[20]

The plural *yaṣûdû (hunts)* agrees *ad sensum* with the distributive "each one (of them)"; the prefix conjugation again indicates a progressive present situation. The parallel "for bloodshed" and the accusative "net" suggest adding "to catch" (with the intent to kill). LXX, Vg, Tg, Syr, Aquila, and Sym identify its root as I *ṣwd* "destruction" (Sym), "death" (Vg), but Lohfink[21] rejects this derivation: "The metaphor of hunting and pursuit in v. 2в supports II *ḥērem* ('net')." It functions as a unique accusative of state or manner with this verb *(with a net)*.[22]

3 Although the general sense of v 3 is clear enough, the text and its details are not. The versions do not represent so much variant readings as bold attempts to make sense of a difficult text. Most commentators, therefore, conjecture emendations, which are surveyed by B. Renaud.[23] After presenting about a dozen emendations, Renaud concludes: "A. George, A. Deissler, and Rinaldi-Luciani refuse to translate. This is doubtless the most honest solution, if it is not the most glorious." In the light of this discouraging history of diverse and unconvincing emendations — and there are even more proposals to improve the text[24] — it seems best to make as much sense as possible of MT as it stands.

kappayim (both hands, lit. "both palms")[25] is best taken as subject of this nominal clause, which demands that the verb *set* be supplied in English, and in the terse poetry the pronoun *their* (i.e., *their hands*). Since the substantival adjective *hāra'* "evil or harmful" describes a state, both hands cannot be upon it literally, and so the adjective is best taken as a metonymy of adjunct for something harmful, such as "the net," the last word of v 2 and the implied object of "weaving" in the last word of v 3. If so, the article signifies that which is vivid to the imagination.[26] BDB[27] thinks that "ethical evil" is in view; in that case, the article

---

17. *IBHS* §11.2.10d, 207.
18. *IBHS* §7.4.1b.
19. BDB 196-97, §1f.
20. *IBHS* §31.3b.
21. N. Lohfink, *"hāram," TDOT* 5:182.
22. *IBHS* §10.2.2d/e.
23. *La Formation,* 349.
24. Cf. Schwantes, "A Critical Study," 180-85.
25. See *IBHS* §7.1b.
26. *IBHS* §13.5.1e.
27. BDB 948, §3.

signifies class. In *lĕhêṭîb* semantic pertinence suggests that *lĕ* signifies purpose, and the hiphil infinitive with the stative verb *yṭb* means "to cause (something) to be good,"[28] that is, do (something) well/thoroughly[29] and fits well the context of making an evil net. The adverbial phrase modifies the copulative "are" (lit. "both hands are upon the evil skillfully"). In sum, I gloss the verset: *Their hands make the evil net skillfully.* Since *raʿ* (bad) and *ṭôb* are precise antonyms, the play upon words ("the hands make the evil good") is probably intentional.

In Mic 7:3Abα/Abβ one may encounter what P. D. Miller[30] labeled "synonymous-sequential parallelism," that is, "cola in which some elements are synonymously parallel and some are sequential or continuous with one another." Here *haśśar (the ruler) . . . wĕhaśśōpēṭ (and the judge)* are synonyms — in fact, a hendiadys, "the judging ruler" — and *šōʾēl (demands)* depends on gapped *šillûm* for its object, and vice versa. The versets read:

> The ruler demands [a reward],
> and the judge [demands] a reward.

E. Z. Melamed,[31] following Cassuto's *Commentary on Exodus* 2:14, quotes a similar usage from Ugaritic, documented from Amos 2:3; Zeph 3:3; Ps 148:11; Prov 8:16, in which *haśśar (the ruler) wĕhaśśōpeṭ (and the judge)* break up a stereotyped hendiadys. The sequence of the predicates, however, is more complex than they suppose, for their appeal to Isa 1:23 is not precise. Their explanation breaks down with *baššillûm* "for a reward"; the *bĕ pretii* (*for* [i.e., "in exchange for"])[32] is not appropriate with *šōʾēl (demands)*. Probably *šillûm (a payment)*, the genus for the species *šōḥad* "bribe," is the gapped object of *šōʾēl*. If so, a zeugma is involved, for *baššillûm* is appropriate only with an elided form of *špṭ*, such as *šōpēṭ (judges)*. The article with these collective singular subjects is generic, signifying class,[33] because "all" in v. 2 indicates that not just one or two magistrates are in view.

Because rulers are "asking" for payment from their subjects, *šōʾēl* takes on the nuance of *demand*. The participle functions as the predicate and so signifies a durative situation.[34] *šillûm (for a payment,* i.e., "a bribe") in its other five uses

---

28. *IBHS* §27.2f.
29. BDB 405, §3.
30. P. D. Miller, "Synonymous-Sequential Parallelism in the Psalms," *Bib* 61 (1980) 256-60.
31. E. Z. Melamed, "Break-up of Stereotyped Phrases as an Artistic Device in Biblical Poetry," in *Studies in the Bible*, Scripta Hierosolymitana 8 (Jerusalem: Magnes, 1961), 131-33.
32. *IBHS* §11.2.5d.
33. *IBHS* §13.5.1f.
34. *IBHS* §37.6.

refers to God's retribution ("repayment"). The article in *haggādôl* precludes taking the singular as a collective. The article is not generic but represents a unique referent.[35] This substantival adjective is a metonymy for the king or for his high official who represents him.[36] The predicate participle *dōbēr (speaks)* is also durative. Perhaps since piel signifies the result of an action, only the durative participle occurs in qal. *hawwat napšô (craving of his soul; see 7:1Bb)* must be a metonymy of adjunct for *šillûm (payment)* or its equivalent (i.e., the bribe he craves), for a word of speaking cannot have a psychological state such as "craving" as its object. The magistrate's depraved appetite is the source of his openly perverse speech. The independent personal pronoun *hû'* stands in apposition to the pronominal suffix *(even he)*, the last one you would expect to stoop so low.

The *wāw*-consecutive (narrative *wāw*) in *wayĕ'abbĕtûhā* summarizes the activity *(and so)*, clarified by the three circumstantial participial clauses.[37] The plural subject looks back to the corrupt magistrates and the greedy great one. The feminine singular verbal suffix does not look back to *ḥērem*, for that noun is masculine, but to the abstract activity of weaving as depicted in v 3Abβ/Ba.[38] The piel is resultative. In sum, the verb may be glossed *and so they weave it*, that is, their rulings and judgings together to gratify their greed.[39] According to this interpretation, the parallel clauses with "rulers," "judges," and the "great one" syntactically and conceptually interrupt the weaving of the evil "net" and are marked off as such by dashes.

4   By connecting *wayĕ'abbĕtûhā* at the end of v 3Bb with v 4 (cf. *BHS*), the versions complicated an intelligible MT. *ṭôbām (the best of them)* refers to their morality, as shown by the parallel "upright," and is in the comparative superlative degree.[40] It too may be a play on words with *ra'* and *yṭb* in v 3A. In this nominal clause *kĕḥēdeq (is like a brier hedge)* is a metaphor for the magistrates and judges who by their conspiracy prevent the plaintiff from obtaining justice, and their skill in obtaining bribes makes approaching them painful and better avoided. The expected suffix *ām* is best supplied by emending *yšr mmswkh* to *yĕšārām mĕsûkâ (the most upright of them is a thorn hedge)*.[41] Vv4Aa and 4Ab are synonymous parallels escalating the simile into the stronger metaphor, as in Isa 40:6.

35. *IBHS* §13.5.1b.
36. *IBHS* §14.3.3d.
37. *IBHS* §33.2.1d.
38. *IBHS* §6.4.2b.
39. *IBHS* §24.3.1.
40. *IBHS* §14.5c, ##31-32.
41. See *HALOT* 2:640, s.v. *mĕsûkāh*.

The construct *yôm (the day of)* is found with the temporal genitive *mĕṣappeykā (your watchmen)*. The piel participle masculine plural construct with second-person singular suffix of the root *ṣph* "to look out or about, spy, keep watch" functions as a substantive for a watchman (distinct from visionary, Isa 21:6; "guards/overseers," 2 Kgs 11:18; Ezek 44:15) and is an incomplete metaphor for prophets (Hab 2:1; cf. qal in Isa 56:10; Jer 6:17; Ezek 3:17; 33:7; Hos 9:8). The pronoun is a possessive genitive for *I AM*'s gift of prophets to see portending dangers and by their oracles to protect the nation's rulers. In sum, the phrase is best glossed by *the day announced by your watchmen* (i.e., prophets). Many unnecessarily emend the text from the *lectio difficilior mĕṣappeykā* to the facilitating reading *miṣṣāpôn* ("from the north")[42] for scribes confuse *wāw* and *yôd*, and *nûn* and *kāp*.[43]

The construct override *pĕquddātĕkā ("of your* [sing.] *visitation")* in this high poetry shows the close connection between the temporal genitives "your watchmen/prophets" and "of your visitation," a metonymy for judgment, that they announced. In this case the pronominal suffix "your" with the verbal noun "visitation" is an abstract subjective genitive (i.e., "when you are punished").[44] Bo Reicke[45] regards the genitive as a genitive of authorship with reference to God (i.e., "when Your visitation comes"), but the change of antecedent from "ruler" to *I AM* is unlikely and he fails to note that the noun normally is passive, not active. Renaud[46] contends that his appeal to an active voice for this verbal noun in Num 3:36; 4:16; Isa 60:17; 1 Chr 24:3 is not convincing. Moreover, he says, "When the word is equivalent to a punitive visit, a punishment, even as the context imposes that sense in Mic 7:4B, it always has a passive sense; it is the punishment undergone by the unfaithful priests and prophets (Jer 8:12), the idols (Jer 10:15; 51:18), the people of Anathoth (Jer 11:23), the false prophets (Jer 23:12), the mercenaries of Egypt (Jer 46:21), the bull of Babel (Jer 50:27; note the formulation so close to Mic 7:4B . . .)." In that light, the pronominal suffix cannot refer to *I AM* (*contra* Lisowsky, Reicke, and Wolff), but to an individual Judean as in v 5 (cf. 6:13), probably "the great one."

The accents combined with the adverb *'attâ (now)* show that *bā'â* is a present perfective ("has come" = *is at hand*), not a future instantiated participle ("is about to come"). *tihyeh (will come)* denotes to come into being in this lively narration.[47] *mĕbûkātām (their confusion;* cf. Isa 22:5) presents a striking

42. See *HALOT* 3:1046, s.v. *ṣāpōn*.
43. See B. K. Waltke, "The Reliability of the Old Testament Text," in *NIDOTTE*, 63.
44. *IBHS* §9.5.1e, 144.
45. B. Reicke, "Liturgical Traditions in Mic. 7," *HTR* (1967) 358-59.
46. *La Formation*, 355.
47. BDB 225, §II.1a.

case of alliteration between *měsûkâ*, the last word of v 4A, and *měbûkâ*, the last word of v 4B, and unifies the verse. The shift from a second masculine singular suffix, with reference to "the great one," to third masculine plural with reference to the rulers and judges of v 3 is acceptable Hebrew, especially in Micah.

5   *'al-ta'ămînû* (*do not rely*, give credence to), a second masculine plural jussive, is presumably addressed to all the citizens of Jerusalem. The hiphil is internal[48] with a tolerative sense[49] = "do not allow yourselves to rely on." The preposition in *běrēa'* (*on your friend*) marks the object.[50] The grammar is the same in the parallel. Instead of MT's asyndetic construction, Mur 88 and LXX link v 5Aa with v 5Ab with a conjunctive *wāw*. This late addition attempts to smooth the text but does not match the elliptical, vigorous, asyndetic style of this pericope with the exception of v 2A.

Placing the adverbial phrase *miššō-kebet* before *šmr*, the verb it modifies, emphasizes the thought signified by *even*. *min* (*from*) is ablative, "away from."[51] The feminine singular substantival participle "who sleeps" is a metonymy for the wife. *ḥêqekā* functions as a genitive of location[52] and designates the breast between the arms. The alternation between plural in Mic 7:5A and singular in Mic 7:5B is acceptable Hebrew (see 2:11).

šěmōr "keep" means "to protect" with objects in the semantic domain of commands in the sense "to preserve them carefully by faithful obedience." But with concrete nouns, such as "mouth," it means "to protect" in the sense of "to keep away from danger so as to preserve someone or something." The probable dual *pitḥê-pîkā* (*doors of your mouth*) is an incomplete metaphor for the "lips of your mouth," as demanded by semantic pertinence (cf. Ps 141:3). "Lips" and "mouth" are both metonymies for what one speaks/says. In sum: "Keep away from even your wife who lies in your bosom whatever you want to say in order to protect yourself."

6   For *kî* (*surely*) see 7:1.[53] *bēn* (*a son*), along with the other family members, "*father*," "*daughter*," "*daughter-in-law*," is anarthrous to underscore the class to which it belongs.[54] The piel *měnabbēl* (*treats with contempt*) with its root *nbl* signifies an estimative/delocative force, and *'āb* (*father*) is in the state denoted by the verb; that is, the son esteems his father a fool and publicly pro-

48. *IBHS* §27.2.
49. *IBHS* §27.5.
50. *IBHS* §11.2.5f.
51. *IBHS* §11.2.11b.
52. *IBHS* §9.5.2f.
53. *IBHS* §39.3.1d.
54. *IBHS* §13.2b.

nounces him to be one.[55] The participle as the predicate of a nominal clause represents a durative, ongoing, situation.[56]

The parallel has the same syntax: *bat (a daughter) qâmâ (rises up,* qal participle) *bĕ (against) 'immâ (her mother)*. The broken-up stereotype merisms of "son~father" and "father~mother" signify that "children rise up against parents."

The identical syntax of *kallâ (daughter-in-law) ba (against) ḥămōtāh (her mother-in-law)* shows that *qâmâ* is gapped. The generic statement *'ōyĕbê 'îš 'anšê bêtô* includes the hostility of all the males within a man's household. The participial form *'ōyĕbê (the enemies)* has no morphemic value[57] and in English needs the article to represent the class. *'îš* is best construed as the objective genitive of an implicitly verbal noun, "enemy." "*'îš* and its plural, *'anšê*, probably denote every male without distinction to rank — at least to judge from the parallels: "son," "daughter," and the like. *bêt* denotes "household," not a physical "house" (see 6:10).

EXPOSITION

The new prophecy is marked off from *I AM*'s reproach oracle against Jerusalem in 6:9-16 by the change of speaker from *I AM* to Micah, who speaks in an autobiographical "I" (v 1, cf. v 7), and by the unified reproach prophecy, including accusation (vv 1-4A) and judicial sentence (vv 4B-6). The use of a lament form ("Woe is me!") and the dropping of direct address ("you") put the reproach under the umbrella of the lament form. The mood is also that of lament. The lament, however, thinly veils that vv 1-4A are in fact an accusation giving the reason for the judgment in vv 4B-6. The startling proclamation that the prophesied day of *I AM*'s judgment is at hand introduces the condemnation to confusion that rips the nation apart down to its most intimate relationships. The unmistakable alliteration between *mĕsûkâ* ("thorn hedge"), the last word of v 4A, and *mĕbûkâ* ("confusion"), the last word of v 4B, tightly unifies the two halves of the oracle in the turning of the pages[58] so that the condemnation must be interpreted in light of the accusation.

The crimes of the nation's leadership in the accusing lament can be analyzed into two parts: an allegory describing a vineyard stripped of its fruit (v 1)

---

55. *IBHS* §24.2f.
56. *IBHS* §37.6b.
57. *IBHS* §5.2b.
58. *Contra La Formation,* 352-53.

and its interpretation (vv 2-4). The interpretation consists of a summary statement that there are no upright men (v 2A), and two metaphors depicting the depraved leadership: (1) hunters (i.e., they prey upon their subjects; vv 2B-3) and (2) hedges (i.e., they obstruct justice; v 4A). The condemnation consists of a general statement that the time of anarchy is at hand (v 4B), and specific illustrations of it are then given (vv 5-6). The reproach represents the evil officials as weaving together a tight conspiracy to plunder their subjects, and the sentence represents the community as unraveling and coming apart at its tightest seams. Presumably, to judge from the other reproach oracles, the threat of exile occasions the social chaos.

As in 6:9-16, Jerusalem's unrighteous magistrates and judges are principally in view. At their head is "the great one." Whereas in 6:9-16 the accusation pertained to deceit in the marketplace, in 7:1-4A the focus is escalated to corruption in the court. Merchants cheat in the marketplace, and when the plaintiff goes to court he is cheated again by having to bribe the officials. Moreover, this prophecy brings to light the extent of the corruption. Not one upright person remains. The entire lump has been leavened. The time of judgment is at hand.

Micah commences his song with an unusual expression of lament, "What misery is mine!" The repetition of liquids in 'alĕlay lî and the placing of the interjection in an anacrusis (i.e., outside of the meter) make the cry more heartrending. B. Renaud[59] explains the unusual meter involving "Woe is me!" (note that I gave it a separate line) as intentional: ". . . it acquires a certain relief. This situation of the exclamation only renders the cry of suffering more heartrendering in its very sobriety. The pause expresses the sigh of him who speaks." His misery is now explained: there is not one upright official left in the land.

The prophet, *I AM*'s voice, enters a vineyard in "summer" hoping to find one cluster of grapes and one ripe fruit that has been left after the harvest has been gleaned (Lev 19:9-10; 23:22; Deut 24:19-22; cf. Isa 17:6; Jer 8:13; Ruth 2:3, 7, 15). Most commentators recognize that Micah is the antecedent of "me," as stated in the superscript and assumed in other oracles (see 1:1; 3:8; 6:10-13) According to Israel's law, harvesters were not to go back a second time and harvest what they missed but to leave those pickings for the poor. Alas, however, the poor prophet finds that the vineyard has been picked over not just once but several times, and not one cluster of grapes, escalated to not even one ripe fig, remains to be eaten and so satisfy his yearnings. The interpretation (vv 2-4A) explains that the fruit trees (cf. 4:4) he looks for and cannot find are righteous rulers and judges. The time refers to the Assyrian invasion and the collapse of either the Northern Kingdom (722-721 B.C.) or of the Southern Kingdom (701

---

59. *La Formation*, 346.

B.C.; see 1:1), for Micah's career is addressed to both kingdoms and embraces the reigns of Jotham to Hezekiah. The important point is to note the cause-effect relationship of sin and judgment in salvation history. In fact, this prophecy from the preexilic period has been preserved in the canon as a paradigm for Israel to interpret her history.

Clusters of grapes were desired because they were delicious for eating (Deut 32:32) or were used in the making of wine (Isa 65:8). The prophet probably chose "cluster of grapes" *'eškôl,* because of its assonance with "to eat," *le'ĕkôl.* Though "soul" is almost an equivalent of the personal pronoun "I" (cf. TNIV), it uniquely connotes appetite (cf. 6:7). The ripe figs at this time of the year are the early fruit of young shoots from the previous year (cf. 6:15). "Yearns for" speaks of strong desires, and by implication the bitter disappointment of finding one's cravings unmet. I recall watching my own fig tree ripening to the point of perfection on the morrow. But the next day, when I went to pick the figs, the birds had already eaten them.

The vineyard is Israel (cf. Isa 5:1-7; Ps 80:9-17[8-16]), the missing cluster of sweet grapes and figs is faithful and upright persons (Mic 7:2), and the first ripe figs are the righteous magistrates whom the righteous God longs for (Isa 56:1; Mic 7:3). Whereas Israel and its leadership failed, Christ is the true vine, and those that abide in him bear the fruit he craves.

The allegory and its interpretation are linked by "not" (*'ên,* construct of *'ayin,* v 1) and "there is not" (*'āyin,* absolute of *'ayin* in v 2). "The faithful" are those who are in covenant with *I AM* and who practice unfeigned love for him, which entails acts of kindness toward humankind, through thick and thin. Such people do his will.[60] The root behind "upright" has the concrete meaning of something that is geometrically upright and/or straight. The metaphorical epithet denotes those whose conduct does not deviate from the divinely revealed order of piety and ethics. The indefiniteness focuses attention on their character and together with the asyndeton enlivens the poem in its terse style. The width of the nation's decadence is underscored by the verb "perish from the land" in v 2Aa, the negative adverb "there is not" in v 2Ab, the nouns of quantity, the aggregate "all" in v 2Ba, and the distributive "each one" in v 2Bb. The singulars "faithful person" and "upright person" match the singulars "cluster of grapes" and "ripe fig." There is not one. Nevertheless, the limits of "all" must be decided by the parameters set up within a discourse. Here, according to v 3, it refers to the masses and their rulers. Micah himself was part of the faithful remnant, one of the "watchmen" warning the city of its plight.

The vile quality of the rulers' decadence is signified by the metaphors "all

---

60. See Waltke, *Proverbs,* 1:226.

of them lie in ambush to shed blood" and "each one hunts his brother with a net." Both metaphors connote that their practices are sinister and deadly. The metaphor "lie in wait," *'rb*, describes the lurking actions of animals or criminals before striking their victims and exposes their crimes as coldly calculated, high-handed, brutish plots against hapless victims, giving them no chance to flee or to defend themselves. "Bloodshed" refers to violent death, a synecdoche for the murdered victim. "Brother" signifies either a person's own blood brother (Gen 4:8-11) or, more broadly, his kinsman (Gen 14:14, 16) or fellow countryman/tribesman (Num 20:3; Josh 1:14-15; Judg 9:18). H. Ringgren[61] notes: "Basic to this latter use of the word is tribes and the nation descended from a common father." Since the Israelites are brothers, they had a responsibility to help each other (cf. Lev 25:35-36; Deut 15:7, 9, 11-12).

The prophet now explains how the hunters weave their deadly net. "Both hands" probably refers to the corrupt officials and the lustful high officials in the rest of the verse. Together they weave the evil *(ra')* net so "skillfully" (*ytb*, lit. "make good") that no one escapes. The play on doing evil well is Micah's "lawyer joke." The corrupt "officials," who are "the judges," perform their duties in exchange for "repayment" (i.e., bribes). The powerful king, "who unashamedly speaks out the craving of his soul," hands down precepts dictated by his lusts. And so the net is woven without a loophole. The arrangement is so smooth and thorough that no one escapes the system. The magistrates and judges not only fail in turning a blind eye to the bribe (Exod 23:8; Deut 10:17; 16:19; 27:25), but they all, even "the great one," conspire together to wring payment out of their brothers.

haśśar denotes rulers and officials of various rank under the king (cf. Deut 1:15; Isa 32:1; Hos 3:4). Here, according to the hendiadys, they are the judges. The Masoretic accentuation system unites "the officials" and "the judges" over against the "great one." H. Wolff[62] helpfully interprets "the great one" as the king's confidants and higher administrative officials, citing 2 Sam 3:38; 2 Kgs 10:6; Jonah 3:7. Here, however, the form is emphatically singular.

The meaning of *hawwâ* "craving" is debated. S. Erlandsson[63] rejects Guillaume's opinion that it means "command, curse" even though Ugaritic *hwt* seems related to Akkadian *awātu/amātu*, "word" and occurs in eight of its sixteen uses with organs of speech or beside a word that denotes speaking. He suggests instead that it means "both the inner root of evil, 'the inordinate desire,' and its consequences, falsehood, perversity, deception, and misfortune." He

61. H. Ringgren, "'ach," *TDOT* 1:190.
62. Wolff, *Micha*, 206.
63. S. Erlandsson, "havvah," *TDOT* 3:356-58.

also notes: "The word *hawwâ* is usually connected with men who are unfaithful and rebellious against God, who are not willing to adapt themselves to the good ordinances of God, but pervert the right according to their evil desires. . . . Ideologically the point is that man must hearken to the voice of God and adapt himself to the ordinance of God in order to be able to act righteously. . . . When he who follows his own thoughts and desires sits on the judgment seat, the result is unjust judgment, oppression, and the shedding of innocent blood." The inordinate desire of the king's soul stands in marked contrast to the appetite (= soul) of the prophet, who represents *I AM*, for righteous officials in v 1. Whereas the prophet is driven by a desire for justice to help the needy (cf. 3:8), the corrupt officials are guided by a policy of injustice to plunder the poor. "Weave" adds to the figure that the ruler and his minions are in cahoots in rigging the system so that no one escapes their reach.

Micah now moves from comparing the depraved officials to hunters with deadly nets to likening "the best of them," "the most upright of them," to brier hedges. The best they can manage is to obstruct justice. These legal sharks have so conspired together that no one can negotiate the tangle of laws and rulings, and to attempt it will result only in painful injury. What a contrast to the sweet grapes and figs they should have been!

The prophet abruptly shifts from accusation in 7:1-4A to "the day" of judgment in 7:4B, perhaps to suggest the suddenness with which judgment strikes. "The day" (i.e., the time) is the subject, qualified by "your watchmen" and "visitation." In construct it often has the sense of "the time of," a forcible and pregnant sense representing the act vividly as that of a single day (see vv 11, 12).[64] This prophetic term has an eschatological thickness embracing both immediate judgment and the eschatological judgment to purify the nation (Mic 4:1; Zech 13:9; Mal 3:1-3). The "your" is masculine singular, perhaps addressed to "the great one" of v 3. "Watchmen" designates the lookouts posted on a city's wall to warn his audience of approaching danger (cf. 1 Sam 14:16; 2 Sam 18:24ff.; 2 Kgs 9:17-20). J. E. Hartley[65] says that failure in this duty "often carried the death penalty." Moreover, as B. Reicke[66] notes, the grammatical form here stands for "prophets" (cf. Isa. 52:7-10; 56:10; Jer 6:17; Ezek 3:17-21; 33:7; Hab 6:17).

Because the nation paid no heed to these faithful sentinels (Isa 30:10; Hos 9:7, 8; Amos 2:12; Mic 2:6-11; 3:5-6), the day God "visits" them in judgment "is now at hand" (Isa 10:3; 22:5; Hos 9:7). According to E. Speiser,[67] "to visit" origi-

64. BDB 398.
65. J. E. Hartley, "ṣāpâ," *TWOT* 2:773.
66. B. Reicke, "Liturgical Traditions," 356.
67. Cited by V. P. Hamilton "pāqad," *TWOT* 2:731.

nally meant "to attend to with care, to take note," and, as expressed by Hamilton, "points to action that produces a great change in the position of a subordinate either for good or for ill." W. Schottroff[68] notes that in conjunction with temporal terms, such as "day," it "pertains to a definite time of Yahweh's judgment within history." The imminent Assyrian invasion will throw the nation into confused "panic" (cf. Isa 22:5).

Specific illustrations of the confusion, the social anarchy, in the besieged city are now given (cf. Isa 3:4-7). In his rhetorical admonitions to recognize that covenant bonds have been completely severed, Micah progressively heightens the relationships involving trust. J. Kühlewein[69] invests "neighbor" with its more narrow sense, "(personal) friend, confidant, companion, comrade." *'allûp* "intimate friend" narrows the broader term *rēaʿ* to a confidante, bosom companion.[70] Its verbal root means "to instruct" and may refer to the intimate fellowship that develops from people sharing and getting to know each other over time. In such a relationship friends become vulnerable to each other because their trust can be misused. Indeed, the seven uses of this word (Jer 3:4; 13:21; Mic 7:5; Ps 55:14[13]; Prov 2:17; 16:18; 17:9) refer to the betrayed confidence of a close friend. The second half of the verse is devoted to one's closest companion, his wife, "who lies in your bosom" and bears your children.

Micah states the commands negatively in v 5A: in the crisis "do not rely on," emphatically, "do not trust," presumably what your most intimate friends tell you. Then he asserts it positively in v 5B: guard what you say even from your wife, for she may use it against you. No one is to be trusted. The bonds of covenant have completely broken down. A society disloyal to verbal agreements quickly unravels and falls apart into anarchy. The judgment fits the crime; the leaders broke covenant with the people; now the ship of state breaks apart in God's judgment. The leaders could not be trusted; now all are suspicious of each other.

The suspicion one should have toward one's closest associate is validated by the individualism and hardened antisocial activity that fractures a man's own household, society's foundational unit. Children, instead of giving honor to their parents (Exod 20:12; Lev 19:3), disdainfully attack them. A man's enemy turns out to be his own household. Each seeks to save his own hide. The phrase "men of his household," according to N. P. Bratsiotis,[71] stands for the male residents within a man's household, his son, son(s)-in-law, adopted males, and ser-

---

68. W. Schottroff, *THAT* 2:483.
69. J. Kühlewein, *THAT* 2:787.
70. J. Kühlewein, "*rēaʿ*," *TLOT* 3:1243-44.
71. N. P. Bratsiotis, "*ʾîsh*," *TDOT* 1:224.

vants with their families. In short, this is a world turned upside down, for parents were to discipline children (Exod 21:15, 17; Lev 20:9), and a man was expected to direct his household (Gen 18:13).

The advent of Jesus Christ into this fallen world brought the same divisions (Matt 10:35-39; Luke 12:53) but turned a world where men hate and are hated (Tit 3:3) right side up.

D. Micah's Confidence in His Saving God (7:7)

7   But I will watch [and trust] in *I AM*;
     I will hope for my saving God.
     My God will answer me.

EXEGESIS

---

7 The conjunction *wa'ănî (but I)* functions as a disjunctive to contrast the prophet's salvation with the nation's perdition.[1] The pronoun is for the logical contrast between the faithful prophet and the unfaithful community.[2] A similar contrast occurs in 3:8. *bayhwh (in I AM)* is elsewhere not attested with *ṣph* and inappropriate, suggesting an ellipsis. As often in Micah, a more appropriate verb such as *bāṭaḥ (and trust)* should be supplied.[3] *'ăṣappeh (I will keep watch)* is a frequentative, iterative piel.[4]

To judge from its unambiguous parallel *'ôḥîlâ*, the form is cohortative, expressing the prophet's strong and determined will;[5] the same is true of *'ôḥîlâ (I will wait)*. It is an internal hiphil (i.e., "I will cause myself to wait").[6] In the phrase, *lē'lōhê yiš'î (my saving God)*, the first genitive is attributive[7] and the suffix, a genitive of relationship,[8] modifies the whole chain.[9]

In a chiastic construction (lit. "my God of salvation, will hear my God," Micah puts "God" in the outer frame and the modifiers in the core. This generic

---

1. *IBHS* §39.2.3b.
2. *IBHS* §16.3.2c.
3. *IBHS* §§11.4.3d; 11.2.6f, #35; see BDB 105, §3.
4. *IBHS* §24.5.
5. *IBHS* §34.5.1a.
6. *IBHS* §27.2f.
7. *IBHS* §9.5.3b.
8. *IBHS* §9.5.1i.
9. *IBHS* §9.5.3b.

title for "God," *'ĕlôhîm*, signifies the quintessence of all divine, transcendent, or heavenly powers.[10] Its antonym is *'ădāmâ*, "earthly" *('ādām)*; *'ĕlôah* is what humanity is not. Thus the term emphasizes God's inhabitance of the heavenly sphere, focusing on his transcendence over human qualities, namely, his immortality and power. The plural form *'ĕlôhîm* does not designate a countable plural, as it would in English (i.e., "G/gods). In Hebrew grammar, unlike English grammar, the plural commonly has other uses than to indicate a countable plural number.[11] For example, the Hebrew plural is used for abstractions (such as "wisdom," or "youth," or "virginity"). The plural is also used for appellatives whose referent is inherently large or complex (e.g., "face" or "back"). Grammarians designate its use with *'ĕlôhîm* as an "intensive plural," a plural that designates a single animate as thoroughly characterized by the qualities of the noun. Thus Leviathan, the sea monster, is in plural form (Ps 74:13-14), and so is the land monster, Behemoth (Job 40:15). When applied to deities, this *intensive plural* is sometimes referred to as the *honorific* plural. In other words, the divine being is so thoroughly characterized by "God-ness" that only a plural is appropriate for his designation. This intensive plural of *'ĕlôhîm* can be distinguished from its countable plural by its modifiers (such as verbs and adjectives). The former use singular modifiers, while the latter uses plural modifiers. The one and only true God is Micah's god, and he depends on this God to hear and save him. *yišmā'ēnî (will hear)*, which sounds like the immediately preceding *yiš'î* ("my salvation"), signifies to give one's ear to the speaker's words externally and to obey them inwardly. What amazing grace that the omnicompetent God will obey the words of his faithful saint!

EXPOSITION

Scholars are about evenly divided whether v 7 belongs to vv 1-6 or to vv 8-18.[12] The dispute can be resolved by recognizing that Micah is editing his book through the rhetorical device known as "janus," which looks both ways, to the back and to the front. He employed the same device in another autobiographical account in 3:8. Micah's autobiographical "I" relates it to 7:1-6 (especially v 1). This connection is further strengthened by the verbal link *ṣph*, found in

10. It is not clear how the meaning of *'ĕlôah* is distinct from that of *'ēl*. The significance of the *h* ending is unknown. Furthermore, *'ĕlôah, ĕlôhîm* can be both an indefinite and a definite noun. When it refers to a specific deity, it is "God," capitalized. However, if it is referring to the essence of divinity, then it is translated "god" — uncapitalized.

11. For extensive documentation see *IBHS* §7.4.

12. See Wolff, *Micha*, 203.

"watchmen" in v 4 and in "I will keep watch" in v 7. These links, however, also contrast the reproach prophecy of vv 1-6 with this confession of faith. In the reproach oracle he was in misery; here he is full of hope; there the prophets watched for judgment; here he watches for the salvation that comes with the morning of the Day of *I AM* after the night of affliction. These differences at the same time link it with the prophecy of salvation in vv 8-16. That prophecy begins with Lady Zion autobiographically confessing her faith that *I AM* will save her from the judgment (vv 8-10).

Micah's brief autobiography has two parts: his faith in *I AM* as a saving God (v 7A) and the prediction that "my God will save me" (v 7B). The same sequence is found with reference to Zion in vv 8-10 and vv 11-13. Faith saves. His determined resolve to watch and wait creates the spiritual milieu of the oracle of hope that follows. Also in the Psalms, the motif of the psalmist's confidence bridges the gap between the psalmist's lament in distress and his praise for salvation, which brings the psalm to a conclusion. "But I" contrasts sharply the black unfaithfulness of the magistrates and the nation, along with their doom (vv 1-6), with the bright faith and salvation of the prophet and the faithful remnant he represents.

Hartley[13] says that *ṣāpâ* "watch for" conveys the idea of being fully aware of a situation in order to gain some advantage. The prophetic expectation of doom was based on the threats of the Mosaic Covenant (Leviticus 26; Deuteronomy 28), and his resolve to hope is based on his faith and confidence that *I AM* will keep his covenant with Abraham and Jacob (see Mic 7:20; cf. Deut 30:1-10). The reason *I AM* lives epistemologically on the earth in contrast to the ancient deities such as Baal of the Canaanites, Ashur of the Assyrians, and Nebo of the Babylonians is that he kept his covenant with Israel's patriarchs (Genesis 15 and 17). To "wait for" (*yḥl;* see Mic 5:6) means to wait in the confident expectation of its realization. Micah's strong resolve to hope for God who saves him entails that he is praying to God for deliverance from the national judgment and so has become part of the remnant (cf. Mic 2:13; 4:6-7; 5:6-7[7-8]). Mic 7:7B assumes and further adds to that entailment: *I AM* will hear him favorably and so save him. *yēša'* "save" means bringing help to the one in trouble in order to deliver him or her from distress because it is their right or due.[14] That hope for salvation is based not on wishful thinking but on the character of God himself: he "will answer me." The personal relationship between *I AM*, the saving God, and his dependent prophet is underscored by the mention of one or the other or both with every word of this verse.

13. J. E. Hartley, "*ṣāpâ*," *TWOT* 2:773.
14. See J. Sawyer, "What Was a *Môšîa'*?" *VT* 15 (1965) 479.

D. Victory Song: Who Is like the Remnant's Pardoning God? (7:8-20)

8   [Zion says,] "Do not rejoice, my enemy, over me.
        Though I have fallen, I will rise;
        though I sit in darkness, *I AM* is my light.

9   I will endure the fury of *I AM* — surely I sinned against him —
        until he pleads my case and executes justice for me.
    He will bring me forth into the light;
        I will gaze on his salvation.

10   And let my enemy gaze [on it] so that shame will overwhelm her,
        the one who said to me, 'Where is he, *I AM* your God?'
    My eyes will gaze on it [i.e., *I AM*'s saving acts];
        now she will become a trampled place, like mire in the streets."

11   In a time to rebuild your walls [Zion] —
        in that time your borders will become remote.

12   It is a time when they will come to you from Asshur even unto
        "Affliction Place,"
        and from "Affliction Place" even unto the River;
        and from sea to sea; and from mountains to the Mountain.

13   And then the earth will become a desolation on account of its
        inhabitants,
        as a result of their evil deeds.

14   Shepherd your people, [*I AM*,] with your rod, the flock of your
        inheritance,
        those who dwell apart in a forest, in the heart of an orchard.
    May they graze in Bashan and in Gilead,
        as in the days of old.

15   "As in the days of your going out from the land of Egypt,
        I will show them [the people] wonderful deeds," [says *I AM*].

16   Nations will see and be ashamed,
        deprived of all their power;
    they will clap their hands over their mouths;
        they will turn a deaf ear [to blasphemers].

17   They will lick dust like a snake, like those who crawl in the earth;
        they will come trembling from their strongholds.
    Unto *I AM* our God they will come quaking,
        and be afraid of you.

18   "Who is a god like you, one who forgives guilt;
        A god who even passes over transgressions for the remnant of his
        inheritance?"

He will not retain his anger forever,
>   because he is one who delights in unfailing love.
19 He will again have compassion on us; he will "vanquish" our
>   iniquities.
>   Yes, you will hurl all their sins into the depths of the sea.
20 You will bestow fidelity to Jacob, kindness to Abraham,
>   which you swore to our fathers in days of old.

EXEGESIS

8 The qal jussive *'al-tiśmĕḥî (do not rejoice)* is second-person feminine singular *oratio variata*,[1] because the personified enemy who was about to bring Zion to her knees is the city of Nineveh. Israel's poets personify cities as women (see 81; Exposition, 451). Jerusalem and Nineveh are both metonymies for their rulers and citizens. The preposition *lĕ* in *lî (over me)* functions as a *dativus incommodi* (i.e., it marks the object against whom the action is directed);[2] the antecedent of the suffix is personified Zion.

LXX and Vg translate *kî* with "because" and connect it to the next clause: "Do not rejoice over me because I have fallen." The parallelism of the rest of the verse, however, favors the majority understanding that it introduces a real conditional clause with a nuance of concession, *although*.[3] The suffix conjugation of qal first common singular *nāpaltî* is present perfect; it denotes Lady Zion's present state as a result of her predicted defeat (3:12).[4] But the suffix conjugation qal first common singular *qāmtî (I will rise)* signifies a future situation because Zion's rising must follow her present fallen state and so is best construed as a prophetic perfective or perfective of confidence.[5]

The syntax of verset B validates this interpretation. The parallel *kî* is also concessive; LXX invests it with both a causative and concessive nuance: *dioti ean* ("for if"). *'ēšēb baḥōšek* (Ba) functions as a protasis (Ba) that expands (*nāpaltî*, Abα) to its apodosis (Bb), which explains Abβ. The parallel apodoses "I will rise" and "*I AM* is my light" indicate that Zion's certainty to rise is based on her confidence in *I AM*'s salvation. The present progressive nonperfective[6] with the

---

1. *IBHS* §34.1b.
2. *IBHS* §11.2d.
3. *IBHS* §38.2a; §39.3.4e; BDB 473, §2b, c.
4. *IBHS* §30.5.2b.
5. *IBHS* §30.5.1e.
6. *IBHS* §31.3b.

constative verb *'ēšeb*[7] underscores the ongoing aspect of the present humiliating situation[8] and as such forms a good parallel to the present perfect *nāpaltî*.[9] The article with the spatial *bĕ*[10] in conjunction with *ḥōšek* denotes a quality that is unique and determined in itself.[11] The metaphor of "darkness" may be a metonymy for a dungeon and is a metaphor of behaviors that are cut off from the moral light that provides safety, freedom, and success (Isa 2:5; 42:6; Prov 2:13; etc.). In the apodosis *yhwh* (I AM) is the subject of this nominal clause *(is)* with the predicate nominative *(light)*. Were the tense future one would expect *wĕhāyâ*. The preposition *lĕ* is either possessive ("I have I *AM* [as] a light") or *dativus commodi* (*my*; lit. *to/for me*, the opposite sense of *lĕ* in the last word of v 8Aa).[12]

9 *za'ap (fury)* denotes an emotional state of extreme anger (cf. Isa 30:30) against someone leading to hostile action against the antagonist (cf. 2 Chr 26:19). Implicitly it is a metonymy of cause that explains Zion's plight. *yhwh* (*of* I AM) is a genitive of inalienable possession; his fury against sinners is something intrinsically proper to him.[13] The qal future nonperfective *'eššā'* (*I will endure*) is a specific future to represent a real situation as a consequence of the situations in the two apodoses of v 8.[14] The concrete notion of the verb "to bear" with anger as its object must be an incomplete metaphor connoting "to endure" (cf. Prov 18:14). Clausal *kî* is better interpreted as introducing another concessive clause. Since semantic pertinence demands that the adverbial phrase introduced by *'ad (until)* modify "I will bear/endure," not "I have sinned," the *kî* clause interrupts the syntax and so is marked off by dashes. The conjunction *kî* is again concessive *(though)*. The qal suffix conjecture *ḥāṭā'tî* (*I sinned*; see 1:15; 6:7, 13) represents a constative situation in past time.[15] In *lô (against him) lĕ* expresses disadvantage (see v 8Aa).

The preposition *'ad* marks the *terminus ad quem (until)*. Inferentially, the clause explains why Zion can endure. After the temporal preposition *'ad* the relative pronoun *('ăšer)* — here independent — means *when*.[16] The qal future prefix conjugation of *rîb*, *yārîb* (lit. "will make an accusation"; see 6:1), with its cognate effected accusative *rîbî* (i.e., *I AM* brings into effect Zion's complaint

---

7. *IBHS* §30.2.1c.
8. *IBHS* §31.3b.
9. *IBHS* §30.5.2b.
10. *IBHS* §11.2.5b.
11. *IBHS* §13.5.1f.
12. *IBHS* §11.2.10d.
13. *IBHS* §9.5.1g.
14. *IBHS* §31.6.2a.
15. See *IBHS* §30.5.1b.
16. *IBHS* §19.3b, c.

against her adversary) is best glossed, *I AM will plead my case.*"[17] The pronominal suffix is subjective genitive.[18] The *wāw*-relative with the suffix conjugation signifies the (con)sequential situation.[19] The root *ʿāśâ* with *mišpāṭ (executes justice)* denotes the responsibility of a person to execute justice for the victim by punishing the oppressor (see 6:8). The pronominal suffix of *mišpāṭî* is a genitive of advantage *(for me).*[20]

The pronominal suffix of the hiphil prefix conjugation *yôṣîʾēnî* signifies "he will cause me to participate in the exodus" (i.e., *he will bring me out;* see 2:13) and is part of the figure begun in v 8Ba, "I dwell in darkness," and strengthens the notion that "darkness" is a metonymy for "dungeon." The future nonperfective shows that her coming out is dependent on the preceding situations depicted in v 8Ba.[21] As for *lāʾôr,* the preposition *lě* is allative *(into),* the article *(the)* denotes class, and *ʾôr (light)* repeats the metaphor of v 8Bb.

In *ʾerʾeh,* the root *rʾh* with *bě* means to look at or into something with interest *(gaze on);* here, more specifically with joy and pleasure.[22] The last phrase, *ṣidqātô,* forms an *inclusio* with the first phrase, *zaʿap yhwh,* its semantic opposite. The pronominal suffix of the last phrase *(his)* is a genitive of inalienable possession. *ṣedeq* or *ṣedāqâ* "never encompasses merely an ethical behavior but . . . a circumstance of sound, unassailed, and favorable success. . . . This aspect occasionally dominates to the extent that translators feel compelled to render the substantive 'well-being' [or *salvation*]."[23]

10   The jussive *wětēreʾ (And let . . . gaze):* expresses implicitly an imprecation addressed to *I AM* (see v 9A and v 10ABα).[24] The verbal form *rʾh* links v 10 with v 9 and supplies the elided object *běṣidqātô (on my salvation).* *ʾōyabtî (my enemy)* links v 10 with v 8. The *oratio variata,* the switch of subjects, is common in poetry, especially with jussives.[25] The presumed antecedent of the first-person singular suffix in *ʾōyabtî (my enemy)* is Zion/Jerusalem, not Micah *(contra* v 7), because Nineveh is Zion's oppressor during Hezekiah's reign (see 1:1). As for *ûtěkassehā,* the form is probably jussive, and the *wāw* introduces a final clause *(Let . . . so that.)*[26] The antecedent of the feminine suffix *(her)* is *ʾōyabtî.*

17. *IBHS* §10.2.1f.
18. *IBHS* §9.5.1g.
19. *IBHS* §32.1.c, d.
20. *IBHS* §9.5.2e, 147.
21. *IBHS* §31.6.2a.
22. BDB 908, §8a(5).
23. K. Koch, "ṣdq," *TLOT* 2:1052.
24. See *IBHS* §34.3b.
25. See *IBHS* §34.3c.
26. *IBHS* §34.6a.

ksh ("to cover") with the subject *bûšâ* (*shame;* cf. 3:7), which denotes a psychological state, is best glossed *overwhelm*"[27] (Ezek 7:18; Obad 10; Ps 55:6[5]).

The definite relative participle *hā'ōmĕrâ* (*those who*) modifies feminine *'ōyabtî*;[28] the tense is present (*say*) because the oracle begins with a command to the enemy to not stop rejoicing or to stay doing so.[29] *'ayyô* (*Where is he?*), the interrogative pronoun *'ayyēh*, with the third masculine singular suffix, anticipates the appositive *yhwh 'ĕlōhāyik* (I AM your God).[30] Some text critics offer unnecessary emendations of *'yw* to *'yh*.[31] Whereas *yhwh* is a proper name identifying God as Israel's covenant-keeping God, *'ĕlōhāyik* in the mouth of pagans, unlike in the mouth of Zion, is a not a unique appellative[32] distinguishing him from all else in the universe he created.

The first-person suffix *'ênay* (*my eyes*) is a genitive of inalienable possession[33] with reference to Lady Zion, showing that she is the speaker, as in the rest of vv 8-10. The pronominal suffix of *'ênay* is a genitive of inalienable possession. The unique *daghesh* in *tir'ênnâ* (*will gaze on it*) alerts the reader to the tautological and so emphatic pronoun *bāh* (*even it*). The expression "to see with one's own eyes" (cf. Num 14:14; Deut 19:21; Isa 52:8; Jer 32:4; 34:3) has the secondary meaning "to feast one's eyes (on)"[34] with joy and pleasure,[35] "to delight (in)." It seems to include a very pronounced contemplation of salvation. The antecedent of *bāh* must be *ṣidqātô*, not *'ōyabtî* (against the English versions), because it has been the object of *r'h bĕ* in its two preceding occurrences and because it is morally reprehensible to gloat over an enemy's affliction (Prov 24:17-18). The shift from the jussive to a future imperfect tense, signaled by *'attâ*, marks a change from an irreal volitional mood to a real indicative, from imprecation to certainty.[36] Zion uses this specific future because the fall of her enemy is certain due to the enemy's defiance of *I AM*, her God.

The deictic, stative, temporal, clausal adverb *'attâ*[37] with the future imperfect *tihyeh. . . . lĕ* (*will become*) denotes the imminent or impending future.[38] As for *mirmās* (*a trampled place*), the root *rms* means "to trample," and

27. BDB 5.
28. *IBHS* §37.5b.
29. *IBHS* §37.5e.
30. *IBHS* §18.4b.
31. E.g., *La Formation*, 359; *BHS*; cf. 2 Kgs 19:13 for the identical syntax.
32. *IBHS* §13.4b, c.
33. *IBHS* §9.5h.
34. E. Jenni, "'*ayin*," *THAT* 2:262.
35. BDB 908, §8a(6).
36. *IBHS* §31.6.2a, b.
37. *IBHS* §39.3.1h.
38. BDB 774.

the preformative *mem* designates a location or an abstraction.[39] The locative *(a trampled place)* makes the metaphor more intelligible than the abstraction "trampling." The simile to intensify the enemy's utter humiliation and defeat under the heel of *I AM* through the enemy's adversaries is marked by *kĕ (like)* and *ṭîṭ (mire)*, which denotes "wet loam" or "mud" on the bottom of cisterns (Isa 57:20; Jer 38:6) or on the muddy streets of ancient towns (2 Sam 22:43/Ps 18:43[42]; Zech 9:3; 10:5; Pss 40:3[2]; 69:15[14]; Job 41:12[20]). The masculine noun *ḥûṣôt* may have the general sense "outside," or the specific sense of what is outside a house or city, that is, *of the streets*, as here.[40] The genitive connotes location *(in)*,[41] and the countable plural connotes an extensive humiliating defeat.

11 The anarthrous construction *yôm* at the beginning of a verset is commonly, as here, an accusative of time *(in)*. *yôm* refers to a state, more than to a precise time in the cultic calendar, inaugurated by *I AM* in the more or less immediate future of the prophet's contemporaries and best glossed by English *that time*.[42] The time in view is specified by *'attâ*. Syntactically *yôm* is probably in construct with the prepositional phrase *libnôt* (lit. "to build").[43] The *lĕ* denotes purpose. The historical context suggests that *bnh* has its more particular sense of *to rebuild*; its object *gĕdērāyik (your* [second feminine singular] *walls)* is a complementary accusative.[44] The feminine suffix of *gĕdērāyik* presumably is addressed to Zion by Micah, giving voice to *I AM's* response to Lady Zion's faith in her God. In v 12 Micah addresses Zion, to judge from the mention of "your [feminine] walls."

The phrase *yôm hahû'* stands in parallel with *yôm libnôt* "in the time of that one," suggesting that the demonstrative pronoun *hahû'* ("of that one") has the parallel infinitive phrase as its antecedent after initial *yôm (in that time)*. K. Elliger unnecessarily emends *hahû'* to *hû'*, presumably to match the initial construction in v 12. Normally one expects *hayyôm hahû'* "that day," as in Mic 4:6; 5:9(10), but that facilitating reading should be rejected because of the parallels in vv 11A and 12A; besides, LXX reads with MT. Probably our poet avoided the most customary collocation for the figure of anaphora, repeating initial anarthrous *yôm* in three successive versets. The relative *'ăšer* in the sense of "when" is elided (see 7:9Ba) in the clause *yirḥaq ḥōq*. BDB defines *ḥōq* as a "prescribed limit, boundary." Most modern versions gloss *ḥōq* simply by *border*, but

---

39. *IBHS* §5.6b.
40. BDB 300, §2.
41. *IBHS* §9.5.2f.
42. Cf. G. von Rad, *"hēmera,"* *TDNT* 2:946.
43. *IBHS* §9.6.
44. *IBHS* §11.4.1.

I. Willi-Plein[45] thinks that *ḥōq* is always about limits imposed by God: to the rain (Job 28:26), to the sea (Jer 5:22; Prov 8:29), to the heavens (Ps 148:6), or to time (Job 14:5, 13), but this may be due to contexts, not to an inherent sense of the noun. Here it refers uniquely to the walls, to judge from the parallel. LXX tied itself up by interpreting *ḥōq* as "prescribed decree." The English lexical structure here demands a plural, "borders." There is no need to emend the form to *ḥuqqēk* on the basis of some LXX[L] manuscripts, Ethiopic, and Armenian. These translations, probably following a common recension within the Greek tradition, may rightly have understood the pronominal suffix at the end of verset A as gapped at the end of verset B. By gapping the pronominal suffix, the author enhances the obvious assonance between predicate and subject. Dahood validated similar gapping, what he calls "double-duty" particles, in the Psalms.[46] There is an obvious assonance of *ḥwq* with the root *rḥq*, which expresses the state of the subject as being "far," "remote," or "distant" from everyone. The inference is that there will be ample space for all in restored Zion. The imperfect designates a specific future situation, referring to the time when Zion's "walls" are rebuilt, and the stative verb may have an ingressive force, "will become far."

12   Mur 88 reads uniquely the more customary *hayyôm hahû'* ("in that day"), the reading anticipated by GKC.[47] Nevertheless, MT's *yôm hû'* should be retained (lit. "a time of it"; i.e., *it is a time of*) for the sake of anaphora and to avoid the technical term "that day" (see v 11). The *wāw* of *wěʾādeykā (when . . . to you)* introduces a circumstantial clause[48] specifying the circumstances contemporary with *yôm. wěʾādeykā* need not be emended to *wěʾādayik*, a form otherwise unattested, to keep the second feminine singular pronoun consistent with v 11; sliding between genders is common in Hebrew poetry (see 1:11 and 4:8). The word order is emphatic, for "to *you*" occurs before the verb. LXX's *hai poleis* "your cities will be leveled" perhaps deliberately corrected *dālet* into *rêš* with metathesis of *yôd* in its desperate attempt to make sense of the passage.

Although *'aššûr* could be the subject of *yābō'*, the verse would make better sense by taking the third masculine singular prefix as indefinite "one will come" or "they will come";[49] there is no need to emend the form to *yābō'û*, appealing to the unique plural in LXX, *hēxousin*. LXX needed a plural to agree with "your cities." Possibly the original reading may have been *yb'w* and contributed to LXX's confusion. But what is the antecedent of "they"? Surely not Israel's ene-

45. Willi-Plein, *Vorformen*, 107-8.
46. Dahood, *Psalms 101–150*, 3:430.
47. GKC §126Aa.
48. *IBHS* §39.2.3b.
49. *IBHS* §4.4.2a.

mies destined for destruction. The only sensible referent is the masculine singular *'ammĕkâ* (*your people,* v 14), which explains *yābô'* and gives coherence to the whole oracle. The compound preposition *lĕminnî* means *from* (lit. "as regards from out of").[50] The LXX's *eis diamerismon* ("for a distribution") derives from its misconstruing the difficult poetic collocation of *wĕ* plus *lĕminnî* (*even unto*). The parallel in v 12Ba strongly suggests that LXX *kai hai poleis (wĕ'ārê),* as often happens, resulted from the unintentional corruption of original *dālet* into *rêš,* making the original reading *wĕ'ădê (and unto).* Vg's *et usque* supports the supposition. *māṣôr* "distress" is a poetic metonymy for Egypt, as also in 2 Kgs 19:24/Isa 37:25 and Isa 19:6 (*"Affliction Place"*).

KBL[51] erroneously thinks that "historical considerations suggest Muri in Arabia"; they have not gained a following. The *wĕ* with repeated *lĕminnî* is emphatic, *yes, from.*[52] LXX, *eis diamerismon apo Tyrou* ("From Tyre to the River"), again confounded *lĕminnî* and vocalized the text, followed by Syr, as *miṣṣôr.* *nāhār (the River)* is often a proper name for the Euphrates in poetry even without the article.[53.]

If the difficult MT *wĕyām miyyām (and from sea to sea)* is retained, probably *wĕ* is emphatic ("even") and *yām* is an accusative of place with gapped *yābô'* ("they will come to the sea");[54] so also Vg. The reading, however, is implausible. Probably initial *min* with the following *ym* is due to dittography from the preceding *ym*. The prepositions of v 12Ba, *lĕminnî . . . wĕ'ad* have been gapped in both Bbα and Bbβ, giving the expected sense, "from sea to sea and from mountains to the mountain" (so LXX[B]). In *wĕhar hāhār (and from mountains to the Mountain) har* may be a nonconventional collective singular,[55] matching the singular *hāhār,* and *hāhār* may be definite to signify Mount Zion, the well-known mountain.[56]

13 The *wāw*-consecutive with the suffix conjugation of *wĕhāyĕtâ (and then . . . will become)* after the prefix conjugation of v 12 signifies both sequence and the specific future,[57] and *hyh* has its active, not stative, sense (*become* or "turn into").[58] After the elect find salvation within Zion, the rest of the earth will become a *šĕmāmâ* (*desolation;* see 1:7). Since nations represent-

---

50. *IBHS* §11.3.3.
51. KBL 557, s.v. IV *māṣôr.*
52. *IBHS* §39.2.4b.
53. BDB 625, §1.
54. *IBHS* §10.2.2b.
55. *IBHS* §7.2.1c.
56. *IBHS* §13.6a.
57. *IBHS* §32.2.1.
58. BDB 226, §II.2e.

ing the entire known world are in view, *hāʾāreṣ* refers to *the earth,* not a specific "land."[59] The article designates a unique referent.[60] The preposition *ʿal* signifies that the desolation happened *on account of*[61] *yōšĕbeyhā* (*its inhabitants; see 6:12*).

Were it attached directly to *maʿalĕlêhem,* the preposition *min* of *mippĕrî* (*as a result of*) would signify "the remoter cause, the ultimate cause *on account of* which something happens."[62] But with *pĕrî* (*fruit*), which is a figure for the consequence of an action, it designates the origin.[63] The cause of the desolation is the inhabitants (v 13A), but more basically and emphatically it is their *maʿalĕlêhem* (*their evil deeds*), a genitive of source or agent after *pĕrî.*[64] This noun is always plural, usually of evil deeds, and is used four other times with this genitive of source or agent (Isa 3:10; Jer 17:10; 21:14; 32:19).[65]

14 The masculine singular imperative *rĕʿēh* (*shepherd;* see 5:3, 5) is addressed, probably by Micah as a representative of the faithful remnant, to *I AM.* The notion of "to feed" inherent in the root is developed in the rest of the verse, which refers to the land, a place of grazing. The object *ʿammĕkâ* with a second masculine singular suffix (*your people*) refers to Israel, for in Micah *ʿammîm* (plural) refers to non-Israelites (1:2; 4:1, 3; passim) and *ʿam* (singular) with the pronominal suffix ("my people," "his people," "your people") refers to Israel (1:9; 2:4, 9; 3:3; 6:2; passim). The metaphor "to shepherd" is continued by *bĕšibṭekā* (*with your rod,* 4:14) to add to the notion of feeding that of protecting.

The direct object accusative *ṣōʾn* (*the flock*), an apposition to "your people," continues the metaphor. In *naḥălāteka* (*of your inheritance;* see 2:2) *naḥălā* essentially refers to an inalienable, and therefore a permanent, possession that falls to an individual or group either through its awarding in the transmission as an inheritance or through its expropriation from the preceding owner. Probably the genitive "your" is a possessive: by betting Israel as his firstborn, *I AM* owns Israel as his permanent possession throughout the generations.[66]

The participle *šōknî* (*those who dwell*) functions as a dependent relative, modifying *ṣōʾn,* and so part of the figure "to shepherd." The final *yôd* is *litterae compaginis* (i.e., a suffixing connective common with nouns in the construct,[67]

---

59. BDB 76, §1.
60. *IBHS* §13.5b.
61. *IBHS* §11.2.13e.
62. BDB 580, §2f.
63. *IBHS* §11.2.11b.
64. *IBHS* §9.5.1e.
65. *IBHS* §9.5.1b.
66. *IBHS* §9.5.1g.
67. *IBHS* §8.2e.

here with a prepositional phrase after the participle).[68] All the versions, lacking a firm oral tradition, naturally read it as plural, but the MT tradition is more difficult, ancient, and grammatically satisfying, for the singular comports better with its antecedent. *bādād* normally occurs either by itself as an accusative of manner or, as here, with *lĕ* signifying "manner" (*apart,* "alone").[69] It occurs with verbs of dwelling, with the connotation of being free from danger (cf. Deut 33:28; Jer 49:31; Ps 4:9[8]). *ya'ar (in a forest)* is an adverbial accusative of place modifying *škn*.[70] *Bĕtôk (in the heart of)* is a complex preposition,[71] a union, though not frozen, of a noun with a preposition,[72] and means emphatically "in the very midst of, in the heart of."[73] The prepositional phrase is also adverbial, modifying *škn*. The version understood *karmel* as a proper name, but in connection with *ya'ar* it is better taken as an appellative, *an orchard* (cf. Isa 29:17; 32:15). The apposition "in the very heart of an orchard" suggests that *ya'ar* and *karmel* are a split-apart collocation: an orchardlike forest is in view.

The subject of *yir'û (may they graze)* is the "flock," identified as I AM's people in v 1Aa, but whereas the initial verb is transitive in v 14A ("shepherd"), here as the initial verb of verset B it is intransitive ("graze, feed"). The parallelism with imperative *rĕ'ēh* suggests that ambiguous *yir'û* is jussive. *bāšān wĕgil'ād (in Bashan and in Gilead)* are again adverbial accusatives of place. In *kîmê 'ôlām kĕ* denotes agreement according to a norm[74] and absorbs the preposition "in," and *'ôlām (of old;* see 5:2) functions as a genitive of measure after the construct *yĕmê*.[75]

15 The catchword *kîmê (as in the days)* links v 15 to v 14Bb and compares the new age with the time God led Israel out of Egypt. As in v 11, *yôm* indicates the general sense of "the time of" in a forcible, vivid way. Normally the form is singular, but the countable plural is used here to emphasize the extended duration of God's miracles in Egypt, when he conquered the Egyptians and delivered Israel. The infinitive construct *ṣē'tĕkā* functions as a genitive of measure,[76] and the pronominal suffix as a subjective genitive.[77] Since the speaker of "I will show him wonders" in verset B is clearly *I AM,* the antecedent

---

68. *IBHS* §9.6a, b.
69. *IBHS* §11.2.10d.
70. *IBHS* §10.2.2b.
71. *IBHS* §11.1.2b.
72. *IBHS* §11.3.1.
73. BDB 1,063.
74. *IBHS* §11.2.9b(2).
75. *IBHS* §9.5.3g.
76. *IBHS* §9.5.3f.
77. *IBHS* §9.5.1a.

of "your" (second singular masculine) in "your people" must be Micah, who, along with the remnant, is reckoned by the covenant-keeping *I AM* as in corporate solidarity with the ancestors who came out of Egypt. The interpretation that *I AM* is addressing representative Micah in v 15 is also supported by the qal stem in "you went out" (cf. Exod 13:3; 23:15; Deut 11:10; Ps 114:1), for if the antecedent were *I AM*, the stem should be hiphil ("you caused the going out of"). In other words, the qal stem of the verb in verset A and the first person with the hiphil in verset B show that *I AM* is the speaker of v 15. LXX *(ex Aigyptou)*, with all other versions, possibly read *mimmiṣrāyim*, not *mē'ereṣ miṣrāyim (from the land of Egypt)*. The addition in MT may be due to dittography, and/or it may be the common idiom, which can be deleted in translation.[78]

LXX's *opsesthe* "you shall see" probably deliberately smooths the more difficult text of MT, *'arĕ'ennû (I will show him)*. Several Greek texts and ancient versions read *deixō* "I will show," conforming the text to MT. Syr and Tg read plural (cf. Sym), but not Vg, probably to smooth the text with "they will graze" in v 14. In any case, with the exception of LXX, they all point to the same consonantal text. Wellhausen's commonly accepted emendation to *harĕ'ēnû* "show us" is unlikely because the second masculine singular pronominal suffix in verset A refers to Israel, not God. As noted above, liturgical hymns commonly switch speakers, for *I AM* meets his people in their worship. The change to third masculine singular in the B verset is consistent with Micah's style (see 2:11). The point is important, for if Wellhausen is right, then v 15 continues the petition of v 14. If MT is right, then v 15 is *I AM*'s promise in response to Micah's petition. The hiphil is a three-place hiphil containing the subject, "I," the object of the causing, "him," and the object of the root, *niplā'ôt (wonderful things)*.[79] The root *pl'* means "wonder," and the denominative verb in niphal means "to be surpassing, extraordinary." Its participle is gerundive, signifying potentiality, that is, capable of producing wonder, "wonderful."[80]

16 The root of *yir'û ([they] shall see)*, *r'h*, has the same sense as in vv 10-11, but whereas there the specific future is replaced by a jussive, here the report of salvation begun in v 15 continues with the specific future in v 16, though the form could be jussive. The *gôyîm (nations, "pagan peoples"; see 4:3, 7; 5:7)* stand in contrast to *'ammĕkâ*. In contrast to *gôyîm, 'am* has a fundamental notion of relationship, as can be seen in the common formula "gathered to a people" and "cut off from a people," and expressions such as "I dwell among a people." The conjunctive *wāw* of *wĕyēbōšû (and be ashamed)* represents two aspects of the

---

78. *IBHS* §9.5.3h.
79. *IBHS* §27.3b.
80. *IBHS* §23.3d.

same situation.[81] The preposition *min* of *mikkōl (deprived of)* is partitive, "it marks what is missing or unavailable," and so means "without" (= "deprived of"). *kôl* in the absolute state stands in apposition to *gĕbûrātām (their power;*[82] see Mic 3:8).

The B verset gives concrete representations of the A verset. *They will clap* glosses *yāśîmû* "they will place."[83] The gloss *hands over their mouths* is not due to a different text, such as the plural of LXX, *cheiras epi to stoma autōn,* and Syr and Tg, but to the fact that the stereotyped singular of Hebrew *yād ʿal-peh* (cf. Job 21:5) does not carry over well to other languages. *'oznêhem teḥĕrašnâ* woodenly means, "their ears will be deaf." The equivalent English idiom is *they will turn a deaf ear* (see Ps 28:1), presumably to blasphemers.

17 The *gôyîm* of v 16 continue to be the subject of *yĕlaḥăkû ʿāpār (they will lick dust),* a sign of abject humiliation in defeat (cf. Gen 3:15; Ps 44:26[25]). *lḥk* connotes "to consume." The piel probably denotes frequentative activity, for in qal *lḥk* is intransitive and denotes the bodily movement of licking.[84] The generic article of *kannāḥāš (like a snake)* marks out the "serpent" as a class unique and determined in itself.[85] In the apposition, *kĕzōḥălê (like those who crawl)* occurs elsewhere only in Deut 32:24, which also refers to the gliding, crawling motion of a serpent. In both cases the form is a plural, independent relative participle.[86] The genitive *'ereṣ (on the ground)*[87] denotes location.[88] No difference is intended between the parallels *ʿāpār* and *'ereṣ* ("ground").

Since the root *rgz* of *yirgĕzû (they will come trembling)* basically means "to tremble/shake/quake physically," *mimmisgĕrōtêhem (from their strongholds)* is inapposite. A verb of motion such as "come" must be supplied: they shall tremble [and come] from their strongholds.[89] A parallel expression is found in 2 Sam 22:46, where the verb is probably *ḥrg*. Micah intends a play between *rgz* ("tremble") and its anagram *sgr* in *msgrh* ("stronghold").

Many scholars want to delete *'el-yhwh 'ĕlōhēnû (unto I AM our God)* and to delete either *ypḥdw (they will quake;* so BHS) or *wyrw (and be afraid;* so Sievers) in order to preserve the 3:2 (so-called *qinah*) meter begun in v 14. In fact, however, the resulting meter is 2:2. Moreover, all the versions agree with

81. *IBHS* §39.2.5.
82. *IBHS* §14.3.1b.
83. See *HALOT* 3:1322-23, s.v. *śîm, śûm.*
84. *IBHS* §24.5a.
85. *IBHS* §13.5.1f.
86. *IBHS* §37.5a.
87. BDB 76, §3a.
88. *IBHS* §9.5.2f.
89. *IBHS* §11.4.3d.

MT. Others think that the text preserves two alternative readings: either "unto *I AM* our God they will come trembling" (v 17ʙa) or "they will be afraid of you" (v 17ʙb). According to the former, Micah is the speaker, and according to the latter, they argue, either *I AM* is the speaker, addressing Micah as in v 15 and thus forming an *inclusio* with that verse, or Micah is the speaker, using the second masculine singular in an address to *I AM*, forming a transition to v 18. However the parallelism of "our God" and "of you," both with verbs of fearing, helps to clarify that "you" has "God" as its antecedent. Moreover, and more importantly, recall that Mic 7:8-20 is a liturgical hymn. In hymns of this sort, poets commonly address God and the congregation of people, first addressing one and then the other, for at the temple God meets his people. Since "they will fear you" (v 17ʙb) is most probably said by Micah to *I AM*, it is best to regard Micah as the speaker of a unified meditation upon "wonders" (the last word of v 16). If so, it forms a smooth segue into his hymn of praise to *I AM* in vv 18-20. Leaving the text-critical issue aside and turning to the syntactical construction, note that according to MT's accents and ancient versions, the prepositional phrase *'el-yhwh 'ĕlōhēnû*, coming before the verb *yphdw* (*they will come quaking;* lit. "they will quake"), is emphatic. *phd* also has the core idea "to shake, tremble" predominantly before something dreadful and reinforces its parallel *rgz*. With both verbs the preposition *min* ("from") and its opposite *'el* ("unto") a verb of motion such as "come" must be supplied[90] (cf. Jer 2:19; Hos 3:5). The chiastic structure of v 17ᴀb and of v 17ʙa supports the fact that v 17ʙa is the original text (see Exposition, 462). The original meaning of *yr'* "seems to some to have been 'to shiver, shake,'"[91] but by the time of Biblical Hebrew it is a stative verb, "to fear."

wĕyir'û (and they will be afraid) adds the pagan nations' inner emotion of fear to explain their outward behavior of cringing, trembling, and quaking. In *mimmēkkā (of you)* the preposition designates the cause or agent of their fearing.[92] The parallelism between "of you" (v 17ʙb) and "unto *I AM* our God" (v 17ʙb) intensifies that the nations recognize *I AM* as the God who does wonders for his people.

18 The interrogative personal pronoun *mî* aims to elicit a person's identification, who then is characterized by the next clause.[93] The rhetorical question anticipates the negative answer, "No one" (cf. 1 Sam 22:14; 26:15; Job 34:7; Eccl 8:1). The prepositional phrase *kāmôkâ (like you)* modifies the verbless

90. *IBHS* §11.2a.
91. H.-P. Stähli, "*yr'*," *TLOT* 2:570.
92. *IBHS* §11.2.11d.
93. *IBHS* §18.2a.

clause *who is a god*.[94] Biblical writers sometimes use *'ēl* as a generic appellative for a divine being in other religions, in contradistinction to a mortal. Gunkel emends *kāmôkā* to *kāmôhû* to agree with third masculine singular verbs in verset B. Syriac reverses this, reading the verbs as second masculine singular, but leaves *'appô* untouched. Semitic style and/or the liturgical hymn form can explain Micah's incongruity of pronouns, and so emendation is necessary. M. H. Pope[95] takes *'ēl* as a vocative ("O God"), but a vocative never stands between the interrogative pronoun and the comparative particle.[96] Moreover, in a similar phrase in Ps 77:14(13) the word is not a personal name.

The indefinite relative participle *nōśē'* *(one who forgives)*, modifying *'ēl*, is the first of two specifying the sphere of *I AM*'s incomparability. The phrase *nōśē' 'āwōn* can have the cultic senses of "bear [i.e., incur] guilt on oneself" or "to take away [i.e., forgive] guilt [from someone, always elliptical]." The parallels suggest the former.[97] Though the accusative by itself can signify the latter meaning (cf. Gen 50:15; Exod 32:32; Lev 10:17; 34:7), the modifying phrase *liš'ērît naḥălātô* ("the remnant of his inheritance") shows that the latter meaning is intended.

In *wĕ'ōbēr (who even passes)* waw is emphatic.[98] *'br* with *'al* (*over*, "by") normally means to "pass along by," to which the English idiom "to pass over" is equivalent (cf. Prov 19:11; cf. with *lĕ* in Amos 7:8). The figure also signifies "forgiveness." Marti, Nowack, Duhm, Smith, and Sellin dubiously omit *metri causa liš'ērît naḥălātô* to reclaim an alleged 3:2 meter. According to Duhm and Sellin, it is a gloss from Exod 15:11. If this prepositional phrase is adjectival, modifying *'āwōn peša'*, it denotes possession ("belong to"); if adverbial, modifying the verbal element of the participles, *nś'* and its parallel *'br*, it signifies either specification ("with reference to") or interest ("in favor of");[99] the latter is preferable. For *šĕ'ērît* "remnant," see 2:12, and for *nahălātô* see 7:14. The disjunctive *ṭipḥā* may suggest that MT understands *šĕ'ērît* ("remnant") as in apposition to *nahălātô*, unlike the genitive construction in v 14. Otherwise, *nahălātô* is a partitive genitive.[100]

Introductory *lō'* (*not*, v 18B), with or without *maqqeph*, negates the entire

94. Cf. *IBHS* 30.3d.

95. M. H. Pope, *El in the Ugaritic Texts*, VTSup 2 (Leiden: Brill, 1955), 13.

96. See C. J. Labuschagne, *The Incomparability of Yahweh in the Old Testament* (Leiden: Brill, 1966), 79 n. 1.

97. See R. Knierim, *Die Hauptbegriffe für Sünde im Alten Testament* (Gütersloh: Mohn, 1965), 50-54, 114-19, 193, 202-4, 217-22, 226.

98. *IBHS* §39.2.1b.

99. *IBHS* §1.2.10d.

100. *IBHS* §9.5.1k.

clause.[101] The two-place hiphil, *heḥĕzîq*, with *I AM* as subject and *'appô* (*his anger;* see 5:4) as object of the causative idea, means, with this qal stative verb, "cause [his anger] to be strong." To make something strong may entail strengthening it, as, for example, a watch (Jer 51:12), or it may mean *retain* "to hold fast" to something, such as covenantal obligations (Isa 56:2, 4, 6). The latter sense is preferable here.[102] The perfective is gnomic,[103] as in Syr, Vg, and Tg, but not LXX. LXX *eis martyrion* misreads *lā'ad* (*forever,* in the sense of "the unforeseeable future"; see Mic 4:5) as *lā'ēd* ("for a witness").[104] *kî* ("because"; see 7:8) *ḥāpēṣ* ([*is one*] *who delights in*) is a verbal adjective or participle and a classifying predicate adjective, which states what he is like, not who he is. This is so because the word order is predicate–subject–*hû'* (*he*).[105] *ḥesed* (*kindness* [to help the helpless]; see Mic 6:8) is the object of *ḥāpēṣ*, though a stative verb.[106]

19 The subject of *yāšûb* continues to be *hû'* (v 18), a reference to *'ēl kāmôkâ* (v 17; i.e., *yhwh* [vv 8-9, 17]). The grammatical matching of *yāšûb* with asyndetic *yĕraḥămēnû* invests *šûb* with an adverbial force that defines its manner as "again" (*he will again have compassion on us*).[107] The piel *yĕraḥămēnû* functions as a productive denominative of *rḥm* (i.e., "he will have mercy").[108] According to H. J. Stoebe,[109] "Four-fifths of all occurrences of *rḥm pi.* have God as subj.: God is always the agent of *rḥm pu.* The Hosea passages demonstrate that the act of Yahweh described by *rḥm pi.* signifies installation (or the reinstallation) in the child-parent relation (Hos 1:6; 2:6, 25 that is not sentimental but thoroughly real." He also notes, "*rḥm pi.* stands in exclusive opposition to God's wrath or replaces it because wrath suspends the proper relationship of the people to God." This leads to its use in relation to sin. The verb occurs several times with *ḥnn* "to be gracious." Stobe goes on, "Thus in a few passages forgiveness, expressed by *rḥm pi.*, constitutes the precondition for the reestablishment of the community with God that was lost through sin (Isa 55:7; Mic 7:19; cf. also 1 Kgs 8:50)." The verbal suffix functions as a direct object accusative via a preposition in English;[110] its antecedent is

101. F. J. Snyman, "The Scope of the Negative *Lō'* in Biblical Hebrew," Acta Academica Sup. 3 (2004) 124.

102. BDB 305, §6d.

103. *IBHS* §30.5.1c, ##19-21.

104. Cf. *IBHS* §1.6.3, esp. k.

105. See *IBHS* §8.4.2a; §37.5a, ##3-4.

106. See *IBHS* §22.2.3b.

107. GKC §120g.

108. *IBHS* §24.4g.

109. H. J. Stoebe, "*rḥm,*" *TLOT* 3:1229.

110. *IBHS* §10.2.1c, d.

liš'ērît naḥălātô ("the remnant of his inheritance," 7:18), with which Micah again identifies himself (see 7:17).

yikbōš (he will tread down): LXX's *katadeusei* ("he will sink [our sins]") is a free rendering of *yikbōš (he will "vanquish")* and is influenced by verset B, as is Peshitta's "he will gather." The root *kbš (vanquish*, "tread under foot," "subdue," "overcome") is usually used with personal objects, suggesting that the poet is personifying *'ăwōnōtênû* and using it as an incomplete metaphor of comparing God's subduing of Israel's sins to his defeat of Pharaoh and his picked troops at the Red Sea. The B verset confirms the inference that the poet is using personification and metaphor. The countable plural (*contra* the collective singular in v 18) *'ăwōnōtênû (our iniquities)* calls attention to Israel's many iniquities. Peshitta adds "all" from *kol* in verset B. The noun may be a metonymy of cause; that is, Israel's iniquities brought the Assyrians upon them. In that case, Israel's political enemies are in view. Verset B, however, strongly suggests that Micah is describing God's forgiveness of his people's sins by the metaphor of his subduing the Egyptian army in the Red Sea.

Conjunctive *waw* adds the second metaphor clearly from that historical background. Our poet returns (cf. *kāmôkā*, v 18) to addressing God, *tašlik (you will hurl)*. This sliding between personal pronouns is perfectly acceptable in Semitic languages, but the Indo-European versions retain the third masculine singular for the sake of smoothness, thereby missing the connection of v 19B with v 20. *šlḥ* ("throw, fling, cast, hurl") always occurs as an unclassified hiphil.[111] This physical act with *biměṣūlôt yām (into the depths of the sea)*, with the direct object accusative as a spiritual reality, *ḥaṭṭō'tām (their sins)*, supports the interpretation of *kbš* as a metaphor from the Exodus. *bě* has its basic spatial sense, "in," and with the verb of motion, "into."[112] *šlḥ* is used in many different connections as a metaphor for forgiveness.[113] *měṣūlôt* is a plural of extension,[114] signifying the inherently large and complex sea, and so connoting the complete removal of Israel's sins. Stade pointed to this word as evidence of the late origin of the text, but it occurs in Exod 15:5 and Ps 68:23(22), now considered among the oldest compositions in the OT (see Introduction, 9). *yām (of the sea)* functions as a partitive genitive[115] further intensifying the complete forgiveness and restoration of the remnant. For the meaning of the root of *ḥaṭṭō'tām* ("their sins") see 1:5. The countable plural in this case is emphasized by the addition of *kol (all)*; not one sin remains. The remnant is now signified

111. *IBHS* §27.4c.
112. *IBHS* §11.2.5b.
113. Cf. *HALOT* 4:1529, entry 2c.
114. *IBHS* §7.4.1c.
115. *IBHS* §9.5.1k.

by the third masculine plural. As expected, all the versions retain the first-person plural of the A verset. M. Dahood,[116] ignoring Semitic style, took the noun as a feminine plural enclitic *mem* and the *nû* as gapped (see 7:17). The shifting of second and third persons is due in part to alternation of supplication and meditation as well as praise in this liturgical hymn.

20 Some Greek MSS, against all other textual witnesses, read third masculine singular instead of *tittēn (you will bestow)*[117] in order to conform the text to v 19. The normal collocation of *ḥesed wĕ'emet* ("kindness and faithfulness") is split apart. Perhaps they have been reversed to *'emet* ("truth") with the nuance "what is reliable" *(fidelity)* . . . *ḥesed (kindness;* see 7:18) because the Ab verset in Hebrew poetry intensifies the Aa, as seen in the intensification of the indirect objects, placing the third and lesser patriarch *lĕya'ăqōb (to Jacob)* before the first and greater patriarch *lĕ'abrāhām (to Abraham).* Because *'emet* is frequent in the Psalms and rare in prophecy before Jeremiah, Jepsen[118] thinks that v 20 is not from Micah. But he underestimates its clear use in Hos 4:1, misunderstands the date of the Psalms, and ignores that Mic 7:20 is part of a praise psalm. LXX reads *kathoti* "even as," which normally represents *ka'ăšer,* but there is no need to retrovert that Vorlage because absolute *'ăšer* can also have that meaning. More probably, however, the undeclinable relative pronoun introduces the attributive clause modifying *'emet* and *ḥesed,* the metonymies for the covenantal promises, and functions as an accusative of direct object after the clausal verb.[119]

The perfective *nišba'tā* has a preterite sense,[120] referring to the particular situations when God swore his promises to Abraham and Jacob. The niphal is unclassified;[121] it may be a productive denominative of *šeba'.* The appellative in verset B, *la'ăbōtênû (to our fathers),* finds its specific definition in *lĕya'ăqōb* and *lĕ'abrāhām (to Abraham)* in verset A. The preposition *min* of *mîmê* is temporal and ablative, designating the time when God's oaths originated.[122] On the one hand, LXX's *kata tas hēmeras* may suppose that it read *kymy* instead of *mymy.* Since *mem* and *kaph* are readily confused in the preexilic angular script, it would attest to a very early textual error. On the other hand, LXX's reading could have been influenced by its *kathōs hai hēmerai* (7:14) and *kata tas hēmeras* (7:15). As to *qedem,* the noun designates that which is before one, ei-

---

116. M. Dahood, "Some Ambiguous Texts in Isaiah," *CBQ* 20 (1958) 46.
117. See BDB 678, §1b.
118. A. Jepsen, "*'ĕmet,*" *TDOT* 1:310.
119. *IBHS* §19.3a.
120. *IBHS* §30.5.1b.
121. *IBHS* §23.5b.
122. *IBHS* §11.2.11b.

ther with reference to space, "front, east," or with reference to time, "aforetime, of old." The duration of time is relative to the topic: of God himself (cf. Deut 33:27; Hab 1:12), of Wisdom's temporal origin in Ur-time (Prov 8:22, 23), of mountains (Deut 33:15), and of the heavens (Ps 68:35[34]) (see 5:1). Here it refers to the time of Israel's Ur-fathers. The genitive after the prepositional phrase of *min* ("from") is partitive (*of old*),[123] not attributive ("ancient days").

EXPOSITION

Micah's concluding prophecy is in the form of a liturgical hymn containing oracles of salvation along with motifs of confidence, petition, and praise. The composite yet coherent prophetic hymn consists of four almost equal stanzas. In the first stanza (vv 8-10), employing the figure of personification, Lady Jerusalem confesses to her enemy — historically Lady Nineveh — her faith in *I AM*. In the second stanza, employing the figure of metaphor, Micah responds, promising Zion, pictured as a sheepfold, that she will become a grand and vast sheepfold offering salvation to the elect from a world under judgment. In the third stanza (vv 14-17) Micah petitions *I AM*, who formerly led his people out of Egypt, to again shepherd them (v 14). *I AM* answers that he will show them wonders like those in Egypt (v 15). In a meditation addressed by Micah to *I AM*, Micah prophesies what those "wonders" will be, leading to the pagan nations acknowledging in their defeat that *I AM* is God. In the concluding fourth stanza Micah sings a hymn of praise to *I AM* for being a God who forgives the sins of his people in order to keep covenant with the patriarchs.

These four stanzas, all of which are spoken in dramatic addresses, logically build one upon the other as they vividly escalate the motifs of Zion's salvation and of destruction of the pagan nations. In the first stanza Zion "rises" phoenix-like from her ruin as she proclaims her faith that *I AM* is her "light" (v 8) and owns that *I AM*'s punishment of her sins is just, but because he executes justice, he will now punish the proud and immoral nations that afflicted her (vv 9-10). In the second stanza, Zion's walls are rebuilt and enlarged (v 11), and the remnant returns from all over the earth to inhabit them (v 12), while the rest of the earth is reduced to rubble. In the third stanza, *I AM* luxuriously provides for Zion (v 14), while the nations come and cower before *I AM* (vv 15-16). Micah responds with his hymn of praise to *I AM*, the pardoning God who keeps covenant.

In another sense the liturgical hymn with salvation oracles has two parts.

123. *IBHS* §9.5.1k.

The first three stanzas in fact function as escalating oracles of salvation (vv 8-17) brought to a climax in the concluding hymn (vv 18-20). These first three oracles are bounded by the *inclusio I AM* (vv 8-9, 17): in Zion's expression of faith in him escalating climactically to the cringing pagan nations acknowledging to *I AM* that he is Victor. This last reference to *I AM* segues to the hymn "Who is a god like you?" (v 18). Note too in three salvation oracles the escalation of Zion's rise (vv 8-9, 11-12, 14-15) and of the pagan's downfall (vv 10, 13, 16-17). In the first stanza of the latter the enemy is trampled like mud in the streets (v 10), in the second the whole wicked world becomes a desolation (v 13), and in the third the pagans acknowledge that *I AM* is the God who defeated and humbled them (vv 16-17).

The rising crescendo of salvation oracles climaxes surprisingly in praising *I AM* as a forgiving God, not as a Warrior as in Moses' Song of the Sea with which it has striking intertextual links (see below). The change is profoundly insightful. *I AM* must rid Israel of sin as decisively as he defeated Pharaoh at the beginning of her history, for the ultimate cause of Israel's repeated defeats and humiliation is her sins and *I AM*'s fury again them (v 9). The first stanza features Zion's sin and *I AM*'s fury (v 9). The last stanza features his grace to forgive and so keep his sworn oath to the patriarchs. That oath explains Zion's victory over Pharaoh at the beginning of Zion's history and her victory over sin, her real enemy, at the end of her history.

The striking intertextual connections with Moses' Song of the Sea, Israel's first victory song (Exodus 15), follow. In both songs the vanquished "tremble" (*rgz;* Exod 15:14; Mic 7:17B), "quake" (*pḥd;* Exod 15:11; Mic 7:15), and become mute (Exod 15:16; Mic 7:16). *I AM* does "wonders" (Exod 15:11; Mic 7:15), shows *ḥesed* "kindness" (Exod 15:13; Mic 7:18-19), and owns Israel as his "inheritance" (Exod 15:17; Mic 7:14, 18). Both hymns celebrate God's incomparability, asking "Who is a god like you?" (Exod 15:11; Mic 7:18), and to make the intertextual connection absolutely clear, the remnant's praise uses picturesque and completely original imagery from the Song of the Sea: *I AM* "again" has mercy: he "vanquishes" Israel's sins and "hurls them into the depths of the sea" (Exod 15:1, 4-5; Mic 7:19). Whereas *I AM* at Israel's origins miraculously threw Pharaoh's picked troops into the sea, he now at Israel's end does the even greater saving deed of hurling Israel's sins into the depths and of giving his true people universal victory.

As in the liturgical hymns in the Psalter speakers change without notice. In Psalm 2 the nations conspire (v 3), *I AM* responds (v 6), the King recites the decree legitimizing his kingship (vv 7-9), and finally the psalm addresses the nations, but the change of speakers is never indicated by a verb of speaking. As in that psalm, so also in Mic 7:8-9 the nations speak, Lady Zion speaks, Micah speaks, and so does *I AM*, depending solely on the pronouns to alert the reader of the change. Was the prophetic hymn originally sung antiphonally.[124]

Micah, prophesying against the historical background of Hezekiah and the Assyrian invasions (see 1:1), presupposes Jerusalem's fall to Nineveh (see Introduction, 3-6, 3:12, and the reference to Assyria in v 12). The oracle may have been delivered during the invasion of Sennacherib, who essentially asked "Where is your god?" (see v. 10). Also on that occasion both Micah and Isaiah lampooned *miṣrayim* ("Egypt") by the nickname *māṣôr* ("Affliction Place"; see v 12). Hezekiah, however, repented (Jer 26:18) and so spared Jerusalem for the moment (cf. Jer 18:7-10). As it turned out, Jerusalem ultimately fell to Babylon. In other words, Micah's book functions in the canon with respect to the fall of Babylon as well as of Nineveh. The prophecy is stated abstractly, never naming the enemy, because it is applicable to the salvation of God's people from any enemy, for that hope rests on God's fidelity to his sworn covenant with Abraham (v 20). Tg interpreted the prophecy as a reference to Rome.

1. The First Salvation Oracle: Zion Confesses Faith in I AM (vv 8-10)

The hymn opens as Lady Zion dramatically commands her enemy, also personified as a lady, to stop rejoicing over her downfall (cf. Psalm 137). Their gender is inferred by the Hebrew feminine singular "you" for the addressee in vv 8-9, 12; it cannot be determined by the common singular "I" for the speaker in vv 9-11. Zion, like all cities, is depicted as a woman because in Hebrew the implied inanimate noun "city" (*ʿîr*) is feminine, and poets personify inanimate and abstract nouns according to their gender in sexually distinguished animate nouns.[125]

The stanza is united in having Zion as the sole speaker, and, like the next two, first features Zion's salvation (vv 8-9) and then the destruction of her enemy (v 10). Each verse mentions *I AM*: in defeated Zion's confession of faith, "*I AM* is 'my Light'" (v 8), in her confession of sin, "the fury of *I AM* I can bear" (v 9), and in the mouth of the blaspheming nation, "where is *I AM*?" (v 10). In addition to employing the catchword *yhwh* in every verse and to the theme of Zion's faith signified by her confessions of *I AM* as her Savior and stern moral teacher, vv 8-9 are linked by the catchword "light." V 10, which presents the countertheme of her enemy's ruin, is connected by conjunctive "and" and by the catchword "see" in demanding that the audience supply "his salvation"

---

124. In the translation I placed in quotes only those addresses by Lady Zion (vv 8-10) and by *I AM* (v 15), not the addresses by Micah, whether to Zion or to *I AM*.

125. *IBHS* §9.3.1e; §9.4.1c, d.

from the last word and object of "see" in v 9 as the object of the first word and the object of "see" in v 10.

The root *śāmah* "rejoice" denotes being glad and merry with one's whole disposition. The enemy's glee exhibits her animus against God and his representative city. The word has a cultic nuance because the enemy would have celebrated its military and triumphant joy in temples to its pagan deities, even as Jerusalem anticipates celebrating *I AM*'s victory over Assyria/Babylon (v 10).

Zion's enemies, presumably Nineveh and then Babylon, are not to make merry over Jerusalem because, though Zion is now fallen in battle, she will rise phoenix-like from the ashes. *nāpal* ("fall") is often used metaphorically for clamity, as in battle (Judg 20:44). When used of a city, it means that it has met a catastrophic end (Jer 51:8; cf. Ezek 33:21), and "rise" in this military context means to rally from defeat (see Prov 24:16). The Hebrew tense form of "rise," a so-called prophetic perfective, vividly and dramatically represents the future situation as both an unanticipated event and complete.[126]

The repetition of concessive "though" signals that verset B will heighten and bring Ab into sharper focus. The concessive clauses suppress Zion's present downfall in order to feature in the main clause her resurrection. The metaphor "I dwell in darkness," sometimes associated with "blindness" (cf. Job 12:25; Isa 29:18; 42:6, 7, 16; 49:9),[127] signifies that she is in a place where behavior is cut off from the moral light that provides safety, freedom, and success (Isa 2:5; 42:6; Prov 2:13; etc.). "To sit in darkness" probably is also a metonymy and metaphor for being in a dungeon (i.e., imprisonment in exile). The unexpected "I will rise" of the main clause is now explained as due to Israel's unique covenantal relationship with *I AM* as "my light." As "darkness" connotes immoral behavior and imprisonment, "light" connotes morality, order, safety, and freedom. The metaphor "*I AM* is my light" suggests that a metonymy of effect is in view: *I AM* brings Zion freedom from her dungeon-like situation through his moral guidance and protection. Whereas in *lî* ("over me"), the last word in v 8Aa, the *lamedh* signified disadvantage, in *lî* ("my [light]" or "[a light] for me") it signifies advantage. This juxtaposition sets Zion's enemy as also against *I AM*.

In contrast to unrepentant Cain, who complained, "My punishment is greater than I can bear," repentant Zion is ready to endure God's wrath because it is just ("surely I sinned against him") and temporary ("until") (v 9A). As for the latter, God will punish Zion's malefactor and bring her "into the light" out of her humiliating captivity; she will see his righteous salvation (v 9B). The

---

126. *IBHS* §30.51e, 490.
127. H. Ringgren, "*hōšek*," *TDOT* 5:253.

faithful interpret the primary cause of her fall as *I AM*'s fury *(za'ap)* against her sin. The enemy's military superiority is merely his agent. *za'ap* ("fury") denotes an emotional state of extreme anger (cf. Isa 30:30) against someone, leading to hostile action (cf. 2 Chr 26:19). Implicitly it is a metonymy of cause that explains Zion's plight. "With this word the community accepts the threats of judgment attested to in 1:6–6:16 as the expressions of Yahweh's wrath which has become a reality."[128] "To sin" *(ḥāṭā')* means "to commit an offense against one with whom one stands in an institutionalized community relationship."[129] Though sin can be an offense against another person in the community, it is normally, as here, against God. Zion directed her sin "against *I AM*" because she despised his Torah and his word by the prophets (cf. 2 Sam 12:9). Micah, along with the other reforming prophets, proclaimed that Zion's situation was untenable: her sin must bring God's judgment (see 3:8).[130] The word becomes a catchword with its use in v 19. The connection explains that God's removal of Zion is essential to her salvation: for her to rise permanently from under God's wrath, God must first remove her sin once and for all.

Zion can endure God's wrath because it is temporary and restorative. The expression "until he pleads *(rîb)* my case" shows that the faithful remnant understood *I AM*'s wrath to be remedial and so temporary, and not penal and so final as in the case of the non-elect. *rîb* (see 6:1, 2) means "to make a complaint/accusation," often a legal one, and sometimes, as here, in the sphere of international relationships. But whereas in Mic 6:1, 2 Micah is the messenger to the people carrying *I AM*'s accusation against them, here *I AM* is pictured as the *advocate for* them.[131] After *I AM*'s fury against Zion's sin is spent, he will act as repentant Israel's advocate and make a legal accusation against her enemy. The goal of the legal process is "justice" *(mišpāṭ)*. G. Liedke[132] says: "*špṭ* occurs in a 'three-cornered relationship': two humans or two groups of humans, whose relationship is not intact with one another, are restored to a situation of peace through the *špṭ* of a third party or parties. . . . *špṭ* happens because the matter that disturbs the relationship between X and Y is righted by the one judging."

Nineveh's unprovoked attack against Zion must be righted. *I AM*'s punishment on Assyria/Babylon is just because Assyria's imperial ambition to gobble up her world is motivated by insatiable lust for wealth and power and is accompanied by joyful gloating over Zion's misfortune and hubris against her God (see In-

---

128. Wolff, *Micah*, 221.

129. K. Koch, *"chāṭā',"* *TDOT* 4:311.

130. Koch, *TDOT* 4:313.

131. Cf. J. Limburg, "The Root *ryb* and the Prophetic Lawsuit Speeches," *JBL* 88 (1969) 303.

132. *"špṭ,"* *THAT* 2:1001.

troduction, 4). God's moral sensibility against cruelty, coldness, smug arrogance, faithlessness, and cynicism toward him and his image, especially his elect people, demands that he punish the greedy gloater and blasphemer. *I AM* will not promote further moral ugliness by maintaining the situation that exacerbates it. His righteousness demands justice against the wrongdoer, and his holiness demands that he punish unfeeling cruelty toward one who is down-and-out (see Prov 24:17-18). He "executes" justice, punishing the oppressor and delivering the oppressed, not just giving a verdict in Zion's favor.

As Koch stresses, the parallel to "justice," *ṣedeq* ("righteousness," "salvation"), encompasses besides ethical behavior a favorable circumstance of success, prompting the translation "salvation" in some contexts. The Lord guarantees that righteousness yields true profit and security.[133] Because *I AM* is righteous, Zion is confident that *I AM* will bring her "salvation." Lady Zion never wronged Lady Nineveh; it is only right that her covenant-keeping God should save her. She describes her salvation by continuing in the parallel the metaphor of her present plight of being in a dark dungeon: "he will bring me forth into the light"; and as a result, she says, "I will gaze on his salvation." This parallel confirms that light connotes freedom.

10 Zion follows her command to her enemy "Do not rejoice" and her boast in *I AM* with a so-called imprecatory prayer, "And let my enemy gaze [on his saving acts]." The elision of "saving acts" demands that the reader link the two aspects of salvation that the first three stanzas feature (see above): Zion's deliverance (v 9) and her enemy's humiliating defeat (v 10). As a result of seeing Zion's salvation, the enemy will be overwhelmed with shame. "Shame"[134] means "someone . . . underwent an experience in which his (or its) former respected position and importance were overthrown. Someone risked something to a power . . . and so undertook a daring venture. Now he receives the consequences of that venture so that he must suffer the opposite of what he thought, viz., dishonor, and be put to shame, not because of some subjective act but because of something that was inherent in the risk he took." Whereas the enemy, trusting its pagan powers, both religious and military, sought social honor and prominence in a daring venture against *I AM* and his city (see v 10Abβ), Zion's rival has been overthrown and so must endure dishonor and shame (see v 10B; 3:5-8). Zion's adversary expressed hubris against God by asking derisively, "Where is he, *I AM* your God?" The rhetorical question expected a very emphatic negative answer, "Nowhere!" and aimed to debase and insult both *I AM* and his city (cf. Isa 36:13-20). The Name the foe aimed to abuse signifies that the only God, *I AM*, chose Is-

133. K. Koch, "*ṣdq*," *TLOT* 2:1052.
134. H. Seebass, "*bôsh*," *TDOT* 2:52.

rael for a unique covenantal relationship to make her a light to the nations, punishing and rewarding her as she kept covenant with him.[135]

Whereas in v 9B Zion confidently anticipated gazing on God's salvation of her, now she just as confidently predicts, because of her enemy's blasphemy, that her own eyes will also gaze on her enemy's abject humiliation, likening Nineveh/Babylon to a trampled muddy street (cf. Isa 10:6; Zech 10:5). "One cannot be brought down any lower," says H. Wolff.[136] The enemy's rejoicing (v 8) has been turned around 180 degrees to the lowest depths of humiliation. The mocker is now mocked.

2. Second Salvation Oracle: Micah's Prophecy (vv 11-14)

In response to Zion's prayer and confession of faith in the preceding, Micah, who is God's messenger, responds with an oracle of salvation. The two stanzas are attached by the initial temporal terms "now" in v 10Bb and "time" in v 11Aa. The salvation oracle has two parts: the restoration of Zion (vv 11-12) and the desolation of the rest of the earth (v 13). The verses pertaining to Zion's salvation are linked by the anabasis of initial *yôm* ("time") in vv 11A, B, 12A. Zion's salvation is now expanded to include the salvation of all the elect throughout the earth within her secure borders (see v 12). A *waw* consecutive links the salvation of Zion with the destruction of the pagans. As Zion's salvation is universal, so the destruction of the pagans is expanded from the particular historical enemy to all the earth.

The prophecy finds fulfillment in the church of Christ, composed of all nations (see Rom 4:16-17), which come to the heavenly Zion, the "true" Zion, represented symbolically by the earthly city (Heb 12:22). It will find its consummation in the eschaton (Revelation 21–22). Before God's revelation to Paul, the complete unification of the nations with Israel in this future salvation that began with Pentecost was unknown to the prophets (see Mic 7:15). The predicted desolation of the earth in connection with Zion's salvation will be consummated at Christ's parousia.

Initial *yôm* "in a time (or day)" forms a nice transition with Zion's hope for "light" (vv 8, 9), for though in Israel's cultus the day officially began in the evening (Exod 12:18; Lev 23:32) and though the idiom represents a state more than a precise date, the day ended with the light and is the emphasis of the term "day." Micah repeats the word "in a time" as the initial word in three successive

135. H. Ringgren, "'ĕlōhîm," *TDOT* 1:276.
136. Wolff, *Micha*, 223.

clauses, an emphatic anaphora (vv 11A, B, 12A). The verb "to rebuild" stands in stark contrast to Lady Nineveh's/Babylon's fate of becoming trampled like mire in the street. "Your walls," *gĕdērāyik*, denotes a "wall of stones (without mortar),"[137] including the enclosures for vineyards (cf. Num 22:24; Isa 5:5; Ps 80:13[12]), for flocks (Num 32:16, 24, 36; 1 Sam 24:4[3]; Zeph 2:6), for temple enclosures (Ezek 42:7), and of a city (Ezra 9:9; Ezek 13:5; 22:30), though "hedge" (KJV) may be metaphorical in this last use. It seems to stand in contrast to *ḥômâ*, the large protective walls around cities and buildings, or parts of them. Possibly the word is used metaphorically to compare Zion to a sheepfold. In any case, the choice of words suggests that Zion lives securely, unthreatened by attackers: they have all been destroyed. The plural of extension indicates that the wall is large,[138] the point elaborated on in verset B.

"In that time" emphatically repeats the initial *yôm* of verset A and introduces verset B, which elaborates on A. "Your borders will become remote" entails that there will be ample space for all the restored elect in rebuilt Zion.

Micah brings the anaphora to a climax with the third initial *yôm*, the glorious time of salvation. The subject of "will come" is indefinite, "*they* will come." Are "they" the remnant of Israel or the converted citizens of those nations? The Tg rightly interpreted it with reference to the exiles. The exile is presumed in Zion's expectation to come out of darkness into light, a figure for salvation from captivity (see vv 8-9). Although the salvation of the nations is in view in Mic 4:1-3, this hymn contrasts Israel's salvation with the defeat of the nations. Zion's walls will be expanded to embrace all the elect, from the ends of the earth (Mark 13:27). The mention of "Assyria," rather than Babylon (see 4:10), suggests that the prophecy was given against the Assyrian invasions (see 5:7[8]; 7:8). The case cannot be pressed, however, because of the reference to Assyria in a similar merism in Zech 10:10, which has a Persian background.

On the basis of *yĕ'ōrê māṣôr* "rivers of Egypt" in Isa 19:6; 37:25 (= 2 Kgs 19:24) most lexicographers identify *māṣôr* "affliction" as another proper name for *miṣrayim* "Egypt." The *mêm* of *ṣûr* can denote place ("place of affliction") as well as an abstraction ("distress," "affliction"). Because of the initial consonance of *mṣr* in *māṣôr*, the nickname is probably a pun with *miṣrayim* ("Egypt"). Egypt, which approaches Zion from the south, versus Assyria, which approaches Israel from the north, constitutes a geographical merism, a figure of speech involving opposites to indicate totality. These two descendants of Ham attacked Israel from the north and the south. Moreover, they constitute a historical merism: Egypt afflicted Israel at her birth, and Assyria brought her to

137. KBL 173, s.v. *gĕdērâ*.
138. *IBHS* §7.4.1c.

ruin at her end, at least in the Northern Kingdom. (They would have done the same to Jerusalem had not Hezekiah repented and *I AM* intervened.) These nations represent the salvation of all who formerly threatened her very existence. Since *māṣôr* is found uniquely elsewhere only in Isaianic material, this choice of name may represent another linkage between the two contemporary prophets (see Mic 4:1-4).

Verset B uses more geographical merisms to emphasize the remnant's universal salvation, reversing the merism in v 12Ba, "and from 'Affliction Place' even unto the River." "The River" stands for the Euphrates, Israel's northern and eastern extremity (cf. Gen 15:18; Deut 11:24; 1 Kgs 5:1[4:21]). "From sea to sea" and "from mountains to the Mountain" not only contain implicit merisms within themselves but together form their own merism: sea versus mountains. "The mountain" is the well-known mountain, Mount Zion (see Mic 4:1-3), the place of salvation in this hymn.

After the salvation of the elect from the nations under God's wrath and their entrance into Zion's secure sheepfold, desolation will fall upon the rest of the earth because of the wicked deeds of its inhabitants (cf. Isa 24:1-6; Obad 16). "Desolation" *(šěmāmâ)*, from the root translated "horror" in 6:13, 16, has its objective sense here; it will become a place of horrible desolation (see also 1:7). The verse will find its consummation at the Second Coming of Jesus Christ (1 Thess 5:1-11; 2 Pet 3:10-13).

3. Third Salvation Oracle: Interplay of I AM and Micah (vv 14-17)

Micah's twofold salvation oracle in vv 11-13 came in response to Zion's twofold expression of faith in *I AM* (vv 8B-10). Now, on the basis of that oracle, he prays for *I AM*'s ample provision (v 14); *I AM* answers: he will show Zion wonders like those at the time of Israel's exodus from Egypt (v 15). On the basis of that answer Micah, in a meditation addressed to *I AM*, responds with another salvation oracle: the pagan nations will be humbled and cower before *I AM*, the Victor (vv 16-17). The verses of this stanza are stitched together. Vv 14-15 are linked by the dramatic interplay between *I AM* and his prophet, indicated by the change of pronouns. V 14 is an imperatival address to *I AM*, presumably by Micah, who represents the remnant; v 15 is addressed by *I AM* (see v 15B) to Micah (v 15A), and v 17B is addressed by Micah to *I AM*. Vv 14-15 are crocheted together by the catchword at the end of v 14 and the beginning of v 15: "as in the days of old" and "as in the days of your going out from the land of Egypt" respectively. Since vv 16-17 is a unity, the whole salvation oracle of vv 16-17 is addressed to *I AM* (see v 17B).

The imperative and jussive forms of initial *rāʿâ* "Shepherd" (v 10) and "May they graze" (v 14), respectively, signal the shift to the next stanza: Micah's petition for the restored remnant within rebuilt Zion (vv 14-15) and for the punishment of the wicked nations (vv 16-17). The approximately fifty petition psalms in the Psalter all ask God for deliverance, and of these, thirty-five add the motif of asking him to punish the enemy, as in this liturgical hymn.

a. Micah's Petition and I AM's Promise to Save Zion (vv 14-15) Micah's petition that *I AM* richly provide for his restored remnant is answered by *I AM's* promise to show him/Israel wonders. These two verses are closely linked by the dialogue between Micah's petition and *I AM's* promise and by the use of "you" with reference to Israel: first in the mouth of Micah and then in the mouth of *I AM*.

(1) Micah's Petition: Shepherd Zion (v 14) Micah's reference to Zion as "your people," "your rod," and "your inheritance" shows that he is addressing *I AM*, and his introductory imperative "Shepherd" identifies the stanza as having the mood and motifs of the petition psalms. H. Wolff[139] says: "Yahweh as shepherd and the people as a flock are motifs of trust that appear frequently in the psalms of prayer (Pss 80:2[1]; 74:1; 28:9)."

"To shepherd" is a common metaphor for rulers (see 2:12; 4:6-7; 5:3[4]). W. White[140] says, "From very ancient antiquity, rulers were described as demonstrating their legitimacy to rule by their ability to 'pasture' their people." Earlier he wrote, "[It is] used as an honorific title in royal names and inscriptions from the time of Sargon of Akkad (c. 2300 B.C.)." "Your people" refers to the remnant of Israel who have now returned from being scattered far away from their homeland to the ends of the earth (v 12). The connotations of the figure for *I AM* as Israel's Shepherd-King are defined in the remainder of the verse: constant security (see "rod" [v 14A], rich provision ["dwell alone in an orchard," v 14Ab], and "graze in Bashan and in Gilead" [v 14B] in perpetuity ["flock of your inheritance," v 14Aaβ]). *šebeṭ* designates "rod" with the figures "shepherd/sheep" and "scepter, mace," with the reality entailed in "rule your people." It is the symbol of authoritative rule and protection. The kingdom is secure because the Ruler in that Golden Age will protect his kingdom against all enemies.

The metaphor "your flock" for the elect represents an idyllic rule. Christ the Good Shepherd (Mic 5:3[4]) will lose none of the elect (John 10:10-30). "In-

139. Wolff, *Micha*, 225.
140. W. White, "*rāʿâ*," *TWOT* 2:852-53.

heritance" combines the notions of family and perpetuity, a possession passed through the generations. A family's inheritance was providentially chosen (Num 26:56), and God chose Israel for his unique possession (cf. Exod 19:6). The metaphor implies that he elected to tie up his life with theirs (Exod 34:9; Deut 4:20). Jesus noted, "God said . . . , 'I am the God of Abraham, the God of Isaac, and the God of Jacob'" (Matt 22:31-32). His name is forever bound up with them. Today his heritage includes both Jews and Gentiles, all who are Abraham's seed through their relationship with Jesus (Acts 15:16-18; Gal 3:26-29; Eph 1:3, 4; 1 Pet 2:9-10). Micah's petition itself is based on this election.

"Dwell" *(šākan)* can indicate an eternal dwelling or a temporary camping (see 4:10); here the former is in view. The qualifier "apart" connotes Zion's unique election, involving her unique diet and freedom (cf. Deut 33:28; Jer 49:31; Ps 4:9[8]). Her dwelling is further qualified as "in a forest, in the very heart of an orchard." *karmel* ("orchard") can be either a proper place name for Mount Carmel on the Mediterranean or a common noun meaning "orchard" (Isa 10:18; 16:10; 29:17; 32:15-16; Jer 2:7; 4:26; 48:33; 2 Chr 26:10). Although the similar passage in Jer 50:19 favors the former, the parallel, "forest," favors the latter. The expanded metaphor reinforces the ideas of security and well-being. Although in Isa 29:17 *karmel* stands as an antonym to "forest" in Isa 37:24, in combination with "forest" it designates an orchard like a forest (i.e., the finest orchard imaginable), here presumably carpeted with grass.

The form *yir'û* that introduces v 14B is ambiguous: is it jussive ("may they graze in") or indicative ("they will graze in")? The parallelism with the unambiguous imperative *rĕ'ēh* favors the former. This interpretation also nicely suits the connection between the closing expression "as in the days of old" and the introduction to *I AM*'s "as in the days when you went out of Egypt." "Bashan" is the fertile country bounded by the Jabbok River on the south, the Sea of Galilee on the west, a line from Mount Hermon eastward on the north, and the Hauran Range on the east. It was well known for its stately trees (Isa 2:13; Zech 11:2) and its well-fed domesticated animals (Deut 32:14; Ezek 39:18; Amos 4:1; Ps 22:13[12]). Gilead refers to the area on Trans-jordan between the Jabbok River and either the Arnon or the Yarmuk. It too was Israel's first land and was known as good pastureland (Num 32:1, 26). By mighty wonders Moses gave these lands to Israel at the beginning of their history (Num 21:33; Josh 13:29-31); they were lost under Jehu (2 Kgs 10:33), regained by Jeroboam II (2 Kgs 14:25), only to be lost to Assyria during Micah's ministry (2 Kgs 15:29). Now Micah prays for the restoration of these fertile expansions of Israel. The extended metaphor for *I AM*'s beneficent rule in the messianic era emphasizes the petition for new Israel's restoration to its original prosperity and security, "as in the days of old," when God chose his inheritance.

(2) *I AM's* Promise: To Show Zion Wonders (v 15)   Picking up the end of v 14, "as in the days of old," with "as in the days of your going out from the land of Egypt," *I AM* responds to Micah's plea with a promise to show him, the remnant's representative, wonders. *I AM* will indeed show the new Israel wonders as when he brought his inheritance out of Egypt at the beginning of their pilgrimage. Those "days" are the paradigmatic time when God displayed his power to Israel (Exod 12:50, 51; 13:3, 9, 14, 16). By saying to Micah "when you [masculine singular] went out," the covenant-keeping God shows that he regards Micah and the restored Israel as in corporate solidarity with their fathers whom he led out of Egypt to establish his divinely willed order in the world and society.

The remnant of Israel, unknown to Micah but made known by revelation to Paul, would come to include the church, which is composed of both Jews and Gentiles, who are equally co-heirs of God's promises to Israel through their common Spirit baptism into Christ (Eph 3:1-11). The exodus that Christ affords his church, bringing them out of a world of sin and judgment and setting them on their heaven-bound journey through the Wilderness, involves far greater "wonders." Israel's Passover, the baptism into the Red Sea, whereby they put Egypt behind them and set out for the Promised Land, and the heavenly manna and the water from the rock all typify Christ and his greater salvation (John 6; 7:38-39; 1 Cor 10:1-4; 2 Cor 5:17).

b. Micah's Meditation: Pagans Surrender to I AM *(vv 16-17)*   Verses 16-17 are linked together by shifting the subject from Israel to the nations *(gôyîm)* and by the escalating predicates: "[they] will see" and "be ashamed," as indicated by their clapping their hands to their mouths and by their turning a deaf ear to blasphemers, to "they will lick dust," as "they crawl out from their strongholds" and "tremble" and "fear you [i.e., *I AM*]."

The conceptual relationship of vv 15-16 corresponds to that of vv 9B-10, as shown in the key word *r'h* ("gaze," "see," "show"). As "my [i.e., Zion's] eyes will gaze on [*I AM*'s] saving acts" (v 9B) is widened in v 11 to "let my enemy gaze," so "I [i.e., *I AM*] will show *(r'h)* him [the restored remnant] marvelous deeds" (v 15) is expanded in v 16 to "May the nations see and be ashamed." As in v 10, where the elided object of seeing *(r'h)* must be supplied from the last word of v 9 (namely, "saving acts"), so also here the elided object of seeing *(r'h)* must be supplied from the last verb of v 15 (namely, "wonderful deeds," a metonymy for saving acts). This expansion of vision, as Wolff noted, is also found in Exod 15:13, 14-16; cf. Pss 98:2; 126:2.

"The nations [plural] will see and be ashamed" escalates the first stanza, "My enemy [singular] will see and shame will cover her" (v 10). For the meaning of "shame" see v 10. When the nations see the display of God's awesome power on Israel's behalf, they will also feel ashamed for having vaunted themselves against *I AM* and his people. They will no longer vaunt themselves because *I AM* will have made them impotent: "deprived of all their [former] power" (cf. Josh 2:9-11). The B verset gives concrete expression to their feeling shamed with two metonymies involving their mouths and ears: they will no longer blaspheme *I AM* nor listen to the blasphemies of others. "They will clap their hands over their mouths" is idiomatic, an equivalent to the demeaning English "Shut up" (cf. Judg 18:19; Job 21:5), not merely "Be quiet."[141] They are to shut up and stop playing the fool in exalting themselves and denigrating *I AM* (cf. Prov 30:32; cf. Job 21:5). In sum, they will no longer taunt *I AM* and his people as they did, saying "Where is he, *I AM* your God?" (v 10). More problematic is the significance of the metonymy, "they will turn a deaf ear." Wolff, translating literally "their ears become deaf," arbitrarily links deafness with the thunder of *I AM*'s mighty deeds, and BDB refers it to judicial deafness (cf. Isa 6:10). More probably it is an aspect of their humiliation and a correlative to not blaspheme. When God performs wonders on Israel's behalf, the nations will not only stop taunting Israel but they will also turn a deaf ear to the vain boasts of others and their blasphemy against *I AM*. Whereas in v 10 Assyria went down in defeat, in v 16 the nations are stripped of their power. This deprivation of their power explains their shame within themselves (v 16) and their cowing before *I AM* (v 17)

The prophetic meditation that the nations will be humbled (v 16) is now escalated by two similes in v 17Aa that are explained in v 17Ab. "They will lick dust like a snake" (cf. Isa 65:25) in this and other expressions involving "dust," such as "eating dust" (Gen 3:15) or "sinking down in dust" (Ps 44:26[25]), signifies abject humiliation, not starvation. The second figure, "like those who crawl on the ground," reinforces the first, clarifies the ambiguity that humiliation, not starvation, is intended, and forms a smoother transition to the explanation in verset 17Ab. Verset 17B adds to their utter debasement their coming and cowering before *I AM*. The vanquished come trembling *(rgz)* from their strongholds (*misgērôt;* its root *sgr* is an anagram of *rgz* [see Exegesis, 443]). The verb rendered "come quaking," *pāḥad,* has the fundamental meaning "to tremble/quake," rarely with joy (cf. Isa 60:5) and mostly with fear (cf. Jer 33:9, where it also occurs in parallel with *rāgaz*). This strong expression of the horror that accompanies fear occurs elsewhere with expressions denoting visible quaking and trembling (Isa 19:16; 33:14; Jer 33:9) and is the opposite of expressions denoting "trust," "to be secure" (Isa 12:3; Pss 27:1; 78:53; Prov 3:24; cf. Isa 51:12-13). L. Derousseaux[142]

---

141. BDB 803, §1b.
142. L. Derousseaux, *La Crainte de Dieu dans l'Ancien Testament* (Paris: Cerf, 1970), 74.

says that this root is found frequently in religious contexts to denote the terror caused by Yahweh's intervention. The chiastic parallel of v 17ʙa reinforces and intensifies v 17ab. A ("they will come trembling") and A' ("they will come quaking") form their outer frame, and B ("from their strongholds") and B' ("unto *I AM* our God") compose their inner core. The compound proper name "*I AM* our God" also occurs in the liturgical prayer of 4:5. Here, too, Micah regards himself as in corporate solidarity with his people. "The fear of you" in v 17ʙb adds their inner state of psychological fear while reinforcing that the pagans recognize that the Power behind Zion's triumph is her covenant-keeping God. Although "fear" of God frequently includes the psychological opposites of "fear" and "trust" (cf. Exod 14:31), this text has in view only numinous dread before the sacred presence (cf. Gen 28:17; Amos 3:8; Job 4:12-15). This is the same sort of terror the nations experienced at Israel's exodus from Egypt (Exod 15:15); it is not the godly fear that leads to repentance and faith.

The prophecy develops the theme begun in the Garden of Eden, that the Serpent will be humiliated in the dust — that is to say, he will be defeated and shamed, a prophecy that finds its fulfillment in the church of Christ and its consummation at the Second Coming, when Christ saves his people and destroys the damned (Rom 16:20; 2 Thess 1:5-10). Jesus promised that the gates of death will not prevail against his church (Matt 16:18).

4. Praise of Pardoning and Covenant-Keeping I AM (vv 18-20)

On the basis of Micah's meditation on *I AM*'s promise to show wonders to his covenant people, the prophet segues into a climactic hymn of praise for *I AM*'s uniquely sublime attributes: he is a God who in his *ḥesed* forgives (v 18), who triumphs over sin by removing it (v 19), and who exercises *ḥesed* (kindness) and *'ĕmet* (reliability) in keeping his covenant promises to the patriarchs (v 20). *I AM*'s *ḥesed* informs both his delight to pardon and his fidelity to keep covenant. At the beginning of Israel's history, *I AM* himself claimed these incomparable attributes to be his true glory (Exod 33:19–34:6). *I AM*'s power to forgive sin (vv 18-19) is essential to the triumph of his attributes to display covenant fidelity and kindness to the patriarchs (v 20).

Micah's question "Who is a god like you?" is not unique in ancient Near Eastern literature. The Egyptians, Sumerians, Babylonians, and Assyrians held a similar view of the incomparability of quite a number of their gods. "The attribute of incomparability," says C. J. Labuschagne,[143] "was originally ascribed to a

---

143. Labuschagne, *The Incomparability of Yahweh*, 53.

limited number of gods, who had proved their supremacy through their struggle against and their victory over powers hostile to the gods, or it was originally bestowed on a few gods identified with the most conspicuous phenomena in nature, who showed unparalleled characteristics." In pagan religion the attribute of incomparability did not imply any trend toward real monotheism. By bestowing the attribute on a particular god, worshippers regarded him as the most important, giving him priority in their devotion and lavish praise. When Israel's prophets imply the existence of other gods, such as Micah does in his question "Who is a god like you?" they are using religious language, not catechetical teaching that recognizes their ontological reality. Pagans represent their gods by manufactured idols, while the prophets and the apostle Paul in their catechetical teaching deny their ontological existence but accept the reality that pagans are so spiritually blind that they worship non-existent "gods" and/or demons (cf. Deut 4:39; 32:16-17; Isa 40:25; 41:5-7, 21-23, 28-29; 44:9-20; 1 Cor 8:4-8).

I AM's incomparability pertains to his unique character to forgive sinners in his intervention in salvation history, not to his surpassing military power as we might expect. "The dominating characteristic causing Yahweh to be incomparable is His miraculous intervention in history as the redeeming God. . . . Through the whole of the Old Testament there is a very real and close connection between Yahweh's incomparability and the fact that *He intervenes in history as the redeeming God* — the references to His qualities as God of the covenant (Deut 4:7; 1 Kgs 8:23; Mic 7:18) and as Creator (Isa 40:18, 25; Jer 10:16) are no exception," says Labuschagne.[144]

The prophet sees behind his saving acts to a greater superiority: his ability to forgive out of his very nature in order to keep his covenant obligations to the patriarchs. Two characterizing modifying clauses underscore this excelling quality of his, the second emphasizing the first. "Who takes away *(nōśê')* guilt *('āwōn)* from someone" is a figure signifying "to forgive totally." By *'āwōn* is meant both the misdeed and its punishment.[145] The second modifier reinforces the first. "Who passes over transgressions" underscores this reality by another metaphor that enables *I AM* to continue his intervention in history on his elect people's behalf. In the human realm also "to pass over transgression" out of love (see Prov 10:12, 19; 17:9) causes people to delight and rejoice in the one who forgives and wins him more fame, honor, praise, and distinction than a warrior (cf. 16:32; 20:3). We should assume that the offended overlooks all sorts of irritating and offensive violations of his rights. His incomparable grace, however, is extended to the repentant "remnant of his inheritance," not to unrepentant sin-

---

144. Labuschagne, *The Incomparability of Yahweh*, 91.
145. R. Knierim, "'*āwôn*," *TLOT* 2:863.

ners (v 9; cf. Exod 34:7; Mic 2:7; see Introduction, 37). For the meaning and significance of "inheritance" see v 14. There may be an intertextual allusion to Exod 34:7 and Num 14:18, where both *ʿāwōn* and *pešaʿ* are objects of *nāśāʾ*. God displayed this amazing glory of his at the beginning of Israel's history when he forgave the repentant nation for their worship of the golden calf. As Moses held the tablets with the Ten Commandments in his hands, Yahweh passed by, proclaiming his grace to forgive sin (Exod 34:4-7). "Transgression," *pešaʿ*, a synonym for "sin," signifies the fracturing of the covenantal relationship by misdeeds entailed in rejecting God's authority.

The parallel B verset reemphasizes the truth yet again by asserting the truth negatively. He does not retain his anger "forever" (i.e., a time of unlimited and unforeseeable duration) because he is a God who delights *(ḥāpēṣ)* in "kindness" *(ḥesed,* see Mic 6:8). Though God's people are unfaithful, yet he amazingly remains faithful to them (2 Tim 2:13).

God's forgiveness in the light of his perfect justice becomes intelligible in the light of Israel's sacrificial system. The expressions involved in "who forgives guilt" are also connected to the great Day of Atonement, when the scapegoat "took away Israel's guilt" (Lev 16:22). The crucial vocabulary of Mic 7:18 is used for the suffering Servant of Yahweh in Isaiah 53: "bear" *(nāśāʾ,* v 11), "iniquity" *(ʿāwōn,* vv 6, 11), "transgression" *(pešaʿ,* vv 8, 11), all in connection with *I AM'*s "pleasure" *(ḥāpēṣ,* v 10). These passages find their fulfillment in Jesus Christ. God does not wink at sin, but provided the sacrifice of Jesus Christ, the only one who kept his covenant obligations (Rom 3:21-26) both to bear and to take away sin. No other "god" ever died in the place of his sinful people to save them from his wrath against sin so that they can live and so that he continues to live in an epistemological sense in their praises. (Of course, he "is" in his ontology.) The other so-called "gods" of the ancient Near East are all dead, but Israel's forgiving God is praised today around the world. With him there is forgiveness, so that he continues to be feared and worshipped (Ps 130:3-4).

The A verset continues the celebration of the pardoning God in the third-person singular "he"; it refers to the elect in the first-person plural as "us" and shows that they are the ones who sing his praise. The B verset heightens the praise by returning to celebrating God in the second-person singular "you" and referring to the elect as "them," forming the transition to v 20. By using "us" Micah again identifies himself as in corporate solidarity with true Israel, the faithful covenant people of God who live forever because their unchanging God always forgives them.

In v 19Aa Israel, on the basis of the preceding oracles of salvation (vv 8-10, 11-13, and 14-17), celebrate *I AM'*s renewed mercy *(rḥm)* to them. The initial "he will again" anticipates the clear allusion in v 19B to Moses' Song of the Sea at Israel's exodus from Egypt, the exodus in v 19B. The root of "he will have compassion/mercy" *(rḥm)* concretely refers to the "womb." This soft spot became the physical locus for the experience of the strong emotion of pity for the needy. The verb is always used with the emotion of compassion/mercy from a superior to an inferior, parents to children, victors to the defeated, and the advantaged to the disadvantaged. The extension of mercy is voluntary, not involuntary. In v 19Ab Israel implicitly personifies her sins as the Pharaoh and his picked troops. Unless *I AM* triumphantly "vanquishes," "subdues," and "tramples under foot" Israel's sin and guilt, "hurls them into the depths of the sea" (Exod 15:4-5), and so totally and finally rids Israel of their iniquity, they have no hope of total and final liberation from the pagan military powers that have enslaved them throughout their history (Rom 7:14). Israel's sin, not the power of pagans, is the real enemy that defeats them. If the wages of sin is death and the gift of God (which is righteous) is eternal life (Rom 6:23), then ultimately the powers to be reckoned with are spiritual, that is to say — sin and righteousness. *I AM* must remove Israel's sin as decisively and effectively as he had Pharaoh and his picked troops. Israel's universal victory over sin both in extent and in time is also indicated by the countable plurals "inquities/guilt" and "sins," by "all," and by the metaphor "hurled into the depths of the sea." No one remains to condemn the elect before the righteous Judge (Rom 8:31-39). In other words, Israel's liberation from the powerful Egyptians at the beginning of her history is a type of Israel's greater spiritual liberation from enslaving sin in her future that outlasts judgment.

As other scriptures testify, Jesus Christ died vicariously on the cross in the place of the elect, satisfying the righteous requirements of God's law (Isa 52:13–53:12; Rom 3:21-26). His substitution for millions of people is not a matter of quantitative equality but of qualitative inequality. All the righteousness of people is nothing more than a pile of filthy rags repugnant to God. But Christ's pure righteousness totally satisfies the holy God. In addition to his vicarious sacrifice for them, through their spiritual baptism into Christ they became one with him (Rom 6:1-18). Even more than that, through sending his Spirit to dwell in them he empowers them to live their own lives in a way pleasing to God (Rom 8:1-17).

Micah's use of "you" shows that he continues to address his praise to *I AM* (v 19B), but now he refers to the elect in the first-person plural "our," making more pronounced and personal the corporate solidarity of the people of God. Israel's hope of salvation rests in God's *ḥesed,* his unfailing kindness to his needy covenant partners who cannot deliver themselves. His *ḥesed* prompts him to forgive their sins (vv 18-19) and to keep his covenantal oaths with their fathers, Abraham and Jacob.

The poet draws his praise to a conclusion by putting aside the Exodus personification and metaphor and returning to *I AM*'s bedrock attributes, "kindness" and "fidelity," applying them specifically to Abraham and Jacob, the original heirs of his promises, covenants, and oaths to bless them: to make them as numerous as the stars in the sky and the sand on the seashore, to give them an eternal land, to enable them to take possession of the cities of their enemies, and to bless all nations through them. The patriarchs are clinically dead and cannot realize these promises by their efforts. They are totally dependent on God's fidelity and kindness to help them in their need (Gen 12:1-3; 15:1-16; 17:1-17; 22:15-18; 28:10-15; 35:11-13).

"Fidelity" (*'ĕmet*) refers to God's faithfulness to his words and in his deeds. Since God is faithful, his worshipping community can rely on his words and deeds even in their deepest distress. *'ĕmet* may be part of a collocation, for *ḥesed wĕ'ĕmet* is a frequent compound. But since the Hebrew writers use the plural, not the singular, attributes for the pair, since "them" (plural) is used when *ḥesed wĕ'ĕmet* is its antecedent, and since the words are elsewhere distinguished and, as here, even reversed (cf. Pss 40:11-12[10-11]; 85:11[10]), the Hebrew poets regarded them as distinct virtues, not as a hendiadys for "faithful kindness." They again recall, for the fifth time in vv 18-20, Exod 34:6-7. God's *rab ḥesed* ("great kindness") exceeds that of mortals because he bestows it on undeserving sinners (see vv 18-19). Nevertheless, God works out these attributes in Israel's history through the repentant remnant, who share the faithfulness of the original recipients of the covenant (see "us" in the B verset), and not through unrepentant, disloyal Israel (Mic 2:7-9; 3:11; cf. Exod 20:6; 34:6-7).

The proper name of Israel's eponymous ancestor, "Jacob," usually functions as a gentilic for the nation (cf. 1:5; 3:1, 8). Here, however, as the parallel "our fathers" shows, the patriarch himself is in view (cf. Gen 28:10-15; 32:23-33[22-32]; 35:9-13). His heirs are the remnant of Judah, including Micah. The blessed destiny of God's elect is assured because God, who is sovereign over creation and history, cannot lie and must keep his oaths. "You swore to us" concludes the trilogy of direct addresses to *I AM* begun in v 18. The remnant identifies itself by faith as the heirs of God's oath to their fathers. Though God swore these promises in "days of old," they are as relevant today as then because his sublime attributes of fidelity and kindness to his needy covenant partners guarantee their fulfillment in the church, which inherits them (Gal 3:29; Eph 2:19).

Index of Authors

Index of Subjects

For the meaning of Hebrew words, see the commentary on their first use in the book of Micah.

472

of, 283; theme of, 234; universal rule of, 295. *See also* Jesus Christ

Micah (book): audience of, 43-44, 343, 373; date and authorship of, 8-13, 35, 140-41, 213-20, 229, 248-49, 251, 296-97; editing of, 87, 110, 124, 144-46, 186, 224, 294; form and structure of, 13-16; grammar of, 11; historical background of, 3-8, 302; history of criticism of, 9-11; place of, 36; relevance of, 44; text of, 16-18; theme, 204-5

Micah (prophet): autobiography, 2-3, 38-40, 165-67, 174, 264, 288, 424, 431; call of, 1-2, 344, 374; corporate solidarity with people, 288, 442, 462, 464; date of, 3; inspiration of, 37, 165-66, 416; name, 1, 34, 38; power of, 166-67, 174; prayer of, 313; precursor of Jesus Christ, 175. *See also* Editing

Miriam, 381

Moresheth: location of, 39

Mountain: symbolism of, 195, 209; as witnesses, 345, 374-76. *See also* Temple

Mourning: ritual of, 85-87

Names: significance of, 88, 203

Nations: converted, 191-220, 285; false securities of, 331; fear of, 443-44; hostility to kingdom of God, 250-59; humiliation of, 442-44, 460-62; rebellion of, 330; punishment of, 252-57, 259-61; under wrath, 341-42. *See also* Assyria

Neo-Assyrian Empire: invasions of Israel, 4-7, 41-43; foreign policy of, 5

New Testament: use of Old Testament, 44

Oil, 413

Omri (House of), 414

Ophel: meaning of, 235

Paronomasia, 88

Peace, 212

Peoples and nations, 196

Perseverance of saints, 126, 213, 434

Priests: feckless, 179; responsibility to teach, 180

Prayer: cry out in, 151; importance of, 156;

unanswered, 151, 157, 165. *See also* Remnant

Prophecy and prophets: certainty of, 212-13; conditional nature of, 38, 57, 186; differences between true and false, 168-71; divine manner of, 43; ecstasy, 111; functions of, 169; interpretation of, 206-8, 298; terms for, 36-37, 111, 158, 160, 163, 220-21, 252, 344; theme of, 204-5

Prophets (false): adversaries of the true, 125; blasphemy of, 181; in cahoots with barons, 2, 110, 130, 172; in cahoots with magistrates, 168; clairvoyance of, 163, 170; judgment of, 162-64, 173-74; marks of, 158-60; methods of, 162-63; motivations of, 159-61, 169-72, 180; preaching of, 124-31, 154-75, 180; sin of, 158; solidarity of, 127

Prophets (true): establish God's kingdom, 126, 174; marks of, 128, 165, 170; as messengers, 158-59, 169; a plurality, 126; Spirit-empowerment of, 175; as watchmen, 427. *See also* Micah (prophet)

Prostitution: cultic, 54-55, 59-60

Rain: symbolism of, 308-9. *See also* Dew

Redactor. *See* Micah (book)

Redemption, 380-81

Remember, 382-84

Remnant: bane and blessing of, 307-9, 316-18; faith of, 310, 317-18; faithful, 126; fear not, 299; heavenly origin, 315; increase of, 302; inheritance of *I AM*, 445; intimacy with *I AM*, 305, 308; notion of, 227; power of, 222, 315; prayer of, 313, 319; regathering of, 226; as rulers, 305, 306-19; as survivors, 132; in time of Hezekiah, 131-42; triumph of, 120-29, 171, 222, 305-18. *See also* Messiah, community of; Perservance of saints

Repentance: godly, 386, 462; necessity of, 88-89, 126, 186, 464

Resting place. *See* Land (Promised)

Revelation: *See* Prophecy

Select Index of Scripture References

477